# Democratizing Finance

*Origins of the Community Development Financial Institutions Movement*

## CLIFFORD N. ROSENTHAL

*With a Foreword by David Erickson*
*Director, Federal Reserve Bank of San Francisco*

Suite 300 - 990 Fort St
Victoria, BC, V8V 3K2
Canada

www.friesenpress.com

**Copyright © 2018 by Clifford N. Rosenthal**
First Edition — 2018

All rights reserved.

No part of this publication may be reproduced in any form, or by any means, electronic or mechanical, including photocopying, recording, or any information browsing, storage, or retrieval system, without permission in writing from FriesenPress.

Publisher's Cataloging-In-Publication Data
(Prepared by The Donohue Group, Inc.)

Names: Rosenthal, Clifford N., author. | Erickson, David James, writer of supplementary textual content.

Title: Democratizing finance : origins of the community development financial institutions movement / Clifford N. Rosenthal ; with a foreword by David Erickson, Director, Federal Reserve Bank of San Francisco.

Description: First edition. | Victoria, BC, Canada : FriesenPress, [2018] | Includes bibliographical references and index.

Identifiers: ISBN 9781525536625 (hardcover) | ISBN 9781525536632 (paperback) | ISBN 9781525536649 (ebook)

Subjects: LCSH: Community Development Financial Institutions Fund (U.S.)--History. | Community development--United States--Finance--History. | Federal aid to community development--United States--History. | Community development credit unions--United States--History. | United States--Economic policy--History.

Classification: LCC HN90.C6 R67 2018 (print) | LCC HN90.C6 (ebook) | DDC 307.140973--dc23

ISBN
978-1-5255-3662-5 (Hardcover)
978-1-5255-3663-2 (Paperback)
978-1-5255-3664-9 (eBook)

1. *History, United States, 20$^{th}$ Century*
2. *Social Science, Social Classes*
3. *Business & Economics, Banks & Banking*

Community Development, Credit unions and banks, Inequality, Financial democracy, Clinton and, CDFI, Progressive populism

Distributed to the trade by The Ingram Book Company

# TABLE OF CONTENTS

| | |
|---|---|
| Foreword | v |
| Preface and Acknowledgments | xi |
| Introduction | xiv |
| List of Acronyms | xix |
| **Part I. Prologue** | **1** |
| Chapter 1. Franklin, Freedman's, Filene | 3 |
| **Part II. The Roots of Community Development Finance** | **21** |
| Chapter 2. The Sixties | 23 |
| **Part III. The Seventies** | **45** |
| Chapter 3. The Chicago Story | 47 |
| Chapter 4. Grassroots Community Development and its Supporters | 61 |
| **Part IV. The Eighties** | **79** |
| Chapter 5. CDCs and Loan Funds | 81 |
| Chapter 6. Community Development Banks and "Banks" | 96 |
| Chapter 7. The Investors | 113 |
| Chapter 8. The CDCU Movement in the 1980s | 125 |
| **Part V. The Nineties: The Visions Converge** | **149** |
| Chapter 9. Coalition-Building: The Road to Trinity | 151 |
| Chapter 10. CDFIs and Congress: First Encounters | 159 |
| Chapter 11. On the Campaign Trail | 176 |
| Chapter 12. Transition | 181 |
| Chapter 13. On Capitol Hill | 194 |
| Chapter 14. The Road to the Rose Garden | 208 |
| Chapter 15. In the Rose Garden | 223 |
| Chapter 16. A Year in Congress | 233 |
| Chapter 17. Home Stretch | 248 |

**Part VI. The Fund is Launched. The Field Grows.** — 263
Chapter 18. Staying Alive: CDFIs and the Newborn Fund — 265
Chapter 19. The Fund Opens for Business — 278
Chapter 20. CDFIs at the Dawn of the New Era — 293
Chapter 21. The Class of 1996 — 326
Chapter 22. The First Crisis — 334

**Part VII. Community Development Financial Institutions in Historical Perspective** — 349
Chapter 23. Twenty Years After — 351
Chapter 24. Reflections on Democratic Finance — 368

**Part VIII. Epilogue** — 383
Appendix 1. Profiles of the "Class of 1996" — 385
Appendix 2. Selected Profiles: The Class of 1996 Revisited — 394
Notes — 402
Bibliography — 455
Index — 459
About the Author — 484

# FOREWORD

David Erickson
Director, Federal Reserve Bank of San Francisco*

## The History of an Idea, a Movement, and an Industry

This book is a master work on the history of community development finance. It traces the history of an idea, a movement, and an industry that sought to meld the "approaches and values of philanthropy and business," according to Clifford Rosenthal. Achieving the right balance between "philanthropy" and "business" was tricky, however. Those who leaned toward more financially sustainable business models were accused of "mission drift." Those who emphasized social goals struggled to get to the scale they wanted. At root was the question: Was this effort a "movement" or an "industry"? Was it possible to be both?

Rosenthal runs a line from Benjamin Franklin's small business loan funds, created at the end of the eighteenth century, to the Freedman's Bank for newly emancipated African Americans in the 1860s, to the credit union movement of the early twentieth century, to a raft of banking and urban reinvestment strategies in the 1980s and 1990s. As Rosenthal suggests in the introduction, those latter unconventional banks, credit unions, and loan funds "might have remained an interesting but obscure footnote if not for the convergence of multiple economic, social, and political events." What was an incipient movement became a permanent fixture of the American finance industry thanks to key policies and political moves in the 1990s that, among other things, created a new entity in the U.S. Treasury Department—the Community Development Financial Institutions (CDFI) Fund—to help foster a wide array of financial institutions dedicated to improving low-income communities. As of 2017, there were more than a thousand CDFIs with combined assets of over $130 billion.

Rosenthal's thorough research is informed by the fact that he was part witness and part architect of this movement. He has conducted scores of interviews and pored over tens of thousands of pages of memos, news accounts, archives of the Clinton presidency, and other sources to weave this story

---

\* The views expressed herein are those of the author and do not represent the views of the Federal Reserve Bank of San Francisco or the Federal Reserve System.

together. He chronicles successes and failures—not only to tell the story, but as a guide to the contemporary CDFI movement.

## From Church Basements and Communes to the White House

The idea that finance and access to capital could improve communities started with a small group of advocates that grew substantially over time. Nothing could dramatize the movement's success more than the 1993 White House Rose Garden ceremony to announce the creation of the CDFI Fund, with the prospect of hundreds of millions of new dollars flowing into the emerging community development finance system.

The early movement was "a river that was fed by many streams," according to Rosenthal, "from campaigns against apartheid, redlining, nuclear power, poverty, and racial discrimination." One consistent source of inspiration and resources, however, came from the faith community. The idea to use finance as a tool for positive social change came from Buddhists to Baptists. Almost all the mainline Protestant churches were active builders of this movement, too. Catholic nuns, however, stood head and shoulders above the crowd as early and consistent advocates.

Another consistent part of the story was leadership, which came from many levels—from the pioneers of the movement, their early supporters in the investment and philanthropic communities, and leaders at the highest levels, especially Bill and Hillary Clinton. Hillary Clinton's college roommate connected the Clintons to Muhammad Yunus, the creator of the Grameen Bank in Bangladesh and a powerful advocate for market-based solutions for low-income people. And Bill Clinton made the idea of access to capital a central part of his 1992 presidential campaign. "This whole business of economic empowerment has got to be at the center of the civil rights movement," he said.

The political coalition that supported the democratizing capital movement achieved great success even though it was attacked by both the left and right of the ideological spectrum. At one point, the Rev. Jesse Jackson Sr. accused this effort of creating "a separate but equal banking system." Ideologues on the right opposed government tinkering with the market. Nevertheless, the coalition was strong because it had national reach and could, over time, demonstrate benefits to most congressional districts around the country.

This new network also had the ability to be flexible and respond constructively to national crises. For example, after the riots in South Central Los Angeles in 1992, community development finance offered the positive message that its tools could be used to create more economic vitality in that struggling city and elsewhere in troubled urban America. And of course, as one of the movement's biggest cheerleaders, Treasury Secretary Robert Rubin liked to remind Congress: "Addressing the problems of our distressed urban and rural communities is critical to the future of this country. That's not a moral judgment. It's not a social judgment. It's a hard-headed business judgment."

Community development finance has consistently demonstrated its resiliency over the past 23 years, including the past two years under the Trump administration. In both years, the president proposed to eliminate the CDFI Fund. Both efforts failed. As of 2018, funding for the CDFI Fund is nearly at its highest level ever.

## Defining Characteristics of the CDFI System

The fact that this approach to community improvement was not a program but rather something more akin to a quasi-market was also a key to its success and support. This was a decisive shift away from the previous generation of centralized, highly bureaucratic, prescriptive, and rigid federal programs. This new approach used incentives to steer capital and make targeted investments. In this policy evolution, the CDFI transition to a decentralized network of players (nonprofit and for-profit) mirrored the same evolution that took place among community development corporations (CDCs) a decade earlier.

The quasi-market had important advantages over a more static government program. It could adapt to changing circumstances, and it allowed customizable solutions for each community and project. However, there were limits to the community development finance marketplace. There were problems of achieving scale, and innovation was often lacking. For example, almost all CDFIs remain vertically integrated small institutions that have failed to develop shared, back-office support and other sector-wide infrastructure or platforms to streamline their business model.

As the community development finance sector grew, it confronted tensions and trade-offs. For example, as the financing got more complex and involved more players and partners, there was a need for more technocratic control over the transactions. This tendency toward more complex and top-down models ran headlong into an older War on Poverty concept that argued for "maximum feasible participation" of the poor. And another related consequence of increasingly complex transactions was that it required communities and community groups to be financially savvy in order to accept investments. This fact skewed federal (and other) resources to communities that were the most ready, versus those with the highest need.

This market was limited by the amount of subsidy that was available. It was not the case that it grew on its own, once some of the biases for investment in low-income communities were removed. Early advocates for access to capital, like Gale Cincotta (often described as the mother of the Community Reinvestment Act), thought the market, if functioning properly, would be enough to bring prosperity to low-income neighborhoods. However, the dream of a robust financial marketplace in those places never materialized. In part that was because the financial transactions were often bespoke and few in numbers. Too few deals of a standard type made it harder to develop the performance and risk data that are necessary to grow a financial marketplace.

## Reflections on the CDFI System

This is the story of a policy success. The incentives provided by the federal government and the ingenuity of the community development finance sector have brought hundreds of billions of dollars of investments into low-income communities. The big question, though, is whether finance and access to capital are effective tools to fight poverty and revitalize those communities.

In what was the first large national CDFI convening in 1994, Paul Lingenfelter, program officer at the John D. and Catherine T. MacArthur Foundation, gave a speech to the assembled activists entitled "The half-truth of community development finance." In that speech he said: "Community development financial institutions in the United States have been built on a half-truth. The half-truth is: Lack of access to capital is a primary factor in perpetuating, if not causing, poverty." He concluded: "Not in my wildest dreams do I think community development financial institutions can end poverty, and I often think that limited access to capital is less significant than many of the other hurdles the poor have to face. In the end, however, I conclude that access to capital has been denied and that it matters."

Many of us thought that access to capital on fair terms would be sufficient to start the economic engines in low-income neighborhoods and reduce income and wealth inequality. Similarly, those who strove to reduce health disparities thought that access to medical care for those who lacked insurance would be sufficient to close the disparities in health outcomes. Education advocates thought that more resources, higher teacher pay, and better classroom technology would reduce the education achievement gap. Across the board, those strategies were well meaning and helpful to a degree, but they did not solve the problems. Defenders will argue that those efforts were never adequately funded, and that is probably true. But even so, we should have seen a few bright spots—a few neighborhoods where economies took off; a few places where health and education disparities narrowed significantly.

The reality is that low-income people need all those sectors to work well together to help create opportunities in disinvested places. Community development finance has been successful in improving neighborhoods through one important strategy: real estate investments in critical assets—especially housing, clinics, and schools. In other words, it is good at financing needed physical capital. It is much less effective in financing positive human capital interventions—investments that improve education, health, and other critical social services. Paul Grogan, president of the Boston Foundation and one of the founders of the Local Initiatives Support Corporation (LISC), tackled this problem in *Investing in What Works for America's Communities* (2012). In looking to the future of community development, he wrote:

> It lies in turning the architecture of community development to meet urgent challenges of human development. How to turn a successful community organizing and real estate development system toward the goal of increasing educational outcomes, employment success, family asset building, individual and community resilience to weather setbacks? As an industry, we need new strategies to face these challenges.[1]

# Foreword

In Rosenthal's account of the community development finance movement, there were moments when there was a desire to finance both "place" strategies, like real estate, and "people" strategies, such as asset building. But people strategies were never the main thrust of the community development finance movement (except for some asset-building efforts of many of the nonprofit credit unions). In a powerful critique of this deficiency in the field, Nancy Andrews, in her 2009 essay "Coming Out as a Human Capitalist: Community Development at the Nexus of People and Place," wrote: "CDFIs capitalize public support—housing subsidies, child care subsidies, health care subsidies—to create long-term assets that serve low-income populations and places for many years. But the most durable asset of all is a change in the life chances of a child."[2]

How do we improve the life chances of a child? Put differently, how do we invest more effectively in both places and people? One strategy that is showing promise is a partnership with the health sector. Those who are interested in improving population health now readily accept that they need the community development sector to help make neighborhoods and social services more health-promoting.

The role community development finance can play in improving populations is substantial, and the potential medical care cost savings are staggering. Dr. Douglas Jutte recently wrote in the *Practical Playbook*:

> The importance of this potential collaboration cannot be overstated. In the U.S. we currently spend at least $3.5 trillion per year on healthcare. Over 85% of those resources are spent on chronic disease, and we know that a substantial portion of chronic disease is preventable, linked to poverty, and concentrated in low-income communities. This translates to at least $1 trillion spent annually on avoidable chronic disease among residents of low-income neighborhoods. These are precisely the places where community development invests its time, resources, and expertise tackling many of the determinants of poor health.[3]

What is necessary is to find a way to spend that $1 trillion in a better way. It may be that we finally have a cash flow from the medical sector to fund the upstream interventions in education, housing, public safety, and recreation that are needed at scale for the over 40 million Americans living in poverty. And the indispensable player in that upstream population-health business model will be the community development finance industry. It will be essential in harmonizing those multiple funding streams and experimenting with new tools, such as pay-for-success financing.[4] In that future state of the world, we will be able to finance the multiple interventions necessary to improve the life chances of all children.

## Conclusion

Historians like the idea that the future is a fixed point and the past is always changing. In part this is because the meaning of past events is open to interpretation, especially how those events and actions add up to themes and trends that shape the world we live in today. A vigorous debate of this type is missing from the work of those who want to use finance and access to capital as tools for positive social change. Very few histories of this movement exist. It may be that too many of those who were involved in this effort are "doers" and don't slow down enough to reflect on the work. It is also true that historians and other academics have overlooked this sector. Too few people know of the amazing accomplishments of the affordable housing, community development, and community development finance fields. Clifford Rosenthal is changing that. We are in his debt for the hard work he put into this analysis. Now more historians need to write their interpretations, so we can have the vigorous debate on this field that has been absent too long.

In the spirit of urging this debate, I would like to make a strong critique of our field and ask this question: Is access to capital our domino theory? In April 1971, John Kerry famously asked U.S. senators in the Fulbright Hearings: "How do you ask a man to be the last man to die in Vietnam? How do you ask a man to be the last man to die for a mistake?" This book is a history of more than 50 years of efforts from well-meaning activists who believed that they could make a better society and do right by communities that have been harmed by racism, disinvestment, and lack of opportunity by creating financial investments in those communities. And yet many of the problems we care about have not improved substantially. The poverty rate, for example, was about 15 percent during the War on Poverty, and it is about 15 percent today. The dominos didn't fall in Southeast Asia, and access to capital has not been the answer to people living in poverty in the United States.

Is it time to radically rethink the strategy to help low-income people? Can we build on the advances and insights that have been achieved in the community development finance industry over the past 50 years? Can we take those accomplishments in new directions with new ideas, new partners, and new resources? We won't be able to take that next step until we interrogate the lessons of the past and incorporate those insights into a better future.

# PREFACE AND ACKNOWLEDGMENTS

As a cofounder of the CDFI movement, I both observed and helped shape the events described in this book. My direct involvement spanned 1980 through 2012, when (from 1983) I led the National Federation of Community Development Credit Unions. The organization was a half-dozen years old when I joined it; I learned from and was inspired by its founders, who had fought for community-controlled capital throughout the 1970s—a largely untold story. Their struggle was the one I subsequently carried on and broadened, planting the seeds for the institution that became the CDFI Fund.

Writing as a participant-observer, I must acknowledge biases that a disengaged historian would not have. I hope that these deficits are outweighed by my own insider perspectives, amplified by those of 200 interviewees who played important roles in CDFI history. Increasingly, members of the founding generation of CDFIs have retired; some have passed away. This has made more urgent my task of capturing their stories. As CDFIs have matured, a new generation of activists have found careers—and, I hope, their life work—in these institutions. Through many dialogues, I have learned that most of this generation have little knowledge of the challenges of movement-building that created their CDFIs, nor of the decades of anti-poverty, reinvestment, and community development initiatives that preceded CDFI.

Thus, I have had a dual goal in writing this book: both to record and honor the contributions of my colleagues of three decades, the co-creators of community development finance; and to inspire those new to the field to see and value their roles as the beneficiaries and makers of an ongoing legacy. For practitioners and others unfamiliar with the details of federal policymaking—particularly, the complexities involved in creating a new institution like the CDFI Fund—I hope my detailed narrative of the journey from grassroots visions and campaign promises to legislation will be an instructive case study.

Interviewing many longtime colleagues and others whom I knew only by reputation was one of the great pleasures of this project and greatly enriched my own perspective on the history of community development finance. Over 2014-17, I interviewed CDFI organizers, foundation and faith-based investors, bankers, Clinton administration and CDFI Fund officials, and former congressional staff. I regret that this book reflects only a portion of those interviews; in their entirety, they provide a foundation for a rich archive for the oral history of community development finance.

I am especially grateful to the people who cofounded ShoreBank, helped launch Southern Bancorp, Inc., and so much more: Ron Grzywinski, Mary Houghton, and George Surgeon. Their hospitality on my visit to Chicago and patient responses to my questions helped me avoid the most glaring errors. My thanks to Martin Eakes, whom it has been my honor to know since the early days of the Center for Community Self-Help, for his days of interviews, decades of inspiration, and breakfasts in Durham's diners. Former Clinton administration officials Michael Barr and Paul Weinstein Jr. educated me about policymaking in the White House and executive branch, while Jeannine Jacokes provided me valuable insights into the working of Congress from her time as a staff member of the Senate Banking Committee and thereafter.

Two foundations provided support that made my years of research and writing possible: the John D. and Catherine T. MacArthur Foundation and the F.B. Heron Foundation. Even beyond the dollars, I am grateful for the encouragement of Debra Schwartz (MacArthur) and my longtime CDFI colleague Clara Miller (Heron). Neither they nor their organizations bear any responsibility for the errors, omissions, or opinions expressed in this book.

I benefited from the files made available by the two organizations that were pivotal in establishing the national coalition of CDFIs: the Opportunity Finance Network (OFN; originally the National Association of Community Development Loan Funds) and my former organization, the National Federation of Community Development Credit Unions. My thanks to Lisa Mensah, both in her current capacity as CEO of OFN and for her years at the Ford Foundation; and to Cathie Mahon, my successor at the National Federation who, years before, coordinated our effort to establish a New York State CDFI Fund. Neither organization is responsible for any errors or omissions in this book.

The Clinton Presidential Library and the Rockefeller Archives, which houses documents of the Ford and Taconic foundations, were indispensable resources for my research. Lyndon Comstock, Dick Jones, and Jeannine Jacokes shared not only their memories, but their files, including documents reclaimed from the pre-digital age. Contemporary articles from the press, including banking trade journals, helped me to trace in almost daily detail the progress of CDFI legislation and the early years of the CDFI Fund, as well as the perspectives of mainstream financial institutions on the community development banking initiative.

My thanks to my CDFI colleagues Jim Clark, Lyndon Comstock, Jeannine Jacokes, Errol T. Louis, Lisa Mensah, Valerie Piper, Steve Rohde, Kerwin Tesdell, Michael Swack, Terry Ratigan, and Pat Conaty for reading portions of the manuscript and offering their corrections and suggestions, as did my friends and colleagues outside the CDFI field, especially fellow historian Marvin Ciporen and Cheyenna Layne Weber, the driving force of the Cooperative Economics Alliance of New York City.

I had the privilege of serving as a Visiting Scholar at the Milano School of International Affairs, Management, and Urban Policy of The New School in New York City from 2014 through 2018. My thanks to the university and to Professor Lisa Servon (currently at the University of Pennsylvania), who helped make my engagement possible.

The San Francisco Federal Reserve Bank has generously provided editorial support for my work and, in the person of David Erickson of the Community Development Department, invaluable advice and encouragement. Many thanks to Kelly Kramer, who toiled persistently and with good humor over the manuscript in all its details. Bill Luecht, who reviewed the manuscript, has served at the

Community Development Financial Institutions Fund since its earliest days and is a unique resource for understanding the history of that institution. Neither institution bears any responsibility for shortcomings or errors in this book.

Finally, but above all, my thanks to and for my wife, Elayne Archer, companion on this long journey and cherished editor-on-demand, and my daughter, Dana Archer-Rosenthal, who progressed from stuffing envelopes for the National Federation at age three, to learning about the Community Reinvestment Act by age seven, and more recently, to working in the fields of philanthropy, community development finance, and social entrepreneurship.

Clifford Rosenthal  
Brooklyn, New York  
June 2018

# INTRODUCTION

Weeks after President Bill Clinton began his first term in 1993, he set out to fulfill his campaign promise: to create a "network of 100 community development banks and 1,000 microenterprise organizations" to expand economic opportunity. The "action-forcing event," as his advisers framed it, was this:

> Across the country, rural and urban communities are starved for affordable credit, capital, and basic banking services. Millions of Americans in low-income neighborhoods have no bank where they can cash a check, borrow money to buy a home, or get a small loan to start a business or keep one going.[5]

The United States has a long history of efforts to make capital and financial services available to people on the economic margins. Benjamin Franklin—the country's first social investor—established revolving loan funds to help poor artisans start businesses. As the Civil War was ending, President Abraham Lincoln signed a bill chartering Freedman's Savings and Trust Company to serve African American war veterans; it grew meteorically, then crashed in 1873. Early in the twentieth century, Edward A. Filene, the Boston department-store magnate and philanthropist, funded a nationwide campaign to organize credit unions for the working class. In the 1960s, the Office of Economic Opportunity fostered hundreds of anti-poverty credit unions; many struggled or failed. In the 1970s, the community reinvestment movement was born, demanding that banks end redlining and racial discrimination. But the problem persisted.

By the 1980s, community activists and a handful of unconventional bankers were forging their own responses. In Chicago, South Shore Bank had pioneered the prototype for a community development bank. Around the country, there were scores of credit unions that served low-income and minority communities, and an emerging group of nonprofit loan funds. These varied institutions were successfully making loans that conventional banks shunned as impossible or simply unprofitable. They might have remained an interesting but obscure footnote if not for the convergence of multiple economic, social, and political events.

From the mid-1980s, hundreds of savings and loan associations (S&Ls) failed, many because of speculative lending and fraud that was facilitated by deregulation earlier in the decade. Bailing them out cost the federal government more than $100 billion and eroded faith in conventional financial

## Introduction

institutions. In 1988, mainstream banking suffered another blow, when "The Color of Money," a Pulitzer Prize–winning series of newspaper articles in the *Atlanta Constitution-Journal*, documented systematic racial discrimination in lending. In Congress, momentum grew for some sort of legislation to address financial discrimination and inequality, especially in the nation's cities. If further motivation was needed, it came on April 29, 1992, when South Central Los Angeles exploded in days of violence following the acquittal of police officers whose brutal beating of motorist Rodney King was captured on home video and went viral worldwide. Urban America was in trouble.

So, when the grassroots lending organizations that would become known as community development financial institutions (CDFIs) brought their stories to Congress, they found a receptive audience. They testified about loans to sharecropper families in Mississippi; loans to start a laundromat in a desolate neighborhood of Camden, NJ; and loans to fishing cooperatives in Maine. These community lenders did all this and more, with loss rates—miraculously!—of about 1 percent. Equally impressive to some legislators, South Shore Bank was making a profit. On October 28, 1992, less than two weeks before the election, President Bush quietly signed into law a modest pilot program to foster community development banks.

Bill Clinton had a bigger vision for community development banking, which he promoted tirelessly in his campaign stops in 1992, reaching popular audiences through an interview in *Rolling Stone* magazine, on the Arsenio Hall television show (where he also played his saxophone), and on MTV in a televised dialogue with young voters. As governor of Arkansas, he had learned about South Shore Bank from its founders. He met Muhammad Yunus—founder of the Grameen Bank, the microlender for the poor in Bangladesh—who, Clinton declared, "should get a Nobel Prize" (which Yunus later did, in 2006). Governor and Mrs. Clinton helped establish the country's first rural community development bank in Arkansas. Clinton visited South Central Los Angeles after the riots in April and saw for himself how check-cashers far outnumbered bank branches. On November 8, he was elected president, and his transition team began the work of translating Clinton's inspiring but still vague vision into reality.

Shortly after the inauguration, President Clinton created two top-level advisory bodies, the National Economic Council and the Domestic Policy Council. They formed a task force to develop legislative options for a new community development banking fund, consulting with the range of stakeholders: CDFIs themselves, now formalized in a national coalition, community reinvestment advocates, mainstream bankers, and congressional allies. Finally, on the morning of July 15, the White House invited these constituents to the Rose Garden for the announcement of its community development banking bill. The president listened delightedly to the stories of "unbankable" CDFI loans: to a worker-owned textile factory in rural North Carolina; to a Ben and Jerry's ice cream franchise employing shelter residents in Harlem; and to a single mother who purchased a stable in Ohio thanks to a microenterprise loan. Their inspiring stories were followed by enthusiastic endorsements from South Shore Bank's cofounder; the CEO of giant NationsBank; and the chairman of the National Community Reinvestment Coalition. "I've never seen so much horsepower behind a banking bill," commented a bank lobbyist."[6] *American Banker* noted that "the sheer magnitude of the ceremony on the White House's south lawn, which ran for nearly an hour, indicated the administration and congressional leaders want to move the package through quickly and without amendments."

It did not move quickly, nor did it escape amendments. But in a ceremony on September 23, 1994, President Clinton signed into law the Community Development Financial Institutions Fund. It was, he declared, his dream fulfilled. It was also a decade-long dream of the grassroots community development financial institutions. Instead of disbursing funding for specified programs, the federal government, for the first time, would be providing capital to help build autonomous *institutions*. The CDFI Fund would supply *equity*—capital grants and investments to enable the emerging CDFIs to build their own balance sheets, make their own lending and investment decisions, and leverage private-sector support.

Seven weeks later, a political tidal wave threatened Clinton's dream. In the mid-term elections on November 8, 1994, Rep. Newt Gingrich's "Republican Revolution" scored a huge victory, winning control of both houses of Congress. Over the next two years, with Gingrich as Speaker of the House, the new majority in Congress repeatedly slashed domestic programs, including the CDFI Fund. The federal government was shut down twice. The Whitewater investigations of alleged Clinton misdeeds in an Arkansas land deal exacerbated the partisan divide. However, Clinton's unswerving support helped the new CDFI Fund, which finally opened for applications in October 1995 and made its first awards the following July.

In the CDFI Fund's first round, 32 of the 268 applicants were chosen to receive $37 million. Among these were banks incubated by South Shore Bank; credit unions from the South Bronx to the Navajo reservation; a venture fund creating jobs in Appalachia; funds serving Latino microenterprises; and loan funds financing affordable housing and nonprofit organizations from Maine to Alaska. Their collective assets barely amounted to a rounding error in the financial universe. Even South Shore Bank was no more than a modest-sized community bank. Many CDFIs had begun around kitchen tables or in church basements, often founded by social activists rather than financial experts. With a few notable exceptions, their seed capital came from the retirement funds of communities of nuns, from community organizing drives, from the occasional foundation grant, and—in the case of credit unions—from the collective savings of the residents of low-income communities.

Scarcely had the CDFI Fund disbursed its first awards when a congressional investigation threatened its future. In 1997, a House of Representatives subcommittee seized on operational deficiencies and missteps in the fund's startup procedures to attack it as an alleged "slush fund" for Clinton's cronies, such as the Southern Development Bank of Arkansas. No corruption was found, but the Treasury Department admitted to some shortcomings, and the first leadership team of the CDFI Fund resigned.

After its early crisis, the CDFI Fund operated free of any hint of scandal, abuse, or waste—no small accomplishment for a federal agency. Except for a short-lived, unsuccessful effort by the Bush administration to virtually eliminate the CDFI Fund in 2005 amid a broader attack on community development programs, the fund faced no serious threats. It expanded the size and scope of its programs, especially through the New Markets Tax Credit Program, created in the final days of the

## Introduction

Clinton administration, the Native American CDFI program, and later the Healthy Food Financing Initiative, the Capital Magnet program, and the CDFI Bond program. "CDFI" became the most valued brand in community development; armed with the Treasury Department's official certification, CDFIs gained access to other federal and state programs, foundation funding, and social investment. During the Obama administration and in the context of the Great Recession, the CDFI Fund received the largest appropriations in its history. By 2017, the CDFI Fund counted more than a thousand certified institutions with combined assets of more than $130 billion.

\* \* \*

At a ceremony in 2014 marking the twentieth anniversary of the CDFI Fund, Gene Sperling, a senior adviser of President Clinton and later President Obama, reflected: "CDFI was a minor story when it passed, but look now: a thousand CDFIs. Look at the role the CDFIs play and the stability role they played during the crisis, when other banks did far worse: the over-$2 billion given out, the multiples of the loans, the lives that are changed because of that."

In many ways, the CDFI initiative is one of the great domestic policy success stories of the past half-century. At a relatively modest cost in federal appropriations, CDFIs have financed hundreds of thousands of units of affordable housing, as well as child care centers, primary care clinics, community facilities, and fresh-food outlets in "food deserts." The CDFI Fund made it possible for Native American communities to establish financial institutions that they, themselves, owned and controlled. Some CDFIs that began in spare rooms or borrowed spaces now boast assets of hundreds of millions of dollars and have done deals in the tens of millions of dollars; aggregate assets of CDFIs are now estimated to be as much as $130 billion. Although the Great Recession took a toll, many CDFIs continued to provide credit where mainstream banks did not.

Yet, success has not come in quite the shape that Clinton envisioned when he called for creating a sustainable, self-sufficient network of community development banks. As one presidential adviser recalled, "What the President had in mind was full-service [institutions]. It wasn't just about investment, it was also about credit, and it was about banking services, because we were heavily focused on the unbanked. That was a big deal for us. We wanted more people to have access to banking services."[7] In a 1997 speech celebrating microenterprise funds, First Lady Hillary Clinton, a longtime supporter of the CDFI initiative, shared her vision of a reinvigorated, locally oriented banking system: "What I would like to see is five [or] 10 years from now, [is] community banks that are free-standing private banks…back in neighborhoods, back on street corners—banks like I used to remember when I was growing up, with people being able, with advances in technology, to get small loans again."[8]

The CDFI Fund has not revived that era, reminiscent of its nostalgic portrayal in the iconic film *It's a Wonderful Life*. Rather, the past 20 years have seen the numbers of banks and credit unions each reduced by more than half; African American–owned institutions have been especially hard hit. Payday lenders charging 300 percent or more on short-term loans have become a multi-billion-dollar industry. The Great Recession brought a massive wave of home foreclosures, swelled by subprime lending, securitization, and "robosigning" of documents that forced people from their homes. Occupy Wall Street erupted in fall 2011 as an outraged response to a financial system favoring the "1 percent"; a million or more customers moved their funds from big banks to local banks and credit unions. Trillion-dollar banks have been fined billions of dollars by the Consumer Financial Protection Bureau for opening millions of phony accounts, selling unwanted services, and other abuses.

As a policy, "community development banking" has been more successful in advancing community development than banking. It would be unrealistic to expect the CDFI Fund to transform the banking universe; it has neither the capacity nor the congressional mandate to do so. Yet, more could have been done, and still may be done. Over the first 20 years of the CDFI Fund, an average of only 20 percent of its grants and investments went to regulated depositories—banks and credit unions; some 80 percent went to loan funds, primarily nonprofits. This was not the outcome the original legislation envisioned. The loan funds have been leaders in financing housing and community development projects; however, they are generally not providers of retail financial services to households, including reasonably priced small loans and savings accounts. The problem is acute: Tens of millions of people remain unbanked or underbanked and depend on high-cost predatory lenders. The asset or wealth gap between white Americans and minorities, always large, grew further because of the Great Recession. The Federal Reserve estimates that half of Americans would be unable to come up with $400 to pay for an emergency without borrowing; two-thirds of black and Latino households lack sufficient savings to fund a poverty-level budget for three months if their income is disrupted. Among CDFIs, credit unions and banks are the best positioned to address these gaps, both to facilitate savings and to provide emergency small loans at a reasonable cost. The CDFI Fund can play an important role in furthering this work.

It will be challenging. In the past 20 years, few new banks and credit unions with the primary mission of community development have been formed. The financial and legal entry barriers for starting banks and credit unions of any kind are formidable, and the challenges are doubly hard for minority and community development institutions. But there are encouraging signs that the CDFI field may be able to expand its impact. Although there has not been a surge of newly chartered mission-driven banks and credit unions, scores of existing institutions, including some serving hundreds of thousands of customers, have obtained CDFI certification, offering the prospect of reaching greater scale than the field has ever achieved.

In 2017–18, there were encouraging signs that the CDFI Fund may remain an important part of the political landscape. Despite a Trump administration budget calling for the virtual elimination of the CDFI Fund and many other domestic programs, the CDFI Fund repeatedly demonstrated strong bipartisan congressional support, winning appropriations at or near its historic highs. After two decades, community development finance has proven itself. The CDFI Fund's prospects for survival are not guaranteed. But there are grounds for hope.

# LIST OF ACRONYMS

| | |
|---|---|
| AEO | Association for Enterprise Opportunity |
| BEA | Bank Enterprise Act |
| CCB | Community Capital Bank |
| CDB | Community development bank |
| CDBA | Community Development Bankers Association |
| CDC | Community development corporation |
| CDCI | Community Development Capital Initiative |
| CDCU | Community development credit union |
| CDFI | Community development financial institution |
| CDRLF | Community development revolving loan fund |
| CDVCA | Community Development Venture Capital Alliance |
| CFA | Consumer Federation of America |
| CRA | Community Reinvestment Act |
| CU | Credit union |
| CUNA | Credit Union National Association |
| CUNEB | Credit Union National Extension Bureau |
| DPC | Domestic Policy Council |
| FCU | Federal credit union |
| FDIC | Federal Deposit Insurance Corporation |
| GAO | Government Accountability Office |
| LIHF | Low Income Housing Fund |
| LIIF | Low Income Investment Fund |
| LISC | Local Initiatives Support Corporation |
| NACDLF | National Association of Community Development Loan Funds (later NCCA) |
| NAFCU | National Association of Federal Credit Unions |
| NCCA | National Community Capital Association (later OFN) |
| NCCB | National Consumer Cooperative Bank |
| NCCED | National Congress for Community Economic Development |
| NCIF | National Community Investment Fund |

| | |
|---|---|
| NCRC | National Community Reinvestment Coalition |
| NCUA | National Credit Union Administration (federal regulator) |
| NEC | National Economic Council |
| NFCDCU | National Federation of Community Development Credit Unions |
| OEO | Office of Economic Opportunity |
| OFN | Opportunity Finance Network |
| PRI | Program-Related Investment |

# PART I. Prologue

From the earliest days of the republic, the United States has wrestled with the problem of providing access to capital to people on the economic margins. The lineage of community development banking can be traced as far back as Benjamin Franklin, the country's first social investor, who endowed revolving loan funds to help young artisans start businesses. It runs through the well-intended and rapidly doomed Freedman's Savings and Trust Company, created by Congress in the last days of the Civil War to serve emancipated African American veterans. By the first decades of the twentieth century, a movement of financial cooperatives—credit unions—spread rapidly among the working class, who were otherwise prey to usurers.

Philanthropy, federal intervention, and self-help—these were the strains that, singly and in combination, produced successive efforts to address financial exclusion over more than two centuries. Their successes and failures alike help to illuminate the challenges and responses of the contemporary community development financial institutions (CDFI) movement.

# CHAPTER 1. Franklin, Freedman's, Filene

## Philanthropy: The Patron Saint of Microenterprise Lending

Benjamin Franklin died rich and famous. The tenth son of a Boston soap maker, equipped with little formal education, he apprenticed as a printer, established multiple businesses, and by the age of 42 was wealthy enough to retire from business for good, pursuing his interests in science, international diplomacy, and more. *Poor Richard's Almanack,* which he first published in 1732, made him famous throughout the country and beyond, with its admonitions to live frugally. He died on April 17, 1790, at the age of 84. Twenty-thousand people attended his funeral.

"A penny saved is a penny earned"—Franklin's didactically immortal advice—pointed the way to one form of capital accumulation. But thrift was not enough to provide startup and working capital for aspiring entrepreneurs of the working class, born and raised—like Franklin—without the advantage of family wealth. Although Franklin warned against the potential dangers of excessive borrowing—especially caused by living beyond one's means—he recognized the need for prudent and productive debt. A year before his death, he prepared a codicil to his will dated June 23, 1789.

> I have considered that, among artisans, good apprentices are most likely to make good citizens, and having myself been bred to a manual art, printing, in my native town, and afterwards assisted to set up my business in Philadelphia by kind loans of money from two friends there, in which was the foundation of my fortune, and of all the utility in life that may be ascribed to me, I wish to be useful even after my death, if possible, in forming and advancing other young men, that may be serviceable to their country in both of these towns. To this end, I devote two thousand pounds sterling, of which I give one thousand thereof to the inhabitants of the town of Boston, in Massachusetts, and the other thousands to the inhabitants of the city of Philadelphia, in trust, and for the uses, intents, and purposes hereinafter mentioned and declared.[9]

Specifically, Franklin's "intents and purposes" were to establish loan funds for aspiring artisans of limited means as he had been. The beneficiaries would be "young married artificers, under the age of twenty-five years, as have served an apprenticeship." The outcome would not only be broader prosperity, but engaged citizens, "serviceable to their country."

Franklin, as the Ford Foundation has noted, "was probably America's first social investor."[10] He was an early proponent of "philanthropy at 5 percent," a concept that became popular at the end of the nineteenth century (for example, through Cecil Rhodes)—and resonated in the Program-Related Investment (PRI) approach of late-twentieth-century foundations. Notwithstanding Franklin's warm concern for the success of young artisans without means, he did not propose to provide them with grants. Rather, they were to receive loans—regardless of extent of need—at an interest rate of 5 percent per annum.

## Peer Group Lending

The poor and the near-poor—then and now—had little collateral to induce a lender to make a loan. Franklin's revolving loan funds would rely on character references and guarantors. Applicants were obliged to

> obtain a good moral character [reference] from at least two respectable citizens, who are willing to become their sureties, in a bond with the applicants, for the repayment of moneys so lent, with interest, according to the terms hereinafter prescribed; all which bonds are to be taken for Spanish milled dollars or the value thereof in current gold coin.[11]

In the centuries before credit reports, and in much of the world today, "character-based" lending in its various forms was the only way that the poor and working classes could obtain credit. It was true of credit unions (as described in the next section), and it is true today of peer-group lenders, such as the Grameen Bank in Bangladesh, which formalized the concept by establishing groups of five women who would be responsible collectively for the repayment of loans taken by any of their members.

## Impact and Sustainability

How best to allocate resources and achieve significant, lasting impact? Franklin wanted to serve as broad a target community as possible—but knew that spreading funds too thinly would give borrowers just enough to fail. He sought to balance scale and impact by specifying both maximum and minimum loan amounts. Loans were

> not to exceed sixty pounds sterling to one person, nor to be less than fifteen pounds; and if the number of appliers so entitled should be so large as that the sum will

not suffice to afford to each as much as might otherwise not be improper, the proportion to each shall be diminished so as to afford to every one some assistance.[12]

Thus, if demand outstripped supply, Franklin decided that more, but smaller, loans would maximize impact.

At first glance, Franklin's "business plan" for his loan funds seems to be deficient or overoptimistic in failing to build in parameters for a loan-loss reserve. But Franklin laid out very specific long-term projections for the sustainability of the funds in Boston and Philadelphia, based on the repayment of principal and lending at the annual 5 percent rate. His horizon was two hundred years: "If this plan is executed, and succeeds as projected without interruption for one hundred years, the sum will then be one hundred and thirty-one thousand pounds." At that point, by the late nineteenth century, he instructed that of this projected sum, 100,000 pounds were to be invested in Boston by the fund managers

> in public works, which may be judged of most general utility to the inhabitants, such as fortifications, bridges, aqueducts, public buildings, baths, pavement, or whatever may make living in the town more convenient to its people.... The remaining thirty-one thousand pounds I would have continued to be let out on interest, in the manner above directed, for another hundred years.... At the end of this second term, if no unfortunate accident has prevented the operation, the sum will be *four millions and sixty one thousand pounds sterling*" [emphasis added].[13]

Thus, for Franklin, sustainability meant more than the continued viability of the revolving loan fund: It encompassed a foresighted concern for the urban infrastructure and environment. It was equally evident in his instructions for his hometown of Philadelphia, which was also to receive a one-thousand-pound seed-money bequest: "At the end of the first hundred years, if not done before, the corporation of the city [shall] Employ a part of the hundred thousand pounds in bringing, by pipes, the water of the Wissahickon Creek into the town."

Were his projections of a 100- or 200-year sustainable revolving loan fund simply fanciful, neglecting the likelihood of poor performance or default by the apprentice-borrowers? In fact, as Franklin's biographer Walter Isaacson writes, the value of Franklin's original bequest to Boston grew in one hundred years to about $400,000, which funded purposes of which Franklin would have approved: "A trade school, Franklin Union (now the Benjamin Franklin Institute of Technology), was founded with three-fourths of the money plus a matching bequest from Andrew Carnegie..."[14]

In the hundred-year picture, Philadelphia seemed to have done less well than Boston: only $172,000 remained. Somewhat defensively, one Philadelphian claimed that his city had more closely followed Franklin's wishes: In contrast with Boston, which had turned its fund into "a savings company for the rich," Philadelphia had focused its lending on poor applicants, and "had not been as successful in getting repayments."[15]

In any case, Franklin's philanthropy had a lasting, prominent effect in Philadelphia. Three-fourths of the sum went to the Franklin Institute, Philadelphia's science museum, "with the remainder continued as a loan fund for young tradesmen, much of it given as home mortgages. A century later, in 1990, this fund had reached $2.3 million."[16] Here, too, the money was used in a way that likely would have pleased Franklin. Under Philadelphia's mayor Wilson Goode, a portion of the corpus went to Philadelphia Academies for scholarships at vocational training programs in city schools—probably as close to the apprenticeships of Franklin's day as could be imagined.

## Federal Intervention: The Civil War and Black Banking

Slavery denied African Americans the chance to accumulate capital in the formal financial system. Mutual self-help was the only recourse. Research has established that many West African societies had mutual savings arrangements in which members made regular payments into a common treasury, withdrawing funds when needed to pay for funeral, ceremonial, and other expenses.*[17] As early as 1693, mutual aid groups appeared among African Americans, as noted by Cotton Mather, and by 1780, the African Union Society was established in Newport, RI. The first black insurance company, the African Insurance Company, was founded in Philadelphia in 1810, and in 1855, the National Negro Convention in New York explored but did not implement a revolving savings and loan proposal. In 1859, African Americans established the Saving Fund and Land Association in California.[18]

The Civil War prompted the federal government to develop banking institutions for the newly emancipated slaves. The Union army made the first efforts in 1864: Union generals established savings banks in Beaumont, SC; in Norfolk, VA; and in Louisiana, the "Free Labor Bank." These banks were extensions of the Freedmen's Bureau, which had broad governmental powers over the civilian population. The military banks were, quite clearly, government-owned and government-controlled institutions. They were crucially different from the efforts that followed.

In January 1865, the abolitionist minister John W. Alvord convened a group of 20 philanthropists and businesspeople in New York to develop a plan for a new bank with national reach. The initial market was black soldiers: They had cash in the form of back pay and bonuses for serving in the Union armies, but with no place to safely deposit their funds, they were vulnerable to swindles, which were widespread. The Alvord group's plans rapidly advanced with the assistance of Senator

---

\* Rotating savings and credit associations (ROSCAs) exist today in various forms among many immigrant groups; for example, the *su su* is common among certain Caribbean immigrants in the United States. The savings in these institutions have been recognized by some banks in qualifying potential borrowers for mortgages.

Charles Sumner of Massachusetts. On February 13, 1865, a bill was introduced in Congress; three weeks later, on March 3, President Lincoln signed "An Act to Incorporate the Freedman's Savings and Trust Company."[19]

Freedman's Savings and Trust Company (often referred to as Freedman's Bank[20]) was chartered by the United States Congress—but in fact, it was privately owned, and Congress viewed it as a philanthropic effort. The federal government retained the right to examine the bank's books. Fifty trustees were charged with oversight, and ownership resembled a depositor-owned mutual institution. Whites controlled it, and initially, few blacks were employed, although this changed later.

The bank grew explosively. Originally headquartered in New York City, it later moved to Washington, DC From 1865 until 1871, branches were organized in Richmond, Charleston, Savannah, New Orleans, Vicksburg, Houston, and elsewhere—in total, more than 30 branches in 17 states and the District of Columbia. It has been estimated that in its brief existence, some 70,000 depositors opened and closed accounts in the bank, which amassed more than $57 million.[21] The gatherings where black veterans received their back wages or bonuses were a prime marketing opportunity for the bank. But the depositor base spread far beyond veterans, including African Americans from every trade and walk of life; schoolchildren as well were encouraged to open accounts with a nickel or even a quarter.

Depositors were issued passbooks, some inscribed with moral instructions "on temperance, frugality, economy, chastity, the virtues of thrift and savings." More problematic, some passbooks carried images of President Lincoln and other high federal officials, giving the impression of government backing for the bank. This misconception was compounded by the illiteracy of many depositors and the promotional meetings that stressed Congress's role in creating the bank. "It is certain," Frederick Douglass wrote, "that the depositors in this institution were led to believe that as Congress had chartered it and established its headquarters at the capital, the government in some way was responsible for the safe keeping of their money."[22]

*Passbook for Freedman's Savings and Trust. Courtesy of Federal Reserve Bank of Cleveland.*

Freedman's Savings and Trust was chartered as a vehicle for saving—capital accumulation, not credit. But a charter change in 1870 allowed the bank to enter real estate lending. Disaster followed. Precious little of the loans flowed to African American depositors: Instead, "white managers often misused funds, including borrowing funds from the bank and not repaying them."[23] The impact of fraud, abuse, and speculation was multiplied by the Panic of 1873, which produced a liquidity crisis for the bank. As the commission charged with closing down the bank observed, "The panic which has just passed over the land has had much to do with this large reduction of deposits."[24]

By March 1874, the bank was in desperate straits. It solicited Frederick Douglass to become its president, a source of no small pride for him: "I could not help reflecting on the contrast between Frederick the slave boy… and Frederick—president of a bank counting its assets by millions."[25] He was impressed by his fellow trustees and overwhelmed by the grandeur of the bank's office in Washington near the Treasury Building: "They accordingly erected on one of the most desirable and expensive sites in the national capital, one of the most costly and splendid buildings of the time," furnished with marble, black walnut, and other expensive fittings. He saw "the row of its gentlemanly and elegantly dressed colored clerks, with their pens behind their ears and buttonhole bouquets in their coat-fronts, and felt my very eyes enriched.... The whole thing was beautiful.... I felt like the Queen of Sheba when she saw the riches of Solomon."[26]

*Frederick Douglass. Brady-Handy photograph collection, Library of Congress.*

He would soon come to regret his awestruck reaction. "The more I observed and learned the more my confidence diminished." He found discrepancies in the books and evidence of dishonesty of employees. The reserves he was told the bank enjoyed had evaporated. "I was, in six weeks after my election as president of this bank, convinced that it was no longer a safe custodian of the hard earnings of my confiding people." In vain, he loaned the bank $10,000 of his own money to buttress confidence in the bank. But when he testified to Congress about the bank's dire situation, his fellow trustees—even those who agreed with him—contradicted his assertions. These same trustees who preached confidence in the bank "had themselves not one dollar deposited there."[27] Humiliated by his experience, Douglass had come to realize that he had been brought in to raise the dead.

> The fact is, and all investigation shows it, that I was married to a corpse. The fine building, with its marble counters and black walnut finishings, was there, as were the affable and agile clerks and the discreet and colored cashiers but the life, which was the money, was gone, and I found that I had been placed there with the hope that by 'some drugs, some charms, some conjuration, or some mighty magic,' I would bring it back.[28]

He did not. He could not. Congress gave credence to his testimony, and on June 20, 1874, it passed an act directing the appointment of commissioners to close the bank.[29]

Closing Freedman's Savings and Trust took months. The commission audited every branch, finding discrepancies and bad bookkeeping in many, and finding liens filed against their assets. "It is doubtful," the commission reported, "whether we shall ever be able to obtain an absolutely correct statement of the liabilities and assets of the company." By the end of the year, some 72,000 accounts were still open; verifying balances by examining the passbooks would be a colossal job.[30]

Closing the branches was a painful process, as depositors feared they would no longer have recourse to their funds: "The appeals and remonstrances addressed to us against closing the branches have been of the most importunate and decided character, and have been made principally on behalf of the poorer and more ignorant classes of our depositors…Sympathizing with them, and knowing their anxieties, and how readily they would fall an easy prey to designing men," the commission empowered modestly paid agents to be available to respond to their concerns.[31]

As bad as the damage was for individuals, it also affected churches, private businesses, and beneficial societies that both maintained accounts there and urged their members and customers to do so as well. The collapse of the bank inflicted great damage to these pillars of black society: "When the Freedman's Bank closed…many of these institutions, particularly the churches and beneficial societies, had to suspend or drastically curtail vital services, thus adding to the social and economic woes of the African American community."[32]

The unwinding of the bank took decades. The bank continued to pay dividends, and half of the depositors eventually received about three-fifths of the value of their accounts. For those depositors with passbooks and for whom bank records provided verification, reclaiming a portion of their funds was relatively straightforward. But for depositors without passbooks, or their relatives or heirs, the process was more difficult. The commission lamented, "We shall be ignorant of the address of depositors; most of them being unable to read, it will be impossible to notify them of the payment of dividends, and thousands of them, if payments are to be made by checks, will find it impracticable to identify themselves in the ordinary manner."[33] Some depositors got nothing. For more than 30 years, they and their descendants petitioned Congress to make good their losses.[34]

## More Than a Bank: The Costs of Failure

The astonishing growth of the Freedman's bank, patronized by formerly enslaved African Americans, powerfully demonstrated their hunger for financial access. With prudent, honest management, adequate infrastructure, and a favorable economy, Freedman's Savings and Trust might well have succeeded. But after it gained lending powers in 1870, Freedman's incurred losses on loans made with insufficient or nonexistent security, loans made to insiders, and speculative investments. The beneficent, philanthropic paternalism of some of its trustees was overwhelmed by those interested in personal gain.

"This was an institution designed to furnish a place of security and profit for the hard earnings of the colored people, especially of the South," wrote Frederick Douglass. "According to its managers it was to be this and something more. There was something missionary in its composition, and it dealt largely in exhortations as well as promises…. Their aim was now to instill into the minds of the untutored Africans lessons of sobriety, wisdom, and economy, and to show them how to rise in the world."[35] Douglass felt the very growth of the bank would convey an important message to the country about African Americans and help build respect. In placing his own funds on deposit and later even making a loan to the bank, "it seemed fitting to me to cast in my lot with my brother freedmen and to help build up an institution which represented their thrift and economy to so striking advantage." The more millions in the bank, he thought, "the more consideration and respect would be shown to the colored people of the whole country."[36]

The costs of the bank's failure were enormous—personally, socially, and politically. Frederick Douglass was devastated, and he felt that his reputation had been grievously harmed. He wrote in his autobiography that his connection with the bank "has brought upon my head an amount of abuse and detraction greater than any encountered in any other part of my life."[37] It is hard to imagine a more bitter, anguished post mortem than that written by W. E. B. Du Bois in 1903.

> Morally and practically, the Freedmen's Bank was part of the Freedmen's Bureau, although it had no legal connection with it. With the prestige of the government back of it, and a directing board of unusual respectability and national reputation, this banking institution had made a remarkable start in the development of that thrift among black folk which slavery had kept them from knowing. Then in one sad day came the crash—all the hard-earned dollars of the freedmen disappeared; but that was the least of loss—all the faith in saving went too, and much of the faith in men; and that was a loss that a Nation which to-day sneers at Negro shiftlessness has never yet made good. Not even ten additional years of slavery could have done so much to throttle the thrift of the freedmen as the mismanagement and bankruptcy of the series of savings banks chartered by the Nation for their especial aid. Where all the blame should rest, it is hard to say; whether the Bureau and the Bank died chiefly by reason of the blow of its selfish friends or the dark machinations of its foes, perhaps even time will never reveal, for here lies unwritten history.[38]

Freedman's Savings and Trust was not a government entity—nor was it *not* a government entity. Chartered by Congress and adorned with the likenesses of President Lincoln, well-known generals, and other "friends" of African Americans, it hinted at governmental endorsement; indeed, it was chartered by the Congress of the United States of America. The bank was designed by white men and, with the brief exception of Frederick Douglass's presidency in 1874, entirely governed by white men. It did have "colored" employees, and moreover, advisory boards in some branches: As an audit of the Richmond, Virginia, branch reported, "They have what is called an advisory board of colored men of the better classes, to whom all questions of interest are submitted, and these men evidently take a deep interest in the welfare of the institution, and promote, in every way, the habits of saving on the part of their people."

---

\* "Report of the Commissioners," 64, by Chas. A. Meigs, National-Bank Examiner. The various summaries of branch audits that the commission submitted to Congress frequently comment in detail about the racial makeup and respective compensation of staff, both the cashiers (generally white) and the clerks and other staff (often, African American), who were generally lower paid. One report on the Louisville, KY, branch by an examiner begins by contemplating the racial characteristics of the cashier, whose competence he commended: "The cashier, Horace Morris, is by birth slightly mixed with African blood, but I should not have known it if I had not been informed: he is as white as I am, with a head of good brown hair, without a kink. He is intelligent, a good penman, and correct accountant" (69).

## Freedman's and Freedom

Banks fail; minority banks face heightened challenges, and they have often failed disproportionately. The loss of a minority bank, conceived in hope and promise, is always especially difficult. The failure of Freedman's bank was more than a business failure. For African Americans, it was a repudiation of the belief that thrift would be rewarded. Faith in the federal government was not vindicated. "An idea that began as a well-meaning experiment in philanthropy had turned into an economic nightmare for tens of thousands of African Americans who had entrusted their hard-earned money to the bank."[39] Perhaps the most poignant and dramatic echo of Freedman's failure was the closure of New York City's Freedom National Bank in 1990, whose depositors faced the loss of precious funds because of an erroneous belief that the federal insurance fund would protect them.[*]

## Populism, Fueled by Philanthropy: Credit Unions

The most extensive movement to bring capital access to the working class of America owed its inspiration to nineteenth-century cooperatives in England, credit unions in Germany, village banks in India, and most immediately, a court stenographer in Quebec.

The first, enduring principles of cooperativism were articulated in England by the weavers of the Rochdale Society of Equitable Pioneers, who formed a cooperative store in England in 1844, although practical experiments date even earlier, to the New Lanark community founded by Robert Owen, the utopian socialist.[†] On the continent, credit associations and cooperatives began to emerge at the end of the 1840s, both in urban areas and among poor farmers. By 1859, there were 183 "people's banks" in Germany with 18,000 members.[40] These German institutions attracted attention and replication elsewhere in Europe. In 1866, Luigi Luzzatti, who had studied them in Germany, started the first

---

[*] Freedom National Bank was cofounded in 1964 by baseball legend Jackie Robinson. It served a local market, but in a sense, it was a national institution based in Harlem—the "Main Street" of black America. Nationally, the demise of Freedom struck a sharp blow to African American pride. Freedom—like Freedman's— held the deposits not only of individuals, but also of numerous churches, nonprofits, and charitable organizations. Some held substantial deposits over the insured limit spread out over multiple accounts, in the mistaken belief that the federal government would cover their funds. For months, their claims for reimbursement were denied, as the FDIC followed its established policy and steadfastly refused to return the uninsured excess funds of Harlem institutional and business depositors. Finally, after months of intense advocacy, special legislation sponsored by New York Senator D'Amato made them whole. In contrast, it took years, even decades, for some depositors in Freedman's Savings and Trust to be made whole, and many never were.

[†] The Rochdale Principles are cited to this day by cooperators in the United States and around the world. Although consumer cooperatives subsequently thrived in Britain, credit unions made little progress until the late twentieth century.

cooperative bank in Milan, Italy.[41] By 1909, the People's Bank of Milan was one of the largest banks in Italy, with 25,000 members and over $32 million in savings.[42]

In the United States, the German successes were enthusiastically noted in numerous scholarly and journalistic works over the last third of the nineteenth century. But no institutions took root until the early twentieth century. The facilitator—and the man whose name the vast, successful Quebec credit union system bears to this day—was Alphonse Desjardins, a court reporter for the Canadian parliament. Through parliamentary hearings to outlaw usury, Desjardins learned that individuals were being charged as much as 1,200 percent on small loans.[43]

Desjardins gathered together a small group of associates, and in December 1900, they adopted a constitution and bylaws for La Caisse Populaire de Levis, to combat usury and help promote economic independence, along with Christian values. The *caisse* opened for business the next month. It grew rapidly, to 840 members, by May.[44] Each member was to purchase at least one five-dollar share, which could be paid on an installment basis of 10 cents weekly, plus an entrance fee. Governance was democratic—one member, one vote—and credit decisions were made by a volunteer credit committee. (In fact, these defining characteristics were largely adopted by the credit union movement that emerged in the United States.)

Desjardins was keenly attuned not only to the liberating economic impact of the *caisse*, but its profound impact on human development.

> The poor people are … brought up to an astonishing level of education so far as economics are concerned. They know what is the nature of capital…. One of the great advantages of cooperation is that it teaches people how to do their own business instead of relying upon a middleman.[45]

La Caisse Populaire de Levis thrived in its early years, showing profits, building reserves, and paying members a 4 percent dividend.[46] The story of its success traveled to New England. On November 22, 1908, at the invitation of Monsignor Pierre Hevey, pastor of the French-Canadian immigrant St. Mary's Church, Desjardins visited Manchester, New Hampshire. The parish promptly organized the St. Mary's Cooperative Credit Association (La Caisse Populaire Ste. Marie), in the absence of any applicable chartering legislation. It was "legalized" on April 6, 1909, through a special act of the New Hampshire legislature, and became known subsequently as St. Mary's Bank.[47] A few days later, on April 15, 1909, Massachusetts passed a credit union law spearheaded by banking commissioner Pierre Jay, who had also met and corresponded with Desjardins.

## Philanthropy Catalyzes Growth

As the building blocks of credit unionism were first being laid, Edward A. Filene provided the indispensable force that made credit unions a mass national movement. The owner of a Boston-based department store, Filene was an enlightened capitalist with a demonstrated concern for employee benefits, which included employee lounges and cafeterias, worker engagement in formulating work rules, paid holidays, and free medical care. Filene "dreamed of someday turning the ownership of the store over to the employees."[48] He was prominent in civic and reformist movements and corresponded with world leaders from Woodrow Wilson, to Gandhi, to Vladimir Lenin.[49]

In 1907, during a trip around the world, he learned about and visited the cooperative movement in the villages of India. He was struck by the widespread poverty and the prevalence of moneylenders who provided credit at exorbitant cost for peasants' agricultural needs and their life rituals. He learned of the Agricultural Cooperative Banks—village associations sponsored by the British government that provided matching capital to be re-lent to members. When Filene returned to the United States in 1908, he corresponded with President Theodore Roosevelt, describing the Indian cooperative credit system and urging that something similar be promoted by the United States in the Philippines.[50] He became acquainted with Desjardins and began thinking about credit unions in a broader cooperative context.

Desjardins aided and inspired the organizing of handfuls of credit unions in the Northeast, but credit union progress was halting, and Filene's own involvement was limited until he joined with other prominent Bostonians to form the Massachusetts Credit Union (MCU) in January 1914.[51] It made its first, tentative efforts to expand the credit union movement nationally in May that year in a presentation to the National Conference on Jewish Charities in Memphis.[52] Jacob de Haas, representing the MCU, met and spoke with a representative of Julius Rosenwald, the prominent philanthropist and president of Sears Roebuck, and later "with leaders of the Southern Sociological Convention to consider the possible use of credit unions among southern Negroes."[53] However, no specific strategy emerged from this meeting.

Meanwhile, the recently established (1907) Russell Sage Foundation in New York City began to address the issue of access to affordable credit. It designed legislation attacking predatory lending nationally and worked in New York on a state credit union law. There its legislative efforts linked with those of New York State Senator Franklin D. Roosevelt, who sponsored a law for the creation of agricultural credit unions.[54]

## Going Viral

In these early years, credit unions appeared to be an idea whose time had come. Credit unions began to spring up almost spontaneously, so readily that a Sage Foundation researcher concluded "one or two experienced organizers could succeed in a comparatively brief period in bringing about the organization of a substantial number of credit unions."[55] There were, in fact, other financial institutions, such as cooperative societies and savings banks in Massachusetts, but they did not reach down into the lowest income groups. Massachusetts Governor David I. Walsh noted in a speech in 1915 that "every banking door in the Commonwealth is barred to the man who wants to borrow $25 without security. That's the greatest thing about this [credit union] movement, it reaches a class the banks cannot reach. It will help all."[56]

*Dane County (WI) Farmers Equity Union Coop Credit Union. Courtesy of CUNA Mutual Archives.*

Despite these enthusiastic beginnings, growth was helter-skelter, with new credit unions rapidly forming and others liquidating when they could not achieve a solid footing. Neither their accounting practices or even interest calculation was standardized.[57] Filene was dissatisfied with the new movement's progress and took steps along with other Boston supporters to develop a broader, more systematic strategy, first in Massachusetts, where they established a state association, and then nationally. In May 1919, Filene invited governors, labor leaders, the eminent historian Charles A. Beard, bank commissioners, Desjardins, and others to help organize a "National Committee on People's Banks." They drafted a bill that year for the organization of "federal people's banks," to be supervised by the Federal Reserve. The bill went nowhere—but the call for creating a central bank or finance facility for popular financial institutions recurred for decades in the credit union movement (where it was ultimately achieved in the 1970s) and even, in concept, among other CDFIs at the turn of the twenty-first century.[58]

The turning point in developing credit unions as a mass national movement came in 1920 when Filene hired a lawyer, Roy F. Bergengren. Bergengren soon was charged with forming and directing the Credit Union National Extension Bureau (CUNEB). He toured the country, attempting to secure local allies to press for state legislation; Filene sometimes joined him. He encountered opposition from installment loan companies, building and loan societies, and some state bankers' associations, although others recognized the value of credit unions as self-help vehicles that would not encroach on their business. Filene did not hesitate to invoke the specter of "Bolshevism," arguing that credit unions and cooperatives would blunt the tendency of the impoverished working class toward socialism—and later, fascism.

Despite the spontaneous enthusiasm for credit unions, an organized national movement would not have developed without Filene's financial support: Organizing and promotion take money. In 1919, Filene started a foundation, initially known as the Cooperative League but later as the Twentieth Century Fund.[59] He provided the entire endowment of the fund, and in 1928 signed over income from his holdings in the Filene department store enterprise. Year after year, the Twentieth Century Fund provided tens of thousands of dollars in operating funds to CUNEB, which both helped organize credit unions and assisted state lobbying efforts. However, Filene and the Twentieth Century Fund engaged in micromanaging to a degree that few contemporary foundations would be comfortable with: It became all but an annual ritual for Filene to reject Bergengren's growing budget and salary requests.

Filene also took issue with Bergengren's strategies and tactics. Bergengren, for example, was very concerned about the plight of small farmers in the South, whom he regarded as needing credit unions more than any other group, but Filene rejected this emphasis in 1924.[60] Bergengren and Filene often were at odds about whether and how to focus on federal credit union legislation. Nonetheless, by the time he died in 1937, Filene had spent more than $1 million of his own funds to support credit union organizing.[61]

Despite their differences, CUNEB's organizing efforts were widely successful. By 1930, 32 states had credit union enabling laws, and 1,100 credit unions were functioning.[62] But the Great Depression brought new challenges. Striving to keep up the momentum, in 1933 Filene made a speaking tour throughout the Midwest, where he experienced the quasi-religious fervor that the young credit union movement engendered. An article by a reporter for the Decatur, IL, *Sunday Herald* provided a first-hand account of Filene's speech of January 14 to a crowd of more than 1,000 at the LaSalle Hotel in Chicago:

*Edward A. Filene. Courtesy of America's Credit Union Museum.*

> I have seen a good many demonstrations but nothing that quite equaled that given the founder of the credit union movement in Chicago. It was not the volume of the cheering nor the duration that impressed. It was the spontaneous love of disciple for a master.... There was a spiritual fervor in the attitude of these folks from parishes and farms, from factories and stores, from railroads and shops, towards a man who, for the most part, had been almost a legendary figure in the background of a movement that promises to become a great economic force in this country.[63]

## Toward a National Credit Union System

By 1934, there were 2,500 credit unions operating in 38 states and the District of Columbia. But many states still lacked enabling legislation, and even where credit union chartering laws existed, the constant opposition of installment lenders made for a rocky path for credit unions. Hence, the need for federal legislation, both to make possible nationwide coverage and to provide a possible alternative to state chartering laws.

Over the course of 1933-34, Filene and Bergengren worked to advance federal legislation. Filene, in contrast and opposition to Bergengren, wanted to go further: Specifically, he pressed Washington at the highest level for a federal appropriation of $100,000 to support credit union organizing and loan capital for new credit unions. This effort failed, but on June 26, 1934, President Roosevelt signed the Federal Credit Union Act. He sent one of the signing pens to Filene, who in turn sent it to Bergengren.[64]

Another critical element in the growth of a sustainable national credit union movement was the development of a permanent infrastructure. Some of this work had taken place over the previous 10 or 15 years, as the credit unions in various states formed statewide leagues to advance their interests and provide support for organizing and operations. But the next stage was the establishment of a national association. In August 1934, delegates from 21 states and the District of Columbia met for four days on the grounds of a YMCA conference center in Estes Park, CO, for what became known as the "constitutional convention" of the Credit Union National Association (CUNA). CUNA became the successor of CUNEB, as well as the nucleus of a complex of credit union organizations, including an office supplies corporation and a mutual insurance company.

The Great Depression did not spare credit unions. Like banks, they were shuttered for four days when President Roosevelt declared the nationwide bank holiday of March 6, 1933.* Many credit unions were subsequently dissolved, but liquidations were not as massive as among the banking industry, and few credit union members lost their deposits. The economic devastation continued to spur the organizing of credit unions despite (and in part, because of) the overall distress of the financial system: As of 1935, credit unions numbered 3,600, and 100 new ones a month were forming; by 1938, there were 6,219 credit unions.[65]

## African American Credit Unions

Facing outright segregation in the South and less formalized exclusion in the north, African Americans found in credit unions a desperately needed alternative. As Jessica Gordon Nembhard has written, "The Great Depression probably saw the rise of more African American-owned cooperatives than any

---

\* President Roosevelt's order prevented panicked "runs on the bank"—withdrawals by depositors who feared their savings would be lost if their institutions failed.

other period in United States history."[66] North Carolina was the epicenter of organizing rural credit unions and other cooperatives. By 1939, an African American federation to develop cooperatives was formed, the Eastern Carolina Council; it was aided by the credit union division of the North Carolina Department of Agriculture and its extension service. There were three black credit unions in the state by 1936; by 1948, there were 98.[67]

African American credit unions emerged in the cities of the North as well, primarily among churches and civic associations. The thirties were "a period in history when black men felt themselves reverting to a status of slavery from which they had been emancipated only a few generations ago. The formation of our (Paragon Association) was the answer to this great socio-economic dilemma," wrote Clyde Atwell, a longtime official of the Paragon Federal Credit Union, which was founded by Caribbean immigrants. In the North, African Americans did not have to deal with the legacy of sharecropping, but rather with economic abuses magnified by their racial and cultural status: "Prices were high. Schemes for fleecing the blacks were rampant. Being poor but ambitious, our people were most vulnerable," Atwell wrote. "With an eye of self-preservation some ventured their life savings in the purchase of two-family brownstones. In many instances the intended investment became a misfortune. Being limited in knowledge on matters pertaining to real estate, the homes were soon reclaimed by the very brokers who sold them."[68] It was this dire situation that led to the organizing of the credit union. As a founder of the Paragon Association, the credit union's sponsor, wrote: "July 18, 1939, marks the day the black historians must emphasize as the beginning of the economic emancipation of the blacks in Brooklyn, New York." In Brooklyn's Bedford-Stuyvesant neighborhood, the "Paragon [association] was founded by poor, dejected and deprived people. They were stalled up by poverty. The order of the day was no work, no money, and no hope. Self-sufficiency meant scheming to get one good meal sometime during the day."[69]

## Finance for the Common Good

In Edward Filene's last months, he summed up his view of the role of credit unions in society. Credit unions were

> the schools for the masses so that they may be educated to establish financial democracy for themselves and free their jobs and themselves from the absolute control of those who … are using money solely for their own profit, without the requisite understanding that they have no right to use money except for the common good and social interest of all the people, and that the wholly selfish use of it will bring with it radical movement, revolution and war.[70]

On September 26, 1937, Filene died in the American Hospital in Paris, at the age of 77. Condolence messages came from President Roosevelt, labor leader John L. Lewis, socialist Norman

Thomas, and many other dignitaries. Except for Muhammad Yunus, who would found the Grameen Bank more than 40 years after Filene's death, no single individual in the history of community finance has achieved such prominence.

## "Mission Drift"

As early as the 1940s, credit union leaders began to contemplate whether credit unions had moved away from their original mission of serving the working poor. At a meeting of CUNA's board of directors in 1942, President William Reid remarked with dismay that many credit unions "don't want to be bothered with $50 or $100 loans for remedial purposes. It now means five or ten loans where one was made before to put the same amount of money to work."[71] This criticism was sharpened in the years that followed: In May 1952, a CUNA leader complained to his fellow directors that some credit unions were losing sight of their original purposes:

> They operate as a cross between a bank and a loan company. The members' welfare and benefit is not their chief purpose. This trend has started in many cases because of the bigness of the individual credit union, but mostly it has started because of the turnover in the Boards of Directors of credit unions. We find many credit unions that have none of the original Board left and somehow we have neglected to tell these new directors about the purpose of the credit union movement.[72]

Some CUNA leaders were increasingly concerned about growing economic inequality. Addressing CUNA executive committee members in May 1954, CUNA President H. B. Yates sounded notes that resonate today: "One of the greatest dangers to democracy is the unequal distribution of wealth. The great chasm between the rich and the poor among individuals, as well as nations, causes distrust, dissatisfaction, and trouble." He added, optimistically, "The credit union movement helps to permanently solve this problem of unequal distribution by enabling man to help himself and permanently improve his condition."[73]

During World War II, many small, weak credit unions were liquidated; organizing of new credit unions slowed; and loan demand—the vital source of income for credit unions—diminished because of the scarcity of consumer goods. But the credit union movement continued to grow: By 1955, credit union ranks had nearly doubled to 16,201, with membership reaching 8.1 million; their share of installment credit share in the United States was 6 percent.[74] By 1960, there were 23,761 credit unions with 21 million members. The number of credit unions peaked at around 25,000, and has steadily declined since then, while the membership has grown to more than 100 million with aggregate assets of more than $1.3 trillion.

## Conclusion

In their various ways, these early initiatives foreshadowed the challenges and trajectory of the CDFI movement of the late twentieth century. Capital access for startup businesses, financial exclusion of minorities, usurious credit—these problems persisted despite the country's growing prosperity in the 1950s. As CDFIs tried to develop alternatives to mainstream banks, they, like Benjamin Franklin, wrestled with melding the approaches and values of philanthropy and business: How could they build sustainable lending institutions while serving needy, asset-poor populations? In the 1960s, the federal government would try a top-down approach to expanding financial access—this time, not specifically for formerly enslaved people, like Freedman's Savings and Trust, but more generally for the inner cities and rural poor. Against the odds, African Americans would establish their own banks. In an ironic echo of Freedman's demise, when Freedom National Bank in Harlem failed in 1990, its depositors faced the loss of uninsured funds. As the credit union movement, established to serve the working poor, became increasingly successful, it would face questions of "mission drift," as would the CDFI movement in its third decade; "movement" or "industry"—the same questions recurred.

# PART II. The Roots of Community Development Finance

The War on Poverty in the 1960s produced the broadest, most concerted federal effort to expand financial access to the poor since the Freedman's Savings and Trust Company one hundred years before. The Office of Economic Opportunity (OEO) established community action agencies (CAAs) to deliver and coordinate services for low-income people. In hundreds of these CAAs, the OEO also established credit unions charged with providing credit and financial education. From the outset, this top-down federal effort was hindered by inadequate training and management support, insufficient capital, and the unrealistic expectation that these new institutions would become self-sustaining within three years.

Alongside the CAAs, with their mandate of "maximum feasible participation of the poor," the Ford Foundation and others fostered demonstration projects, such as a promising new entity, the community development corporation (CDC). By the end of the decade, recognizing that foundation grants were too limited to meet the development needs of poverty communities, the Ford Foundation, Taconic Foundation, and several other philanthropies developed a new financial tool: Program-Related Investments (PRIs). The many hard-earned lessons of the Sixties, from the War on Poverty to the new age of philanthropy, all played large roles in the later development and expansion of the CDFI movement.

# CHAPTER 2. The Sixties

## The "Rediscovery" of Poverty

The plight of the poor was not top-of-mind for Americans after World War II. By the 1950s, there was yet another war in Korea, and the "cold war" with the Soviet Union, which brought the threat of nuclear war to every school, as children were instructed to huddle under their desks in the event of an atomic bomb attack. The United States anxiously began a "space race" following the Russian launch of the Sputnik satellite in October 1957. Still, the country as a whole prospered: Consumer goods became more available, and incomes rose—for some households.

Then came *The Other America*. Michael Harrington's book, published in 1962, laid bare the underbelly of growing American prosperity. A year later, David Caplovitz published the seminal book, *The Poor Pay More*, hailed as a "pioneering work… [that] delineated with uncompromising, scientific evidence the brutal economic facts of existence for a group of low-income families in four New York City housing projects."[75] Both books influenced Washington policymakers, including the Assistant Secretary of Labor, Esther Peterson, and found broad readership.[76]

The seeds of the War on Poverty were just being planted in the days before the assassination of President John F. Kennedy on November 22, 1963. On November 19, Kennedy instructed Walter Heller, chairman of the Council of Economic Advisers, to make anti-poverty policy "a major component of his 1964 legislative program."[77] Days after assuming the presidency, President Lyndon B. Johnson directed Heller to proceed with his plans. On January 4, 1964, in Johnson's first State of the Union, he sounded the call for an "unconditional war on poverty."

The War on Poverty moved quickly from rhetoric into reality. On February 1, 1964, Sargent Shriver was named to direct the antipoverty program.[78] By February 24, the hotly contested term "maximum feasible participation" of the poor first appeared in draft legislation. On August 20, the Economic Opportunity Act of 1964 was signed into law.[79] The OEO in Washington would be the general headquarters for the "war."

The OEO funded a network of local CAAs (also called community action programs, or CAPs) to deliver a variety of programs in poor communities. The OEO leadership in Washington saw these "outposts" of the War on Poverty as a means to empower poor communities, the embodiment of "maximum feasible participation" through which the poor would participate in shaping the programs and policies that affected their lives.

That such an approach from Washington would draw right-wing fire was unsurprising. But many big-city Democratic mayors, motivated by self-interest, were also vigorously opposed: OEO funds were designated to bypass municipal governments and instead flow directly to and through the CAP agencies, over which mayors had no control. These CAP agencies were potentially independent power bases for poor and minority communities. Mayoral opposition was clothed in apocalyptic terms. On June 2, 1965, the United States Conference of Mayors debated (but did not adopt) a resolution accusing the OEO of "fostering class struggle."[80]

Notwithstanding the hyperbole, it was true enough that the proponents of the War on Poverty wanted to give voice to poor and minority communities, who were generally marginalized at City Hall. Before long, in the face of political opposition, the Johnson administration beat a reluctant retreat. On September 18, 1965, Budget Director Charles L. Schultze proposed "abandoning the goal of organizing the poor politically." And President Johnson agreed.[81]

This, then, was the context for the birth of the ill-fated OEO credit union initiative.

## Poverty and the Credit Dilemma

Caplovitz's book, *The Poor Pay More*, documented the painful and destructive credit dilemma for low-income inner-city residents. Credit was becoming more widely available in mainstream America, but in inner-cities, it often was supplied by local merchants and door-to-door salesmen peddling inferior merchandise at elevated prices with obscure credit terms. "Because of the diverse and frequently misleading ways in which charges for credit are stated, even the highly-educated consumer has difficulty knowing which set of terms is most economical," Caplovitz observed.[82] Further, he notes, "the system is not only different from the larger, more formal economy; in some respects, it is a *deviant* system in which practices that violate prevailing moral standards are commonplace.... The system is extraordinarily flexible. Almost no one—however great a risk—is turned away."[83]

"Almost no one is turned away"—and so, especially for the most marginal, the cycle of poverty was exacerbated and perpetuated. Caplovitz summarized the dynamic this way.

> Underlying the credit problems of many families is the emergency that sharply curtails income: The breadwinner becomes ill or loses his job; suddenly the family finds that the 'easy payments' are no longer easy. When this happens, they are apt to learn about the complex set of conditions governing their credit transactions.[84]

Caplovitz identified a systemic economic disease, one that would persist, spread, and evolve over the next half-century. The lack of emergency savings among vast sections of the American public has given rise to widespread, predatory "payday lending."[85] Caplovitz asserted that the provision of credit by local merchants was an integral part of a larger financial ecosystem: "Unscrupulous [local] sellers could not exist without the finance companies and banks that buy their paper. These financial institutions must share the blame for the exploitation of the poor, for they know all too well (and if they don't they should) that they are buying dishonestly obtained contracts."[86]

How to address the problems of the poor, especially in urban areas? Better information and consumer education could help people to avoid bad choices in local markets, but that was not enough: Better alternatives were needed to give people real choices. Hence, credit unions, nonprofit organizations that offered reasonable loan rates and emphasized member education, appeared to the OEO as a logical, and possibly cost-effective, federal response. And the existing network of local CAP agencies were viewed as the ideal platform through which to implement that strategy.

Unlike CAP agencies, credit unions did not directly threaten the municipal power structure. Although closely connected with CAP agencies, they were legally separate. They had enemies of their own—especially banks and installment lenders—but their history and ethos of self-help and nonpolitical nature tended to minimize opposition.

## Credit Unions and the Poor

In fact, during the 1960s, the universe of low-income credit unions was broader than the OEO network. In its 1963 annual report, the Bureau of Federal Credit Unions identified more than 400 credit unions "serving groups comprised predominantly of low-income people…. Many others have some low-income people in their fields of membership."[87] The bureau reported that it had "recently increased its effort" to reach low-income groups, working with various governmental and credit union trade organizations in establishing "experimental" credit unions.

In the first decades of the twentieth century, CUNEB carried on a nationwide campaign with missionary zeal to spread the credit union gospel among the working class. But by the 1950s, its successor, CUNA, was growing uneasy with "mission drift," a departure from the earliest principles of voluntarism and self-help, along with misgivings about growing inequality.[88] In 1958, CUNA's directors launched a study of the problems of low-income communities, which was followed by the launch of several demonstration credit unions among the poor. Two such projects were established in 1961, one in Nebraska and another in Texas, among Spanish-speaking low-income communities.[89] In May 1964, under the leadership of CUNA's managing director, Orrin Shipe, a strong advocate of serving the poor, CUNA approved an appropriation of $50,000 to begin demonstration projects in Chicago, Washington, and New York.

The low-income credit unions of that era were barebones, grassroots institutions, some with funding, others purely volunteer. Pete Crear began his long and illustrious career in the credit union movement working in his hometown of Detroit with some of these credit unions as an auditor and a field representative for the Michigan Credit Union League.[90] Crear, an African American, joined the credit union movement fresh out of college, after encountering subtle but unmistakable discrimination when he attempted in vain to use his accounting background in the corporate sector. At night and on the weekends, he visited some of the smallest credit unions, many of which were based in churches. Decades before automation, bookkeeping was sometimes sketchy in these tiny, volunteer-run institutions. He recalls one such credit union recording its transactions on the cardboard sheets that came with laundered shirts. Bank reconciliations were often months out of date, and Crear had to help volunteers laboriously reconstruct and balance the accounts.

Crear recalls a different atmosphere for credit unions based in Detroit's tougher housing projects. The word on the street was "'don't screw with them,' so the gangbangers left the credit union alone. These were cash operations, but nobody screwed with them."[91] Services from these low-income credit unions were basic, but as Crear pointed out, there was "no great outpouring of financial institutions looking for minority customers." Where they could, African Americans borrowed from small loan companies, but "access to credit was fairly well blunted. There was nobody who was looking to serve you. And so, the credit union was a very significant player in those projects."[92]

## The Government/Industry Alliance

The OEO recognized it could not build its CAP agency/credit union system alone. It found allies in the Credit Union National Association and the Bureau of Federal Credit Unions, the federal regulator for the industry.

From 1966, CUNA received a series of OEO contracts to support its work. It had already launched demonstration projects in the minority communities of Chicago—Pilsen Neighbors Federal Credit Union (which was largely Hispanic) and Prairie-Halsted Federated Churches Credit Union (largely African American). CUNA's work became more systematic when it established an Economic Opportunity Department and began to develop a regional infrastructure of training and technical assistance specialists. The OEO extended and expanded its funding of CUNA, reaching a total of $593,000 for the period ending June 30, 1970.[93]

Initially, the Bureau of Federal Credit Unions was optimistic both about the progress of credit unions and its partnership with OEO and CUNA. It highlighted credit unions established in low-income housing projects in New York City: "These credit unions have made satisfactory progress since they were organized in 1963 and 1964, demonstrating that such credit unions can successfully provide financial assistance to low-income people."[94] Notably, the bureau commended credit union efforts with some of the most excluded low-income people in the country: "Several credit unions have been established to serve groups of handicapped persons whose income generally is lower than average.... Efforts have been made and are continuing to establish credit unions to serve Indians on some of the reservations."[95]

The bureau's 1965 report elaborated on its new partnership with the OEO.

> Significant in 1965 was the wide-spread movement sponsored by the Office of Economic Opportunity and other agencies and organizations to establish credit unions for the benefit of low-income people in community action programs. Some of these new credit unions have been funded for major operating expenses, including a full-time, paid staff of from one to three employees.... The Bureau has actively cooperated with the program with a view to evaluating the merits of this experimental procedure.[96]

Still, the bureau hedged its bets.

> The experience of these credit unions is still too limited to justify any broad conclusions.... It appears that some of these credit unions have grown more rapidly than they would have without the funding for full-time, paid employees. Others, however, have shown no more rapid development than would normally be expected of a credit union without funding in such a group.[97]

The bureau acknowledged that progress was likely to be slow in view of the limited ability of low-income people to save, though it believed "they can, however, save small amounts regularly and thereby accumulate a cash reserve that will be available as needed for emergencies, self-improvement and other purposes."[98] Notably, the bureau once again highlighted the engagement and empowerment of persons with disabilities in credit unions. More than 5 percent of credit unions were serving

> physically handicapped people. These credit unions are not only providing much-needed thrift and loan service to the physically handicapped, they are also being operated and managed by such people. These physically handicapped people have been successful in providing themselves with services that otherwise would not be generally available to them. At the same time, they have been learning good management principles.[99]

Examining the finances of OEO credit unions, the bureau's survey of 21 selected credit unions in 1965 found that member savings accounts averaged only $171, and that even that number was slightly inflated by the accounts of some middle-income members; in fact, about a third of the accounts had balances of $10 or less. On the positive side, the bureau found that one-quarter of the credit union members were saving regularly and benefiting from their access to loans: "A vast majority of these loans, made generally to low-income members with little property to pledge as security, were a source of substantial assistance to these borrowers.... It is evident that these FCU's are not only serving the loan needs of their low-income members but are also promoting thrift among that segment of the members."[100] Sargent Shriver, Director of the Office of Economic Opportunity, was even much more expansive: "Through credit unions, it is possible to build up the strength of the poor and give them some small means of power so they can withstand the force of human greed and gain for themselves a new dignity and justice."[101]

## The Movement Spreads: New Credit Unions and Project Moneywise

In the early decades of the credit union movement in the United States, the regulators were often active partners in organizing new credit unions. In the 1960s, the Bureau of Federal Credit Unions continued this practice: Working alongside the OEO, it found that "the greatest potential for extending credit union services to those in need of them exists today in limited-income areas."[102] The bureau issued 98 charters to limited-income groups in 1966—14 percent of all the charters it issued that year. By year-end, there were 526 federal credit union charters "whose average income is considered substandard."[103] Examiners were given specialized training to improve their skills in working with these groups.

The bureau's signature effort was Project Moneywise, an initiative to build the capacity of the credit unions that served the poor—a forerunner of the capacity-building effort of the CDFI Fund three decades later. The bureau held Project Moneywise training programs lasting up to four weeks in major cities, with a curriculum that included consumer education, family financial counseling, and credit union operations and management; the OEO provided funds through an interagency agreement, while the bureau provided instructors. Echoing Caplovitz's book, Project Moneywise instructors discussed "why the 'poor pay more' and what can be done to reverse this trend…. The importance of credit in helping people to break the chains binding them to unethical sections of the market-place was stressed."[104]

In its 1967 report, the bureau noted proudly that Project Moneywise had reached more than 200 leaders of local communities in 10 cities. It conducted programs for CAP agency staff on Indian reservations and for Mexican American citizens in Phoenix and Chicago.[105] A bureau writer, BFCU's Jo Ellen Jennette, highlighted the impact of the federal effort to end "the vicious cycle of poverty."[106] She cited the testimony of a member of the St. Bridget's-St. Leo's Federal Credit Union of St. Louis, where typical wages were $2,400 a year or less: "I used to live in the project, had no steady income, and was actually going nowhere. Then the credit union came into my life and things changed…. Today I own my own business and am buying my own house and store. I have an income. I am a respected leader of the community."

Washington took note. Senior administration officials, Congress, and the media enthusiastically commended the Project Moneywise campaign. Esther Peterson, Special Assistant to the President for Consumer Affairs, keynoted a Washington, DC, Project Moneywise program.[107] Congresswoman Barbara C. Jordan, the first African American woman from the South elected to the United States House of Representatives, promoted credit unions as a "bootstrap," a "cooperative small-loan bank" that could "drive the loan sharks out of business."[108]

Although the curriculum of Project Moneywise provided a heavy dose of consumer education training—equipping the trainees to provide "development services," in the contemporary language of the CDFI Fund—it also promoted institution-building by developing credit union organizers and leaders.[109] In Boston, for example, Project Moneywise yielded 11 new credit unions operating in low-income areas.[110] As Jennette's pamphlet asserted, "The poor must be offered workable alternatives if they are to escape from the vicious circle binding them to this kind of exploitation….The creation and successful operation of such credit unions are the goals of Project Moneywise."[111]

## Credit Unions for the Poor: Who Owns Them?

The term "OEO credit unions" is often used as shorthand—typically an uncomplimentary one— for the low-income institutions of the 1960s. Yet hundreds of low-income credit unions already existed outside the OEO network: Indeed, the entire credit union movement had originated among the working class. These other credit unions often collaborated with the "real" OEO credit unions that were based in CAP agencies but remained distinct from them.

OEO credit unions were primarily government-created entities. To the degree that widespread failure of these OEO-sponsored financial institutions was attributable to federal design, it is important to understand their structure. Every credit union in the United States—then and now—is a separate legal entity, with its own board of directors; members, and only members, own the credit union—one person, one vote—regardless of the amount of deposits ("shares") the member invests. Every credit union has a field of membership, approved by the regulator and specified in the credit union's charter; only those persons or organizations who fall within the specified parameters can become members.

This was true for OEO credit unions as it was for other credit unions. Beyond these basics, there were two different models for OEO-sponsored credit unions. About 55 percent had charters "which permitted any person who lived or was employed in a designated neighborhood to become a member of the credit union." The other OEO-financed credit unions were "restricted to persons who were enrolled and participating in a community action program."[112] The second type was obviously more restrictive, tending to limit participation to the poor; under the first model, membership could include employees of local businesses and organizations, as well as residents who were not poor—thus providing at least an opening for attracting people with greater saving and borrowing potential. To create an institution with a narrow field of membership—or in later CDFI terms, a "target market"—restricted to the poor did not necessarily guarantee failure. But it certainly did not help.

## Operating Support and Its Perils

The OEO began providing financial assistance to credit unions sponsored by CAP agencies in January 1965, a few months after the Economic Opportunity Act became law. Some credit unions received direct funding; others did not. Financial support typically included salaries for one to three employees, funding for rent, and other operating expenses.

The CAP agency network of credit unions grew to 245 by October 1968, later reaching more than three hundred. About one-fourth of them received modest annual subsidies from the OEO, ranging from $10,000 to $30,000. A few demonstration credit unions received more than $100,000. By December 31, 1969, toward the end of the OEO credit union experiment, 125 credit unions were receiving OEO funding to subsidize employee salaries, space rental, or other operating expenses. Total OEO support was $3.2 million, of which $1.1 million went for technical assistance, consultants, and other expenses.[113]

As a federal agency, the OEO was subject to the annual appropriations process in Congress. At best, an OEO-funded project lived year-to-year. Operating support was crucial during the startup period of a credit union, as it took years to build a loan portfolio and generate income. Depending on short-term operating support did not make for a smooth route to self-sufficiency. When the CDFI activists of the 1990s later pressed for a federal fund, they emphatically rejected a model that would provide operating funds. Rather, they demanded equity investments—permanent capital that a CDFI could use to obtain additional debt, build its balance sheets, and eventually become self-sustaining.

## Waning Support, Growing Opposition

In the early, optimistic years of the War on Poverty, the OEO and its initiatives encountered relatively light resistance, although the mayoral administrations that did not control anti-poverty agencies continued to protest vigorously. The OEO supported credit unions as "an essential way to break the cycle of poverty"; they were sources of low-cost credit and excellent examples of community action. The credit union regulatory agency was also supportive. On the community side, the chairman of the Chicago Congress on Racial Equality (CORE) praised credit unions as a means of keeping money in the local community and "creating a new value system for our people… a new people-centered economic framework, a new morality."[114] But optimism and harmony did not last very long.

The Watts, Los Angeles, uprising of 1965 replaced media images of the beleaguered poor, worthy of assistance, with scenes of angry African American rioters. Poor black communities erupted in Detroit, Newark, and elsewhere in 1967. The sources of rage were economic as well as social. That year, as Caplovitz noted, "the investigations of the recent riots in Negro ghettos in various parts of the country have suggested that resentment against consumer exploitation is one of the many grievances that find expression in riots."[115] But this did not lead typically to renewed support for credit union development (although a credit union was formed in Watts shortly after the uprising). The great polarization in American society was now openly recognized, famously summarized in a quote from the Kerner Commission report on the 1968 Detroit riots: America was moving toward "two societies, one black, one white, separate, and unequal."[116]

## Chapter 2. The Sixties

The political landscape changed dramatically in 1968. On March 31, Lyndon Johnson announced that he would not seek re-election. On April 4, Rev. Martin Luther King Jr. was assassinated, triggering riots around the country. On June 5, Senator Robert F. Kennedy was slain. The civil rights movement brought an explicitly economic dimension to the struggle with the Poor People's Campaign, culminating in the erection of the Resurrection City encampment on the mall in Washington, DC, in May and June. Meanwhile, the OEO was coming under attack for poor management. It became a favorite target of the Nixon Republican campaign. Many legislators who had supported the original OEO legislation were defeated in midterm elections.

Optimistic early assessments of the progress of newly formed credit unions began to fade. There had been numerical growth: By fall 1968, there were 672 credit unions operating in recognized poverty areas, including some 245 that were related to CAP agencies. The 106 OEO credit unions that were federally chartered (others were state-chartered) totaled 65,900 members, who accounted for $4.2 million in deposits and $4.2 million in loans. Cumulatively, they had made $14.2 million in loans.[117] But by 1969, only seven OEO-related credit unions had achieved assets of at least $100,000, and the average member savings were only $44.[118]

The stereotypical view was that the OEO had dumped substantial sums of money on poverty credit unions. But in fact, only a minority received any funding at all. As early as 1967, Caplovitz observed the situation with distress.

> Efforts to establish credit unions and other types of self-help institutions have been set back by the absence of seed money. Neither the Federal Government nor the State Credit Union Leagues have been eager to provide the capital and leadership to get these institutions established, and until such funds and leadership are available, there is little chance that these programs will get off the ground.[119]

The Government Accounting Office* (GAO) made an in-depth study of eight selected OEO credit unions and found that "delinquency was not a major problem and that relatively few loans had been written off as uncollectible," but the credit unions had "relatively high operating deficits and… little success in attaining OEO's goal of becoming self-supporting."[120] The GAO noted that OEO guidelines had anticipated providing grants to cover operating deficits for only one or two years. Savings had not grown sufficiently, which was "attributable primarily to the very limited savings that low-income families have available for deposit in the credit unions."[121]

Given the bleak choices in poor communities, it would have seemed that credit unions would grow wildly among poor communities. But there were psychosocial as well as economic barriers. Caplovitz observed the barriers credit unions faced:

---

\* Now the Government Accountability Office

> Since many low-income people have for years been victimized by unscrupulous merchants, high-rate money lenders, and house-to-house salesmen, they have sometimes looked upon credit union leaders as they do upon other strangers—as just someone else who seeks to gain at their expense. Gradually, their skepticism is being overcome and they are beginning to realize that these programs and plans can and do benefit them.[122]

At best, the task was daunting. Orrin Shipe, the managing director of CUNA for the OEO initiative, noted the limited financial progress of the new credit unions. He called the effort "the biggest, toughest job the credit union movement has ever taken on. Yet no other organization can help the poor to help themselves like we can."[123]

Despite the limited progress of the credit unions, OEO officials continued to make the case that they provided valuable services, even if they were not yet self-sufficient. The credit union regulator, as well, "believed that credit unions were an effective instrument in helping poor people to help themselves and that the social benefits that accrued were worth some expenditure by the Government to assist them."[124] But the election of President Richard M. Nixon in November 1968 began the trajectory toward the elimination of the OEO. Donald Rumsfeld, who as a congressman had opposed the creation of the OEO, reluctantly succeeded Sargent Shriver as head of the OEO, serving only briefly before joining the White House staff. The upper ranks of the OEO were filled with others who also opposed it.

The credit union movement had never unanimously supported the War on Poverty, even though CUNA had obtained repeated OEO contracts to support credit union development. Orrin Shipe, CUNA's chief executive, faced opposition from other leaders who thought that any government investment in low-income credit unions was a "boondoggle" and rather should go to the "non-poor" elements of the credit union movement.[125] In its August 1970 report to the OEO, CUNA concluded that

> community-type credit unions in low-income areas have had a good deal of trouble accumulating sufficient capital to be able to support the necessary full-time operations without some subsidy.... The slow growth of membership and of members' shares has led to a low level of loan services, which in turn implies limited usefulness of the credit unions.[126]

That fall, CUNA turned its back on Washington-led efforts to spread credit union services among poor communities.

> The low-income credit union as such offers little or no opportunity for us to bring forth dynamic ways of improving in an outstanding manner our present approaches for bringing credit union services to poor people.... [There are] more non-poor people than poor people who need but do not benefit from credit union benefits.[127]

## The Anatomy of Failure

On June 17, 1971, the GAO reported to Congress on "Progress Being Made and Difficulties Being Encountered by Credit Unions Serving Low-Income Persons." It studied eight OEO credit unions in depth and diagnosed critical problems: operational deficits with limited prospects for breaking even; insufficient growth of deposits; high salary and space costs; and a lack of formal goals or financial projections for achieving financial self-sufficiency.[128] But it found hope in a development that could bring additional lending capital to low-income credit unions, which they urgently needed if they were to break the vicious cycle of smallness and move toward self-sufficiency. On October 19, 1970, the Federal Credit Union Act had been amended to provide deposit insurance for state- and federally-chartered credit unions, in parallel to Federal Deposit Insurance Corporation (FDIC) insurance for commercial banks. The GAO noted the new opportunity for credit unions.

> Low-income credit unions had demand for loans in amounts which exceeded the available deposits…The insurance of deposits would permit low-income credit unions to attract more funds. It was anticipated that organizations would be willing to deposit funds in low-income credit unions if the funds could be insured against loss.[129]

Deposit insurance would indeed prove critical in providing access to capital. But federal insurance was not so easily won for low-income credit unions, as will be discussed in the next chapter.

## Credit Unions and Civil Rights: Organizing in the South

In rural areas in the South, the denial of wealth-building opportunities took insidious forms. The fight for economic equity was closely linked to the civil rights struggle. Earnest Johnson, a legendary credit union organizer and trainer and the son of a farmer, recalled his attempt to borrow from a white-owned bank.

> I tried to get a loan to get a car, and they approved that loan within ten minutes at a bank. But I changed my mind on the car and wanted to borrow the same amount of money to buy forty acres of land that was being purchased from my mother's brother.
> And that man turned around in his chair, and he told me that that was a horse of a different color. And he didn't let me have the money. The only thing I [heard was that] he went and tried to buy the land himself. So that led to the idea that we need a financial institution that we controlled, and that led me into organizing the East Alabama Federal Credit Union.[130]

Johnson recalled a visit from the manager of nearby Tuskegee Federal Credit Union when people were organizing demonstrations for voting rights. "He was telling us that you need your own financial institution. And that made me fall right in love with what he was saying, and that led me into the credit union industry. And I'm still there."[131]

*Earnest Johnson, legendary credit union organizer. Courtesy of National Federation of CDCUs.*

Carol Zippert, a longtime civil rights and cooperative leader, was introduced to the cooperative movement in the early 1960s through the efforts of Father A. J. McKnight in Lafayette, LA. He was, Zippert recalled, "the first black priest to come to our church parish, which was all black; the churches were segregated as well."[132] With the literacy classes McKnight organized came engagement with the civil rights movement for high-school students like Zippert: "We were the same ones that would go out to integrate places, like the lunch counters at the five and dime stores. [We learned that] these were not our restaurants, our hotels; we don't have any businesses. So, Father McKnight got us talking about our community assets." Families saved for three years to raise capital, $300 each—"it was a lot of money in the early 60s, so people would pay about $2 a month, towards their $300." At Father McKnight's church, they organized the St. Paul Federal Credit Union. In 1975, aided by the Federation of Southern Cooperatives, Zippert helped to organize the Federation of Greene County Employees Federal Credit Union (FOGCE FCU) in Alabama. When the credit union later ran afoul of the regulators because of high delinquency, the community banded together—physically and financially—to save their institution. When examiners from the National Credit Union Administration came to shut down FOGCE, she said, "We stood in the door. We had the people, we stood in the door, and we blocked it. We got the whole community involved in raising the money. Even the school system. Because at that point in Greene County, we had a black superintendent and a black school board."\*

Elsewhere in Alabama, Eddie Ayers, a teacher and the son of sharecroppers, joined with six other people to organize the Demopolis Federal Credit Union in 1966. He recalled the inextricable link between the legacy of slavery and economic retaliation against civil rights activists. "People were getting put off the land, they had to move because they were participating in the demonstrations in the sixties. And the idea was born that we needed a credit union."[133] Like many other credit unions in the South, Ayers said, "We had no place to house a credit union. The treasurer was a barber, he owned a barber shop, so he carried the books to the barber shop and that's where we operated, right out of the barber shop." After years of being denied credit by banks to start small businesses, "with the coming of the credit union I could feel a change, and I could see it that it was a different attitude."

Although barber shops were not the typical locations for credit unions, Earnest Johnson recalled that many "were in people's houses—that's where the offices were. In houses that didn't even have indoor plumbing. But they made a big difference in people's lives. People would get off work and go to do business at the credit union on the table at someone's house, after they finished eating supper. All of this was volunteer work." Sadly, though, "they were set up to fail" because they lacked resources, Johnson recalled.[134]

## Beyond OEO: The Ford Foundation and the "Gray Areas"

Even before the OEO initiative, the Ford Foundation was investing heavily in another anti-poverty approach: the Gray Areas, a project conceived and developed by Paul Ylvisaker, Ford's public affairs director.[135]

As the name implies, Gray Areas suffered from a certain lack of definition. Although this was a Ford Foundation project, the term came from an economist, Raymond Vernon, who studied the project. Generally, Gray Areas described communities that were not quite fully deteriorated, but on the cusp. Neither the target population nor the methods were clearly defined; nor were the specific goals, which made evaluation more difficult. "Everything about Gray Areas was nebulous," wrote Mitchell ("Mike") Sviridoff, who ran the New Haven project, later becoming a senior Ford Foundation official and the first head of the Local Initiatives Support Corporation (LISC).[136] It was, he wrote, "a comprehensive,

---

\* FOGCE FCU ended 2016 with $1.4 million in assets. Carol Zippert, PhD, is an educator, poet, and publisher of a local newspaper. She and her husband, John, a longtime staff member of the Federation of Southern Cooperatives/Land Assistance Fund, were inducted into the national Cooperative Hall of Fame in May 2016. In order to marry in 1967, they had to sue the State of Alabama to remove the state's "miscegenation statute," which prevented marriage of interracial couples.

coordinated human-service, education, and employment strategy. There was no mention in the early days of the Gray Area program of physical, economic, or empowerment objectives—issues that later became touchstones of the antipoverty movement, and eventually of community development."[137]

Five cities were selected—Boston, New Haven, Oakland (CA), Philadelphia, and Washington, DC—as well as the state of North Carolina. The project was formally launched on March 30, 1961, after a two-year planning process. The initial allocation was $4.75 million, and over the course of 1961–64, $26.5 million was distributed in stages to the various sites.[138]

## Reinventing Service Delivery

Newly established private nonprofit organizations led the projects. Their ambitious goal was "the planned reinvention of service delivery systems to the poor,"[139] and specifically, to improve assimilation of new arrivals (especially African Americans) to the cities. By facilitating central coordination of City Hall, multiple social welfare institutions, and other local players, the Gray Areas projects would alleviate the multiple, interrelated problems of the cities.

The Gray Areas were emphatically not about redistributing power or wealth: There was no neighborhood-style community organizing in the manner made prominent by Saul Alinsky in Chicago. At Community Progress, Inc., in New Haven—generally acknowledged as the foremost project of its kind— "Sviridoff and his associates spurned such unruly and ill-defined goals as 'community organizing' and 'citizen participation.'"[140] Other sites were perhaps more open to those efforts, but none were full-throated partisans of "maximum feasible participation" of the poor. None dealt with the centrality of race and racism. Rather, their notion was more in line with the older, settlement-house attempts to assimilate, acculturate, and uplift new community residents. In New Haven, the school became a focal point—a morning-to-night community institution that went beyond educating children to bringing services and activities to adults, everything from pre-kindergarten to remedial education.

By 1967, Ford had provided $27 million in funding to the Gray Areas initiative.[141] Its record of accomplishment was mixed, limited in part by "a hesitation to tackle the important racial dimensions of urban problems."[142] It had spawned some solid programs that produced incremental improvements, such as those in New Haven, especially in education, and even influenced federal strategies. Some Gray Areas projects, such as those in Boston, became prominent players in the OEO network. Others foundered in the swamp of local politics and power struggles, not to mention the lack of clear direction or adept program management.

Thus, the Gray Areas were not the "game changer" to which philanthropy aspired. Nonetheless, "together with Michael Harrington's *The Other America*, Gray Areas made poverty *visible* to America."[143] The lessons learned and the individuals involved were important to the continuing search for more effective strategies—strategies that stand more directly in the lineage of the contemporary CDFI movement: community development corporations (CDCs) and Program-Related Investments (PRIs).

## Community Development Corporations (CDCs)

The Ford Foundation was not extensively involved in local community-based development efforts prior to the 1960s. However, as early as 1955, it provided support for ACTION-Pittsburgh, a local development corporation and forerunner of the CDC movement.[144] Although Bedford-Stuyvesant Restoration Corporation is customarily described as the first CDC, Progress Enterprises, founded in 1962 by Rev. Leon Sullivan, pastor of Zion Baptist Church in North Philadelphia, could arguably claim that title.[145] Progress Enterprises pioneered an extraordinary approach that has rarely, if ever, been replicated: Parishioners contributed $10 a month for 36 months—the "10-36 plan"—with the proceeds divided between a charitable trust for social services and a fund for enterprise development. In this way, Progress Enterprises was able to build housing, a shopping plaza, and various business enterprises.

In 1966, McGeorge Bundy, former national security adviser to President Johnson, assumed the presidency of the Ford Foundation. Bundy proceeded to initiate new urban strategies that would occupy increasing attention and support over the next decades. CDCs would be a key to these strategies.

## "Bed-Stuy, Do or Die"

With 400,000 residents, Bedford-Stuyvesant in Brooklyn, NY, was second only to the South Side of Chicago as the largest African American neighborhood in the country. It was hard hit by riots (as was Harlem) in July 1964, following the shooting of a 15-year-old African American, James Powell, in Manhattan by an off-duty policeman. Deterioration, rampant unemployment, and violence plagued Bedford-Stuyvesant, hence its dire, "do or die" moniker. But it had certain core assets, including gracious housing stock and many concerned, if disunited, community organizations, such as the Central Brooklyn Coordinating Council.[146] Despite its size and prominence, Bedford-Stuyvesant was greatly overshadowed in influence by the "capital of black America," Manhattan's Harlem, which had much greater political influence in the person of Congressman Adam Clayton Powell.

## RFK Meets Bed-Stuy: "Brooklyn Negros Harass Kennedy"

No early forerunner of the CDFI movement had a more prominent godfather than Robert F. Kennedy. As attorney general in his brother's administration, Robert Kennedy had headed the President's Committee on Juvenile Delinquency and Youth Crime, becoming a passionate anti-poverty advocate. After he was elected senator for New York in 1964, the problems of urban America were no longer his national portfolio, but rather the issues of his constituents.

In 1964, the Central Brooklyn Coordinating Council commissioned the Pratt Institute to develop a plan for government collaboration with neighborhood residents to rehabilitate Bedford-Stuyvesant, which was delivered in 1965.[147] Pratt's Ron Shiffman suggested that Senator Kennedy be invited to tour the neighborhood and meet with local leaders, which he did on February 4, 1966.[148] His door-to-door canvassing did not always find a warm welcome. A subsequent community meeting brought him face to face with anger and frustration born of repeated, ineffectual government efforts. Thomas R. Jones, a prominent African American civil court judge, summarized the mood: "I'm weary of study, Senator, very weary. The Negro people are angry, Senator. And judge that I am, I'm angry too."[149] On February 5, a *New York Times* article summarized Kennedy's day as "Brooklyn Negros Harass Kennedy."[150]

Over the course of 1966, Senator Kennedy elaborated a plan with four pillars: employment, education, housing, and a "sense of community." He raised the national profile of his vision in August, testifying before a Senate committee: "The heart of the program should be the creation of Community Development Corporations, which would carry out the work of construction, the hiring and training of workers, the provision of services, and encouragement of associated enterprises."[151]

Over the following months, Kennedy put the organizational and political pieces together for the launch of the new community development corporation (CDC). Politically, this meant bringing on board Mayor John Lindsay—a potential rival to Kennedy's presidential aspirations—and the senior senator for New York, Jacob K. Javits, who also had higher aspirations. Organizationally, Kennedy's team came up with a dual structure for the new CDC.

- The Bedford-Stuyvesant Renewal and Rehabilitation Corporation, charged with delivering programs and services, was the community arm. Judge Thomas R. Jones would initially head it.
- Alongside it was to be the Development and Services Corporation (D&S), which would help access resources, recruit investors, and provide high-level managerial assistance. To say that this body comprised the "A" list (or "C" suite) would be no exaggeration: It was chaired by Andre Meyer of Lazard Freres investment company and included Chairman of IBM Thomas Watson Jr.; former Secretary of the Treasury Douglas Dillon; and other prominent figures that Kennedy recruited from politics, finance, and industry.

Depending on one's viewpoint, D&S was either a "dream team" or, as some residents believed, an arm of "colonialism," enlisting the white elite to ride herd on the residents. The dual structure embodied the persistent tension between community empowerment (in the tradition of "maximum feasible participation" of the poor) and a results-oriented, business-driven approach.

On December 10, 1966, at a conference sponsored by the Central Brooklyn Coordinating Council, one thousand community residents filled the auditorium of Public School 305 on Monroe Street in Bedford-Stuyvesant to hear Senator Kennedy announce the formation of the dual corporations. Mayor John Lindsay, Senator Jacob K. Javits, and officials of the United States Department of Housing and Urban Development joined Senator Kennedy, underscoring the bipartisan, nationally significant nature of the event.

As reported by the *New York Times* on December 11, Kennedy said, "Our past efforts to deal with the problems of our cities have not worked; their promise failed, their purpose failed."[152] He was, on the one hand, sensitive to the issue of community ownership and empowerment. Kennedy argued

## Chapter 2. The Sixties

that previous programs failed because they "don't have their origin in the community, but are imposed from the outside, and the community has no stake in their success."[153] On the other hand, he saw an overwhelming need both for investment and other financial resources on a large scale, as well as managerial talent—hence the high-level D&S.

The *New York Times* reported that "housing experts believe [Bedford-Stuyvesant Restoration Corporation] could become a prototype for corporations in other cities. The aim is for the corporations to become eventually self-sustaining."[154] Its editorial board enthused that the new corporations "represent a start in what could become the country's most exciting endeavor to give the people in racial ghettos meaningful participation in reviving their decaying neighborhoods."[155] It could be a "promising vessel for meshing the imagination and sense of urgency of Negro and Puerto Rican citizens of the slums with all the public and private resources New York and the nation can bring to bear."[156]

### Building the Community Development Corporation

There was tension between the two corporations and internal conflict within each of them. The search for an executive director who could navigate these complex waters was lengthy and difficult. Eventually, the new organization selected Franklin A. Thomas. Born in Bedford-Stuyvesant and educated at Columbia University, Thomas was a lawyer who had become deputy general counsel of the New York City Police Department. With his credibility in the community, New York City politics, and the business world, Thomas—who later became president of the Ford Foundation—was uniquely qualified to lead the effort; indeed, the whole enterprise might have foundered had he not been willing to become CEO.

Despite Senator Kennedy's emphasis on engaging the private sector, he and his colleagues saw clearly the fledging CDCs' need for major federal support. In June 1967, Senators Kennedy and Javits secured a pot of money for CDCs through an amendment to the Economic Opportunity Act. Although the pot was for CDCs nationwide, over the next seven years the Bedford-Stuyvesant Restoration Corporation received nearly one-third of the entire $106 million distributed from this fund.[157]

In its early years, under Frank Thomas's leadership, the Bedford-Stuyvesant CDC achieved many successes, albeit none on the grand scale of transformation that Kennedy might have hoped. IBM built a cable-reconditioning plant in Bedford-Stuyvesant, a shining example that, unfortunately, other corporations did not follow. The D&S helped the CDC raise much of a $100 million mortgage pool, a mechanism that spread risk among 85 banks. It started summer programs to engage youth in rehabilitating exteriors of homes, repairing sidewalks, and other highly visible projects that proved very popular in the community. Projects like this also engaged residents themselves, who were asked to pledge a modest amount, $25, to fix up the interiors of their homes.

The Ford Foundation was an early supporter of the effort, although initially at the modest level of $25,000. But the CDC's supporters were looking for much more, and that required going to the top levels of Ford—namely, President McGeorge Bundy. This is where the role of the high-powered D&S board came into play. According to Eli Jacobs, interim director of the D&S, overcoming Ford's skepticism required the personal intervention of Senator Kennedy and two D&S board members: the eminent financiers Benno Schmidt and Andre Meyer.[158] By the end of 1968, the Ford, Astor, and Rockefeller foundations had provided several million dollars to the new CDC, supplementing the millions that came from the Department of Labor under the "Title VII" funds for CDCs.

## The Origins of Program-Related Investments (PRIs)

If the federal government could not win its "unconditional war on poverty," certainly philanthropies with their limited grant budgets—even the Ford Foundation, the nation's largest—could not. To expand the impact of their funding, Ford, the Taconic Foundation, and a handful of others began to look to their endowments as a source of additional resources. Thus, the strategy of Program-Related Investments (PRIs) was born. Over the decades, PRIs by foundations have become an invaluable source of patient, below-market capital for CDFIs. But before foundations could make PRIs a permanent part of their toolbox, certain legal questions had to be resolved.

For decades, foundations were regarded with suspicion in Washington. In the 1950s, there were congressional investigations aimed at determining whether foundations were funding communist fronts or being used to evade taxes.[159] In the 1960s, reports of self-dealing, below-market loans to business associates, and speculative practices by trustees triggered investigations by the Select Committee on Small Business of the United States House of Representatives, chaired by Wright Patman, and later the Treasury Department. The policy debate in Washington would "embroil Ford in a fiery debate about the role of foundations in American society."[160]

In the early 1960s, Ford and a few other adventurous foundations made charitable investments for such purposes as minority businesses in urban areas. But these were still relatively rare and—as time would show—mostly unsuccessful. Seeking a more systematic approach, in the mid-1960s, Ford's public affairs associate director, Lou Winnick, proposed a strategy to create a "continuum" of funding mechanisms, positioned between grants and market-driven investments.[161] To carry this out, he proposed establishing a $10 million fund, which Ford's trustees initially rejected. But as city after city erupted in riots—Watts, Los Angeles, in 1965; Detroit and Newark in 1967—the increasingly desperate urban situation "made the case that the social needs revealed by the [uprisings]…and subsequent demands on philanthropic resources required extraordinary responses."[162] By 1968, with a new board chair and his own elevation to become the Ford Foundation's national affairs deputy vice president, Winnick's PRI strategy was adopted.[163]

The Ford Foundation found an important ally in the Taconic Foundation—a small, progressive philanthropy that had actively supported the civil rights movement and other causes. In November 1967, John Simon, a Yale Law School professor and the president of Taconic, published a seminal paper entitled "Foundation Debt and Equity Investment in 'High Risk, Low Return' Enterprises Providing

Economic and Housing Opportunities for Minority and Poverty Groups." In it, "Simon suggested that the physical and cultural separation between traditional providers of capital and minority-backed enterprises exacerbated the problem" of poverty in the United States.[164]

In December 1967, Simon and Winnick of Ford organized a meeting of six foundations to create a pool to make what they called "program-related investments."[165] In May 1968, they established the Cooperative Assistance Fund for "combating poverty, prejudice and community deterioration through assisting members of minority and poverty groups to improve themselves economically and to have access to improved and integrated housing."[166] Meanwhile, the Ford Foundation on its own established a $10 million loan fund and began investing separately. On a smaller scale, Taconic started to invest as well, making investments of a few thousand dollars in the Baltimore Community Investment Company and Union Settlement Federal Credit Union in East Harlem, NY.

For program-related investing to become an accepted practice, it was still necessary to overcome lingering congressional suspicion and gain the approval of the Internal Revenue Service. In February 1969, the United States House Ways and Means Committee began hearings on tax reform. Ford Foundation President McGeorge Bundy went to Washington to testify. A Senate amendment clarified that

> a program-related investment—such as low-interest or interest-free loans to needy students, high-risk investments in low-income housing, and loans to small businesses where commercial sources of funds are unable—is not to be considered as an investment which might jeopardize the foundation's carrying out of its exempt purposes.[167]

In fall 1969, John Simon went to Washington to explain the PRI concept to the staff of the Joint Committee on Internal Revenue Taxation. "Language was included in the bill that recognized that unlike a grant a PRI could be structured with a provision for repayment, and it could be made to a for-profit entity whose business advanced an exempt or charitable activity or goal."[168] The clarification that a PRI could be made to a for-profit entity—not only to tax-exempt charities—was important: Without it, Ford and other foundations would not have been able to invest in South Shore Bank, other community development banks, or certain other CDFIs.

## Conclusion

The shortcomings and missteps of the "unconditional war on poverty" declared by President Lyndon Johnson have long made the Sixties an easy target for critics. Yet, by the end of the decade, pieces of a viable new strategy were emerging, including a new institutional model—the CDC—and new financial tools, especially PRIs. Moreover, the decade yielded important—if painful— lessons that would help shape later, more successful initiatives, such as community development banking.

The OEO credit union experience is an important case study as a government-driven initiative to plant financial institutions in poverty communities. The comfortable default assessment is that the OEO effort was an unmitigated failure. Indeed, most of the credit unions it established failed, eventually. Critics readily blame the poor and lament the money being spent on them: Too few community members volunteered for the credit unions; they didn't know what they were doing, and they relied too much on paid staff; members didn't save enough; too much money was being spent to rent space in anti-poverty agencies; there was no planning. But there was more than enough blame to go around, starting at the top.

Simply put, the policymakers in Washington were vastly unrealistic in their notion of what could be achieved and how fast. As Adolfo (Al) Alayon, president of the National Federation of CDCUs, remembered with some bitterness, "The whole War on Poverty program was of that nature. They threw money at the problems, and by the time we learned what to do with it, they took the money away."[169] Washington's timetable for the credit unions to achieve self-sufficiency strains credulity. As the GAO noted, "OEO guidelines dated August 1969 state that certain operating and administrative costs of a credit union can be financed by OEO but that such assistance cannot be expected to be provided for more than a year or two."[170] The Credit Union National Association (CUNA) did its own financial modeling, projecting that an urban low-income credit union would need at least five years to become self-supporting at a level of about $300,000 in member deposits, assuming substantial volunteer labor.[171] In any case, neither the OEO nor CUNA pushed the credit unions to develop formal self-sufficiency plans.[172]

Connected to this, of course, was the crucial and obvious problem of lack of access to capital. As the GAO, CUNA, and OEO all recognized, the poor could not save much. OEO credit unions received operating subsidies, but no core capital to build reserves and leverage additional deposits. Moreover, the restrictive fields of membership under which some OEO credit unions operated—that is, only participants in CAP agency anti-poverty programs could join—was virtually a recipe for disaster. Still, a minority of these credit unions survived and went on to serve low-income communities for decades, while others eventually merged with other, more mainstream credit unions, to which they sometimes transmitted a portion of their DNA.

## Lessons of the War on Poverty

The OEO shortcomings were consequential, in ways bad and good. For decades, the OEO experience soured much of the mainstream credit union movement on serving the poor: When advocates for community development credit unions (CDCUs) approached their peers for assistance, they had the OEO failure thrown into their faces and were told that "poverty is not a common bond" for credit union development. When the National Federation of CDCUs and its allies went to Capitol Hill in the 1990s to argue for a federal CDFI Fund, they still encountered congressional members and staff who remembered or else knew of the experience of the OEO credit unions.

But the lessons of the Sixties helped inform the community development banking campaign of the 1990s. The OEO experiment provided a handy "don't do" roadmap. Policymakers and advocates agreed that annual operating subsidies in the manner of the OEO were not the way to go. Instead, the CDFI Fund would invest equity capital, which institutions could use to leverage and grow. The CDFI Fund—unlike the OEO—would require rigorous financial projections that, according to its legislative history, would point toward self-sufficiency. Wisely, the OEO had bypassed City Hall, which often "hijacked" funding for its own purposes; similarly, the CDFI Fund legislation made government entities ineligible (although certain exceptions were made for Native American communities). Whereas the OEO credit unions typically restricted services to the poor, the CDFI Fund set a more realistic standard specifying that 60 percent of a recipient's financial activity had to be directed toward "target" populations or communities.

In the War on Poverty, there was a tension between partisans of community empowerment—"maximum feasible participation" of the poor—and those whose goal was simply to improve the delivery of services to the community. This tension would echo in the evolution of CDFI Fund legislation: Early drafts emphasized community ownership and governance of CDFIs; successive iterations diluted this concept to unspecified "accountability" to the target community.

## Creating a National Network: The Role of Government

The OEO rapidly incubated hundreds of urban and rural credit unions, building on its network of anti-poverty community action agencies. With its government partner, the Bureau of Federal Credit Unions, the OEO actively assisted the development of new credit unions—although it did not build an infrastructure or provide sufficient capital to ensure their viability. In contrast, although draft CDFI Fund legislation emphasized that it was to serve as an information clearinghouse and the federal "voice" of community development banking, the fund would not finance the establishment of new CDFIs. From the standpoint of credit union development, this was a lost opportunity. To obtain a credit union charter, a community group had to demonstrate sufficient commitments of startup capital. However, the CDFI Fund would not make such commitments until the credit union was already chartered—a kind of "Catch-22."

Clinton's vision called for the establishment of a "network of 100 community development banks and 1,000 microenterprise programs." But there was no strategic plan to focus on the areas of greatest poverty; need was one of the multiple factors that the CDFI Fund considered in making its awards. Consequently, as some advocates feared, the poorest communities with the fewest human and financial resources generally had the hardest time competing for funding.[173]

# PART III. The Seventies

There was no grand War on Poverty in the 1970s. The Nixon administration dismantled the OEO's initiatives, sapped its spirit, and dispersed its anti-poverty warriors. The dominant economic concerns of Americans were not about inequality nor the plight of the poor: They were the cost of gasoline and the long lines at local stations resulting from the 1973 oil embargo by Arab oil-producing countries. The new "war" was not against poverty—it was against inflation. In 1974, President Gerald Ford introduced a campaign to "Whip Inflation Now," symbolized by the much-derided WIN button that the president wore and urged others to as well. There were no urban uprisings to rival the widespread events of the Sixties—no flaming reminders to prompt big strategies from Washington.

As the War on Poverty receded, its supporters fought a rear-guard battle to preserve what pieces they could. New strategies and institutions to facilitate the flow of capital to low-income communities emerged—strategies that would be vital to the evolution of community development finance. The Seventies witnessed:

- The birth and flowering of the Community Reinvestment Act (CRA) movement, which won major legislative victories
- The first community development bank: South Shore Bank of Chicago
- The emergence of community development corporations (CDCs)
- A long campaign by low-income credit unions to create a federal fund to help capitalize their operations
- Growing private-sector investment from foundations and the faith-based community.

# CHAPTER 3. The Chicago Story

## The CRA Movement: Community Reinvestment in the Seventies

As Dan Immergluck has succinctly written, "The history of U.S. banking and credit markets is filled with systemic exclusion and segmentation based on race and geography."[174] Ironically, the modern roots of "redlining"—denial of credit to the residents and businesses of a neighborhood—can be traced to the federal housing policies of the Great Depression.

In the 1930s, the federal Home Owners Loan Corporation established a neighborhood risk-rating system, which produced "residential security maps" of cities that coded neighborhoods on a spectrum from green for the most desirable, through blue and yellow, and finally down to red, for the least desirable. Redlined neighborhoods included those that had "undesirable"—i.e., African American— concentrations of residents. Banks and savings and loan institutions obtained these maps and avoided the redlined areas.[175]

The Federal Housing Administration (FHA), also established in the 1930s, insured the loans of mortgage lenders up to 90 percent. For the first few decades, it focused on lending in the suburbs, to the detriment of lending in the cities. But when under the presidency of Lyndon Johnson in the 1960s the FHA began insuring city properties, it unleashed a Pandora's box of abuse: Unholy alliances of lenders, brokers, and appraisers preyed on racial fears through "block busting"—essentially promoting panic selling among white homeowners anxious about black families buying in "their" neighborhood. This enabled scavenger investors to buy low; sell to black families—many of whom subsequently defaulted; collect on FHA insurance; and continue their profitable strategy of "flipping" properties. There was another, insidious financing technique that worked to victimize blacks and other low-income people: the land contract installment sale. Under this arrangement, a family made monthly payments in hopes of owning a home. But if they missed payments—sometimes even a single payment—they would lose everything they had paid in, rather than steadily building up equity, as they would in a standard mortgage.

## Community Organizing in Chicago: Enter Gale Cincotta

Mortgage lending discrimination became the target of a growing movement in the 1970s, nowhere more sharply than in Chicago. Community organizing had roots in the nineteenth century with Jane Addams and Hull House on the North Side.[176] In the 1930s, Saul Alinsky began a mode of community organizing that has continued vigorously to this day, through the Industrial Areas Foundation. But the woman who, with her organizing colleague Shel Trapp, a former Methodist minister, became a towering figure in the community reinvestment movement was Gale Cincotta—born Aglaia Angelos, of Greek and Latvian background, a proudly working-class housewife who lived in the Austin neighborhood on the West Side of Chicago.[177]

Gale Cincotta didn't want to move. Not in the face of neighborhood deterioration, fueled by FHA polices and accelerated by block busting. Not when confronted by the deterioration of Chicago city services, when the neighborhood was "written off." And especially not in the face of the deteriorating public schools, where she sent her children to classrooms jammed with 75 students. Cincotta described her early trajectory this way:

> My active community involvement began with issues of education at the local and citywide levels. I was instrumental in the formation of the Organization for a Better Austin [OBA] and I worked my way up through the ranks at OBA, between 1966–71, chairing the Education Committee, the Real Estate Practices Committee, and the Finance Committee before becoming its President for two years.[178]

Although volunteering in the Parent Teacher Association (PTA) was a common route for women to develop leadership skills, when Cincotta became president of the OBA, women's leadership in broader organizations was still quite unusual.

## The Early Bank Protests

The OBA joined forces with the Northwest Community Organization (NCO) and other neighborhood groups in gathering anecdotal stories and data about the difficulty of getting mortgages from banking institutions in Chicago; they then progressed to imaginative, disruptive, nonviolent protests. In 1971, the NCO conducted the first "bank-in" at a local bank: Groups of activists entered the bank; dumped pennies at the teller stations to make deposits; demanded that tellers recount the "deposits"; withdrew the deposits; and sometimes "accidentally" dropped bunches of pennies on the floor. In other actions, neighborhood groups went to the homes of bank officials or regulators. Often, they succeeded in obtaining meetings, at which they negotiated lending commitments. For example, the NCO action led to a meeting with the bank's board and a commitment for $4 million in mortgage lending in the neighborhood.[179] (This, it should be noted, preceded by several years the passage of the Community Reinvestment Act of 1977.)

The activists did not limit their targets to the banks: They also pursued the FHA and the U.S. Department of Housing and Urban Development (HUD). Cal Bradford, an early colleague of Gale Cincotta and longtime activist and researcher, paraphrased Gale Cincotta's view this way: "Really, we hate the government. We don't want the government in our neighborhood. We're trying to get FHA. We want the private economy to come in our neighborhood and do what it does—except with us."[180] As Bradford characterized the community reinvestment movement, "it acted radically, but what it had in mind was pretty conservative."[181]

The religious community provided vital support in the early stages of the movement. The Catholic Church, including especially Catholic Charities, provided funding, as it had for Saul Alinsky's efforts with The Woodlawn Organization. The support was not unanimous: Although there were many young priests who participated in the multi-ethnic, multi-racial organizing efforts, some Catholic congregations and pastors were conservative, even opposing the black in-migration. The Campaign for Human Development of the Catholic Church funded and provided national exposure to Cincotta's efforts. Msgr. Geno Baroni, who founded the National Center for Urban Ethnic Affairs, was a major supporter.[182] Protestant ministers—including Shel Trapp—also participated in organizations such as the OBA.[183]

## National People's Action (NPA) Is Born

Cincotta and Trapp moved beyond the OBA and NCO to form an ad hoc citywide coalition that became the Metropolitan Area Housing Alliance (MAHA). The next step was taking the movement national. The issues they had confronted, such as FHA abuse, were widespread across the United States. On March 18–20, 1972, activists from across the country came together at St. Sylvester's Church in the Palmer Square neighborhood of Chicago, attracting the attention of prominent government officials. "The Fed had heard the term 'redlining' before they came," recalled Michael Westgate, "but they recognized that what was happening in their cities was destroying them."[184] Presidential candidates George McGovern, Eugene McCarthy, and LaDonna Harris attended, as well as Senator Percy and Mayor Richard J. Daley.

A month later, several hundred delegates followed up the Chicago event with a meeting in Baltimore. A two-pronged structure—one that enabled maximum freedom of action—was formed. One arm was National People's Action on Housing (later, National People's Action [NPA]), chaired by Gale Cincotta. NPA was a loose coalition, a forum and mechanism for like-minded community organizations, churches, and others to build collective strength and formulate strategies; its methods were lobbying and direct action. The other arm was the National Training and Information Center (NTIC; initially, the Housing Training and Information Center). A tax-exempt charity, HTIC/NTIC carried out programs for which it could win grants from philanthropies like the Taconic Foundation, a small but vigorous funder of progressive causes, including later CDFIs.

While a national force for community reinvestment was forming, the local advocacy coalitions in Chicago achieved a breakthrough, one that inspired replication across the country. In 1974, they won from Mayor Daley's administration a local version of community reinvestment legislation, three years before the federal Community Reinvestment Act. That June, the Chicago City Council passed a disclosure ordinance, which obliged banking institutions that did business with the City of Chicago to disclose data on their deposits and lending.[185] Other local disclosure ordinances around the country followed.

## HMDA and CRA: Disclosure and Reinvestment

The name of the game for community activists, and for NPA's publication, was disclosure. Cincotta wrote a monthly column, "The Next Move," for *Disclosure,* and in the publication's first issue (August 1974), she declared, "Full mandatory national public disclosure is our primary demand today."[186] NPA drafted an extensive document that had—according to Shel Trapp—"farm loans in, everything, business loans" as well as housing loans.[187] Senator William Proxmire, the Wisconsin Democrat who chaired the Senate Banking Committee, became NPA's chief ally. With his staff, Proxmire pared down NPA's draft legislation in order to overcome opposition. Cincotta was a star witness at the hearing in May 1975, providing research on the history and pattern of mortgage discrimination in Chicago. On September 4, 1975, S. 1281 narrowly passed in the Senate, and on October 31, 1975, a companion bill passed the House. The two versions were reconciled, and the Home Mortgage Disclosure Act (HMDA) of 1975 was signed into law on January 2, 1976, by President Gerald Ford.

Disclosure of redlining was necessary but not sufficient to change mortgage lending: The practices had to be affirmatively prohibited. NPA ramped up the pressure in 1976—the year of the nation's bicentennial. On June 13–14, two thousand supporters came to Washington for NPA's convention. Large numbers of delegates circled around the Washington Hilton, where the American Bankers Association was meeting; dozens "visited" the home of the acting chairman of the Federal Home Loan Bank Board.

At Senate hearings in November 1976, Cincotta called for additional regulations to put teeth in HMDA, earning from Senator Proxmire the honorary title of "Mother of CRA"—the Community Reinvestment Act—even though NPA had not specifically provided him with draft legislation.[188] The banking industry—with support from prominent regulators—was strongly opposed: They railed against the bill as being "credit allocation," the ultimate sin (according to bankers) of the government, directing to whom they were to lend. Arthur Burns, who headed the Federal Deposit Insurance Corporation (FDIC) and then chaired the Federal Reserve Board, declared, "This is the road to serfdom."[189] Nonetheless, Proxmire prevailed, finding a housing bill to which he attached CRA, thus smoothing its passage. With his persistent support, CRA was passed and then signed into law by President Jimmy Carter on October 12, 1977. It became effective on November 6, 1978.

CRA, despite the tremendous passions it roused, was really a rather vague piece of legislation that simply obliged banks to make an affirmative effort to serve the "entire community, including its low- and moderate-income neighborhoods." But it became a potent tool for communities seeking to expand bank lending. When a bank applied to regulators for permission to merge or to open or close a branch, community groups had an opening to protest by submitting a CRA challenge, asserting that the bank had not provided credit equitably to low- and moderate-income segments. To win approval for its application, the bank needed to defend its record. If it could not persuade regulators that it had, indeed, served the entire community fairly, its application could be denied or delayed, pending a public hearing. Even a delay could be very costly to a bank. Consequently, banks were motivated to seek settlements with protesting community groups. Some bankers denounced CRA as an instrument for blackmail by community groups. But it certainly was not credit allocation; banks firmly retained their discretionary lending powers.

In the early years of CRA, there were relatively few challenges. Branch closings and openings and mergers and acquisitions provided the primary opportunities for challenges. But merger and acquisition activity were limited for the balance of the 1970s. Only later did community reinvestment coalitions win multi-billion-dollar commitments from banks to increase their lending and, sometimes, their grant-giving.[190] As the CDFI movement expanded in the early 1990s, CRA facilitated a flow of capital into the hands of these community lenders.

## Reconciling Advocacy and Community Development

It has become accepted wisdom that community organizing and community development are difficult to combine in a single organization. Community development typically requires outside funding, often in substantial amounts, from banks, government, and/or corporations—but these institutions are often the targets of community organizers. Michael Westgate describes how the tension was resolved in Chicago: "The best solution may be, as there was between NHS [Neighborhood Housing Services] of Chicago and NTIC, a relationship where a Bruce Gottschall [of NHS] and a Gale Cincotta could call on each other to take those actions or make those phone calls which might be unseemly if made by the other."[191]

Ed Williams of Chicago's Harris Bank recalled the close relationship between the two organizations. "The NHS, after NTIC, was an organization that Gale loved and supported the most. That's where she spent her time and her energy. She was a drum major for that organization as much as she was for any organization. People could easily confuse her between the two."[192] In fact, Cincotta served on the board of NHS of Chicago, working to choose sites for its neighborhood offices, and she actively supported the national expansion of NHS programs and the establishment of the Neighborhood Reinvestment Corporation. Ted Wysocki, who worked for and with Cincotta in the 1970s, recalls that "Gale always appreciated that there needed to be nonprofit intermediaries to channel capital to the communities."[193]

It would be inaccurate to assume that the vigorous confrontations by Cincotta and the CRA advocacy organizations with the banks were motivated by class hatred and aiming for destruction of the old order. In fact, as Cincotta said, "We weren't talking about overthrowing the government, but how we needed banks. We weren't asking to nationalize the banks. We said we needed them—and their brains—to stabilize our cities."[194]

## South Shore Bank

While Cincotta, Trapp, and their colleagues on the West Side were "inventing" community reinvestment, a team on the South Side was creating the prototypical community development bank. The CRA advocates were working to redirect the lending of mainstream banks to the neighborhoods they had ignored. In contrast, the founders of South Shore Bank sought to aggregate neighborhood deposits and funds from sympathetic foundations, institutions, and individuals in an institution that *they* controlled.

ShoreBank did not play an active role in the coalition-based CRA advocacy efforts (although it did testify in favor of the law). Rather, it provided "proof of concept," refuting the assertion of mainstream bankers that African American and other low-income communities were simply unworthy of credit. As Bruce Gottschall, the first executive director of Neighborhood Housing Services of Chicago, wrote:

> Certainly, ShoreBank's efforts inspired those of us who developed the Neighborhood Housing Services (NHS) of Chicago partnership in 1974–75.... Those of us engaged in this process believed that, following ShoreBank's example, it would be possible to create a partnership among banks, neighborhood residents, and the government to address community lending and investment issues.[195]

The roots of South Shore Bank go back to the 1960s. Recalled Ron Grzywinski, "I remember when Martin Luther King came to speak in Joliet [IL, June 4, 1965]. For some reason, I went there, to a big outdoor stadium; hardly anybody was there, [but] a handful of Catholic nuns. Something drove me to go there."[196] Early in his career, Grzywinski—white and of Polish extraction—translated his commitment to civil rights to the problems of access to credit for minorities and minority-owned businesses. After working for IBM, selling computers to banks, he went to work for a bank in Lockport, IL, an hour's drive outside Chicago, and became its president. The bank had been on a downslide, losing deposits.

"The person they originally put in to run it was himself a racist. He was a longtime employer there," Grzywinski recalled. "He was an older man, didn't understand this neighborhood, and at that time this community was going through all the dynamics of Federal urban renewal." Grzywinski familiarized himself with the changes in the local economy resulting from black in-migration. He describes an experience that could have been drawn from *The Poor Pay More*.[197] Grzywinski recalled visiting a furniture store that was a customer of the Lockport bank.

> The owner was talking to a customer. I walked around and saw that he was selling no-name refrigerators, stoves, television sets, other stuff like that—but the prices all seemed to be brand-name prices....I started asking him about his business. It was pretty clear that this was a schlock operation.
>
> I began leading him on, saying 'You must have a lot of losses, right? Well, how do you finance this store?' He said, 'We finance it all ourselves.' Then he reached into his coat pocket with this sort of snaky smile and he said, 'Interest rates start at 36 percent and they go up from there. We have some losses, but it doesn't really matter, because we get our cost back in the down payment.' I left there saying, 'I've got to do something about this.'

In June 1967, Grzywinski moved on from Lockport to the South Side of Chicago, intending to purchase the Hyde Park Bank. Located near the University of Chicago, the bank was struggling with "white flight" and deterioration. Grzywinski took his vision of a bank with a social mission to the public sector. He met the Illinois state treasurer, Adlai Stevenson III—the son of the former governor of Illinois and twice Democratic candidate for president—who was troubled by the lack of credit available for minority-owned businesses. Stevenson offered a challenge: "I'll tell you what—you're going to see if you can make those loans. I will put a $1 million deposit in your bank for one year at the market rate of interest, see what you can do, and if it works out, renew it."[198]

Grzywinski took the challenge: "Without any advertising at all, it was clear that there was significant good loan demand. For the first seven or eight months, we did all the loans off the corner of my desk." Stevenson renewed the deposit and brought additional deposits through a state fund. Grzywinski described the breakthrough nature of their business lending.

> We started doing minority small business lending at the Hyde Park Bank in 1967. We were the first bank in Illinois, the second in the country to set up a special department for that. In the beginning of '68, I got the board at the Hyde Park Bank to approve us creating a separate department to do that and to support itself by raising deposits for that purpose, deposits from outside the market.

The out-of-market deposit strategy later became the "development deposit" program of South Shore Bank.

## The South Shore Quartet

It was at Hyde Park Bank that the unique team, which would later guide South Shore for decades, took shape. Grzywinski was joined by Mary Houghton, a program officer of the Johnson Foundation; Milton Davis from the University of Chicago Business School and a leader of the Chicago Chapter of the Congress of Racial Equality (CORE); and Jim Fletcher, who grew up in public housing in Chicago and had been director of the OEO's Midwest office. One would be hard-pressed to find in the CDFI movement an enduring team like ShoreBank's, let alone one with multiracial leadership.[199] Together, they touched many bases crucial to the success of South Shore Bank—state and local policymakers, bankers and corporations, academia, anti-poverty circles, and the civil rights movement.

*From left: Mary Houghton, Milton Davis, James Fletcher, Ron Grzywinski. Photograph by Jonathan Becker.*

After successfully turning around the flagging Hyde Park Bank, Grzywinski took a detour from his duties as bank president to become a fellow at the Adlai Stevenson Institute at the University of Chicago.[200] It was there that he focused on designing what would become South Shore Bank. An early collaborator was Michael Bennett, an African American community organizer from Ohio.[201]

The history of the CDFI movement would have taken a different turn if their initial plans had been implemented. Early on, they envisioned "a neighborhood financial institution along the lines of a credit union." As plans matured over 1971–73, "the idea of a credit union as a centerpiece was replaced by a bank, whose role became more central to the process." There were several reasons for the shift. The public would more readily understand a bank; it would convey an image of economic stability, provide better access to the business community, and be seen as trustworthy because of its extensive regulatory oversight. Early plans included a measure of community ownership through the purchase of shares, but that part of the vision was never implemented.[202]

Still, a bank in itself was not a perfect vehicle for reviving a distressed community, as Grzywinski recalled: "All we knew was that we needed to create a self-sustaining organization that could take a comprehensive approach to neighborhood development, and that a bank by itself was inadequate. We started out thinking that it could be anything, but a bank was too limited. It's a passive institution."[203]

However, an expansion in banking powers offered a possible solution. The Bank Holding Company Amendments of 1970, which was implemented two years later through Federal Reserve regulations, permitted banks to invest in community development corporations, to the degree that these were designed primarily to aid low- and moderate-income populations. "Our 'aha' moment was this: If the Fed would allow a bank holding company to invest, could a bank holding company *be* a community development corporation? That is how we then were able to design ShoreBank."[204]

South Shore Bank's founders would use this power to create a "family" of institutions under the umbrella of a holding company, the Illinois Neighborhood Development Corporation (INDC). With a constellation of for-profit and nonprofit entities, they would have multiple tools to address neighborhood deterioration and poverty. South Shore Bank would not have to simply wait for deals to be brought to it: Rather, through its affiliates, it could acquire property, develop job training programs, seek foundation grants, and do just about anything required for a strategy of comprehensive community economic development. This vision of a multifaceted holding company structure would not be fully built out until 1978. But first, the challenge was capitalizing South Shore Bank itself.

## Raising Startup Capital

The first step in 1972 was to raise money for a feasibility study—only $50,000, but even this was not an easy lift, Grzywinski recalled: "It took a year, and the money came from 13 sources," gathered from a combination of foundations, a conservative insurance company (which placed a matching requirement), and various individuals, including a contribution as small as $100 from a director of the Hyde Park Bank.

The bigger goal was $4 million. Grzywinski wryly recalled that they raised capital based on an "original offering circular…to purchase an unknown bank in an unknown neighborhood someplace in Chicago for demonstrating an untested idea." An investment unit was priced at $160,000. An initial unit was purchased by Edison Dick, the scion of the A.B. Dick Company (the dominant manufacturer of mimeograph machines). South Shore Bank, like so many CDFIs that followed it, turned to the faith community for investments. With the assistance of Stanley Hallett, a former Methodist minister and one of the original board members of South Shore Bank, they successfully pitched the Board of Homeland Ministries of the United Church of Christ.[205] Other early investors included the Executive Council of the Episcopal Church, the Wieboldt Foundation of Chicago, the Joyce Foundation, and the Cummins Engine Foundation.[206]

The Ford Foundation would become a major, repeat investor in ShoreBank—but not immediately. Ford was not asked for, nor did it fund, ShoreBank's initial feasibility study. When Grzywinski asked Ford to purchase two investment units totaling $320,000, he was initially rejected: "They said, 'Ford has a policy that it will only invest in one community development corporation per city and we've already invested in TWO, The Woodlawn Organization,' which was in the next neighborhood over from us."[207]

The door was partially reopened a few months later. The foundation offered to purchase the two investment units, but on the condition that South Shore Bank would extend its work to the Woodlawn neighborhood. Grzywinski demurred: "I said, 'I've made a commitment to all the other shareholders that we would work only in South Shore, so I can't commit to Woodlawn without getting their approval.'" And in fact, the other shareholders, particularly the United Church of Christ, would not go along with Ford's condition: They believed that the capital goal was barely enough to serve a single neighborhood.[208]

The bank's team returned to Ford with this news. Ford agreed to invest but reduced its commitment to $160,000 for the South Shore neighborhood alone. But the path was still not easy. What South Shore needed—like any other bank—was equity, a cushion of capital to absorb any losses. Without equity, it would be unable to raise deposits. The Ford Foundation was not prepared to invest equity, especially not in a for-profit entity, which South Shore Bank certainly was. The negotiations went on for a year and involved much wrangling over the structure and funding of the investment.

> First, they wanted us to pay our legal costs. We said we couldn't do that. They said, 'Okay,' and they drew up an agreement that was [actually] a loan, but was like equity in every other way: It had no maturity date, it had no interest payment. It was equity. We even convinced the Feds that it was equity. Later when the Fed got tougher, they even grandfathered it in.[209]

In the end, the Grzywinski and his colleagues raised a modest amount of equity capital to purchase South Shore Bank: $800,000. Grzywinski invested $100,000 of his own borrowed funds. Much of the startup capital to purchase the bank derived from a $2.4 million loan from the American National Bank, with a guarantee by Grzywinski and his wife.[210]

## Why South Shore?

Grzywinski and his colleagues knew they wanted to buy a bank. They did not start with the notion of purchasing a bank on the South Side of Chicago, but the South Shore neighborhood had certain advantages: There was physical deterioration and crime, but it was not as bad as some other neighborhoods; there was some good housing stock. There were neighborhood organizations, including the South Shore Commission (although some of its members wanted to "stabilize" the neighborhood by keeping blacks out). Most important: The neighborhood had an existing bank that wanted to depart the declining neighborhood for a location in the prosperous downtown.

In 1972, the CRA was not yet a gleam in the eyes of Gale Cincotta and Senator William Proxmire. But residents opposed the relocation plans of Hyde Park's bank; they feared it would be a symbolic death blow to the community. The weapon of a CRA challenge did not yet exist. But the residents did have some leverage: Bank regulators could weigh "convenience and need" in ruling on a bank's application to relocate. The Office of the Comptroller of the Currency held hearings in 1972 on the bank's application. The Legal Aid Society of Chicago helped the community to prepare its arguments, and on December 5, 1972, the Comptroller of the Currency denied the bank's application, citing the needs of the South Shore community as a factor in his decision.[211]

In contrast with later CRA campaigns, Richard Taub wrote, "It is important to note that this was not a mass community mobilization. It represented the efforts of a few concerned citizens who could mobilize some expert resources to make its case. It is also doubtful that they would have succeeded" if a competitor bank in the proposed downtown location had not also voiced its opposition.[212] Thus, the path was cleared for the opening of the nation's first community development bank. In August 1973, the new South Shore Bank was born.

South Shore Bank's founders did not take over a thriving concern: The bank had $38 million in deposits, down by about half from a decade before. The founders did not have deep pockets—some $800,000 in equity and $2.4 million in debt. The heavy proportion of debt would drag down profitability for much of the 1970s. In addition to the debt burden, the new bank faced another big challenge to sustainability. Its goal was to demonstrate the viability of a for-profit, market-based approach in a low-income community. But by its nature, the banking business in low-income neighborhoods is dominated by an abundance of depositors with small savings balances and customers who mostly need small loans or need to pay household bills. Small transactions are expensive, especially in terms of teller time; small loans are often as costly to underwrite as much larger loans. South Shore Bank confronted the dilemma faced by any depository dedicated to serving a low-income population.[213]

How, then, would South Shore Bank become sustainable and also achieve its mission of revitalizing the South Shore neighborhood? First, it had to increase its deposit base so that it had sufficient funds to lend. But this would be difficult, if not impossible, without increasing its equity capital—the cushion to absorb losses. Insured banks and credit unions are required by their regulators to maintain a certain ratio of equity capital or net worth to their total assets; they cannot raise unlimited deposits.

From the outset, it was not easy for South Shore to raise either deposits or equity. Although the bank's founders could point to their previous successes in lending to minority businesses, South Shore Bank itself had a limited track record. Nonetheless, a capitalization campaign in 1973-74 brought in $1.381 million in additional equity to fuel expansion. On the deposit side, by 1974, the bank had developed a signature product aimed at going beyond its limited local base: "development deposits." Susan Davis, who had run a newsletter on women's rights, spearheaded this early effort, which used "state-of-the-art" technology: an electronic typewriter, to personalize appeals to institutional investors, including religious organizations, foundations, corporations, and other "social investors." To document South Shore's accomplishments and keep investor interest strong, the bank started issuing an annual report highlighting the impact of its development deposits.

This, then, was the formula: Use large institutional deposits to cross-subsidize the profit-squeezing base of small neighborhood deposits. Although deposits were essential, they were not really the focus for the South Shore team of Grzywinski, Houghton, Davis, and Fletcher. "None of us were operations people," Houghton recalled. "We didn't actually care about deposits. We were totally focused on lending, and getting as much money out in the neighborhood in investment as possible. We didn't really have a lot of talent on the deposit side. It all just took a while."[214]

## Retail Banking vs. Development

South Shore Bank did not have the luxury of ignoring the mundane side of banking. If its goal was to revitalize a neighborhood, it needed something better than its legacy second-class facility and operation; the new bank had to generate local pride and energy. The bank set out to update its obsolete computer system, provide a decent parking lot, and make the bank customer-friendly. But even these measures were not an overwhelming success: As Taub wrote, "The combination of increasing hours, simplifying procedures, reducing minimum balance requirements, and proving parking and drive-up teller facilities should have increased bank deposits. The bank did attract new depositors by lowering the barriers, but the total amount of money in deposits did not discernably rise."[215]

Moreover, the bank did not successfully deepen its relationships with the neighborhood, despite the efforts of Milton Davis, the bank's president and chief community liaison. "What is striking," Taub wrote, "is that it has kept the community at a distance. Its efforts to generate formal relations with community groups have been ambivalent."[216] Thus, despite the idealism of its founders, their civil rights roots, and links to the anti-poverty movement of the Sixties, South Shore Bank in the end was a *bank*, a privately owned, for-profit development entity, not a vehicle for direct "community empowerment" or ownership. It was not a cooperative, a credit union, or a minority institution—it was a *community development bank*.

South Shore's innovative national campaign to raise development deposits from sympathetic institutions brought in the funds it needed to expand. But the challenge remained: how to make profitable loans in its market? The team did not inherit a good portfolio from its predecessor: It included many uncollectable FHA loans. One option was to specialize in small consumer loans, which would yield an interest rate sufficient to provide a reasonable profit margin. These loans would be appealing in a low-income and minority community that lacked other good choices. But automobile or other consumer loans did not build a compelling narrative that would attract social investors interested in community development. It is unlikely South Shore Bank would have become nationally prominent if its "story" to socially responsible investors was, "We make car loans."

The management team established a "development division" for commercial lending, headed by Mary Houghton. This built on the expertise that Grzywinski and Davis had developed in minority enterprise lending.[217] It also provided a lending destination and marketing rationale for South Shore's growing development deposit campaign, yielding inspiring stories for the bank's annual reports to social investors. Still, its commercial lending was not an unmitigated success: Even with guarantees from the federal Small Business Administration (SBA) for some loans, the bank found the lending process costly.

What did become a much greater success, providing a great story for the bank to tell its national audience, was *real estate lending*, especially for multifamily dwellings purchased, owned, and rehabilitated by small, "mom-and-pop" entrepreneurs. Of course, this was not the bank's only line of business: Working with local corporate and foundation partners, South Shore was also able to play a financial role in much larger projects, although these efforts had mixed results.

## Filling Out the Holding Company

South Shore Bank made progress in its first five years, despite its initial heavy burden of debt, the expense and difficulties in upgrading its retail operations, and the challenges of lending in a low-income, credit-starved neighborhood. But as reactive institutions, saying yes or no to the loan applications that came through the door, banks had limited ability to drive an agenda of community development.

South Shore found the answer in using the liberalized powers provided by the Bank Holding Company Amendments of 1970. In 1978, it created a series of affiliates and subsidiaries to fill out the family of its holding company, the Illinois Neighborhood Development Corporation (INDC):
- The City Lands Corporation, a 100-percent-owned, for-profit subsidiary that initiated and managed real estate rehabilitation projects
- The Neighborhood Institute (TNI), a tax-exempt charitable affiliate that initiated and managed social and economic development projects
- The Neighborhood Fund, also a wholly owned INDC for-profit subsidiary, licensed by the SBA as a Minority Enterprise Small Business Investment Corporation.[218]

Although the other new members were for-profit, TNI was founded as a charitable organization, which provided a vital channel for foundation and government grants, tax-deductible contributions, and other funding. Such a structure could readily be used for programs and services that would otherwise drag down the bank's profitability. This could create problems with examiners, who did not share the bank's enthusiasm for costly, non-income-generating services, such as financial counseling, advising business borrowers, or job training—not to mention community organizing. TNI received crucial, ongoing support from the Mott Foundation and the Chicago Community Trust; it could provide a kind of engagement with the predominantly African American community that was not as readily done by the bank itself.[219]

# CHAPTER 4. Grassroots Community Development and its Supporters

## The "New Hope": CDCs in the 1970s

After a decade of urban experiments with dubious success, in 1971 the Twentieth Century Fund released a study of community development corporations, entitled "CDCs: New Hope for the Inner City." The fund—which was, in fact, the organization founded in 1919 by Edward Filene, the patron of the credit union movement—had assembled a task force that included a Senate subcommittee staffer, businesspeople, academics, and several CDC directors, including Franklin Thomas of Bedford-Stuyvesant. Notably, the author and compiler of its report was Geoffrey Faux, who had a "front seat" to the programs of the Sixties as the former director of the Division of Economic Development of the Office of Economic Opportunity (OEO).[220]

Broadly speaking, there were two opposing poles in the social policy of the 1960s during the War on Poverty: There were those who believed in the primacy of community empowerment—"maximum feasible participation" by the poor; and there were those who, like Mitchell ("Mike") Sviridoff at CPI in New Haven, disdained community control and espoused a more top-down notion of development that sought to remedy the "deficits" of the poor through education and other programs. Faux, likely shaped by the OEO experience, was initially skeptical about CDCs:

> Like most other professionals trying to fight the war on poverty, I believed that it could be won only by providing the poor with services such as training and education, which would cure them of their economic disabilities. I was particularly doubtful about the capacity of the people in ghettos and barrios to develop their own opportunities. I am no longer skeptical.[221]

CDCs were the bearers of hope—a rare commodity in 1970. This was, after all, three years after the bloody uprisings of 1967 with the stunning, if obvious, verdict of the Kerner Commission ringing in Americans' ears: "Our nation is moving toward two societies, one black, one white—separate and unequal."[222]

There was a vigorous debate about whether the ghetto, with its predominantly black and Latino residents, should be broken up and its inhabitants "dispersed" to the suburbs or "developed." The Twentieth Century Fund's task force allowed that some combination of strategies might be necessary, but it came down more heavily on the side of development, in near-apocalyptic terms: "If the nation has nothing to offer the alienated, hostile masses of the inner city but a welfare check and a vague hope that some day they may be transplanted to the suburbs, it will face a confrontation with these masses long before a dispersal strategy can be effected."[223]

By the turn of the 1970s, there were, according to the task force, about 75 urban CDCs in operation, although there were also some rural entities, and—as Faux noted—the definition of a CDC was so nebulous that various other entities might call themselves or be considered CDCs. The track record of CDCs was still relatively limited and brief. Nonetheless, the task force found that CDCs were a much more promising creation than the Model Cities agencies or community action agencies (CAAs) of the War on Poverty: "Community development corporations, because they are conceived and designed locally, are more flexible and responsive to local needs and conditions than are organizations which have been designed in Washington."[224] Praising the engagement of local residents, the task force noted that "their efforts have been made despite national apathy and even hostility at times from those whose help they expected."[225]

## The "CDFI Fund" That Wasn't: Stillborn Legislation

Even while CDCs were in their relative infancy, their supporters began fashioning legislation to nurture and expand their network. As early as summer 1968, the Community Self-Determination Act was introduced in Congress. The bill's provisions foreshadowed, and even went beyond, many of the ideas that re-emerged with the efforts to establish a CDFI Fund in the 1990s, including the following.

- Federal chartering of CDCs and community development banks
- Creation of a nationwide community development bank as a secondary financing institution
- Authorization of favorable tax status for CDCs
- "Turnkey" tax incentives for cooperating with outside businesses
- Managerial and technical assistance money for CDCs through the SBA.[226]

The bill was endorsed by Senators Humphrey and Muskie, both Democratic presidential candidates; even Republican presidential candidate Richard Nixon found it worthy of consideration. But it was an election year, and for various reasons, the proposed initiative languished. It was revised and revived in 1970, prepared under the auspices of the Senate Subcommittee on Employment, Manpower, and Poverty, as the Community Corporation Act of 1970. It gathered 33 Senate sponsors and 48 in the House; although not formally introduced, it was circulated for comment. As described by Faux, the principal points were these.

- National community development corporations could be chartered by various anti-poverty organizations: CAAs, Model Neighborhood Corps, local and community development

corporations, tribes, and others. They would have the power to raise capital by selling shares with a par value of $5.
- These corporations could be established in poor urban and rural areas with population less than 100,000.
- A National Community Corporation Certification Board would grant charters for these organizations and make grants to them.
- CDCs would be authorized to "raise debt capital on a 20-to-1 ratio to initial equity capitalization, to assist in the financing of business enterprises. Using this capital, CDBs would be true development banks and would not engage in consumer financing or accept deposits."[227]
- A national community development bank would provide secondary financing for local community development banks and could perform the functions of these banks where none existed.
- An existing organization would be permitted to start a CDC, or else convert to one.

Had these legislative concepts become law, a federally sponsored community development banking network, much like that created in the 1990s, would have emerged nearly 25 years earlier. A comparison with the later CDFI Fund legislative language is instructive. The National Community Corporation Certification Board, like the later CDFI Fund, would provide capital to eligible institutions, with the purpose of enabling them to leverage additional debt. The proposal recognized the need for *equity capital*, the shortage of which was a major obstacle to business development in the ghetto and to the sustainability of CDCs—an obstacle that would be no less formidable in the 1990s.

The proposal strongly endorsed the need for a national support structure for CDCs: "What now exists is a hodgepodge of small, scattered efforts by a variety of Federal and local agencies, foundations, business corporation and church groups to finance inner-city development."[228] Its very language foreshadowed candidate Clinton's: "The Federal Government and concerned people in the private sector should establish as a minimum goal the provision of enough resources to assure that there are *at least one hundred urban community development corporations* [emphasis added] with the capacity to handle large-scale development programs by January 1973."

The similarities of context are also striking. The push for CDCs followed shortly after a wave of urban uprisings, which heightened urgency about finding some sort of feasible initiative to address the massive problems of inequality and racial discrimination. The 1992 campaign of Bill Clinton and his promise to create a "network of 100 community development banks and 1,000 microenterprise programs" followed by a few months the uprising in South Central Los Angeles in April 1992, resulting from the acquittal of the police officers who brutalized Rodney King. This coincidence is hardly surprising: Nothing so invigorates the search for a federal urban initiative as riots in the inner city.

Even more than the later CDFI initiative, "CDBs [community development banks] would be true development banks and would not engage in consumer financing or accept deposits." This explicit refusal to foster basic banking services in low-income communities is surprising, given the difficulties those consumers faced, as documented years earlier in *The Poor Pay More*. Although candidate Bill Clinton highlighted the need to fuel businesses' development, his visits to South Central Los Angeles sensitized him to the scarcity of bank branches and affordable basic banking services in inner cities. The CDFI Fund would support community development "banks" of all types.

The 1970 proposal envisioned a national community development bank to serve as a source of "secondary financing" for local CDCs or community development banks. In various ways, this notion appeared in the later CDFI policy debates and legislative language. For example, Alfonse D'Amato, Republican senator from New York, negotiated his grudging support for a CDFI Fund in exchange for a secondary market for business loans.[229] The CDFI legislation had a provision for supporting institutions that enhance the liquidity of CDFIs (although this has not been systematically pursued).

How did the respective community development banking initiatives address the question of community ownership and engagement? It is striking that the 1970 proposal envisioned a form of community ownership through sales of shares with a par value of only $5; the one-person, one-vote rule was to ensure democratic control, perhaps a vestige of the community empowerment and ownership philosophy of the 1960s. Although CDFI legislation directed the fund to consider "the extent to which the applicant is, or will be, community-owned or community-governed,"[230] in practice, the fund required only that an applicant ensure "community accountability," a standard that was vague at best.

The question of "ownership" arose in another form as well. The 1970 proposal put in the hands of a National Community Corporation Certification Board the power to grant charters to community development banks. The CDFI Fund, in contrast, certifies CDFIs, although it does not charter them.[231] In both cases, the national body—presumably a federal entity—controls the designation: who is "in" and who is eligible for investment.

Amid the efforts to develop systematic national support for CDCs, a new organization to represent their interests was formed in 1970. The National Congress for Community Economic Development (NCCED) was spearheaded by those CDCs that had been funded by the OEO under its Title VII program. Throughout the late 1960s and 1970s, CDCs multiplied, but modestly. "The main reason the industry seemed stuck in small numbers was that projects, even if successful, rarely produced enough excess revenue to pay the overhead costs of a successful CDC."[232]

The 1970 bill might have gone far to develop a national support system, but it did not advance through the legislative process. Despite considerable congressional support, it lacked what later CDFI legislation had: the support of a popular, newly elected president.

## Community Development Credit Unions (CDCUs)

Too little capital: The Government Accounting Office (GAO),* the regulators, and the credit union movement itself all agreed that this was a primary reason why the anti-poverty credit unions of the 1960s failed to thrive. The Nixon administration's attack on the War on Poverty reduced government

---

\* Since 2004, the Government Accountability Office.

funding. Many low-income credit unions were forced to liquidate; others were unable to expand their services and membership; and few new credit unions were started.

A potential game changer came in October 1970, when the Federal Credit Union Act[233] was amended to provide deposit insurance in the amount of $20,000 per account for credit unions. The insurance fund would be comparable to the FDIC, but it would be administered by a newly established independent agency, the National Credit Union Administration (NCUA).[234] In its June 1971 report, the GAO optimistically pointed out that deposit insurance would make it easier to attract institutional capital to supplement the modest savings pools of anti-poverty credit unions: Organizations would be more willing to deposit funds in low-income credit unions if the funds could be insured against loss.[235] More deposits meant more funds to loan; more lending would mean more income; more income would improve the prospects for sustainability.

Deposit insurance brought with it a grand trade-off: the security of federal guarantees versus a fundamental principle of cooperation. Before share insurance, credit unions were "pure" cooperatives. That is, they were democratically owned entirely by their members, each of whom had one and only one vote; deposits were called "shares," which accurately reflected the reality that if the credit union became insolvent, its members risked some or all of their deposits. The advent of federal insurance transferred risk to the government-controlled fund. To this day, deposits in credit unions are called "shares," but since they are federally insured, they do not represent the kind of equity stake that previously characterized credit unions. Credit unions remain democratic in the sense of one member, one vote—but the federal government is a major "stakeholder," which acts to protect the interests of the National Credit Union Share Insurance Fund.[236]

In fact, credit unions were sharply divided on the new deposit legislation. Federal deposit insurance—backed by the "full faith and credit" of the United States government—promised to bring additional members to credit unions (indeed, it did, by the tens of millions). But some credit unions believed that the movement was doing fine without federal deposit insurance. They feared that it would inevitably bring increasingly intrusive regulation and supervision by Washington (and indeed, many would argue that this is precisely what happened).*

## The Crisis for Low-Income Credit Unions

Federal share insurance was not automatically provided to all credit unions: They needed to meet certain regulatory standards to qualify. Specifically, they needed sufficient equity capital, or net worth. Not surprisingly, many low-income credit unions had struggled to build adequate net worth as a cushion against losses. Already decimated by the loss of subsidies, many OEO credit unions confronted the denial of federal deposit insurance.

---

\* Decades later, a similar concern about regulation echoed within the community development loan fund movement, as it debated whether to join the campaign for a federal CDFI Fund.

Failing to gain deposit insurance would have been a death sentence for those credit unions. It is hard to conceive of a viable two-tier system in which some credit unions were insured, but others were not. The threat of mass extinction brought together the group of grassroots leaders that became known informally as the Federation of Limited Income Credit Unions. Over the course of 1971–72, the group successfully advocated for infusions of federal capital from the OEO. The support of the regulator, the NCUA, enabled many of the at-risk credit unions to obtain transitional share insurance. Moreover, low-income credit unions won the exclusive privilege of insuring deposits from nonmembers: Other credit unions could provide deposit insurance only to their members.*

Surviving the share insurance crisis did not ensure smooth sailing for low-income credit unions. Support from the OEO for credit union operations was vanishing. By December 1972, only 274 of the more than 400 OEO credit unions still existed, according to the Credit Union National Association (CUNA).[237] CUNA's study noted that "low income communities continue to face enormous problems in attempting to achieve viability. Despite a decade as the object of national attention, these communities are still unable to follow a traditional path to self-development."[238] On the other hand, despite their declining numbers, many of the OEO-related credit unions hung on, "long after many predicted their certain demise."[239]

In fact, studying 1973 financial data, CUNA found that the vital signs for many community development credit unions (CDCUs) were encouraging. The low-income credit unions increased their deposits and loan portfolio far more rapidly than credit unions in general. But the robust growth rates were concentrated among the credit unions with higher assets. The smallest credit unions were having a particularly hard time. CUNA found that 73 of 155 credit unions it studied were

> not making significant progress toward self-sufficiency. While there is no doubt that these credit unions have provided valuable services to their communities, it would appear that many of them *exist only because of the subsidies they receive rather than have the subsidies supplement their income during the growth process* [emphasis added].[240]

Size mattered. To achieve sustainability, it was necessary (although not sufficient) to aggregate enough deposits to meet the credit needs of the community. There were scattered, modest efforts to obtain outside "nonmember" deposits to supplement those of low-income members. But ensuring the survival of the low-income credit union movement would demand a broader, more systematic national effort.

---

\* The issue of capital adequacy would return in 1998, when Congress mandated capital standards for credit unions; those that fell short of the required capital ratio faced an increasingly rigorous regime of sanctions—"prompt corrective action," up to and including liquidation. Again, low-income credit unions were disproportionately vulnerable.

## Creating the National Federation of CDCUs:
## The Quest for Community-Controlled Capital

After winning transitional share insurance, in spring 1974, the grassroots leaders of the informal Federation of Limited Income Credit Unions decided to form a permanent national organization. That year, they incorporated and became the National Federation of Community Development Credit Unions. In November 1974, they held their first annual meeting.[241]

The federation would remain an all-volunteer operation for several years, housed in "the left side of my desk," recalled Al Alayon, the federation's president, whose "day job" was CEO of the Consumer Action Program of Bedford-Stuyvesant, Inc., in Brooklyn, NY. "We had no staff. Our board members would be our technical staff," he recalled.[242] It was only in 1977 that the organization was able to open offices of its own in downtown Brooklyn, and James N. Clark became its first paid executive director.

Thinking big, the newly minted National Federation of CDCUs launched a campaign for a federal fund to provide capital and technical support to its member credit unions. In 1974, the federation laid out its vision and strategy for creating a federal fund in a document that became known as "The Blue Book" because of its cover. It articulated the theory of change at the heart of the CDCU movement:

> Low-income areas have generally not been able to develop the economic infrastructure needed to reinvest earnings and thereby promote internal growth and self-sufficiency. They continue to be characterized by a constant negative flow of income. Income inflows from salaries, transfer payments and business activities are matched and often exceeded by income outflows produced by consumer purchases outside the area and profits extracted by outside owners of community businesses and housing stock. Community savings, deposited at local branch banks, do not serve to build up the community because they are often drawn to higher-profit, shorter term investments in areas perceived as more stable and productive.[243]

It was bad enough that banks extracted and exported deposits from low-income communities—they left residents at the mercy of high-cost creditors. Without access to affordable credit, the "lack of savings signifies that the low-income person possesses no buffer against the fluctuations of the economy. He has no extra resources in a time of crisis. Facing a crisis, he is forced to turn to a finance company or a loan shark for even more money."[244] (Substitute "payday lender" for "finance company," and the analysis readily applies to the dilemmas of the poor and other unbanked people in the twenty-first century.)

The solution, argued the National Federation, was to create a strong, federally supported CDCU movement that would address the root causes of poverty. The movement would work "to inhibit chronic negative flows of income which now drain low income areas … and provide an indigenous source of capital for minority and low income business development."[245] CDCUs would pool savings;

recirculate them as reasonably priced loans; mitigate capital outflows; and even, in the best-case scenario, provide a channel for outside capital to flow *into* poverty communities, thus enhancing an economic multiplier effect. They would expand their provision of the day-to-day financial services low-income people needed: check-cashing at low or no cost; sales of food stamps; and more.[246] They would expand nonfinancial services, including consumer education and counseling and assistance to small businesses. (In the CDFI era, these would be known as "development services" and would be a requirement for winning awards from the CDFI Fund.)

With federal investment, CDCUs would avoid the trap of remaining second-class financial institutions—"poor men's banks": Their members would receive a return on their savings comparable to that of other financial institutions, "considering the value of the extra services provided by the credit unions."[247] In fact, the CDCU would become the "vanguard" of the credit union movement, bringing its benefits community-wide rather than restricting services, as other credit unions did, to specific employee groups, religious organizations, and associations.

Boldly, the National Federation argued that the federal government should create a fund controlled by the CDCU movement itself. Specifically, the federation proposed "that it be granted $18 million over a three-year period by the Office of Economic Opportunity," to develop "an innovative program designed to stabilize and strengthen eligible community development credit unions."[248] The bulk of this program—$16.1 million—would go a Credit Union Development Fund, while the remainder would go for personnel costs, especially technical assistance, planning, and management support.

The resulting financial system would be accountable to low-income people and communities from bottom to top. A board of trustees would be created, whose members would be appointed by the National Federation with the approval of the OEO. The trustees, which included the federation's president ex officio, would review and approve requests for operational subsidy and capital, based on a business plan and written agreement between the credit union and the fund.[249] Although the federation's proposal called for a one-time, three-year grant, the new federal entity was to be an ongoing revolving fund that would be replenished as deposits flowed back from credit unions that had achieved self-sufficiency.

Applicants to the Credit Union Development Fund would be required to develop comprehensive business plans—unlike the OEO initiative (but quite like the later requirements of the CDFI Fund). The fund would assist with operations, lending, marketing, and obtaining additional capital from the private sector. Credit unions would receive subsidies in diminishing amounts as they increased their lending volume and hence their income. Importantly, the credit unions would be supported in adding data processing capability. This was not only to increase operational efficiencies; it would be

> especially important in assuring that these credit unions will be able to receive the direct deposit of members' transfer payments, a new development which is sure to affect many community development members. The Treasury Department is already experimenting with the direct deposit of all transfer payments (social security, disability, veterans and public assistance payments).[250]

What would the federal government get for its money? A network of capable, sustainable community-owned and managed institutions: "[CDCUs would] become full-service neighborhood financial institutions whose momentum will insure continued growth and sufficient income over the long run."[251] The infusion of funds would enable credit unions to meet their loan demand, increase income, increase dividends to members, and increase membership and service, thus generating a virtuous cycle. The federation projected that most recipient credit unions would achieve self-sufficiency by 1980.[252]

It was an ambitious vision, especially for a volunteer-run movement that still was struggling to survive. Hampered by a lack of resources and Washington beltway expertise, the federation was unable to bring its proposal to fruition, as the federation's executive director, Jim Clark, wrote to its membership several years later.

> In 1975, we came close to having our proposal funded. Congress at that time looked favorably upon our comprehensive CDCU development proposal. Working with CSA [the Community Services Administration, successor to the OEO], we lobbied but as a result of our lack of sophistication in the appropriation process, others were able to move their agendas and we lost our opportunity.[253]

## CDCUs and President Carter's "Comprehensive National Urban Policy"

In November 1976, Jimmy Carter was elected president, ending eight years of the Republican Nixon and Ford administrations and raising advocates' hopes for greater federal support for urban issues. On March 21, 1977, President Carter instructed cabinet secretaries to form an interagency working policy group on urban and regional development, spearheaded by HUD Secretary Patricia Harris. On March 27, 1978, in his National Urban Policy Message to Congress, Carter submitted his proposals for a comprehensive national urban policy—a "New Partnership involving all levels of the government, the private sector, and neighborhood and voluntary organizations in a major effort to make America's cities better places in which to live and work."[254]

The goals were impeccable, and the means numerous. The policy would "increase access to opportunity for those disadvantaged by economic circumstance or a history of discrimination."[255] There would be a National Development Bank, an Urban Volunteer Corps, increased aid to state and local government, expanded Community Development Block Grant funding, and much more. President Carter proposed that an additional $20 million be appropriated to the Community Services Administration as "venture capital for the most effective Community Development Corporations."[256] A "self-help development program"[257] would be established in the Office for Neighborhoods in HUD. Near the end of his policy message, he pledged support for the CDCU movement.

> Some urban communities are not served by any financial institutions. Community Development Credit Unions address this problem by investing their assets in the communities in which they are established. This type of credit union was first established under the poverty programs in the 1960's. About 225 exist today, and many are the only financial institutions in their communities.
>
> I am proposing a $12 million program to provide $200,000 in seed capital for new Community Development Credit Unions, to provide them with an operating subsidy for staff, training and technical assistance.[258]

So, CDCs and CDCUs were both to be partners in rebuilding urban neighborhoods. The National Federation's advocacy had reached the highest levels. But already, the prospective budget for the Credit Union Development Fund had shrunk by one-third, from the National Federation's proposed $18 million program to $12 million.

## Hijacked!

The reduction in funding—even before the Carter proposal made its way to Congress—was painful enough. But for the National Federation, the greater disappointment was that the CDCU movement would be marginalized; its vision of a community-controlled capital was subsumed and subverted by federal control. In a memo to the federation's board of directors on March 31, 1978, shortly after the president's announcement, Executive Director Jim Clark wrote: "To our surprise, the National Credit Union Administration submitted a proposal which contained many of the elements of the Federation's proposed work plan."[259]

> When we approached NCUA after discovering this submission [to the White House], the response provided was 'This was a government initiative.' NCUA obviously decided that there was no need to confer with the Federation, although it had no problem adapting our comprehensive proposal in its CDCU proposal. ... In effect, NCUA saw itself not only as the agency to carry out the total initiative with a complete disregard not only for the Federation and other organizations that have worked to strengthen CDCUs but also for the Community Services Administration.[260]

The "power grab" by the NCUA did not stop there. Not only were CDCUs denied a role in managing the funds or setting policy, the NCUA proposed stringent new procedures for chartering those credit unions that would receive funds: These credit unions alone would be qualified to be called "CDCUs." As Al Alayon recalled, "The NCUA tried to redefine the name that we coined, we created, and we defined. *We* defined who we were."[261]

The National Federation was furious. It denounced the NCUA's plan as "selective, exclusionary and demeaning, requiring the very credit unions that put [the] community development credit union movement in the forefront to qualify officially under a new NCUA chartering policy.... It also appears that the initiative is more slanted to new credit unions" than existing credit unions.[262] The federation and its allies could take some comfort in the Carter administration's rejection of one NCUA prerogative, namely allocation of capital: "The Office of Management and Budget made it very clear that NCUA would not administer the capitalization fund."[263]

## The Bittersweet Fruits of Victory

On November 20, 1979, P.L 96-123 created the Community Development Revolving Loan Fund for Credit Unions (CDRLF). It did not provide $18 million or even $12 million; only $6 million was appropriated. The National Federation did not run it: It was jointly administered by the NCUA and the CSA, the much-diminished successor to the OEO. There were no grants to subsidize operations, nor to automate credit unions; some provision was made for technical assistance.

Even that victory was short-lived. In 1981, the Reagan administration set out to eliminate the CDRLF, along with other vestiges of federal anti-poverty policies and programs. The National Federation would fight throughout the 1980s to keep the fund alive and make it useful. By the close of the 1980s, the federation did achieve that limited victory, but by then, the fund was exclusively administered by the NCUA—a potential conflict of interest for that regulatory agency.

## Raising Private Capital

Along with their lengthy, concerted efforts to create a federal fund, CDCUs individually and collaboratively sought to expand private-sector and institutional deposits, even before such deposits were insured. The CABS Federal Credit Union (named after Consumer Action for Bedford-Stuyvesant) in Brooklyn played a prominent role. Starting in 1968, it obtained a $10,000 deposit from the National Council of the Churches of Christ, followed by deposits in amounts of $10,000–$30,000 from corporations (the advertising agency Doyle, Dane & Bernbach; Standard Oil of New Jersey), religious organizations (Union Theological Seminary), and other credit unions (Schaeffer Brewery Employees Credit Union).[264]

After CDCUs won the privilege of acquiring insured nonmember deposits, it became easier to attract outside capital.[265] The National Federation gained an important ally in the National Center for Urban Ethnic Affairs (NCUEA), which was founded in 1971 by civil rights and social activist Monsignor Geno Baroni, later assistant secretary of HUD. Monsignor Baroni was a prominent advocate for CDCUs, urging the Campaign for Human Development of the Catholic Church to work both with community and church-based credit unions. As NCUEA's literature explained, "These efforts focused on expanding the horizons of the credit unions associated with religious institutions to include the economic revitalization of the entire community."[266] With the NCUEA's assistance, the "New York Four"—credit unions located in four low-income neighborhoods—formed a coalition to solicit nonmember deposits.[267]

CDCUs are routinely stereotyped as exclusively consumer lenders. It is certainly true that the OEO-era credit unions and many of their successors were motivated by and focused on household-level problems of poverty. But some, like the "New York Four," expressly sought outside capital to supply liquidity for loans to local businesses. For example, the Lower East Side FCU's business plan was entitled "Plan for SBA Guaranteed Business Loans and for Growth thru Non-Member Deposits."[268] It stated, "The Credit Union is an integral part of the LESEDAC program of economic development. LESEDAC's goal has been to create alternative institutions on a cooperative format to provide the entrepreneurial and credit structures missing in the area."[269] Similarly, the CABS Federal Credit Union was integral to its parent nonprofit's broader agenda of community development. "Its activities and the implied stability and credibility it gives to the activities of its parent corporation, the Consumer Action Program of Bedford-Stuyvesant (CABS), have created jobs, expanded area income and provided for essential services.[270] With its parent, the credit union had

- Cosponsored a $2.2 million housing development, with space for a daycare center
- Provided "stability and credibility" needed for CABS to obtain a $6.5 million loan to construct a nursing home and health-related facility for the elderly
- Provided seed capital for a community-owned housekeeper service that employed 300 area residents.

Thus, despite its relatively small assets—$624,578.14 as of December 31, 1973—the credit union had substantially leveraged its impact on a minority poverty neighborhood.

## Beyond the War on Poverty: A New Generation of Credit Unions

Although the Sixties left a troubled legacy for anti-poverty credit unions, it did not discredit the underlying concept—community control over capital—nor did it discourage a new breed of credit unions. North Side Community FCU (Chicago, 1974) grew out of the Hull House social service agency. In two university towns, credit unions with roots in the alternative and cooperative cultures emerged: Santa Cruz Community Credit Union (California, 1977) and Alternatives FCU (Ithaca, NY, 1978). Both credit unions were founded with a vision of local control of capital and a broader community development agenda, with less emphasis on consumer credit and household poverty and more on nurturing local businesses, housing, and cooperatives.[271] New faith-based and rural credit unions emerged as well. The Federation of Greene County Employees (Eutaw, AL, 1975), with deep roots in the civil rights movement, served a predominantly African American community; the Sisseton-Wahpeton FCU (Agency Village, SD, 1978) and the Central Appalachian People's FCU (Berea, KY, 1979) served Native American and low-income white communities, respectively.

## A Cooperative Central Bank for the Credit Union Movement

From the 1970s through the proposals to establish the CDFI Fund in the 1990s, policymakers and practitioners put forth concepts for a central financial institution to support a network of specialized community lenders.[272] In 1974, the mainstream credit union movement founded U.S. Central Credit Union. Statewide wholesale "corporate" credit unions had emerged to meet the liquidity and investment needs of local credit unions; U.S. Central was a top-tier wholesale credit union for these statewide corporate credit unions, forming the apex of a three-tier national pyramid for financial cooperatives.[273]

U.S. Central was important financially, politically, and psychologically. It meant that credit unions would not be dependent on banks for certain "correspondent" services, such as check-clearing and investments; they would be better insulated from the political opposition of the bank sector (which regarded credit unions as a competitive threat, although their market share was less than 10 percent); and finally, they could take pride in a cooperative, self-help system that credit unions and credit unions alone owned. This system proved highly serviceable until the Great Recession, when investments in subprime securities brought the system crashing down.*

## The Supply Side: Social Investment in the Seventies

Local congregations and national entities, including the Catholic Campaign for Human Development and several Protestant organizations, were important sources of grant funds for community organizing and local development efforts. But beyond grants and donations, the early *investments* of faith-based organizations were vital to the birth and early development of the CDFI movement. Numerous ecumenical and denominational groups put their funds in service to their ideals, at a time when the nascent CDFIs had more vision than track record to offer. In the 1980s, many CDFIs literally owed their start to faith-based groups. But the foundations of faith-based investing were laid earlier.

One of the original and most influential investors was the community of Adrian Dominican Sisters, headquartered in Adrian, MI. Notwithstanding the ethos of humility, they rightly claimed that "the Adrian Dominican Sisters were on the cutting edge of socially responsible investment" in the 1970s. In 1968, the congregation held its General Chapter meeting to examine and renew its vision.[274] In 1974, the order took the next step with an Enactment establishing the Portfolio Advisory Board [PAB], which was operationalized in 1975 as "a way for us to connect with and support people and groups who share our commitment to justice and social responsibility.... Firmly rooted in the tradition of Catholic social justice, the PAB followed two paths: shareholder advocacy and community investing."[275]

---

\* In the early 1990s, Professor Hyman Minsky proposed making the emerging CDFI Fund a central bank for the CDFI field, but the idea never achieved traction.

Women's congregations lacked the full financial resources of the Catholic Church; they had to provide for their sustenance and retirement themselves. Gospel-driven ideals had to be joined with a pragmatic concern for the real-life needs of the congregation itself—"balancing Christian ethics with fiduciary responsibility. While the Congregation certainly wanted to work for justice and be an advocate for the poor, it also faced the very real task of needing to finance its own future wisely and take care of its retired Sisters."[276]

Sister Louise Borgacz, one of the early leaders of the PAB, reflected that "religious women must be on the cutting edge of the Church…. As Dominicans, as Adrian Dominicans, we have a history of courage, daring, dedication and holiness."[277] Choosing between providing outright grants or loans, the Sisters chose low-interest loans, "because loans create partnerships between the Congregation and the organizations involved…. The Congregation keeps them accountable and works with them if they encounter challenges."[278]

In 1976, the Adrian Dominican Sisters joined the Interfaith Center on Corporate Responsibility, an ecumenical coalition of hundreds of institutional investors focused primarily on shareholder advocacy. Through their research, the Sisters learned about bank lending practices including "redlining."[279] In 1977, the Sisters made their first "alternative" investment, a deposit of $100,000 in South Shore Bank. In 1978, they formally established their Alternative Investment Loan Fund with a $350,000 commitment to provide low-interest loans, deposits, and other investments. Their early borrowers included the Ecumenical Coalition of Mahoning Valley, Youngstown, OH, which borrowed in a failed effort to purchase a closed steel mill; the Immaculate Heart of Mary Federal Credit Union in Houston, TX; the St. Mary Human Development Center in Ridgeland, SC, for "working capital"; housing groups; and the Ecumenical Development Cooperative Society in the Netherlands (later Oikocredit), among others.[280]

Although the Adrian Dominicans played a seminal role, Mary Houghton of South Shore Bank recalled that many other congregations joined the growing movement.

> The most important resource by a long shot were the Catholic nuns. [Susan Davis of ShoreBank] befriended all these treasurers, and they moved a lot of money to ShoreBank. They were the bulk of the support for ShoreBank. It was incredibly important…to our early survival. We bought the bank in 1973, and we were really not out of the woods until 1983.[281]

The Adrian Dominicans and other faith-based investors took the finances of their borrowers very seriously, but their impact assessment had, above all, a human face: "We measure the effectiveness of our investments by the number of people whose lives were improved and whose communities were positively impacted—our original General Chapter vision in action."[282]

## Program-Related Investing: Foundations Finding Their Way

As noted in the previous chapter, program-related investing as a field began to take shape in the second half of the 1960s. In 1968, the Taconic Foundation, led by John Simon, launched the Cooperative Assistance Fund, which pooled the resources of multiple foundations. Even before the 1969 legislation that solidified the statutory basis of Program-Related Investments (PRIs), the Cooperative Assistance Fund (CAF) invested in for-profit banking institutions. In 1972, it purchased $100,000 worth of common stock in the first black-owned bank in Indianapolis, Midwest National Bank. In 1974, it bought $160,000 worth of stock of South Shore Bank, and in 1977, it purchased an additional $80,000.[283]

In the mid-1970s, the CAF's capacity expanded with the addition of a $1 million investment from the Rockefeller Brothers Fund, which enlarged the consortium from eight to nine foundations. In December 1975, John Simon wrote to Dr. Landrum R. Bolling, executive vice president of the Lilly Endowment, Inc. in Indianapolis:

> CAF has just taken its most substantial action to implement an earlier [decision] to devote special attention to the field of southern and/or rural economic development. [Last week the Trustees approved] very substantial participation in a major new entity, the Southern Agricultural Corporation… with special attention to the land-retention problems facing many black farmers.[284]

Despite these promising developments, the CAF was still finding its way. In 1976, Simon wrote optimistically to a prospective investor, the Veatch Program North Shore Unitarian Society, that the "CAF has developed—often with considerable growing pains!—into what we believe is a highly useful instrumentality for foundation work in a number of fields."[285]

Specifically, a new management structure was developed for the CAF through a contract with the Opportunity Funding Corporation, an arrangement "that greatly increases its capacity to identify and to generate investment opportunities that can 'make a difference' in the development process—an arrangement that also makes it easier for CAF to participate in investment packages that combine philanthropic resources with those provided by financial institutions and the government."[286] The OFC, Simon wrote, "was created to test ways of using risk-reduction techniques to increase the flow of capital into low-income communities."[287] Apart from the financial and programmatic advantages of this emerging approach, Simon and his colleagues saw another important dimension of the program-related investing strategy. It was, he wrote to Landrum Bolling, a "less patronizing way to use the charitable dollar."

The "less patronizing way" meant treating the borrower as a responsible counterparty in a business transaction. Although recipient organizations appreciated this more respectful approach, they often found themselves subjected to a rigorous, lawyer-intensive negotiation with a foundation—a far more demanding process than grant-seeking. Even a sophisticated organization like South Shore Bank had to wrestle at length with lawyers representing the Ford Foundation.[288] In the following decades, CDFIs with limited legal in-house capacity and experience often found themselves frustrated, but most came to recognize that the process and the discipline of borrowing rather than simply receiving grants built their capacity and made them more capable and confident in seeking other investments.

Despite efforts to improve the approaches to program-related investing, the early experience of the Ford Foundation and others was not promising: "Within two years the PRI staff had made loans to ventures ranging from cattle feeding, fruitcake banking, and steel joist manufacturing to fast-food franchising, publishing, public transportation, and catfish raising. Not surprisingly, some of the enterprises supported by PRIs failed." A Ford staff member recalled, "We were making substantial loans to small enterprises run by inexperienced entrepreneurs in the poorest neighborhoods. It's surprising that we lost only 35 percent." As an outside consultant reported, "Original projections [were] absolutely unfounded and overly optimistic."[289]

Apart from the poor performance of investments, the economy took a toll on the Ford Foundation and other philanthropies in the 1970s. Financial crises drastically diminished Ford's asset base in the 1970s, which meant that its annual payout to grantees dropped from about $200 million in 1970 to only $119 million by 1979.[290]

## Conclusion

From 1972 to 1976, the Republican administrations of President Richard Nixon, and then after his impeachment and resignation, Gerald Ford, held power in Washington. The War on Poverty was terminated; after efforts to impound its funding were successfully challenged in court, in 1975 the OEO was reauthorized in weakened form as the CSA.

Nonetheless, there were important legislative victories during these difficult years for the community development movement. In 1975, the Home Mortgage Disclosure Act provided access to data that advocates and regulators could use to spotlight potentially discriminatory lending patterns. In October 1977, the Community Reinvestment Act provided a crucial, if vague, legislative mandate for banks to affirmatively serve all sectors of their communities. These laws were crucial to the development of the CDFI movement. It is important to recall, as well, that the Equal Credit Opportunity Act was signed into law in 1974. Known as "Reg B" and applicable to all creditors, its purpose was

> to promote the availability of credit to all creditworthy applicants without regard to race, color, religion, national origin, sex, marital status, or age (provided the applicant has the capacity to contract); to the fact that all or part of the applicant's income derives from a public assistance program; or to the fact that the applicant has in good faith exercised any right under the Consumer Credit Protection Act.[291]

If the Community Reinvestment Act and the Home Mortgage Disclosure Act were more focused on *place*, the Equal Credit Opportunity Act was more focused on *people*. All these laws together are indispensable to ensuring access to credit and capital for historically excluded communities and populations.

Two initiatives in the 1970s to obtain federal capital foreshadowed the CDFI movement. The Community Corporation Act of 1970 called for establishing local community development "banks"; a national certifying body; and a National Community Development Bank to provide supplemental financing. Despite gathering a significant number of sponsors, the legislation stalled in Congress. The National Federation won a federal fund for low-income credit unions—but the victory was dimmed by diminished funding and a lack of community control. This mixed outcome made the federation more determined than ever to demand full-fledged public-sector support to capitalize institutions serving poverty communities, a theme for its efforts throughout the 1980s.

Neither of these two initiatives focused on actual banks: The former aimed to build upon community development corporations, the latter on credit unions. South Shore Bank was still in the early stages of inventing the concept and practice of a regulated depository dedicated to community development, a full-fledged community development bank—or more precisely, a bank holding company, with several subsidiaries and affiliates to take on work that a bank alone could not.

As institutions serving high-poverty communities, South Shore Bank and low-income credit unions shared a structural dilemma: Low-wealth, low-income customers typically meant large volumes of small, unprofitable transactions—small savings accounts, small loans, bill-paying, and check-cashing. To increase their impact and improve their bottom line, it was essential for them to seek larger deposits and investments that could cross-subsidize their low-margin core business. Faith-based investors, especially Catholic women's orders, were at the forefront of the nascent social investment movement. South Shore Bank pioneered "development deposits," marketing nationally for funds from social investors. "For a while," Mary Houghton recalled, "we had [the investors] all to ourselves, we thought. But after seven or eight years of essentially having a very strong focus on ShoreBank, lots of other social investment groups figured [this approach] out."[292]

Faith-based and philanthropic investment were indispensable in nurturing CDFIs in the 1980s. But it would take another decade before the emerging movement would achieve the track record, self-confidence, and allies to press for a national policy to support the financial institutions that served the financially excluded.

# PART IV. The Eighties

The election of Jimmy Carter in 1976 had brought renewed hope for federal support for community economic development. President Carter's "New Partnership," announced in 1978, offered "venture capital" and support for CDCs, funding for a Credit Union Development Fund, and more. But these initiatives were reduced or eliminated after Carter was roundly defeated in 1980 by Republican Ronald Reagan, who parlayed the Iran hostage crisis and the combination of inflation and high unemployment—"stagflation"—into a stunning victory: 44 states and 489 electoral votes.

Reagan evoked an image of America, the shining "City on a Hill," that contrasted sharply with Carter's portrayal of a country that had lost its self-confidence.[293] But Reagan's radiant city had no place for the poor or minorities: His campaign speeches stirred up racism with images of "welfare queens" driving Cadillacs and "young bucks" eating T-bone steaks, presumably thanks to government food stamps. He had nothing but contempt for the War on Poverty and its partisans. He further eviscerated the Community Services Administration—the bloodless successor to the OEO—by transferring it to the Department of Health and Human Services as the Office of Community Services (OCS).

Banking was "disrupted" in the 1980s—mostly not in a good way. The prime rate rose to 21 percent, putting tremendous pressure on financial institutions—especially savings and loan associations (S&Ls)—that had lower-yielding, fixed-rate portfolios. By the end of the decade, hundreds of S&Ls had crashed and burned, at a cost of hundreds of billions of dollars in federal bail-out funds.

And that was not all that was changing with banking. Automated teller machines (ATMs) appeared and began to spread for the first time, prompting banks to dream of a future without human tellers. Citibank was slightly ahead of its time: Its new, unpopular policy of charging customers for the privilege of seeing a teller was virtually dead on arrival. Banks began "pruning" unprofitable (or "suboptimally" profitable) branches in low-income neighborhoods.

Although the Community Reinvestment Act (CRA) was passed in 1977 and came into effect in 1978, only in the 1980s did community groups learn how to use CRA challenges to exact major settlements from banks that were seeking to merge, acquire, or relocate branches. Still, rampant racial discrimination in lending persisted, and the decade closed with a journalistic bombshell: "The Color of Money," a Pulitzer Prize–winning series of articles in the *Atlanta Journal-Constitution* that documented the unfair lending treatment of African Americans.

## Laying the Foundation for the CDFI Movement

Meanwhile, the infrastructure for the CDFI movement was taking shape.
- CDCs continued to multiply, aided by the formation of two major national intermediaries, the Local Initiatives Support Corporation (LISC) and the Enterprise Foundation. By the late 1980s, they gained a major new financial tool—the Low-Income Housing Tax Credit.
- ShoreBank strengthened financially, increasing its capacity, influence, and visibility.
- The first efforts at "replicating" ShoreBank took place: Southern Development Bank in Arkansas, which won the support of then-Governor Bill Clinton, and Community Capital Bank in New York.
- In North Carolina, the Center for Community Self-Help was born—an innovative, ambitious model that combined a loan/venture fund, a credit union, and a nonprofit under one umbrella.
- A handful of recently organized loan funds came together to form a national association.
- The National Federation of CDCUs came back from a near-death defunding experience, developed a new financial intermediary, and framed the first concepts for state and federal funds to support community development lenders.
- Program-Related Investments (PRIs)—previously, the domain of the Ford, Taconic, and a few other intrepid foundations—received a big boost when the John D. and Catherine T. MacArthur Foundation of Chicago entered the field.
- Faith-based investors, especially Catholic women's orders, expanded their pioneering investments in nascent community development lenders.

# CHAPTER 5. CDCs and Loan Funds

Two sets of unregulated institutions joined credit unions and banks in laying the foundation for CDFIs in the 1980s.

CDCs, which had emerged from the War on Poverty, had to adapt to an era of diminished federal support. As they turned to private-sector partners and local government, they were aided by the emergence of new intermediaries to help them marshal support. Community development loan funds did not share the War on Poverty heritage. Mostly grassroots organizations, they were typically started by activists from social movements or religious organizations. In the middle of the decade, they formed their own intermediary association.

## CDCs in the 1980s: From Advocacy to Development

In a 1988 study (published in 1992) of CDCs, Avis Vidal encapsulated the generational evolution among CDCs.[294] A portion of the earliest, pre-1973 cohort were organized by community action agencies. These CDCs "were born of the activist spirit of the '60s—products of the War on Poverty and the civil rights movement, and reactions to the negative effects of the federal urban renewal program." In contrast, Vidal concluded, those formed from 1973 to 1980 were, as their predecessors

> connected to neighborhood organizing and advocacy, but were more likely than older CDCs to respond to distinctly local circumstances rather than to national events. For these CDCs, public-sector funding generally came from single-purpose programs established to address specific problems, rather than from comprehensive programs such as Model Cities.[295]

Regardless of their origin, by the 1980s most CDCs reflected a cultural shift, "away from a confrontational or polemical style to one that is more cooperative or businesslike."[296] Especially as federal support shrank, corporate America became an increasingly visible, crucial partner for community development efforts, especially for CDCs and the new national intermediaries. For better (as pragmatists would assert) or worse (as some in the advocacy community believed), CDCs became "dealmakers." Even the most vigorous advocates, like Gale Cincotta, understood well the difficulty of combining the advocacy and development cultures in a single organization—hence, she strongly supported the nonprofit Neighborhood Housing Services (NHS) as a vehicle to use the monetary fruits of her CRA advocacy battles with banks.

## The Reagan Revolution

After coming to power in 1981, the Reagan administration launched systematic, draconian cutbacks in funding for the range of community development and associated activities—not only for CDCs, but for the credit unions' long-sought federal fund, the Legal Services Corporation, housing programs, and other assistance to distressed communities. The Community Services Administration (CSA) was folded into the Department of Health and Human Services (HHS) as the Office of Community Services (OCS), with much-diminished influence and mission. David Stockman, Reagan's first director of the Office of Management and Budget (1981–85), notoriously led the charge for tax and spending cuts—"Reaganomics," "supply-side" economics, or "trickle-down" economics.

First-generation and even some second-generation CDCs had benefited from significant federal support, especially from dedicated Title 7 OEO/CSA funding. However, those that followed—and even the early CDCs themselves—faced tougher going in the 1980s. CDCs formed in the Reagan years were characterized more by "reliance on state and local government, the establishment of public/private partnerships to support local development, and regional and national nonprofit organizations."[297] In the 1980s, the most prevalent activity of CDCs was residential housing—especially rehabilitation, but also some new construction. Some CDCs carried out commercial real estate and/or business development and support. But for most, housing was primary, and it was often quite successful: By Vidal's estimate, CDCs around the country were producing up to 27,650 units annually, more than the federal production of new public housing.[298]

It is not surprising when new federal money (for example, the CDFI Fund in the 1990s) spawns many new nonprofits. But in the 1980s, CDCs multiplied even as federal funding was decreasing: from about 1,000 CDCs in 1980 to 1,750 by 1988.[299] Unsurprisingly, more organizations meant increasingly intense competition for funds. So, what accounts for this flowering of the CDC movement in the 1980s—in numbers, size, complexity, and sophistication?

One factor was the growth of intermediaries—support organizations that raised the visibility of CDCs, provided technical support, and sometimes channeled or helped secure funds. Another factor was the diversification of the funding base: Increasingly, CDCs won support from local and regional funders—foundations, corporations, and state and municipal government. Although targeted anti-poverty funding decreased, the federal Community Development Block Grant program provided opportunities for enterprising local CDCs.

## Ford and the Dilemma of "Mature" CDCs

In the late 1960s and early 1970s, the Ford Foundation had invested heavily in a small group of urban and rural CDCs, primarily serving African American and Chicano/Mexican American communities. It made long-term, multimillion-dollar grants, such as an $11.08 million grant to Bedford-Stuyvesant Restoration Corporation in 1969 for 17 years and $4.47 million in 1970 to Mississippi Action for Community Education, Inc. From the 1970s, some of these organizations received PRIs and guarantees of as much as $3 million from the Ford Foundation.[300]

These first-generation CDCs typically pursued comprehensive strategies of economic, housing, and commercial development, along with social services and advocacy. The next generation focused more narrowly on housing, to the regret of the Ford Foundation. One program officer wrote summarized the issue this way.

> The [1980s] has been a difficult period for mature CDCs. The decrease in federal funding has made it difficult for some to maintain programs and has prevented others from increasing the scale of their impact. Despite a recent increase in funding for nonprofit housing development and the emergence of a national intermediary support infrastructure, few new resources have reached mature CDCs. Most of the newer resources and assistance have been targeted to emerging CDCs with a housing focus rather than the mature groups that employ comprehensive program strategies.[301]

In the age of Reagan, community development moved on. Many mature CDCs cut back their operations, laid off staff, reduced programs, and liquidated assets. These CDCs were "the very bedrock of the community development field… [and were] isolated from emerging forces in the field."[302] Nonetheless, the Ford Foundation, which had invested heavily in them, continued to support them into the 1990s.

## The Intermediary Strategy: LISC and Enterprise

After seeing many of their direct investments in business and projects fail, Ford and other funders shifted their strategy to intermediaries, whether local, regional, or sectoral. In the 1980s, this strategy flowered: Some intermediaries were created by funders, while others arose from grassroots organizations coming together to establish state and national associations. These intermediaries added value in several ways: They spread risk among multiple funders; mitigated risk by working through organizations with specific expertise; and helped build the capacity of the CDC field.[303] Philanthropy created two prominent national intermediaries, LISC and the Enterprise Foundation. Although they did not lead the emergence of the CDFI movement, both grew to be giants in the community development field and used the financial tools and resources of the CDFI Fund extensively.

## LISC and CDCs

Michael Rubinger joined the Ford Foundation in 1970, his first "real job" after graduate school, working as an assistant to Mike Sviridoff, the veteran of Ford's Gray Areas initiative in New Haven.[304] "CDCs were a big thing for Ford then," Rubinger recalled. "It had adopted 10 CDCs for 10 years and committed themselves to a 10-year program. It was all the rage. It was exciting, and so I just sort of gravitated to that."[305] Later in the decade, after reviewing the progress of the "first generation" of Ford CDC grantees, Rubinger recalled that "the consensus [was] that those 10 groups did well. Some were better than others, but that's to be expected, and [the thought was] that there must be a lot of other organizations out there like these groups."[306] The task was to seek out other organizations that would be good candidates for Ford support: "The original target was 'Could we find 100 organizations who were doing the kind of work that those 10 groups that Ford funded all those years were doing?'"[307] Ford, although the largest foundation, was not in a position to increase its funding of CDCs tenfold.

Toward the end of the 1970s, senior Ford Foundation leaders, including Lou Winnick, Sol Chafkin, and Mike Sviridoff, formulated a new community development strategy. They spelled it out in a discussion paper, "Communities and Neighborhoods: A Possible Private Sector Initiative for the 1980s."[308] Ford would create a new entity, with the working title "Local Initiatives Support Center." (Soon "Corporation" was substituted for "Center.") "Armed with the discussion paper, Sviridoff embarked in early 1979 on a whirlwind round of fundraising talks with a choice list of blue-chip corporations."[309] By May 23, 1980, when LISC's formation was officially announced, Ford had recruited an "A-list" of partners, including Aetna, Richfield, Continental Illinois Bank & Trust, International Harvester, Levi Strauss, and Prudential Insurance Co. These funders put up almost half of the $10 million that launched LISC.

Despite impressive corporate backing, the new entity was by no means a sure thing. Sviridoff did not want to run it. At Ford, he had incubated and spun off various organizations, like Public Private Ventures, and he envisioned the same path for LISC. "His notion was that…he would find somebody to run [LISC]. He went to several people who he thought would be good [for the job]. They didn't want to do it. They didn't think it would work, so he did it himself."[310]

The original notion, according to Rubinger, was that "LISC was going to sunset after three years." Originally, the plan was that Ford staff would be "itinerant program people," finding groups to support and then moving on. But by about 1982, "we began to realize if we were really going to have any impact, we couldn't just come and go. We couldn't just find groups, give them a grant or make them a loan and then go home. That wasn't going to work. We had to commit ourselves to these organizations over a longer term." The strategy that emerged was "raising local money, matching it, and creating a fund that was earmarked for some local geography." Chicago, Boston, the Bay Area, and other sites succeeded in funding permanent offices.

In some cities, LISC's entry was greeted as "Greeks bearing gifts." Often, local organizations feared that LISC would cannibalize their own local funding sources. LISC argued that it was raising local foundation and corporate funds that would not have been available otherwise; besides, LISC contended, it was not exporting the funds back to other areas or supporting its headquarters operation.

"When [Sviridoff] left in '84 or '85," Rubinger recalled, "I would say in retrospect that LISC was successful, but it was small and very boutique-y. Paul Grogan turned it into a national organization. A genuine national organization. We were already doing things nationally, but the volume of our investments increased leaps and bounds." Grogan, who had gained prominence for his community development work in Boston, served as CEO of LISC for 14 years. Rubinger left Ford for Public Private Ventures in 1989, where he worked for eight years, returning to LISC as deputy, and then a year later, when Grogan departed, as CEO.

## Enterprise Foundation

Enterprise grew neither from a federal initiative, nor from a foundation. It was the creation of James Rouse, a famously successful developer of shopping malls and "festival marketplaces," like Faneuil Hall in Boston and Harborplace in Baltimore. Rouse was directly inspired by Jubilee Housing, a church-based group in northwest Washington, DC, that acquired and rehabilitated housing. Although the early concept involved supporting nonprofit development through the Rouse company's for-profit businesses, this strategy did not prove out. However, Enterprise Community Partners (as it later became known) did obtain substantial support from Ford, other foundations, corporations, and government.

## Origins of the Community Development Loan Fund Movement

In the 1970s, there were a scant few community-oriented loan funds. The attendance list of the First National Conference of Community Loan Funds in 1985 showed five with origins before 1980: the Cooperative Fund of New England and the Fund for an OPEN Society (both 1975); Common Space (1977); the North Country Loan Fund; and the Institute for Community Economics (ICE, 1979). One organization, ICE, played a seminal role in incubating the broader loan movement. And one charismatic leader, Chuck Matthei, became the moral compass for the movement in its early days.

## Gandhi, Dorothy Day, and ICE

An orientation package for new ICE board members laid out the core values of the organization: "Motivated by Gandhi's village development movement and the experience of the American Civil Rights Movement, ICE's founders recognized the basic connection between economic justice and political democracy."[311]

ICE was born in 1967 as the International Independence Institute, cofounded by the longtime peace activist Bob Swann, who had been imprisoned as a conscientious objector during World War II. Among his influences was the Gramdan ("Village Gift") land reform and lending movement in India—an approach, he noted, that was like that of the Grameen Bank, which developed later in Bangladesh.[312] In 1969, Swann cofounded New Communities, Inc. in Lee County, GA, a community land trust for African American farmers.

ICE was the foremost advocate and proselytizer for community land trusts (CLTs). Ownership of the land was vested in the community, not individual residents, effectively removing it from the speculative marketplace. Residents had limited opportunity for property appreciation (for example, improvement of their dwelling), but they benefited from stability of tenure and affordability—as would those who came after them. In 1972, ICE published the definitive guide to organizing community land trusts. Throughout the decade, it tirelessly promoted the CLT concept.

## The Making of an Organizer

On a hot afternoon in Connecticut in August 2002, shortly before his untimely death from thyroid cancer on October 1, Chuck Matthei was interviewed by his longtime colleague, Professor Michael Swack.[313] Matthei grew up in a largely Republican, suburban community of Chicago. His early political experience was organizing a team of volunteers for Donald Rumsfeld's first congressional campaign.[314] But before long, "the civil rights movement affected my view of the world, and my place in it," as did his opposition to the war in Vietnam. He encountered the Gandhian view of nonviolent change, which was based on personal commitment and individual integrity, as well as a "constructive program… what we could call community economic development."[315]

*Chuck Matthei.
Courtesy of OFN.*

Matthei finished high school in 1966. He decided not to go to college. "On a Honda 50 motorbike… I left the suburbs of Chicago for the rest of my life, with a clear idea what was important to me, but no idea how to pursue it." After the Draft Board rejected his application as a conscientious objector, he refused induction. He went to trial in Chicago, but the charges were dropped. His travels took him to rural communities across the Northeast and to a Catholic Worker community, where he met Dorothy Day (1897–1980), a revered, lifelong peace activist.[316] His activism extended to protests at nuclear power plants: After occupying the Seabrook nuclear plant in 1977, he was arrested and went 11 days without food or water.[317] Through this campaign, he met with a number of people who subsequently joined ICE and otherwise became prominent in the loan fund movement, including Julie Eades and Chuck Collins.

## From Land Trusts to Loan Funds

ICE remained focused on community land trusts throughout the 1970s. Matthei and ICE staff toured the country tirelessly, spoke at conferences and to local groups, wrote guides, and provided technical assistance to aspiring CLTs. In 1979–80, ICE underwent a reorganization, with new board and staff members. As it delicately put it to funders and prospective board members, "Outstanding financial and management problems were resolved."[318] There was a doubling down of focus on "practical work."

Like most of the early CDFI activists, "I didn't set out to be a banker," Matthei recounted to Michael Swack. "I didn't have a bank account or a steady income of my own." He became one through experience, while working in a small community in northern Maine. The group had an opportunity to acquire a property at a favorable price from a sympathetic local resident. "They needed a place to borrow, and there was no conventional financial institution available to them." So, Matthei and his colleagues pondered, "Wasn't it possible to build a bridge between the rich and the poor?" He recalled:

> We set up a very simple revolving loan fund mechanism. We began to go to individuals, religious institutions, and others whom we knew, and began to say, 'If you have savings beyond your immediate personal needs, lend it to us, and we'll pool it with the investments of others and we'll use it to finance projects like these, to take advantage of these opportunities.'[319]

Accordingly, the ICE Revolving Loan Fund was established in 1979 to bridge the perceived gap between community groups and potential lenders. Structurally, the revolving loan fund was a restricted fund within ICE, but closely integrated with other ICE programs. The loan fund closed its first year, 1979, with $15,000 in borrowed funds under management. Thereafter, it increased its assets rapidly. By 1985, it was bringing in more than a half-million dollars in new loans from investors each year. Although by that time, "ICE's revolving loan fund has been capitalized primarily by ecumenical sources and by individuals seeking socially responsible investments."[320] It had received a PRI from the Mary Reynolds Babcock Foundation and had an offer of $250,000 from the Consumer Cooperative Development Corporation.

Thus armed, ICE took the major step of approaching the Ford Foundation. The Ford Foundation investment would be a quantum leap. By 1985, ICE's capital under management had grown dramatically, but it still had reached only $1.5 million. From Ford, it requested a $1 million, seven-year PRI "to expand the low-income housing development activities of its Revolving Loan Fund," along with a $50,000 grant for ICE's loan loss reserve, $35,000 for technical assistance, $30,000 for a computer system, and funds for the standardization of loan documentation.[321] The key problem was affordable housing; the key deliverable: "300–400 units of low- and moderate-income housing." In making the case for approving the grant, Ford staff noted: "ICE's program is unusual among financial and technical intermediaries, and is generally difficult to achieve for housing providers. As such, ICE's efforts are complementary to those of other intermediaries, since it is able to assist organizations in preparing themselves to receive larger-scale and longer-term financing from the Enterprise Foundation, LISC, and others."[322]

Ford had made larger bets on community economic development organizations, notably LISC. But its support for ICE was certainly a groundbreaking one.

## The "First" Community Development Loan Fund: A Financial Snapshot of ICE

Technically, ICE was not the first community-based revolving loan fund. But it was undoubtedly a seminal institution, incubating and breaking ground for the movement that emerged. ICE's proposal in 1985 to the Ford Foundation provides a view of this pioneering institution.[323] By 1985, as ICE reported to Ford, it had made a cumulative total of $1.503 million in loans, of which $1.045 million was outstanding. "To date, the RLF has incurred no losses and has never been late in a payment to its lenders."[324] It reported one loan at risk for $2,661, "which, if lost, would result in a loan loss rate of less than .002 percent."[325] Its $1.5 million balance sheet was supported by a fund balance of $40,097 as of December 31, 2014 (a net-worth ratio of about 2.7 percent).[326]

Housing-related loans made up about 60 percent of its portfolio, with business loans at 30 percent. Its portfolio included not only community land trusts, but other limited-equity co-ops, nonprofit housing corporations, emergency shelters, and worker-owned businesses. According to its Policies and Procedures (dated September 21, 1985), "The [Revolving Loan Fund] does not make venture capital investments." Moreover, with certain exceptions for loans of $5,000 or less, "All loans to borrowers shall be secured," generally by mortgages or liens on property or equipment.[327]

The revolving loan fund had a "matched book" portfolio of investments: "The RLF receives loans from individuals and institutions on terms proposed by the lender and accepted by ICE. … No funds are loaned for a longer time than ICE has use of them, or at a lower rate than ICE must pay the lender."[328] Lender terms ranged from several months to 20 years. In 1985, ICE's average cost of funds was 6 percent, while its borrowers paid an average of 8 percent, a spread of 2 percent that covered operating expenses.

Perhaps ahead of its time, ICE reviewed the social impact of its loans by studying a random group of 16 revolving loan fund housing borrowers. It found that 41 percent of the households housed were very low income, 45 percent low income, and 14 percent moderate income. Demographically, 36 percent were black, 40 percent Caucasian, and 23 percent Hispanic. The Ford Foundation routinely asked grantees to report on the composition of their boards and staff. As noted by Ford's program officer, ICE acknowledged a lack of diversity in its staff and board:

> ICE is concerned about the underrepresentation of minorities among its employees and on its Board.… It is committed to proportional representation by minorities on its staff and its Board and is taking concrete steps to correct this deficiency. ICE has agreed that the second disbursement of PRI loan funds should be conditioned

upon review of its progress in addressing underrepresentation at both board and staff levels.[329]

For community development loan funds, the issue of diversity would persist through the CDFI era.

## ICE Organization and Culture: Collective Living and Personal Sacrifice

The issue of sustainability and self-sufficiency has been a central theme through the CDFI era. Somewhat surprisingly, ICE declared its revolving loan fund self-supporting by the mid-1980s. As new board members learned in their orientation to the organization, "The RLF is financially self-sufficient, covering all of its operating expenses from net earnings (mark-up on loans and income from permanent loan capital)."[330] The secret, of course, lay in the group's philosophy, which strongly echoed Catholic Worker themes. As Gregg Ramm, an early staff member and later executive director, put it, "We had the most extraordinary compensation package: Come live in this house in Greenfield, Massachusetts, and we'll all share cars."[331] Or, as Ramm recalled Chuck Matthei's approach, "We're all here to sacrifice." As Matthei and his colleagues explained to potential board members and funders:

> As a matter of philosophical principal and economic practicality ICE deliberately tries to keep its overhead and operational expenses as low as possible—in order to make limited resources go as far as possible. Compensation policies reflect this: Most staff live at ICE and receive room and board, health benefits, and a modest monthly stipend.[332]

The 1985 operating budget of ICE was $21,648. Obviously, without an austere, collective lifestyle, break-even would have been impossible. The lifestyle of ICE, though not explicitly religious, resembled a secular version of the lifestyle of Catholic women's orders. It was *not* replicated elsewhere in the CDFI movement, and in fact did not prove indefinitely sustainable for ICE.

More than other early CDFIs, Chuck Matthei's personality played a key role in keeping such an unconventional organization together. Lean and ascetic-looking, prematurely bald and bearded, and customarily attired in jeans, he was charismatic, preaching a powerful gospel of peace activism, eliminating poverty, and of course, the community land trust as a vehicle for economic justice for the poor. Profoundly spiritual, Matthei was not a cult leader, and ICE was not a cult.

## Building Capacity

ICE's growth was robust, and its early track record was encouraging, with losses hovering around zero. Still, ICE, like other startup loan funds, was learning while doing. As Chuck Collins put it, "We would make appalling mistakes. We would do a budget and we would leave out something obviously critical. We were all learning together. I remember [using] the old Lotus 1-2-3 primitive spreadsheets."[333]

Greg Ramm joined ICE in 1984 after three years in the Peace Corps, teaching math and science in a village in Zaire. He returned to the United States not knowing what he wanted to do, armed with an undergraduate degree in computer science and a commitment to social justice deepened by his time in Africa. When he came to ICE as executive assistant to Matthei, he found there "a real fight whether ICE should have computers or not."[334] Ramm wrote a report about what new computers could do, and "ICE moved into the new technology era."[335]

Although the lifestyle of ICE was not worldly, the skills it required were. Even from its early days, ICE required loan officers who could package sophisticated loan packages, just as LISC and Enterprise did. But ICE did not deal with conventional products—single-family homes or established small businesses, for example—nor did it have conventional, well-heeled borrowers conversant with the banking system.

## "The Time is Right": Organizing the National Community Development Loan Fund Movement

By 1985, there were at least several dozen loan funds in operation or soon to be in business. ICE had provided technical assistance to many of them, and there were informal links among them. That fall, ICE put out the invitation to the "constitutional convention" of the community development loan fund movement.

The conference built on an early wave of public attention. Matthei was fresh from a socially responsible investment conference of 250 people in California, sponsored by the Vanguard Foundation of San Francisco. The loan funds, especially ICE, had begun to attract mainstream attention. An article entitled "Lending to Charities Can Allow Investors to Combine Flexibility and Generosity" appeared in the *Wall Street Journal*.[336] The article cited Wayne Silby, cofounder of the Calvert Group and a pioneer of socially conscious investing. Silby invested $10,000 of his own money with ICE, although he stressed that it would be irresponsible of him to invest other people's money in Calvert the same way. The *New York Times* published an article entitled "Social-Issue Funds Growing."[337] Sounding the call for the conference, Matthei sent potential participants "A Proposal for Communication and Cooperation among Community Loan Funds":

> With public and investor concern over conditions in South Africa, the arms race, environmental problems, and the crying needs for decent affordable housing and new employment opportunities for low- and moderate-income people also growing, the [loan fund] movement should flourish.[338]

## Chapter 5. CDCs and Loan Funds

The First National Conference of Community Loan Funds opened on the morning of October 16, 1985, at the austere Espousal Center of the Diocese of Boston in Waltham, MA. The attendees represented 35 existing and emerging funds—to Matthei's knowledge, "almost every loan fund in the country that looks for capital from multiple sources and provides loans to multiple community development groups."[339] He opened the conference wearing "my button-down striped Brooks Brothers shirt. I got it from a thrift shop in Forest City, Arkansas."[340] The civil rights movement, the peace movement, the women's movement, the environmental movement, the anti-poverty movement, cooperatives—activists from all these were represented. "We are," he said, "a people with a political heritage."[341] The loan fund movement's key job was "somehow to graft a conscience on the capitalist." The loan funds must clearly constitute a *movement*: "We have to understand that the performance of any one will ultimately reflect on all the others. None of us can afford serious mistakes on the part of the others. We will, in the old figure of speech, sink or swim together."[342] (Within a few years, the question of "movement" versus "industry" became a heated topic for debate among loan fund practitioners.)

Among the dozens of practitioners were many who continued to work in and influence the CDFI movement for decades.* The faith community was well represented, including participants from the Interfaith Center on Corporate Responsibility, the Campaign for Human Development (Sr. Corinne Florek), the McAuley Institute (JoAnn Kane), the United Methodists, the Marianist Sharing, and the Housing Fund of the Archdiocese of New York.[343] The conference drew funders and social investors, including notably Kirsten Moy from Equitable Life (later the first appointed director of the federal CDFI Fund) and Nancy Andrews (Ford Foundation PRI officer, later CEO of LIIF), Joan Bavaria (Social Investment Forum), George Pillsbury (The Funding Exchange), and Barbara Cleary (Affirmative Investments). Another "wing" of the emerging CDFI movement—the regulated institutions—was represented by South Shore Bank's Joan Shapiro, who served as a resource person.†

In preparation for the conference, ICE sent out a questionnaire that was completed by 18 existing and emerging loan funds. Collectively, these institutions totaled $9.442 million in capitalization in 1985; since their origin, they had amassed $9.873 million in loans and endowments from 794 lenders. They had loaned out $6.747 million to 464 borrowers, with a loss rate of 0.9 percent.[344] The "senior" members of the cohort—active loan funds that dated to the late 1970s—were the Fund for an Open Society (1975; $1.8 million in capital), Common Space (1977; $50,000), the Cooperative Fund of New England (1975; $190,000), North Country (1978; $160,000), and the ICE revolving loan fund (1979; $1.63 million). Many others had emerged since 1980. Several of the loan funds that became

---

\* These included Julie Eades (New Hampshire Community Loan Fund), DeWitt Jones (Boston Community Loan Fund, later Boston Community Capital), Jeremy Nowak (Delaware Valley Community Reinvestment Fund, later TRF), Dan Liebsohn (Low Income Housing Fund, later Low Income Investment Fund), Dave Lollis (Federation of Appalachian Housing Enterprises [FAHE]), and Michael Swack (New Hampshire College and a founder of New Hampshire Community Loan Fund).

† Author's note: I also attended, representing the National Federation of Community Development Credit Unions.

leaders in the field—Boston Community Loan Fund, Delaware Valley Community Reinvestment Fund, Low Income Housing Fund, and New Hampshire Community Loan Fund—were in their first 18 months or still under development.[345]

On October 18, at the conference's closing plenary session, participants agreed to "establish a national association of community loan funds," and identified a list of projects and concerns. The ambitious action agenda included ideas that would soon be implemented, and others that would be fulfilled many years later:

- Information sharing
- Technical assistance
- Joint response to public policies
- "Development of a capital fund or capital-sharing mechanism"
- Cooperation in financial packaging and loan participations
- "Approach to major institutional sources of capital…particularly regarding the availability of long-term or take-out financing, and the possibility of a 'secondary mortgage market' in community investments."[346]

ICE proposed that "the Conference declare itself to be 'in session' for a period of one year, or until a Second National Conference is convened, thus constituting an informal national association of CLFs." An executive committee would meet periodically and begin to implement the action agenda. Aided by contributions and registration fees, ICE reported that it had enough money to undertake follow-up work, supplying several ICE staff people to provide part-time support to a coordinating committee.[347]

## ICE/NACDLF

As of 1986, the new National Association of Community Development Loan Funds (NACDLF) had 21 full member loan funds, with $29 million in loan capital under management. Over the next five years, it grew to a reported 40 member funds and $73 million under management, with cumulative lending amounting to more than $88 million. Housing continued to account for the bulk of lending dollar volume—80 percent, compared with 20 percent for business—though the number of loans stood at 53 percent and 47 percent, respectively. Total losses to investors cumulatively totaled $20,480, or 0.02 percent of all dollars loaned.[348]

ICE continued its role as incubator through the end of the decade, with Chuck Matthei serving as executive director. Greg Ramm, who served in multiple roles in ICE—as resident computer expert, conference coordinator, technical assistance provider to emerging loan funds, and executive assistant and deputy director to Matthei—also assumed the interim role of coordinator of the new NACDLF until a permanent executive director was named.

The austere communal model of ICE under Matthei's leadership showed increasing strain in the late 1980s. As Matthei himself wrote later in a 1994 article, "A few organizations have experimented with compensation based solely on need"; he mentioned the Catholic Worker movement but not

ICE, which nonetheless seemed clearly on his mind. "[It's] often hard to sustain such a practice," he continued. "Policymaking and administration can be time-consuming and complicated. Age and family life may begin additional pressures and concerns.... The organization mentioned above is now moving toward a more conventional salary scale."[349]

In 1990, Matthei resigned, leaving Ramm to move up from deputy to executive director. Ramm has described the growing tension in ICE that led to a parting of the ways. "We were all torn," he said. Did ICE need to evolve into a more traditional nonprofit, or could it remain more of a commune-based structure? Ramm recalled that some people were pushing him to move faster to the nonprofit model, while others were saying he was selling out. "I tried to keep one foot in each world," he remarked. "We did have the communal house, and still kept salaries low. We would have been more successful if we had made a clean change. It was not tenable to have a foot in both camps."[350]

In 1991, Matthei went on to found and direct the Equity Trust, Inc. in Voluntown, CT, the home of the Community for Nonviolent Action, which also developed a loan fund. Ramm managed ICE until 1997, when he resumed the international aid work that largely defined his career.

## A Legacy... and New Directions

Matthei left an indelible mark as a "north star" for mission-driven, values-based practice above all. As Rebecca Dunn, longtime executive director of the Cooperative Fund of New England, put it, "I wished I could channel him when he was speaking. He verbalized my thoughts."[351] Julie Eades, first manager of the New Hampshire Community Loan Fund, met Matthei at training for civil disobedience at the Seabrook nuclear plant. "A month doesn't go by," she recalled, "without me thinking, 'Gee, what would Chuck do in this situation?'…. I think he was a great thinker. There are many things that I learned from him about process, both as a civil disobedience trainer and someone in economic development."[352]

Despite the respect and even reverence that Matthei inspired, he would not and could not be the leader for the CDFI era. "ICE never took federal money when Chuck was associated with it," Ramm recalled. Indeed, given Matthei's insistence on moral "engagement" with investors, advocating and negotiating with the federal government would not have been easy roles for him. Moreover, as Dick Jones of the Boston Community Loan Fund recalled, working in a coalition—essential for a national political strategy—was not his natural mode. "Chuck on some level didn't want to play with anyone else. He was nervous about everything. Some of it was principle, some of it was practical…. We tried to address his legitimate concerns, and he would pull the rug out."[353]

From 1986 to 1990, the NACDLF grew robustly, while intensively working to define itself—its core principles, membership, governance, and operating procedures. Financially, loan funds showed strong, continuous growth. In its annual reports to the membership, the association reported strong year-over-year rates of increase in median capital under management: 55 percent as of mid-year 1987, followed by 33 percent (1988), and 42 percent (1989).[354] The number of loan funds in the association did not increase dramatically: By October 1990, it had grown to only 37 full member funds.

From its earliest years, the association stressed "peer review" of loan fund policies, operations, and performance: The 1987 Report to the Membership noted, "While initially voluntary, a satisfactory peer review might eventually be a condition for a member fund to be eligible to receive the financial services of the NACDLF."[355] Indeed, the association evolved in this direction, as it strove to develop its standards. "Eventually" came quickly: In 1987, NACDLF received a commitment for a $1.5 million loan from the progressive Funding Exchange to capitalize a "Seed Fund," which would enable it to provide capital to new or young loan funds.[356]

During NACDLF's "incubation" period, from 1986 through 1989, it operated under ICE's wing, which provided NACDLF part-time staffing and space in its Greenfield, MA, home. Matthei served as board chair and was the new organization's most prominent voice; however, in 1986, its initial, interim board included individuals who became leading figures in the movement for decades to come—in particular, Julie Eades (New Hampshire Community Loan Fund), Jeremy Nowak (Delaware Valley Community Reinvestment Fund, later TRF), Sarah Smith (Catherine McAuley Housing Foundation), and Michael Swack (New Hampshire College, later Southern New Hampshire University). Its public profile grew, through presentations at social investment conferences and articles in mainstream media, as well as co-op publications.

On July 5, 1989, the period of incubation ended, when Martin Paul Trimble became the first full-time executive director of NACDLF. It was not the career trajectory he had planned.

> I went to the University of North Carolina to play soccer. I thought I wanted to play professional soccer, but I got injured. My world was turned upside down. I couldn't play soccer anymore, and I didn't know what I wanted to do. I spent a year on the road. Ran out of money in Florida, Texas, California, Idaho. Worked, saw the country. It was great!
>
> Then I became a teacher in rural Maryland. But I went to graduate school at Harvard Divinity school thinking that I wanted to go in the 'family business.' My dad's an Episcopal minister.[357]

In the end, he didn't go into the "family business," nor did he pursue a brief "career" as a roofer (the union job "paid good money"). In 1985, he was hired for a job that would bring him to the threshold of the CDFI world. He became a grants manager for the Pew Charitable Trusts in his hometown, Philadelphia.

> For me, it opened up a whole different world about the American religious experience. At that time, I got involved in the anti-apartheid movement. Started doing some stuff in Central America. I started raising issues at Pew around the consistency of its investment policies and its grant making. We had made some stealth grants to support the role of religious institutions and community development. While I

was at Pew, I led an effort with my father to raise $5 million of Episcopal money for [the Delaware Valley Community Reinvestment Fund]. It was called the Episcopal Community Investment fund. We raised 5 million bucks. It was great! [Then] I got booted.[358]

Somewhere along the line, Trimble had met loan fund leaders Jeremy Nowak and Julie Eades. He also met Amy Domini, a leader in socially responsible investment generally and faith-based—specifically Episcopal—investment in particular. But his hiring, he recalls, was "just serendipitous. My dad gave me an office in his church at Second and Market Street and we built it from there. It was in Philly, because that's where I was and I didn't want to leave."[359] In its October 1989 report to its membership, NACDLF enumerated the reasons to put down roots in Philadelphia: halfway between Washington (for policy) and New York (for capital markets); proximity to a strong local fund (Delaware Valley Community Reinvestment Fund); reasonably priced office space; affordable living costs for prospective staff; and, finally, "the opportunity for the new director to remain active in community development work."[360]

## "Movement" or "Industry"?

Even in its first few years, when NACDLF consisted of fewer than 50 organizations, there was a spirited debate about what precisely was the nature of these organizations. Clara Miller, then of the Nonprofit Finance Fund, recalls one conference at which there was "a gigantic floor fight between the people who said we were a movement, and those who said we were an industry."[361] Miller, who was elected to the board in 1992 and later became chairwoman, interpreted the debate as between those who wanted the organization to focus on performance—the "industry" camp—and those who wanted NACDLF to be "a big tent, a marginal protest organization"—that is, a movement. Jeremy Nowak, of the Delaware Valley Community Reinvestment Fund, argued that NACDLF partook of both; it was not an either/or choice.

In any event, the emphasis on performance became a defining characteristic of NACDLF. In contrast, the National Federation of Community Development Credit Unions followed more of the "big tent" approach, steadfastly adhering to the principle that it was a movement: Credit unions that met the threshold of serving predominantly low-income people or communities would qualify for membership, regardless of their financial profile. (Of course, depository institutions, such as credit unions, would not remain in existence if they did not meet minimum financial and other regulatory requirements.)

These differences were expressed in the different cultures and operations of the CDCU movement and loan movement, respectively. The National Federation frequently had to devote substantial resources and attention to assisting troubled or weak credit unions, both in terms of technical assistance and regulatory advocacy. With its stated emphasis on "high-performing" institutions, NACDLF was freer to pursue other priorities.

# CHAPTER 6.
# Community Development Banks and "Banks"

There were many banks and credit unions that had long served African American and other minority communities, but it was ShoreBank, with its multi-part holding company model and motto, "Let's Change the World," that defined "community development bank" through the early 1980s. In the second half of the decade, ShoreBank helped incubate its first offspring: Southern Development Bank in Arkansas. Outside this nascent family, a Buddhist commercial banker began a years-long process to organize and capitalize a startup bank in Brooklyn, NY. Meanwhile, activists in Durham, NC, developed a kind of nonprofit "holding company" that they called a statewide development bank. It included a parent nonprofit, an unregulated loan fund, and a state-chartered credit union (no actual bank). It was these four institutions—ShoreBank, Southern, Community Capital, and Self-Help—that were cited in the first community development banking legislation in 1992.

### ShoreBank in the 1980s[362]

In the 1980s, ShoreBank progressed gradually to financial stability. As Mary Houghton recalled:

> We bought the bank in 1973, and we were really not out of the woods until 1983. We had been grossly under-capitalized. We bought this bank with $800,000 of equity, and a $2.4 million bank loan. We didn't have a lot of room. It turned out that running the deposit operation of the bank was really difficult. None of us were operations people. We didn't actually care about deposits. We were totally focused on lending and getting as much money out in the neighborhood in investment as possible. We didn't really have a lot of talent on the deposit side. It just all took a while.[363]

With ShoreBank on sounder footing by 1983, the team was thinking about expanding. People were questioning whether their "experiment" was replicable, or simply a one-off: Did it work only because the South Side neighborhood really wasn't as deteriorated as others in Chicago, since it had a stock of salvageable, attractive housing? Other than proving critics wrong, there was another motivation for

## Chapter 6. Community Development Banks and "Banks"

an expansion, familiar to enterprises that need to draw on philanthropic or social investment capital: What have you done lately that's new and interesting? As Houghton reflected:

> At some level, the push to expand at ShoreBank was partly influenced by the fact that you couldn't raise more capital unless you had some initiative that was going to get funded. None of the existing investors or new investors just wanted to put more money in to grow the South Side of Chicago.... The internal motivation to expand was probably, 'Well, if we can come up with a really exciting new initiative, then we can raise some more capital. Some of the capital can help support the existing institution.'[364]

So, ShoreBank looked to the West Side of Chicago, where potential opportunities included apartment-building rehab projects of a type it was familiar with. The Austin neighborhood office opened around 1986, but it never really took off. "We did a couple of big real estate developments in Austin that did a decent job. We had a nice office. [But] we never really built a really thriving business in Austin. I think you would have to say, with hind-sight, it was not terribly successful."[365] Nor did the Austin expansion "solve" ShoreBank's capital constraints. Initial public offerings of stock (IPOs) were not feasible at the time. "The difficulty raising capital was a chronic problem for ShoreBank," Houghton recalled. "The pool was really pretty modest."

Meanwhile, the ShoreBank company was exploring another kind of expansion. "In 1983," Ron Grzywinski recalled, "Mary got a phone call from the Ford Foundation saying, 'We've been supporting this guy in Bangladesh who's got this idea that he can make loans, very tiny loans to women in rural areas, and he's been doing this, and we've been putting in a little bit of money, but now he thinks he's going to get a bank charter and he's asked us to find him an American or an Indian banker that would be willing to come there and talk to him about banking.'"[366]

Thus began ShoreBank's relationship with the Grameen Bank of Muhammad Yunus—the economics professor who, beginning with $27 from his own pocket, provided loans to impoverished villagers in Bangladesh, thereby founding a microenterprise movement that eventually achieved global scale. Grzywinski and Houghton began to visit Bangladesh—frequently, and at length. They were "oriented" to Bangladesh by a friend of Houghton, Jan Piercy, who was working with Planned Parenthood in Dhaka, Bangladesh, and who later was a human bridge to the Clintons and the Southern Development Bank. "We were going more than once a year. We were acting as financial analysts and bankers to the Grameen Bank. It was three or four weeks every nine months. It took a fair amount of psychic energy," recalled Houghton.[367]

ShoreBank's international vistas expanded some years later, with the downfall of the Soviet Union in 1989, by which time ShoreBank had built a consulting practice. "We were approached about managing a small business loan program in Poland." The program proved a success: "We were very proud of the fact that we booked $25 million of loans in two years," mostly in loans of about $25,000, for which there was great pent-up demand. Later, ShoreBank was invited to take on United States

— 97 —

Government projects in Bulgaria (moderately successful) and Russia (less so). In later years, especially after the bank's downfall, ShoreBank's far-flung interests would provide ready fodder for its critics.

## Managing ShoreBank

For several years, Houghton played a key role in upgrading the retail operation of the South Shore Bank, which meant both reducing staff size as well as developing and attracting middle managers.[368] In 1983, Houghton changed her role, moving into the bank's holding company to work with Grzywinski on expansion plans. Jim Fletcher succeeded her on the operational side. Milton Davis, the fourth member of the group, worked at the holding company.

South Shore Bank was not a conventional bank, and its management style was not conventional, either. "I was the person," Houghton remembers, "who would always pick up on a new idea when it was half-baked, and withstand all sorts of internal hatred because, 'There goes Ron and Mary again, running after some stupid idea.' I was the early change-maker." Still, she emphasizes the full, crucial involvement of the management "quartet." It was not the "Ron and Mary" show; Jim Fletcher and Milton Davis were essential throughout the first quarter-century of ShoreBank. Milton Davis, born in the South, was a civil rights leader, active in the Congress of Racial Equality; "he could be relied on to think of the values-based reason of how we should solve a difficult problem, whether it was business or racial." In contrast, Jim Fletcher, who had a background in the anti-poverty movement "was a business guy. He loved deal-making."[369]

This diverse set of skills and orientations was a source of strength for dealing with the complex political, social, and economic environment in which ShoreBank operated. For the staff, however, it could be frustrating, as Houghton recalled.

> You have to believe that from 1973 to 1998 we didn't make a decision unless the four of us agreed. It was a real thing. Ron and I would have lost our shirts, or lost everybody's shirts, without two strong black guys.... It did drive the rest of ShoreBank nuts, because they couldn't figure out who had the most power. They couldn't figure out who they should go to when they wanted to get a decision made. They'd say, 'What are you guys talking about? What's going on? It would be easier if there was just one of you.' It wasn't too popular inside ShoreBank.[370]

While growing in deposits, profitability, and operational efficiency, ShoreBank expanded its scope as well through its local affiliates, formed in 1978. The Neighborhood Institute (TNI) was the non-profit arm of ShoreBank's holding company (the Illinois Neighborhood Development Corporation, INDC). Charged with non-income-generating functions, it was run by Jim Fletcher in its early years. TNI benefited from significant support from the Mott Foundation and the Chicago Community Trust, although—like most nonprofits—its income streams were not guaranteed. It is important to note that TNI was not financially supported by the bank holding company: Their funding could not be commingled.* TNI won grants and contracts from federal and state agencies to support job training and counseling, tenant advocacy, weatherization and building renovation, and other activities. It successfully rehabilitated many multifamily buildings and facilitated the emergence of low-equity co-ops.[371]

The City Lands affiliate of ShoreBank, initially capitalized with only $150,00, was betting on the profit-making potential of the real estate market in a neighborhood that ShoreBank was working to improve. It struggled early with its strategy of rehabilitating bank-owned buildings, but in 1980 it joined the Parkside Partnership project, a major, coordinated rehabilitation effort. By 1985, City Lands had been profitable for four years, with hundreds of units in multiple buildings either under construction or in the works.[372]

## "Replicating" ShoreBank: Southern Development Bank

Although ShoreBank became nationally known by the early 1980s, it was still *sui generis*: There had been no replication, no proof of concept beyond the confines of the South Side of Chicago. That changed in the second half of the decade, when ShoreBank became midwife and adviser to the first rural community development bank, and when it intersected for the first time with the Arkansas governor, Bill Clinton, and his wife, Hillary Clinton.

There were other prominent Arkansas names involved in the birth of Southern Development Bank, including the Walton Family Foundation, established by Walmart, and the Winthrop Rockefeller Foundation, spearheaded by its president, Tom McRae IV.[373] Walter Smiley, a board member of the foundation and later of the bank for many years, recalled McRae's great passion for the project.

> [McRae] probably, more than any single person, deserves credit for forming Southern. As he ran that foundation, we were having real trouble doing anything good. We would give money to people, and you'd look three years later, and they can't find the records, and you don't know what happened to the money and the president quit. It was very frustrating to Tom and to me as a board member. He got two ideas. One was for a community foundation and the other one was for a development bank. Those two ideas were Tom's.[374]

---

\* Similar regulatory issues have affected community development credit unions that operated alongside a sponsor or affiliated nonprofit. Examiners insist that books be strictly segregated and all transactions—such as allocation of shared staff time—be scrupulously documented. Implicitly or overtly, examiners are suspicious that a credit union is "upstreaming" its income for the benefit of its sponsor.

David Ramage, who headed the New World Foundation in New York City in the early 1980s, was asked to help sell the idea of the new bank to the Winthrop Rockefeller foundation. As a board member of ShoreBank, he was well positioned to reinforce McRae's pitch.[375]

But how to translate these ideas into reality? McRae was no banker. Neither was Smiley, although he knew a lot about one side of the business from his experience running a company that did data processing for banks. Smiley's passion for the project came from his upbringing: "I was a Baptist from a small town. In small Baptist churches, that's what you're told, you're supposed to go do [good]." To get the necessary expertise, it was McRae who first learned about and reached out to ShoreBank, according to Smiley. "We trusted ShoreBank. They knew a lot more about it than we did. We knew nothing." With the help of Grzywinski and Houghton, they designed a structure for a new bank, one that included the Good Faith Fund, a microenterprise lender, and the for-profit Opportunity Lands Corporation.

The ShoreBank team provided more than technical and design assistance for Southern. "They were a huge help in raising money," Smiley recalled. "In fact, they basically raised most of the money for us, after the Rockefeller Foundation contribution."[376] In particular, Grzywinski and Houghton were responsible for attracting out-of-state funders, which came to include the Ford Foundation. In all, more than $10 million in grants and capital were raised for the various entities that would make up Southern Development Bank. The out-of-state funding was critical, because apart from the Winthrop Rockefeller and Walton Family foundations, plus a small amount from the state, the local business community was skeptical. Grzywinski recalled, "We went and called on one of Walter [Smiley's] good friends who had a big corporation, and the guy just doubled over laughing at what we were proposing to do."[377]

The Catholic women's communities did not laugh. Encouraged by their experience in supporting ShoreBank, the Dominican Sisters in Springfield, IL, stepped up to help launch Southern—despite Grzywinski's cautionary note.

> When we started the bank in Arkansas, Southern Development Bank Corporation, there was one order of nuns who insisted on putting in equity. We said, 'No, no, no, you don't want to do that. Why would you ever put your money in an equity instrument? It has no liquidity. We don't want to take your money.' They insisted, and I'm sure they're still owners.[378]

With more than $10 million raised, Southern began its life much better capitalized than South Shore Bank had been. This was a big advantage. South Shore Bank began in 1973 with somewhat more than $2 million, primarily debt. As discussed earlier, this debt was a heavy drag on ShoreBank's profitability for the better part of a decade.

## Southern Development Bank and the Clintons

While the Winthrop Rockefeller Foundation was examining the ShoreBank model, the Clintons became engaged on a parallel track. Jan Piercy, a close college friend of Hillary Clinton at Wellesley, spent one Thanksgiving dinner with the Clintons in the mid-1980s. She sparked the governor's interest by sharing a report that had profiled ShoreBank.[379] Some months later, Clinton invited ShoreBank's leaders down to explore how the ShoreBank model might be applied in Arkansas. Ron Grzywinski recalled the governor's lively interest: "I have a memory of some Saturdays going to the governor's mansion. Clinton and his cowboy boots and his feet up on the sofa.... He was a very smart man and he knew a lot of stuff."[380]

Still, despite the enthusiasm of Clinton and the foundations, the plan to start a new community development bank in Arkansas was by no means a sure thing.* "What we had done was all urban," ShoreBank's George Surgeon remembered. "Would there be enough activity? Would there be enough impact to really make a difference?"[381] The plan that evolved was not to start a *de novo* bank—that is, from scratch—but rather to acquire an existing bank, as had been done in Chicago. However, as Walter Smiley recalled, "We couldn't find a bank in the Delta. Everybody wanted banks in the Delta and we couldn't find one that was priced anywhere near what we could afford, and they were real skeptical of it." Coming down from Chicago, ShoreBank's Surgeon "learned that everybody was very pleasant and very charming and loved to visit with us, but nobody in their right mind wanted to sell their bank."[382]

After considerable searching and with help from Rob Walton, they focused on a bank in Arkadelphia. It was not the prime target area for the bank, but its owner, James Harrington, was amenable to the deal and the mission. (He later served on Southern's board for many years.) The closing was scheduled for early May 1988. As Surgeon recalled, it almost didn't happen.

> The Ford Foundation's money got lost somewhere on its way to Arkansas. The wire transfer didn't hit the books. We're sitting at the closing table, we had all the money lined up to go—except we needed the two-million-dollar PRI from the Ford Foundation. Somehow it just didn't want to come to Arkansas.[383]

Finally, after storytelling and time-buying, the money came through, and the deal was done. Elk Horn Bank and Trust Company became the heart of Southern Development Bancorp.

Surgeon, who had been staffing the bank organizing effort part-time under ShoreBank's contract with the Winthrop Rockefeller Foundation, soon found himself in a far more prominent position than he had imagined. Shortly after the purchase, he was meeting with the president of the bank, offering

---

* In fact, ShoreBank had been approached by the Spanish Speaking Unity Council in Oakland, CA, for help in taking over a failing thrift. ShoreBank actually did put together an offer for the bank, which was in conservatorship; however, it was rejected, and the bank was sold to another group (which proceeded to lose it several years later). Source: Surgeon interview.

to volunteer his assistance for year-end matters. The president, Larry Whitley, promptly announced that he was leaving in two weeks—and that the FDIC was going to start its examination of the bank the Monday after Whitley's departure. "I think I started off as vice chairman and chief executive officer of the bank. I moved down to Arkansas at the end of 1989 and became officially president and CEO of the holding company on January 1, 1990," Surgeon recalled.[384]

## A Holding Company Like ShoreBank's

Southern's structure—a bank holding company, Southern Development Bancorp—resembled ShoreBank's. Southern Development Bancorp had a bank; a venture fund, Opportunity Lands Corporation; and the Arkansas Enterprise Group (AEG), an umbrella nonprofit. Unlike ShoreBank, Southern had a microenterprise subsidiary under the AEG, the Good Faith Fund.

Hillary Clinton served on Southern's board, and as Walter Smiley recalled, "Hillary became very involved to the point that she really understood it."[385] Hillary Clinton was especially enthusiastic about microenterprise. "Bill and I invited the bank's founder, Dr. Muhammad Yunus, to Little Rock to discuss how microcredit lending programs might help some of the poorest rural communities in Arkansas," she wrote in one of her autobiographies. "I helped set up a development bank and microlending groups in Arkansas, and I wanted to promote microlending throughout the United States, modeled on the success of Yunus and the Grameen Bank."[386]

The Good Faith Fund modeled itself after Grameen's peer-group lending; from his conversations and visits in Arkansas, Dr. Yunus became convinced that the model would work there.[387] Based in Pine Bluff, with several satellite offices in southeastern Arkansas, it specialized in making small loans to African American and women entrepreneurs. ShoreBank brought in Julia Vindasius to run the fund. Its work attracted national attention[388]; after several years, it became a major recipient of funding from the SBA Microlending Demonstration Program.

Although Southern followed the basic structural template of ShoreBank, over time the inherent tensions of the model became apparent. Tom McRae left the Winthrop Rockefeller Foundation in 1989 and joined Southern, overseeing the nonprofit side. As Smiley recalled:

> Bill Brandon, who was our first bank CEO, and Tom McRae, [if you] put them in this room together, there is no way in hell they would ever understand one another. They just simply could not do it because you had Brandon with 30, 40 years ingrained of banking experience of what a bank model looks like. You had Tom over here who was completely ignorant of that, but he wanted to do good so badly. Then you've got to figure out whom do you put in charge.

Smiley recalled, with much frustration, the early troubles of Southern. Arkansas wasn't Chicago, nor was it Bangladesh; intellectual firepower did not readily translate into sound lending.

[Southern's venture fund] lost virtually all of [its capital] in eighteen months, twenty-four months. It didn't take long.... We screwed up because what we didn't understand is that these bright young people had the right motivation, [but] they didn't have the right skills to be investing eight million bucks, or to be trying to figure out how do you take a Grameen model and move it to Pine Bluff.[389]

Notwithstanding the sinkholes and missteps on the path, the company grew, making more acquisitions. When in 1992 candidate Bill Clinton vowed to create a "network of 100 community development banks and 1,000 microenterprise programs,"[390] his inspiration clearly came from Southern as well as ShoreBank.

## Community Capital Bank

*[In the] summer of 1978 in Berkeley, I had the sudden inspiration that I wanted to start a 'good' bank, one that would actually put our resources back where they're needed, into the community, rather than the Fortune 500.... I was in the Shambhala Training program, sitting on my zafu [meditation cushion], and it simply hit me, very clearly, this is what I want to do. I want to start a bank.*[391]

The founding generation of the CDFI movement was an eclectic lot. That Lyndon Comstock—Buddhist, activist, commune resident, housing rehabber—would go on to start a community development bank was perhaps a bit out of the ordinary, but not bizarre. The biggest piece of serendipity (or fate) was something else. As Comstock told it:

I'm literally an offspring of the South Shore Bank.... My father was a bank examiner in the Chicago area at the start of his career. South Shore was one of the banks my father was in charge of examining. My mother worked for a while at the South Shore Bank, of all banks. In fact, my mother and father met at the South Shore Bank.[392]

Although banking was in Comstock's blood, he "never had any interest in banking. As a kid, I thought it was just very dull, and as an adult I thought it was worse than dull, I thought it was poisonous." Shaped by the political movements of the 1960s and early 1970s, Comstock saw banks as "the enemy." Nothing in his own experience prompted him to embrace banks. Seeking financing for a housing cooperative, he found that "there was no bank that was even interested in talking to us about it. It wasn't just that they thought the loan wasn't an acceptable loan, or it was too risky; they simply didn't want to talk to a not-for-profit housing cooperative in 1974."[393] Even a decidedly liberal credit union in Berkeley turned him down.

In 1974, Comstock's views shifted from implacable enmity to banking, to pragmatic frustration, and ultimately, the determination to use the tools of banking to advance community development. Having met dead ends and disappointment, over the next few years Comstock gradually came to the notion that it would take a new type of institution to provide capital access for cooperatives, small businesses, and other "unbankable" organizations. Although he was making an adequate living as a remodeling contractor, he decided to acquire the skills he would need to become a "real" banker: "I had had this inspiration, I had realized that I was someone who could do this, I could use my… middle-class educated background to do something useful. I came up out of a banking family, I'm not intimidated by the idea of banking, I had just always felt it was very boring, but I was not intimidated."

He enrolled in a two-year program at the business school of the University of California–Berkeley. Immediately after graduating in 1981, he entered Wells Fargo's training program, which prepared him to become a commercial lender. In 1984, he moved to First National Bank of Chicago. By the end of 1985, he had logged nearly five years in the world of major banks, acquiring the skills and credentials that would serve him in his pursuit of starting a "good bank."

About that time, Comstock happened on an article in the *Wall Street Journal* about the Institute for Community Economics. "It sounded like just what I wanted to be involved in except that it wasn't a bank, it was a loan fund," he recalled. At various events, he met Chuck Matthei and Chuck Collins of ICE, and other CDFI pioneers, including the author. As exciting as he found the work of ICE and the community development loan funds, he said, "My instinct [was] to use the commercial bank model, which is more widely recognized and gives you access to a lot more money than a loan fund does." His journey of discovery took him back to his family's roots, although the South Shore Bank of the 1980s—a community development bank—was quite different from the bank where his parents met. "I arranged to go visit with the South Shore people, and it was great, I loved it," he recalls. "I thought what they were doing was just terrific. Real live people who were doing exactly what I wanted to do."[394]

Comstock no longer felt able to pursue his vision while he spent his days as a First Chicago commercial banker. He left the bank, without a "fallback" plan to make up for the income that had supported him. "Maybe that's the advantage of growing up in a middle-class background, that you assume that you're not going to end up homeless or have nothing to eat." So, the Buddhist/activist/contractor/mainstream banker began devoting himself full-time to establishing a "good bank."

Other than his banking credentials and self-confidence that this was something he could and would do, Comstock did not enjoy many assets. If people like Matthei radiated charisma, Comstock did not. Low-key, even diffident in his speaking style, he did not project the evangelical fire of the others; instead, he impressed quietly with his grasp of the task, his single-minded pursuit of his goal, and his sharp, occasionally acerbic, insight. Financially, he lacked the access to the philanthropic capital that Southern Development bank had enjoyed, and he did not have the extensive network of connections and potential supporters that South Shore Bank had been able to call on. He had moved to New York City, but he had no roots there, and no ready access to the foundation capital of the country.

Organizing the money and people to start a new bank took every bit of Comstock's persistence for some five years. He recruited several young people to assist him full-time, using whatever meager resources he was able to raise. "We started with the assumption that we just couldn't go the usual small bank route, of assembling a small group of millionaires and going to an underwriter who sells the stock of small banks and saying, 'Sell us like you would any other small bank.'" He continued:

> We want a group of shareholders who bought the stock exactly because of our planned lending program…. It takes a lot of effort to find shareholders who feel that way. On the institutional side, it's a combination of religious institutions, foundations, labor unions, and a few other organizations, like some insurance companies. On the individual side, it means trying to find individuals who have enough money to buy, say, $5,000 worth of stock in a bank and like the idea of what we're doing at the bank and want to support the idea by buying stock.[395]

Wanted: prospective shareholders interested in affordable housing lending, small-business lending in lower-income neighborhoods, quality job-creation in fields like health care, and "outside of the box" initiatives like community land trusts.

Despite formidable obstacles, by the late 1980s trends favored Comstock's efforts to start a new bank. Socially responsible investment was gathering momentum, spurred by the movement to divest in South Africa. Economic justice and civil rights were being linked by Rev. Jesse Jackson, among others. Comstock could point to the growing success of ShoreBank, which had become profitable. Southern Development Bank was generating excitement as a rural replication of ShoreBank. Community development loan funds had multiplied and expanded. The community development credit union movement had begun to attract growing attention as banks deserted low-income areas. In short, although Comstock's proposed *de novo* Community Capital Bank was a relatively untested concept, in many ways, the time was right.

The time was right—but the capital barrier was high. "It was just so difficult to even reach this minimum threshold of six million dollars," Comstock recalled. "It took every last dime I could scrape from anybody to just get to that six million."[396]

## Wall Street and Its Environs: Faith and Finance

Like many CDFI startups, Community Capital Bank was aided by crucial help from the faith community. Attracted by the new bank's "greenlining" mission, a local activist organization, Brooklyn Ecumenical Cooperatives, used its networks of connections in the faith community to promote early investment in the bank by 13 orders of nuns. Another crucial connection was the historic Trinity Church, which sits on Broadway at the mouth of Wall Street. Trinity had an active, progressive grantmaking program, then run by Georgianna Gleason, who became a strong supporter of Comstock's campaign. In addition to providing small grants, "she helped us meet other people in the Episcopal world. That became part of our entry into the church world generally," Comstock recalls, "which is a lot of what helped convince J.P. Morgan & Co. to eventually get involved."[397]

> At the end of day, we couldn't have gotten a bank charter without Morgan's help. The New York State Banking Department thought CCB [Community Capital Bank] was a crackpot idea that was virtually certain to fail…. [Despite political pressure from community organizations,] they were trying to stall us to death, until Morgan created the avenue. Morgan quietly let them know they supported the idea. Bingo, the regulators now had an out if it failed. Not only would they go to Morgan to say that they should prop it up if CCB got in trouble, but, more importantly, to everyone who mattered, they would tell them that Morgan was backing it. That's why they let it go ahead; it meant that they were off the hook for this 'bad' decision. We got the charter almost instantly after that.[398]

In seeking grants to support its organizing work, Comstock's campaign was not organized as a tax-exempt charity. This meant it had to rely on "fiscal sponsors," other nonprofits with compatible missions that could receive and accept responsibility for the expenditure of funds. The National Federation of Community Development Credit Unions played this role, in particular, for a grant from the Rockefeller Brothers Fund.[399]

*National Federation of CDCUs places deposit in Community Capital Bank. From left: author, Amy Nolan (CCB), Lyndon Comstock. Courtesy of Lyndon Comstock.*

The Ford Foundation had invested in South Shore Bank and Southern Development Bank, and Comstock hopefully proposed that they invest in a community development bank in their own backyard, New York City. Ford disappointed him. A letter from a program investment officer on January 19, 1990, stated that CCB's plan "does not fit within those program strategies of the Ford Foundation that most closely parallel the mission of CCB and its current focus on housing." Specifically, Ford's Urban Poverty program "is based on a community or neighborhood centered approach to urban problems, and CCB's city-wide focus does not fit within this program." Another rationale for Ford's turndown foreshadowed a concern that the CRA advocacy community had about the CDFI initiative. Although acknowledging the importance of a "capital markets" approach to increasing the capacity of nonprofit housing developers, "the creation of a new bank such as CCB would not directly address that approach, and might even reduce the likelihood that [other] banks would increase their community development lending."[400] In its way, Ford was questioning whether a new community development bank could have the unintended consequence of "letting banks off the hook." Ultimately, launching the CDFI Fund would depend on allaying this concern, which was voiced by CRA advocacy groups.

Comstock looked elsewhere to raise the $6 million in startup capital the regulators required before they would issue a charter. Over nine months, the bank succeeded in raising the funds from 250 shareholders, of which 60 were institutions and 190 individuals. Among the institutional investors, about one-third were faith-based organizations; others included corporations, foundations, labor union affiliates, and banks.[401] There was another mountain to climb as well: assembling a management team. Most commercial bank startups have boards composed of wealthy, profit-seeking investors and their associates. CCB, in contrast, required board members who were firmly committed to community development; had significant time to spend on board duties (without fees, unlike other banks); and whose business acumen was sufficient to gain approval by bank regulators. So, early directors included representatives of the IBEW union, the United Methodists, Brooklyn Ecumenical Cooperatives, First Women's Bank, and sympathetic investors, notably a cofounder of the Calvert funds, John Guffey.[402]

Community Capital Bank finally received its charter approval in November 1990 and formally commenced operations in January 1991. Although its scope was citywide, CCB did not, and could not, afford a presence in all the five boroughs of New York City. Like ShoreBank and Self-Help, it minimized its retail operation, trying to avoid the heavy costs of servicing small transactions. It opened a single headquarters office in downtown Brooklyn, a few blocks from the Brooklyn Bridge. Structurally, it was not quite like the other two community development banks or Self-Help. It did not have a holding company structure, but it did start a nonprofit affiliate, LEAP Inc., which began workforce programs and provided financial advice to startup health care and food processing businesses in low-income New York communities.[403]

For five years, Comstock had been the visionary and driving force to establish the Community Capital Bank. Despite his tireless labors and experience in conventional banking, he did not get regulatory approval to serve as CEO. Rather, he was chairman of the board of CCB for a decade, during which time he played an active role in national and state CDFI coalitions. The bank leveraged its initial capital to reach more than $100 million in assets. Comstock went on to start yet another community development bank, Community Bank of the Bay, in Oakland, CA.

## The Center for Community Self-Help

North Carolina was losing manufacturing jobs. Especially hard hit was the largely African American population of the rural eastern part of the state, where textile mills had provided a crucial, if modest, livelihood for low-income residents. It was this problem that Martin Eakes and Bonnie Wright set out to address in 1980 when they founded the nonprofit Center for Community Self-Help in Durham.[404] The two graduates of Davidson College—followed by Yale Law School and Princeton for Eakes, Yale School of Management for Wright—sought to convert endangered manufacturing enterprises to employee ownership. Their first office was a trunk in the couple's car. They upgraded to an office in downtown Durham in 1981 when Self-Help got its first grant from the Mary Reynolds Babcock Foundation. By 1982, it was able to pay staff; by 1983, it had founded or converted more than a dozen employee-owned firms.

In 1984, the Center for Community Self-Help founded the dual financial units that formed the pillars of its statewide "development bank"—for that's how Self-Help saw and called itself, notwithstanding the lack of a banking charter. The depository was the state-chartered Self-Help Credit Union; alongside it was the nonprofit Self-Help Ventures Fund. The initial equity capital for the credit union, $77, came from a bake sale held in the town of New Bern.[405] Thus, a structure more or less parallel to ShoreBank's holding company model was put into place, consisting of:

- A regulated, insured depository: the state-chartered Self-Help Credit Union
- An unregulated nonprofit loan fund, able to make loans and investments that could not be readily made by the regulated credit union
- A nonprofit, charitable organization that could obtain foundation and government grants.[406]

The differences between ShoreBank and Self-Help are worth noting, however. The entire Self-Help structure was not-for-profit. Unlike ShoreBank, Self-Help did not have to labor for years to retire initial debt. Its focus was statewide and rural, whereas South Shore Bank in its early years focused on a single urban neighborhood. Self-Help rapidly established itself as a major player in the national market for "development deposits," a field that ShoreBank formerly had virtually to itself.

The Self-Help Credit Union had a major strategic advantage over South Shore Bank: Although the Self-Help Credit Union brought in thousands of individual, organizational, and church depositors, for years it was more of a wholesale institution. The credit union, of course, needed to have full-fledged systems to process deposits and withdrawals, but it operated largely by mail and had virtually no walk-in traffic, sparing it the heavy day-to-day costs that South Shore Bank encountered in a neighborhood of customers with small transactions.

The Self-Help Credit Union also differed from the typical credit union. Credit unions historically were restricted to serving a well-defined field of membership, whether of geography, occupation, or association (e.g., a church or labor union). The Self-Help Credit Union could draw funds nationally, because its field of membership included anyone who joined the sponsoring nonprofit, the Center for Community Self-Help. This basically opened membership to any person or organization that paid the modest membership fee of a few dollars. It also brought a very significant regulatory advantage. Among credit unions, only designated low-income institutions are allowed to raise insured deposits from *nonmembers*. But the National Credit Union Administration (NCUA), as the federal insurer for credit unions, looked with some suspicion on such deposits. After a scandal in fall 1988, the NCUA restricted low-income credit unions from holding more than 20 percent of their deposits in nonmember funds.[407] Since virtually all of the Self-Help Credit Union's deposits were *member* deposits, the restriction did not hamper it.

Like the credit union, the Self-Help Ventures Fund was born in 1984. Bob Schall came to Self-Help from the food co-op movement, managing a cooperative distribution network. Arriving at Self-Help in 1985, he recalled, "By the time I got here, they had just started making loans. They had more deposits in the credit union than they had loans. The Ventures Fund, I think, had $50,000 in assets."[408] One of Schall's first jobs after he was hired was to write a Program-Related Investment (PRI) proposal to the Ford Foundation. The reality, he recalled, was that "we didn't have enough money to keep me on staff for very long if I did not raise my own money." Within a year, however, major investments began to roll in.

Self-Help rapidly expanded in size, scope, and recognition. By 1985, it had opened an office in Charlotte, NC. That year, the United Nations selected it as one of the 20 most successful rural development groups in the United States. The young institution's portfolio included an impressive range of cooperative enterprises: a worker co-op hosiery manufacturer, a consumer food co-op, a nonprofit housing cooperative, a community-owned rural newspaper, and a nonprofit cultural center, among others.[409] Still, Self-Help was evolving away from being the "bank" for employee ownership conversion.

> We didn't really change our mission, but we changed our strategy radically. When I came, we were only working with the worker-owned businesses, consumer co-ops and non-profits.... We used to call this 'shadow management.' We helped these employee groups start businesses and we stayed with them. We happened to make them loans. But I think our biggest value-add was the management assistance we provided. But that model just was not working very well. And we were pretty much the only promoter of these businesses in North Carolina.
>
> It is not like we had a market that was coming to us. We were out there trying to create the market, which financially wasn't sustainable. It had to be grant-supported because our employee groups couldn't pay us. Businesses were not successful enough that we could get a big fee out of it. Many of them had trouble staying in business without our continuing support.[410]

Financing for worker-owned enterprises was not abandoned, but it was no longer the singular focus for Self-Help.[411] Paradoxically, the very success of the credit union in bringing in deposits meant that Self-Help had more money than it could use—at least for cooperatives. It needed to find a way to use its expanding financial capacity, and thus it turned to financing single-family homes—especially for low-income, minority, rural, and/or female-headed households. As Schall recalled, "We decided that that would be a good way to expand, because it was compatible with our mission. It built ownership. It was a different model of building ownership—it was individual ownership rather than cooperative ownership—but it was a way of building ownership." Reinforcing this strategic argument, home ownership tied in well with Self-Help's goal of promoting business ownership. "The typical path for a person to get into small business lending is to borrow against their house," Schall noted. "And the folks we were working with did not have home equity" to borrow against.

There was also a pragmatic ancillary argument: "Our regulators wanted us to do something conventional. You know, either car loans or mortgage loans. And they didn't like that we were focused on business lending."[412] So, in 1986, the credit union made its first homeownership loan, entering the field in which it would ultimately measure its impact in hundreds of millions of dollars of financing, especially for low-income, minority, and female-headed households. By July 1989, the credit union—managed by Bonnie Wright, assisted by Thad Moore—had grown to more than $15 million in assets, making it one of the largest community development credit unions in the country.[413]

Self-Help laid out its goals for 1989 in its newsletter: $2.5 million in new credit union housing loans; $2.5 million in commercial loans originated by the credit union; and $750,000 in loans by the Ventures Fund.

> Our goals are that at least 40 percent of the businesses we give loans to should be in rural areas, that 40 percent should be women-owned, and that 40 percent should be minority-owned. Additionally, we'd like to have at least 20 percent of our loans go to worker-owned businesses, housing cooperatives, and democratic organization (like many nonprofits).[414]

## Access to Capital: Philanthropy and State Funds

As foundations expanded their program-related investing and grantmaking for community development in the 1980s, Self-Help became an early, top-tier recipient. In 1986, the Ford Foundation made a $1.5 million PRI; in 1989, Ford invested $2 million to scale up the credit union's lending capacity, while making a grant of $250,000 to support Self-Help's Partnership Lending program.[415] The John D. and Catherine T. MacArthur Foundation invested. The Z. Smith Reynolds Foundation provided the Ventures Fund a $750,000 grant in 1989 to expand its lending to minority-owned businesses and cooperatives.[416] When the National Federation launched its Capitalization Program for CDCUs, the Self-Help Credit Union was one of the first to be awarded deposits.

More than almost any other nascent CDFI of the 1980s, Self-Help blazed a path in statewide advocacy. In 1988, the North Carolina General Assembly granted Self-Help $2 million to support its higher-risk lending to minorities, women, and rural residents. The next year, Self-Help won $2 million for its North Carolina Homeownership Program.[417] Despite the exceptional success Self-Help enjoyed in leveraging state funds, Martin Eakes found that "the North Carolina legislative appropriations for [Community Economic Development] starting in 1988 were largely dependency-creating operating grants." Consequently, when CDFI Fund legislation was being developed, Eakes argued strongly "that the CDFI awards should be all capital, with a matching requirement, and with little to no operating funding."[418]

## The Self-Help Model

In a speech in 1992 to the annual conference of the National Association of Community Development Loan Funds, Martin Eakes summarized the rationale for Self-Help's model.

> *The development bank's structure must combine a non-profit subsidy entity with an insured depository institution* [emphasis in original]. When you look at Self-Help's or ShoreBank's organizational chart, the multiple development entities you see really boil down to two functional pieces. The depository institution has the incredible power of converting ordinary savings into development credit. It is the financial engine for the development bank, and gives the development bank enough size to attract and retain sophisticated staff. A depository institution alone, however, would simply be a second-rate bank. When you add a non-profit development entity that can be the recipient of subsidy dollars, the development bank takes on a new depth.[419]

There were other ways, as well, in which the Self-Help "holding company" provided a vital advantage. With the nonprofit charity to fall back on, Self-Help could take on more costly programs (including smaller loans), assume greater lending risk, launch experiments to see "what works" in low-income communities, and—crucial to Self-Help's mission—advocate with large financial institutions for social change. Self-Help could shift to the Ventures Fund certain types of loans that if made by the credit union might incur regulators' objections. More dramatically, in fall 2008, Self-Help faced a potentially devastating liquidity crunch in the wake of the panic spurred by the fall of Lehman Brothers, when its short-term line of credit was summarily called on a few hours' notice by a Wall Street bank. The Self-Help Credit Union, however, had sufficient liquidity to help the organization avert the crisis.

## Managing Self-Help

Neither Self-Help nor any other early CDFI had anything like the quartet that managed ShoreBank and its affiliates. From the beginning, Self-Help was a unified structure, in which Martin Eakes was the ultimate authority. As described above, the Eakes/Wright couple were cofounders of the organization; Bonnie Wright became the manager of the credit union, and others came to head the affiliated units, but Eakes was the CEO of Self-Help as a whole entity.

The CDFI movement has attracted and developed any number of talented, mission-driven leaders, but only a few charismatic figures, like Chuck Matthei. Martin Eakes has played a unique role in the movement. His speeches over the years are replete with implausible self-deprecation ("I am the world's worst manager," for example, and "lots of people could do what I've done")—except when it comes to describing his high school exploits as a boxer and basketball player. He won a MacArthur Foundation "genius" award and was appointed a Trustee of the Ford Foundation, recognition not only for his role as an innovative institution-builder, but as a fierce and fearless advocate, who has taken on the biggest banks and predatory lenders in the country, fought regulators (for example, over efforts to close minority credit unions in North Carolina), and led other causes as well.

Despite Eakes's pre-eminence, Self-Help has never degenerated into a cult of personality. It has attracted and retained extraordinary talent, individuals who have remained for decades, becoming industry leaders in their own right—this despite a unique salary structure that limits the top salary to a multiple of about three times that of the lowest-paid employee. Thus, the CEO of the $2 billion enterprise that Self-Help has become had a salary slightly above $80,000 in 2016.[420] The integrated structure of the Self-Help "holding company" has meant that the organization has largely avoided the friction that other complex CDFIs with multiple affiliates have encountered.

## Mainstream Banking: Scandals and Exposés

By the end of the 1980s, Congress was wrestling with losses of hundreds of billions of dollars from S&Ls, for which the taxpayers bore ultimate liability. Banking suffered further reputation risk from a journalistic bombshell: A series of *Atlanta Journal-Constitution* investigative articles, "The Color of Money," provided irrefutable evidence of mortgage-lending discrimination against African Americans in the Atlanta area. Community groups had learned how to use Community Reinvestment Act (CRA) challenges to exact settlements in the billions from banks that were seeking to merge, acquire, or relocate branches.

Conditions were ripening for a new kind of banking. The nascent CDFI movement found receptive ears in Congress and growing energy for change at the grassroots.

# CHAPTER 7. The Investors

Throughout the 1980s, religious organizations, especially orders of nuns, continued to play a seminal role in the startup of CDFIs, usually investing modest amounts—tens of thousands of dollars—but achieving huge moral and practical leverage. National denominational offices began to play a larger role as well. The socially responsible investment movement became more formalized in the 1980s, and the first tentative connections with community investment were forged.

Among foundations, the Ford Foundation continued to play a leading role in funding community economic development. It remained the largest source of Program-Related Investments (PRIs) in general, and emerging CDFIs in particular. Indeed, it was one of the few foundations so engaged, but it was joined by another major actor.

## The John D. and Catherine T. MacArthur Foundation

The MacArthur Foundation made the occasional PRI in the early 1980s, but it was only in 1986, according to Paul Lingenfelter, who directed its initiative, that the foundation began to use PRIs systematically.[421] Lingenfelter, who joined the foundation in 1985 as director of program evaluation, was neither an investment nor a community development specialist. A generalist with a PhD in higher education, he came to the foundation after being deputy director of fiscal affairs at the Illinois Board of Higher Education. He was dispatched to the Ford Foundation, where he learned about program-related investing from the leaders of its PRI office, Tom Miller and Jan Jaffe. They suggested that he learn about organizations like ShoreBank, Enterprise, LISC, NHS, and the National Federation of Community Development Credit Unions (CDCUs). "I became intrigued with the concept," he recalled. "I was impressed with South Shore Bank, impressed with the idea of using capital as a tool for addressing poverty."[422]

Lingenfelter developed a financial model for a prospective PRI program. It was "easy to show that it made great economic and philosophic sense to do so," he recalled, since the foundation would receive modest interest payments and receive repaid capital—it would largely pay for itself. "Interest-bearing recyclable grants" was the term Lingenfelter used. Nonetheless, "frankly, we expected to lose the money, or lose some of the money with this," he recalled.[423] He took the proposed plan to a MacArthur board member, a lawyer, who was intrigued by the program, and he presented a draft application reduced by half from Ford's 16-page application. His board member declared it "a crock" and told Lingenfelter to simply ask for the last audit: "Don't make people jump through hoops," he said.[424] Lingenfelter then had no problem selling the program to his bosses and the board.

Over the course of the decade, the MacArthur Foundation made a total of $40 million in PRIs. These were broadly divided between Chicago-specific and national investments (with a single international investment), some of which had a Chicago-specific component. "Through a conscious decision," Lingenfelter wrote, "nearly all of the Foundation's community development PRIs are to intermediary organizations." In a 1991 paper, Lingenfelter systematically laid out the case for investing in intermediaries.

The MacArthur Foundation had a multi-billion-dollar endowment, but it was nowhere near the size of the Ford Foundation. Its staff was also far smaller than Ford's. In its early years, MacArthur staffed its PRI initiative with a half or less of one professional's time, part of a secretary's time, and a small portion of an in-house attorney's time. An intermediary-based PRI initiative leveraged the foundation's staff. This was certainly cost-efficient for the foundation, but more than that, "without using intermediaries," Lingenfelter wrote, "both our programmatic scope and our experience and understanding would be far narrower." As Lingenfelter recalled, "My board could not conceive how a grant program could have much of an impact on the problems of poverty" by national grantmaking.[425] PRIs were an attractive way to leverage the foundation's dollars, since they often triggered investments or funding by other organizations. Summing up five years' experience, Lingenfelter wrote: "With few exceptions we have been extremely pleased with the results. …We believe we have made a useful contribution to the work of these intermediaries, but it is even more certain that we would have fallen far short of their contributions had we attempted to make such investments directly."[426]

MacArthur's portfolio, built from 1983 through 1990, included many of the familiar names in the emerging CDFI movement. A partial list included:

> Chicago: LISC (also for its national program), NHS, ShoreBank and its affiliate, The Neighborhood Institute, the Chicago Capital Fund
> Nationally and regionally: Enterprise, Housing Assistance Council, ICE, the Low Income Housing Fund, the National Federation of CDCUs, NHS of America, Self-Help, First Nations Financial Project (Oweesta), the Industrial Cooperative Association (ICA), Northeast Ventures, and Southern Development Bancorporation of Arkansas

PRIs typically ranged from $1 million to $3 million, although LISC received $7 million.[427]

For organizations like the National Federation of CDCUs, the MacArthur investment was an enormous breakthrough. For several years, the National Federation had received a growing number of investments of $10 to $30,000, primarily from women's religious orders. In 1986, the MacArthur Foundation's investment of $500,000 put the federation's Capitalization Program on the verge of one million dollars under management. It gave the organization confidence, credibility, and recognition;

MacArthur's small, un-bureaucratic approach was a great benefit for nonprofit recipients, especially small and relatively inexperienced ones.

## The Ford Foundation

Tom Miller traveled a very different route to the foundation world than Paul Lingenfelter. He had managed community development venture capital investment in Appalachia, worked in a national CPA firm in Washington, DC, and then done pro bono work in Washington's Adams-Morgan neighborhood.[428] "I just fell in love with the people who were doing that work. I decided I didn't want to reach for the brass ring of partnership."[429]

Instead, a job search brought him in 1972 to Kentucky Highlands, one of the earliest and most successful community development venture capital organizations. He shortly became head of the organization, leading its expansion beyond job training and development to social investment, fueled by the Title VII funding that had been created for community development corporations in the War on Poverty. "It was absolutely clear to me that to achieve the job strategy, you needed ventures," he recalled, "and that meant entrepreneurs." Miller, the CPA, became convinced that "investments can achieve commercial goals as well as social ones. A nonprofit can manage it."[430]

Although Miller was hugely excited by his work, he recalls, "I was burnt out by the end of 1980. I couldn't stand to hear the telephone ring" with pitches for "crazy" ideas by aspiring entrepreneurs. Instead, he went off on his own entrepreneurial adventure, oil-well wildcatting. That brief chapter of his life ended when he was recruited to the Ford Foundation in 1982, then run by Franklin Thomas, formerly of the Bedford-Stuyvesant Restoration Corporation, whom Miller had known previously.

Miller came to Ford with the mission to "make the PRI program work." The portfolio was just recovering from heavy losses—up to "60 percent or 70 percent"—and had barely avoided being cut off by the trustees. The reason had been poor "retail" investments (i.e., investments directly in enterprises). The solution, Ford had concluded, was to invest through intermediaries, like the Cooperative Assistance Fund and the Institute for Community Economics. Under Miller's leadership, Ford's PRI portfolio increased incrementally from about $40 million to about $100 million when he left in 1992. Ford's trustees strongly supported the initiative. A dedicated trustee committee operated "like a stockholder meeting every year," Miller recalled. Targets were set for annual lending and for target percentages of recoveries. We "took it out of the shadows so they could see everything that was going on," he said, and it became so popular that trustees regularly asked whether Miller needed more money.[431]

Miller was explicitly tasked with spreading the PRI concept to foundations and other social investors. Paul Lingenfelter and the MacArthur Foundation, he recalled, were among the first to seek Ford's advice. "It was wonderful, a lot of fun," he recalled, spreading the PRI gospel to community foundations and others; it was "interesting that it was the religious organizations [that] first picked up on the idea." One element of the Ford Foundation approach that the MacArthur Foundation did *not* replicate was the role of the lawyers. Miller had to please house counsel, which, he noted, "was the source of considerable internal tension."[432]

## Investing in Equity

Equity grants to build the net worth of organizations were one of Tom Miller's favorite innovations: "How else do you get equity in this business" of social investment, he asked rhetorically.[433] It was true for almost all small businesses, especially those in low-income and minority communities; it was equally true for CDFIs, which in their own right were typically thinly capitalized startup businesses aspiring to sustainability. A decade later, equity grants would be the crucial *federal* innovation of the CDFI Fund.

The Ford Foundation began providing equity grants to accompany PRIs in the early 1980s. In August 1988, the Brody & Weiser consulting firm delivered an "Equity Grant Review" commissioned by Ellen Arrick of Ford's PRI department. Billed as "preliminary findings" rather than a full evaluation, the report examined for the first time Ford's five-year history of providing these funds. It identified the five goals of the equity grant program:

1. Reduce the level of risk borne by PRIs
2. Encourage borrowers to take appropriate risks to meet social goals, and to account for these
3. Build capacity for nonprofits to develop social ventures
4. Fill gaps that debt could not meet in social venture financial structures
5. Provide incentives to meet Ford's goals.[434]

The consultants interviewed many early CDFI recipients of equity grants, including Self-Help; Coastal Enterprises, a CDC in Maine; First Nations, which supported indigenous development in the United States; the Industrial Cooperatives Association, a leader in worker-owned enterprise development; ICE, LISC, and South Shore Bank, along with all of Ford's PRI program officers as well as senior officials.[435]

From 1983, when Ford began providing equity grants to intermediary borrowers, through 1987, Ford approved 30 grants for $2,171,738 in conjunction with PRI loan commitments of $24,048,672.[436] Some of the funds went to the costs of projects, but more than half went to capitalize loan loss reserve pools, reflecting PRIs' significant investment in financial intermediaries. "These intermediaries served needs including low-income housing, refugee microenterprise, rural water and wastewater, employee ownership, and overall community development."[437] Typically, equity grants were about 10 percent of the amount of a PRI, although the maximum was 20 percent.[438]

The report framed two related questions: What was the appropriate *ratio* of equity or net worth to assets for a PRI recipient? *How much equity* would the recipient require, and how much would it be appropriate for a funder to provide? The consultants noted that housing-related and business- or enterprise-related CDFIs had different needs.

With regard to loan funds, the major learning is that there is significant data indicating that the equity grants have not been sufficiently large to accomplish all the purposes intended. In retrospect, it appears that the risk involved in loan funds that are involved in enterprise development is greater than either the borrowers or the Foundation had anticipated. Several enterprise development loan fund interviewees indicated that the current level of equity grant funding leaves them with difficulty in balancing the need to fund the risks associated with social goals, against the need to build permanent equity in order to be able to continue operations when the PRI loan has been repaid.[439]

Based on interviews with enterprise lenders, the report offered the preliminary conclusion "that the equity portion of many loan funds may need to be as high as 30 percent in order for the fund to take the level of risk appropriate to its social goals, and even higher for some funds."[440] Business lending funds had "less predictability" than real estate–focused loan funds, which had the advantage of access to collateral; still, equity grants to the latter might still need to be higher than 10–20 percent. (Needless to say, many PRI recipients argued that Ford could or should have provided larger amounts.)

There was a fundamental difference between unregulated loan funds, on the one hand, and regulated depositories—i.e., banks and credit unions—on the other. The 20 percent or 30 percent equity (net worth) ratio that the consultants recommended for higher-risk loan funds was not generally appropriate for depositories: It would translate into insufficient leverage and reduced profitability. On the other hand, a depository was required by regulation to meet equity or net worth standards (usually, 7–10 percent).

In any case, the potential supply of equity grants was limited. By the late 1980s, the Ford Foundation had, intentionally or not, provided an important innovation: a hybrid, equity-like loan that anticipated the emergence of other capital tools for CDFIs, including "EQ2" for loan funds and secondary capital for low-income credit unions. Equity grants went into a CDFI's net worth; PRIs or loans were generally liabilities. But a Ford Foundation PRI to the recently formed Southern Development Bank blurred the line.

> The combination of low interest (1 percent), long term (14 years) and deferred principal repayments served an important equity function, even though the PRI was structured as a loan. The terms were so generous that the federal regulatory agency counted the loan as primary capital for some purposes, which effectively rescued a $2 million Winthrop Rockefeller Foundation common stock investment that otherwise would have been lost. Although this example is somewhat complex, the important issue is that the combination of very low interest rate, term in excess of ten years, and generous principal repayment schedule may cause a PRI loan to be treated as quasi-equity, with equity-like usefulness.[441]

As to the appropriate amount of equity, the consultants wrote that "one loan fund projected that a rise to ten million dollars in equity is the amount required for a small loan fund to obtain enough conventional debt and attain self-sufficiency."[442] In fact, many loan funds ultimately did attain this level of equity, but it was not—could not—be primarily due to a foundation like Ford, as large as it was: Almost always, reaching $10 million in equity would be achievable only with the boost that would later come from the CDFI Fund. In the meanwhile, even the 10 percent equity grant that accompanied many Ford PRIs would be invaluable in building the balance sheets of CDFIs.

## Faith-Based Investment in the 1980s

The circles of social investment, faith-based activism, and the early CDFI movement were relatively small in the 1980s; relationships among individuals and organizations were only at one or two degrees of separation. Among those who bridged these worlds was Amy Domini, who started her career as a broker and later founded Domini Social Investments.[443]

As a stockbroker in the early 1980s, she found that some of her clients wrestled with balancing their values with their investment objectives. In 1984, she addressed these questions in her work, *Ethical Investing*. Domini was active in the national Episcopal Church, including on its Socially Responsible Investment Committee, and she represented it at the ecumenical Interfaith Center on Corporate Responsibility (ICCR). As the Episcopal Church looked to move beyond filing shareholder resolutions, she recalls, "I was asked by the Church to move over to the endowment side, from the socially responsible investment side, to be a kind of advocate to make the kind of loans" that it was seeking to direct to communities.[444] Her writing and speaking brought her in contact with Chuck Matthei of ICE, who recruited her to the board of the newly formed National Association of Community Development Loan Funds.

Foundations had elaborated the concept of "program-related investments"; for many church bodies, the operative term was "mission-related investments." Over the course of the 1980s, the advisory and governing bodies of the Episcopal Church increased their commitment to such investments.[445] In October 1987, the letter "Economic Justice and the Christian Conscience,"[446] developed by the Urban Bishops Coalition and signed by 80 bishops of the Episcopal Church, was broadly distributed throughout the church. The letter, which was actually a lengthy, footnoted paper, focused on the "frightening paradox" of poverty and prosperity in the United States. It noted with distress that "the gap between these two groups, the well-to-do and the poor, is widening daily and at an alarming rate. In the United States, it is now larger than it has been since the late 1940s."

The letter rejected "trickle-down" economics and "quick-fix" remedies as band-aids, declaring that "only a major re-orienting of society's operational values can make possible the laying of a new foundation on which a truly just economy can thrive."[447] It noted that the Roman Catholic Church, the Presbyterians, the United Church of Christ, and the World Council of Churches were working on similar documents. The letter concluded, "Martin Buber was right in holding that the only way truly to reconstruct a culture of community is to begin in the here and now to build community-based economic and social institutions."[448]

Translating these values into practice, in 1988, the General Convention of the Episcopal Church called for "more community economic development efforts on the part of the Society."[449] In November 1989, the Executive Council approved placing $3.5 million into an Alternative Investment Portfolio managed by the Committee on Trust Funds, with $3.5 million more to be held in a loan fund "pending recommendations from the Economic Justice Implementation Committee." In 1990, the church's Joint Advisory Council on Alternative Investments attempted to ground alternative investments in an analysis of *stewardship*, the church's proper role in managing its financial and other resources.[450] In its analysis, it concluded, "Especially, we should recognize that people who are not housed properly, or fed properly, or educated properly haven't the ability to fulfill their purposes."[451]

The Committee on Trust Funds defined its strategy as

> to promote community-based development by supporting community-based financial institutions. These institutions make credit available for housing and job creation and benefit low-income persons who are unable to access traditional sources of capital. *The Society's funds are invested with the full expectation that (1) principal will be fully repaid and (2) a reasonable rate of interest will be earned* [emphasis in original].[452]

Thus, the committee was quite clear that it was in the business of providing debt or deposits, and not equity. (Notwithstanding the committee's stated aversion to making equity investments, it noted that it had purchased $25,000 of equity in South Shore Bank in the 1970s, of which it was proud.) It was chastened by bad memories of the Sixties: "A predecessor program of the late 1960s efforts to address the issues of community economic development through venture capital had resulted in financial loss to the Society."[453] Its investments were to be made generally "at close to the market rate for short-term interest… [recognizing] that the Society is giving up the potential growth that common stocks might offer."

Referring indirectly to the earlier failures, the Committee on Trust Funds "elected to seek out intermediaries of intermediaries."[454] It repeatedly emphasized *building a sustainable infrastructure* for CDFIs, citing the National Association of Community Development Loan Funds and the National Federation of CDCUs as examples of what it was trying to support. Among other CDFI intermediaries, the church had also invested in the Industrial Cooperative Association, which promoted worker cooperatives.

A related strategy involved a deliberate effort to mobilize local and regional bodies of the church. Part of the committee's goals were to provide "a mechanism for challenge funds to local Episcopal sponsors, intermediaries, and agencies, [and to] establish credibility in this process so that others will be willing to take similar risks at a later time."[455] In other words, the strategy provided a framework and impetus for local CDFIs to approach their respective diocesan and related organizations for matching funds. From the late 1980s, various Provinces of the Church invested in community development loan funds and credit unions from New England to California, often working with and through their national associations. When the New Hampshire Community Loan Fund was struggling to get on its feet, it found a strong ally and advocate in Douglas E. Theuner, Bishop of New Hampshire, who, according to Amy Domini, embraced the loan fund as his cause, "pounding on parishes" and on other Episcopal bodies to support it.[456]

## Women's Congregations and CDFI

Among the earliest CDFIs, it is difficult to find an organization that did *not* receive investments from one of the many Catholic women's communities. By the late 1980s, some CDFIs listed dozens of congregations among their investors.

## Sisters of Mercy

The New Hampshire Community Loan Fund was one of the many fledgling CDFIs that received an early investment from the Sisters of Mercy. Julie Eades, longtime CEO of the fund, recalled the no-nonsense and no-excuses loan transaction: "The Sister hands me a check, and she doesn't let go of it. So, the two of us are kind of awkwardly holding on to this check. She looks me square in the eye, and says: 'You'd better do something good with it. And you'd better pay it back.'"[457]

The Sisters of Mercy played many roles in the development of the CDFI movement. Over the course of three decades, it invested in fledgling CDFIs like the New Hampshire Community Loan Fund, and sometimes sisters helped staff them. The religious community established Mercy Partnership Fund as part of its Mercy Investment Program, to make and manage its community investments.*

In 1984, the community's Omaha province hired Sarah Smith to develop a structure that would support its new Mercy Housing ministry, which extended to 18 states. Smith became the CEO of the Catherine McAuley Housing Foundation (later the Mercy Loan Fund),[458] which was originally capitalized with low- and no-interest investments from faith-based institutions and provided loans to affordable housing projects. "We built it one loan at a time," she recalls, "and we valued every one of them as if it were gold." It was a time of sky-high interest rates, she recalled, and the focus was "access to capital, not just affordability."[459]

The Sisters of Mercy were prominent in developing both national and regional structures. Sister Patricia Wolf, RSM, a founding member of the Mercy Investment Program and cofounder of the Leviticus Fund, was executive director of the Tri-State Coalition for Responsible Investment (New

---

\* The work of the Fund continues today as part of Mercy Investment Services, the socially responsible investing program of the Sisters of Mercy of the Americas.

York, New Jersey, Connecticut) and also served as executive director of the Interfaith Center on Corporate Responsibility.

## The Leviticus Fund

One product of the Tri-State Coalition was the Leviticus 25:23 Alternative Fund, Inc. Founded in 1983, the nonprofit fund drew its name from a section of the Book of Leviticus in the Hebrew Scriptures, reading: "Your land must not be sold on a permanent basis because you do not own it; it belongs to God, and you are like foreigners who are allowed to make use of it"—a biblical injunction that sounded very much like the guiding faith of the community land trust movement. The Leviticus Fund drew its investments from organizations and individuals and had voting members from varied faith denominations. A tripartite focus emerged: affordable and supportive housing; child care facilities; and not-for-profit facilities in the New York metropolitan area.[460]

## Adrian Dominicans

From the 1970s, the Adrian Dominicans were vigorously engaged in corporate research and shareholder resolutions, targeting apartheid, weapons production, the environment, labor practices, corporate governance, equal employment, and more. However, especially in the early years, Sister Carol Coston wrote, they had to deal with

> [the] collective frustration... of ever effecting real change in the corporations in which we held stock. We dutifully filed shareholder resolutions, voted proxies, initiated dialogue with corporate management, and spoke up at annual meetings. It was hard to feel any great sense of victory. So the idea of doing something more proactive with our investments was quite appealing—to know specifically where our money was being used and who benefited from it.[461]

Hence, the appeal of community investing. The Adrian Dominicans played a leading role among faith-based community investors in the 1980s. In 1982, they loaned $30,000 to the National Federation of CDCUs, the first investment in its new Capitalization Program for CDCUs. By 1984, the congregation's social investment fund had increased to $1.5 million, and by 1991, to $2 million.[462]

Among community investors, the Adrian Dominicans were distinguished by their strong engagement with their borrowers: They wanted to see the impact of their investments first-hand, and where needed, to try to help with workouts when organizations ran into trouble. One of their principles was that "there would be ongoing communication so that a relationship was begun" with investees. The

Adrian Dominicans made deposits in nine CDCUs in the 1980s, including Quitman County FCU in Marks, MS, which Sister Carol Coston and Sister Maureen Fenlon visited. The visit made plain the

> commonality of mission we felt with them. It was easy to see the long history of segregation that the founders of the credit union faced.... The small town was clearly divided by race, the blacks living, literally, on the other side of the tracks. The white power structure refused to give the credit union organizers a zoning permit to construct a building.[463]

The Adrian Dominicans certainly expected their loans to be repaid, but they realistically understood the risks. Their borrowers were "often members of minority communities, women who have no business experience, or persons trying to establish different forms of business structures, such as cooperatives, that banks do not understand or choose to refuse loans."[464] Some of the worker cooperatives, in particular, had experienced hard times and had to close, causing losses to their investments. But failure, for the Adrian Dominicans, was not a reason to abandon the humane principles that had motivated an investment: "When all bailout or regrouping strategies have failed, we try to help the workers or directors close down with a minimum of financial loss to us and the organization, and to do it in a way that respects the dignity of the participants."[465]

The "alumni" of the Adrian Dominican congregations were active in bringing their experience and expertise to other faith-based investors: the Ecumenical Development Cooperative Society (Maureen Fenlon), the Women's Initiative Fund for micro-entrepreneurs (Corinne Florek), Christian Brothers Investment Services (Carol Coston), and Catholic Healthcare West (Judy Rimbey), which was an especially active community investor.

## The "God Box": The Interfaith Center on Corporate Responsibility (ICCR)

Overlooking the Hudson River at 475 Riverside Drive in Manhattan sat the "God box," as it was colloquially known, a neighbor of Riverside Church, Columbia University, and Union Theological Seminary. It housed the Interfaith Center on Corporate Responsibility (ICCR), as well as denominational and other faith-based organizations. ICCR began in 1971 with a membership of a few Protestant denominations but soon grew to include Roman Catholic organizations, women's orders, and associated health care organizations. ICCR became a forum and a voice for hundreds of faith-based and other institutions concerned with corporate, environmental, social justice, and governance policies; it was a place where shareholder resolutions and other strategies were forged.

ICCR's engagement in community economic development, according to Tim Smith, executive director for 24 years, began with visits by religious investors to South Shore Bank, which obtained equity investments from the United Church of Christ and other denominational bodies over the years.[466] Although corporate responsibility always remained the core of ICCR's work, proactive social investment gradually drew increasing interest among ICCR and its member organizations. In the 1980s, ICCR formed its Clearinghouse on Alternative Investments, which became a channel for distributing information packets about CDFIs to its large membership.[467] For many startup CDFIs, the search for operating funds began with a pilgrimage to the various denominational offices at 475 Riverside Drive. Some, like the Methodists, had small grant programs: As the National Federation of CDCUs was struggling to rebuild itself in the early 1980s, it obtained a precious $30,000 grant from the Methodist program. ICCR periodically hosted meetings at which CDFIs could introduce themselves and make their case.

On the investment side, ICCR was not itself a funder, but some of its members—like the Methodist Pension Board—controlled large sums, with as much as $1 billion available for market-rate investments. The Presbyterian Church (U.S.A.) Foundation became an active social investor over the course of the 1980s, making a major investment in the National Federation's Capitalization Program for CDCUs.

## Socially Responsible Investment

The socially responsible investment (SRI) movement grew dramatically and took new organizational shape in the 1980s. Along with shareholder advocacy, portfolio managers significantly expanded their social screening of investments. It was no longer limited to excluding the traditional "sinful" tobacco, alcohol, drug, and military producers: Divestment from companies doing business in apartheid South Africa became a huge cause. Student activists (including some future CDFI leaders) prominently pressed university endowments to divest, but the movement was much broader, joined by dozens of cities and pension funds across the country. By the mid-1980s, church pension funds alone had at least $8 billion in screened investments, even apart from the traditional exclusions of tobacco, alcohol, and drug companies.[468] The business of SRI expanded as well. Investment companies began adding socially screened mutual funds and money market funds.[469] Investment professionals, institutional investors, researchers, and other active investors came together to form the Social Investment Forum (SIF), which documented and promoted the growing SRI movement.

While women's congregations like the Adrian Dominicans and the Sisters of Mercy had fearlessly invested in relatively untried community development lenders, the broader SRI community was making its first, tentative steps. Two prominent CDFI leaders paved the way, serving in the leadership of the SIF—Joan Shapiro of South Shore Bank and Chuck Matthei of ICE. Shapiro, who headed South Shore's development deposit program, made the case for SRI to move to a new stage, arguing for the dual dimensions of social investment: "Social investing involves deciding where *not* to invest. It also involves deciding where *to* invest" [emphasis in original].[470]

South Shore Bank continued to be the most prominent community development lender and the most successful seeker of social investment. By 1984, as it reported in a press release, it held $32 million of its $68 million loan portfolio in "development loans," mostly for multifamily homes and small businesses. These were funded by $30 million in development deposits the bank had gathered. Meanwhile, the bank's own socially screened money market fund provided returns of 9.53 percent, compared with the average of 9.28 percent returned by large bank funds.[471] The community development loan fund movement, still in its infancy, had just begun to attract new investors: SIF's 1985 "Social Balance Sheet" cited the work of early funds, which typically had assets in the hundreds of thousands, although one (MACED) held as much as $3.5 million.[472] The report did not mention community development credit unions, which had received investments from faith-based organizations for several years.

Although SRI grew significantly in the 1980s, community investing was still modest. In 1989, the Ford Foundation PRI department funded a report by the SIF identifying the scope, practices, and obstacles to "alternative investments."[473] The report, which was based on a survey of SIF members, noted that socially responsible investing "has gained widespread acceptance in recent years…. Socially screened assets now measure in the hundreds of billions of dollars. Less well known and funded are alternative investments, or investments in projects that are specifically designed to deliver a socially beneficial product or remedy a social ill."[474]

The authors determined that "the median commitment to alternative investments among responding financial professionals is 0.1 percent of their firms' social assets."[475] Meanwhile, the assets held by community development loan funds, credit unions, and banks that were SIF members totaled only about $125 million.[476] Among the obstacles to greater investment were concern about risk, lack of liquidity, and noncompetitive rates of return. High on the list, and a perpetual concern for financial managers and investors, was the *information* challenge: "The due diligence process is beyond the scope of most investors and investment professionals who lack both the time and expertise necessary for such an evaluation. An easier way of investing in alternative projects is by using a financial intermediary that specializes in community development investments."[477]

Unsurprisingly, given the concern about risk and return, financial professionals and investors indicated that they were quite willing to invest in a (hypothetical) development bank (92 percent), while fewer—though still a majority (75 percent)—were willing to invest in a hypothetical loan fund.[478] Reputation and personal interaction with a development lender helped increase the comfort level of potential investors.[479]

As the 1980s ended, social screening was well established, including among institutional investors and their clients. Still, "individual investors and religious organizations are currently the largest investors in alternative investment vehicles…"[480] The disparity in volume between screened and "alternative" investments, and the need to increase support for the latter, was and would be a continuing concern within the social investment movement.

# CHAPTER 8. The CDCU Movement in the 1980s

I joined the National Federation of Community Development Credit Unions in October 1980, a month before Ronald Reagan won the presidency in a landslide.* The "Reagan Revolution" initiated a two-front battle for the federation. On the one hand, our member credit unions affiliated with anti-poverty agencies suffered from devastating cuts in their sponsors' budgets, as well as the shredding of the social safety nets their members depended on. As to the federation itself, we saw our own federally funded budget obliterated, putting our existence in question.

## The Birth and Brief Life of the CDCU Revolving Loan Fund

The National Federation's decade-long quest for community-controlled capital had ended in a muted victory—much reduced in scale and scope—with the passage of legislation establishing the $6 million Community Development Revolving Loan Fund for Credit Unions (CDRLF). The fund was launched in fall 1980, with the selection of 30 organizations to receive loans or deposits of $200,000 at 2 percent interest; one-third of these were startup institutions. The National Federation and the National Center for Urban Ethnic Affairs (NCUEA) were awarded contracts to provide technical assistance in business planning and community development strategies. The National Federation also secured a small training contract from the newly created National Consumer Cooperative Bank.

The federation hoped against hope that the credit union commitment to self-help in low-income communities would enable it to survive the Reagan administration's profoundly conservative policies, marked by contempt for anti-poverty efforts of all kinds. But after taking office in January 1981, the new administration set about liquidating the vestiges of the War on Poverty. The enemy was not *poverty*, but rather the "entitlement" programs to aid the poor, such as welfare (Aid to Families with Dependent Children, or AFDC)—and the infrastructure of organizations that existed to defend them. By the close of the fiscal year, September 30, 1981, the OEO's successor, the Community

---

\* After graduate studies as a Russian historian, I volunteered and later worked throughout the Seventies organizing food cooperatives and training Native American and migrant farmworker organizations. I learned of the National Federation in 1979, when I became the president of a small credit union in Washington, DC, for farmworker organizations.

Services Administration (CSA), was terminated; its remaining functions were transferred to the new Office of Community Services (OCS) of the Department of Health and Human Services (HHS). Harvey R. Vieth, a dentist from Colorado who had been active in the Republican campaign, came to Washington to head the office. Little was left in body, and nothing in spirit, from the OEO of the 1960s. In November 1981, the federation's elected president, Al Alayon, assessed the landscape.

> As we come together for the Federation's Sixth Annual Meeting, once again CDCUs are faced with a grim and uncertain future. The recently enacted budget cutbacks will have a devastating effect on the lives of the poor people throughout the country. This in turn will have a negative impact on the continued growth and development of community development credit unions. Job losses and reduction in services and benefits such as food stamps, social security and unemployment insurance, will greatly reduce the amount of income available to poor people to meet their obligations and will completely eliminate their ability to save.... Delinquencies will increase, savings will decrease, cash flow problems will arise, and the ability to pay dividends and meet obligations will be greatly diminished. Survival once again becomes the key word.[481]

*Adolfo (Al) Alayon and board of National Federation of CDCUs, c.1980.*

The $6 million CDRLF was not even a rounding error in the federal budget. It was a *revolving loan fund*, not even a "give-away" program for the poor. Nonetheless, it was targeted by Reagan's Office of Management and Budget (OMB), under David Stockman. The administration took a hard line: Not only was the CDCU revolving loan fund to be discontinued, but "one million dollars in funds allocated to the CDCU program but not obligated for 1981 was to be returned to the Treasury, along with funds obligated to specific CDCUs but not yet disbursed."[482] The federation engaged a lobbyist and was able to beat back these forays, ensuring that all that remained of the originally allocated "$6 million Fund"—as CDCUs called it, in brief—would go to credit unions; in addition, there was renewed authorization for the program under the Community Economic Development Act of 1981.[483]

But the battle with the administration did not end there. If the administration could not end the revolving loan fund outright, it could plant a "poison pill" that would make the fund unattractive to low-income credit unions. In a letter to federation Executive Director Jim Clark on August 20, 1982, the director of the Office of Community Services, Harvey Vieth, wrote:

> We discovered that a critical provision of the existing CDCU regulations contained a maximum interest rate of 2 percent on capitalization loan funds awarded under this program. I am concerned that such a rate, based on a five-year loan period, is restrictive and unreasonably low compared to the prevailing market rates. During a time when interest rates are unusually high, coupled with a substantial Federal budget deficit, a regulatory-fixed 2 percent maximum interest rate on loans under the CDCU is unjustified. We are currently exploring with the Department ways in which a more reasonable interest rate can be set for new capitalization loan agreements.

So, even a low-cost *loan* exceeded the administration's tolerance for aiding the poor.[484] Community development credit unions were to help bear the cost of reducing the federal deficit.

Even while playing defense, the federation pursued its long-held campaign to gain control of the federal funds appropriated for CDCUs. We managed to get New York's Republican Senator Alfonse D'Amato to recommend to the Department of Health and Human Services that the federation serve as an intermediary to manage the yet-undisbursed remainder of the CDRLF. Jim Clark wrote optimistically to David Ramage, head of the New World Foundation, "We are very close to getting control of the $6 million Federal capitalization fund for CDCUs. By September 30, 1982, or soon after, we believe that approximately $1.9 million of uncommitted funds will be turned over to us as an intermediary to administer under contract or cooperative agreement."[485]

Had the federation succeeded, it might have been a turning point in its history—a huge boost in its credibility and prospects for continuing its work. But Clark's optimism was misplaced. The proposal failed.

Meanwhile, the federation was fighting for its own survival. In 1981–82, Clark valiantly and fruitlessly attempted to persuade the Office of Community Services to continue to fund the federation's technical assistance program: After all, CDCUs represented the best tradition of self-help by the poor.

At best, he obtained a dollop of funds that enabled the federation to conduct an orderly close-out of its operations. But the clock was ticking. With $500,000 of its former federal funding gone, all the federation could count on was $5,000 a year in member dues. Reflecting our desperate need for cash, Clark asked our credit unions to sell raffle tickets to raise funds.

## Origins of the Capitalization Program for CDCUs

Even when—especially when—the federal government dashed the federation's hopes to establish a CDCU-controlled fund, the federation doggedly pursued its goal by other means. Over 1981–82, we explored with our membership the creation of a central private-sector fund to aggregate capital and "downstream" it to local CDCUs.

There were numerous, thorny design questions. If the federation succeeded in raising millions of dollars to invest in CDCUs, how—as a membership organization—could it insulate its investment decisions from internal political tensions and pressures? Could it, and should it, become a regulated, insured depository, a place where credit unions and others could place their funds—or should it simply become a broker or clearinghouse? Should it, could it become a vehicle for long-term investment—and/or a place where CDCUs and investors could place liquid funds at competitive rates? Should it allow investors to choose where the federation reinvested its money? What performance standards or evidence of financial stability should the capitalization fund demand from applicants? Would the broader credit union movement invest in a fund for CDCUs? Indeed, would the "mainstream" credit union movement, with which CDCUs at best enjoyed an uneasy relationship, tolerate a new institution for its poor cousins?

At the federation's annual meeting in November 1981 in New York City, a working group of its members developed this goal statement:

> The proposed capitalization fund will, on a revolving, self-sustaining base, provide capital to CDCUs at the lowest possible rates for stabilization with self-sufficiency, community economic development, and some market rate lending. All fund participants will be required to make a fair share investment in the fund.[486]

Following this guidance, on March 18–21, 1982, the federation's board met at the rustic, state-owned Asilomar conference center adjoining the ocean in Pacific Grove, CA.* The board finalized ambitious plans for the Capitalization Program for CDCUs: raising $20 million over three years in borrowed private-sector capital to channel as insured deposits in CDCUs, which would attempt to raise matching deposits locally. At the same time, the board had to make plans for closing shop, since federal support—except for close-out expenses—would end by September 30, 1982.

---

\* The location was so peaceful that one inner-city attendee complained he found it hard to sleep.

That summer, we sent proposals and requests for capital to nearly 200 corporations, foundations, church organizations, credit unions, and others. In particular, we appealed to the Credit Union National Association, Inc. (CUNA), the umbrella organization for credit unions in the United States, requesting $500,000 to fund Capitalization Program deposits and a contribution of $20,000 for operations. We also requested an operating grant of $40,000 from the associated CUNA Mutual Insurance Group.[487] Ultimately, CUNA agreed to only a minimal donation of a few thousand dollars.

Like many nonprofit organizations that depended on federal grants, the federation was altogether unacquainted with the foundation world. I recall learning about a "new" concept: Program-Related Investments (PRIs). We made many unsuccessful cold calls—unsolicited inquiries of foundations whose generic description and progressive orientation seemed to make them candidates. Fortunately, we found a foundation leader who was both responsive and knowledgeable: David Ramage Jr., formerly of the Center for Community Change and the board of South Shore Bank.[488] In a letter of August 31, 1982, federation Executive Director Jim Clark wrote to Ramage:

> Our private-sector capitalization program, which is the subject of our proposal to you, has aroused the interest of a number of foundation staff. However, there appears to be reluctance and much conservatism on the part of foundation boards to use funds as Program-Related Investments. We especially need your assistance to build understanding and interest in PRI's.

The New World Foundation agreed to host a luncheon on October 8, 1982, to introduce the federation to the foundation world. The dozen or so attendees included several smaller foundations but also the Ford Foundation. The PRI field was still not highly developed, and so the meeting did not yield any investment prospects, including from Ford.[489] But it did produce some small grants from the New World Foundation and the Norman Foundation, as well as placing the federation on Ford's radar, if distantly.

## First Investments: By Faith Alone

Hope came in the form of grants from the faith community. Protestant denominational offices provided modest, but precious, assistance: The Board of Global Ministries of the Methodist Church and the Coalition for Human Needs of the Episcopal Church provided grants that added up to some $20,000. The federation laid off all its full-time staff. The grants supported part-time work for Executive Director Jim Clark and minimal hours for me as deputy director. Unable to pay rent, the federation's skeleton operation moved from an old, high-rise office building in downtown Brooklyn with views of the Manhattan skyline to the fourth floor of my home (also in Brooklyn, so that we could maintain some appearance of continuity). Our operations consisted of an answering machine and the remnants of the federation's multi-user, MPM-based computer system. Thus began a migration that would take the federation to borrowed space in East Harlem, then to a series of low-rent offices in the financial district of Lower Manhattan.

With virtually no net worth, no funding prospects, and no track record as a borrower, in fall 1982 the federation submitted its ambitious plans for the Capitalization Program for CDCUs to the Adrian Dominicans. "On November 6," the federation announced to the world, "the Portfolio Advisory Board of the Order approved a three-year, $30,000 loan—the first of its kind in the NFCDCU Capitalization Program."[490] In the first half of 1983, a half-dozen other women's communities followed, including the Sisters of Mercy; the Sisters of St. Joseph, Nazareth, MI (February); the Sisters, Servants of the Immaculate Heart of Mary; the Sisters of Mary Reparatrix; and the Sisters of St. Francis. The amounts ranged from $5,000 to $30,000; the terms, three to five years; the rate, 6–8 percent.[491]

The federation was now a capital intermediary, one of the first in the country. Still, the faith-driven investments of the women's orders were still "other people's money." We now set about exploring another source, one totally aligned with the movement's basic principles: the pooled funds of low-income communities vested in CDCUs themselves. The membership had specified this approach by calling for credit unions to make a "fair share" investment in the proposed Capitalization Program—investments that would be recirculated within the movement. In effect, this would become a kind of "central bank" for CDCUs. In credit union terms, it would be

> a specialized corporate credit union, which concentrates on the financial and technical needs of CDCUs.... Our ultimate goals include helping CDCUs to expand their lending impact locally, and also moving NFCDCU toward self-financed operation. When Community Development Central develops an adequate capital base, it may begin doing loan participations with local credit unions, enabling them to take on larger development projects.[492]

There was one big problem: Credit unions were not permitted to place funds in an unregulated institution, such as the emerging Capitalization Program. Consequently, on August 4, 1982, the federation began discussions with the federal regulator, the National Credit Union Administration (NCUA), on the possibility of setting up a regulated institution—a "corporate central" credit union, which would serve as a kind of "bankers' bank" for CDCUs. This would be the highest expression of community-controlled wealth, a national institution for recycling capital within the CDCU movement itself.[493]

Meanwhile, another kind of central financial institution had been established. In August 1978, Congress created the National Consumer Cooperative Bank (NCCB) and the affiliated Office of Self-Help and Technical Assistance. The bank and office officially opened for business on March 21, 1980. Just as the Reagan administration attempted to terminate the Community Development Revolving Loan Fund for Credit Unions, it attempted to smother this institution in its infancy by canceling the bank's charter. The bank's supporters fought off this death threat and finally reached a compromise with Congress: On December 31, 1981, President Reagan signed a bill that officially privatized the NCCB as a cooperative financial institution owned by its customer-stockholders.[494]

The legislation that created the Co-op Bank excluded credit unions from borrowing, thus denying another capital channel to CDCUs. "We lost the opportunity to borrow from the Bank and [its] Self-Help Development Fund because we were ill prepared and not sufficiently organized," wrote Jim Clark to the federation's board in 1980. "We hope to work in the immediate future to change the legislation that excludes CDCUs from borrowing from the Bank."[495] That effort never materialized.

## Regime Change

By spring 1983, the National Federation was scraping by with Jim Clark as executive director, paid for a few days a week, and me working as his (mostly unpaid) deputy. We had made our first, modestly successful efforts at reinvention, raising small grants and the first Capitalization Program investments. But the federation was far from sustainable.

The old era ended in April 1983, when I got some life-changing news: I was selected for a year-long Charles Revson Foundation Fellowship for the Future of New York City at Columbia University. I hoped to assist Clark in keeping the federation alive without drawing a salary. But Clark, with a large family to support, decided he could no longer continue the arduous struggle to keep the federation alive on a part-time salary. One afternoon, we met in the Bedford-Stuyvesant offices of the federation's elected president, Al Alayon. He remarked that the federation had "had a good run" and that the CDCU movement could hold its heads high even as the federation left the stage. I offered to keep the organization going as a volunteer, on one condition: that I be given the title of executive director for the first time in my career. With nothing to lose, Alayon agreed. Thus, I inherited leadership of an organization with a net worth of $27.17 as of March 31, 1983—actually an improvement from the deficit of $2,164.55 on December 31, 1982.[496]

My Revson fellowship literally meant the difference between life and death for the federation. It was not only the stipend that enabled me to sustain the organization: In summer 1983, I took a week-long seminar in the management of financial institutions, where I learned the basics of banking, particularly asset and liability management. This grounding, with subsequent coursework in areas such as housing finance, gave me the tools and self-confidence to pitch the grand vision of the National Federation—establishing a "central bank" for the CDCU movement.

Returning from class in fall 1983, I picked up a message from the federation's answering machine in my study: "You may not remember me, but I'm Annie Vamper. I've been working for the regulator, the National Credit Union Administration, but I can't do that anymore. They really don't care about these small credit unions. If you know of something in the credit union movement, let me know." One of the first African American women to head a credit union in the Southeast, Vamper had served two tours of duty with NCUA, focusing on small and community development credit unions. I called her back that evening and offered her the grand title of associate director at the modest, part-time salary the federation could afford. She accepted.

For months, Vamper commuted two hours each day to work in my home office while I was at class. In 1984, our member credit union, Union Settlement Federal Credit Union in East Harlem, offered us rent-free space, an 8- by 10-foot office on the second floor of the social service agency, directly above the credit union. As additional grant funds trickled in, we moved into a "real," if somewhat shabby, office in Lower Manhattan, within sight of the fortress-like Federal Reserve Bank of New York.

From fall 1983 until Vamper's illness and premature death in 1990, the federation's senior management—really, its entire management—consisted of Vamper and me: she, the African American woman from the Deep South, and I, a white, Ivy League–educated northeasterner. Members sometimes called us "the odd couple." I was the CEO, the public face of the federation; Annie was the deputy, the chief fiscal officer, the staff of the Capitalization Program, and the technical assistance provider who helped organize new credit unions and advised existing ones on their regulatory and bookkeeping issues.

## Survival Strategies

One obvious lesson stood out from the federation's near-death experience: Never build an organization on a single revenue source—in our case, the federal government, although the principle could easily be applied to other donors or clients. Building capital intermediaries—the Capitalization Program and the proposed Community Development Central Credit Union—remained key to the federation's vision. But our need for operating support led us to launch several small programs that could be aligned with the specific interests of funders. What made it possible was this: The CDCU concept (and reality) was of a multifaceted institution—an anti-poverty vehicle; a vehicle for community organizing and community empowerment; a stable, regulated financial institution that could provide a range of credit and banking products for individuals and small local businesses; a trusted counselor providing financial advice for its members; a local employer; and an adult education institution—a "school" for community members to learn about their own finances and the financial system in general. Thus, in the 1980s, the federation won contracts for affordable housing finance; for promoting small business lending, and for our Community Credit Union Job Training Program, funded by the federal Job Training Partnership Act (JTPA)[497]; later, the federation was an early and active player in the growing financial education movement.

We also had a crucial strategic asset: our New York City location. In the 1980s, New York had liberal state and city administrations with a commitment to address problems like housing and unemployment. It had the nation's highest concentration of foundations. (The Ford Foundation was a 10-minute cab ride up the FDR highway adjoining the East River.) Crucially, New York was also the headquarters for the nation's largest banks—which, not coincidentally, were visibly shedding branches in low-income neighborhoods and upscaling their services. For the first time, the growing deficit in banking services for the poor became a public-policy concern.

Thus, New York was where the money was, and where the action in banking was. We tried to use New York City as a laboratory and as the financial infrastructure on which to rebuild our national organization. Member credit unions around the country sometimes grumbled about our New York focus. But the reality was, our New York programs provided the operating funds for us to" keep the lights on" while we pursued our national goals. By 1984, we succeeded in getting significant support from two prominent local foundations, the New York Foundation and the New York Community Trust. Our upward trajectory began.

The glaringly public "debanking" of New York City's low-income neighborhoods provided an opportunity for the federation to reach a broad, influential audience. An article in the *New York Times* on December 5, 1983, described the situation: "Deregulation Alters Banking: Many Losers and Winners." It noted that "the poorest people are faring the worst. Other losers included small businesses, low-balance depositors, old line industries, home buyers, while the winners included high-balance depositors, money funds, and convenience seekers."[498]

Midway through my fellowship year, newly armed with the vocabulary of banking and finance, I walked the few blocks from our office in Lower Manhattan to the Federal Reserve Bank of New York, where I delivered an address to 200 regulators, bankers, and community activists at a conference, "Financial Services in the 1980s," sponsored by the Regional Interagency Committee. In my remarks, entitled "The New Era in Financial Services: Implications for Low- and Moderate-Income Neighborhoods," I argued that CDCUs could be an important part of the solution for neighborhoods abandoned by the banks.

> I would suggest that the forces and the factors which produced these 'losers' in the initial phase of deregulation are likely to intensify—that more people may lose out, and they may lose more badly. We don't believe the clock will be turned back, that there will be a major 're-regulation' of banking.... Federal policies, if they continue in the present direction, will further accentuate the differences between the rich and the relatively poor markets.... Distributing food stamps, cashing welfare or SSI checks—you can bet that these won't be growing businesses for most banks.[499]

Moreover, technological change might make matters worse: "If computerized credit scoring spreads, we think it will work to the disadvantage of most low-income, and many moderate-income, people."

I positioned CDCUs as the best successor in the neighborhoods that banks were abandoning physically or by upscaling their services. "Community development credit unions can and do address many of the needs which have become relatively unprofitable for banks in certain areas." Given the limited capacity of individual CDCUs, for the first time, I laid out the federation's vision:

> a central 'back office' operation, or technical support center, which will provide a shared capability for data processing, marketing, loan evaluation and processing, management assistance, and other operational necessities for credit unions.... We plan to link, or 'horizontally integrate,' credit unions with other community service and development agencies.

> [Finally], we are in the process of seeking a charter for a new national financial institution, a central credit union for community development credit unions—similar to a 'banker's bank'—which will be able to channel financial and technical support into local credit unions.[500]

The agenda I sketched would, in fact, inform the federation's work for the next decades.

## Taking It to the Street: Organizing the Lower East Side People's FCU

The logic was apparent: Instead of banks, with their lofty overhead and disinclination to serve the poor, why not give the task to institutions whose DNA fitted them for the job? CDCUs were nonprofit, community-controlled cooperatives, willing captives of their neighborhood, geared to small depositors and borrowers. All they needed was adequate support and subsidy—hopefully, from the banking industry and the public sector. But in fact, there was only a handful of longstanding CDCUs in New York City, notably Union Settlement FCU in East Harlem, which had provided the federation a temporary home when we could not afford to pay rent. New credit unions would have to be developed to serve unbanked neighborhoods. The concept was all very well, but was it practical? There had to be some proof of concept.

The journey from concept to reality began in the first days of May 1984, as I was finishing my fellowship year. I found myself on a street corner in Manhattan, dialing the federation's answering machine from a pay phone. There was a message from a housing organization on Manhattan's Lower East Side: "Manufacturers Hanover Trust [MHT] is going to close its branch on Avenue B and East Third Street, over our protests. They say they can't find another bank that's willing to take over the branch. Someone suggested maybe we should consider a credit union. We don't really know what that is. Can we talk to you?"

*Loisaida*," or Alphabet City—the area including avenues A, B, C, and D—was a "port of entry" for generations of immigrants. Deteriorated housing, homelessness, open-air drug "supermarkets"—the neighborhood faced all of those. But it had a strong infrastructure of experienced, sophisticated community organizations, and they were beginning to make progress in their fight against the drug trade. A bank closure would be a body blow to their efforts, the visible symbol of a neighborhood being written off. Protesting the decision of MHT, or "Manny Hanny," as it was familiarly known, they took to the streets at the bank's Midtown Manhattan headquarters to protest.

After learning more about credit unions, the representatives of the neighborhood's Joint Planning Council (JPC) became convinced that a credit union owned by and responsive to the community was worth a try. That summer, they won a commitment from MHT to fund a feasibility study for a "community financial center" anchored by a credit union, with a conditional promise of additional financial support. The federation began working under contract to the JPC to survey community support. By spring 1985, the JPC had collected $900,000 in nonbinding pledges of deposits—not equity investments, which a new bank would have required. Despite the demonstration of community support and a favorable feasibility study by the federation, MHT rejected JPC's request for seed funding of a credit union. Negotiations broke down.

## Chapter 8. The CDCU Movement in the 1980s

*Demonstration at site of bank branch closing Avenue B and East 3rd Street, c. 1983. Courtesy of Lower East Side People's FCU.*

### Showdown at the Federal Reserve Bank

"Convinced that MHT had violated its commitment to the Lower Est Side, the JPC decided to use its last available weapon: a challenge under the Community Reinvestment Act."[501] The bank wanted to open a new facility in prosperous Midtown Manhattan. The community argued that the Federal Reserve should deny MHT's application: Its departure from 37 Avenue B would leave a 100-square-block neighborhood without a bank. MHT's own figures demonstrated only $25,000 in loans outstanding from a $10 million branch deposit base. This suggested that it had not, in fact, served the needs of low-income communities. The Federal Reserve agreed to consider the challenge.

On the eve of Columbus Day weekend—Thursday, October 10, 1985—the two sides met at the Federal Reserve Bank of New York. MHT grudgingly put forth a new offer of financial assistance. The JPC angrily rejected it, and the meeting ended with no plans for further negotiations. The next step would be a public hearing, after which the Federal Reserve would either sustain or reject the community's challenge.

The two sides cooled off over the Columbus Day holiday. On Monday, MHT offered to reopen negotiations. On Tuesday, the sides assembled for a session that was brief and to the point. MHT presented a revised, more generous proposal; JPC offered a counter-proposal. The differences were resolved, and a draft agreement was adopted. MHT would provide $100,000 in interest-free seed deposits for the proposed credit union; spend up to $150,000 to repair the aging, deteriorated branch; and allow the credit union to use it rent-free for three years, after which it would have a bargain-price purchase option of $90,000 for the building, which included six apartments above the bank branch.

The last, significant hurdle was to actually obtain a federal credit union charter. In December, the JPC submitted its application; on January 16, 1986, NCUA approved the charter.[502]

On May 1, 1986, the Lower East Side People's Federal Credit Union held an open-air celebration to mark its grand opening. Manhattan Borough President David Dinkins, later New York City's first African American mayor, cut the ribbon. Rev. John Kennington, one of the organizers who worked in a drug and alcohol rehabilitation program, presided. "This is a potential financial power base for the people living on the Lower East Side," he said.[503] "We're a very besieged community. Our defeats far outnumber our victories. But this [credit union] charter is one of our biggest triumphs.... It holds much promise for picking up this community."[504] Amid the debris and noise of renovation, with boards on the doors and a roof that still leaked, the Lower East Side People's FCU was open for business.[505]

*Celebration at Lower East Side People's Federal Credit Union. Courtesy of the credit union.*

It is impossible to overstate the importance of the Lower East Side People's FCU in the history of the CDCU movement. It was the first fruit of the Community Reinvestment Act (CRA)—not as a means to convince a bank to make more and fairer mortgages, as important as that was, but to provide seed capital for a startup, nonprofit financial institution. CDCUs were now on the policy (and philanthropic) radar, at least in New York. The Lower East Side People's FCU was a visible demonstration that a credit union could provide financial services and loans where a bank would not. The new credit union had *street presence*—it looked like a bank, even if a bit of a ramshackle one, with its venerable wooden teller stations and its vaults and safety deposit boxes. In New York City, Lower East Side People's FCU became a stronghold of the CDCU movement, taking in through mergers with other low-income credit unions areas such as Central and East Harlem, which otherwise would have lost their institutions. Over the years, as the credit union grew, banks provided grants to help it expand its products and services—for example, adding an ATM.

By 2017, the credit union—the winner of multiple CDFI awards—had more than $50 million in assets; a loan portfolio of some $40 million; a membership of 8,000; operations in the New York City boroughs of the Bronx, Queens, Manhattan, and Staten Island; a mobile service center; an active VITA tax preparation site; and much more. In 2011, activists in the Occupy Wall Street movement in New York City deposited the funds their supporters had collected in the Lower East Side People's FCU.*

## The Quest for Capital: Seeds of a CDFI Fund

As much as the federation put on a brave front arguing for CDCUs as successors to banks that would actually make loans to low-income people, we recognized that serving this population without subsidy effectively transferred a heavy financial burden to a small nonprofit with no economies of scale. If the banks were to be allowed to shed these unprofitable customers, then they should provide support to CDCUs; if the public sector was concerned about the costs of an unbanked sector, it, too, should bear responsibility for helping these credit unions survive.

In 1984, thanks to support from the New York Community Trust, the federation launched a state advocacy campaign to secure the investments and subsidy CDCUs would need to make an impact. That year, New York State–chartered banks won expanded real estate investment and other powers, conditional on making "qualifying community investments" in low- and moderate-income neighborhoods. The federation seized on this opportunity. In 1985, we developed model legislation for a "New York Corporation for Community Banking" (Assembly A-8145). This entity would provide a centralized mechanism for banks to meet their CRA obligations by funding deposits in "community-oriented financial institutions, in low- and moderate-income communities"—primarily, credit unions.

---

\* In 2017, the credit union went to federal court to challenge the appointment of an avowed opponent of the Consumer Financial Protection Bureau, OMB Director Mick Mulvaney, to serve as acting head of the bureau.

The proposal, halfway through Reagan's two terms, reflected well-founded pessimism about any federal action. I wrote that "the [Corporation for Community Banking] is an important precedent in an era when initiative has shifted from the Federal government to the individual states. If this project succeeds, the CCB Act could well become a piece of model legislation to be duplicated in other states."[506] The bill had 26 sponsors but ultimately did not advance from the Democratic-controlled state Assembly to the state Senate. But we continued our state advocacy, reviving and expanding the concept in the mid-1990s after passage of the federal CDFI Fund legislation.

## "Community Development Central"

Thus, by the mid-1980s, the federation was pursuing capital aggregation on multiple tracks. The proposed New York State Corporation for Community Banking was the statewide forerunner of a national CDFI Fund initiative. We were continuing our efforts to revive the Community Development Revolving Loan Fund for Credit Unions, frozen by the Reagan administration.[507] We were managing our own Capitalization Program for CDCUs.

Finally, there was the federation's campaign for "Community Development (CD) Central," the "bankers' bank" for low-income credit unions. By early 1985, more than 40 CDCUs had pledged 1 percent of their assets to capitalize CD Central, amounting to some $7 million, later growing to almost $10 million. We engaged a consultant with experience in the mainstream corporate credit union world. The challenge was to obtain a federal charter and, with it, deposit insurance. The broader credit union movement was not supportive; its response, whether explicit or implicit, was that "there are enough existing corporate centrals out there" that CDCUs were eligible to join.[508] The NCUA had no appetite for the federation's proposed innovation, and it rejected CD Central's charter application. Deterred but unwilling to concede defeat, we continued to pursue this objective until the end of the decade.

## The Capitalization Program: The Federation's First Million

Meanwhile, our Capitalization Program made steady, if undramatic, progress in 1984 and 1985. We expanded and diversified our sources beyond the religious investors that had provided the crucial first dollars. We obtained our first significant corporate investment from the RCA Corporation.[509] After 18 months of negotiation, we obtained an investment from the Cooperative Assistance Fund (CAF), the PRI intermediary that had been created by the Taconic Foundation and others. The Consumer Cooperative Development Corporation of the National Cooperative Bank committed to match CAF's deposits.[510]

The breakthrough came in 1986, bringing the prospect that the federation's Capitalization Program would become a significant player in social investment. Several Catholic women's orders and the

McAuley Institute rolled over their original investments; new investments came from the United Methodist Church Community Economic Development Program, the Seton Enablement Fund, the Gerbode Foundation, and the National Council of the Churches of Christ. It was the John D. and Catherine T. MacArthur Foundation's investment that marked the turning point for the federation.

In the middle of 1986, I received a call from someone in Chicago—"Paul Lingenfelter," although I'm sure I mangled his name at the time. He was very friendly, very low-key. Sitting in my two-person office in Lower Manhattan, I was rather casual in my response; we often received phone calls like this, and usually they never led anywhere. He mentioned that his foundation was contemplating an expansion of its Program-Related Investments. He asked me about the federation's work, how we fit into the community economic development scene.

To my surprise, Paul followed up some weeks later and invited me to write a proposal. I spent my few weeks of vacation that August drafting a proposal in WordStar, using my industrial-strength, 20-pound Kaypro microcomputer that was the height of "portability" at the time. I sent in the proposal by September. We then entered the world of lawyers with MacArthur, which proved remarkably quick and painless. By November, we had a draft agreement. On December 6, 1986, the board of directors of the federation resolved to borrow $500,000 for five years at 3.5 percent interest from the John D. and Catherine T. MacArthur Foundation of Chicago.

We started 1986 with Capitalization Program assets of $100,224. We closed the year with $970,078 in total assets, although our net worth remained minute in comparison.[511] Apart from the financial impact, we believed that the MacArthur investment had brought us to another level of national credibility. As I reported to our membership, "The investment put NFCDCU in select company: Other MacArthur investment recipients included the South Shore Bank, the Enterprise Foundation, and the Local Initiatives Support Corporation, all nationally prominent actors in the community development arena."[512]

MacArthur's quick, relatively painless process left me with a mistaken notion of what it took to raise major investments from the foundation world, as our later experience with the Ford Foundation would show.

## First Trip to the White House

There was more good news on the policy front.

At the federation's annual meeting in Washington in April 1986, we met Morgan Doughton, a senior policy analyst at the White House Office of Policy Development, which was charged with reviewing public assistance systems and formulating welfare reform strategies.[513] The Reagan administration was not contemplating any sort of War on Poverty or expansion of federal programs. Rather, Doughton—a gracious, somewhat elderly man—showed great interest in CDCUs as self-help vehicles for low-income communities. In June 1986, the White House Office of Policy Development asked the federation to provide information about the role of credit unions in serving these populations, particularly their role in promoting savings to generate economic activity.

The federation launched a major study, drawing on the official financial statistical data of all federally insured, low-income-designated credit unions from 1980 to 1984—more than 300 institutions.[514] We added a questionnaire that we developed in consultation with a sympathetic staff member of the Department of Health and Human Services, as well as the White House Office of Policy Development; we also included case studies of individual CDCUs. The rest of the credit union industry—that is, the national credit union trade organizations, CUNA and the National Association of Federal Credit Unions (NAFCU)— were not pleased with our initiative, but they did not wish to be left on the sidelines of a project that had engaged the White House; reluctantly, they provided several thousand dollars in financial support for our work. We finished the report, entitled "An Analysis of the Role of Credit Unions in Capital Formation and Investment in Low- and Moderate-Income Communities," and submitted it to the White House on December 17, 1986.[515]

The federation's annual report for 1986 declared that we had "demonstrated decisively that CDCUs—which are often stereotyped with the failures of the 1960s—in fact represent a dynamic, growing movement." Our findings showed a modest increase in the number of these credit unions (10 percent over 1980–84), while their membership had climbed to 245,907. The survivors of the War on Poverty that were associated with federal anti-poverty agencies represented about one-third of the total; faith-based credit unions, especially those based in Baptist and Catholic congregations, were common. CDCUs were still tiny—median assets had grown considerably, but the median size in 1984 was only $191,082; in aggregate, assets totaled some $318 million. The report noted that "million-dollar CDCUs more than doubled in four years, during a period when public resources for low-income communities were declining."[516] Member shares (deposits) grew at a compound annual rate of 24.9 percent, while loan growth grew comparably. Remarkably, annual loan charge-off rates were 1 percent or less.[517]

Our report to the White House offered a list of recommendations, including a call for the creation of Community Development Central—a "National Community Development Federal Credit Union." It also called for a national CDCU Service Corporation, "to provide both financial and technical assistance to new and fledgling CDCUs to enable them to achieve self-sufficiency more quickly"; the model cited was the Neighborhood Reinvestment Corporation, which "franchises" local affiliates through its network. We recommended transferring the Community Development Revolving Loan Fund for Credit Unions away from its unwelcome home in the Department of Health and Human Services to a proposed new entity, along with startup capital of $7 million. An earlier draft had called this new entity a kind of national "Neighborhood Financial Corporation"[518]—the core concept that we would develop into a proposal for a CDFI Fund. Other recommendations included facilitating the formation of new credit unions; removing regulatory restrictions on business lending by credit unions; allowing access to the Minority Bank Depository program; and "piloting programs aimed at promoting savings among [public assistance] recipients."[519]

On April 24, 1987, the federation brought its annual meeting to the Old Executive Office Building adjoining the White House. (Not without irony, the session was held at the Indian Treaty Room.) Morgan Doughton praised the federation's study and "indicated strong White House interest in disseminating the report to state agencies and community groups involved in welfare-reform demonstration projects."[520] Demonstration projects, he emphasized, were "not a cop-out" or substitute for other legislation; they were a way to "give the people the opportunity … to be the driving engine behind the process in their neighborhoods, by which people make progress out of poverty. And to the extent we do that effectively, they're going to need financial vehicles that can be applied in these neighborhoods."[521]

The credit union trade organizations, CUNA and NAFCU, were not happy with our finished product. CUNA, which had provided several thousand dollars, asked to remove its name from the report as a funder. It opposed the establishment of Community Development Central: "We think it duplicates the services of U.S. Central," said a CUNA spokesperson.[522] NAFCU opposed any new regulatory framework to recognize the special role of CDCUs, and it refused to support the report's recommendations.

The Reagan administration sent to Congress the Low-Income Opportunity Act of 1987, which provided for state-run demonstration projects in low-income areas, while encouraging self-help. But it did not translate into a program to support the development of CDCUs in poverty communities. Meanwhile, the National Credit Union Administration (NCUA) issued regulations that would make it *more* difficult to start CDCUs and promote economic development in low-income communities, issuing restrictions on credit union business lending; stiffer requirements on chartering new credit unions; a new rating system for credit unions (CAMEL, modeled closely on bank examination procedures); and stiffer reserve requirements. On the positive side, the Community Development Revolving Loan Fund for Credit Unions was transferred over to NCUA, and preparations were made to resume lending at a rate approaching the original 2 percent; however, funds were not disbursed.

## First Draft: Creating a National Neighborhood Banking Corporation

Although our "Report to the White House" did not yield helpful initiatives from the Reagan administration, we continued to pursue and refine our call for federal investment. On March 8, 1988, the federation issued a concept paper directed to "community banking advocates" calling for the creation of a "Neighborhood Banking Corporation." Over the next few years, we would use the paper to rally the allies that formed the CDFI Coalition.

With that concept paper, the federation enlarged its view beyond CDCUs. In brief, we argued for the creation, "with the financial contributions of banks, [of] a new national corporation which will support non-profit, community-based financial institutions serving low-income people."[523] This network would include not only CDCUs, but also "community development loan funds and other non-profit financial entities."[524] We linked our position to the push by banks to acquire expanded powers:

"NFCDCU believes *bank support for CDCUs and other community financial institutions should be greatly and systematically expanded, as a condition for any expansion of bank powers*" [emphasis in original].[525]

Ours was a "small-government" proposal, relying heavily on the private sector—namely, banks. Although the Neighborhood Banking Corporation would be established by an act of Congress, it would be seeded with a minimal federal contribution: $2–$5 million for startup expenses, with the possibility of phasing in $6 million from the Community Development Revolving Loan Fund for Credit Unions. At least $25 million in permanent capital would be raised from bank donations, along with at least $250 million in working capital in the form of low-cost loans or investments. The national Neighborhood Banking Corporation would reinvest these funds at a spread, which would enable it to cover its administrative expenses.[526] The new entity "would function in a manner generally parallel to the Neighborhood Reinvestment Corporation"; we envisioned a *network* of institutions located in and serving "unbankable" or underserved populations. The Neighborhood Banking Corporation would invest in existing institutions and help start new ones; it would provide equity contributions, operating grants, loans and deposits, and access to secondary markets. It would be a public corporation, with a board composed of various financial regulators, or alternatively, a mixed corporation that also included representatives of banks and low-income consumers. It would deliver technical assistance through existing organizations, such as the National Federation of CDCUs, the National Association of Community Development Loan Funds, and the Woodstock Institute.

With this proposal, we had clearly begun to reach out to colleagues in the nascent CDFI field. But we retained our emphasis on *neighborhood-based* financial institutions that would fill banking gaps for low-income people; we were not calling for sectoral or regional CDFIs. In our eagerness to craft a solution that would have some chance with a miserly, disinterested White House and Congress, our "big vision" asked for a *de minimis* federal investment—not even a rounding error in the budget, and not even a continuing appropriations stream. The proposal would not be achievable without a *quid pro quo* from banks that were thirsting for additional powers. (When the CDFI fund was established half a dozen years later, there would be no *quid pro quo* to engage banks: Rather, they received the "carrot" of the Bank Enterprise Award Program and CRA credit for investing in CDFIs.)

We circulated the proposal among our member credit unions, loan funds, and advocates but received little feedback. The exception was a response from a CRA advocate, concerned that the Neighborhood Banking Corporation might "let banks off the hook" of their community lending responsibilities. It was 1990 before the federation's concept began to gain traction.

## The Federation and Ford

Even though the federation's Report to the White House had not altered federal policy, it did much to raise the federation's national profile, especially among funders, and particularly the Ford Foundation. We had first met Ford staff five years earlier, at the introduction to the funding world arranged for us by the New World Foundation. Thereafter, I had numerous private meetings and luncheons with

Ford—pleasant, educational, and unproductive. I struggled to make the case with Tom Miller, the head of PRI, and other staff. Our "community development" credit unions seemed to have little to do with community development as Ford understood it. Ford, of course, had a long history with place-based community development, including physical revitalization, especially as practiced by CDCs. CDCUs, though they supported local minority business development and did some housing finance, primarily focused on *people*, the residents of poor communities. The federation's argument was that CDCUs performed a vital community development function by retaining and recycling capital in these communities, helping low-income individuals to save money and preserve their disposable income by providing reasonably priced credit. These, we argued, were indispensable elements of a robust community development strategy.

In 1987, Ford began to warm to the federation's approach, prompted in part by our report to the White House. First, it commissioned a study of CDCUs, which the federation's former and future staff member Errol T. Louis conducted. In a memo to Ellen Arrick of the PRI department dated November 1, 1987, I outlined a series of objectives that included establishing a "national support corporation" to provide back-office underwriting, loan packaging, and other servicing for CDCUs; a specialized secondary market for CDCU housing and small-business loans; continuing work to charter Community Development Central; an expanded Capitalization Program, to move beyond liquidity deposits to include risk-sharing investments; and a national CDCU Management Institute.[527] On November 2, Louis and I met with Ford's PRI, urban poverty, and rural poverty staff. I described the meeting in a memo to the federation's board the following day.

> If I described the meeting as other than 'frustrating,' I would be misleading you. I think there is a definite appreciation on the part of some of the above-mentioned personnel that CDCUs are doing some good things…. [But] I heard some of the most discouraging words of all about one or two discussion points: 'that sounds interesting, maybe we should study it in more depth.'
>
> The basic problem, I think, is that—in Ford's words—it doesn't know how to 'get a handle' on our movement, where we fit—whether they should accept us the way they are, or should try to 'steer' us toward development, whether we serve the people they are interested in—the 'poor,' etc.[528]

Although an overarching strategy did not emerge from these discussions, in spring 1988 Ford funded the federation's national Community Development Credit Union Demonstration Project, an attempt to build or strengthen CDCU networks in rural North Carolina, Philadelphia, Chicago, and New York City. As stated in the federation's final report to Ford on the project (January 23, 1989):

> The purpose of the grant was to determine ways in which low-income or *community development credit unions (CDCUs)* could develop their potential as *banking institutions* [emphasis in original], to compensate for the withdrawal of mainstream banks

from the low-income market; and as agents for *financing community development* [emphasis in original], in an era of shrinking public resources.

Thus began Ford's major, long-term support of the National Federation of CDCUs, both grants and investments. By the middle of 1989, Ford committed a $225,000 grant and $1 million in investments for the expansion of the federation's work with the four CDCU networks.

The difficulties the federation faced in making the case for CDCUs as vehicles for community development arose repeatedly as we engaged with policymakers and social investors. The patchy connections between the development of the individual and of the community became somewhat more explicit later, when Individual Development Accounts (IDAs) emerged as a key tool, thanks in large part to the Corporation for Enterprise Development (later CFED; from 2017, Prosperity Now). But for much of its history, we in the CDCU movement felt that the CDFI Fund—which we had helped to create—never really "got it" about credit unions, as evidenced by its disproportionately low funding of our sector.

## No Help from Washington

In 1987, the National Credit Union Administration (NCUA) began to restart the Community Development Revolving Loan Fund for Credit Unions, which it had inherited from the Department of Health and Human Services partly through the federation's efforts. It even began accepting applications. By January 1988, there was yet another reversal. A letter to the federation from NCUA stated: "We regret to inform you that, in compliance with the bipartisan Budget Summit Agreement between the Administration and Congress, the National Credit Union Administration cannot disburse any funds from the Community Development Credit Union Revolving Loan Fund in fiscal years 1988 and 1989."[529]

Thus, this relatively tiny program to supply capital to low-income communities—by now, simply a matter of disbursing previously appropriated funds, with no new outlays—had once again became the victim of "budget-balancing" austerity.

## Scandal in Omaha: Sex, Drugs, Money... Politics

Distant in geography but not in its connections to Washington, a tawdry, unprecedented scandal unfolded in fall 1988. Lawrence King Jr. was the longtime CEO of the Franklin Community FCU in Omaha. A Democrat until the Reagan presidency, he transferred allegiance and became vice-chair of the National Black Republican Council. As described in an investigative journalism piece in New York's *Village Voice*, King was "one of the most influential blacks in the Republican Party.... The 44-year-old King walked the glitzy corridors of power and established himself as a rising star. He threw lavish parties, [and] produced a stirring political video urging blacks to support George Bush."[530] Republican strategists viewed King as an important channel to increasing the party's support in the African American community: "By giving blacks direct access to capital, GOP strategists reason, the party has a chance at winning their votes."[531]

The election of November 8, 1988, continued Republican dominance in Washington, as George H.W. Bush overwhelmingly defeated Governor Michael Dukakis of Massachusetts. Despite his prominence in the party, King was in no position to enjoy it. On Friday, November 4, the FBI, IRS, United States Treasury Department, and Omaha police raided and shut down King's Omaha credit union. By Thursday, November 10, they had determined that at least $30 million allegedly on Franklin's books were missing. On November 14, the authorities sued, claiming King had diverted $34 million for his personal use.

The country had witnessed scandals at hundreds of S&Ls, many that would have dwarfed the Franklin credit union case. But there were political and personal details that put the Omaha scandal in a different league: King's mansion with 26 acres, his multiple diamond rings, his $65,000 watch, his private jet allegedly purchased on his $16,000 credit union salary. There was more: stories of cocaine-heavy parties for Omaha's secretive gay community.[532] His national political entertaining was done in the $5,000-a-month townhouse he rented near Embassy Row in Washington. He marketed his idea for "Franklin USA," an entity to obtain HUD funding to set up credit unions in black communities across the country, and pitched the idea to HUD Secretary Samuel Pierce, the only black member of Reagan's cabinet. During the Republican convention in New Orleans in 1988, King held a party at the Mardi Gras warehouse that was attended by 1,000 people, including former President Gerald Ford; four years earlier, at the 1984 Republican convention, King had sung the national anthem.

King had established an affiliate for the credit union, the Consumer Service Organization, where low-income residents could send their assistance checks and be referred to accounts at the credit union. King and his organization were highly respected in the black community and Omaha generally.[533] He had expanded his operation in the 1980s, aggressively soliciting "nonmember deposits"—the power that only low-income credit unions enjoyed—at rates 2 percent higher than market. "As the cash rolled in, King spent it on young men," according to investigative reporters; King entertained them in various hotels as well as in a private office adjoining the credit union, where he had installed a brass bed.[534]

By September 1988, however, an unnamed whistle-blower had communicated information that King was converting credit union deposits to his personal use. The federal authorities soon discovered that there were two sets of books: The credit union had about $2.5 million in actual assets, while a second set of books showed that Franklin had raised up to $38 million in phony certificates of deposits. The personal details got grosser still, with charges that King was involved in the sexual abuse of children, including transporting teenagers from foster care to parties for the sexual edification of his guests.[535]

King was charged with 40 counts of embezzlement and fraud.[536] On February 12, 1991, Lawrence King Jr. pleaded guilty to embezzlement and misapplication of credit union funds.[537] On June 18, 1991, he was sentenced to prison for 15 years.

## The CDCU Movement Suffers

Where did the money allegedly for "credit union deposits" come from? To be sure, some came from King's extensive circle of business and political acquaintances in Omaha. But what was most damaging was that substantial amounts came from religious and other philanthropic investors—the kinds of sources that had been crucial in building the National Federation's Capitalization Program. For example, among Franklin's victimized depositors in Franklin's Ponzi scheme was the Sisters of the Presentation of the Blessed Virgin Mary in Aberdeen, SD, which had placed $2 million with Franklin.[538]

King and Franklin Community Credit Union had left the National Federation of CDCUs in the late 1970s, rejoining only in August 1988, shortly before the bubble burst.[539] For the federation, the optics were terrible: Here was a CDCU ostensibly in the same business as the National Federation, raising "nonmember deposits" nationally—and what's more, on a larger scale than the federation had reached. Eventually a copy of a Franklin solicitation for deposits found its way to me—with my forged signature. We were forced to carry out damage control, assuring social investors of our own transparency, stressing our role and reputation as a trusted intermediary, and offering to provide information and assistance.

Apart from potential reputation damage, the CDCU movement suffered regulatory attack. NCUA was governed by a three-member board, under Chairman Roger Jepsen, a Republican former senator. NCUA took an unprecedented action: In December, it issued an "emergency" regulation that limited the ability of low-income credit unions to acquire nonmember deposits totaling more than 20 percent of their deposits.[540] Wounded and furious, we contacted a civil rights advocacy organization in Washington to explore a suit against NCUA, arguing that its regulation would harm low-income, predominantly minority financial institutions, shutting off their access to badly needed capital. Ultimately, their lawyers advised us that we stood little chance of winning: Absent a clear finding of "arbitrary and capricious" action by a federal agency, the courts were inclined to defer to the agency's judgment.

Meanwhile, CDCUs suffered from NCUA's efforts to ensure that it would not be embarrassed again. Over the next year, NCUA purged its official listing of low-income credit unions, reducing the number from 325 to 195[541]; it denied low-income designation to credit unions that apparently qualified for it. We heard from our African American members that they encountered thinly veiled suspicion from their examiners, anxious that there not be another Lawrence King on their watch. They suspected any CDCU that had an affiliated nonprofit, as Franklin had.

Despite our fears, the National Federation's Capitalization Program continued to grow. Religious organizations continued to be stalwarts, and on an increasing scale: The federation obtained a $500,000 loan from the Presbyterian Church (U.S.A.) Foundation and a $300,000 loan from the Dominican

Sisters of Springfield, IL. Most encouraging was a breakthrough with money-center banks: Chemical Bank, through its community development corporation, funded $250,000 in interest-free deposits in CDCUs through the Capitalization Program.

In January 1989, the federation got a significant boost in national visibility and credibility when I was appointed to a three-year term on the Consumer Advisory Council of the Federal Reserve System. In my address at the October 1989 meeting, I introduced CDCUs, presented the case for national policies to provide capital to CDCUs and other nonprofit community lenders, and put CDCUs on the radar for regulatory approval of CRA credit for bank investment, grants, and other support.

## Conclusion

The Eighties were a decade of struggle for the National Federation of CDCUs—struggle for the survival and recognition of our credit unions and struggle for our own survival as an organization. By the decade's end, we could point to some hard-won successes. Our Capitalization Program for CDCUs, launched with a $30,000 loan from the Adrian Dominicans, had grown to more than $2.3 million. The top-tier foundations—Ford and MacArthur—had provided grants and investments. The federation's membership—demoralized and decimated during the Reagan years—had reached a new high. We had helped organize the Lower East Side People's Federal Credit Union, proof of the concept that CDCUs could serve neighborhoods abandoned by banks. The federation had brought our story to the highest reaches of government—even though the White House had not followed up on the federation's recommendations.

On the federal front, the federation fought a decade-long defensive battle to revive the Community Development Revolving Loan Fund for Credit Unions—the precious, if diminished, victory of its campaign of the 1970s. Throughout the Eighties, we advanced other, more ambitious proposals for public-sector access to capital for CDCUs and other community-based lenders. In 1984, we launched a campaign to establish a New York State Corporation for Community Banking; from 1986, we extended our approach to the federal level, promoting the concept of a "Neighborhood Banking Corporation" that became a rallying point for the campaign to establish the Community Development Financial Institutions Fund.

Financial stability and capacity would come only in the next decade: The federation's net worth remained a minuscule $26,850 as 1990 began.[542] But by the beginning of the new decade, the federation had made its way into the national community development arena. It was poised to make an impact.

# PART V. The Nineties: The Visions Converge

The journey had been long, but the transformation of "community development banking" from aspiration to reality was achieved in a few short years.

As the decade began, a half-dozen activists from credit unions, loan funds, a community reinvestment organization, and a newly formed bank were meeting in borrowed space in lower Manhattan to sketch a vision of inclusive finance. Meanwhile, a long-shot presidential candidate from the South was urging voters to share his enthusiasm about a microlender to poor women in Bangladesh and a neighborhood bank on the South Side of Chicago.

By July 15, 1993, President Bill Clinton was announcing legislation on the south lawn of the White House, as borrowers from grassroots community lenders told their stories to an audience of Congressmembers and Cabinet secretaries, bankers, foundation executives, and civil rights advocates. Although community development banking was a top priority of the president, the path to final legislation was not straight. CDFIs had good stories to tell, but they were inexperienced in the ways of Washington and employed no lobbyists. Mainstream banks had their own legislative goals, including interstate branching and securing appropriations for the Bank Enterprise Act, which rewarded conventional financial institutions for supporting community development. Midway through the legislative process, the Whitewater investigation of alleged Clinton misdeeds in an Arkansas land deal threatened the president's plans.

Finally, on September 23, 1994, President Clinton signed the bill creating the CDFI Fund. He declared it his dream come true—a dream shared by CDFIs as well.

# CHAPTER 9. Coalition-Building: The Road to Trinity

Two organizations were pivotal in assembling the coalition that successfully advocated for the CDFI Fund: the National Federation of Community Development Credit Unions and the National Association of Community Development Loan Funds (NACDLF).

By the late 1980s, both the National Federation and NACDLF had been increasingly successful in making the case for socially responsible investment. But the two organizations were still living on the edge in terms of their own operations. As NACDLF noted in October 1989, "Until grant monies can be secured, the NACDLF must operate with an austere budget."[543] The federation's situation was, if anything, more fragile. Although the federation had a "real" office in downtown Manhattan, after its earlier migration from borrowed space in Brooklyn to East Harlem, it was still living hand to mouth, sometimes struggling to make payroll. Worse, its second in command, Annie Vamper—half of the federation's management team—died on May 19, 1990, after a long illness.

By the end of 1990, the tide was turning for both national organizations.

## The "New" NACDLF

The "new" NACDLF was taking shape. No longer was it headquartered in a small city in Western Massachusetts; now it was in the crossroads of the Northeastern corridor—Philadelphia, a city with the full set of urban problems. Chuck Matthei, the charismatic early leader of the loan fund movement, had moved on—still prominent, but less the "face" of the movement now. He was succeeded by Martin Trimble. Strongly rooted in faith, if differently from Matthei, he was no less a fierce, passionate advocate for social change. Trimble described the tension embodied by the two leaders in this way.

> I think [Chuck's] strength was he had a vision of economic justice. I shared that vision. I think I understand better, now, where the tension lay. In organizing, we have a paradigm: the world as it is, and the world as it should be. Chuck operated in the world as it should be. I think what I understand now, although I didn't have the language for it then—and I think this is where the tension was with the next generation, which I considered myself part of—is that the path to the world as it should be is through the world as it is.[544]

The transition in NACDLF's leadership to Trimble in 1989 was critical to the alliance that gave birth to the CDFI Coalition. I recall a meeting in the National Federation's office in Lower Manhattan around 1990 with a leadership group from NACDLF, including Trimble and Matthei. As we discussed the federation's plans to advocate for a national Neighborhood Banking Corporation, Matthei was unenthusiastic, to say the least. Raising federal capital, with the likelihood of federal regulation, was not how he built ICE; his powerful personal style, which was founded on engagement with investors, morally and politically, was not a recipe for dealing with a Washington bureaucracy. Trimble, in contrast, was willing to join with us, and bring NACDLF along with him. Like the federation, he was willing to take on the federal government to demand resources for our communities.

But before NACDLF and the National Federation could pretend to lead any movement, they both needed to expand and strengthen themselves internally.

In its annual report of October 1990, NACDLF announced that it was financially strong; it hired three new staff that year and relocated from donated space in a church to an office building in Philadelphia's Chinatown, where it shared space with the Delaware Valley Community Reinvestment Fund. It noted that Mark Pinsky had begun working with NACDLF as newsletter editor and "also to help the Association develop a public affairs strategy." In 1991, NACDLF made significant advances in becoming a national capital intermediary. Its earlier investment of $1.5 million from the Funding Exchange had been designated for "new and younger" loan funds. But demand proved lower than anticipated among this sector, so consequently NACDLF opened capital access to all its members. "With this change NACDLF created the Central Fund, a vehicle to aggregate large blocks of national/international, institutional capital to be redistributed to all its members."[545] It also reinforced NACDLF's focus on equity:

> Most NACDLF member funds are too heavily debt capitalized and operate without sufficient permanent capital and loss reserves to protect investors. This financial imbalance will become more evident as member funds are adversely affected by the declining economy, mounting bank failures, continuing real estate deflation, and worsening government fiscal crises. [Consequently, NACDLF set the goal of raising] an equity grants pool of $20–$30 million over the next five years. These monies would be allocated by formula to enable funds to achieve optimum levels of permanent capital and loss reserve (e.g., 20 percent total capitalization exclusive of loss reserves and 5 percent of total monies loaned to a fund, respectively).[546]

NACDLF's diagnosis was accurate: Loan funds needed more equity. Its goal, at least in the short run, was overly optimistic, if it was predicated primarily on investments from foundations and religious organizations. Thus, NACDLF was primed to consider the National Federation's approach: Look to the federal government.

## The National Federation: Capital Breakthroughs

Throughout the 1980s, the federation had fought to loosen the strings of federal capital, even while expanding its own Capitalization Program. Finally, in 1989, after a series of advances and setbacks, the Community Development Revolving Loan Fund for Credit Unions was reactivated, this time for good. It was not the community-controlled fund the federation had sought from the 1970s; rather, it was under the control of the regulator, the National Credit Union Administration (NCUA), a dubious commingling of powers. The federation did not welcome this arrangement—but given the indifference and unsuitability of other federal agencies, reviving the fund under NCUA was the best available outcome.

Still, the money did not immediately flow. Under President George H.W. Bush, there had been no fundamental change of heart by the Republican administration regarding financial services in low-income communities.[547] Rather, NCUA purged credit unions from its official roster of low-income institutions—those that were exclusively permitted to accept philanthropic and other "nonmember" capital. The ranks of low-income credit unions shrank from more than 300 to a low of 142 by 1990. Moreover, not a single new CDCU in the entire country was chartered by NCUA in 1990, 1991, or early 1992.[548]

The news for the federation's own Capitalization Program was better. After the federation's years of advocacy, the Ford Foundation vindicated the organization's hopes with a $1 million Program-Related Investment (PRI) in 1989. The path was not particularly easy. The federation's negotiations with the MacArthur Foundation in 1986 for a PRI had been relatively quick and painless. Ford was another matter entirely. The federation learned about covenants, positive and negative, warranties, and representations. Most frustrating, it had to obtain opinion of counsel on the most basic matters.* Many CDFIs, especially small and young organizations, had a similar experience. Dealing with Ford was an education—exasperating at times, but ultimately helpful in building the organization's capacity. It forced the federation to think hard about its financial and organizational structure, and better equipped the federation to work with other investors.

New investors came, and earlier ones increased their investments. The MacArthur Foundation increased its investment by $450,000 and gave the federation our first-ever grant for reserves, $50,000. Other commitments came from the Calvert Social Investment Fund and the Episcopal Church. By year-end 1990, the federation's Capitalization Program for CDCUs was managing approximately $3.8 million, all of which was channeled into federally insured deposits. Our ambitious vision of a fund owned by and for the CDCU movement itself—one that could generate income to advance the federation toward financial stability—now appeared to be more than an unlikely distant dream.

---

\* For example, Ford required a lawyer's opinion that the National Federation was duly incorporated and existed. To its amazement, the federation's pro bono counsel—the very same one that had incorporated the federation 15 years before—declined to provide this for reasons of liability. Fortunately, the federation found the necessary assistance elsewhere.

The Ford Foundation's support helped the federation expand its footprint. The federation was "national" primarily in name: With our limited resources, we could not possibly provide much service to our members across the country. Our Ford-funded CDCU Demonstration Project brought both grant and investment dollars that we used to deepen our engagement with networks of CDCUs in rural North Carolina, Philadelphia, Chicago, and New York City itself. Aided again by Ford, as well as the Trinity Church grants program, the federation reached out to another important subsector of the CDCU movement: African American church-based credit unions. These typically volunteer-run credit unions were important to the black community far beyond their relatively meager assets. For decades, they had been the source of credit and financial services denied to African Americans by white-owned banks.

In March 1992, we held an unprecedented event: the first national conference for faith-based credit unions. Early on a rainy Saturday morning, we traveled to a historic church in Midtown Manhattan. We had no idea what to expect—perhaps a group of local church credit union volunteers. When we arrived at 8:00 a.m., we were amazed to find church credit union volunteers from credit unions we never knew existed, from Baltimore and from as far away as California, waiting for us to open the doors. Rita Haynes of Faith Community Credit Union, later the chairman of the federation, came from Cleveland; Lucia Moreno, from a Latino credit union in Wilmington, CA, traveled across the country to present. Rev. Floyd Flake, Congressman from Queens and a prominent community developer whose church had a credit union, was keynote speaker.[549]

The federation published the proceedings of the conference and held multiple follow-up events for church-based credit unions in the 1990s. In the second half of the decade, we expanded our sectoral approach to CDCUs serving Latino communities.

## The Federation and the "Mainstream" Credit Union Movement

Unlike NACDLF or other emerging CDFI trade organizations, the federation operated in a space populated by multiple credit union associations. There were credit union "leagues" in each state; in Washington, there were two competing organizations, the National Association of Federal Credit Unions (NAFCU) and the Credit Union National Association (CUNA), which represented thousands of state and federally chartered credit unions through the system of statewide leagues. For a decade, CUNA had provided the National Federation with minimal, grudging support and recognition—typically, a $5,000 annual donation, which did not go far during the years when the federation was struggling to survive.

In 1989, the stakes were raised when a bank-driven battle to abolish the federal tax exemption of credit unions heated up. This political Armageddon spurred a call for unity within the credit union movement. But bitter at the years of stingy support from CUNA during our hard times, now feeling our own growing strength and recognition, the National Federation balked at joining CUNA in the tax-exemption battle, which we believed would primarily benefit large credit unions. After contentious exchanges, the federation and CUNA agreed to a formal strategic alliance. On Tuesday, February 26, 1991, the federation and CUNA signed an agreement that provided the National Federation of CDCUs with formal recognition as "the leading trade association for credit unions serving members with low incomes in the United States."[550] On Thursday, February 28, 1991, the federation's board joined some 15,000 credit union activists on the Capitol mall for a historic "Operation Grassroots" rally to oppose taxation.

Over the next five years, CUNA provided substantially increased financial support to the federation, funds that were critical in helping the federation stabilize financially, add staff, and expand its programs. But the alliance between the large, "mainstream" CUNA and the much smaller, minority-dominated federation was always uneasy. By the mid-1990s, as CUNA was going through its own crisis brought on by problems in its credit card and mortgage operations, the two organizations moved apart.[551]

## Confronting Federal Banking Policy: Two Approaches

In 1991, in their respective ways, both NACDLF and the National Federation stepped up their advocacy to highlight dysfunctions and inequity in the financial system.

In February, while the federation's board was in Washington, finalizing its agreement with CUNA and participating in the Operation Grassroots "Rally on the Mall," we used the opportunity to raise the profile of CDCUs in Congress. On February 27, the federation presented a briefing session on "Preserving Financial Services in Low-Income Communities" at the Rayburn House Office Building. Moderated by federation staff member Errol Louis, the session highlighted the obstacles CDCUs faced both in raising and deploying capital. Robert Jackson, from Quitman County FCU, explained "How 'Non-Member Deposit' Restrictions Halt the Flow of Capital into Low-Income Communities" like his own in the impoverished Mississippi Delta; Karen Zelin, of the Santa Cruz Community CU in California, the foremost CDCU business lender, discussed how proposed NCUA business lending restrictions would deny capital to low-Income, minority, and cooperative entrepreneurs. The federation used the opportunity to present our proposal for the creation of a National Neighborhood Banking Corporation.[552] About 10 congressional offices were represented, including that of the chair of the Congressional Black Caucus, Rep. Edolphus Towns (D-Brooklyn, NY).[553]

In a follow-up memo to the federation's board on March 18, I reported the following.

> Various Congressional staffers have expressed interest in our concept for a national 'Neighborhood Banking Corporation,' which would provide operating support and deposit capital for our credit unions—a much expanded, improved version of the NCUA [CDCU] Revolving Loan Fund. The basic motivation is this: Many of us feel that if Congress is appropriating tens of billions to bail out the savings and loans, from which our people couldn't borrow anyway, then there should be some sort of

appropriation to assure that low-income communities get some sort of financial assistance for the provision of 'banking' services.

I noted that other groups were working on parallel tracks to create something similar. "At some point, it seems to me likely that we will need and want to strike an alliance with them, since there is no chance that multiple concepts will be funded."[554]

## From Practice to Politics: Origins of the CDFI Coalition

Although the federation was the earliest and foremost advocate for a federal fund to support CDFIs, there was little possibility that we alone could carry our proposal to fruition. The federation's prime targets in Washington were *regulatory*—the fight against NCUA's burdensome restrictions on access to nonmember deposits, business lending, and low-income designation; the barriers to chartering new CDCUs; the need for crisis intervention to save troubled credit unions. With a staff of three or four people in the early 1990s, none of whom were lawyers or regulatory experts, the workload was virtually all-consuming. The work was essential; the federation's membership depended on it. But it was a huge drain on the organization's limited capacity. Alone, we lacked the bandwidth to take on a full-scale campaign to establish a "National Neighborhood Banking Corporation."

NACDLF's buy-in was crucial. As an association of unregulated, non-depository lenders, it did not have to wrestle with the kinds of problems that absorbed the federation. NACDLF dove into the largest questions of banking policy. In 1991, Martin Trimble presented a paper entitled "Banking Crisis and Public Purpose Lenders" at a colloquium organized by the University of Rhode Island, funded by the Fannie Mae Foundation. NACDLF developed a close relationship with the Financial Democracy Campaign and its codirector, Tom Schlesinger, who also served as the director of the Southern Finance Project. Trimble and influential progressive critics of the banking system, including Jim Hightower, William Greider, and Jane Arista, made a presentation that appeared on C-Span.[555]

Throughout 1991, NACDLF and the National Federation worked to engage other community lenders and advocates in our efforts. Attempts early in the year to assemble a nucleus were not particularly fruitful; moreover, as NACDLF noted, "a joint policy initiative on banking deregulation would not be appropriate given the fragile nature of their respective members."[556] As the year progressed, participants in the embryonic coalition debated whether to press for a far-reaching, comprehensive banking policy. In fall 1991, Lyndon Comstock, the founder and chair of the newly chartered Community Capital Bank in Brooklyn expressed his reservations.

> Most of the people at this [upcoming] meeting are practitioners, not just theoreticians, in the community development finance world. We're institution builders much more than we are public policy advocates. I, for one, feel that public policy advocacy is only of peripheral significance to our main work. I see that our agenda is almost

totally dominated by national level public policy issues. Frankly, we're not likely to have any influence on that debate. I'd rather see us using more of our time to talk about how we can expand the alternative banking system that most of us are already part of.[557]

In Comstock's view, it was more crucial to develop management talent for a growing CDFI industry. "I do feel," he wrote in a memo of November 18 to Martin Trimble and Jeremy Nowak, executive director of the Delaware Valley Community Reinvestment Fund and a leader of NACDLF, "that training/management development is the single most important need for CDFIs going forward—even more important than capital. So, management development programs have everything to do with expansion of the different types of CDFIs." In a subsequent series of memos to Nowak and Trimble (December 5, 10, 27, 1991) he presented at length a vision and plan for a "CDFI educational program," including recruitment, intensive training, and curriculum development. His approach (similar to one used by NACDLF) included peer-group education—"cosponsoring the creation or expansion of new CDFIs or [community development venture organizations] by having teams from the CDFI network program assist those initiatives."[558]

Comstock also focused on the need to expand the cross-sectoral representation of the nascent coalition. In a letter to Trimble dated December 9, 1991, he wrote that "a trade organization is getting underway for the microenterprise funds. (Our affiliate, LEAP, is joining this new trade association, Association for Enterprise Opportunity, even though we don't specialize in microenterprise.) …. I bring this to your attention because there's an obvious tie-in with the CDFI network." In addition, reflecting the work of Community Capital Bank's nonprofit affiliate, LEAP, he suggested including representatives of the emerging field of community development venture capital, to be represented by Nick Smith of Northern Ventures (Duluth, MN) and Ron Phillips of Coastal Enterprises in Maine.[559] (In fact, AEO and the Community Development Venture Capital Alliance would soon join the coalition.) Despite the diverse sectors and business models of these various organizations, Comstock reflected, "Perhaps, there's certain events that could happen at a national level. (Actually, it's kind of interesting to think about having a national CDFI convention someday, rather than separate ones for loan funds, credit unions, micro-credit programs, etc.)."[560] Two years later, exactly such an event—the CDFI movement's "Woodstock"—would be held.

In early December, the last meeting of 1991, the participants of the aspiring coalition defined issues for further discussion. Among these was the need for "synthesizing ideas advanced in Financial Democracy Campaign's Public-Purpose Banking Proposal and National Federation of Community Development Credit Unions' National Neighborhood Banking Concept Paper."[561] Other federal policy issues included Community Reinvestment Act challenges; federal and state legislation to support and expand the CDFI sector; human capital development; and constituency outreach "to educate CDFI staff, board, borrowers, and investors as well as community activists about [the] Public Purpose Banking agenda."[562]

The group planned to get an early start on election year 1992 by holding a follow-up meeting on January 10 in the library of an office building owned by Trinity Church, at the foot of Wall Street. The location was not fortuitous. Georgianna Gleason, grants officer at Trinity, had been an early supporter of Comstock's Community Capital Bank, as well as of the National Federation, providing funding for its outreach to minority faith-based credit unions. Given the seminal importance of faith-based organizations in nurturing the newborn CDFI movement throughout the 1980s, it was especially fitting that the CDFI Coalition was born under Trinity's roof.

## Naming the Newborn

The "charter" members of the loose steering group that met at Trinity included two trade organizations (NACDLF and the National Federation), as well as individual organizations: Community Capital Bank; Self-Help (which had both a loan fund and a credit union); the policy/action organization Woodstock Institute; and other occasional participants. Although the other organizations either were, or represented, financial practitioners, Woodstock occupied a unique and valuable position: A veteran, respected research organization and policy advocate, it was an important bridge to the CRA advocacy world. The neutrality, if not active support, of the CRA community would prove critical in any bank-related legislative campaign. ShoreBank was *not* one of the charter members; coalitions were "not ShoreBank's style" (an attitude that others in the movement sometimes found standoffish or even arrogant), and the bank was by no means sold on the group's strategy.

During the early months of 1992, the informal organization half-jokingly referred to itself by the ungainly name of the "Ad Hoc Coalition of Public Purpose Lenders." Earlier, Woodstock had done studies of the various types of lenders—credit unions, loan funds, banks—and tagged them "community development financial institutions." After the election of Bill Clinton, the CDFI name stuck, and the "Trinity Group" became the CDFI Coalition.

# CHAPTER 10. CDFIs and Congress: First Encounters

In 1991, the Community Reinvestment Act (CRA) came under attack. The country was still digging out from the bills and political fallout of the savings and loan scandal. In 1988-89, mortgage lending discrimination against African Americans became another type of national scandal through "The Color of Money," a series of investigative reports in the *Atlanta Journal-Constitution*.* Subsequently, the Federal Reserve Bank of Boston had published research further documenting discrimination that was not limited to the South.

But the banking lobby and its supporters were not shy. On May 23, 1991, the House Subcommittee on Financial Institutions voted "to virtually gut the Community Reinvestment Act, as part of the markup on H.R. 1505, a sweeping proposal supported by the Bush Administration to revamp the nation's banking system." Specifically, it adopted an amendment to exempt from CRA banks with less than $100 million in assets and rural banks with less than $250 million. It also provided a "safe harbor" to shield banks from CRA protests if they had received at least a satisfactory rating from federal regulators in the previous two years.[563]

CRA advocates rallied enough support to defeat these amendments. On June 21, the *Wall Street Journal* reported that "many [Congressional] committee members said that they had received more reaction—mostly negative—from constituents on the amendments exempting banks from the Community Reinvestment Act than on any other part of the banking bill."[564] Republican Representative Marge Roukema of New Jersey noted the "intense emotional protests" in her district and the press. Meanwhile, Treasury Secretary Nicholas Brady assured reporters that "the Bush Administration had no role in drafting" the defeated anti-CRA amendments.[565]

## Carrots and Sticks: Origins of the Bank Enterprise Act

While rallying support to defeat the proposed CRA amendments, the Washington-based Center for Community Change called out another threat to the CRA: It reported that Pennsylvania Republican Rep. Tom Ridge[566] was preparing to offer an amendment to reduce federal deposit insurance premiums for banks that made loans to distressed communities and offered basic banking accounts. More

---

* Bill Dedmon, the author, won the Pulitzer Prize in 1989 for his articles.

than this financial reward, the Bank Enterprise Act (BEA) "would guarantee a satisfactory or better CRA rating and a permanent safe harbor under CRA for banks that invest 0.5 percent of their assets in a community development corporation, a community development bank, or a community development credit union."[567]

Bill Zavarello, legislative director for Democratic Representative Maxine Waters whose district included South Central Los Angeles, recalled the opposition to BEA from Washington advocacy groups and progressive members of Congress. "'They were all aligned against the BEA. Those of us from the progressive point of view felt like, 'Don't give the banks a break. Don't bribe them to do what they are supposed to do.' It was pretty simple. We're all for incentives, but we felt like you're letting them off the hook. We lost that battle. Floyd Flake, to his credit, as a politician was incredibly tenacious."[568]

Ridge's cosponsor in the House was the Rev. Floyd H. Flake, who became the most visible, dogged promoter of the BEA. Rep. Flake bridged several worlds. Trained as a social worker and educated for the ministry, he worked as a marketing analyst for Xerox, then as dean of students and director of the Afro-American Center at Boston University. Appointed pastor of the Greater Allen A.M.E. Church (later Greater Allen A.M.E. Cathedral) in Jamaica, Queens in 1976, he grew its membership from 1,400 to more than 23,000, making it one of the country's largest churches and bringing him a national reputation. Under his leadership, the church became a driving force in community development, sponsoring commercial and residential development, other enterprises, and a private school.[569] Although Rev. Flake was elected to Congress in 1987 as a Democrat representing Queens, NY, throughout his career he did not hesitate to endorse and build ties with Republicans locally and in Congress. He moved easily in New York City financial circles, building strong relationships with money-center banks, which financed his major projects. In his career, Rev. Flake was invited to numerous advisory boards, including of banks and the FDIC.

Rep. Flake knew well the benefits and limits of the CRA. Community development on the scale he practiced it required significant bank financing.[570] The New York banks that supported his projects were sophisticated CRA investors. But the banking industry was not enamored with the CRA, which was generally—at best—a break-even proposition. As for the advocacy community, although CRA deals with banks had grown substantially in the late 1980s, the flows and impact of the CRA were still limited. What if there was a "carrot," Flake asked, to incentivize CRA investment, instead of only the CRA "stick" of delaying or denying mergers, acquisitions, and expansions? Could "good CRA citizens" be rewarded for their efforts?

With the S&L bailout still fresh, the economy sliding into recession, and the federal budget being cut back, Flake could not plausibly have asked Congress to directly appropriate funds to line the pockets of banks. Instead, he developed an apparently ingenious approach that would not tap the federal budget: reduce the FDIC deposit insurance premiums for banks to reward their CRA activity. This would be a "win-win": more money for community development and reduced cost (as good as cash) for banks.

Over the course of 1991, Reps. Flake and Ridge drafted and promoted legislation for the Bank Enterprise Act (BEA). They gathered support from both sides of the aisle in Congress. Vicky Stein, who worked for the subcommittee headed by Democratic Rep. Ben Erdreich from Alabama, recalls "there was a bi-partisan atmosphere at the time and many of us working for Democrats actually worked with and socialized with Republican staffers. There was a positive and open dialogue and while we respected our differences we were still able to find common ground."[571] That would change drastically after the 1994 elections, marked by Newt Gingrich's "Republican Revolution."

On December 19, 1991, Public Law 102-242 enacted the Bank Enterprise Act of 1991 (Subtitle C), part of the "Federal Deposit Insurance Corporation Improvement Act of 1991." Among its provisions were these.

- **"Reduced assessment rate for Deposits Attributable to Lifeline Accounts"** (Sec. 232), which were defined in terms of "basic transaction services for individuals," taking into account balances of less than $1,000, fee structure, withdrawal, and other factors. Deposit premium assessments for a bank's holdings of such accounts would be reduced by 50 percent.
- **"Assessment credits for qualifying activities relating to distressed communities"** (Sec. 233). A Community Enterprise Assessment Credit Board would be established to determine availability and assessment credit for qualifying activities, including increases in new originations of qualified loans and other financial assistance provided for low- and moderate-income persons or enterprises in distressed communities and increases in the amount of deposits from residents. The credit for such increases would be 5 percent, but up to 15 percent if it consisted of investments through or in a qualified *"community development organization"* [emphasis added].
- **Designated distressed areas** were to meet at least two of three criteria: 70 percent or more of families having less than 80 percent of the area median; a poverty rate of 20 percent; and an unemployment rate 150 percent of the national average.
- **"Community Development Organizations"** (Sec. 234) included community development banks, community development corporations, community development credit unions, and community development units within insured depositories.

Conceptually, CDFI advocates welcomed many of the bases the legislation covered. It addressed not only bank investment but "lifeline accounts"—basic financial services for bank customers with limited resources. It recognized and provided enhanced rewards for investing in "community development organizations," specifically listing community development banks and credit unions, as well as Neighborhood Reinvestment Corporation affiliates. In its way, it was quite innovative, as cosponsor Tom Ridge argued.

> For the first time, the federal government is sending appropriations to banks to achieve a social goal.… The federal government has decided, again for the first time, that incentives may be an important track alongside the contentious Community Reinvestment Act system of community investments.… The enterprise act provides

strong incentives for banks to locate or stay in distressed communities. And it places extraordinary emphasis on bank-controlled community development corporations.[572]

There were several problems, however, with the structure of the bill. First, it reduced the inflows into the FDIC deposit insurance fund—a cause for concern just a few years after the catastrophic and expensive S&L crisis. Although the BEA ostensibly was intended to amplify the CRA, it came at a time when the CRA was, in fact, just beginning to make a greater impact: As Dan Immergluck wrote, "The effectiveness of CRA was most pronounced from 1989 to about 1992, after Congress chastised regulators for failing to enforce the law and passed important amendments to CRA and HMDA."[573]

Where would the money to launch this initiative come from? The legislation specified that "the provisions…shall not take effect until appropriations are specifically provided in advance."[574] But Congress did not provide appropriations. Ridge was disappointed but hopeful.

> The Bank Enterprise Act stands a good chance of at least partial funding in 1992. It is a bipartisan provision that seeks to redress the mortgage discrimination found in a Federal Reserve report. Legislators are keenly sensitive to this report and to the fact that our nation's distressed communities need more than just rhetoric.
>
> While battling for appropriations is never easy, and the appropriators make no promises at this point in the process, I am more optimistic about funding than I was about enactment of the enterprise act itself. I think the hardest part has been done.

Ridge was right, and he was wrong. True, the appropriations battle was *not* easy. But the hardest part had not been done. There were no appropriations in 1992, or 1993 either, although in a July 1992 report, the House Committee on Appropriations recommended $1 million "to begin preliminary study, design, and development of the Bank Enterprise Act."[575]

But Rep. Flake persisted. In the end, he won.

## Educating Congress: South Central Los Angeles Raises the Stakes

The Bank Enterprise Act of 1991 aimed to advance community development finance, and it recognized a variety of "community development organizations." But, as its title indicated, its primary thrust was to incentivize and reward banks; CDFIs would be collateral beneficiaries. CDFIs were still relatively unknown on Capitol Hill. In 1992, through a series of Senate and House hearings, CDFI leaders educated Congress about their relatively new, small, innovative institutions.

The stakes were raised dramatically that spring. On April 29, 1992, South Central Los Angeles erupted in six days of violence in reaction to the acquittal of police officers who had been captured on video brutalizing driver Rodney King a year earlier. It could not have been closer to home for Rep. Maxine Waters, whose district included South Central. "Maxine was sitting there watching the TV when the riots began," recalled Zavarello, her legislative director. "At one point she literally said, 'Bill, there's my office.' They didn't torch it, but the wall to the bank next door collapsed on our district office."[576] Waters was acutely aware of the need for financial services; she would be a key advocate and ally for Bill Clinton in making community development banking a reality. "The pivotal support she afforded Clinton helped him a lot," Zavarello recalled.

## In the Senate

Early in 1992, the National Federation redoubled its efforts to direct congressional attention to the endangered status of low-income credit unions. In March, the federation wrote to Banking Committee staff member Jeannine Jacokes, highlighting the regulatory concerns of CDCUs and calling for a new national fund.

> As I mentioned to you, regulatory pressures are rendering CDCUs an endangered species. Congressional concerns to avoid taxpayer expenditures on financial institutions have, in our view, pushed the pendulum too far in a restrictive direction. The consequence of these trends…is a decrease in banking services to the urban poor at precisely the time that services should be dramatically expanded. We think Congress could reverse this trend at relatively modest cost by establishing a national **Neighborhood Banking Corporation** [emphasis in original].[577]

Following up, Errol Louis, associate director of the National Federation, and Martin Trimble, of NACDLF, met with Jacokes in early May. On May 15, Louis wrote to Jacokes, reiterating the federation's concern to roll back the NCUA's limitations on nonmember (philanthropic and other) deposits in CDCUs. He urged increased chartering of new CDCUs; a moratorium on "the liquidation or forced merger of institutions serving predominantly low-income or minority communities"; and the establishment of the "National Neighborhood Banking Corporation."

Meanwhile, Jacokes was working toward the development of pilot community development banking legislation, gathering information on other segments of the emerging CDFI industry, including ShoreBank, Southern Development Bancorporation, and Self-Help. She drafted a lengthy list of questions, exploring issues including loan losses and delinquency, profitability, income levels of borrowers, housing units and jobs created, use of government subsidies, and much more. On June 5, a community development banking bill was introduced. In fact, as Jacokes recalled, the Senate Banking Committee refrained from tagging this with the "banking" name, lest the bill become encumbered by contentious banking-related provisions.[578] (The term "community development financial institution" had not come into common use.) The markup of the bill was set for June 18.

As described by the Senate Banking Committee's majority staff director, Steven B. Harris, in a letter to the Board of Governors of the Federal Reserve on July 8, "This proposal would create a small-scale pilot program to facilitate the creation of community development banks." He traced the interest in the issue to the Rouse-Maxwell National Housing Task Force in 1988, which recommended a federal program to seed banks like South Shore, noting that "Community Development Banks, like South Shore Bank in Chicago, have proved extraordinarily successful at making capital available for community and economic development in low-income and minority communities."[579]

## In the House

On July 22, two subcommittees of the House Banking Committee held a joint hearing entitled "Traditional and Non-Traditional Lenders' Role in Economic Development." Rep. Erdreich, chairman of the Subcommittee on Policy Research and Insurance, opened the hearing and framed the context.

> The recession, the budgetary crisis at every level of government has placed considerable burden on all of us, and certainly on our Nation's economic resources. The recent riots in Los Angeles and unrest in New York brought to the forefront the economic and social problems of our distressed communities. We have to stop this steady decline by stimulating real economic development.[580]

His colleague, Democratic Rep. Carper from Delaware, chairman of the Subcommittee on Economic Stabilization, noted that even before the Los Angeles riots, his subcommittee held hearings in Philadelphia, which it described as "in dire straits.... Like most of our cities [Philadelphia] needs institutions which enable it to build from the ground up, and from the inside out. What these cities need is entrepreneurship run amok. What they lack is access to capital." Carper also urged that attention also be "focused on distressed rural areas, [as] their needs are equally critical."[581]

The congressional hearings provided an important opportunity for CDFIs to tell their story on a bigger stage. Each major subgroup of the emerging CDFI movement was represented in the hearings, along with a "conventional" banker and a federal housing agency. They made brief oral presentations to congressional panels, responded to initial questions from members, then had the opportunity to submit fuller, written statements for the record, which was published some weeks after the hearing; often, congressional staff asked for written responses to follow-up questions, which were also printed in the record. Thus, these hearing records provide helpful insight into the state of the CDFI movement in 1992: how CDFIs saw and presented themselves, and the aspects of their work that prompted congressional curiosity or required elaboration.

## Community Development and Mainstream Banks

ShoreBank's Mary Houghton and George P. Surgeon (Southern Development Bancorporation and Elk Horn Bank & Trust Co.) represented community development banks. Houghton described ShoreBank's decade-long effort to "stabilize a community that was suffering from the disinvestment that invariably follows racial change in American cities." The key to its eventual success was "through the orderly transfer of the housing stock from white to black ownership," as well as finding a niche specifically among "black entrepreneurs [who have] rehabbed one out of every three units of rental housing in South Shore to an excellent quality standard." Houghton highlighted the gaps in working capital that plagued small businesses, compounded by gaps in information and technical assistance gaps.[582]

ShoreBank was not yet part of the emerging CDFI Coalition, and Houghton argued—as ShoreBank always did—for the "particular vehicle of a bank holding company [that] can be used as a form of permanent local economic development institutional activity… [which] has the staying power to implement large-scale, long-term strategies which are needed to impact on poverty…. I would assert that a financial institution has unusual credibility with investors, funders and local residents and superior staying power and capacity." ShoreBank was on the verge of a significant expansion: She announced its new joint venture with a university in the upper peninsula of Michigan, and feasibility studies to expand to Cleveland, Portland (OR), and Detroit.

Despite her wholehearted espousal of the bank holding-company structure, Houghton agreed that "localities have differing economies, institutional infrastructures, and cultures… [and that] efforts will differ dramatically from place to place." Moreover, in her written statement, she called the legislators' attention to another type of institution that she supported and chaired. Houghton described one of the earliest, most prominent microenterprise organizations, the Women's Self-Employment Project in Chicago, which used the peer group lending model through its Full Circle Fund. This and other funds, like MICRO in southern Arizona, were inspired, she noted, by the self-sustaining international models of Accion in Latin America and the Grameen Bank in Bangladesh.[583]

Surgeon presented the rural side of community development banking. Surgeon had come from ShoreBank to serve as president and CEO of Southern Development Bancorporation and its wholly owned subsidiary, Elk Horn Bank & Trust Co. in Arkadelphia, AR. The company's core strategy was to assist "the creation and expansion of small, locally owned businesses" in order to diversify the local economy "and thereby provide some insulation from economic dislocation during periods of recession that are inevitable in a free market economy." In addition to banking services, Southern provided "development services—nonfinancial assistance [ranging] from seminars for welfare recipients about self-employment to custom designed, national product marketing, and brokering campaigns."[584]

Surgeon identified national trends "that support the need for development banks and other financial intermediaries that promote economic development." These included the continuing decline in manufacturing by major corporations and consolidation of the banking industry, which had made access to small-business loans and equity investments more difficult. He decried inequality, which highlighting the increasing divergence in incomes and net worths of Americans at the extremes of the socioeconomic spectrum. During the 1980s, the incomes of the wealthiest 1 percent of the American population almost doubled while the incomes of the bottom 20 percent languished.... Southern's programs are uniquely geared to help the poor and middle class not only enhance their incomes, but also increase their ownership of wealth.[585]

Like ShoreBank, Southern had several affiliates, some of which provided "non-bankable financial services, such as long-term, subordinated, fixed-rate loans," working capital, and equity. In particular, he mentioned its associated microenterprise fund, which had attracted the attention and support of the Clintons early on: the Good Faith Fund, which was inspired by the Grameen Bank peer lending model. The fund's clientele was about 80 percent African American; half of its borrowers were women.[586]

Gail Snowden, division executive of First Community Bank, Bank of Boston, represented innovative mainstream banks. She described their unique model as "a bank within a bank created in 1990 to serve selected major inner-city urban markets in New England." The bank's initiative, which had grown to 12 branches in Boston, Providence, and New Haven, was "modestly profitable." She specifically warded off criticisms of the Community Reinvestment Act (CRA): "I think that CRA does not say do stupid things. It does say to take a new eye to your products and see how you can change them to make them work."[587] Snowden urged Congress to provide appropriations for the "Greenlining Bill"—that is, the Flake/Ridge BEA legislation. She acknowledged that CRA was needed "because you do need to slap people's wrists from time to time, but also to create a productive incentive-based system."[588] Specifically, she urged an immediate appropriation of $100 million to provide incentives to banks.[589] (The bill's cosponsor, Rep. Tom Ridge, used the opportunity of the hearings to add his pitch for BEA: The Senate Appropriations Committee was meeting the next day, and Ridge was pressing for a $50 million allocation.)

William C. Perkins, director of the Federal Housing Finance Board (FHFB), highlighted his agency's response to the South Central riots, which, he wrote, demonstrated the importance of community revitalization. Through the FHFB's Community Investment Program (CIP), its member banks were committed to offering $600 million in CIP "advances" (i.e., loans) for the areas affected.[590] This, he stated, "may well serve as an excellent example that engenders successful models for economic development and commercial revitalization in other areas of the country."[591]

## Community Development Corporations

Ron Phillips was president of Coastal Enterprises, Inc. (CEI), a 15-year-old, statewide community development corporation (CDC) headquartered in Wiscasset on the mid-coast of Maine. With $20 million in assets, it lent extensively to small businesses in rural areas. CEI's philosophy and mission were "concentrated on development strategies that maximize local resources and value-added production, support for indigenous entrepreneurs and creation of quality jobs and self-employment for all Mainers, including women, AFDC recipients, and other low-income people."[592] Borrowers ranged from fishing enterprises and manufacturing to child care. CEI, like other organizations represented, had several distinct financing vehicles that varied by size (from microloans up to $200,000) and financial structure, providing equity as well as debt. Phillips emphasized the importance of bank partners, including Fleet and Key banks, for CEI's work.

Phillips and CEI were bridges to the earlier era of community development. He was a relentless advocate for CDCs as vehicles for filling credit gaps: "Banks, credit unions, and sometimes even traditional government programs operate under tighter credit rules." In his written statement, he noted the disappointing trajectory of public support for CDCs since early Economic Opportunity Act of 1965 legislation: "What remains of that ambitious undertaking now resides in the Office of Community Services of the Department of Health and Human Services, a small token to a profound and idealistic legacy in our history." He quoted a 1990 study by Neal Peirce and Carol Steinbach that CDCs were "an absolute national necessity."[593]

## Community Development Loan Funds

Jeremy Nowak was executive director of the Delaware Valley Community Reinvestment Fund (DVCRF), one of the premier community development loan funds in the country. He was also the chairman of NACDLF. At the time of the hearing, the association represented 40 loan funds, which had raised $68 million from 3,100 socially responsible investors, plus $14 million in grant funds or equity investments. Nowak provided a helpful profile of the investors in community development loan funds: Individuals made up 28 percent of the investors, religious institutions 26 percent, foundations 27 percent, government agencies 5 percent, and financial institutions 7 percent. The loan funds claimed a loss rate of less than 1 percent.

Nowak emphasized his loan fund's focus on entrepreneurs and community-based organizations, especially CDCs, as integral to its mission of "strengthening the civic infrastructure of low-income areas." To illustrate the reality, he cited the example of financing the last laundromat in North Camden: "Of all the bad neighborhoods and of all the disinvested neighborhoods, North Camden probably beats the rest outright."[594] Without his organization's financing, the laundromat would have been unable to find the insurance it needed.

Like other CDFI representatives, Nowak stressed that "capital, by itself, in and of itself, is never enough.... It is all of the costs of capacity building that go along with capital." Because "our capital is never enough," DVCRF had to bring in capital from conventional banks. Nowak pointed out the limitations of CRA, which, he argued, was "largely a housing culture.... Banks are simply not as aggressive with respect to economic development lending as they are to housing lending."[595] Community development loan funds thus had a crucial role—but their lending should catalyze, not substitute, for bank lending.

Nowak highlighted the departure of banks and S&Ls in many low-income neighborhoods and the implications for community development banking: "There is an opportunity for the emergence of an infrastructure of loan funds, community development banks, and credit unions to play—to kind of reinvent banking in those neighborhoods." Nowak made the case for a "nonsectarian" approach to the range of CDFIs, urging Congress to "support the infrastructure of community development loan funds, community development banks, credit unions, and CDCs through equity investments and through subsidy for the kinds of technical assistance that are so important, given the kinds of transaction costs that we are talking about."[596] He argued that two main directions in public policy—carrots or sticks—"are not mutually exclusive; in fact they are linked by necessity."[597] Conventional institutions needed to invest more in low-income areas; the infrastructure of community development financial intermediaries needed to be strengthened as well. To achieve the latter, he recommended "money for technical assistance and equity (or subordinated debt), direct loan pool contributions…. A national trust fund, for example, capitalized by the public sector and financial institutions, could offer equity grants and stock investments into new and existing development banks and intermediaries."[598]

## Community Development Credit Unions

Santa Cruz Community Credit Union, on the Northern California coast, was one of the most innovative CDCUs, specializing in lending to small businesses and cooperatives. Its vice president for community development, Jeff Wells, was a board member of the National Federation of CDCUs and testified on its behalf as well as that of the federation's recent ally, the Credit Union National Association (CUNA).

The $18 million Santa Cruz Community Credit Union had compiled an outstanding record of small-business and farm loans, with a charge-off rate of 0.64 percent since 1985. Its portfolio included loans for affordable housing and social service agencies, battered women's and homeless shelters, halfway houses, and low-income elderly facilities. A full-service retail institution, 25 percent of the credit union's members had less than $100 in their savings accounts. The Santa Cruz area was ravaged physically and economically by the Loma Prieta earthquake in October 1989. Although all the credit union's business loans were current, federal examiners applied harsh regulatory pressure, demanding that the credit union "immediately cease all small business lending activities."[599]

Like other witnesses, Wells emphasized the link between changes in the banking system, poverty, and civil unrest.

> The riots in south central Los Angeles, where one of [the National Federation's] CDCUs is located in Watts, have demonstrated the tragic consequences of the changes in our banking system over the last decade. These changes affect rural areas,

inner cities, African-Americans, Hispanics, Native Americans, and low-income white communities. A combination of deregulation, consolidation, economic recession and outright redlining have led banks to systematically withdraw credit and other financial services from low-income areas that most need economic growth.[600]

There were 14,000 credit unions in the United States, but Wells testified that most served predominantly middle-income members and were not adequately positioned to serve lower-income households. There were 400–500 CDCUs whose mission was to serve this market; they served 350,000 members and had aggregate deposits of $500 million. Despite their mission, he emphasized, the CDCU movement had suffered from NCUA's regulatory pressure in the wake of the S&L crisis. More low-income and minority credit unions had been closed, while almost no new CDCU charters had been granted; regulations had restricted philanthropic and other investments in CDCUs.[601] "I agree that we need a top priority of safety and soundness," Wells testified, "but at what expense? Certainly not at the expense of curtailing the fundamental mission of providing credit to those who desperately need it. We must seek a balance."[602]

Wells presented to the committee the National Federation's position paper, "A National Program to Preserve and Expand Banking and Credit in Low-Income Communities."[603] The federation's five-point plan included:

1. A three-year moratorium on liquidation or forced mergers of low-income or minority credit unions
2. A three-year program of chartering new credit unions
3. Repealing regulatory restrictions on nonmember (philanthropic and other) deposits
4. Encouraging the extension of low-income designation—and with it, the ability to accept nonmember deposits— to additional minority institutions
5. Establishing the "National Neighborhood Finance Corporation" to "support and expand nonprofit financial institutions (especially credit unions and loan funds) which specialize in serving low-income communities." The corporation would be established through a $1 billion trust fund and would attract Community Reinvestment Act and Bank Enterprise Act award contributions and investments from financial institutions.

## Needed: A Secondary Market

Frank Altman, president of the nonprofit Community Reinvestment Fund (CRF), described his unique, emerging CDFI as striving "to demonstrate and hopefully operate on an ongoing basis a secondary market for community and economic development loans." CRF's business was "purchasing economic and community development loans from public agencies, private nonprofit revolving loan funds, and banks and bank lending consortia whose lending is for charitable purposes"; its clients included "even a community development credit union on the north side of Chicago."[604] Philanthropy played a critical role in making this possible, he testified, but it was not enough: CRF "relies heavily on foundations to capitalize its Credit Reserve Fund… [but] unless other sources of credit enhancement can be found, CRF's growth will be constrained."[605] Altman was concerned with facilitating bank investment in entities like his: "While banks must play a central role in financing community development, they cannot be expected to assume the role of risk-capital provider, particularly in light of the losses experienced in the thrift and banking industries, or to subsidize interest costs—the Community Reinvestment Act notwithstanding."[606] He called on Congress to "enact a pilot program to develop appropriate, limited federal credit enhancements for secondary market instruments such as those offered by CRF."[607]

## Philanthropy

Paul Lingenfelter, of the John D. and Catherine T. MacArthur Foundation, provided a short course in the theory and practice of Program-Related Investments (PRIs). The Ford Foundation had led the PRI field for 20 years, and remained the largest, with about $150 million in PRIs. Few foundations had followed: "Most of them are intimidated for some reason or maybe they simply have a grant making culture that finds it difficult to believe that a loan could do even more good."[608] In contrast, he wrote, MacArthur had learned from Ford's experience and was working with Ford and other foundations to spread the PRI strategy.

The MacArthur Foundation, with $3 billion in assets, had a six-year history of PRIs. Its portfolio was a "who's who" of the young CDFI field. The foundation had provided equity capital, long-term debt, and deposits for institutions including South Shore, Southern Development Bancorporation, and CDCUs around the country; it had funded pre-development, bridge loans, and home improvement loans to organizations like LISC, Enterprise, LIHF, the Housing Assistance Council, and NHS of America. No loans were delinquent on principal or interest payments, and the cumulative losses out of a $50 million portfolio were only $300,000 from two loans. "We are pleased with the financial performance of our PRIs," which yield on average 3.5–4 percent, "but we are even more pleased with the programmatic returns from our investments."[609]

Although acknowledging that MacArthur's history of PRIs was too brief to draw definitive conclusions, Lingenfelter noted that the foundation was sufficiently pleased with the program that it was planning to expand its portfolio by $7–10 million a year. He refuted the notion that PRIs were either "a stingy grant or a soft loan"; rather, they were "a serious effort to use capital to create public goods. We consider both the philanthropic and the financial goals of equal importance."

Lingenfelter focused on the key constraint on CDFIs: "The development lending institutions that we have supported…are hampered by the lack of permanent capital. I think all of us with a stake in their work should be thinking about ways of endowing economic and community development institutions, just as in the society we have endowed hospitals and educational institutions."[610] His written testimony emphasized "the need for permanently capitalized economic development institutions."

He noted that many PRI borrowers carried a large amount of debt, "and it would be intolerable without patient creditors.... These organizations need permanent capital and more actively involved social investors in order to achieve greater flexibility for lending and greater liquidity for investors." CDFIs should not be expected to solve the problem of capital access for distressed communities alone; there would be a continuing need for CRA, the Low-Income Housing Tax Credit, federal Urban Development Action Grants, and other public funds. "Private foundation PRIs have helped substitute for the lack of permanent capital.... This has been a useful role, but PRIs have no meaningful function without these other sources of significant capital. Currently such programs are being threatened or curtailed due to budgetary pressures and regulatory concerns. They need to be continued and expanded."[611]

## Dialogue: Lending, Regulators, Structures, Capital

As legislators were learning about the variety of CDFIs, they focused on questions about lending standards, portfolio performance, and the stance of regulators. The panel posed a key question to Mary Houghton: "Are South Shore's credit/underwriting standards lower than those of other commercial banks? If so, does this result in criticism from regulators?" She assured the subcommittee that the bank's underwriting standards were not lower than its peers, stating that "net loan losses have generally been the same as the national peer group" of banks its size. How was this accomplished? Houghton noted the ability of South Shore's borrowers to figure out how to make a profit. Still, other banks tended to shy away from such borrowers because of high transaction costs.[612]

George Surgeon responded that Southern Development Bank could make loans that other banks were unwilling to, because it tried to "box the risk" through technical assistance loan guarantees.[613] He explained the different loss rates among various affiliated companies: Its small business investment company (SBIC), Southern Ventures, Inc., which specialized in venture capital and equity investments, was responsible for most of Southern's development investment losses, which amounted to 3.1 percent on $14.1 million invested. In contrast, Elk Horn Bank had lost less than 1 percent on its development loans. The bank, and Southern in general, "are both profitable," he wrote, and its profit outlook for 1992 was good—possibly even a "record year."[614]

Other CDFIs cited comparable performance. Jeremy Nowak testified that the aggregate loss rate for community development loan funds was less than 1 percent, while his own institution had not suffered a single loan default. "That is incredible," remarked subcommittee chairman Erdreich.[615] Ron Phillips, of Coastal Enterprises, Inc. in Maine, acknowledged a somewhat higher default rate: "just under 5 percent.... I think losing money is a cost of our business and we ought to face it and face it very gallantly."[616] Santa Cruz Community Credit Union reported losses of less than 1 percent.

The subcommittees tried to understand the differences between regulated institutions—i.e., banks and credit unions—and nonprofit community development revolving funds. As Nowak explained, although the Delaware Valley Community Reinvestment Fund fell under nonprofit law and state securities law, "we are not regulated in the sense that a bank or credit union is regulated in the sense that someone comes around and says you have got to expense this amount for loss reserves or your capital asset ratio has to be this much… We have, however, shown that we can self-regulate."[617] When the committees remarked upon Delaware Valley's capital ratio of 11 percent—about twice that of banks—Nowak responded: "Honest self-regulation forces you to ask tough questions…. Capital levels and reserve levels…are based on an internal assessment of asset valuation and risk tolerance."[618]

Houghton claimed that South Shore "[does] not suffer from excessive scrutiny from regulators," because South Shore's capital ratio, loan portfolio, and earnings were good. Moreover, she lavished praise on the Federal Reserve Board, which had been "exceptionally helpful…. If the regulators were all more like the Federal Reserve, that would be one thing" that could help community development banks.[619] It was not the examiners that were the problem, Surgeon added, but the regulatory burden: Banking rules were becoming more difficult through greater appraisal requirements, lender and environmental liability, and other regulations.[620] Regarding credit unions, Jeff Wells presented a list of regulatory issues in NCUA's examination practice, policies, and regulations. Frank Altman's complaint was not with regulations per se, but rather the policies of agencies in preventing local loan funds from selling their loans to CRF.

Chairman Erdreich probed to understand the relationship and differences between ShoreBank and Southern Development. Surgeon replied that Southern was entirely independent of ShoreBank; its mindset or "attitude" was its main borrowing from ShoreBank, while "the programs that we are running in rural Arkansas are actually borrowed or modeled after programs in Europe and in some Third World countries more than those in the South Shore Bank of Chicago."[621] Although Southern Development's nonprofit arm, the Arkansas Enterprise Group, did not generate sufficient earnings to meet operating expenses and fuel growth, Surgeon testified that "Elk Horn Bank does not absorb any of the operating costs of its affiliated companies, nor has the Bank made any loans to any of its 'direct' affiliates."[622]

The witnesses widely agreed that there was no universal model for meeting community development needs. Surgeon put it this way.

> Economic development in low- and moderate-income communities requires a multi-dimensional strategy utilizing the resources of financial institutions, local and federal government agencies, and nonprofit community organizations and intermediaries. There is no 'silver bullet' that will cure the ills of our inner city or struggling rural communities.[623]

The subcommittees inquired whether additional investment vehicles might be formed to stimulate development lending. Lingenfelter noted that "the only option with security is a federally insured deposit in a community development credit union or bank such as South Shore bank, and most people lack the information needed to make such deposits even if they were prepared to spend the time and trouble it would take to do so."[624] He suggested exploring changes that might make it possible for people to invest a portion of their retirement funds through a mutual fund, for example.

Subcommittee chairman Carper inquired about trends in funding CDFIs. Nowak responded that investments in loan funds from religious institutions and individuals had remained stable, and that corporations were looking increasingly to intermediaries. Although Delaware Valley was about to get a $1 million investment from Metropolitan Life, he noted that insurance companies "don't have the institutional will to invest in CDCs or loan funds because CRA did not apply."[625] The subcommittee chairs wondered whether the lack of an independent source of funds, like deposits, would constrain unregulated community development loan funds. Nowak replied that "growing loan funds into depository institutions is clearly a key institutional challenge over the next 5–10 years."[626]

## The Pitch: What Federal Role?

When questioned about existing demand versus capacity, Gail Snowden claimed her bank's resources were adequate; however, she repeated her pitch to fund the Bank Enterprise Act with $50 million or $100 million. Her issue was not available resources, but rather the tension between satisfying CRA and safety-and-soundness examination standards. In contrast, Houghton and Surgeon stressed the magnitude of the work they faced with limited resources, and they urged support for the draft community development banking legislation that was working its way through the Senate Banking Committee. Surgeon suggested that

> [it] would be a model program…available for direct equity investments by a new government agency, or maybe it would be by an existing agency, into community development banks across the country. Those funds would have to be leveraged with private equity capital with the idea of creating more development banks in other parts of the country.

He went on to describe the tremendous challenge of covering much of rural Arkansas—"to get out there like I was, and get stuck in the piney woods, is no fun."[627]

Ron Phillips, rather than supporting the community development banking legislation or the Bank Enterprise Act, urged support for a Senate bill (S. 1866) to support community development corporations: the National Community Economic Partnership Act. Asked about an independent funding base like deposits for loan funds, he took the question in another direction, with possible implications for the establishment of a federal CDFI Fund, agreeing that "an independent funding source could be an attractive addition… [but] expanded funding among existing federal agencies would be more immediate and practical." He enthusiastically endorsed the Farmers Home Administration (FmHA) Intermediary Relending Program and cited the SBA Micro Loan Program, which was just getting off the ground, but which he found expensive at the borrowing rate of 6.75 percent.[628]

## Key Messages for Congress

The subcommittee members had heard that CDFIs improbably seemed to be serving a population banks didn't want with loss rates as low as 1 percent. There were multiple types of CDFIs—not only banks—and different communities might be best served by different types of CDFIs. CDFIs could not do the job alone; public and private support—including from banks—would still be needed. There were problems with existing regulatory constraints (especially for low-income credit unions), but there was no call for a new type of charter.

Were the subcommittee members convinced by what they heard? At a minimum, they were intrigued. If community development banking were to achieve a legislative victory, a change in perspective, such as Democratic Rep. Moran of Virginia offered, would be crucial:

> I think this is fascinating. It is this kind of idealistic effort that we normally would suspect is never going to work and, in fact, we have some real live models of it working, and I can't help but find myself somewhat skeptical, but you have clearly documented a success that can be applied to other efforts.... You are a catalyst, clearly, the kind of catalyst for change in depressed urban and rural communities that is necessary throughout the country.[629]

Chairman Carper added, "What we are hearing from you is one of the most encouraging testimonies that I have come across in my 10 years as a member of the House of Representatives."[630]

## The First Community Development Banking Bill

In the waning weeks of summer 1992, versions of a community development banking bill passed the House and Senate in turn. On August 5, the bill passed the House, and on September 10, with certain changes, the bill made it through the Senate on a voice vote. A conference report resolving differences between the House and Senate versions was agreed to by the House on October 5, and by the Senate on October 8, again by voice vote.[631] On October 28, 1992, Congress enacted Public Law 102-550: the "Housing and Community Development Act of 1992." Senator Riegle was its chief sponsor.

The voluminous bill encompassed a host of housing-related issues: housing assistance, public housing, preservation of low-income housing, mortgage insurance and the secondary market, housing for the elderly and persons with disabilities, community development block grants, and more. Its Title VIII, Community Development, contained "Subtitle C—Miscellaneous Programs" (Sec. 853). Among these miscellanies was the "Community Investment Corporation Demonstration." The South Central riots were addressed in funding for "Emergency Assistance for Los Angeles" (Sec. 854).[632]

The purpose of the act was to "improve access to capital for initiatives which benefit residents and businesses in targeted geographic areas; and ... test new models for bringing credit and investment capital…through the provision of assistance for capital, development services, and technical assistance."[633] The federal government "needs to develop new models for facilitating local revitalization activities; [and] indigenous community-based financial institutions play a significant role in identifying and responding to community needs."[634] Four specific examples were mentioned: South Shore Bank, Southern Development Bancorporation, the Center for Community Self-Help, and Community Capital Bank.

Although the law, as framed, was couched as "community investment corporation[s]" rather than "banks" for political considerations, eligible recipients included depository-institution holding companies and nonprofit organizations that were "affiliated with a nondepository lending institution; or …affiliated with a regulated financial institution but …not a subsidiary therof."[635] Banks and federally insured credit unions were included. Applicants had to have a primary mission of revitalizing an area, maintaining "through significant representation on its governing board and otherwise, accountability to community residents."[636] The corporations were to match federal assistance dollar-for-dollar with nonfederal funds.

As to the form of assistance, "equity" meant nonvoting common stock, equity grants, or contributions to capital reserves or surplus; depository-institution holding companies were eligible for loans, and nonprofits were eligible for grants or loans.[637] Recipients were expected to demonstrate capacity, comprehensiveness, extent of need, background of the principals, and past success; there was to be "an appropriate distribution of eligible organizations among regions of the United States."[638] The law authorized $25 million for FY 1993 and $26 million for FY 1994 for capital assistance. There were separate authorizations for development services and technical assistance ($15 million for FY 1993 and $15.6 million for FY 1994) and for a training program ($2 million for FY 1993 and $2.1 million for FY 1994).

## A Joyless Signing

On October 28, 1992, President George Bush issued a "Statement on Signing the Housing and Community Development Act of 1992." He noted approvingly changes to the regulatory structure of government-sponsored enterprises (GSEs), the money laundering provision, and regulatory relief for depositories. He regretted, however, "that the Congress chose to attach these important reforms to a housing bill that contains numerous provisions that raise serious concerns," especially alleged "constitutional difficulties" that touch on HUD.[639] Nothing was mentioned about community development banking.

The act's Community Investment Corporation Demonstration (CICD) would live a short but fruitful life. Within two weeks, the Bush presidency would enter its twilight, as Governor Bill Clinton was elected on November 8—and with him, a commitment to make community development banking a reality. The Clinton campaign had set forth a vision in broad terms; Senator Riegle's CICD program provided a template for the newborn Clinton administration to work with. It had the further considerable advantage, as Jeannine Jacokes has noted, that "we had already proven that the proposal could get bipartisan support."[640]

# CHAPTER 11. On the Campaign Trail

While Congress was formulating various modest proposals to direct more capital to disadvantaged communities, candidate Bill Clinton was formulating his own, more expansive vision.

The Clinton presidential campaign of 1992 was unlike any other. On June 3—the day after he secured his nomination—Bill Clinton in his wraparound sunglasses played Elvis Presley's "Heartbreak Hotel" on his tenor saxophone in an appearance on the late-night Arsenio Hall television show. Interviewed by Hall, he spoke of his long involvement with the nation's critical urban issues. South Central Los Angeles was on his mind.

> I'm talking about things in this election that I've been working on for years, that I really care about. I was in South Central LA three years before the riot occurred.... I gave a speech three years ago and I asked to go to South Central LA and meet with people from…those community organizations, because I could see how terrible it was, and how things could get out of hand.

In the 1990s, he continued, "This whole business of economic empowerment has got to be at the center of the civil rights movement."[641]

On June 16, Clinton was interviewed on MTV, with a live audience of some 200, mostly young people, 18 to 24 years old, many who were attending colleges in the Los Angeles area. Planned for 60 minutes, the interview ran to 90, as Gwen Ifill reported to the *New York Times*, and "continued even when the taping stopped for commercial breaks and other delays, cover[ing] a range of subjects, including deficit reduction, environmental protection and abortion rights."[642]

Clinton was deliberately reaching out to the audiences and demographics that were beyond the reach of the incumbent president, George H.W. Bush; as one reporter wrote in the *New York Times*, "Mr. Bush might well have thought Arsenio Hall was a building at Andover."[643] Clinton's stops along the campaign trail included South Shore Bank in Chicago and a community development organization, Common Ground, in Dallas. Along the way, he communicated his vision for community development banking, delivering a message that had never been heard from a presidential candidate.

The Clinton campaign had prepared a book-length document, *Putting People First*, that outlined the range of policy proposals that would guide the Clinton administration. In one section, "Investing in Communities," Clinton called for the creation of "a *nationwide network of community development banks* [emphasis in original] to provide small loans to low-income entrepreneurs and homeowners in the inner cities." In July, as the Democratic Party formally nominated Clinton, it issued a platform, entitled "A New Covenant with the American People," which proclaimed a "new partnership to rebuild America's cities after 12 years of Republican neglect." It laid out, side by side, two policies that would advance in tandem in the early months of the Clinton presidency.

> While cracking down on redlining and housing discrimination, we also support and will enforce a revitalized Community Reinvestment Act that challenges banks to lend to entrepreneurs and development projects; a national network of Community Development Banks to invest in urban and rural small businesses; and microenterprise lending for poor people seeking self-employment as an alternative to welfare.[644]

This linked approach—community development banking and a new, improved CRA—would remain integral to Clinton's approach.

With fewer than 60 days until election day, the Clinton campaign amplified his plan for community development banking. On September 16, the campaign issued a press release, "Creating Jobs, Helping Entrepreneurs and Building Communities. The Clinton/Gore Community Development Plan."[645] The press release and fact sheet, which referred back to Clinton's economic strategy, *Putting People First*, spelled out in somewhat greater detail what Clinton had in mind.

- Create a national network of *100 community development banks and 1,000 microenterprise programs* [emphasis in original] to provide capital and technical assistance to individuals who want to start or expand small businesses and help revitalize communities....
- Strengthen the *Community Reinvestment Act* [emphasis in original] to emphasize performance over paperwork and stop the practice of 'redlining' in economically disadvantaged communities [emphasis in original].[646]

Although the "credit crunch" for small businesses was a prime driver of the community development banking plank—"Small businesses are the key to vital communities"—the campaign's fact sheet noted that community development banks "lend for the community's housing and commercial space needs."[647]

The scope of the program envisioned "enough grants to adequately capitalize 100 community development banks," all of which would be required to obtain a match through charitable or equity investments; money would be distributed on a competitive basis. Critically important, the plan envisioned allowing "commercial banks to fulfill a *small portion* [emphasis added] of their Community Reinvestment Act requirements by depositing money directly in community development banks."

Structurally, Clinton's notion of a community development bank was considerably narrower than that of the emerging CDFI movement, and narrower than what would later emerge from policy discussions. As described in the campaign's fact sheet:

> There are several models for community development banks. Those currently operating are generally holding companies consisting of several subsidiaries, including a

federal depository institution providing traditional banking services, a for-profit real estate development company, an SBA-approved small business development investment company, and one or more non-profits that provide development services such as business counseling or job training.[648]

At the time, of course, there was a grand total of three community development banks: ShoreBank, Southern Development, and Community Capital Bank. ShoreBank and Southern did have holding companies that resembled Clinton's description; Community Capital Bank in Brooklyn did not, although it had one nonprofit affiliate, LEAP. Among nonbanks, only Self-Help had a structure and lending approach that resembled the three community development banks.

Bill Clinton was personally familiar with community development banks and microenterprise funds, but he was not familiar with the potential role of credit unions. Martin Eakes, of Self-Help, set out to broaden his vision.

> I remember following Bill Clinton from campaign stop to campaign stop in 1992, getting someone at each stop to ask him questions about Self-Help Credit Union as a model for his Development Banking agenda. This was when we were fearful that the ShoreBank connections in Arkansas would narrow his program to banks only. By the end of the campaign, he was routinely talking about ShoreBank AND Self-Help, which we thought was important to opening up the eligibility gateway.[649]

The Clinton campaign's understanding of microenterprise programs was for enterprises that served businesses with "five or fewer employees, with owners that have incomes no higher than twice the poverty level."[650] Although the loans were "not profitable for commercial banks because they are small and don't net big gains," they were vital, "especially for people on welfare who are trying to fulfill the American Dream and start a business." The plan specifically envisioned a model like that pioneered by Grameen Bank and used by the Good Faith Fund in Arkansas: "Competitors will have to show that they can…set up peer groups effectively."[651] Thoughtfully, the plan aimed to ensure that self-employment training would be provided through federal programs.

## On the Cover of Rolling Stone

> I have just returned… as you know, from a top-secret *Issues Conference* in Little Rock with our high-riding Candidate, Bill Clinton…the only living depositor in the Grameen Bank of Bangladesh who wears a Rolling Stone T-shirt when he jogs past the hedges at sundown.
>
> Hunter Thompson[652]

## Chapter 11. On the Campaign Trail

On September 17, "The *Rolling Stone* Interview: Bill Clinton," hit the newsstands, some six weeks before the election. This was not *Time*, nor *Newsweek*, nor the *New York Times*: It was a mass, popular publication, read more faithfully by rock-and-roll enthusiasts than "serious" policy students. It was more evidence of Clinton's genius for reaching out to different demographics, as he did with television variety and talk shows where he demonstrated his (middling) saxophone expertise. In the lengthy article, he gave the back story and his vision for community development banking.

The interview had been conducted weeks earlier, in late July, at Doe's Eat Place in downtown Little Rock, AR. Of the three interviewers, William Greider was the expert on the financial system. Greider had written extensively about the S&L bailout and, voluminously, about the Federal Reserve System in his groundbreaking 1987 best-seller, *Secrets of the Temple*. Greider remarked, "You've staked out a very different idea of a banking system, very different from what anybody—either Democrat or Republican—has been talking about for the last fifteen or twenty years." Clinton responded, "I think every major urban area and every poor rural area ought to have access to a bank that operates on the radical idea that they ought to make loans to people who deposit in their bank."

Clinton went on to cite South Shore, Southern Development Bank in Arkansas, and the "vast markets for all kinds of small businesses in a place like South Central Los Angeles that could be owned and operated by the people who live there." He was especially inspired by the Grameen Bank and Muhammad Yunus—"I think Muhammad Yunus should be given a Nobel Prize"*—and went on to describe the Good Faith Fund in Arkansas, a peer-group microenterprise fund operating under Southern Development Bank's umbrella. Clinton had become acquainted with Yunus through a college friend of Hillary's.[653] In Arkansas, he said, "the South Shore Bank's Good Faith Fund [sic]—loans to real low-income people, mostly for self-employment ventures—was based on the work of Muhammad Yunus at the Grameen Bank, in Bangladesh."[654] Clinton had met Yunus himself in Washington and spent 90 minutes with him. He recalled:

> I was just blown away. It was obvious what the parallels were. He made enterprise work. He promoted independence, not dependence. The idea struck me that whenever the power of the government can be used to create market forces that work, it's so much better than creating a bureaucracy to hire a bunch of full-time people to give somebody a check. I mean, I just loved it. I loved it.[655]

Community development banks were not a poll-tested, focus-group-analyzed plank tossed onto the Democratic platform. These singular institutions were an informed passion of Bill Clinton—and not incidentally, one that had equally engaged Hillary Clinton, who had assisted the Southern Development Bank and the Good Faith Fund in Arkansas.

On November 3, 1992, the unlikely candidacy of Governor Bill Clinton was consummated with a victory over incumbent President George H.W. Bush and an independent candidate, Ross Perot.

---

\* In fact, Yunus won the Nobel Prize in 2006.

Eighteen months before, in March 1991, after the first Persian Gulf War rapidly ousted Iraqi forces from Kuwait, Bush's approval rating in a Gallup poll was the highest a president had ever received: 89 percent. By summer 1992, it was 29 percent. The economy was nearly two years into a recession. The Clinton campaign's mantra—"It's the economy, stupid"—had guided it to victory.

# CHAPTER 12. Transition

On October 28, a week before Clinton's election, his predecessor signed into law a prototype for community development banking legislation, the Community Investment Corporation Demonstration (CICD). Within days of Clinton's victory, the process of creating a CDFI Fund moved into high gear. Three sets of actors would shape the emergence of the fund: the Clinton administration; Congress, especially the Senate Banking Committee; and the CDFI movement, in the form of the CDFI Coalition.

The CDFI Coalition, formalized and with a defined platform, increased its visits to Washington, seeking to influence both Congress and the Clinton administration. The Clinton Transition Team was charged with translating campaign rhetoric into actionable Washington strategy. Meanwhile, the Senate Banking Committee worked on shaping a legislative initiative that drew on the recently passed CICD, as well as a year's worth of input from CDFIs.

## The Senate's Questions

The Clinton platform presented a vision—a sketch rather than a blueprint. The hard work of actually *designing* a major "community development banking" program now began. The Senate Banking Committee had spent many months learning from CDFIs themselves about their realities and aspirations. The committee had organized a staff symposium on affordable credit in low-income communities, held hearings, and corresponded with various CDFIs individually. On November 9, days after the election, Banking Committee staffers Matt Roberts, Jeannine Jacokes, Rick Carnell, and Konrad Alt faxed a memorandum to "experts on community development banking." The six-page compendium of detailed questions went to CDFI leaders, advocacy groups, bankers and their associations, and the Clinton Transition Team.[656] In the memo, the committee framed broad policy concerns amplified by numerous specific questions.

- Feasibility: Was it realistic to create 100 community development banks in four years, as Clinton envisioned?
- Definition: What did it take to be a "community development bank"? What activities and institutional models should characterize these institutions? Was it necessary that they replicate the holding company model of ShoreBank or Southern?

- Regulation: Should there be a special charter for community development banks? What agency or agencies should administer the program?
- Financial assistance: Was matching private capital available? What form should government assistance take? Should community development banks be permitted to be either for-profit or nonprofit? Would continuing operating subsidies be required?
- Other assistance: Other than capital and operating assistance, what sort of aid would be needed? How much expertise existed, and how should more be developed?
- Relationship to other community development efforts: How could this new program avoid diminishing or duplicating the efforts of existing traditional lenders?

If this was "sausage making," as the legislative process is often picturesquely described, it was carried out with careful attention to ingredients and preparation. It required both CDFIs and the administration to work assiduously to flesh out the inspiring vision of "100 community development banks and 1,000 microenterprise programs."

Various leading CDFI organizations responded to the Senate Banking Committee's call for information. Their responses, although not centrally coordinated, were basically aligned on key points that would become the core principles of the CDFI movement

## Community Capital Bank: Startup Challenges, Structural Issues, Chartering

Community Capital Bank of Brooklyn was one of the named institutions in the Riegle CICD bill—one of only three operating community development banks in the country. Lyndon Comstock had spent some five years organizing the bank and was uniquely qualified to address "a network of 100 community development banks" from scratch. In a memo dated November 20, 1992, he drew on his own experience to extrapolate the cost and feasibility of establishing 100 community development banks.

> The organizing process for a bank is complex, difficult, and not widely understood.... To give a sense of the enormous effort that this type of equity raising can require, the paid organizing staff at Community Capital Bank spent approximately one person-year per million dollars of equity raised, not counting the volunteer help from the board of directors, advisory board, and others. At Community Capital, the minimum equity requirement was $6 million.

Comstock noted, as well, the scarcity of management talent available to engage in this "new" kind of banking. He estimated that realistically, "an additional 15 actual new community development banks in the United States over the next four years [would] be a major, major accomplishment"; perhaps the figure of 100 could be reached by existing institutions (including, but not only, minority banks) redefining their missions. Comstock thus added a dollars-and-cents argument to reinforce a concern of the various CDFIs: A community development banking initiative should build upon the hundreds of existing institutions.

Comstock's experience led him to question Clinton's emphasis on the bank holding company structure, which the candidate viewed as a defining characteristic of ShoreBank and Southern Development Bancorporation.

> Presumably because ShoreBank Corporation and Southern Development Bancorporation are both holding company models, the plan put forward by President-elect Clinton calls for the use of a bank holding company model for new community development banks. The Community Investment Corporation Demonstration Act signed into law earlier this month…follows a similar logic, and defines an 'eligible organization' as a bank holding company or a specialized type of nonprofit.
>
> In my comments on the draft version of [the CICD] legislation, I suggested this approach was a mistake, and I still hold that view. Two of the four models that are cited…namely Community Capital Bank and the Center for Community Self-Help, are not bank holding companies. Community Capital Bank does not even qualify as an eligible organization under the statute(!), and it's not clear to me whether Center for Community Self-Help does either.[657]

The Senate Banking Committee correctly understood that capital alone was insufficient to address the unmet needs of community development bank borrowers, who typically required technical assistance in management, financial planning, and more. But, Comstock argued, it was not necessary to add complexity by launching holding companies: The necessary services could and should be delivered without that further step. Community Capital Bank had addressed the need for supportive "development" services by establishing an affiliated nonprofit, LEAP, Inc., without implementing a holding company.

Comstock and others specifically rejected the notion of creating a special federal charter for a community development bank.

> There may be situations where a special charter would be helpful, on a case-by-case basis. For example, a regional entity could be created to help channel capital to local CDFIs in a low-income region…. In general, however, I think that creation of a new category of federally chartered institution called a 'community development bank' would be a mistake…. I'm inclined to believe that a new class of charter called a 'community development bank' would rapidly become a second-class charter. The three existing commercial banks that are devoted to community development, South Shore, Elk Horn, and Community Capital, have demonstrated their value while operating under the same regulatory framework as all other commercial banks.[658]

Although Community Capital Bank had an advantage—it was already a full-fledged community development bank, and it had been cited in legislation and in Clinton's policy papers—Comstock rejected the notion of restricting the proposed CDFI Fund to banks like his own. He argued emphatically that "support be made available to all categories of CDFIs, not just community development banks, and that ... assistance be provided to *existing* [emphasis in original] community development financial intermediaries, and not just newly created CDFIs."[659] Moreover, he urged consideration for other emerging types of CDFIs, including "venture development organizations." ("Community development venture capital" funds had not yet been christened.)

## Self-Help: Depositories, Inclusiveness, Underwriting Independence, Incremental Funding

The Center for Community Self-Help in Durham, NC, was one of the four institutions cited in the Riegle CICD legislation. It described itself as a "statewide development bank," although it was not, in fact, a bank in the legal sense. Rather, it was an organization composed of nonprofits alongside a state-chartered credit union. This was the model that Self-Help advocated.

> The structure of a full-fledged community development banking institution should combine an insured depository entity with one or more non-profit entities. The depository entity—whether a commercial bank, a credit union, an S&L, or a savings bank—serves as the financial engine for the development bank.... The non-profit entity or entities—whether a revolving loan fund, micro-lending program, community development corporation, or technical assistance affiliate—are able to receive subsidy in the form of grants for operations and capital.[660]

By gathering philanthropic and other capital, the entity would be able to undertake higher-cost or higher-risk programs and lending, conduct research and development, and more effectively engage commercial banks in community development. As to the form of depository, Self-Help was partial to the community development credit union (CDCU) model, because such institutions afford "additional assurances of long-term adherence to a CDB mission." But the key point was that there be a regulated, insured depository of some kind.

Self-Help's structure had enhanced its ability to use public credit enhancement programs, access secondary markets, and leverage development credit from traditional lenders. One notable success: Self-Help had obtained significant appropriations from the North Carolina state legislature—$6 million since 1988—to promote ownership of businesses and homes for low-income and minority communities across the state. Accordingly, it suggested that "state governments are potential large-scale investors in [community development banks]."[661]

Self-Help agreed that a program limited to banks would never achieve the Clinton administration's goal:

> We believe a strategy to build CDBs [community development banks] must be very *inclusive* [emphasis in original]. It must include CDBs based around credit unions as well as banks. It must include assistance to organizations that are not now full-fledged CDBs, but have potential to become CDBs.... Only through such an inclusive approach is the goal of 100 development banks feasible.[662]

Self-Help's memo laid out various scenarios for infusing assistance into existing depositories, non-depository lenders, CDCUs, and community development corporations, among others. It strongly emphasized "an inclusive, incremental, performance-based strategy.... One trap is the danger that a large number of community development banking experiments will fail, discrediting the strategy.... [An incremental strategy] should also help avoid the overly rapid growth that we believe could be dangerous for the field."[663] At the same time, Self-Help pointed out the dangers of a federal program "micro-managing" the investment and lending activities of community development banks, by requiring federal sign-offs on loans or imposing uniform underwriting guidelines.

If its recommendations were followed—incremental funding, agnosticism with respect to institutional type but favoring a compound depository/nonprofit structure—Self-Help believed the emerging CDFI program could "result in as many as 50 full-fledged community development banks within four years."[664]

## CDCUs: Structuring a Fund, Addressing Banking Deficits

For half-dozen years, the National Federation of CDCUs had promoted the concept of a CDFI Fund in various forms, while also pressing for concerns specific to low-income credit unions. On July 9, 1992, during the campaign, it had circulated the latest version of its concept paper, "The National Neighborhood Finance Corporation (NNFC)," to the Senate Banking staff and others. More than its CDFI colleagues, the National Federation emphasized bank branch closings and the lack of financial access in poverty communities, like South Central Los Angeles, where the federation had been working intensively with local groups to start a new CDCU. The NNFC was needed to address "problems which we believe have proven resistant to CRA mandates"[665]; however, this should by no means relieve banks of CRA responsibilities.

The federation envisioned a new entity that would support an "infrastructure of community-owned financial institutions" across the country: CDCUs and community development loan funds would become the "new bankers" in low-income neighborhoods. The proposed entity could parallel the Neighborhood Reinvestment Corporation, with its nationwide network of Neighborhood Housing Service organizations. To avoid the need for annual appropriations, the federation called on Congress to create a $1 billion trust fund, mixed-ownership or quasi-governmental in form, which would be self-sustaining through annual interest received (estimated at $50 million annually). It would be supplemented by contributions and investments from banks, which would receive credit under CRA and the Bank Enterprise Act of 1991.

By fall 1992, after passage of the Riegle CICD legislation, the election, and the intensifying dialogue among CDFI leaders, the federation refined its thinking. On December 4, 1992, it submitted a response to the Banking Committee's questions in a memo entitled "Community Development Banking: The Credit Union Option." The memo repeatedly cited Self-Help, one of the federation's most prominent members: Specifically, it proposed $10 million in capital "to create 10 full-fledged community development banks based on the CDCU+nonprofit model pioneered by Self Help." Moreover, the federation urged providing $20 million capital to 200 CDCUs "that will be… the next wave of full-fledged Self-Help-style development banks."[666] Finally, it asked for a $10 million increase in the Community Development Revolving Loan Program for Credit Unions, the fund the federation had fought for throughout the 1970s and 1980s.

At this point, the Federation "strongly support[ed] the Bank Enterprise Act (the 'Greenlining Bill'), which proposed that banks pay reduced deposit insurance premiums if they make investments in certain CDFIs."* Another source of capital, the federation suggested, could come from tax deductions provided to investors who made below-market deposits in CDCUs and other CDFIs.

Like its colleagues, the federation argued that the Clinton administration could meet its goal only if it built on existing institutions. There were 400 CDCUs across the country that had been providing financial services and loans to poor people for decades. These were a proven, effective base for a new wave of community development banks. Like Self-Help, the federation estimated that 50 "showcase" institutions along the Self-Help credit union/loan fund model could be created in four years. The federation echoed the key needs identified by its colleagues: equity capital, human capital, and removing regulatory barriers that impeded the proliferation of CDFIs.[667]

## The Loan Fund View: Not Just for Small Business; Levying the Financial System

NACDLF confined its initial comments to a preliminary memo of November 18, believing "it would be premature to advance our specific agenda before discussing it with our colleagues."[668] It highlighted certain key concerns.
- The program should *not* be "primarily, if not entirely, business oriented"—as the Clinton platform seemed to suggest—but should address a range of credit needs.
- Other sources besides federal grants would be required.
- There should be an explicit commitment that credit would be, and would remain, affordable.

---

\* The federation's position and that of other CDFIs would later change when a portion of the CDFI appropriation was diverted to the BEA.

- A CDFI program should recognize that community development lending was not necessarily more risky than other lending, if properly executed.

However, NACDLF adopted a broader, more aggressive approach than its colleagues in demanding that the conventional financial system bear the costs of supporting a community development banking network. NACDLF linked funding for a new CDFI Fund to the S&L bailout, as well as the CRA. Equity, it asserted, should be derived from
- Congressional appropriations
- A percentage recapture levy on the profits and/or appreciation of, for example, bailed-out S&Ls, merged commercial banks, and Resolution Trust corporation properties
- A *quid pro quo* for any federal help to conventional financial institutions
- The end product of all negotiated CRA challenge settlements.[669]

To address the need for long-term, below-market capital, NACDLF proposed that individuals receive tax-free treatment for below-market investments in CDFIs, and that "financial institutions that receive and/or profit from public subsidies, guarantees, or contracts make available .05 percent of their total assets as long-term, below-market loans to community development financial institutions or to participation pools managed by these entities."[670]

## The Coalition Goes to Washington

In the weeks following the election, the ad hoc CDFI leadership group that was born in Trinity Church's library coalesced into a more formal coalition. It understood that achieving its goal in Washington would require the diverse group—banks, credit unions, loan funds—to speak with one voice. If they needed any additional impetus to develop a unified "industry" approach, it came from the foundation community. Early in November, Greg Ratliff of the John D. and Catherine T. MacArthur Foundation, a longtime supporter of CDFIs, asked NACDLF's Martin Trimble for a memo on the group's direction, in preparation for meetings that MacArthur and the Ford Foundation were scheduled to have with Vernon Jordan, the civil rights leader and close adviser of Clinton who headed the transition effort.[671]

On Friday, November 20, at 11:00 a.m., NACDLF convened a meeting of the "Public Purpose Banking Participants" in Washington, DC, at the United Methodist Building. The venue was more than simply convenient: As the only nongovernmental building on Capitol Hill, since the 1930s it had "served as a witness at the center of government power to the church's beliefs—a reminder that the church is concerned for people and all that affects them. Through its halls and in its offices have begun some of the most widespread justice movements of the 20th century."[672] (Moreover, the United Methodist Church was one of the early financial supporters of the CDFI movement.)

The November 20 meeting was convened to review the Clinton plans and begin to shape a long-term public policy agenda for CDFIs.[673] The invited participants included the existing community development banks; the National Federation and NACDLF; individual community development loan funds and microlenders; the microlenders represented by CFED/AEO; and policy advocates, including the Woodstock Institute. Later that day, representatives of the group met in person with Jeannine Jacokes and Matt Roberts of the Senate Banking Committee, exploring such questions as the necessary scale for community development banks; whether CDFIs dealt exclusively with "unbankable" loans; and mainstream bankers' concerns about potential competition and subsidy for community development banks.[674]

## The Transition Gears Up: Roadmap for a Revolution

In December 1992, as Bill Clinton was preparing to take office, the Presidential Transition Domestic Policy Staff emphasized the urgency of an urban initiative.

> When you came back from touring the streets of South Central L.A. in the wake of the riots, you predicted that despite all the media attention, Presidential fanfare, and Congressional breastbeating, a year would pass and nothing in South Central would change. You were right. We must find a way in your Administration to arrest the deterioration of America's great cities and close the gap between the urban poor and the rest of the country.[675]

The staff prepared an ambitious, optimistic document, "The Clinton Revolution: A Domestic Policy Agenda for the First 100 Days."[676] In its chapter on community empowerment, it proposed "three major strategies to restore the American dream to our cities": One was the creation of a network of community development banks; the others called for comprehensive enterprise zones and housing initiatives.

"Of all the ideas you talked about in the campaign," the memo reminded the president, "development banks have perhaps the greatest potential to radically improve conditions in our cities." To achieve this, the policy staff urged "a single independent institution—the National Community Development Trust."[677] An independent entity would be key to the president's vision of "reinventing government." This would rule out placing the trust in the Department of Housing and Urban Development (HUD), which was described as "perhaps the most poorly managed department, [which] would guarantee that HUD's pathetic management ethic would be transferred to your program—perhaps with fatal results." As well, rural constituencies would feel "slighted" by placing the program in HUD. Treasury, on the other hand, would be a logical choice since CDFIs were financial institutions; the downside was that the agency had "no community development orientation."[678]

The administration should seek an authorization of $850 million over five years. There were various options to capitalize CDFIs: capital and technical assistance grants; loans and loan guarantees; membership in the Federal Home Loan Bank System; tax credits for investors in CDFIs; and CRA credit for banks that aided CDFIs.[679] Community development banks would be the preferred structure, but they would require large amounts of capital. The transition staff, like the CDFI leaders, believe that "attempting to build a network of similar institutions in a few short years would be extremely risky." Thus, the staff urged a network that included all the various types of nonbank community institutions: loan funds, CDCUs, CDCs, microenterprise funds, and other nonprofit groups. Still, "the federal program would favor CDBs [community development banks] as the highest form of community development financial institution on the evolutionary chain… [with] the greatest ability to leverage funds, the greatest potential to realize economies of scale, and the ability to attract and retain sophisticated lending and management staff."[680] CDFIs would be encouraged, though not required, to become depositories when they grew sufficiently large and sophisticated.

The staff set a high bar for funding institutions that had a "primary, explicit and very public commitment to community development in a targeted area"; more than 75 percent of an institution's loans and investments would have to be directed to such an area. If they were to succeed, CDFIs would also need to help their borrowers succeed. And as for running the Trust itself, "we suggest tapping members of the ShoreBank and Elk Horn staffs to run and staff the operation."[681]

The transition staff was optimistic about passing a community development banking bill, finding "strong support in Congress for non-traditional community development strategies, and for community development banks in particular." Senator Riegle would be the administration's "strongest backer." CRA was likely to be the most controversial area. Democratic Rep. Barney Frank would potentially oppose subsidies for for-profit institutions (an argument that the transition staff found "a bit specious—obviously, deposit insurance, which every bank receives, is a similar subsidy)."[682]

The presidential transition staff consulted individually with a number of CDFI leaders—Martin Trimble, George Surgeon (Southern Development Bancorporation), Bob Weissbourd (ShoreBank Advisory Services), Bryan Hassel (Self-Help), Sarah Kovner (Community Capital Bank), and me.[683] The transition team's early thinking reflected some of the key concepts of CDFIs themselves. But given the fluid nature of the transition process—and of the CDFI movement itself—the coalition leaders explored every channel possible to establish a direct route to the key policy advisers.

In December, coalition members met with the Brookings Institute, whose Robert Litan was on the Transition Committee. It reached out to federal officials co-opted to work on the team; it got Harvard Law School colleagues of Chris Edley Jr., who was overseeing the Transition Team's work, to relay CDFI requests for an in-person meeting.[684] On December 9, representatives of the coalition met with staff of the Senate Banking Committee to continue their dialogue, then headed over to the nondescript offices of the Transition Team on Connecticut Avenue, NW, a half-mile from the White House, hoping to follow up a faxed request from the National Federation for an in-person meeting with Edley.

We waited and waited, well into the evening; Mark Pinsky, then a consultant to NACDLF, remembered eventually leaving to catch a train home to Philadelphia.[685] Finally, a tall, very young-looking aide, Courtney Ward, emerged and informed the few remaining CDFI leaders that we would not get a meeting that night. To salvage their effort, I and a few members of the CDFI delegation arranged to meet Ward the next morning to present our case.

Ward was on loan from the office of New York Democratic Rep. (later Senator) Charles Schumer, where he worked on banking issues, including the aftermath of the S&L crisis. The Clinton campaign had put forth an abundance of policy proposals. Coming to the Transition Team, as Ward recalled, "you felt like a small fish in a big pond, in the sense that you were tasked with putting together thoughts, ideas, policy approaches.... There were so many issues and topics that they were trying to cover."[686] On December 10, Ward met with representatives of the National Federation and Self-Help.[687] We perceived that CDFI was the center of our universe, although not theirs. Still, Ward was able to provide reassurance on some of our key concerns: Funding would *not* require that the institution be an actual bank, although Clinton liked that structure and saw it as viable ("We don't necessarily seek to favor one type over another"). Partnerships would be encouraged. The administration wanted to emphasize a community role rather than a top-down approach.

Ward pointed out some of the potentially contentious issues and political pitfalls. There was a danger that banks would use the issue to get into a full-scale CRA discussion, but the administration explicitly rejected the notion that CDFI support would provide banks an "out" from CRA obligations. Ward advised us that some Hill players "have their knives sharpened for us. [We need to have] all our ducks in order."[688] On the congressional side, Senator Riegle was the logical person to carry the proposal, but it was necessary that there be a single proposal that all agreed upon, including Democratic Rep. Henry Gonzalez, of Texas, chair of the House Banking Committee.

The CDFI camp was encouraged. Although the incoming administration was far from submitting its own legislation, there did not seem to be any insurmountable obstacles. The path to actual legislation would nonetheless be a long one.

## The Little Rock "Summit"

On December 14–15, the incoming Clinton administration convened an Economic Summit in Little Rock, AR. The event provided a sense of both the style and general direction of its policymaking; as various commenters reported, it did not provide a setting for getting concrete work done. The guest list ranged from a gaggle of economists; to the CEO of Apple Computer, John Sculley; to Marian Wright Edelman, CEO of the Children's Defense Fund (which Hillary Clinton had once worked for); to Brenda Shockley, executive director of Community Build in South Central Los Angeles. Among the 300 invited participants at the televised event was Caryl Stewart, who had worked closely with Vermont Senator Patrick Leahy and was the founder and board chair of the Vermont Development Credit Union, a statewide institution that sought to replicate Self-Help. She was the only credit union participant; Mary Houghton attended, representing ShoreBank.

The "summit" focused on macro-level issues and did not deal specifically with community development banking, although Stewart heard one or two mentions of it. After the event, she submitted a brief concept paper arguing for community development credit unions to play a prominent role in the proposed community development banking initiative.[689] Noting President Clinton's passion for education and early childhood development, she offered the notion that "community development banking can be the 'Head Start' of community economic development."[690]

## Other Visions, Other Interests

The CDFI Coalition members were not the only ones attempting to shape a new community development banking system. Professor Hyman P. Minsky was a prominent progressive economist from the Jerome Levy Economics Institute of Bard College (Annandale-on-Hudson, NY). With his associates, he published papers in December 1992 and January 1993 proposing a community development banking system that was at once larger, more comprehensive, more federally managed, and more attentive to the needs of the lowest income segment and small businesses than some other concepts.[691]

At the heart of Minsky's vision was a Federal Bank for Community Development Banks, to be launched with an initial appropriation of $1 billion. The bank "will combine the functions of a central bank, a correspondent bank, and an investor for the CDBs."[692] It would acquire equity in local community development banks by providing funds to match up to $10 million in private investment. Moreover, it would have regulatory and supervisory power over the local community development banks. The central Federal Bank, as well as the individual community development banks, would be designed to make a profit. Community development banks, Minsky argued, "can be a significant part of a new economic and social environment in which opportunity replaces deprevation [sic], stagnation and despair in urban and rural communities that have been left behind."[693]

Minsky was particularly concerned with two failings of the financial system: the lack of access to business loans smaller than those banks could or would make and the prevalence of for-profit check-cashers in low-income communities. Bank consolidation had fueled a decrease in small community banks, which meant less access to loans for small businesses; community development banks could fill this gap. In low-income communities, he saw check-cashers, which specialized in small transactions, as the foundation for community development banks: Profits from this business could fund other basic banking services, including savings, payment services, and remittances. "An inner-city Community Development Bank may well have a set of store front offices which are service centers where cash checking and supplying money orders are the major businesses."[694] These would be "narrow" banks providing basic services; separate affiliates in a bank holding company structure would provide home mortgages, credit cards, and loans to small businesses.[695]

Robert Litan, of the Brookings Institute and the Presidential Transition Team, advanced a private-sector funding approach. He rejected the notion of creating a new kind of bank charter and a new federal agency in favor of using community credit unions, conventional banks, or subsidiaries of existing banks. Capital would come not directly from the government, but from conventional banks in exchange for some relief from CRA. Litan, whose ideas found support among bankers, thought that $1 billion in private capital could readily be raised in this way. However, he echoed a concern that Lyndon Comstock and others had expressed: "The human capital will be more of a problem. Few people know how to do it…. It might work better to train community activists to be bankers than bankers to be community lenders."⁶⁹⁶

In addition to these competing concepts, there were other interest groups and stakeholders in Washington who could not be ignored. In November and December, Martin Eakes, Caryl Stewart, and National Federation staff made a round of visits to the federal credit union regulator and the major national trade organizations, CUNA and NAFCU. The notion of federally capitalizing credit unions was not necessarily a popular one in the credit union industry. Credit unions were perpetually fighting against the banking industry to preserve their federal tax exemption; the trade organizations were wary of credit unions taking any sort of appropriated federal funds. NAFCU represented primarily large credit unions, few of which served low-income communities; it was unenthusiastic at best.⁶⁹⁷ CUNA supported its recent ally, the National Federation of CDCUs.⁶⁹⁸ On December 3, CUNA's president, Ralph Swoboda, wrote to President-elect Clinton highlighting the National Federation and calling attention to some of federation's long-pursued issues, including restrictions on new CDCU charters and restrictions on nonmember philanthropic and other deposits in low-income credit unions.⁶⁹⁹ The federal credit union regulator, NCUA, in the person of the liberal member of its three-person board, Robert Swan, and his senior staff, was cautiously supportive; at the same time, it pointed out that the Clinton proposal was too focused on small business lending, a problematic area for credit unions, partly because of bank opposition.

## Early Reactions

Several weeks later, key points in the transition staff's memo found their way to *New York Times* reporter Robert Pear. His article, "A Lending Plan for the Distressed," cited "confidential documents from the transition team [that] show that Mr. Clinton's advisers have recommended that he ask Congress for $850 million to aid community development banks over the next five years, with the money to be distributed through a new national trust." The article stated that "existing banks and credit unions could apply for Federal aid. But…the selection criteria would favor new institutions."⁷⁰⁰

A tilt favoring new institutions aroused concerns both from the banking industry and from CDFIs, although with different motives. The article quoted the executive director of government relations for the American Bankers Association, Edward L. Yingling, as saying, "We support the concept of community development lending, but we have a lot of concern about the idea of setting up a network of 100 new banks." Instead, he remarked, "You ought to build on the current system, which is showing great promise…. What you really need is a lot of flexibility to experiment, to see what works and to adjust to local needs." In this respect, the ABA's position paralleled that of the CDFI Coalition. Interviewed by Pear and speaking for the National Federation, I stated: "We feel very strongly that the Federal program should build on existing experience and institutions."

Other bank organizations also weighed in. A coalition of six groups, including the Savings and Community Bankers of America, offered support for the emerging initiative. Paul Schosberg, its president, drew explicit connections to the War on Poverty, but with a difference: "When Clinton talks about moving Americans into the mainstream, you're hearing echoes of what we heard from LBJ and his administration."[701] The difference, of course, was that banking institutions—some of them for-profit—would be the delivery channels for community development, not anti-poverty agencies.

Amid early support for the Clinton concept were hints of future tensions and political problems, especially with respect to CRA, which had a broad, mobilized activist constituency. Litan's suggestion that having "conventional banks invest capital in the development banks in return for relief from some provisions of the Community Reinvestment Act"[702] drew support from bankers but would almost certainly rouse opposition from CRA advocates. Other difficulties loomed once a CDFI Fund was launched. "If you have 100 charters," the ABA's Yingling stated, "the decision about who gets one will be highly politicized."[703] In fact, his observation foretold a congressional attack on the CDFI Fund in 1997 after it made its initial awards.[704]

# CHAPTER 13. On Capitol Hill

There was a festive atmosphere in the Capitol on the days leading up to the inauguration of Bill Clinton on January 20, 1993. There was a bell-ringing ceremony with electronic links as far as South-Central Los Angeles, a massive fair on the Mall in Washington, concerts, and an inauguration ceremony for young people.

The supporters of the new administration were optimistic—but the future of community development banking was by no means assured. On January 17, Neil R. Peirce, a journalist who had studied and reported on the community development corporation (CDC) movement for the Ford Foundation, wrote:

> If the Clinton camp thought it would be easy to deliver on the president-elect's promise to create 100 community development banks for poor, capital-short communities, it's learning otherwise. Ideas on how to do it have been ricocheting back and forth among fiscal gurus on the Clinton transition team, the Senate Banking Committee, grass-roots credit unions and loan funds, big national intermediaries for low-income housing, and lobbyists for mainline banks.[705]

A host of critical details needed to be resolved before the White House could put forward a bill. Where to house a CDFI fund? Existing institutions and/or newly established ones? Bank holding company or not? How much money, and in what form—annual appropriations or "trust fund"? For months, the very likelihood of a fund was up for grabs, as momentum ebbed and flowed. Rumors from "confidential sources" trickled out frequently—some well-founded, others speculative or based on the unofficial, "predecisional" memoranda of the new administration.

## The Coalition: Taking Shape, Defining Principles

With Clinton's victory and bright prospects for major legislation, the ad hoc CDFI Coalition formalized and expanded, although it did not yet incorporate as a separate entity. By early 1993, the original members—-the National Federation of CDCUs, the National Association of Community Development Loan Funds, Self Help, Community Capital Bank, and the Woodstock Institute—were joined by the First Nations Development Institute, representing indigenous communities, and the relatively new Association for Enterprise Opportunity (AEO), representing microenterprise funds. However, ShoreBank and Southern Development Bancorporation, the most prominent names in the field, were not yet members; neither was the National Congress for Community Economic Development, which represented community development corporations (CDCs).[706]

By mid-January 1993, the CDFI Coalition had drafted the position paper that would be the foundation for its advocacy: the detailed, somewhat ponderous "Principles of Community Development Lending & Proposals for Key Federal Support." Thus, the coalition was now prepared to "speak with one voice"—a precondition for getting anything done in Congress.

First, the movement had to convince policymakers that CDFIs filled needs unmet by the existing financial system. The symptoms of social and economic distress were obvious, as the "Principles" stated: increasing poverty, recent riots in South Central Los Angeles and New York, and an unsavory brew made up of "the recent recession, astronomical government deficits, the savings and loan bailout, and the health care crisis."[707] Trends in banking magnified the problem: Bank consolidation diminished the appetite for lending to new and small borrowers, and "most conventional lenders are further restrained by class and cultural barriers, the high cost of operations, and their commitment to profit maximization."[708]

The coalition advocated six "Key Principles in Meeting Credit Needs in Lower-Income Communities.[709]

- **Not just banks.** Community development "banks" should include a spectrum of institutional types, reflecting the diversity of local credit needs.
- **Not only small business credit.** The paper rightly noted that the Clinton campaign platform emphasized small business. There was nothing wrong with that, but the coalition strongly recommended that a new fund should also support housing lending, consumer lending, retail banking, and other credit needs in working-class and low-income communities (for example, working capital and facilities-development loans for nonprofit social service providers and tribal organizations).
- **CDFIs should be consulted.** Legislation should be informed by the practical experience of existing CDFIs.
- **No massive campaign to establish new development banks.** The program should emphasize expanding existing CDFIs. "An attempt to franchise or otherwise mass-produce CDFIs is not likely to be able to meet" the large, unmet demand for affordable credit.[710]
- **No overnight strategy: Development finance takes time.** South Shore Bank and Self-Help in North Carolina had taken one to two decades to develop their capacity, which "cannot be bought with massive federal appropriations but must be built over time through sound lending and borrower capacity-building programs. Any other approach invites repetition of past federal antipoverty initiatives that produce fraud and abuse."[711]
- **"Clarify the different interests and responsibilities of conventional lenders, public agencies, and CDFIs."** The coalition argued that all these actors should have a role in the new program.

- Above all, a new CDFI network must not become a substitute for CRA; rather, CRA should be extended.⁷¹² The federal government should make any subsidies and new powers for financial institutions contingent on supporting CDFIs and meeting community borrowing needs.

By urging that the CDFI Fund build upon existing institutions, the coalition sought to avoid the danger that the administration would put its stamp on a "proprietary" program of establishing *de novo* banks and microenterprise funds. (The National Federation had bitter experience with such an effort in the 1970s, when the credit union regulator co-opted the federation's proposal for a federal fund and attempted to restrict it to new and handpicked institutions.)⁷¹³ The CDFI Coalition argued that

> an emerging industry of community development financial institutions (CDFIs) offers a solid foundation for this bold [Clinton] initiative, which might include new institutions, community organizations, conventional lenders, and others, in addition to CDFIs....To date, with almost no public support CDFIs have proved that it is possible to mobilize and lend significant amounts of capital for development in low- and moderate-income communities. Our track record and experience can and should serve as a foundation for growth.⁷¹⁴

The "Principles" described the various species of CDFIs—community development banks, credit unions, loan funds, microenterprise funds, as well as "hybrid" institutions like the First Nations Development Institute's Oweesta Fund and venture funds. In their various ways, all served important public purposes: They provided credit to the poor and those with unmet credit needs; helped individuals become self-sufficient; and spurred community-wide economic development. The coalition endorsed multi-unit, multi-service CDFI models, like bank holding companies and the nonprofit version that Self-Help had pioneered in North Carolina. Whether for-profit or not-for-profit, a CDFI holding company could deliver intensive technical assistance to borrowers, develop housing, provide job training, or engage in other community revitalization activities. Moreover, when the model included a nonprofit, charitable arm, the CDFI could obtain foundation and public grants to support its work. The coalition urged that new legislation provide a "growth ladder" for various CDFIs to grow into or develop these institutional models.

The coalition asserted that CDFIs provided a path to community empowerment in ways that mainstream banks could not: They used "the lending process in a way that encourages borrowers to participate in decision-making within their organizations and communities."⁷¹⁵ (The language recalled, if faintly, the theme of "maximum feasible participation" of the poor from the War on Poverty.)

## The Nature of Federal Support: Equity, Debt, Human Capital

Indisputably, the greatest need of CDFIs was for equity or net worth. The coalition noted that "only four development banks have been created in the past 20 years, primarily because of the difficulty in raising equity or net worth capital."[716] Equity enabled CDFIs to take greater risks, offer flexible pricing, provide longer-term loans, attract and protect private-sector investors, and increase their income. Each dollar of equity would enable a CDFI to leverage multiple additional dollars of debt for relending.

Federal appropriations ought not be the sole support for an emerging CDFI network. Echoing, if less assertively, the proposals of NACDLF, the coalition urged that "institutions which benefit from public subsidy of their lending or other financial services (e.g., deposit insurance, insurance, and pension fund guarantees) could reasonably be expected to contribute in various ways."[717] Potentially, hundreds of millions of dollars could be made available from these sources. Another possible source: tax deductions or credits for individuals who made below-market investments in CDFIs.

Developing human capital was crucial. The "Principles" called for training a "new generation of community development lenders"—a particular concern of Community Capital Bank's Lyndon Comstock. The coalition linked this to President Clinton's proposal for a new National Service Corps, as well as suggesting three-year internship and apprenticeship programs at CDFIs and collaborations with universities. CDFI borrowers, too, needed aid in developing their human capital: The coalition called for supporting technical assistance to borrowers, especially in business planning, financial management, and marketing.

The coalition argued against a "strict selection process" that would exclude much of the CDFI movement; rather, a CDFI Fund should "seed the existing industry broadly and then…allocate resources to those organizations that meet negotiated performance targets."[718] Importantly, the federal government should focus on *outcomes*: As Self-Help had pointed out, the worst-case scenario would be for a federal agency to micromanage all CDFI lending by requiring sign-offs on individual loans or imposing rigid standard underwriting or loan servicing guidelines. Federal CDFI program administrators should take a broader, longer-term look at CDFIs, assessing indicators such as lending volume, portfolio performance, capacity-building, and program results over a sufficiently long time.

The "Principles" paper "helped create a sense of unified action among the participants," as Comstock noted.[719] It was quickly endorsed by the Social Investment Forum, the Calvert Social Investment Fund and Calvert Social Investment Foundation, and Co-op America.[720] The coalition's "Principles" was a tangible, detailed document suitable for circulation among the policy specialists on Capitol Hill and in the Old Executive Office Building. By February 1993, the coalition representatives were engaging directly with the White House. In a memo to the "Ad Hoc Coalition of CDFIs" and its members, Mark Pinsky reported:

> The White House does not yet have any specifics on program…. I have had several conversations with the guy in the White House Domestic Policy Office…[and] he told me that a copy of our paper is being distributed as part of a small packet to various federal officials.

> I suggested that it would be worth their while to spend an hour or two listening to us (that is, the Coalition members)—à la our Congressional briefing—*while* they are settling on an agency [to house the program].[721]

## Community Development Banking in the Senate

In the first months of 1993, much of the congressional action focused on or was driven by the Senate Banking Committee. On January 6, Jeannine Jacokes and Matt Roberts of the Senate Banking Committee staff went on fact-finding visits to CDFIs. In New York City, they visited the National Federation of CDCUs and Community Capital Bank; the bank's founder, Lyndon Comstock, arranged a tour to projects in Brooklyn and West Harlem, where they saw a Ben & Jerry's ice cream franchise funded by the bank.[722] They visited the Delaware Valley Community Reinvestment Fund in Philadelphia and saw its work in Camden, NJ, one of the most economically devastated cities in the United States.

The Senate Banking Committee set a hearing on community development lending and the role of community development banks for February 3, at 10:00 a.m. The coalition began to prepare: "Fringe Lenders Unite to Seek Central Role in Clinton Program," as *Banking Week* reported on February 1.[723] This terminology offended CDFIs: "Fringe lenders" commonly referred to high-cost, usually unregulated lenders, which were part of the problem, not the solution.

Prior to the Senate hearing, coalition members met with other national advocacy organizations to enlist their support. The broad-based National Neighborhood Coalition advised on political strategy.[724] On February 2, CDFI leaders held a luncheon meeting with a dozen representatives of national Protestant, Catholic, Friends, and ecumenical bodies at the Methodist Church Building. Martin Trimble of NACDLF laid out the coalition's principles and its goal of "recreating banking institutions."[725] A representative of the Methodist Church questioned whether a CDFI program would "let banks off the hook," voicing a potential concern shared by other advocates. Comstock, of Community Capital Bank, stressed that the coalition supported full enforcement of the Community Reinvestment Act (CRA), even though CRA had failed to produce significant lending. All the participants worried that the Clinton proposal was losing momentum and might fall off the table.

Meanwhile, the Subcommittee on Financial Institutions of the House of Representatives was attempting to claim a role in the emerging CDFI program. The hearings had been called on very short notice, reflecting turf competition between two Democrats, Reps. Joseph Kennedy of Massachusetts and Stephen Neal of North Carolina. On February 2, 1993, Comstock and Self-Help's Brian Hassel testified, along with representatives of a Neighborhood Housing Services (NHS) affiliate and a CRA officer. Comstock summarized his impressions of the House hearing in a later memo to his CDFI colleagues.

The House Banking Committees seem to have a relatively uninformed and unsympathetic approach to community development banking. It was unfortunate that we didn't have a single advocate among the 17 representatives attending the Financial Institutions Subcommittee hearing on February 2. In general, the Republican reaction could be characterized as: 'You folks are doing a good job, but this has nothing to do with the federal government.' The Democratic reaction at the House level might be characterized as: 'We need the major banks to do the lending in low income neighborhoods and any federal support for you could turn into an excuse to weaken CRA.'[726]

In fact, community economic development had a strong advocate on the committee. Congresswoman Marcy Kaptur from Toledo, OH, had long supported community development corporations (CDCs), as well as credit unions. Kaptur was a human link to the initiatives of the 1970s: As an adviser in President Carter's White House, she had been an ally of the National Federation as it sought to establish the Community Development Revolving Loan Fund for Credit Unions.[727] On February 3, Kaptur testified glowingly about the New Community Corporation, a CDC in Newark, NJ, which had built nearly 3,000 apartments; operated early childhood and infant daycare programs; built commercial space; brought a large, new supermarket into the poverty-stricken Central Ward of Newark; and much more. In a vastly different community, Santa Cruz Community CU in California had saved or created hundreds of jobs and assisted after the 1989 earthquake. There were many other important success stories, too, including ShoreBank, Delaware Valley Community Reinvestment Fund, LISC, and the Neighborhood Reinvestment Corporation. "Let's not lose 10 years of learning…by overlooking the network of community development lenders and developers already in place," she urged. Kaptur endorsed the Bank Enterprise Act (BEA) legislation, as well as the National Federation's calls for regulatory changes to ease chartering and operations of CDCUs. Finally, she called for establishing an assistant secretary of Neighborhood Development and Finance at the Department of Housing and Urban Development (HUD), along with a national training institute on community development finance.[728]

On the evening of February 2, after meeting with its faith-based allies at the Methodist Church building, coalition members crossed the street and walked a hundred yards to the Senate office building to conduct a briefing session in preparation for the next day's Senate Banking hearing. Although this was not an official congressional event, Senator Riegle had circulated a written invitation to the briefing. CDFIs were still not widely known in Congress, although they had testified in 1992. But President Clinton's plans had raised the profile of the CDFI movement dramatically. The room was filled with congressional staffers, community advocates, and others.

The National Federation's Errol Louis moderated a panel of presentations by CDFI Coalition members, as well as Milton Davis of South Shore Bank, which had not been a member of the coalition but undoubtedly enjoyed the greatest name recognition.[729] ShoreBank, as always, advocated specifically for the bank holding company model, but Davis acknowledged that all types of CDFIs had a role: "Need dictates structure and strategy."⁷³⁰ Was South Shore replicable? A resounding "yes," Davis replied: ShoreBank was currently consulting with 12 or 14 cities.

What was the relationship of CDFIs to conventional financial institutions? Jeremy Nowak, of the Delaware Valley Community Reinvestment Fund, pointed to the unprecedented instability in conventional finance that had contributed to the need for CDFIs. He stressed that CDFIs served as intermediaries for banks, helping to bring capital into communities where banks otherwise would not invest. It was not an either/or proposition, he explained: CDFIs and increased direct bank investment were both needed.

A surprise presentation put the role of CDFIs into global perspective. Muhammad Yunus, founder of the renowned Grameen Bank of Bangladesh who had met and profoundly influenced Governor Bill Clinton in the 1980s, told how after several years of successful microlending, he had tried in vain to persuade bankers to serve the poverty population. Rebuffed, he started the Grameen Bank in 1983. "Tiny bits and pieces are important," he said, "but first you have to decide what rules to play by." Those rules and procedures should not—could not—be those of ordinary banking; Grameen had to be designed from the ground up. "You're making a start today," he remarked. "The whole world is watching."⁷³¹

## The Senate Banking Committee Hearing

The next day, February 3, the official Senate hearing opened to an overflow audience of 150. The timing of the hearing—a scant two weeks after President Clinton's inauguration—sent a signal that this was a significant event. "This is an important hearing," Committee Chairman Don Riegle declared in his opening statement, "I think [it's] one of the most important that is likely to happen this year with respect to the new direction that the country needs to take and is preparing to take with respect to revitalizing our urban communities particularly." He noted, as well, "that this is a very high priority for the new administration, and the committee will move forward very promptly as soon as they have put their proposal on the table for us."

The urgency prompted by the riots in South Central Los Angeles was still fresh. Senator Riegle called for "new strategies to address neighborhood disintegration and inadequate access to capital. This need was clearly demonstrated by the riots in Los Angeles and is obvious from the general condition of many of our communities where homelessness, unemployment and crime are on the rise." Like the CDFI Coalition, Riegle endorsed building upon existing institutions, while improving and strengthening CRA.⁷³²

Several other senators offered opening statements. Connie Mack, Republican from Florida, expressed "some skepticism." Senator Alfonse D'Amato extended "a special welcome" to Lyndon Comstock and Brooklyn's Community Capital Bank, his New York constituent, but did "not believe that we need new kinds of banks or new Government spending programs." Instead, he proposed that every bank invest up to 5 percent of its capital in a community development bank, while noting that "there are those who say this idea would enable banks to buy their way out of CRA." (Indeed, this was precisely the fear of CRA advocates.)[733]

The committee had framed several broad questions for the CDFI witnesses.
- What is the need for community banking institutions?
- What is a community development bank (CDB)?
- How are CDBs different from other banks?
- What have CDBs accomplished?[734]

## Community Development Banks, Existing and Aspirational

Milton Davis of ShoreBank led off, explaining its holding company model, which was required because "community development requires more than credit, and delivering credit successfully in disinvested communities requires more than a bank." He addressed the banking industry's concerns by arguing that community development banks were not competitors but "natural partners" of mainstream institutions. He concluded, "After many years of experimentation, we know something that works. The difficult challenge is to carefully design a program which translates this knowledge into public policy."[735]

Lyndon Comstock of Community Capital Bank stressed the need to help existing CDFIs of all types expand, rather than focusing solely on creating new CDFIs. To expand their capacity and impact, CDFIs had three critical needs: equity capital; grants for technical assistance; and professional training programs. The CDFI Coalition, he testified, supported strong CRA regulations and enforcement and rejected the notion that bank support for CDFIs could or should substitute for federal investment: Banks already received CRA credit for such investment, but that had yielded only modest support, mostly in deposits rather than crucial equity. Comstock closed by making the case for CDFI organizations with affiliates, like Community Capital Bank's LEAP, Inc., "a nonprofit venture development organization" (the term "community development venture capital" had not yet been adopted), which he had established to provide risk capital for small businesses.[736]

At least partially in deference to the chairman, two Michigan speakers closed out the first panel. Steven Lopez, president and CEO of Southside Bank in Grand Rapids, emphasized the extreme disadvantages of African Americans in accessing capital, while Wayne County Executive Edward H. McNamara discussed plans to start a development bank in the Detroit area.

In the dialogue that followed the testimony, Senator D'Amato bemoaned the "volumes of paperwork" required of banks and repeated his alternative proposal: Why not have conventional banks deposit up to 5 percent of their capital in community development banks? ShoreBank's Milton Davis supported that idea "110 percent." Although Davis did not address granting a CRA waiver for such banks, he noted that South Shore had been the only bank to testify in support of CRA.[737]

Although some Republican senators lauded ShoreBank's social impact, they were especially impressed by its profitability. Senator Robert Bennett (R-UT) welcomed Davis as "kind of a hero…

[but] my interest comes from the fact that you have made money."[738] For Senator Pete Domenici (R-NM), too, profitability was key to replicability.

> How are we going to…duplicate [ShoreBank's] kind of activity across this land?…. Right up front, I truly believe the concept of building profit into it as a motive is very, very important….There may be a nonprofit role, but I truly believe the heart of this activity ought to be accumulating capital and equity from across America that wants to invest.[739]

On the Democratic side, Senator Richard Shelby from Alabama emphasized the need for management talent as equal to the need for capital. Democratic Senator Sarbanes of Maryland raised the key question: Would banks be "let off the hook" by investing in CDFIs? Would legislation produce a two-tier banking system, leaving community development banks the burden of serving poor communities, while mainstream banks were free to walk away?[740] Absolutely not, replied ShoreBank's Milton Davis: "I have heard nothing here today…nor am I saying that an investment in a development bank [should] let the banks off the hook…. All that I am saying is it is another way to help them meet that CRA requirement."[741] Both "normal" banks and community development banks are needed to restore functioning in a marketplace. Davis explained:

> You must have an institution whose primary objective and goal is development. That simply is not the case with the large institutions…. Their primary objective is profits. They do not know the markets in these neighborhoods. The last thing I would [like] to happen is to have them forced to make investments in the neighborhoods, have them all go down the tubes, and then for the banks to say we tried this but it did not work.[742]

Ending the morning panel as it opened, Chairman Riegle repeated his pleas for urgent action.

> I do not think we have a lot of time here to work with. We are seeing examples of cities that catch fire and burn down, and we can see a lot more of that happen. Lives and opportunities are being squandered and I think destroyed in effect every day…. So, we have to have a concept that will work, but it cannot take forever and it cannot string out over a long, long period of time because we are playing catch-up as it is.[743]

In its afternoon session, the Senate Banking Committee heard testimony from the nonbanks—credit unions, loan funds, and microenterprise lenders—that could fulfill the Clintonian vision of 100 community development banks and 1,000 microenterprise programs. Several witnesses highlighted the needs of rural America. Pauline Nunez-Morales was executive director of the New Mexico Community Development Loan Fund in Albuquerque, a constituent of Banking Committee Member

Senator Pete Domenici. (The coalition followed the basic lesson that it is always good to have a senator's constituent testify.) Created in 1989, the fund's capital came from socially responsible investors. As the state's only CDFI, the loan fund financed a variety of needs in a primarily rural state: for example, health facilities, organic agriculture, transitional housing, and a small logging business. Ron Phillips, president of Coastal Enterprises, Inc. (CEI) in Wiscasset, ME, described its statewide portfolio, which ranged from microenterprises to manufacturing, with loans of up to $400,000. An ardent, indefatigable advocate for community development corporations (CDCs), Phillips emphasized that local banks were major partners in CEI's development lending.

Banks were important partners in major cities as well. Jeremy Nowak, the CEO of Delaware Valley Community Reinvestment Fund in Philadelphia, testified about his fund's structuring of formal loan-participation pools with banks, becoming a "wholesale" channel for them. "The way that you build community development financial institutions," he said, "in part is by getting banks to meet CRA regulatory requirements."[744]

But banks were hardly allies in the impoverished Mississippi Delta town: Rather, they carried on the legacy of slavery. Robert Jackson provided compelling testimony on behalf of the Quitman County Federal Credit Union in Marks, MS, 80 miles south of Memphis.[745]

> Until 1977, there was only one bank in the Marks area, and it was owned by a local family that also controlled much of the land and political machinery in the county. Since loans are routinely denied to many poor people, including my parents who were sharecroppers, they did not even bother to go to the local banks.
>
> Out of pure desperation, we organized a grassroots movement for equality that led to the creation of the Quitman County Development Credit Union, which is also a community development corporation.

Jackson described his credit union's typical loan. A farm family had lived on a plantation their entire lives, until the farmer got sick in 1989 and could no longer work. The family was told to move out of the plantation-owned house. With nowhere to move, no credit history, and no breadwinner, they turned to the credit union for a $10,000 loan to purchase a modest home. "This is not an exception," Jackson testified; "this is the rule. Families are being displaced from large plantations with nowhere to go, no money to move anywhere else, no sympathy from the landowners, no severance pay, nothing." Jackson said, "[If a credit union like mine] had a $100,000 infusion of equity, I can guarantee you that we would make $1 million worth of loans in Quitman County, MS, the poorest section of the United States."[746]

Professor Michael Swack—academic, practitioner, policy advocate—played many roles in the emerging CDFI movement, founding and/or serving on the boards of the Institute for Community Economics and the New Hampshire Community Loan Fund. He codirected the Institute for Cooperative Community Development, in Manchester, NH, which had developed a peer group microlending program called Working Capital, modeled after the Grameen Bank.* Banks were valued partners, as they were for Coastal Enterprises: Working Capital funded its lending through lines of credit from three banks, establishing small loan loss reserves at the banks to compensate for risk.

Swack connected microenterprise with anti-poverty policy. Starting a microenterprise was a path out of poverty for some recipients of public assistance (which had made them attractive to candidate Bill Clinton, who was very concerned with welfare policy), but asset and income restrictions prevented them from doing so. Swack urged policy changes to eliminate such restrictions. He also proposed a policy that he had championed as chair of the quasi-public Community Development Finance Authority of New Hampshire: tax credits for businesses investing in community development.

To help convince the panel that a potential infrastructure for community development banking already existed, several speakers provided profiles of the various sectors. Swack reminded the committee, "It is not just the South Shore Bank. There is a lot of expertise. There are probably 500 institutions represented by the various groups that are involved in this. That experience has been gained over the 15 years."[747] He cited the Association for Enterprise Opportunity, which represented over 150 microenterprise programs. Ron Phillips introduced into the record a listing of 325 CDCs across the country. Pauline Nunez-Morales mentioned the 41 member funds of the National Association of Community Development Loan Funds, which had made more than $100 million in loans, leveraging $760 million in public and private capital to finance 15,000 housing units, and created 3,500 jobs. And Robert Jackson, a board member of the National Federation of Community Development Credit Unions, noted that there were more than 300 credit unions serving low-income urban, rural, and reservation-based communities across the United States.

## Follow-Up

The hearing record included documents to provide policymakers a fuller picture of the CDFI movement. The CDFI Coalition's "Principles of Community Development Lending & Proposals for Key Federal Support" was included in its entirety, thus becoming the official public platform of the CDFI movement. There was detailed information about the financial status and achievements of CDFIs. The Woodstock Institute added its working paper, "Banking on Communities: Development Banking in the United States," while Neighborhood Housing Services of New York City, Inc., described its work and that of the "NeighborWorks Network – A National Community Development Lending System." The First Nations Development Institute, a member of the CDFI Coalition, described its Oweesta Program for investing in reservation-based economic development.

---

\* In this model, a small group (typically five people) essentially served as a guarantor for loans to any one of its members.

Advocacy organizations submitted their own statements and position papers for the record. The Consumer Federation of America (CFA) highlighted an aspect of community development banking that had gotten less attention in the testimony.

> Tragically, today, millions of households are non-participants in our nation's subsidized, regulated and insured banking system....CFA strongly believes that the community development banks that the President has proposed must be a *supplement* to existing banking facilities for low- and moderate-income and particularly minority consumers and neighborhoods, and *not* [emphasis in original] a replacement.... Basic banking is the first step of including the poor, working poor and elderly in the nation's publicly subsidized banking system.[748]

CFA also emphasized the need for consumer and community engagement—even ownership—of CDFIs, echoing themes from the War on Poverty.

> We recommend that consumers be actively consulted, represented and involved in the development and day-to-day operations of community development banks.... The only way community development truly takes hold is when the residents of a community believe they have a real stake in their communities' growth.... Credit unions and cooperatives are the epitome of financial empowerment from the ground up. They deserve a significant role in ultimate legislation and should have substantial funds earmarked for their development.[749]

CFA vigorously opposed relieving banks of their CRA responsibilities, and it rejected the proposal by Senator D'Amato of providing a waiver or "safe harbor" for banks that invested up to 5 percent of their core capital. ACORN, the Association of Community Organizations for Reform Now, stated a similar position more vividly and bluntly. In a letter of February 17, Deepak Bhargava, legislative director, wrote:

> I wish to make clear that ACORN strongly opposes any initiative that would dilute the community reinvestment obligations of existing insured depository institutions. In particular, we oppose efforts to allow existing institutions to receive 'credit' under the Community Reinvestment Act (CRA) for equity investments or loan participations with community development banks.
> As always happens when a new program is created, the vultures appear on the scene to grab whatever advantage possible. The banking trade groups are clearly seizing on the community development banks as a backdoor means of escaping their responsibilities under the CRA. They want to contribute a few pennies to the new

banks—maybe a desk blotter and handful of ballpoint pens—and then get an 'outstanding' CRA rating.[750]

Like the Consumer Federation of America, ACORN urged legislation to "maximize participation of residents in the creation and governance of new institutions in low-income neighborhoods.... Community ownership, control, and governance must be at the heart of any community development bank proposal." While the Clinton initiative required a private-sector match for all federal awards to CDFIs, ACORN argued that a ratio of 1:1 or 2:1 might be unrealistic, especially for low- and very-low-income communities without access to social investors.[751]

After a congressional hearing, committees often direct follow-up questions to witnesses for written responses, which become part of the printed hearing record. Would a new CDFI network "create a two-tiered banking system—one that serves the needs of poor communities and the other that serves anyone else?"[752] Couldn't the unmet needs of distressed neighborhoods be met simply by improved enforcement of CRA? What about Senator D'Amato's proposal that mainstream banks should receive a pass on CRA requirements if they invested 5 percent of their capital in community development banks? Were community development banks a "panacea"? Uniformly, the witnesses answered no to all these questions (although ShoreBank acknowledged that it certainly would welcome additional equity investments).

Asked why so few community development banks had been formed since South Shore Bank, Lyndon Comstock stressed the difficulty of raising equity[753]: It had taken his Community Capital Bank team the equivalent of one person-year for every $1 million in equity capital raised. Milton Davis elaborated on the difficulty of starting a new community development bank.

> Compared to most community development institutions, development banks are complex and large scale, requiring commensurate amounts of organizational resources and capital ... [as well as] patient and dedicated investors who are willing to take greater risks associated with start-up and a new institutional model; who have been willing to forgo dividends and liquidity... and who support a development agenda.

The universe of potential investors was small, although Davis was hopeful that "with new Federal programming and appropriate incentives," the task might become easier for the next wave of community development banks.[754]

On March 8, a month after the hearing, Banking Committee Chairman Riegle and Senator Paul Sarbanes (D-MD), chairman of the Subcommittee on Housing and Urban Affairs, wrote to President Clinton to outline the principles that they hoped to see guide the administration's legislation. "The testimony we heard in these hearings was disturbing," they wrote. "Credit and basic financial services—which are integral to strong, vibrant economies—are often unavailable in many inner-city and rural communities. Discriminatory practices remain prevalent." They drew the following conclusions.

- The administration should make strong implementation of CRA, the Fair Housing Act, and the Equal Credit Opportunity Act the cornerstone of efforts to increase community lending in underserved areas.
- Banks certainly should not get regulatory exemptions or safe harbors for investing in community-oriented financial institutions.
- Government-sponsored entities—the Federal Home Loan Bank System, Fannie Mae, and Freddie Mac—should "vigorously pursue" their affordable housing and investment goals.
- A national community lending initiative "should build upon the existing network of community-oriented financial institutions, including community development credit unions, community development loan funds, microenterprise lenders, community development banks, minority-owned financial institutions and community development corporations."[755]

Thus, the CDFI Coalition had allies in high places to press for its core principles and recommendations.

# CHAPTER 14. The Road to the Rose Garden

*During the first six months of the William J. Clinton administration in 1993, disorganization, disarray, confusion, and general chaos were the rules rather than the exceptions.*[*]

On February 17, 1993 President Clinton delivered his first State of the Union address. Along with the big issues—the economy and jobs creation, health care reform, the North American Free Trade Agreement, education, welfare, and more—he did not neglect his campaign promise: "With a new network of community development banks, and one billion dollars to make the dream of enterprise zones real, we will begin to bring new hope and new jobs to storefronts and factories from South Boston to South Texas to South Central Los Angeles."[756]

## The New Policy Shops: The NEC and DPC

President Clinton fulfilled another campaign promise with an executive order establishing the National Economic Council (NEC), along with the Domestic Policy Council (DPC); these would parallel the National Security Council as top-level advisory bodies.[757] Robert Rubin, Assistant to the President for Economic Policy (later Secretary of the Treasury), became the director of the NEC. The NEC and DPC established the Interagency Working Group on Community Development and Empowerment, which included members of cabinet agencies. This working group would vet competing ideas and consolidate recommendations to the president on a range of issues, including community development banking. On February 15, the working group held its first meeting.[758] Over the following months, the group translated the president's ambitious but vague campaign promise into the administration's community development banking bill.

Paul Weinstein Jr.[759] was one of the bridges from the Clinton campaign to the White House. He had worked on the Clinton campaign almost from the very beginning: "I was of one of two 'deputies' to Bruce Reed, who was the deputy campaign manager for policy. I went to Arkansas and actually served as the point person and the policy person in the War Room. You had somebody from

---

[*] George E. Shambaugh IV and Paul J. Weinstein Jr., *The Art of Policymaking*, 2nd ed. (Thousand Oaks, CA: SAGE/CQ Press, 2016), 1.

every office, and we were the rapid response group. My job was to coordinate with everybody."[760] This included helping draft the chapter on community development—which included the creation of a network of community development banks—in the Clinton policy manifesto, *Putting People First*.

Weinstein recalled that "essentially, the Domestic Policy Council and the National Economic Council were given joint control over the…so-called community empowerment agenda, [under] Gene Sperling and Bruce Reed, who were both at that time, Deputy Assistants to the President." Weinstein worked as a team with Sheryll Cashin and Paul Dimond of the NEC, splitting up the issues. "We all worked on all these issues, but I would say Paul Dimond was focused more on the empowerment zone piece. I was more focused on the CDFI. We were all focused on CRA reform."[761]

## "Pin the Tail on the Community Development Bank"

With the Clinton administration committed to some still unspecified community development banking program, legislative proposals proliferated on both sides of Congress—so much so that the president of Savings and Community Bankers of America, Paul Schosberg, wryly compared the situation to the children's party game Pin the Tail on the Donkey.[762] Perhaps the most compelling, comprehensive proposal came from Senator Bill Bradley (D-NJ), the former professional basketball star. On March 18, he released an impassioned statement on urban policy.

> It was less than a year ago that we watched Los Angeles explode in disorder across our television screens, followed by the parade of people saying it was time to do something about our cities. And of course, nothing happened.…
>
> Last year I spoke on this floor to paint a picture of America's cities. I described places that were poorer, sicker, less educated and more violent than ever in my lifetime.… Today I want to show a new picture of the same places. It is a more hopeful picture, though there has been no real change.…
>
> Life loses its meaning where there is no community.… Where there are ten check-cashing shops for every bank or credit union that lets people borrow and save for tomorrow, there is no community.[763]

Bradley presented an eight-part initiative, including a neighborhood-based reconstruction corps, community schools, community policing, increased transportation to suburban jobs for inner-city residents, and more. He included a proposal that embodied an emerging anti-poverty strategy: the Assets for Independence Act (AFIA), which would help people escape poverty through restricted, matched savings accounts for specified "wealth-building" purposes—home ownership, education, or starting a small business.

Bradley's "Community Capital Partnership Act" contained his community development banking proposal. He told the story of the New Community Corporation in his home state, New Jersey:

Formed after the Newark riots in 1967, this community development corporation had developed 2,500 housing units, an extended-care facility, a shopping center, and more. Bradley quoted Monsignor William Linder, the legendary founder of New Community: "I have seen bank branch after bank branch close because the bank did not find serving our community profitable.... Frankly, no one in authority cared about our community." But instead of giving up hope, Bradley remarked, Monsignor Linder and his colleagues founded a credit union to provide basic banking services, the New Community Federal Credit Union, which had grown in a few years to $1.7 million in assets.[764]

On the Republican side, Rep. Jim Leach from Iowa introduced the "Community Development Banking Act of 1993" (H.R. 238) which, like Senator D'Amato's earlier proposal, would essentially allow banks to buy their way out of CRA by investing a very small percentage of their assets in community development. On the left, Rep. Maxine Waters and other members of the Congressional Black Caucus introduced H.R. 1699, the "Community Banking and Economic Empowerment Act." On April 28, Democratic Rep. Bobby Rush, whose Chicago district included ShoreBank, announced his draft "Community Development Financial Institutions Act of 1993." Meanwhile, Rep. Floyd Flake held a hearing to "discuss how the BEA [Bank Enterprise Award program] can be a legislative vehicle for funding and development of community development banks."[765]

On April 26, Senator Bradley keynoted a symposium on community development banking in Princeton, NJ, where he had starred in basketball at the university.

> I have heard some people say that the federal government would be wasting its money investing in community development financial institutions. They say that poor people do not save, and our distressed urban communities do not have the basic resources needed to support economic development.
>
> I disagree. The point is that some people in poor communities manage to save money. If we harness this money and put it to work for the benefit of distressed urban areas, our cities will be much better off.[766]

To an audience that included many CDFIs, he highlighted features of his community development banking proposal: accountability to the community, matching requirements, and diversity in institutional types. He reiterated that "traditional banks should not be relieved of their CRA responsibilities when they invest in community development financial institutions."[767]

## Bradley, the White House, the Coalition: Navigating Among Allies

On March 25–26, 1993, Mark Pinsky and I went to Washington for a series of meetings with the key policymakers. Invited by Paul Weinstein to "bounce ideas off us," we met with him in the Old Executive Office Building next to the White House and briefly greeted his colleague, Paul Dimond, of the NEC. It seemed to us that the administration did not have a clear idea of where and how a

CDFI program would be housed, how it might be governed, and how it might meet the crucial need of CDFIs for equity capital. Weinstein emphasized that the Clinton administration was not considering a CRA "safe harbor" that would essentially exempt banks from CRA strictures; however, it would allow a certain small portion of CRA credit for investment in CDFIs—perhaps 5 percent, a level that the CDFI advocates seemed comfortable with. Structurally, he remarked that the administration was contemplating the creation of a national trust for CDFIs; this, I noted, resembled the National Federation's proposal for a National Neighborhood Banking Corporation.

By this time, the administration was no longer talking about $1 billion or even $850 million for community development banking. It appeared that only $354 million was possible, which distressed the administration: It was "not a lot of money," Weinstein said, making it even more crucial to raise additional money for CDFIs elsewhere. Providing tax credits for investing in CDFIs was not to his taste, although he was interested in the notion of tapping a portion of the profits of the government-sponsored housing entities, Fannie Mae and Freddie Mac (an idea that NACDLF had vigorously promoted). Weinstein assured us that although many Clinton administration proposals had fallen by the wayside, CDFI was not one and would not be one of them: The president was committed![768] Pinsky was not very reassured, as he reported back to the CDFI Coalition: "My greatest concern, frankly, is that all of the positive points of the plan Weinstein laid out may be nothing more than Weinstein telling us what we want to hear."[769]

Immediately after the meeting at the Old Executive Office Building next to the White House, we traveled up Pennsylvania Avenue to Capitol Hill to meet with Jeannine Jacokes and her colleagues on the Senate Banking Committee. They were eager to hear what we had learned from Weinstein. Jacokes emphasized that the administration needed to submit a bill as soon as possible, if it wanted to move legislation that fiscal year. They "want to downplay Sen. Bradley's bill," Pinsky reported to the coalition; they were also concerned with keeping municipal and other governmental units from capturing a piece of the CDFI pie for their own revolving loan funds. We then met with Senator Bradley's staff, who informed us that Bradley had lined up strong bipartisan cosponsorship for his proposal. Bradley's initiative was "a mixed bag," Pinsky wrote. "Bradley includes various CDFIs in his bill, but he has a clear preference for loan funds."[770] We presented the CDFI Coalition's view that legislation should support all types of CDFIs.

Although the Bradley and White House initiatives were potential competitors, they were on parallel tracks with similar goals. In an April 19 memo to the president, Bruce Reed and Gene Sperling noted that "our community Development Banking, Community Policing, and enterprise initiatives incorporate *many* [emphasis in original] central components of the Bradley bills: incentives for personal savings and investment in the community… [and] a CD Bank fund to nurture a network of community development financial institutions."[771]

On April 30, Senator Bradley and a dozen colleagues formally introduced S. 861, the Community Capital Partnership Act of 1993. His bill expanded on Senator Riegle's pilot CICD legislation of the previous October, which never was implemented.[772] Bradley's bill proposed $400 million in funding over four years, to help community development banks expand and to aid community development loan funds, credit unions, and community development corporations that wanted to become community development banks. Senator Bradley asked the CDFI Coalition to endorse his proposal. As attractive as it was, the CDFI Coalition refrained, as Jacokes of the Senate Banking Committee had recommended, since President Clinton's own proposal was nearing completion.[773] "We are stalling," Pinsky wrote, "so as not to annoy either the President or Sen. Riegle, chairman of the banking committee."[774]

While the administration's working group was preparing policy options for the president, the CDFI Coalition was doing its own, detailed scenario-planning. Kate McKee[775] and Bryan Hassel of Self-Help took the lead in developing a detailed matrix of the capital needs of various CDFIs, depending on their stage of development, institutional type, and products. Their scheme was far more complex than anything that could get into legislation, but it helped shape the coalition's recommendations on the best uses for federal funding for the diverse universe of CDFIs.[776]

## The CRA Minefield

Even during the campaign, the Clinton team was very concerned with reassuring CRA advocates about its plans for a network of community development banks. It was a "minefield," Paul Weinstein recalled.

> I remember during the campaign we were talking about that. I remember getting crucified by ACORN and others who totally misunderstood us.... We were sort of your classic new Dems, right? We were saying, 'We actually want this program to be *more* vibrant, we want *more* lending, we want *more* investment, we want *more* presence of banks. In order to do that, we are willing to simplify and reduce the paperwork [for banks].... A lot of the community groups thought that we were trying to gut it. Obviously, the record shows that was *not* what we were trying to do. We were trying to actually make it stronger.[777]

Shortly after the administration assumed power, Weinstein, Paul Dimond, and Sheryll Cashin held a tense meeting with ACORN. Weinstein recalled,

> As with any interest group, there was a nervousness—'What role will we have in the future?' They were, I think, legitimately concerned about it.... A lot of tension built up over the years, because obviously, the community groups had fought a lot of hard fights to get doors opened. .... I think at one point, [Rev.] Jesse Jackson maybe even said we were trying to create a separate but equal banking system—which, of course, was not our intent at all.[778]

Of course, the CRA advocacy community was not solely ACORN: It included Gale Cincotta's National People's Action and the recently formed National Community Reinvestment Coalition

(NCRC), led by John Taylor. Aided by allies in Congress, the CRA advocates could have obstructed or outright killed a community development banking initiative that weakened bank investment or "let banks off the hook" from their CRA responsibilities.

## Where to Put the Fund?

Apart from CRA, there were big tactical and program-design issues to decide. How much money, what kind, and who would be eligible—all these were obvious questions. But in turf-conscious Washington, it was equally important to decide *where* to house a new, high-profile CDFI fund. The maneuvering to "own" the president's favored program began even before the inauguration.

There was no obvious answer. In his *New York Times* article of January 18, before the inauguration, Robert Pear wrote that some advisers to the president-elect regarded HUD as "poorly managed," but that on the other hand, a program would be "'a fish out of water' at Treasury because that department has 'no community development orientation.'"[779] On February 4, Ronald Brown, the new head of the Commerce Department, wrote a memo to the president expressing his enthusiasm for the program and arguing that "Commerce knows how to provide assistance for economic revitalization… and Commerce can help community banks get going…. By contrast, other possible locations would not equally well serve the mission of CDBs [community development banks]."[780]

The CDFI Coalition tended to favor "none of the above." As we went down the list of potential agencies to house the fund, I recall that the various coalition members chronicled in turn their problems with each. Our preference was clearly for an independent agency, perhaps something like the Neighborhood Reinvestment Corporation. We certainly didn't think that Treasury was equipped for the business of handing out money for a new program.

Despite the arguments against the Treasury Department, the administration's Interagency Working Group decided that the new fund belonged there. "We didn't want to create just another economic development program at HUD or USDA, or even Commerce," Weinstein recalled. "We wanted to create something that was unique. Something that would eventually become self-sustaining."

> A number of us, including myself, were adamant: 'This *has* to go to Treasury.' This is about banking. This is about basically extending and bringing financial thinkers to this problem. …What the President had in mind was full-service [institutions]. It wasn't just about investment, it was also about credit, and it was about banking services, because we were heavily focused on the unbanked. That was a big deal for us. We wanted more people to have access to banking services.[781]

Congress was unenthusiastic about placing the fund in Treasury, and the issues would be revisited as legislation made its way through Congress in the second half of 1993 and 1994. "I got a lot of push-back from the Hill," Weinstein recalled. "It was amazing. There were a lot of folks who did not want to stick it at Treasury."⁷⁸² (For that matter, when the CDFI Fund was launched, it did not find a warm welcome within Treasury.)

## Options for the President

On April 20, after sorting through various alternatives, the Interagency Working Group sent a memorandum to the president that reflected ideas from the cabinet departments of HUD, Treasury, Agriculture, and Commerce; OMB, NEC, and DPC; community groups; and the banking industry. They summarized the situation this way.

> Across the country, rural and urban communities are starved for affordable credit, capital, and basic banking services. Millions of Americans in low-income neighborhoods have no bank where they can cash a check, borrow money to buy a home, or get a small loan to start a business or keep one going. Perhaps more than any other proposal, the network of community development banks you promised in the campaign—coupled with reform of the Community Reinvestment Act (CRA)—have the potential to transform these communities by empowering people and businesses to join the economic mainstream.⁷⁸³

It noted that discrimination had compounded the chronic banking and credit problems in minority communities. The memo advised against mandating any single model for community development banking; there were too many different types of CDFIs, operating in varied geographies and circumstances, for a "one-size-fits-all" approach. However, "the program should encourage CDFIs which have reached a certain size and level of sophistication to eventually become chartered depository institutions."⁷⁸⁴

The working group was acutely aware of budget realities. Its goal was to "dramatically expand the amount of capital available for CDFI startup and expansion without creating enormous financial liabilities for the federal government."⁷⁸⁵ It offered three funding options.
- One was to use appropriations for "direct federal support to CDFIs—equity capital with a reasonably firm but patient expectation of returns over time," along with "more venturesome investments" and grants.
- A second approach would use $300 million of a proposed $382 million appropriation to leverage a loan of up to $1 billion from Treasury. The appropriated funds would cover expected losses and subsidize below-market interest rates and returns on equity investments.
- The third option was to provide incentives for mainstream banks to capitalize CDFIs in return for liberalized interstate bank branching.

The working group did not recommend one option over the others, and it stressed that they were not mutually exclusive. However, it considered the first option—direct appropriations—to be the least controversial and the most likely to pass in 1993. It also offered three legislative strategies of varying intensity: "go all out" with Congress; "test the waters" with Congress, consulting with leadership; or engage in a two-stage process. Its recommendation: test the waters before submitting a bill.

The memo envisioned structuring a CDFI Fund as a "federally-chartered, quasi-public enterprise," governed by an 11-member board, including Cabinet members, representatives of CDFIs and community groups, mainstream bankers, and regulators. It would "serve as a corporate board of directors to establish policy and would retain a full-time President/CEO to manage operations of the Fund."[786] The fund would have a proactive role, serving "as a national information clearinghouse and support system to help prospective CDFIs get off the ground and existing ones to expand, better meet their mission, and operate soundly."[787]

The working group spent Saturday, May 8, drafting the Clinton administration's bill, line by line. When they were satisfied with their draft, the next step was sending it to the Office of Management and Budget (OMB), prior to transmitting it to Congress.[788]

## The White House Goes to Capitol Hill

Much work was required to align the president's initiative with Congress. The *Washington Post* reported that "the administration is bringing potential congressional allies into the creation of the plan in hopes of building momentum that will enable both the White House and lawmakers to claim credit for keeping the president's campaign promise."[789] Weinstein met repeatedly with House and Senate Banking Committee staff, especially Senator Riegle's staff.[790] He noted that "Senator Sarbanes' staff was somewhat leery of the CDFI concept."[791] Weinstein highlighted the need to reach across the aisle from the Democratic side: "The politics of the Banking Committee tend to be parochial rather than partisan." It was vital to get support from African American lawmakers—Representatives Flake, Mfume, and Waters, as well as Senator Carol Moseley-Braun of Illinois. Weinstein planned to provide a draft to ShoreBank and Southern Development Bancorporation "to make sure they are comfortable with our approach." Finally, in his memo of May 10, Weinstein emphasized the urgency of meeting with appropriations staff in Congress, "because word is they are getting pressured to spend the $60 million [for the CDFI legislation] on other initiatives. **WE MUST DEAL WITH THIS MATTER THIS WEEK** [emphasis in original]."[792]

The draft administration bill soon leaked out.[793] On May 18, Under Secretary of the Treasury Frank Newman, along with Secretary Robert Rubin and White House policy adviser Bruce Reed, met for 90 minutes with the House Banking Committee's Democratic caucus. Speaking to the press, Newman downplayed the status of the administration's proposal, stating that "there isn't even an acronym" for the proposed new entity.[794] But in fact, some of the key elements were hardening into place.
- $382 million over four years for a "Community Banking and Credit Fund"
- A matching fund requirement

- Support for building on the existing system rather than funding a new community development bank network from scratch
- A national information clearinghouse
- An oversight board composed of cabinet secretary offices and community representatives.[795]

Despite the White House's vigorous efforts to work with Congress, Deepak Bhargava of the advocacy organization ACORN predicted that it would not be an easy battle: "The Administration is going to have to do a lot of work to hold the Democrats and it will meet substantial Republican opposition."[796] Some observers saw the administration's draft plan as a partial retreat, since the proposed funding was reduced from an earlier trial balloon of $850 million to $382 million. In fact, some supporters welcomed this reduction. "It's small, but that's the way it ought to be," said Rep. Charles E. Schumer (D-NY). "We ought to see what works."[797]

The Interagency Working Group was eager to resolve the structure and governance of the fund before finalizing its bill. In a May 25 memorandum, Paul Dimond outlined five possible models for the fund, envisioned as a private entity with varying options for presidential selection of board members. White House adviser Bruce Reed wrote a comment to Dimond on the margins of the memo, saying, "Any model will do, as long as the Pres. puts Elk Horn [Southern Development Bancorporation] and South Shore on the board."[798]

The CDFI Coalition would have been surprised at how seriously the administration was contemplating a mixed public/private structure. The National Federation of CDCUs had put forth the idea of a trust fund, possibly seeded with a $1 billion, one-time federal appropriation; the progressive economist Hyman Minsky had also proposed a similar structure. This approach would have the advantage of avoiding annual congressional appropriations battles. Some CDFI Coalition leaders also wanted to encourage or mandate bank contributions to the fund. But we didn't really contemplate a mixed-ownership model in the way the administration was exploring.

## Community Empowerment: Echoes of the War on Poverty

On June 3, 1993, as the administration was finalizing its proposal, a group of four influential national advocacy organizations—the Center for Community Change, the Consumer Federation of America, the National Council of La Raza, and ACORN—jointly submitted an extensive comment letter to Paul Dimond of the National Economic Council. The policy issues and tensions they highlighted in fact echoed those of the War on Poverty, which had largely receded in the succeeding decades, when anti-poverty initiatives were shunned or rolled back.

"We strongly endorse the objectives of the legislation to spur capital investment into communities that have suffered the economic consequences of abandonment and neglect by insured depositories," declared the advocates.[799] They pointed out the problem of discrimination in credit, although they did not focus on CRA—indeed, they did not mention it directly. Rather, they focused on the fund

design and, especially, how it would impact and respond to the needs of poor communities. Their letter highlighted three major areas of concern:
- Representation of low- and moderate-income people and community-based nonprofits in governance both of the fund and its awardees
- Accountability of the fund, should it become a mixed, public-private entity
- Equal consideration for all types of CDFIs
- Match requirements, which had to be flexible so as not to disadvantage low- and very-low-income communities.

In their concern for community empowerment, the advocates were in the line of descent from the left wing in the War on Poverty, those who argued for "maximum feasible participation" of the poor, in contrast with the expert/technocratic strain.[800] The advocates drew on Clinton's own campaign rhetoric from his manifesto, *Putting People First*: They reframed it as "Making Sure People Are Put First at the Fund's Board." Specifically, they urged that the new fund's governing board include "at least three … volunteer board members of nonprofit community-based organizations, while the input of commercial bankers should be minimized." This would help ensure that local communities had an ownership stake in the new community development banks' goals and mission. To avoid the conflict with city mayors that had plagued the War on Poverty, the advocates called for excluding state and local government entities from access to the fund.[801]

Often, well-intentioned, ostensibly fair and objective policies result in disproportionately denying services or access to minority or other disadvantaged groups. The group of advocates called attention to administration proposals that threatened such a disparate impact. They agreed that there should be a competitive funding process, but they emphatically—and prophetically—argued that a complex application would hurt resource-poor communities and organizations: "We are generally concerned," they wrote, "that the competition not disadvantage applicants who may have strong community development financing backgrounds and commitment but may lack administrative resources necessary to compete with larger and more well financed applicants."[802] The proposed matching requirement was a good example of potential disparate impact: "We have a general concern that applications from more distressed communities may be disadvantaged if application reviews tend to favor large external commitments….[Specifically], a 2:1 match requirement…will likely cut these [particularly distressed] communities from the possibility of receiving assistance from the Fund—irrespective of community need or proposal merit."[803]

The argument about disparate impact was well founded. Philanthropic resources and bank CRA programs were unevenly distributed; many were concentrated in New York, Chicago, San Francisco, Philadelphia, and other large cities. Few foundations were located in or focused on the poorest rural areas. The largest, most sophisticated banks in the big cities often provided grants and loans to organizations in their CRA assessment areas. In the rural South, small African American organizations did not have access to this kind of money. To address the imbalance, the advocates argued for the CDFI Fund to give weight to the extent of economic distress in applicants' communities.

The administration intended to fund institutions with the potential to become self-sustaining. It was a reasonable objective, but as the advocates agued, "If 'self-sustaining' is interpreted to mean that applicants must generate income, the requirement will tend to disadvantage many successful community-based nonprofits and community development credit unions who do not, by their corporate nature, generate income (e.g., fees) more than operational expenses."[804*] They offered support for community development credit unions by suggesting that they be allowed to meet match requirements by raising member deposits, instead of hard-to-get equity. On the other hand, like the CDFI Coalition, the advocates rejected the notion of a set-aside or a higher funding maximum for banks and credit unions, arguing that mission, not insured status, should determine funding.

Ultimately, the outcome for the advocates' proposals was mixed. Insured depositories would receive no preference over nonprofits. The matching requirement would be reduced to 1:1, with limited exceptions permitted. The new CDFI Fund would be a fully government-owned—rather than mixed-ownership—entity. But representation by low-income communities and their advocates in governing CDFIs and the Fund itself would be diluted. And in the tension between prioritizing the poorest communities, on the one hand, and rewarding a strong application and performance on the other, the latter approach predominated. After the first round of awards, when the National Federation of CDCUs saw few of its very poor, minority credit unions funded, we clashed vigorously with the CDFI Fund exactly on this question.

## The Administration's Final Draft

In June, the Treasury Department completed its draft bill for transmittal "up the Hill" to the Democratic Speaker of the House, Thomas S. Foley. The "Community Banking and Credit Fund," as it was called, "would provide financial and technical assistance to community development financial institutions and serve as a national information clearinghouse for community development financial institutions." All types of CDFIs would be eligible. The bill resolved a key structural issue, clarified eligibility, and filled in other details of the new fund.

- **Structure.** The White House abandoned the notion of a mixed-ownership, public/private corporation, thus sparing considerable complexity and controversy: "The Fund shall be a wholly-owned government corporation in the Executive branch…." [Section 4(e)]. A nine-member board would govern it, including the secretaries of Agriculture, Commerce, HUD, and Treasury; the Administrator of the SBA; and four private citizens. Like a corporate board, it would appoint a CEO.
- **Matching Requirement.** To engage the private sector, the administration (as well as the CDFI Coalition) had earlier envisioned a 2:1 non-federal match. The administration's bill now

---

\* In fact, this argument was unclear or partially untrue: Low-income credit unions, like all credit unions and banks, had to cover their expenses and generate reserves, lest they be put out of business.

required "no less than one dollar of private equity or private deposits for each dollar provided by the Fund." [Sec. 7 (d)(1)]. Selection criteria included "the amount of legally enforceable commitments at the time of application to meet or exceed the matching requirements" [Sec. 6(a)(9)].
- **Forms of Assistance.** The CDFI Fund would provide "equity investments, loans, loan guarantees, deposits, and grants" [Sec. 7(b)(1)]. This was crucial for the CDFI movement, whose biggest objective was to obtain a source of equity and grants; without these provisions, CDFIs would almost certainly have struggled to grow.
- **Total Funding.** The bill requested $382 million over four years—down from the president's original hopes of $1 billion.
- **Preference for Depositories.** Although all types of CDFIs were eligible, the preference for insured depositories remained, specifying that awards would be "up to $5,000,000 of assistance per year to any one qualified insured community development financial institution and up to $2,000,000 per year to any other qualified community development financial institution" [Sec. 7(c)].
- **No Quota.** There was no quota governing allocations between insured depositories and uninsured nonprofit lenders. However, several proposed criteria reflected the administration's preference. The fund was to consider "whether the applicant is, or will become, an insured community development financial institution" [Sec. 6(a)(13).] It was to assess "the likelihood of success of the applicant in forming and operating a community development financial institution that is, or will become, an entity that will not be dependent upon assistance from the Fund for continued viability" [Sec. 6(a)(2)].
- **Empowering Communities.** The fund was to consider "the extent to which the applicant is, or will be, community-owned or community-governed" [Sec. 6(a)(12)]. But the language was soft: A CDFI was defined as one that "encourages, through representation on its governing board or otherwise, the input of residents in the investment area or the targeted populations" [Sec. 3 (a)(2)]. This was no mandate for Sixties-style "maximum feasible participation" of the poor.
- **No Mayoral Power-Grabs.** The bill avoided the potential power struggles with mayors that had undermined the community action agencies in the War on Poverty. It clearly stated that "the term 'community development financial institution' does not include an agency or instrumentality of the United States or an agency or instrumentality of any State or political subdivision thereof" [Sec. 3(a)].
- **Not Just Money.** CDFIs were to provide not only loans and investments, but also "development services," including business planning, financial counseling, and marketing and management assistance.
- **A Pro-Active Role.** The CDFI Fund was to serve as an information clearinghouse and, in effect, a promoter of CDFIs. It was to become the "Institutional Voice for Community Development" [Sec. 10(a)(2)].

- **Not a Regulator.** The CDFI Fund was not to be some sort of central bank or regulatory agency for CDFIs, as Professor Minsky had envisioned.[805] It had "No Authority to Limit Supervision and Regulation" [Sec. 7(h)] by the bank and credit union regulators, though it "should" consult with them before assisting an insured CDFI [Sec. 7(e)(2)]. There would be no special CDFI charter for banks or credit unions, which CDFIs, the National Federation of CDCUs, and the banking lobby all would have opposed.
- **Timetable.** The administration was eager to get the CDFI Fund up and running. The proposed board of the fund was to publish regulations and application forms within 180 days after the act became law [Sec. 5(a)]. (As it turned out, it took about 15 months to pass legislation, and the CDFI Fund did not open for applications until fall 1995.)

As the administration's bill evolved in June, before the draft went public, the CDFI Coalition continued to press the White House for changes. The administration's June 4 draft distinguished between depositories (banks and credit unions), which would be eligible for up to $5 million in funding, and non-depositories (primarily nonprofit loan funds), which would be capped at $2 million for each award. Although the preference for depositories was weaker than in previous versions, the coalition continued to argue that "this differentiation is not necessary or justified.... We have urged...a single cap for all types of institutions."[806] The CDFI Fund ought to be agnostic as to institutional type, concentrating instead on an applicant's performance, capacity, and soundness. The coalition supported the bill's reduced matching requirement, no greater than 1:1. It emphasized the importance of rural and reservation-based communities both in funding and in the governance of the fund. Finally, the coalition requested various technical clarifications.

The June 15 "final" administration bill strengthened emphasis on "the extent to which the applicant will concentrate its activities on serving low- and very-low-income families."[807] The differentiation between depositories and non-depositories remained, although diluted. Also diluted was the role of the target communities. As CDFI Coalition coordinator Mark Pinsky reported:

- The June 4 version read that a CDFI "*maintains*, through representation on its governing board or otherwise, *accountability* to residents in the investment area or the targeted populations."
- In contrast, the June 15 draft read that a CDFI "*encourages*, through representation on its governing board or otherwise, the *input* of residents in the investment area or the targeted populations." [emphasis added]

De-emphasizing depositories and community accountability did not please the National Federation of CDCUs. Credit unions, of course, were federally insured depositories. CDCUs were member-owned and democratically governed—one member, one vote. Moreover, the CDCU movement had roots in the War on Poverty, with its banner of "maximum feasible participation" by the poor in the governance of community action agencies. Now, in 1993, the administration's community development banking legislation—one of the most important federal initiatives since the 1960s—promised nothing more than "input of residents." Nonetheless, to preserve unity, the federation submerged its own interests in the CDFI Coalition's consensus.

## Two Non-Starters: Good Idea, but...

As the administration's bill took final shape, at least two program ideas to complement and enhance CDFIs emerged but did not become part of the legislative package. In September 1992, during his campaign, Clinton endorsed the concept of Individual Development Accounts (IDAs)—matched savings accounts for restricted, "asset-building" purposes (postsecondary education, small business startup, home purchase) that would help low-income people grasp a ladder out of poverty. IDAs were part of Clinton's program to "end welfare as we know it." Senator Bradley had also promoted this proposal. Despite this support, legislation for an IDA program would not pass for five years.[808]

Another creative initiative would link CDFIs to President Clinton's proposed national service program for young people. This would help address an important need identified by all parties—the CDFI Coalition, members of Congress, and the Clinton administration. Experienced community development bankers were extremely rare; the CDFI Coalition ranked human resource development second only to access to capital in its priorities. Perhaps a robust national service program could develop and train a stream of recruits for CDFIs.

On June 20, Paul Weinstein submitted a memo on this subject to Shirley Sagawa, deputy chief of staff to First Lady Hillary Clinton.[809] He suggested that undergraduates could meet their community service requirement under the national service proposal through apprenticeships at CDFIs of any kind. "Some students might even continue to work at CDFIs, or even start one," he offered. "Even better, however, would be for these individuals to take positions at banks and other financial institutions. If loan officers trained at CDFIs took jobs at mainstream banks, we could see an unprecedented amount of lending activity in lower- to moderate-income communities."[810]

CDFIs would have enthusiastically supported this intriguing, if overly optimistic, approach. The Corporation for National and Community Service did get established, but it was not part of the Clinton CDFI bill. The linkage between CDFIs and national service never became federal policy. However, the National Federation of CDCUs implemented the concept on its own. The federation operated a nationwide VISTA (Volunteers in Service to America) program. Some of the young people who passed through this program did, in fact, go on to work in CDCUs or elsewhere in the CDFI movement.

## Invitation to a Ceremony

At last, the White House was ready to go public: On Thursday, July 15, at 11:00 a.m., President Clinton would announce his plans both for community development banking and community reinvestment in the White House Rose Garden.

On July 7, at 5:15 p.m., the White House requested a "comprehensive list" of foundation and bank supporters of CDFIs to invite to the upcoming Rose Garden ceremony on July 15. Each coalition member could bring up to five people (to be invited by phone on Tuesday, July 13). Meanwhile, the coalition developed a list of CDFI borrowers to make presentations at the ceremony.

The coalition did not see the final language for the CDFI bill until Tuesday, July 13. On the 15th, members of the CDFI Coalition assembled in the grand lobby of the historic Willard Inter-Continental Hotel, across from the Treasury Building, to prepare for their day in the sun.

# CHAPTER 15. In the Rose Garden

> *This event is the culmination of months of planning, drafting, policy development and delicate negotiations with constituent groups and Members of Congress.*[811]
> *Memorandum for the President, July 14, 1993*

The Clinton administration finalized its bill in mid-June—not a week too soon. The congressional calendar and political dynamics demanded urgency. On June 22, a memo from staff of the National Economic Council (NEC) and Domestic Policy Council (DPC) made the case: "A public, 'Rose Garden' variety event covering both the CDFI and CRA initiatives would be very helpful, if not imperative, to our legislative strategy for the CDFI initiative.... This strategy is particularly needed to bring on Maxine Waters and solidify Bobby Rush's commitment to be a foot soldier for the bill."[812]

Representatives Waters and Rush, both members of the Congressional Black Caucus, each had a personal connection to the emerging initiative. Rush represented the South Side of Chicago, and ShoreBank was in his district. "Maxine Waters was the first progressive black federal politician to endorse Bill Clinton," her legislative director, Bill Zavarello, recalled. Waters had delegated Zavarello to meet with the Clinton transition team. Zavarello recalled that initially, "this idea was really not baked. It was always theoretical because we're basing it on a very small number of institutions and so really my job then was to say, 'whenever you get to this, we want to be part of it.' I was just putting in a place marker for Maxine to be part of this."[813] Both would support the administration's initiative, although both were concerned that it did not go far enough.

On June 24, the Interagency Working Group sent a memo to White House senior advisers pressing for the president to announce the following week. The congressional window for moving legislation and appropriations was narrowing, and the "stakeholders" who supported the initiative—CDFIs and community groups especially—"have been waiting for months for an Administration announcement that it is moving forward with these efforts."[814] It was crucial to keep control of the news cycle, to "keep the Hill ahead of the press on the curve. Nothing hurts us more than members [of Congress] learning details of our plans from reporters for the first time."[815]

Despite the staff's urgency, delay was unavoidable. The president was about to head off to the 19th G-7 summit in Japan of the richest industrialized countries, returning on July 14. This made scheduling difficult: Senators would be returning home for a summer recess, and July 15 was the only day the Banking Committee had available in July. As White House staff noted, "A hearing by mid-July is critical to garner full Committee support and to transmit the bill to the Senate floor in time to secure the requisite appropriation."[816]

So, July 15 would be the big day: first, a White House ceremony in the morning, then the Senate Banking Committee hearing in the afternoon.

## On the Threshold

Although the coalition still had some differences with the administration's bill, the most important thing was simply to get the legislation out and moving. The White House's hesitancy and delays increased the coalition's anxiety, as Mark Pinsky reported to its steering committee.

> The major concern is that the White House seems unwilling to fight for its own CDFI legislation.... Several people, most notably the Senate Banking committee staff, have told the White House that it is a big mistake to introduce this bill without putting the full weight of the Administration behind it. However, the staffers I have talked to are pessimistic that the White House is listening.[817]

On June 25, Pinsky spoke to Paul Dimond of the National Economic Council. He reported back to the coalition that "the White House expects to release its bill this week. Will it really happen? Will the Budget sidetrack the effort? Will the Iraqi bombing distract the President? Tune in and find out!"[818]

Meanwhile, the coalition was laying the groundwork for a major campaign to support CDFI legislation. The coalition would develop materials explaining the "Why & What of CDFIs"—a necessary information piece, since CDFIs were little known.[819] It would conduct a public relations campaign and plan a national conference. At the local level, it would mobilize its membership of several hundred CDFIs to contact their representatives. In Washington, the CDFI Coalition would take its case to Congress and the White House, CRA advocacy groups, minority banks, and trade associations.

## The Two-Track Strategy: CRA and Community Development Banking

On July 14, the eve of the Rose Garden ceremony, White House advisers Gene Sperling and Bruce Reed reminded the president of the administration's agreed-upon strategy. The CRA and community development banking initiatives would both be rolled out on July 15, but they would move on separate tracks: A community development banking bill would be sent to Congress, while CRA reform would come through regulation. "Tomorrow," they wrote, "you will send a memorandum to the four bank regulators asking them to issue performance-based regulatory reforms by January 1, 1994."[820]

A two-track strategy was necessary to avoid political landmines. Throughout 1993, White House staff had worked to keep the support of CRA advocates, who preferred strengthening CRA through regulation, rather than running the risk of seeking legislation in Congress that instead might wind up weakening CRA. However, the advocates needed "constant reassurance that they will be full participants in the development of CRA regulatory reforms with the Bank regulators."[821]

Not only would CRA itself have a rough ride if legislation were introduced in Congress: Adding CRA reforms to a community development banking bill would threaten the latter as well. Above all, the administration's goal was to keep the community development banking bill as narrow as possible, avoiding not only a CRA fight but also the "Christmas tree" effect—that is, a piling-on by the banking lobby of their own favored provisions, especially interstate branching. "We have been warned," the Domestic Policy Council staff reminded the president, "that if our CDFI bill becomes such a 'Christmas tree,' there will be no chance for passage."[822]

## July 15, 1993: Making History

On the morning of July 15, CDFI representatives from around the country made their way to the East Gate of the White House, bypassing the tourists and entering the building for security clearance. "I remember having to give my social security number, and they did an identity check right then and there," recalled Errol T. Louis, "which I thought was amazing."[823] One by one, the CDFI contingent made their way through the White House to the South Lawn—the Rose Garden, although no roses were evident—to take their places on folding chairs on the soft turf. A podium and low platform for speakers sat under a large shade tree. Mercifully, the mid-summer Washington sun had not reached its peak when the ceremony began.

"This is an historic occasion," White House staffers briefed the president, "in which the major banks, community groups, the CDFI industry, and members of Congress stand together on the same platform."[824] For the community activists, after 12 years of indifference or hostility under the Reagan and Bush administrations, it was a glorious moment that they had barely dreamed of. "I remember being shocked that it was even happening," recalled Louis.[825]

It was hard not to be a little star-struck, even for New Yorkers who prided themselves on their sophistication. Among the CDFI allies present was Anita Nager, a grantmaker who had supported the National Federation of CDCUs and other community economic development efforts for a decade, through the Fund for the City of New York and the New York Community Trust. Nager, who was certainly accustomed to working among the philanthropic elite of New York, recalled thinking:

> This is a big deal. Even I, who was working for a foundation, felt like I was pretending to be a grown up. The institutionalization, the recognition, of this movement with serious legislation and the promise of serious resources was such a marker and a point of recognition. Shaking Clinton's hand, oh my goodness! It was truly thrilling!

> It certainly was a legitimization of the scrappy movement that we had seen develop over time. We had great hopes that we pinned on the Clintons for this movement and others. Some were met and others weren't, but it felt like the dawn of a new day.[826]

Vice President Gore opened the program by recalling President Clinton's longtime support for community development: "It has from the very beginning of the president's economic plan been an important cornerstone." The trouble in many communities, Gore stated, was that they didn't have a bank. The president's plan "will begin to redress the balance. It will provide rural and urban communities affordable credit, capital, and basic banking services…" Everyone who had visited a community where a CDFI was at work shared the residents' excitement, for one reason: "It works. The idea works."[827]

For many in the audience—perhaps including the beaming president—the program's highlight was the trio of success stories from CDFI borrowers. The CDFI Coalition had recruited three borrowers—one woman and two African American men, reflecting the coalition's and the president's shared commitment to diversity. All the borrowers came from small businesses, again a key part of the president's initiative.

Shaded by a large tree but basking in the spotlight, Timothy Bazemore, an African American man in his sixties from rural Eastern North Carolina, came up to the podium. Standing nearly close enough to touch President Clinton, surrounded by Cabinet secretaries and other dignitaries, Bazemore told the story of the Workers Owned Sewing Company (WOSCO), the employee-owned manufacturer of women's and children's clothes located in Bertie County, which Bazemore organized and led. "When we started, we had five people. Most of us were willing to work for nothing until such time that we could pay ourselves. With money from churches and foundations, we grew to a point where we had enough to go to K-Mart [a chain department store] and say, 'We know that we can manufacture for you.'"[828]

K-Mart was receptive, but WOSCO lacked working capital to keep operating until customers paid for their shipments. A small local bank had cut off WOSCO's modest line of credit, so Bazemore turned to Self-Help. Its credit union and Ventures Fund provided both a $50,000 loan and—an important service of CDFIs—assistance in marketing and financial management. The working-capital loan enabled WOSCO to obtain contracts with Sears and K-Mart. It grew to 80 workers—predominantly women—making it the second-largest employer in Bertie County. Each year, it distributed profits to its worker-owners. "Many times," Bazemore concluded, "we failed to re-apply to local banks, because we knew the answer before we applied…. I am frightened that I don't have the words to convey to you the importance of funding in rural low-income communities throughout this Nation."[829]

Beverly Ross's story illustrated the importance of microenterprise lenders. Ross had taken a major step in buying the Lakeview Stables in Mineral Springs, OH, where she worked. But, like many small-business owners, she lacked working capital. A single parent with subpar credit, her only recourse for a loan was the Athens Small Business Center. She received a loan of $5,780, which enabled her to buy equipment and horses; as well, she received intensive technical assistance in financial planning and preparing a loan application.

Joseph Holland was not a typical low-income entrepreneur, nor was his enterprise typical. A graduate of Harvard Law School, in 1982 he gave up a law practice to return to Harlem and help the homeless. He founded a nonprofit shelter, the Harlem Ark of Freedom, and in 1992 turned his energy to starting a business to employ shelter residents. Community Capital Bank of Brooklyn provided a $100,000 construction loan to fund a partnership between Holland's organization and the Ben & Jerry's corporation, renowned for its social engagement. The 10-person ice cream shop in Harlem provided employment for eight shelter residents and returned much of its profits to the organization.

## The President Speaks: From Tokyo to South Central

The president had returned only hours before from his trip to the economic summit in Japan, followed by a visit to South Korea. At a stopover in Hawaii, "More than 20,000 people responded to Clinton's open invitation to a July 11, 1993, speech on the beach of the Hilton Hawaiian Village."[830] Back in Washington, Clinton linked community development banking to the global themes of the economic summit: "From Harlem to the South Side of Chicago, to South Central Los Angeles, there is a feeling shared from Tokyo to Toronto, people want more control over their lives...." He made a pitch for his plan for "the largest deficit reduction plan in our history." This provided context for his CDFI proposal, which required that every dollar invested be matched by "at least" another dollar of private capital.

After thanking the CDFI speakers—"Joe, Beverly, and Tim," as he called them—President Clinton set about recognizing the assembled dignitaries: Cabinet secretaries and undersecretaries from Treasury, Agriculture, and HUD; the Small Business Administration; the Comptroller of the Currency and other regulators; and "41 or 42" members of Congress. He thanked congressional committee chairs, Senator Riegle and Rep. Gonzalez, as well as multiple subcommittee chairs. He gave "special recognition" to Rep. Joseph Kennedy for his work on the Community Reinvestment Act (CRA), and to three members of the Congressional Black Caucus who had submitted legislation and whom he needed to have on board—Representatives Floyd Flake, Maxine Waters, and Bobby Rush. He introduced Rev. Jesse Jackson, seated at the front, who rose and took a bow.

President Clinton pointedly contrasted the performance of young CDFIs with that of the failed banks and savings and loan associations that had produced a multi-billion-dollar government bailout. To the delight of (much of) his audience, he declared, "I can tell you this, most of the enterprises that we are talking about helping, that were in existence in the 1980s that made loans to poor people who lived in their community or to struggling small business people, had a lot lower failure rate than some of the high flown financial schemes that were subsidized by other government policies in the last decade." He singled out ShoreBank, the Self-Help Credit Union, and the Elkhorn Bank of Arkansas, on whose board First Lady Hillary Clinton had served, and for which he helped raise funds when he was governor of Arkansas.

Moving on to the CRA, President Clinton reminded the largely (but not entirely) supportive audience that "we would all admit that it hasn't lived up to its potential. The current enforcement system relies too much on public relations documentation and not enough on real lending performance." To reinforce his argument, he then turned the podium over to NationsBank Chairman Hugh McColl of North Carolina.

"It's an honor to speak today, on behalf of the banking industry," began McColl. (This line would almost immediately get him into trouble with his peers.) "The creation of a fund to provide assistance for community development financial institutions will expand a critical element in the nation's credit network. Because they are less regulated, these institutions have proven themselves to be effective in reaching the neighborhoods most in need of credit."* Addressing implicitly the concerns of banks about competition, McColl emphasized partnerships with CDFIs: "NationsBank and the Durham-based Self-Help Credit Union worked hand-in-hand referring customers to each other to ensure that all needs are met."

McColl went further out on a limb by embracing the new CRA direction of the Clinton administration. "A new rule, one that sets tougher, more objective, more quantifiable standards would send a clear message to banks that we will be measured by results, no excuses. Mr. President, your proposals are in the best interest of both banks and our communities." He concluded, optimistically: "I think you'll find NationsBank and other banking companies are eager to work with regulators and community groups in the formation of policy that sets measurable, objective standards and makes true partners of all of us involved."

Irwin Henderson—like Timothy Bazemore and Hugh McColl—was from North Carolina, where he was president of the Gateway Community Development Corporation. Henderson spoke on behalf of the National Community Reinvestment Coalition (NCRC), which he chaired and which represented over 250 member organizations across the country. Although some bankers later griped about the "bank-bashing" at the event, Henderson's remarks really were quite restrained. He noted that NCRC "from the very beginning ...[has] stressed performance in lending as the true measure of a financial institution's compliance with the Community Reinvestment Act." He supported reducing unnecessary or duplicative paperwork, while not sacrificing necessary data "in the name of regulatory relief." He supported CDFI legislation as "an important beginning for federal investment" in low-income communities.

## ShoreBank's Dream

Ron Grzywinski was the final speaker. Despite ShoreBank's national prominence and his acquaintance with President Clinton dating to the late 1980s, Grzywinski and his bank were not Washington

---

* Presumably, McColl had in mind community development loan funds, since community development banks and credit unions were, in fact, regulated like any other depositories.

insiders. As he recalled years later, "We were always so apolitical. I probably knew that [my colleagues] went to Washington, but I had no idea" that they testified.[831] Grzywinski was not overly awed by the occasion, as his colleague, Bob Weissbourd remembered: "You know, I'm drafting all these speeches, Ron is sitting on the plane just scribbling some notes. Ron is a great extemporaneous speaker and it comes out great."[832]

Grzywinski remarked, "This is truly the day of the impossible dream.... A quarter century ago, my closest and oldest colleagues and I concluded that to seriously rebuild communities for low-income people, this nation had to create permanent, self-sustaining institutions.... Mr. President, your proposal to the Congress is just one more step in this nation's long journey to focus major private financial resources on making the world's most powerful economy work better for the benefit of all its citizens."

The president closed the ceremony by thanking all the CDFI representatives for their years of work advancing the community development banking field. He recalled learning of South Shore Bank when he was governor of Arkansas, and through them, meeting "a remarkable man named Muhammad Yunus, who told me how he, through the Grameen Bank, had made market rate interest loans to poor village women in Bangladesh, and over 95 percent of them had actually paid the loans back." He thanked Rep. Floyd Flake (his congressional adversary on the Bank Enterprise Award amendment) for showing him the businesses Flake and his megachurch had built in Queens, NY, and he thanked Hugh McColl, who "stayed up half the night one night talking with me about the Community Reinvestment Act and how we could make it work." Finally, he thanked Charles Stith, national president of the Organization for a New Equality (ONE).

When the ceremony ended, the out-of-towners as well as Washington insiders seeking face time flocked to the president, who remained to shake hands and pose for the photos that would make their way to the hometown papers of CDFIs across the country. "I remember that everybody wanted to touch the hem of Clinton's garment," recalled Errol Louis. "Everybody crowded around him.... [Clinton] wants to shake every single hand, and he means that literally."[833] Louis had organized a new institution—which became nationally known as the "hip-hop credit union"—to serve the African American community of Bedford-Stuyvesant, Brooklyn. His CDCU organizing partner, Mark Winston Griffith, attended the ceremony as well: "I remember there was a line of people shaking Bill Clinton's hand," Griffith recalled, "and I was on that line. I thought, 'This is for the banks.' I remember walking off the line, and he came behind me and grabbed my shoulder and shook my hand. It was one of those moments!"[834]

Meanwhile, Vice President Gore stood on the sidelines, eclipsed by the charismatic Clinton. "I said, 'What the hell, I'll get a picture with him,' recalled Louis. "I took a picture of him and I got a picture of Mark with him."[835] It served Louis and Griffith well in their effort to promote their soon-to-be-opened credit union. "What we were doing by getting that buy-in and being at that ceremony, it wasn't just for us. It was really for the whole government," recalled Louis. The government audience, of course, included the financial regulators, including the National Credit Union Administration (NCUA), which would charter, regulate, and supervise the new Bedford-Stuyvesant credit union.

Thad Moore, Self-Help's vice president, captured the feeling of so many CDFI practitioners who had labored, unrecognized, for years. "I had the president of the United States stand up and thank me for all the work I had done," Moore said. "That was something!"[836]

Immediately after the White House ceremony, some of us made our way east up Pennsylvania Avenue to the Dirksen Senate Office Building, where Senator Riegle's Banking Committee was holding its hearing on the administration's bill. Meanwhile, the two bankers, Ron Grzywinski and Hugh McColl, headed south. The two had met for the first time in the White House, waiting impatiently for the beginning of the ceremony. Grzywinski recalled:

> Clinton kept all of us waiting. We were in some anteroom for several hours. I didn't know who Hugh McColl was. He kept looking at his watch. I went up to him and said, 'You must be Hugh McColl.' I introduced myself, and he grumbled about Clinton keeping us waiting. He said, 'I've got to get to Dallas.' I said, 'Well, I've got a board meeting in Arkadelphia, Arkansas.' He said, 'Would you like a ride?' I said, 'Are you going there?' He said, 'Yeah.' I said, 'You got a plane?' He said, 'Yeah.' He and I bonded.
>
> He turned to his assistant and he said, 'Call the pilot and see if they can go there.' It took 30 minutes and she came back and said, 'Yeah, they just lengthened the runway.' It was he and I in this nine-passenger jet, two pilots with us. His self-image was of a loan officer driving the back roads of North Carolina with a notepad, finding farmers or anybody who needed $25,000 loans.
>
> As we were getting closer to Arkadelphia and starting to land, he said, 'God, isn't this an amazing country.... There we were just a few minutes ago...in the White House with the president of the United States and now here we are in the middle of Arkansas.' There was something that really just struck him about that.[837]

It was a productive business trip. Later, NationsBank became a major shareholder of ShoreBank, and engaged it to create and manage the National Community Investment Fund (NCIF).

## First Reactions

Despite several disagreements with the bill, the CDFI Coalition immediately announced its endorsement, declaring it "will build on the pioneering work these institutions [CDFIs] have done over the past several decades."[838] Citing its own cornerstone document, "Principles of Community Development Lending & Proposals for Key Federal Support," the coalition approvingly noted that the bill supported all types of CDCUs, both established and new. Many of the features advocated by the CDFI Coalition were included: grants and equity investments; incremental funding based

## Chapter 15. In the Rose Garden

on growth; and support not only for business lending, but also for housing and other community development lending.

For the National Federation of CDCUs, the legislation was particularly gratifying. Writing for our newsletter, I reminded our members that as early as 1986 we had first formulated the concept of a National Neighborhood Finance Corporation, an idea remarkably like what the president introduced. "After years of being a lone voice for federal support for financial institutions that serve low-income and minority communities, it is wonderful to see so many top policymakers offer their support."[839]

The Consumer Federation of America (CFA) applauded the community development banking proposal and urged quick congressional action. "President Clinton's initiative on community development banks is the brightest beacon of hope in years for low- and moderate-income communities long neglected by our nation's commercial banking industry," said Chris Lewis, CFA's director of banking policy. Lewis warned against a "backdoor heist" of the program by banking interests, which would constitute a "gross waste of taxpayer resources" by allowing commercial banks to substitute federal money for what they should be doing anyway. CFA's only regret was that the program's funding was too meager.[840] Ted Wysocki, a longtime ally of the legendary CRA advocate Gale Cincotta and executive director of the Chicago Association of Neighborhood Development Organizations (CANDO), struck a positive note, praising the proposed legislation for recognizing the expertise of the range of CDFIs and community development organizations. The bill, he remarked, "transforms the 20-year-old public debate over redlining into a call for communities, regulators and banks to collaborate on financing community development."[841]

But there were mixed messages from the banks. Hugh McColl's endorsement of the Clinton legislation and claim to be speaking for the banking industry drew a quick, furious scold from Kenneth A. Guenther, executive vice president of the Independent Bankers Association of America. Guenther declared that McColl had sinned by giving away the banking industry's negotiating position in advance. "I don't know how he can say he speaks for the banking industry."[842] *American Banker* sounded a worried note: The ceremony represented

> a show of political strength that suggested banks may have trouble gaining regulatory relief through legislation…. The sheer magnitude of the ceremony on the White House's south lawn, which ran for nearly an hour, indicated the administration and congressional leaders want to move the package through quickly and without amendments.

The article quoted a banking lobbyist, Jim Butera, who said "I've never seen so much horsepower behind a banking bill."[843] Although McColl incurred the industry lobbyists' wrath for "speaking for the banking industry," his was not a lone voice. A press release of July 20 announced, "Fleet Financial Group Chairman Terrance Murray Endorses Clinton Community Development Landing Initiative." While the $45 billion bank hedged its support with a call for further study, Fleet praised the program as "an integral measure in providing additional capital and credit to small businesses and consumers in low- and moderate-income areas." Murray welcomed reform of CRA as well, but added a pitch to permit interstate branch banking, a high priority for the banking industry's largest institutions.

The bankers' trade associations were somewhat consoled that the administration did not entirely shun existing banks by proposing to fund an altogether new system.[844] But that was not enough for the banks' vocal supporter in the Senate, Alfonse D'Amato, the ranking Republican on the Banking Committee and a major power broker. Senator D'Amato demanded a greater role—and share of CDFI money—for mainstream banks, delivering a thinly veiled threat: Unless commercial banks were given incentives to participate, the president's plan was "only a pipe dream."[845]

The most blistering, hyperventilating attack came not from the banking trades—who, after all, had to work with Congress and the administration—but from Cornell University law professor Jonathan R. Macey, whose opinion piece was published in the *Wall Street Journal*.[846] Clinton's plan would

> force banks to compete with a new breed of socialized financial institutions… and represent the sacrifice of sound economic policy on the altar of political expediency…. [It would] require banks and other financial institutions to lend money to targeted areas—providing patronage to the constituents of favored politicians…. The federal government will be left with the tab when these loans cause banks to fail.

He claimed that more than $400 million of "pork" would be directed to "the right places…by a board dominated by Clinton Administration officials." He conjured a vision of CRA advocacy groups using CDFI Fund money to compete with banks; instead, he demanded, banks ought to be freed of CRA obligations.

For its part, the press frequently emphasized the shrinking of Clinton's proposal from an early goal of $850 million to $382 million. Community development banking was "a scaled back loan program… not nearly as ambitious as the plan he spoke of during the campaign," noted one Associated Press writer.[847] As a *Washington Post* editorial noted, "There shouldn't be any pretending here: This is not a vast program; it only barely begins to address the credit needs of the country's inner cities… [but it is] a modest step in the right direction."[848]

# CHAPTER 16. A Year in Congress

Assessing the political landscape, the Domestic Policy Council offered a bright, best-case scenario: If the administration succeeded in "strengthening CRA through regulatory reform and enact[ing] a straightforward CDFI bill, we will have laid the foundation for substantial reinvestment in distressed communities across America." Mainstream banks, thrifts, CDFIs, "and even the unregulated financial industry on a voluntary basis" would join the reinvestment chorus. But this picture came with a strong caveat: "Because of the highly partisan atmosphere and the narrow Democratic majority in the Senate, there may well be difficult negotiations in the Senate. In addition, we may face challenges in the House to keep the CDFI bill straightforward and clean."[849]

In fact, despite the administration's urgency, it would take some 14 months for community development banking to become law.

## In the Senate

July 15, 1993: 2:15 p.m.: Almost immediately after the close of the White House ceremony, the Senate Banking Committee convened a hearing on the Clinton plan. Senator Bradley and Rep. Rush appeared on the first panel, while Treasury Secretary Bentsen, Agriculture Secretary Espy, Commerce Secretary Ronald Brown (by satellite), and Eugene Ludwig, Comptroller of the Currency, also testified.re admin

July 21, 1993: Senator Riegle introduced S. 1275, "a bill to facilitate the establishment of community development financial institutions," with Democratic cosponsors including Senators Sarbanes, Dodd, Kerry, Boxer, Campbell, Moseley-Braun, and Bradley. The bill defined the potential universe of CDFIs:

> The term "community development institution" means any bank, savings association, depository institution holding company, credit union, micro-enterprise loan fund, community development corporation, community development revolving loan fund, minority-owned or other insured depository institution, or non-depository organization that—

(1) has as its primary mission the promotion of community development through the provision of capital, credit, or development services in its investment areas or to targeted populations; and

(2) encourages, through representation on its governing board or otherwise, the input of residents in the investment area or the targeted populations.[850]

Most of the administration's draft bill appeared in S. 1275. The basic financial parameters of the program were unchanged from recent proposals. Congress would authorize $382 million over four years, and the forms of assistance continued to be "equity investments, loans, deposits, membership shares, and grants," as well as technical assistance.

Contrary to the CDFI Coalition's position, depositories and non-depositories would be treated differently: "The Fund may provide up to $5,000,000 of assistance per application to any one qualified insured community development financial institution and up to $2,000,000 per application to any other qualified community development financial institution." Selection was to take into consideration "whether the applicant is, or will become, an insured community development financial institution." However, there was no quota or set-aside for depositories, only a "soft" preference for insured institutions: "The allocation of awards of assistance between insured and uninsured community development financial institutions shall be in the discretion of the Board, provided that consideration shall be given to the allocation of funds to insured community development financial institutions."

Self-sufficiency—or at least independence from further CDFI Fund investment—was to be an important consideration: An applicant would be required to demonstrate that it "has become or is about to become an entity that will not be dependent upon assistance from the Fund for continued viability." Thus, nonfederal matching investments were essential, a tenet of Clinton's community development banking plan since the campaign in 1992. Selection would take into consideration "the amount of legally enforceable commitments available at the time of application to meet or exceed the matching requirements." However, in a change from the earliest concept, the match would be "no less than one dollar of equity, deposits or membership shares for each dollar provided by the Fund," except for awards less than $100,000.

At least two provisions seemed to favor institutions like CDCUs and lightly echoed the War on Poverty: Selection criteria included the extent to which the applicant is, or will be, community-owned or community-governed, and whether it was providing "basic financial services to low-income people or residents of a targeted area." The bill directed the board of the CDFI Fund to seek "to fund a geographically diverse group of applicants, which shall include applicants from nonmetropolitan and rural areas." In addition, it was to consider "whether the applicant is, or will be located, in an empowerment zone or enterprise community…," thus reinforcing another key initiative of the Clinton empowerment agenda.

Structurally, any notion of a mixed public-private trust was gone: The "Community Development Banking and Financial Institutions Fund" was to be a wholly-owned government corporation in the executive branch, with a nine-person board. It was not to be a regulatory or supervisory entity (diverging from the concepts of Professor Minsky and others). The board was directed to consult with the appropriate banking and credit union regulators in making its decisions and, if necessary, considering any sanctions. There would be no separate charter for CDFIs, a position shared by the CDFI Coalition.

The Senate version called for a 210-day time frame for issuing regulations, a modest increase from the Clinton draft of 180 days. The CDFI Fund was to be the "institutional voice" of the federal government about community development finance, serving as an information clearinghouse and playing an active role in educating about CDFIs and disseminating information to help groups start new institutions.

## What Role for Banks?

The Republican minority did not go so far as to reject the creation of the CDFI Fund. Rather, led by Senator D'Amato—who had proposed a CRA safe harbor for banks that financed CDFIs—they sought a larger role for the banking industry. They were favorably disposed to Rep. Flake's Bank Enterprise Act, of course, which provided for cash awards to banks that increased their investment in community development. But beyond that, they were trying to direct CDFI Fund money to bank-owned community development corporations and banks in general. They were opposed by the CDFI Coalition, which worked with the Senate Banking Committee and the White House to reinforce the argument that funding (apart from the BEA, which was a done deal) should go *only* to CDFIs, the institutions with a primary mission of serving underserved populations.

On behalf of the coalition, Mark Pinsky worked closely with the White House's Paul Dimond and the Senate Banking Committee in the days after the introduction of the administration's legislation. He laid out five arguments for excluding banks and their CDCs from the program.[851]

- First of all, "the greatest possible bang for each taxpayer buck." An additional million or two to a bank would not leverage any substantial additional lending; banks already had ample resources to make those investments on their own.
- Banks and CDFIs served different markets: Banks made "bankable" loans; CDFIs made loans that generally did not meet conventional banks' standards.
- CRA already required banks to do the kind of lending that CDFI legislation promoted. Why should they be given additional subsidy to comply with the law?
- Funding was limited, and the president's goal was to provide it to a diversity of institutions—not to open a pool of money to hundreds of conventional banks.
- Banks and their affiliates could participate by partnering with CDFIs—for example, by establishing loan pools.

With Jeannine Jacokes of the Senate Banking Committee, Pinsky strategized about ways to reinforce this message. She suggested that additional educational efforts might be helpful in persuading D'Amato and others that CDFIs would not constitute a new banking system, nor take away business from banks. In the end, she advised Pinsky, a deal would have to be struck between Senator Riegle and Senator D'Amato.[852]

The administration's bill had not even been formally introduced when the skirmishes began. Senator D'Amato sniffed that the program was too small (a criticism shared, for different reasons, by Democratic Representatives Waters, Rush, and others on the left)—thus, mainstream banks should have a larger role. "The only thing innovative about this proposal is that the president is going to make good on a campaign promise."[853] Rep. Tom Ridge, co-author with Rep. Flake of the BEA legislation, derided it as "just another government handout," while extolling his own legislation.[854]

## The First House Hearing

July 21, 1993: In an auspicious and flattering beginning, Chairman Gonzalez opened the hearing on H.R. 2666: "The members of this committee know the magic of a so-called community development financial institution and what it can bring to a neighborhood." However, as he noted, the magic only goes so far: "It is not the elixir for our Nation's dying, literally, communities"—like his home district of San Antonio, which "cannot even absorb credit because the rates of unemployment are so high, and the job creation [is] so low."[855]

Rep. Jim Leach of Iowa, the ranking Republican member of the committee, praised the community development banking proposal as "one of the more creative ideas" to come out of the presidential campaign,[856] but declared Republicans "a little bit disappointed" that the Clinton administration had not adopted some of the other concepts in play: "In fact, Congressman Flake and I are working on just that kind of legislation at this time." The administration's bill achieved "inadequate leveraging of private sector investment. Therefore, we would expect to see some significant amendments proposed." Nonetheless, in contrast with the bitter partisanship that would roil Congress after the midterm elections, Leach struck a mild tone: "The minority wishes to be cooperative with the majority on this issue," despite some philosophical differences.[857] All sides needed to be concerned with the "lagging" of economic opportunity.

As Chairman Gonzalez noted, the cabinet secretaries "were the star attractors of one of the biggest turnouts that we have had at a hearing of the full committee."[858] Agriculture Secretary Espy, from the Mississippi Delta, highlighted the problems faced by rural America in accessing credit and job creation, citing the testimony of Timothy Bazemore and the role of Self-Help at the White House Rose Garden ceremony the previous week. As well, he cited Southern Development Bancorporation as a prime example of combining a depository with nonprofit affiliates to achieve comprehensive impact. His testimony closed with his personal anecdote about visiting a microenterprise program in Canton, MS, and its impact on helping a single mother "get off of welfare."[859]

Secretary Bentsen cited his own rural credentials: "born and reared in rural south Texas, and I know the poverty of that area."[860] CDFIs, he stated, helped fill "a financial services vacuum…The CDFI looks beyond what a transaction can do for the institution. Instead, they make decisions based on what benefit will flow to the entire community." He reiterated the administration's position that the CDFI program was not and could not be a substitute for CRA. He laid out five principles that should guide the program, stressing especially that there should be a new entity "that is focused exclusively on revitalizing distressed areas" (a premise that some Republicans did not agree with) and that organizations funded by it should have the flexibility to develop the most effective programs.[861] In his written statement for the record, Bentsen emphasized another point that had not been fully discussed with the panel.

> In view of the numerous and conflicting demands for scarce public resources, it would be a serious mistake to view this program as the primary, permanent source of funding for nontraditional lenders. Therefore, to the maximum extent possible, we should be more encouraging of those community development financial institutions adept at securing long-term, non-Federal equity and working capital than others.

Among the criteria for selection that Bentsen cited, the first was "the likelihood of success in becoming a self-sustaining CDFI."[862]

Treasury Undersecretary Newman explained that insured depositories would be eligible for larger amounts of funding, "partly because of [their] ability to lever[age] and make better use of the funds and partly because the regulatory apparatus provides a little bit more safety in terms of the ultimate use."[863] In a follow-up letter to the committee responding to Rep. Ridge's concern, Assistant Secretary (Legislative Affairs) Michael B. Levy of the Treasury Department provided a "rough estimate" of leverage under various scenarios for funding of insured and uninsured institutions. He noted that "it takes time for the CDFIs to acquire the matching private sector capital and to fully leverage their total seed capital… at least 3-5 years for new insured CDFIs to become a significant, but not fully leveraged, loan presence in their communities, and longer to attain full funding/leverage."[864]

In his written statement, Democratic Rep. Paul E. Kanjorski of Pennsylvania underscored that any new banks and credit unions created because of the legislation "will be full-fledged banks and credit unions. They will be subject to all of the same capital and other safety and soundness standards as other banks and credit unions. They will not be inferior or second-class financial institutions."[865] Several committee members were concerned about potential liability of the federal government for losses, but Undersecretary Newman reassured them that once the appropriated money was disbursed, "there would be no hidden liability to the government whatsoever." To avoid the complications of government liability, Newman explained, the bill also did not allow for credit guarantee structures or enhancements.[866]

The proposed administrative costs of the program—$10 million annually—raised concerns more than the proposed $382 million spread over four years; even the bill's supporter, Chairman Gonzalez, found it "rather high." Rep. Leach seized on this point to make his case for the Flake-Ridge Bank Enterprise Award act, which he claimed would produce higher leverage from the private sector.

Several Republican committee members probed the witnesses to determine whether and how much mainstream banks could participate in the programs.

Democratic Rep. Joseph P. Kennedy from Massachusetts emphasized that the president's initiative would have a positive impact on CRA negotiations across the country, which he strongly supported. He also raised a key procedural point, arguing for "a so-called clean bill that would keep the details of this [bill] pertaining only to community development needs."[867]

## "Need" or "Grantsmanship"?

Democratic Rep. Lucille Roybal-Allard, the first Mexican-American woman elected to Congress, raised an issue that was and would continue to be a sore point for anti-poverty advocates—including especially community development credit unions—in the years to come. Her Los Angeles congressional district had "the lowest per capita income of any district in this country… Will communities with the greatest need be given priority in terms of being able to receive assistance or will assistance be given to those communities that are in need but who are also better able to put together the package more quickly?"[868] Agriculture Undersecretary Nash, who had worked under Clinton in Arkansas, assured her:

> It is not going to be a game where those with the best proposals on their own will be successful in acquiring these investments. The priority will be set so that those areas that are the greatest in need with the highest unemployment and ones where we think nothing will happen unless we come in with this program. So I think I can allay your fears by saying that this will not be a grantsmanship game.[869]

(However, after the fund was launched, disappointed applicants from small institutions in high-poverty areas would draw precisely this conclusion: The CDFI Fund was indeed a "grantsmanship" game.)

A somewhat related concern was raised about the size of the awards and the possibility that they might be concentrated in relatively few hands. Treasury Under Secretary Newman acknowledged the issue: "We would want to be very careful about not utilizing too large an amount of the money in any single institution when, in fact there are probably going to be scores and scores of applicants from all around the country and it would be judicious to spread the money a little bit more widely." The House hearings were notable for elevating the concern for Native American populations and Indian reservations. Democratic Rep. Bruce Vento from Minnesota urged their explicit inclusion in the program; Republican Rep. Doug Bereiter from Nebraska echoed his interest.[870] These concerns would find their way into modified bills in the fall.

The administration envisioned a far more proactive role for the proposed CDFI Fund than it subsequently played. "Even before a grant was made," testified Newman, "we would send a team of people to work with a local group who wanted to put together an institution and help them put together a plan that utilized the existing government programs as soon as possible."[871]

Rep. Bobby Rush, who represented ShoreBank's congressional district, had introduced his own legislation earlier, H.R. 2250, which, he reminded the committee, had obtained "strong support from the members of this committee."[872] Chairman Gonzalez offered Rush his praise: "Even though he is a freshman, he has come aboard running very fast."[873] Rush raised an issue that anti-poverty advocates had highlighted: namely, that some rural and urban poor communities would have difficulty meeting the 1:1 matching requirement.[874] Nash assured him that in some—not all—cases, the fund would have flexibility.

Rush had been in amicable discussions previously with Cabinet departments. In his written statement, he said, "I intend to offer some perfecting amendments to this bill, and I have and will continue to work with the Administration in this regard. But I believe…the heart and soul of this bill are healthy and sound." Finally, he noted, "the real significance of this legislation is that it is not just about credit or banking: it is about genuine, comprehensive, *permanent* [emphasis in original] community development."[875] Although bills introduced by Representatives Rush and Waters had sought substantially greater funding, they supported the administration.

## Banks and BEA

Democratic Rep. Nydia Velazquez from New York City emphasized that "existing conventional lenders, especially the large, healthy institutions, do not need Federal Government assistance to raise equity"; rather, the scant funding should be reserved for community development lenders.[876] Treasury Secretary Bentsen reaffirmed the administration's position that the legislation was not a substitute for the CRA obligations of banks, while Frank Newman rebuffed the Republican arguments. "It's difficult to propose giving money to Citibank, NationsBank or Bank of America," he said, "which already have very substantial resources."[877]

But Republican members of the committee continued to urge the administration to assure a greater role for commercial banks. The hearings provided a platform for the supporters of the Bank Enterprise Act program to elevate their own proposal. Rep. Floyd Flake acknowledged that he was "overwhelmingly in support of the community development bank initiative," which was a step in the right direction. But "I still have a great deal of concern as it relates to, first of all, putting some $10 million into an administrative cost factor," compared with the BEA bill that he and Rep. Ridge had sponsored the previous year.[878] Ridge reinforced the criticism of administrative costs and laid out the math underpinning his argument that BEA produced greater leverage—$10 for every $1 in federal expenditure. Moreover, he pointed out the lack of bipartisan support for the administration's bill, compared with BEA: Of the 41 or 42 congressional attendees at the White House Rose Garden ceremony, he was the only Republican attending. In responding to Reps. Flake and Ridge, Undersecretary Newman claimed that BEA "will be implemented," although he was not specific about plans.[879]

Before the month was out, the challenge to the administration's bill from the supporters of the BEA alternative became much more concrete. The Flake-Ridge BEA bill had been an appropriations "orphan"; it had never received the funding it needed to provide incentives to banks. Administration officials had met with Flake—whom they described internally as "an early opponent of CDFI legislation of any kind"—and persuaded him that he would have a role in CRA reform. In turn, "out of his personal respect and support for [the president], he also agreed to hold off on pressing his BEA funding request, pending completion of the CRA regulatory reform."[880]

Evidently, the administration team overestimated their powers of persuasion. On July 22, the Flake-Ridge team, now joined by Rep. Leach, introduced H.R. 2707, which laid claim to half of Clinton's proposed $382 million to fund the Bank Enterprise Act. Initially, the press reported, the Treasury Department was angry, although Flake claimed several days later that they had smoothed over tensions.[881] Treasury spokespersons made conciliatory comments, and Flake predicted compromises would be found. But at a press conference on July 28, the Flake-Ridge-Leach triumvirate announced that their bill was a more feasible bipartisan alternative to the administration's CDFI bill, since some Republicans were already on board. To CRA advocates, the Flake-Ridge-Leach approach was not simply a benign bipartisan compromise, but a deal-killer, a CRA "safe harbor" for banks.

## Backlash

Flake's initiative immediately alienated some of his previous supporters. Members of the CDFI Coalition had previously supported the BEA initiative. As late as June 9, the National Federation of CDCUs announced that it "strongly support[s] the Bank Enterprise Act (the 'Greenlining Bill') which allows banks to pay reduced deposit insurance premiums."[882] But that was before Flake proposed to siphon money from the administration's CDFI bill. Lyndon Comstock of Community Capital Bank reacted immediately and sharply to the Flake-Ridge-Leach initiative. In a letter faxed to Flake's office on July 29, he wrote:

> I am writing to express my great personal disappointment with your bill.... Since your [Flake's] church is the founder of a small credit union itself, I am astonished that you feel that a credit on FDIC insurance or any other form of Federal financial assistance will be likely to have any effect on bank CRA lending practices whatsoever.... I can tell you that it's naïve to think that the types of Federal support you propose could cause them to mend their ways.

Instead, he urged Rep. Flake to support the administration's "excellent bill," embodied in H.R. 2666.

Crucially, Rep. Rush withdrew his support. "I have determined that I cannot support this legislation," he wrote in a letter to Flake on July 27.

> By permitting all United States financial institutions—depository institutions already backed by the taxpayer—access to scarce public funds allocated to this initiative, your bill would greatly dilute the efficiency of the President's focus on building the capacity of the non-traditional but highly successful CDFI's. This result would benefit no one…. H.R. 2707 effectively jeopardizes the President's bill by making it vulnerable to amendment regarding a whole host of issues which would be better reserved for consideration by the [Banking] Committee until after H.R. 2666 is signed into law.

As one writer observed, "The legislative dynamics of the community development bank bill are not yet clear, but one thing appears certain: There will be no quick rubber-stamping of the Clinton plan by the House."[883] In early August, I had a conversation with an aide to Rep. Nydia Velazquez, whose district included parts of Brooklyn and the neighborhood that was home to the Lower East Side People's Federal Credit Union in Manhattan. I learned that Flake's bill was putting a brake on the progress of legislation. Flake and the administration were in communication, but there was "ill feeling" because the Clinton bill had nothing in it for BEA. For her part, Rep. Velazquez would not cosponsor or support BEA legislation because of the safe harbor it offered banks. As for the Senate, Senator D'Amato was apparently negotiating the price for his support: a secondary market for small-business loans.[884]

## The Senate Writes Its Bill

On September 8, 1993, the Senate held additional hearings on the "Community Development Financial Institutions Act of 1993." HUD Secretary Henry Cisneros and Frank Newman of the Treasury Department represented the administration. Although various coalition members had testified at previous hearings, this was the first time the Coalition of Community Development Financial Institutions was officially represented as such, through remarks delivered by Jeremy Nowak, who also served as chair of the National Association of Community Development Loan Funds.

Nowak testified that the coalition represented 300 established CDFIs in 42 states; Washington, DC; Puerto Rico; and American Samoa. He reiterated the coalition's endorsement of the administration's proposal, while reserving the right to urge changes: "Where there are aspects of S. 1275 that fall short of what our experience suggests is necessary, we have offered and will continue to provide our suggestions for ways to strengthen the network." He listed 10 key legislative recommendations, among which were a high bar for CDFI status, requiring that applicants "document that at least 75 percent of their resources are used for community development financing and related program activities." He urged increased funding; a 10 percent cap on administrative costs; and equal maximum funding levels for all types of applicants, insured depositories or not. To help build the field, the coalition supported a comprehensive training program; he argued, as well, for performance-based lending and investment standards.[885]

Paul S. Grogan testified for the Local Initiatives Support Corporation (LISC), the national intermediary created by the Ford Foundation in 1979 to support community development corporations. LISC was not a member of the CDFI Coalition, but his position largely supported the coalition's. He placed the CDFI initiative in historical context.

> [It] represents a sea change, a decisive shift away from the previous generation of centralized, highly bureaucratic, prescriptive and rigid Federal programs to a new opportunity system in which the Federal Government has a critical role to incentivize, to steer capital, and to make targeted investments.... [M]ainstream institutions are not going to make the loans that are too small, too risky, too early stage, too idiosyncratic that the alternative network is willing to make and that will in turn create opportunities for mainstream lending.... We reject the idea that this should be a safe harbor for CRA or that mainstream financial institutions, without a sole community development mission, should be applicants for this funding.[886]

Deepak Bhargava, legislative director of ACORN, spoke for his organization and other prominent national advocacy groups: the Center for Community Change, Consumers Union, Consumer Federation of America, and National Council for La Raza.* Bhargava rejected any effort to drive a wedge between the CRA and CDFI advocates, while re-emphasizing concern for the neediest areas and reinforcing the link to basic banking services:

> We warmly endorse S. 1275 and urge its swift passage by the Senate. We would like to make absolutely clear, however, that we will vigorously oppose any initiative that would delete the landmark Community Reinvestment Act.... The poorest communities, where there are no alternatives, is where these institutions should be created first.

To be sure, low-income communities lacked access to credit, but the initiative should address "the availability of banking services including bank branches and low-cost transaction accounts."[887]

## Aftermath: White House Strategy

On September 10, Christopher Edley Jr. of the Office of Management and Budget (OMB) met with Frank Newman and the Comptroller of the Currency, Gene Ludwig, to formulate the administration's strategy on overall financial reform issues and the CDFI bill in particular. Edley summarized the CDFI strategy this way.

---

\* In July 2017, the National Council of La Raza rebranded itself as UnidosUS.

[The bill] will move forward in the Senate only if linked to some modest set of generally unobjectionable regulatory relief provisions, plus Damato's [sic] proposal to foster securitization of small business loans—a proposal we basically support.... I still haven't heard a convincing story about how we get CDFIs through the House and to conference in a timely way....

So, how to move ahead on a reform agenda while recognizing that CDFIs are the President's first priority in the area, and that the White House must force itself to have a focused legislative agenda?[888]

Following the September 8 hearing, the Treasury Department and the Senate Banking Staff framed and vetted a host of questions and answers that could derail the legislation—the role (or lack of it) of commercial banks; subsidies; which states would get money; federal liability for bad investments; and much more.[889] Some large issues threatened to diffuse the focus of the administration: interstate bank branching, consolidation of the regulatory agencies, and small business securities powers. Nonetheless, as the *Wall Street Journal* reported, on September 21, the Senate Banking Committee "reached a bipartisan compromise, basically approving a Clinton administration proposal to provide $382 million for special community-lending institutions over four years."[890]

## Keeping a "Clean Bill"

The legislation contained something for most of the major players, though none were dancing in the streets. Senator D'Amato got one of his priorities: a private-sector secondary market for small-business loans. The banks got regulatory relief: The American Bankers Association declared it a good beginning, although the Independent Bankers Association of America grumbled that the relief was "scant." Advocates, including Public Citizen's Congress Watch, founded by Ralph Nader, were pleased by provisions to rein in abusive, high-cost home equity loans.[891] The bill was approved by the Senate Banking Committee on an 18–1 vote, with only Republican Senator Phil Gramm of Texas, the irreconcilable opponent of CRA and anything closely associated with it, voting against it. Two senators, Shelby and Mack, reluctantly voted for the draft legislation, while continuing to urge a safe harbor for bank investments in community development and blasting community groups' "intransigent position on CRA."[892]

Bringing Senator D'Amato on board was vital. "I have always said the concept of community development is one I support,' the senator said following a hearing. 'So I am not going to take a contrary position just because there is a section of the bill I disagree with.'"[893] D'Amato echoed the administration's concern about keeping the focus on the community development banking piece, rather than trying to attach interstate branching and other legislation: "'The more you add to the bill, the more controversial it becomes,' he said."[894] Although acknowledging the likelihood that there would be pressure to add controversial amendments, the trade press confidently asserted that "President

Clinton's community development bill will probably be the most important banking bill adopted by Congress this year.... It is sure to clear Congress in some form before year-end."⁸⁹⁵

Once again, optimistic forecasts proved wrong.

## The House Bill: H.R. 3474

On November 9, House Banking Chairman Henry Gonzalez introduced H.R. 3474, a bill to "reduce administrative requirements for insured depository institutions" and facilitate the establishment of CDFIs. In most respects, the bill did not differ materially from the Senate and Clinton versions. But there was one major exception. On November 10, by voice vote it incorporated the Flake proposal, setting aside one-third of the proposed CDFI appropriation for the Bank Enterprise Act program.⁸⁹⁶

This was a major blow to the administration's strategy, and to the CDFI Coalition's. As Mark Pinsky reported to the CDFI Coalition Steering Committee on November 11, Paul Dimond of the National Economic Council conceded in a conversation that "Flake 'handed our heads to us on a platter.'"⁸⁹⁷ The administration's last-minute efforts were too little, too late; the banking press reported a "furious morning of lobbying by the Clinton Administration," which did not head off the committee's 36–14 vote in favor of the Flake amendment, including 16 Democrats.⁸⁹⁸ Pinsky recommended to the coalition that "we call for full funding to CDFIs independent of making judgments about the BEA," while attempting to ensure that BEA investments flow to CDFIs as much as possible.⁸⁹⁹

Although the White House and the national advocacy groups opposed the BEA provisions, on November 21 the House approved H.R. 3474. Putting the best face on the outcome, staff of the Domestic Policy Council and National Economic Council—Weinstein, Dimond, and Cashin—reported to the president that the full House of Representatives adopted "your community development bank and financial institutions initiative (H.R. 3474) by voice vote.... We are hopeful the full Senate will take up this legislation upon its return in January."⁹⁰⁰

## Back to the Senate

The legislation began to undergo alterations on November 24, when H.R. 3474 moved back into the Senate's Committee on Banking, Housing, and Urban Affairs. The next iteration of the legislation made certain material changes and elaborations.
- There was an important change in the maximum funding available to a CDFI. Instead of $5 million at one time, the bill stated that "the Fund may provide a total of not more than $5,000,000 of assistance to an organization…during any 3-year period."
- The bill expanded attention to the specific needs of Indian tribes and reservations, directing that a study be done of their financial needs and that the fund's board include "1 individual

who has personal experience and specialized expertise in the unique lending and community development issues confronted by Indian tribes on Indian reservations."
- Also addressing board composition, the bill added specifics to guide the selection of other nonfederal board members, to include persons who worked in CDFIs, insured depositories, and national public-interest organizations.
- There continued to be a soft, discretionary emphasis on funding institutions that were or would become depositories and that would not be dependent on continued support from the fund.
- The role of retail financial services was reinforced. One selection factor was to be "the degree of availability of basic financial services"; elsewhere the bill urged consideration of "the provision of basic financial services to low-income people or residents of a targeted area." This emphasis seemed to favor banks and community development credit unions.
- The concern for geographic diversity became more explicit: "The Board should seek to provide funding for applicants which are serving nonmetropolitan and rural areas and small cities with no less than one quarter of the funds available to the Board in any year." The link to enterprise zones and empowerment communities remained strong.
- The legislation proposed capitalization assistance to enhance the liquidity of CDFIs.

## Need vs. Performance

Within the CDFI Coalition, there was a latent tension between the National Federation's concerns for the least of its members, on the one hand, and the emphasis on performance that had for years been a core principle of the National Association of Community Development Loan Funds.[901] Despite their common mission and strong sense of solidarity, the constituencies of the two associations differed significantly in their cultures, contexts, and characteristics. Credit unions were highly and transparently regulated, reporting regularly to federal and/or state bodies on dozens of performance indicators—portfolio characteristics, delinquency, net worth, earnings, and many more. Loan funds came in many different sizes and shapes, with no common charts of accounts, delinquency calculations, or mandatory ratios; hence, NACDLF as a trade organization was concerned with setting standards. Most loan funds could not survive or grow without raising grants; with very few exceptions, credit unions survived on the retained earnings generated from their operations.

The tension between the two leading voices in the CDFI movement persisted, but never tore apart the coalition. However, it emerged strongly between the National Federation and the CDFI Fund after the fund was established: As the federation feared, small institutions and those serving some of the neediest communities never obtained more than a minor portion of CDFI Fund awards.

## Confronting the Ghosts of the War on Poverty

As Congress debated the launch of a major new program, long, unpleasant institutional memories on Capitol Hill were revived. The War on Poverty had attempted to address the capital and banking gaps in low-income communities through a top-down effort of the Office of Economic Opportunity (OEO) to establish and support low-income credit unions. Was this new CDFI program bound to repeat the same mistakes?

The Woodstock Institute attempted to allay concerns. Woodstock had done a comprehensive study of OEO's credit union program, which it summarized in a memorandum to Jeannine Jacokes of the Senate Banking Committee.[902]

> It is our conclusion that the OEO program was a poorly-designed, top-down government program implemented with little understanding of the credit and financial services needs of low income communities or the credit unions organized to address those needs. The failures of that program do not reflect a failure of credit unions serving low income members or of community development credit unions in general.... We believe that the current legislation avoids the mistakes of the past and builds on the successes of the present.... The proposed CDFI legislation bear almost no resemblance to the OEO credit union program of the War on Poverty.[903]

Among the salient differences: The OEO program provided operating grants for staff, unlike the CDFI movement's emphasis on equity to build balance sheets and promote self-sufficiency. The OEO program "sought to mass produce new credit unions," unlike the current proposal to build on existing institutions. The Sixties-era program demanded neither comprehensive business planning nor non-federal matching support.

Woodstock's research and analysis helped avert any effort to exclude community development credit unions from the CDFI program. For the National Federation of CDCUs, which had been the first and most persistent advocate for the CDFI program, exclusion would have been the most bitter outcome imaginable. It would have tested the solidarity of the CDFI Coalition, possibly resulting in the withdrawal of the National Federation's support and complicating, if not destroying, the possibility of passing legislation.

The legislation's progress was also threatened by another development. Senator Riegle, the foremost supporter of the CDFI legislation, was about to become a lame duck. Riegle faced a re-election battle in 1994, which would have resurrected his sharply criticized role in the "Keating Five" S&L scandal.[904] Although he was reportedly confident he could win, he announced that he had decided not to run again. As the banking trade press reported, this "did not exactly cause massive gloom in bank board rooms.... Riegle was considered hostile to bank causes in Congress."[905]

As 1993 drew to a close, the Clinton team contemplated a response to the disappointing outcome in the House—and in general, to the shrinking of this key presidential initiative. The transition team had started out with a goal of obtaining $850 million for community development banking; by the time the budget was submitted, it was only $382 million. "Many of our supporters in Congress criticized this small amount of funding for what had been viewed as a major Presidential initiative," Paul Weinstein, of the Domestic Policy Council, wrote. "The news media stated that the President was retreating on his campaign promise."[906] Rather than acknowledging defeat, Weinstein proposed that counting uninsured loan funds, CDCs, and others among the new CDFIs, as well as counting the matching funds that would be raised, it was possible to assert that $382 million would, indeed, create 100 new community development banks and result in a larger volume of investment. "Since community development banks [are] a high profile presidential initiative," he continued, "and because it is politically popular with certain Members of Congress who have been critical of the Administration's initiatives in the area of community development, I recommend that we increase the budget for the [CDFI] program to $500 million through FY 97 with approximately 25 percent going to fund the BEA."[907]

# CHAPTER 17. Home Stretch

Senator Riegle had hoped to get the full Senate to consider his marked-up bill by the end of 1993, but the calendar ran out on his effort. Although there had been setbacks, including the reduced level of appropriations and the major "haircut" courtesy of Rep. Flake's Bank Enterprise Award program, many design issues had been resolved, and the crucial elements were intact: A range of institutions serving distressed communities would be eligible for investment—community development banks, credit unions, loan funds, and microenterprise funds. Investments would not be restricted to loans, but would include equity and grants, so critical to the growth of CDFIs. In January 1994, S. 1275 was "being cued up for consideration in the full Senate sometime in February," Paul Weinstein reported to senior White House advisers and staff. "This raises the possibility that we will have legislation on the president's desk sometime in late March, assuming that any outstanding issues such as the Flake Amendment can be resolved quickly."[908]

But "passage is not certain," the CDFI Coalition reported to its constituents. "U.S. Senate Plans February Action on CDFI Bill, Obstacles Expected," its newsletter announced.[909] Certainly, the BEA issue was a major challenge: The House bill allocated one-third of CDFI funding for the BEA; the Senate bill did not; and the two would have to be reconciled before final legislation could be passed. Senator Riegle, the White House, and the CDFI Coalition were arrayed in opposing the insertion of the BEA into the legislation. But, Mark Pinsky, the coalition's coordinator, wrote:

> The Administration is unwilling to take on Flake because he is important to the President on a host of issues, including welfare reform, health care, and others. The Administration's primary goal at this point is getting some version of the CDFI legislation passed so that it can claim victory. We (NACDLF and the CDFI Coalition) hope to raise a ruckus about BEA in coordination with the CRA advocates, though in some respects they should be leading the ruckus-raising. We may not force the Administration to act, but we need to let Administration officials and others know that we are serious about our opposition.[910]

The banking lobby posed another obstacle, renewing its push for regulatory relief for banks, including elimination of the Community Reinvestment Act (CRA). As 1993 ended, the Clinton administration released proposed regulations, with a comment deadline of February 22, 1994 (subsequently extended to March 24).⁹¹¹ The Center for Community Change released an analysis identifying seven "steps forward" and 16 "major questions to resolve." The CDFI Coalition's position was clear: "The CDFI Coalition has strongly opposed a provision to give a significant rating boost to banks that do little or no lending but that make investments in CDFIs."⁹¹²

Proceeding on the optimistic assumption that the CDFI Fund would survive these obstacles, Paul Weinstein and Paul Dimond urged steps "to get this program off the ground running." They asked the Treasury Department to prepare a draft funding application, and they urged the administration to "start to focus on who we want to run the Fund." They posited that "an ideal Administrator of the [CDFI] Fund would be someone who has experience in banking, community development, knowledge of the foundation world, and a background in government at the local and State level."⁹¹³ Such a candidate was Mahlon Martin, head of the Winthrop Rockefeller Foundation, a board member of Southern Development Bancorporation, and an experienced hand in Arkansas government, including as chairman of Governor Clinton's state cabinet. Although Martin was happy in Arkansas, they thought that he would accept the position if the president asked.

## "CDFI Woodstock": Look at Us Now

No naked dancing, no mud, no drug overdoses, no unforgettable music—but early in 1994, the CDFI movement held an exuberant coming-out party in Durham, NC: the First National CDFI Institute, January 31–February 2, 1994.

Previously, the CDFI Coalition's work had focused on advocacy. But now it took a major step to raise the visibility of the CDFI "industry," as they called it. Durham was a prime location for the institute: It was the home of Self-Help, which provided extensive logistical support. More than 400 people registered, from as far away as Hawaii. They came from existing and aspiring CDFIs, anti-poverty organizations, foundations, municipal governments, banks of various sizes, regulators and federal officials, and more. The coordinators were unprepared for the demand: The sole downtown hotel, which adjoined the Civic Center, was filled to capacity; an overflow facility some distance away was booked—and still, people were turned away.

As Kate McKee, of the conference host organization Self-Help, put it in her opening remarks, "No one would have expected a little more than a year ago that the CDFI industry would come together as it has." McKee, who would later serve as the first interim director of the CDFI Fund, observed that "CDFI" was not even a term used when the coalition formally met in November 1992. "Look at where we are now," she exclaimed.⁹¹⁴ It was an exhilarating, validating experience for those of us who attended. We met people we had only heard about. We bounced from one encounter in the hallways to another, only gradually making our way to the workshops.

The opening day was dedicated to policy issues, including CDFI legislation, CRA, and partnerships with conventional financial institutions. The first panel, moderated by McKee, included George Surgeon, president and CEO of Southern Development Bancorporation; Connie Evans, executive director of the Women's Self-Employment Project, a prominent microenterprise organization; Jeremy Nowak, executive director of the Delaware Valley Community Reinvestment Fund; and Judy Samuelson, director of Program-Related Investments for the Ford Foundation.

Samuelson's comments helped put the CDFI movement in perspective. She noted that there seemed to be viable permanent niches in the financial system, but she cautioned against external pressures for CDFIs to achieve self-sufficiency too quickly: Subsidy would be needed for the foreseeable future. Like the Ford Foundation itself, CDFIs were in the business of institution-building, and this would not happen overnight. Although Ford had devoted as much as $75 million in grants and loans to CDFIs, it was disappointed that more foundations hadn't joined it. In any case, the foundation world hoped that new federal resources would dwarf their own funding of CDFIs.

The coalition waged an unsuccessful "full-court press" to secure Vice President Gore as a keynote speaker.[915] Instead, Eugene Ludwig, Comptroller of the Currency, fulfilled that role. Apart from being the highest-ranking administration official to attend, his presence was important in restating and reinforcing the relationship of CDFI to CRA, which—as Ludwig had testified to Congress—were to be complementary: CDFIs would not and could not be a substitute for a vigorously enforced CRA. Speakers from the Senate Banking Committee (Jeannine Jacokes), the Department of the Treasury (Bryan Mathis), and the office of Rep. Bobby Rush (Robert Walsh) painted the Washington picture for the attendees.

The second and third days offered practitioner-led training sessions that dealt with operational and organizational issues for existing and emerging CDFIs. There were tracks for different institutional types, regulated and nonregulated; other sessions dealt with specific loan products (such as community facilities financing), capital tools, government programs, capital-raising, and more.

## The "Half-Truth" of CDFIs

On February 1, toward the end of the conference, Paul Lingenfelter of the John D. and Catherine T. MacArthur Foundation provided a bookend to Samuelson's opening comments: "The Implications of the 'Credit Gap' For Community Development Financial Institutions." MacArthur, with Lingenfelter managing its portfolio, had been second only to Ford as a funder and investor in CDFIs, and there was no other way to take his comments than as a collegial critique—sobering and challenging as it was. "My true confession—our true confession—is this," he began.

> Community development financial institutions in the United States have been built on a half-truth. The half-truth is: Lack of access to capital is a primary factor in perpetuating, if not causing, poverty. The capital gap is an important problem, and providing access to capital will alleviate poverty and improve the quality of life for the poor.

> Where is the truth in this half-truth? The lack of credit can compound the effects of poverty and racism. The lack of credit can subtly make jobs disappear. It can turn poor, but functioning neighborhoods into areas of abandonment and despair. Without credit it is difficult to accumulate even the modest wealth of the lower middle class.
>
> Sounds compelling. Why is this only half true? We all know that capital must be combined with other things in order to sustain itself or grow. Without certain essential partners, capital will not grow, it will dissipate. When the poor have access to capital, plus knowledge, energy, skills, support systems, adaptive capacity, a tendency to be thrifty, access to economic opportunities, and time to become more prosperous, they will become less poor.
>
> The people who believe there is no capital gap believe that the poor lack one or more of these critical preconditions of greater prosperity. They think the capital markets function rationally, that those who do not have access to capital will lose any capital they get because of their deficiencies. Some who believe there is no capital gap try to address these deficiencies; others blame the victim.
>
> In a nutshell, the community development banking industry is a gamble that the capital gap is real and important.... How can we prove that conventional financial markets discriminate against the poor, that the capital gap is real and important? The most powerful evidence I can imagine to prove the point is to develop a strong, well-built institution that fills the capital gap. Such an institution will not function as a conventional bank, but it will look more like a bank than a comprehensive social service agency. Community development financial institutions need to demonstrate that their 'sentimental, irrational, high risk lending' is anything but.
>
> Not in my wildest dreams do I think community development financial institutions can end poverty, and I often think that limited access to capital is less significant than many of the other hurdles the poor have to face. In the end, however, I conclude that access to capital has been denied and that it matters.[916]

Interviewed by the author years later, Lingenfelter recalled, "Some of my colleagues didn't like it"; some in the audience wanted to take on all the burdens of eliminating poverty. "What I said was that this is a really important idea, the core is access to capital as a powerful lever in increasing economic mobility and reducing poverty, but there are a lot of other associated issues. CD finance can't do it all. We need to focus on where access to capital is the primary issue. Others have to deal with education."[917]

## Solidifying the Coalition: Funding and Advocacy

Flush with the success of the conference and looking forward—if anxiously—to passage of CDFI legislation in 1994, the coalition submitted a proposal to the Ford Foundation that would expand and solidify its role.[918] "The CDFI industry now has a rare and challenging opportunity to build a vibrant and sustainable national network of CDFIs serving distressed communities," the proposal read. With a grant of $175,000 over two years, it would:

- Assess the need for and feasibility of a comprehensive initiative to recruit, train, and retain a strong and diverse corps of leaders and staff members [for] the rapidly expanding community development financial institutions (CDFI) industry
- Maintain a modestly staffed, full-time operation.[919]

The coalition had operated for nearly two years with NACDLF as its fiscal agent, and Mark Pinsky serving under contract as its coordinator, supported by grants to NACDLF from a variety of foundations (Surdna, Joyce, Mott, Mary Reynolds Babcock, the Trinity Grants program, and the Alida Rockefeller Trust). But support from Ford, the pre-eminent supporter of various CDFIs, would send an important signal to the CDFI movement, its supporters, and policymakers.

Ford, in its deliberate fashion, did not jump at the opportunity to fund the coalition. Its response of April 13 indicated that "the proposal has substantial merit," but the foundation needed to understand more fully a number of issues. Among these: How would cross-sectoral training add value to the training efforts of the individual trade associations, namely the National Federation and NACDLF? How would the coalition go beyond "feasibility" work to prepare for real collaboration among organizations? What role would CDFIs, such as ShoreBank and Southern Development Bancorporation, play in implementation?[920] A follow-up meeting of CDFI leaders and Ford was held on June 28, 1994, at the foundation, but no further action came until fall 1994.

## CDFIs and the "New" CRA

The Clinton administration's changes to CRA were in the works. The coalition emphatically continued its opposition to giving banks a "free pass" for investing in CDFIs. In its comment letter of March 17, 1994, the coalition acknowledged that the CDFI movement, the banking industry, and the government itself could not on their own ensure "a reliable, affordable form of credit and capital" in disinvested communities. The letter went on to say:

> While we welcome and encourage bank investments in CDFIs and other community-based organizations, no institution should be able to effectively buy its way out of its direct lending obligations. The investment test [under CRA] gives undue value to investments in CDFIs and other community development and investment vehicles.

Banks should be eligible for a limited CRA rating boost only for investing in CDFIs—one grade up. The letter urged the regulators to "explicitly recognize all CDFI types as successful financial intermediaries," rather than mentioning only community development banks and CDCs.[921]

Meanwhile, a budget battle threatened to derail the CDFI legislation altogether. The White House had expected the Senate to take action on its bill, S. 1275, by February. But, the Interagency Working Group reported, "Despite our best efforts, we still have not been able to secure floor time in the Senate for consideration [of the legislation].... We almost had a vote this week, but apparently the Republicans are playing hardball on any [sic] allowing any Presidential initiatives to reach the floor, including bills with bipartisan support" like the CDBFI bill.[922] There was real urgency, they said, because of the coming crush of a crime bill, budget, and other major legislation: "We cannot afford to let this window of opportunity pass." There was also a symbolic benefit to quick passage: "By the way, if we can pass S. 1275 in the next month and a half, the President could sign the bill on the anniversary of the Los Angeles riots."[923]

On February 23, 1994, the VA, HUD, and Independent Agencies Subcommittee of the House Appropriations Committee voted to rescind (annul) all the prospective funding for the CDFI Fund, along with as much as $9 billion in "take-backs" from various other programs. It was the first such attack, but it would not be the last. In itself, it was not a fatal blow, because ultimately, a rescission would require Senate approval and that of the president—unlikely, but possible.

As Senate action loomed, the National Federation of CDCUs remained concerned that the bill would disadvantage the rural and poorest segments of the CDFI movement, a point that CRA and consumer advocates had raised in their congressional testimony. The legislation was still calling for matching funds that would be equivalent in form and value to federal investments—that is, equity for equity. The problem, as I wrote to Mark Pinsky, was this.

> *Equity capital* [emphasis in original] is the most vital financial resource for community development financial institutions.... But equity capital is also the scarcest commodity. The poorest communities—those with the least disposable household income—are precisely the ones with limited ability to generate equity capital from within. Unfortunately, they are also the ones least able to go to the private sector [for] these funds. Private institutions like banks, foundations, and corporations often concentrate their giving in urban areas and favor the more established groups, with sophisticated staffs and lengthy track records.[924]

Accordingly, the National Federation sought to modify the proposed matching requirements for small institutions. Specifically, in January 1994, we had pressed the coalition to support an amendment that would allow applicants to match small equity grants—$100,000 or less—with any combination of deposits, loans, or grants. This became known within the coalition as the "Rosenthal Amendment." The coalition won the support of Democratic Senator Harris Wofford from Pennsylvania, whose constituency included many rural communities; the "Rosenthal Amendment" became the "Wofford Amendment," with an eased matching provision, although in weaker form than I had proposed. The Coalition Steering Committee attempted to rally support.[925] I attempted to secure the support of Senator D'Amato, but on March 8, his staff member [Ray Natter] called me to discuss Wofford's amendment: The Senator opposed using deposits as matching funds, "because they did not meet a 'market-based test,' in that they are federally insured." Loans would be acceptable, or deposits that were interest-free could count, he acknowledged.[926]

The Republicans rejected the Wofford Amendment. It was a frustrating and bitter irony for the CDCU movement. The savings of low-income people themselves, deposited in a self-help, cooperative institution, would be accorded less value than money leveraged from the private sector. Ultimately, the legislation would provide some discretion to the fund in accepting matches in other than like-to-like, dollar-to-dollar form. But for years to come, the National Federation continued our fight to ensure that the CDFI Fund would adequately support small CDFIs in poor communities.

## The Modified Senate Bill

Finally, on Wednesday, March 16, the Senate began consideration of the legislation. (Its own bill, S. 1275, had been inserted into the House version, H.R. 3474, by which it would be known henceforth.) Senator Shelby, a Democrat from Alabama, and Senator Mack, a Republican from Florida, added amendments to increase regulatory relief to banks; these were included in a leadership amendment that passed on a voice vote.[927] The secondary market for small-business loans—dear to Senator D'Amato's heart—was included.

The proposed appropriation of $382 million was unchanged. No amendments eviscerated the heart of the community development banking provisions. The CDFI Coalition described the amendments as "minor"; most, in fact, were positive, recognizing the particular difficulties in rural areas and on reservations, as well as the challenges faced by small and new CDFIs. Other amendments
- Made limited provision for public agency participation in the program if there were no viable CDFIs in the state
- Required CDFIs to record gender, race, and other key demographic characteristics of borrowers
- Allowed the CDFI Fund to relax matching requirements for CDFIs with "severe constraints" and provide a waiver for new and very small rural CDFIs
- Required CDFIs serving reservations to consult with tribal governments
- Mandated a study of barriers to lenders on reservations
- Adjusted the selection criteria to recognize rural areas that had suffered significant employment losses
- Modified the investment area definition to include rural areas with substantial population losses.[928]

Passage of the legislation seemed imminent. However, on the way to a vote, the bill hit a major, if unrelated, bump in the road. As the banking press reported, although "community development bank legislation is hardly controversial in the Senate…for a few hours it looked to some bank lobbyists as though the bill might be in trouble."[929] As the Senate was preparing to put the finishing touches on its bill, it "began a long debate over whether Congress should hold hearings on the Madison Guaranty/

Whitewater affair."[930] (It would indeed hold such hearings, commencing an investigation that expanded and dragged on for many months.) Despite this major distraction, on March 18, the Senate approved the legislation by unanimous consent, which "makes it likely that the President will sign a federal CDFI program into law this year," the coalition's *CDFI News* reported to its mailing list of more than 2,000.[931]

Although the Whitewater sideshow did not derail the Senate's passage of the CDFI bill, it did present a tactical dilemma for the Democrats.

> [Some] Democrats favor quick passage of the CDFI bill to present President Clinton an achievement at a time when he is under intense bombardment by the Republicans for the propriety of his personal investment decisions in the Whitewater affair before becoming President. On the other hand, other Democrats are leery about moving toward final action at this time because of the possibility it could be used by Republicans to further exploit the Clinton investment controversy, in which an Arkansas savings and loan was involved.[932]

## It Takes Two Houses: Toward Reconciliation

April 4, 1994: "President's CDFI Bill with Assorted Amendments Nears Final Action," announced the *Banking Policy Report*. What remained was to put the "finishing touches on President Clinton's legislation… [which is] now largely noncontroversial except for one issue."[933] That issue, of course, was how much, if any, would go to conventional financial institutions—that is, funding for the BEA, which was included in the House's bill but not in the Senate's.[934]

The next step in the legislative process was to reconcile the House and Senate bills through a conference committee. The Senate chose three Democrats (Riegle, Sarbanes, and Dodd) and two Republicans (D'Amato and Gramm); the House was slightly delayed in naming its conferees. The coalition's coordinators informed the Steering Committee that "Dodd is important because he could be Flake-friendly. …Our saving grace may be that Courtney Ward—the former Schumer aide/former Clinton Transition aide who bought into our policy paper early on—is now Dodd's aide for banking issues."[935] The coalition's coordinators reported to the Steering Committee that they had had "long, productive discussions" with Jeannine Jacokes of the Senate Banking staff and Amy Friend of the House Banking staff. "On BEA, they agree that the Administration is going to have to cut a deal with Flake, or he is going to get a healthy chunk of the pie."[936]

The tension between Rep. Flake and the Clinton administration continued. On May 10, Flake released a statement indicating "he found 'disturbing' reports that the Treasury Department would not support the Bank Enterprise Act provisions of the House community development banking bill." Treasury's position, he argued, was flawed, because it erroneously believed that the BEA would tap the bank and thrift insurance funds, which were not yet fully funded; rather, although the BEA was predicated on reducing deposit insurance premiums, funding from the CDFI bill would make up for that lost revenue.[937]

As the time for the crucial House/Senate conference committee approached, members of the CDFI Coalition tried to rally their troops on several issues:
- Opposing inclusion of BEA in the final legislation
- Limiting the amount of awards for those CDFIs that franchised new institutions outside their own investment area
- Establishing a supervisory board (not simply an advisory board) for the CDFI Fund, one that included CDFI practitioners
- Requiring CDFIs to document that they used at least 70 percent of their resources for community development finance.[938]

The banking industry had its own priorities—especially interstate bank branching. The result was a kind of legislative "logjam," which appeared to last until early June.

Rep. Flake held strong cards going into the Senate-House conference committee: The House had roundly supported BEA, giving it one-third of prospective CDFI appropriations. The Senate did not. Flake found the path to victory by "hammer[ing] out a deal with Sen. Christopher J. Dodd (D-Conn), the swing vote among [the five] Senate conferees."[939] This ensured that the House version, with a modified BEA provision, would prevail. Banks would be eligible for a "rebate" of 15 percent for equity investments made in a CDFI; CDFI banks and conventional banks alike could receive 5 percent rebates for expanding lending and related services in low-income communities.[940] BEA rebates would *not* reduce FDIC premiums—a touchy subject, given the politics of maintaining strong deposit insurance funds—but would be paid as cash awards directly to the recipient banks.[941] So, as one reporter noted, "banks not only get the money, [but] they don't have to worry about establishing a precedent of using insurance premiums for social and political purposes."[942]

Senator Riegle, who had opposed BEA, agreed to partially fund it, and the Clinton administration reportedly went along.[943] But no deal could be final until the conference committee worked out final details. And the July 4 recess, when members of Congress returned to their home districts, delayed action further. By mid-July, the urgency increased—especially because of the Whitewater investigation. "The importance of getting these bills [interstate branching and community development banking] up before all hell breaks loose has not been lost on people," commented Karen Shaw, president of the Institute for Strategy Development.[944] Still, the days passed without action. Finally, "in a seven-hour session that ran past 10 p.m. Tuesday [July 19], the conferees worked their way through a number of controversial issues in the community development bill and appeared to be within striking distance of wrapping up the talks."[945]

July 25, 1994: The two houses of Congress completed a broad legislative package, henceforth to be known as the Riegle-Neal Community Development and Financial Modernization Act of 1994, honoring Senator Riegle and Democratic Rep. Stephen Neal of North Carolina, who had also been a prominent supporter. Along with the community development banking provisions, the legislation authorized interstate branching and provided regulatory relief, leading the trade press to label it "a big win for the banking industry."[946]

## Chapter 17. Home Stretch

It was a big win for Rep. Jim Leach, the moderate Republican and ranking minority member on the House Banking Committee who had joined Flake and Ridge on the BEA. On July 25, just as the conference committee was reaching final agreement, *American Banker* published a profile of Tony Cole, the House Banking Committee's Republican staff director: "Leach's Point Man Relishes Role as Coalition Builder." It was true that with Flake, Rep. Leach had forged bipartisan support for their position. But, as Cole seemed to crow, "We have scored major legislative successes because these people in the White House don't seem to know what they are doing," thereby enabling their opponents "to roll the administration on an issue near and dear to the heart of President Clinton: community development banks."[947]

The Conference Report laying out the final CDFI bill, H.R.3474, was approved overwhelmingly in the full House of Representatives, 410–12 on August 4; unanimous Senate passage came on August 9. "Industry Wins Big as Senate Approves Lending Bill," *American Banker* reported.[948] It quoted Edward L. Yingling, executive director of government relations for the American Bankers Association: "It's not everything on our list, but this is a major step. It's the first time I can remember that we got a bill that eased regulation, rather than increased it." (In contrast, smaller banks, represented by the Independent Bankers Association of America, lamented, "It has nothing in it for small banks.")[949]

The banking industry had been chastened by the S&L crisis and bailout. But now, it had successfully revived its perpetual campaign to roll back regulations.

Meanwhile, the legislation would mean little without an actual appropriation. Accordingly, on August 5, Senator Riegle wrote to the two subcommittee chairpersons whose approval was needed, Senator Barbara Mikulski, Democrat from Maryland, and Rep. Louis Stokes of Cleveland: "The Administration has asked that the Fund be appropriated $144 million in FY 1995. The Senate-passed version of S. 4626 provides $125 million for the program. I ask that you appropriate not less than the amount in the Senate bill."[950]

The Clinton administration's response to passage of the bill was less exuberance than relief. On August 10, 1994, the president's office issued a press statement noting that the "passage of this act fulfills another major campaign commitment.... Since my days as Governor of Arkansas, where I helped to establish one of the nation's first community development banks, community development banking has been one of my signature economic development ideas, therefore I am particularly pleased by the passage of this legislation."[951]

### The Signing: Bill Clinton's Dream

*Let me say to all of you that I have dreamed of this day for a long time.*
*President William J. Clinton*[952]

Passing the CDFI bill was a personal victory for Bill Clinton. "The possibility to sign this act into law and, more importantly, to unleash the energies of millions of Americans too long denied access to the mainstream economics of our country was one of the things that drove me into the campaign of 1992," he remarked. "Anyone who ever heard me give a talk anywhere probably knows that in almost every speech I talked about the South Shore Bank in Chicago."[953] It was ShoreBank, Southern Development Bancorporation in Arkansas, and Yunus's Grameen Bank in Bangladesh that shaped Clinton's vision of a network of community development banks and microenterprise funds. In his 1992 campaign, he visited "an awful lot of places where I thought these same things would work."

"The President and Mrs. Clinton request the pleasure of your company at a ceremony to be held at The White House on Friday, September 23, 1994, at ten-thirty o'clock." The mailed invitation from the White House Social Secretary invited CDFIs and others to appear at the Southwest Gate of The White House, "giving date of birth and social security number."

On that date, inclement weather denied CDFI practitioners another chance to go the Rose Garden: We were moved to a drab auditorium of the U.S. Department of Agriculture. There, we mingled with dozens of senators, representatives, Treasury Secretary Lloyd Bentsen, Agriculture Secretary Michael Espy, and SBA Administrator Erskine Bowles. Two speakers from the CDFI movement warmed up the crowd: the Rev. Philip Lawson, president of the Northern California Ecumenical Council and founder and director of Community Bank of the Bay, and David Lollis, director of Appalbanc in Appalachia.

*President Clinton signs the bill creating the CDFI Fund.*

Community Bank of the Bay in Oakland, CA, was one of the first of the emerging generation of community development banks. It was organized by Lyndon Comstock, the founder of Community Capital Bank in Brooklyn. Now dividing his time between the two coasts, Comstock brought his years of experience in raising capital to the California startup. The bank's supporters included foundations (Levi Strauss), banks (Wells Fargo, Citi, and J.P. Morgan & Co.), corporations (Apple), and faith-based organizations (the Episcopal Church and the Vesper Society). But as Rev. Lawson noted, "Those of us who work in community development financial institutions—the hundreds of community development banks, community development credit unions, loan funds, and microenterprise funds across the country—have created our organizations without any federal help," said Lawson. "We've been successful, but it has been very difficult. There are not enough of us, and we're not making as many loans as we want to make. Thankfully, we're now going to get some help from the federal government.... Well done!"[954]

Dave Lollis of Appalbanc had a long history as a civil rights activist. During the 1960s, along with Bob Moses and Medgar Evers, he had worked to create what became Mississippi Freedom Summer. By the 1980s, he was working in Berea, KY, the home of Berea College—the first interracial and coeducational college in the South, founded in 1855 by abolitionists and radical reformers. Berea was home to the regional headquarters of several community development organizations, including HEAD (the Human Economic Appalachian Development community loan fund); FAHE (the Federation of Appalachian Housing Enterprises); and CAPFCU (the Central Appalachian People's Federal Credit Union). "By the time I'd have said those names," Lollis recalled, "the President's eyes would have glazed over. We've got to come up with something. That's when we came up with calling [our organizations] Appalbanc."[955]

Lollis provided a perspective from one of the poorest rural areas of the country, Eastern Kentucky. "The poor pay the most for and have the least access to capital,"[956] he stated. He described the $400 loan the credit union made to a couple who were forced into bankruptcy by high medical bills and were denied a loan from a local bank. FAHE, the housing organization, had provided a mortgage with a monthly payment of $88.77 for a new house for a woman whose home was literally falling down around her. HEAD had made a microenterprise loan to a manufacturer in Rural Retreat, VA, who had been denied financing by 26 banks—and whose loan from HEAD enabled him to double his receipts in two years. Together, these Appalachian organizations made up a kind of nonprofit "holding company," the structure much admired by the Clinton team.

At 11:29 a.m. on September 23, 1994, President Clinton delivered his remarks on the signing of the Riegle Community Development and Regulatory Improvement Act of 1994, Public Law No. 103-325. Clinton praised the "all-American effort, that this [legislation] had broad bipartisan support in the country, from traditional banking institutions, traditional business institutions, and community organizers who for years felt that no one noticed the efforts they were making." "All-American" was clearly on the president's mind. The audience included football stars and future Hall of Fame members who had pledged their support: Richard Dent, the all-pro defensive player for the Chicago Bears, on leave and seated in the auditorium because of an injury, and Reggie White, "the all-time NFL defensive leader in sacks, [who] has now gone on the offensive, investing his earnings in community development banks."[957]

Among a dozen others, the president graciously called out "Congressman Flake, who had so much to do with this legislation" (not all of it positive, from the administration's standpoint); Representatives Rush and Waters (who had also advanced their own bills); and of course, Senator Riegle, the namesake of the legislation. Validating Clinton's comments about the broad support for the CDFI Fund, banks came bearing money: The president announced a $25 million commitment from NationsBank and $50 million from Bank of America over four years.[958]

President Clinton concluded, "This is the sort of thing we ought to be doing up here, helping people out of the grassroots to chart their course into a brighter future." Surrounded on the stage by members of Congress and a few CDFI representatives, he signed the law opening the new era in community development banking. Bill Zavarello, legislative director for Rep. Maxine Waters, recalled "standing behind the president and [White House adviser] Gene Sperling at some point after the president had signed the bill. I remember Clinton turning to Gene, holding it, and saying 'This is the kind of stuff I want to work on.' It animated him."[959]

## Aftermath

For Senator Donald W. Riegle Jr., the legislation bearing his name was a bittersweet triumph. It was "Riegle's Last Harrah," as *American Banker* reported several days earlier.[960] Scarred by a congressional reprimand for his role in the Keating Five S&L scandal, Riegle decided not to subject himself to another campaign in 1994.

Congress appropriated $382 million for the CDFI Fund, with $125 million in the first year—not $1 billion, not $850 million, as had been floated nearly two years earlier. Thanks to the BEA amendment, not all of the appropriation was even designated for CDFIs themselves. Naysayers abounded, both among banks and among advocates, some of whom viewed it as no better than a watered-down version of grander hopes and dreams. John Bryant, chairman and CEO of Operation Hope, added, "Three hundred million dollars spread over the entire country is no more than planting the seeds of hope." Added a Washington-based financial consultant, Richard F. Hohlt: "If somebody else can do it through federal dollars, more power to them, because it helps take the pressure off banks."[961]

Martin Trimble, NACDLF's executive director, welcomed the fund while reiterating his organization's long-held vision that went beyond the federal fund, and even commercial banks: namely, tapping the "parallel banking industry" of finance companies, insurance companies, mutual funds, and other nonbank financial firms.[962] Mark Pinsky, CDFI Coalition coordinator, acknowledged that it "may be all the money that is available right now, but it is just a drop in the bucket when it comes to addressing the need for credit and investment to pay for affordable housing and business development in this country."[963] Nonetheless, for CDFIs it was the largest pool of money that the CDFI movement had ever seen. More than that: It was the most valuable kind of money—equity and outright grants, which

CDFIs could leverage to build their balance sheets. Now, for the first time, they had the prospect of federal support that would do more than fund projects: It would help build *institutions*. It was not *the* solution to poverty, nor could it be. But it was a necessary element.

As for the Clinton administration, it was under no illusions that it had solved the problem dramatized by South Central Los Angeles and other American cities and rural areas. The day of the signing, Paul Dimond of the National Economic Council wrote a memorandum, "CDFI and Campaign to Invest in Rebuilding America."[964] "Congratulations, again! But, enough back-patting, already.... We need to get back to work." The administration should work to:

- Catalyze a larger, complementary private fund (or funds) from the unregulated financial institutions
- Catalyze a national campaign to invest in local CDFIs that are safe, sound, [and] effective and for regulated and unregulated financial institutions to use CDFIs as intermediaries and partners to find good credit and investment opportunities
- Make the CDFI Fund (and the related National Economic Partnership Act and similar HUD programs) work—not only to expand existing CDBs and CDCUs, and start new ones, but also to challenge the larger number of CDCs and revolving loan funds to become more entrepreneurial, establish profit-making bank holding subsidiaries or allies, and become better bridges to the larger resources in the regulated and unregulated financial institutions.[965]

Dimond urged his colleagues to begin thinking "among ourselves and with a few key players in the CDFI, banking, and various financial services industries" about how to use CDFI and the new CRA approach to engage the private sector.

But in a matter of weeks, a legislative landslide shifted the ground under the administration's feet. The issue would no longer be whether the CDFI Fund was too pitifully small to matter—but whether the new institution would be smothered in its infancy.

# PART VI. The Fund is Launched. The Field Grows.

As Paul Dimond pointed out, passing the legislation was only the first step, and not necessarily the hardest. The CDFI Fund was not conceived to be just another window for federal grants. "Standing up" this innovative institution required selecting suitable leadership; translating statutory language into regulations; addressing hundreds of questions far more specific than Congress could have envisioned; and producing policies that would, crucially, determine what, where, and how funding would flow. Because Congress was concerned with minimizing administrative costs, the CDFI Fund was launched with a scant staff of six charged with fulfilling the myriad of institutional duties required to make a new federal entity operational.

As if the technical and administrative challenges were not enough, the newborn CDFI Fund's survival was threatened by the bitter partisanship that followed the Newt Gingrich-led Republican Party's triumph in November 1994. The Whitewater investigation continued to throw a shadow over the Clinton administration. There were repeated efforts to rescind the appropriation for the fund, which was especially vulnerable before it had disbursed its first dollar. Initially conceived as a quasi-independent entity, the CDFI Fund was instead placed in the Treasury Department, a compromise necessary to save it.

Amid intense pressure to "put money on the street," in the fall of 1995 the CDFI Fund opened its first funding round. Nearly 300 organizations applied, and in July 1996, 31 were chosen to receive $35.5 million. But a year later, the CDFI Fund faced a new threat to its existence. In 1997 a Republican-led congressional oversight committee alleged that irregularities in the fund's selection process proved that it was a "slush fund" for Clinton cronies. The politically motivated charges were unfounded, but the fund implemented necessary improvements in its systems and procedures. The director and deputy director of the CDFI Fund both resigned in the summer of 1997. The fund put the crisis behind it.

The creation of the CDFI Fund was an enormous victory for the Coalition of Community Development Financial Institutions. The coalition enlarged its membership, obtained additional foundation funding, and made ambitious plans for a broader permanent role, despite growing organizational tensions. With federal investment now a reality, CDFIs multiplied. New community development banks were formed. Community organizations of various kinds reconfigured and rebranded themselves as CDFIs. The "CDFI era" in community development had begun in earnest.

# CHAPTER 18.
# Staying Alive: CDFIs and the Newborn Fund

Since early 1994, when passage of CDFI legislation seemed likely, Clinton administration staff had begun to consider organizational questions for the future CDFI Fund, including who should administer it.[966] In August, when passage was finally assured, Treasury Secretary Lloyd Bentsen wrote a memorandum for the president, "Implementation of the Community Development Banking Act." Bentsen highlighted the prominent role Treasury would assume in "standing up" the fund.

> In anticipation of passage, we started the search, in coordination with Presidential Personnel, for candidates for the key position of Administrator, as well as potential Advisory Board members, with emphasis on strong backgrounds in community development and banking.... In addition, the bill provides for a special transition role for Treasury to start many of the administrative functions, including hiring limited staff, before the Administrator is confirmed.... We plan to set this process in motion immediately, so that the program can get off to a running start once the Administrator is officially on board.

Bentsen hoped that the Fund would begin investing in CDFIs in the 1995 fiscal year.[967] But signing the CDFI bill into law ended neither the critiques of the CDFI initiative nor the administration's political challenges.

For example, in a *New York Times* op-ed article of October 12, 1994, banking experts James R. Barth and R. Dan Brumbaugh Jr. declared that their own plan would render CDFIs obsolete: All that was needed, they claimed, was some kind of federal mutual fund to serve the bill-paying needs of the poor. I responded with a Letter to the Editor published in the *Times* on October 17, "Credit Unions Throw a Lifeline to the Poor." Denouncing the Barth-Brumbaugh concept, I wrote: "Their understanding of community development banks is flawed, their animosity misplaced and their proposed Federal mutual fund a big-government nightmare." Defending the CDFI legislation, I pointed out that the critics' proposal did not begin to address the credit gap in low-income communities and the proliferation of high-cost and predatory lenders.

A month later, on November 8, 1994, America voted for change. It was not simply a matter of jamming on the brakes—the country slammed the gears into reverse.

In the weeks before the 1994 midterm elections, the Republicans had issued a manifesto—their 10-point "Contract with America." Virtually all Republican congressional representatives and many candidates pledged their support. Drawing heavily from Reagan's 1985 State of the Union speech, the "Contract" demanded a balanced budget, smaller government, fiscal austerity, welfare cuts, and changes in the way Congress did business. Led by Rep. Newt Gingrich from Georgia, the Republicans successfully pounded away on their message, capturing majorities in the House of Representatives, Senate, and state houses. They gained eight Senate seats, 54 House seats, and 10 governorships. (In a telling sidelight that also reflected the sea change, on the day after the election, Democratic Senator Richard Shelby of Alabama—never one of the strongest supporters of CDFI legislation on the Senate Banking Committee—changed parties, becoming a Republican.)

The "Republican Revolution" encouraged the banking lobby to intensify their push-back against regulations. "CRA, Red Tape Lead Lobbying Agenda, Optimism Reigns in Aftermath of GOP's Congressional Landslide," the headline in *American Banker* trumpeted. In the article, Robert Garsson wrote, "And when the bell sounds, the banking industry will be pounding away at consumer regulations in general and the Community Reinvestment Act in particular."[968] Banks had won some regulatory relief in the Riegle CDFI bill, but they had more targets in mind—not the least, requirements to report gender and race data on their lending. Moreover, the new CRA regulations were not yet set in stone; the first round of comments had resulted in a new proposal on October 7, 1994. "The new proposal is much weaker than last year's," reported the CDFI Coalition, "and is unlikely to significantly increase community development lending and investing by banks."[969] Realistically, under the Clinton administration, banks could not hope to totally eliminate CRA, but with their congressional allies, they could confidently go after "fixes."

At the end of 1994, Lloyd Bentsen stepped down as Treasury Secretary, as he had planned. Robert Rubin succeeded him. A former co-chairman of Goldman, Sachs & Co., Rubin had come to Washington to head the new National Economic Council. He was popular in banking circles—"Industry Cheers Choice of Rubin at Treasury," *American Banker* reported.[970] As well, Rubin would prove to be a strong supporter of CDFIs. And his support would be sorely needed as the Gingrich-led "Republican Revolution" unfolded in 1995.

## The CDFI Transition Team

Before the new Congress was in place, the administration assembled a team to translate the CDFI Fund legislation into regulations.

In the congressional hearings, members on both sides of the aisle had expressed concern about the CDFI Fund's potential administrative costs. Consequently, the act strictly limited the fund to six fulltime equivalents in its startup phase. The initial team was drawn from Capitol Hill, nonprofits, and the ShoreBank circle. In the summer of 1994, Kate McKee recalled, the Clinton administration had approached her to be the interim director;[971] in December 1994, the administration officially appointed her as transition director, in which capacity she served until June 1995, reporting to Deputy Assistant Secretary for Financial Institutions Policy Fé Morales Marks.

McKee was a felicitous choice. She had been a senior manager with Self-Help in North Carolina since 1986. Earlier, she worked for eight years at the Ford Foundation, first in rural development and women's programs in West Africa, then in Ford's Rural Poverty and Resources Program. She also was experienced testifying before Congress.[972] Erskine Bowles, deputy chief of staff to the president, knew McKee well from North Carolina, where he had a long history in politics. He sent McKee a handwritten note, saying, "I'm thrilled you will play a big part in the creation of the CDFI Fund – *No one* is better equipped" [emphasis in original].[973] The CDFI movement, too, was delighted.

To take the position, McKee had to resign from Self-Help, where her husband, David McGrady, worked as well: "Being married to someone at Self-Help and [having been] a longstanding staff member of Self-Help, I had to be very careful," she recalls. The balancing act was personal as well as professional: "I had just had a baby," McKee recalled. "Charlie wasn't one year old, so I said, 'I will do this for 3 months and I'll be the Transition Director, I'll get it up and running.'"[974] So, with one infant at home in Durham and the "newborn" CDFI Fund in Washington, McKee divided her time, commuting home to North Carolina on the weekends. She recalled

> I went up to Washington about a week before the Gingrich revolution. I started my job, and very shortly—I imagine within the first two weeks, even maybe within the first three days—the hunt was on to find federal programs and agencies to eliminate. The fund…was to be a separate small federal agency. We had started doing some leg work, even before I arrived, looking for examples from the workings of other federal agencies.[975]

Jeannine Jacokes had joined the CDFI transition team as its first member, at the end of November 1994. A former staff member of the Senate Banking Committee, she had been involved in virtually every stage in the emergence of the CDFI Fund, going back to Senator Riegle's Community Investment Corporation Demonstration legislation. Moving over to the executive branch, she played a crucial role both in writing the regulations, but also on the legislative front. She recalled, "I was spending a lot of time working with the folks in Treasury Legislative Affairs, the White House, and talking to people on the Hill to keep the thing alive long enough that you could actually launch the program."[976]

## The Little Program Up in the Attic

The CDFI Fund did not find a particularly warm welcome from the Treasury Department staff below senior management; many viewed the fund as a temporary guest with an uncertain future. The CDFI Fund was born in the uppermost reaches of the historic Treasury Building on Pennsylvania Avenue. As Kate McKee recalled, it was

> a garret space up in the top of the Treasury building.... Not real windows, not a real ceiling. To get into it, you went through a little—actually, a very nice—library with a conference table in the middle of it, with all these economics books.
>
> There are six of us. We're trying to get this thing up and running. We're consulting madly across the country. We need to do some planning. We had some flip charts. We had some diagrams. We probably even had some matrices. They were—respectfully, but nonetheless—taped up all over this library.
>
> One morning I arrive and the door is locked. There's a note saying, 'This is [Deputy] Secretary Summers' private library and you are not allowed to put anything on the walls.'[977]

The CDFI transition team did manage to retain access to its modest space in Treasury, and steadfastly kept at its work amid the political turbulence.

## How Do You Spell "Rescission"?

In mid-January 1995, Paul Weinstein of the Domestic Policy Council and Paul Dimond of the National Economic Council met with the CDFI transition team to discuss policy and congressional strategy. "It is suspected that the CDFI Fund will be a target of Republican rescission proposals," White House staffer Carol Rasco reported to Chief of Staff Leon Panetta.[978]

"Rescission," recalled Kate McKee. "R-E-S-C-I-S-S-I-O-N, I never knew that word before."[979] Put simply, it meant reversing appropriations that had already been approved by Congress. This was the cloud that McKee and her team labored under, as they worked to draw up the regulations that would implement the Riegle Act.

The CDFI Fund was a small piece of the domestic budget: $125 million out of a proposed $9.4 billion in spending cuts. But it was certainly not under the radar, since it was so identified with President Clinton. On February 23, 1995, "A House Appropriations subcommittee [took] a first step toward turning President Clinton's cherished community development bank program into an empty shell," reported *American Banker*.[980] McKee, who was hoping to get the regulations drafted and the program launched before the end of the fiscal year (September 30), if not before the end of her six-month tenure, tried to put an optimistic face on it. She told the press, "We feel that this has been caught up in the budget-cutting fervor. This bill passed with strong bipartisan support in both the House and the Senate last year, and we feel we have strong support in the Senate."[981]

Coming so soon after the signing of the bill, the "Republican Revolution" dealt a harsh blow to the ambitions and hopes of the CDFI movement. Although the president remained a potent and engaged supporter, the fund's congressional allies had been weakened or else (like Senator Riegle) departed the Hill. Without abandoning its positive agenda, the CDFI movement had to develop and implement a defensive strategy. The CDFI Coalition was not an experienced player on Capitol Hill, Jeannine Jacokes recalled: "Working with the CDFI industry at that point, except for an exceptional few like Ron Phillips [Coastal Enterprise], or others used to dealing in the Federal program sector, nobody had ever talked to their congressman. Everybody was completely green and didn't even know how to approach it."[982] But what the CDFI Coalition could do—and the CDFI Fund team could not, by law—was mobilize the grassroots for legislative action.

During the first half of 1995, the CDFI Coalition repeatedly rallied its constituents to avert the elimination of the CDFI Fund. On January 2, 1995, even before the rescissions battle was in full swing, NACDLF sent a "CDFI Fund Letter Campaign Reminder" to its members, with a template to be used with their respective senators and representatives. The letter claimed that the emerging CDFI industry included more than 300 institutions working in 45 states. On February 22, the coalition sent an "Urgent Action Alert: CDFI Fund on Rescission List" to all its members and colleagues, calling on them to contact the appropriations subcommittee in the House of Representatives.[983] That intervention failed: The subcommittee voted to rescind the entire $125 million appropriation for the fund; the full House Appropriations Committee later rubber-stamped that action. The coalition next turned its attention to the Senate Appropriations Committee. On February 27, the coalition sent out another urgent appeal, seeking to generate as many as 1,000 phone calls from CDFIs to senators.[984] The memo cited support from Senator Domenici of New Mexico, Chairman of the Senate Budget Committee who also served on the Senate Appropriations Committee; it reported, as well, that Senator Judd Gregg, a New Hampshire Republican, had agreed to organize a letter of support from the entire New Hampshire delegation.

But the CDFI Fund was caught up in the larger battle between the Clinton administration and the Republican-controlled, Gingrich-inflamed Congress. "House Expected to Ax $125 Million for Community Development Banks," *American Banker* reported on March 15.[985] By the rules of the new budget-cutting game, sparing the CDFI Fund would mean finding offsetting cuts elsewhere in the domestic budget. Reportedly, "saving CDFI funds may be difficult because orders to rescind the CDFI funds have come directly from Senate leadership."[986]

By March 20, the coalition staff reported that "our calls and letters are having an impact.... We believe we can win, *if* we can get one or more Republican Senators to speak up in committee and support the Fund publicly."[987] As the battle surged back and forth, the CDFI Coalition continued to work in parallel with the White House: On May 10, representatives of the coalition and ShoreBank met with Paul Weinstein Jr. to discuss the rescission.[988] But by mid-May, House and Senate committee members agreed on a rescissions package that cut the entire $125 million previously designated for the CDFI Fund. The Senate subsequently approved an overall $16.4 billion rescission package by a substantial margin—61 to 39—but six votes short of the two-thirds majority that would be necessary to override a presidential veto.

"We tried not to take it personally," McKee told the press, "But we certainly have been doing some contingency planning."[989] The lack of animus was a small consolation. A Senate Appropriations Committee staffer admitted, "There is a lot of support for providing additional capital for these community development banks, but we figured, why create a new agency when we're thinking of killing all these other agencies?"[990] However, the Senate was willing to allocate about $36 million to the FDIC to administer the Bank Enterprise Act program—a bitter irony for the Clinton administration and the CDFI movement. In her weekly report to White House Chief of Staff Leon Panetta for April 28 through May 5, Carol Rasco wrote: "This represents a complete loss for the program in FY 95. Paul [Weinstein] drafted with the CDFI transition team at Treasury language that would move the Fund to Treasury rather than have it operate as an independent agency. This would alleviate some Republican concerns about creating a new agency at a time of budget austerity."[991]

The administration retained one trump card: President Clinton announced that he was preparing to veto the entire $16.4 billion rescission package that included the CDFI Fund cut. And in fact, on June 7, 1995, Clinton exercised the first veto of his presidency. Despite Republican strength in Congress, they lacked the necessary votes to override the veto. "I can't say the veto came as a surprise," McKee told the press. "The White House was quite concerned about the fate of the CDFI funds."[992]

The battle was still not over, however. Toward the end of June, the House approved a new package of spending cuts. A scant $50 million was approved for the CDFI Fund, with one-third to be used for the Bank Enterprise Award program. "This $50 million at least keeps the programs alive," commented Rep. Flake.[993] Fé Morales Marks, deputy assistant Treasury Secretary, tried to make the best of it as well: "We're very happy about this. With [a] few federal dollars, we can leverage private dollars to bring much-needed economic development to distressed communities."[994]

## Settling into Treasury

So, it was not a resounding victory, but a victory against the odds, nonetheless: The Republican majority would have been delighted to claim credit for eliminating a federal agency—in particular, one that didn't really exist yet. But one price of the compromise was the independence of the CDFI Fund: Instead of being a separate agency, as originally envisioned, it would be housed in Treasury—not as a temporary visitor, but as a regular program. That never was the goal of the CDFI Coalition, which had sought an independent entity. Nor had it been the first choice of the Clinton team: Even during the presidential transition, it had been skeptical about placing the CDFI Fund in an agency with no history of running programs—especially programs that involved *distributing* money (think: IRS). But what started as a compromise with the administration's opponents proved to be a strong advantage for the CDFI Fund's survival.

"It turned out to be just a brilliant stroke," recalled Michael Barr, who served as special assistant to Treasury Secretary Rubin and later as deputy assistant secretary for community development. Admittedly, it was an unusual cultural fit, but "the Treasury Department was insulated from the political [dynamics] on the Hill; it was protected from other encroachments by other agencies or dissolution, because the Treasury is such a powerful institution. And it was embedded in a place that has responsibility broadly across the economy."[995] It was not only the institutional placement that protected the fund, but the personal support of the secretary himself. Rubin recalled "being called to the Senate by a senior senator and being told, 'Community development isn't part of the Treasury. You should worry about monetary policy and the dollar.' I said, 'Senator, I appreciate your views but I actually think community development is critically important to the economy for all us.'"[996]

Barr recalled that Rubin "didn't know about CDFIs when he came into the Treasury Department, but he knew about community development, and he cared about economic development, particularly in inner cities. And so you had someone who was supportive and who had broad credibility, who was not seen as, you know, a 'do-gooder,' saying, 'Hey, this makes good sense, it's like a smart business program.' I think it made a difference."[997]

What made Rubin a strong advocate for CDFIs, as it did for others, was visiting CDFIs. "If I wanted to convince Rubin to be a supporter of the CDFI Fund, I didn't tell him how cool it might be if the CDFI Fund worked, I took him to Kentucky Highlands, and the Enterprise Corporation of the Delta, and Boston Community Capital, and LISC, and all these places around the country. He just saw the amazing work being done, and I remember he was kind of blown away, he said he didn't understand how big an impact CDFIs were already making. We went to the South Bronx, to South Central LA together, to see Juanita Tate," a leader of Concerned Citizens of South Central Los Angeles who, along with her environmental and housing advocacy, was a cofounder of a community development credit union after the riots in 1992. Years later, Rubin recounted his early visit to a neighborhood that had served as a backdrop for presidential candidates decrying urban devastation (including candidate Ronald Reagan in August 1980).

> In early 1995 just shortly after I came to Treasury, I received an invitation to go and visit the South Bronx. What I thought I would see was a few blocks of renovated housing and then the rest of the blight that all of us so identified with the South Bronx. Instead, what I found was a Charlotte Gardens neighborhood that had block after block after block of restored housing, retail establishments, the beginnings of development of new businesses and job creation. It was a remarkable tour, and that tour showed to me the immense power and potential of community development that can come when you have CDFIs working together, in this case with a city that was committed and with the private sector.[998]

Although the Secretary was a strong supporter, the Treasury relationship presented challenges for McKee and her team, as she recalled.

It was a bit constraining because we had to figure out how we could go and educate Congress, on behalf of the fund, but in a way that was acceptable to the Treasury Department, [which] never had a program before.... I always felt like I would've liked to have done a lot more direct outreach to congressional members than we were really allowed to do. [Instead] it was really more intramural; I would go engage with the White House because they were the ones fighting the battle. Through them, the Treasury had certain positions it was taking, including an agreement to provide a more permanent home for the fund.[999]

During the time that the fund was envisioned as an independent entity, the CDFI team had been working to find models of other independent agencies. But when the deal to house it permanently in Treasury was struck, "We had a…different relationship with Treasury then: How were we going to get the regs issued, how were the different aspects of the program design going to work?"[1000] McKee's initial three months became six months. Despite the transition team's very limited resources, "It was all very exciting," McKee remembered. "We were trying to think through where did microenterprise fit? Where did the different types of CDFIs fit? What about finance on Native American reservations? So, pretty cool stuff."[1001]

The relationship of the CDFI transition team to the CDFI Coalition was delicate. The CDFI Fund lacked a strong congressional protector with a stake in the program; Senator Riegle was no longer chair of the Senate Banking Committee, and anti-Clinton forces were in the ascendance. But as federal employees, the transition team was not permitted to lobby Congress. Of course, the CDFI Coalition *could* work to educate Congress. The coalition regarded McKee, former staffer at Self-Help, as "one of us"; it had also developed a mutually productive relationship with Jeannine Jacokes from her work on the Senate Banking Committee. But as McKee put it, the fund's transition team had to maintain "a certain formality" in its dealings with its core CDFI constituency: "It was pretty constraining all the way around." Nonetheless, as Jacokes recalled, although the CDFI movement was not very experienced at lobbying, "the CDFI trade organizations were very helpful" in taking the message to Congress.[1002]

Sometimes, personal connections and an anecdote helped save the day. Jeff Wells was vice president of the Santa Cruz Community Credit Union and a longtime progressive activist who had testified in the earlier legislative hearings.[1003] On a trip to Washington, he decided to visit Rep. Jerry Lewis, a conservative Republican from California who, after the Gingrich victory, became chairman of the Veterans Affairs, Housing and Urban Development and Independent Agencies Appropriations subcommittee, which had jurisdiction over the CDFI Fund. Without an appointment, Wells managed to convince Lewis's staff to let him have a brief meeting—"no more than five minutes," he was told—with the congressman. He gave his prepared speech, urging support for the fund and highlighting his credit union's financing of small business. Then, Wells recalls, "I got up to leave. But he wouldn't let go of my hand. He asked me, 'Have you heard of Odwalla?'" This California company was a small business started by three local musicians who needed to supplement their income and decided to produce and sell fresh juice. Not only had Wells heard of Odwalla, but the Santa Cruz Community Credit Union had financed it as a startup and throughout its growth into a thriving small business with sales that had grown into the millions. Coincidentally, one of Odwalla's founders was the son of Lewis's college roommate.

Lewis, who was surprised that the credit union made small-business loans, asked: "'Are you saying that if I support this CDFI legislation, there will there be more Odwallas in the country?' Yes, Wells replied, "that's exactly what I'm saying.'"[1004] Lewis did not forget. A bill to kill the CDFI Fund came up before Lewis's subcommittee. "They were going to make a motion to kill the program," Wells recalled, "but Lewis wouldn't recognize the congressman who was going to make the motion. This was a lucky encounter with a Congressman who had been a first-hand witness to the success of CDFIs."[1005] If so, it was just the kind of luck the fragile new CDFI Fund needed.

## Preparing to Launch

The regulation-writing process took some months—certainly not unusually long by business-as-usual standards in Washington. But having endured many months of the legislative process, CDFIs bemoaned the delay. The transition team shared their urgency: "We knew," Jacokes recalled, "that on the Hill, their best chance of killing a program is before it gets off the ground. We were racing to get it done as quickly as we could. Once you get money out, then it becomes much harder [to kill a program] because [members of Congress] start to have an investment; they've got constituents that have an investment. That first year [we were] running on fear as much as anything else."[1006]

In early 1995, the CDFI Fund's transition team held several briefing sessions around the country. They reported to the anxious CDFI practitioners that the fund hoped to begin soliciting applications in April, to avoid the threat of rescission. "The transition team will also be looking to ensure that training and technical assistance will be available to CDFIs and groups seeking to organize CDFIs. They will not be providing this assistance themselves, but will instead look to existing technical assistance providers," the New York audience was told.[1007] Potential applicants were encouraged to begin preparing their applications immediately; the final regulations would closely track the legislation itself. They should pay particular attention to raising matching funds with terms that mirrored those of CDFI Fund awards.

There remained the question of who would lead the fund. "An ideal Administrator/Chair of the [CDFI] Fund would be someone who has experience in banking, community development, knowledge of the foundation world, and a background in government at the local and State level," administration advisers mulled.[1008] The administration's prime candidate, Mahlon Martin, was unavailable, so the White House identified and recruited someone who—with one significant gap—met their wish list.

Kirsten Moy had a compelling background. After obtaining degrees in mathematics and operations research, she spent most of her career with The Equitable insurance company; as of 1995, she was serving as vice president of Equitable Real Estate and Investment Management, Inc. She had a long, prominent career in social investment and was familiar with key players. She had become acquainted with the National Federation in 1982, when she edited *Investing in America: Initiatives for Community and Economic Development*, a collection of essays on social investment and community development.[1009] The Equitable had supported the first national conference of NACDLF. Moy was experienced in the foundation world as well, having spent a year at the Ford Foundation.

On February 24, 1995, the White House sent her nomination to the Senate Committee on Banking, Housing and Urban Affairs.[1010] Although "the Senators, Republicans and Democrats, have been impressed by her knowledge of the CDFI industry as well as by her private sector background in financial services and real estate," White House staff acknowledged that her path was not clear. "Because of the proposed rescission by the Republicans, she was becoming increasingly concerned whether there would be a viable program to run."[1011] To help Moy overcome her uncertainty about the prospects of the CDFI Fund, President Clinton himself called to reassure her. In the first days of May, she met with senior White House officials and Treasury Secretary Rubin. In preparing Carol Rasco, senior domestic policy adviser, to meet with Moy on May 5, Paul Weinstein recommended that Rasco "reiterate the President's commitment to the program.... You also may want to let her know that [White House Chief of Staff] Panetta apparently brought the CDFI rescission issue up at his meet with hill appropriators yesterday."[1012]

Moy had worked extensively in the private sector, but she was short on government experience. On the other hand, her key hire as deputy director, Steve Rohde, had considerable public-sector experience: He had served on the staff of the Senate Banking Committee during Senator William Proxmire's tenure; worked for the Federal Home Loan Bank; served in California Governor Jerry Brown's administration on financial and community reinvestment issues; and had directed policy and programs at the Michigan Strategic Fund. Moy and Rohde had known each other professionally for many years.

Rohde's familiarity with community development dated back to the early days of ShoreBank in the 1970s. In 1991, he studied the history of ShoreBank and spent time with its founders, Ron Grzywinski and Mary Houghton, and others. He had formulated his own ideas about how a CDFI initiative could work, and when Clinton on the campaign trail started talking about community development banks, "I had the idea that if he won the election, then maybe I could be hired to put together" a CDFI Fund.[1013] In summer 1995, when Moy was the presumptive but not yet official director of the fund, she recruited Rohde, who was then directing state and local policy for the Local Initiatives Support Corporation (LISC). On October 19, 1995, the Treasury Department issued a press release announcing Moy's appointment; in December, Rohde became the third employee of the CDFI Fund, serving as deputy director, chief of policy, and chief investment officer. As he described it, Moy would be the "outside" person, while he would be the "inside" person.[1014]

## The Coalition: High Hopes, Big Plans

The establishment of the CDFI Fund validated the years of work of the CDFI Coalition. In 1995, its ranks expanded: After several years of standing apart, ShoreBank joined, followed by the Southern Development Bancorporation and the Community Development Venture Capital Alliance (still unstaffed, represented by its board chairman, Nick Smith of Northeast Ventures in Duluth, MN). With a membership of 11, the CDFI Coalition's Steering Committee was a hybrid—a coalition of trade associations representing the major subsectors of the "industry" (credit unions, loan funds, microenterprise funds, CDCs, venture capital, Native American CDFIs); three banks (ShoreBank, Community Capital, Southern), who formally represented only themselves, since there was not yet a trade association to represent their subsector; and an activist research organization (Woodstock Institute). The coalition hired a new coordinator, Christine Gaffney, to join Laura Schwingel, in time to plan for its second major national conference, scheduled for March 1996, in Philadelphia.[1015] (Among the planning team for the conference was Kate McKee, now the "interim director emeritus" of the CDFI Fund.)

Having helped win the battle for a CDFI Fund, what role would the CDFI Coalition play? In the heady days after the signing of the CDFI bill, the CDFI Coalition had begun to think more ambitiously about its—and the field's—future.

Capital—raising it, aggregating it, and channeling it—was the biggest, most challenging question for the CDFI Coalition. In spring 1994, the coalition had begun discussing whether to conduct a capital campaign to raise $500 million in equity and long-term debt for the CDFI industry from banks and the "parallel banking system" (insurance companies, investment banks, government-sponsored entities, and others). The coalition shared its plan with the Clinton administration in the days after passage of the legislation, setting its sights high: "We plan to ask The President to serve as honorary chairman of the CDFI Capital Campaign. If protocol prohibits this, we would ask the Vice President to serve."[1016] (Even had this idea been appropriate, the Gingrich revolution would have shortly dashed this dream.) The coalition was also contemplating developing an industry-wide training program, a longstanding concern that had also been suggested at congressional hearings, both by supporters and skeptics of the CDFI initiative.

The coalition enjoyed increased visibility, enhanced credibility, and expanding opportunities. With these came heightened organizational challenges. First, it had come together as the "Trinity Group," then the Ad Hoc Coalition of Public Purpose Lenders. By 1994, it was "officially" the Coalition of Community Development Financial Institutions. In June 1995, the coalition held an important planning session. In preparation, Mark Pinsky framed some of the key questions that had begun to surface in the previous year: "Is the Coalition to remain primarily an advocacy organization? Is it a training organization? Is it a networking association? Should it ever become a financial intermediary? Do we want it to be an industry Association or an umbrella group for inter-related industries?"[1017] There were issues of staffing and budget, membership, and governance. Underlying all of these was a sensitive organizational issue as well.

Up to this point, the organization had been staffed by NACDLF, which solicited and used grant funds for coalition work. Pinsky had initially been hired as a consultant to coordinate the coalition. But after the CDFI bill was signed into law, NACDLF Executive Director Martin Trimble departed, and Pinsky was selected to succeed him, while still playing a major role in coordinating the coalition. The landscape had changed. The members of the coalition had a common interest in securing the CDFI Fund and expanding the CDFI pie, but once the fund opened its doors, there would be intense competition for investment. This would exacerbate the tension regarding roles between NACDLF, which staffed the coalition, and the coalition as the representative of the entire CDFI field.

Both NACDLF and the members of the coalition felt the need to clarify their mutual relationship—especially since the coalition was on the verge of getting a major grant from the Ford Foundation, which would impose formal expectations and obligations on NACDLF as the fiscal agent for the grant. Meeting in New York City on June 27, 1995, the coalition's Steering Committee decided to develop a formal memorandum of understanding with NACDLF, spelling out fee arrangements, administration, and grants management.[1018] The coalition was not yet ready to become a separate 501(c)(3)—that question would hover for several years to come. One important strategic decision was clarified at the June 27 meeting: Although previously the coalition had envisioned a major joint capital-raising drive (including inviting President Clinton to serve as its honorary head), "Members agreed that … the Coalition's purpose was not to act as a financial intermediary."[1019] This was a crucial point: The trade organizations for CDCUs and loan funds had their own capital-raising programs, and a coalition-run effort would clearly have created competitive tensions.

What, then, would be the role of the CDFI Coalition? The Steering Committee decided on five primary goals:

- Preserve, protect, and monitor the CDFI Fund
- Conduct a CDFI human capacity-building initiative
- Identify and explore new private and public capital sources
- Provide advocacy and public education
- Explore ways to collaborate across CDFI sector boundaries (cross-pollination) and innovate in new products, services, and institutional structures.[1020]

During 1994–95, NACDLF had received several mid-sized grants for the coalition's operations, including from the New York–based Surdna Foundation (which funded an "on-line computer forum" for the coalition), the C.S. Mott Foundation, and others. On May 24, 1995, following earlier proposals, the coalition submitted to the Ford Foundation a request for a $350,000 grant "to tackle the most pressing issue facing the industry—building human capacity through training, recruitment, and retention."[1021] It proposed cross-sectoral training, market assessments, curriculum development, outreach to minority-led financial and community development organizations, and more. After many months, the coalition finally won the two-year grant for an industry-wide program known as "Building the CDFI Field through Training and Human Capacity Building." As part of this grant, it now had the resources to conduct its Training Assessment and Demonstration Study (TADS) and implement pilot training projects. It enlisted the Corporation for Enterprise Development (CFED) to conduct the assessment and plan the projects.

## Who Will Speak for Community Development Finance?

Energized by the establishment of the CDFI Fund, a growing constituency of aspiring beneficiaries, and the interest of funders, the CDFI Coalition was growing in confidence as the nominal leader of an expanding movement. But through many iterations of the legislation, the CDFI Fund was described as being the "institutional voice" of community development banking. Now, as the fund was writing regulations and preparing to issue awards, an inherent tension would develop between these two "voices" for the CDFI field.

# CHAPTER 19. The Fund Opens for Business

The CDFI Fund opened under a cloud. It survived the first efforts to strangle it through rescission, salvaging $50 million from the FY 1995 appropriations to expend by September 30, 1996 (with one-third earmarked for the BEA). But the budget war continued: On July 31, 1995, the House of Representatives passed the following year's appropriations bill, which provided nothing for the CDFI Fund. Thus, the fund had a prospective life expectancy of one year. Saving it would require support from the Senate.[1022]

Meanwhile, preparations for starting up the fund continued. By August 1995, the CDFI transition team had drafted proposed regulations in the form of "policy option papers." They presented these for review by the incoming director, Kirsten Moy, who began working with the fund as a consultant on August 7. The next stops were obtaining approval within Treasury and then by the Office of Management and Budget (OMB).[1023]

The fund's transition staff and the CDFI movement shared a sense of urgency. Ordinarily, proposed regulations and a public comment period would precede the release of regulations and a Notice of Funding Availability (NOFA). But the fund's transition staff planned to release these simultaneously to save several months. As the CDFI Coalition noted, "The sooner money is allocated the better, as any money left unspent is vulnerable to rescission."[1024]

By October 1995, the long-sought Community Development Financial Institutions Fund of the U.S. Department of the Treasury was fully operational, if sparsely staffed. Moy was officially in place as its first director. On October 19, the CDFI Fund published an interim rule, effective immediately, and a NOFA in the *Federal Register*. It rejected procedural objections to the lack of a comment period, noting that unless the regulations became effective immediately, the fund would be unable to implement the program by the following September, as Congress had intended.

> The Department for good cause finds that notice and public comment prior to effect are impracticable and contrary to the public interest. The statute authorizing the programs was enacted over a year ago. As part of that Act, Congress set up special procedures to make the CDFI Fund operational as soon as possible.[1025]
>
> The CDFI Fund's programs are designed to facilitate the flow of lending and investment capital into distressed communities and to individuals who have been unable to take full advantage of the financial services industry.... The initiative is an important

step in rebuilding poverty-stricken and transitional communities and creating economic opportunity for people often left behind by the economic mainstream.[1026]

The rule recognized that CDFIs "while highly effective—are typically small in scale, too few in number, and often have difficulty raising the equity capital needed to meet the demands for their products and services."[1027] Up to $31 million would be available for awards to CDFIs and $15.5 million for BEA awards; the balance of the $50 million appropriation would be used for administrative expenses. As to the BEA, the program's purpose was "to encourage insured depository institutions to increase loans, services and technical assistance within distressed communities and to make equity investments in CDFIs."[1028] The fund would base its awards on a bank's year-over-year increase in community investments; the type, as well as the size, of the bank's increase would determine the award, with the greatest weight given for *equity* investments in CDFIs—15 percent of an applicant's anticipated increase in such investments.

Letters from President Clinton, Treasury Secretary Rubin, and CDFI Fund Director Kirsten Moy accompanied the release of the rules and application. The president's letter lauded the BEA as "representing a new generation of community development programs."[1029] Secretary Rubin's letter declared that "addressing the problems of our distressed urban and rural communities is critical to the future of this country. That's not a moral judgment. It's not a social judgment. It's a hard-headed business judgment."[1030] CDFI Fund Director Moy noted that "the timing of the CDFI initiative is critical"; linking with the public sector, 300 CDFIs would work as allies with traditional financial institutions "to increase capital formation, fill market gaps, and build self-sustaining institutions that can help communities help themselves."[1031]

Through the last few months of 1995, the fund—and the CDFI Coalition—had much work to do to educate the CDFI community and clarify the many questions unresolved by the rule. Meanwhile, the appropriations battle continued. Moy was determinedly optimistic even in the face of the possibility that the fund would be zeroed out of existence. She told the press, "This program continues to be a presidential priority.... If I weren't optimistic about this, I wouldn't have left my old job."[1032] She cited the outpouring of interest—more than 600 applications mailed to interested institutions—and noted that because of the limited funding, awards were likely to be far less than the anticipated $2 million maximum per award.

## The Coalition Gears Up

The initial deadline for applications was December 22, 1995, for the first CDFI Fund award round. This would allow a scant two months for CDFIs to master the regulations, develop suitable comprehensive business plans, and amass potential matching funds, among other critical tasks. Bank Enterprise award applications were due on December 15. However, on December 8, the fund extended the deadline to January 22, 1996 for the CDFI program and to January 16, 1996 for the BEA program.[1033]

Even before the regulations were released, the coalition began preparing its constituents for a compressed application period. Preparation was vital, because many CDFIs—certainly, almost all the depositories and many small organizations—were new to the daunting process of applying for federal funds. In fact, most credit unions and banks lacked experience in writing what was essentially a grant proposal: Unlike nonprofits, this was not the business they were in, and most had little or no staff grant-writing capacity. In August 1995, following the framework of the legislation, the coalition advised its constituents to begin preparing the essentials for what would be an extremely competitive application process, including the following.[1034]

- Evidence that the institution qualified as a CDFI, based on these eligibility criteria:
    - Having a primary mission of promoting community development
    - Serving one or more investment areas or targeted populations
    - Providing both loans or equity investments and "development services"
    - Maintaining accountability to residents of the target area or population
    - Not being a public agency or institution
    - A comprehensive five-year business plan, which would include financials, a description of development services, and a plan to coordinate with other community development programs
    - Analysis of community needs and a strategy to respond to them
    - Demonstrated ability to raise dollar-for-dollar, like-kind matching funds
    - Annual performance objectives.

Once the regulations were published in October, the coalition analyzed them, prepared comments, and began educating its constituencies about the new program. In October and November 1995, it sponsored regional briefings in Chicago, Seattle, New York, Dallas, and Atlanta; the CDFI Fund itself conducted briefing sessions in Washington, DC, and Los Angeles in November.[1035]

For a federal agency, issuing rules and launching new programs is typically a complex, imperfect process: Squadrons of agency lawyers, no matter how experienced, rarely can foresee how their logical Beltway constructs accord with local realities. Had there been a staged, deliberative process—Announcement of Proposed Rule Making, Proposed Rule, Final Rule, accompanied by public comments along the way—the result may have been a clearer, more comprehensive end product. But the CDFI Fund—a sparsely staffed, startup agency launching an innovative program under congressional budgetary threat—did not have that luxury. So, on December 18, 1995, the fund issued "Questions-and-Answers About the Community Development Financial Institutions Program and the Bank Enterprise Award Programs."[1036] The document was a hefty 70 pages—276 questions on the CDFI program, 39 questions about the BEA. The CDFI questions were divided into questions of eligibility (program requirements, organization types, certification, community partnerships); target markets and populations; matching funds; award amounts, terms, and use; the selection process; and miscellaneous issues. The BEA questions were fewer, mostly addressing eligibility, timing, and relationship to the CDFI program.

## Defining Eligibility

The fund made it clear that not all organizations that were engaged in community development would be eligible for investment: An applicant's "predominant business activity must be the provision of loans or Development Investments."[1037] This was a long-held position of the CDFI Coalition, despite tension with some representatives of the community development corporation (CDC) movement, who had argued that the 2,000 CDCs in the United States should be automatically eligible.[1038] The coalition also had opposed blanket eligibility for microenterprise organizations, since some made very few loans but rather were primarily technical assistance providers. As to what percentage of an applicant's finances must be dedicated to loans or development investments, the fund declined to specify: "The Fund's regulations do not establish a specific percentage of an Applicant's assets, liabilities, or net worth that need to be dedicated to lending or Development Investment activities. Instead, the Fund will evaluate the information submitted."[1039]

Excluding government entities from eligibility as specified in the legislation was an important, complex matter. The community development landscape included a wide variety of public and quasi-public entities. The fund's task was to draw as bright a line as possible, lest it be besieged by hundreds of agencies, many of which could mobilize political support. What, exactly, was a government entity? The key question was *control*: The fund decided an applicant would be disqualified if it primarily carried out functions of government, or if government entities controlled the choice of executive director or specific investment decisions. But what about *quasi-public* entities, like housing finance agencies? Simply receiving substantial government funds would not be a disqualifier. The fund would rule on these applications on a case-by-case basis.[1040]

Another important threshold question concerned the eligibility of community action agencies (CAAs), organizations with histories going back to the War on Poverty's strategy to bring capital access to the poor. Hundreds of these agencies had sponsored low-income credit unions. These agencies drew much or most of their support from public funds for federal and other programs (such as energy and food assistance). They were not disqualified from the CDFI program: "If such an organization administers public-sector programs, the Fund will need to evaluate the nature of the activities carried out and whether the Applicant exercises independent decision-making power over its activities." Thus, their eligibility would hinge on case-by-case determinations.[1041]

Tribal governments were a different matter. The fund's document stated that "Indian tribes are considered 'domestic dependent nations' rather than agencies or instrumentalities of the government of the United States or any state."[1042] The legislative history provided ample evidence of the legislators' concern for extending the benefits of CDFIs to reservations and other Native groups; disqualifying tribal-related entities would have severely hampered the development of CDFIs for those populations.

The fund made the important policy decision that credit unions with low-income designation from the National Credit Union Administration (NCUA) would *not* automatically meet CDFI eligibility requirements.[1043] The fund's target market and population criteria were different from NCUA's, and low-income designation did not require a credit union to provide "development services," as the fund did. In another decision that would adversely affect the CDCU movement, the fund determined that a group seeking a credit union charter could not be selected for CDFI Fund assistance unless it had "a high degree of confidence that the credit union would obtain a charter."[1044] Moreover, no money could be disbursed until a charter was granted. This had the effect of limiting the growth of new credit unions in low-income areas. Organizing and chartering a new credit union is a demanding process, typically taking several years, much of which depends on obtaining funding commitments; although capital requirements were much lower than for a bank, low-income credit unions rarely could draw on prosperous donors or investors to provide funds.[1045] Had organizing groups been able to obtain funding commitments from the CDFI Fund, their path to chartering would have been shortened enormously. But the fund would not commit funds to these groups. Given the delays and regulatory hurdles that organizing groups encountered, few groups could plausibly demonstrate "a high degree of confidence" that they would obtain a charter.

The fund attempted to address the issue of CDFI intermediaries. Several of the leaders of the CDFI Coalition, particularly the National Federation and NACDLF, had established central funds to help capitalize their members; they were "wholesale" intermediaries for CDFIs in their respective sectors. "The regulations do not explicitly prohibit such organizations from applying for assistance," the Fund grudgingly admitted. But it believed that working directly with CDFIs was the most effective way to carry out its statutory mandate.[1046]

(In fact, two organizations that the fund classified as intermediaries would receive awards in the first round, LISC and Tlingit-Haida Housing of Alaska.[1047] In subsequent rounds, both the National Federation of CDCUs and NACDLF obtained substantial grants from the fund, enabling them to leverage millions of dollars from private sources and build a sustainable infrastructure for their sectors. For the National Federation, in particular, these resources made it possible to distribute capital to small institutions that had little chance of success by applying directly to the fund.)

On the question of accountability to the community, the fund was intentionally vague: "The regulations do not prescribe a specific manner in which an Applicant should satisfy this requirement."[1048] The vague, subjective standard for "community accountability" disappointed advocates for strong community influence or control. For example, it would be possible for a for-profit bank to demonstrate "accountability" by simply sitting on the advisory board of a local charity. Perversely, the vague standard sometimes proved problematic for credit unions: These institutions, above all, were entirely accountable to their membership, who elected the board of directors. But there were instances in which a credit union could not necessarily demonstrate accountability if it added to its target market a low-income neighborhood that did not have a representative on the credit union's board. In any case, there was no hint of Sixties-style "maximum feasible participation" of the poor. The democratization of finance had its limits in the CDFI movement.

## Chapter 19. The Fund Opens for Business

## Investments and Matching Requirements

The law and regulations permitted the fund to provide equity investments, grants, loans, deposits, and credit union shares, with no stated preference or priority in funding. However, "the Fund anticipates that in many cases the most effective use of its resources will be to provide assistance in a manner that enhances an Awardee's net worth."[1049] This, of course, was exactly the point that the CDFI movement had stressed from the beginning. The CDFI Coalition and the policymakers were basically in accord that the CDFI Fund had to avoid becoming an ongoing annual grant program. Nonetheless, "the Fund's authorizing statute and regulations establish no prohibitions on the use of Fund assistance for operating expenses. However, the Fund is required to ensure that Awardees are not dependent on subsequent Fund assistance for future viability."[1050] The fund retained considerable discretion: "The Fund does not expect all Awardees to be self-sufficient from their operations.... The Fund will seek to ensure that all Awardees will be self-sustaining to the maximum extent practicable consistent with the mission of the institution."[1051] This broad discretion clearly worked to the benefit of nonprofits, which were dependent on grants. Depository institutions (credit unions and banks) were by their nature self-sufficient—persistent unprofitability or diminished net worth would put a depository out of business.

From the earliest days of the Clinton campaign, raising private-sector matching funds was an essential element. Initially, plans called for a 2:1 match, but as the legislation made its way through Congress, the requirement was diluted to 1:1—largely in response to advocates' and CDFI concerns that a steep match would disadvantage the poorest communities with the least access to bank, corporate, and philanthropic funding. The language for the match also softened over successive iterations: Instead of "legally enforceable" commitments, the fund looked for "firm" commitments. Although the original concept clearly envisioned a private-sector match, the fund determined that "state or local government funds could be used as matching funds,"[1052] federal funds would not qualify.

One principle that did not change was that matching funds must be "at least comparable in form and value"—that is, equity for equity, debt for debt. This was particularly a concern for community development credit unions, although it also applied in various ways to other CDFIs. Equity was in scarce supply for all small institutions, especially those outside major urban markets; raising it was doubly hard for credit unions, which, with few exceptions, built their net worth through retained earnings from operations. In what the National Federation of CDCUs regarded as a significant victory, the fund's Q-and-A provided a detailed, helpful response. The fund noted that it had "received numerous questions regarding the use as matching funds by an Applicant of 'available earnings retained from its operation.'"[1053]

> The Fund has determined to provide special consideration for how credit unions may use retained earnings as a source of matching funds. Credit unions appear to face unique barriers in raising capital to enhance net worth... The Fund has determined that special consideration is warranted for such institutions, at least for this first round of funding, and perhaps longer.[1054]

Finessing the issue of attracting outside investment, the fund allowed nonprofit and for-profit CDFIs to meet the match requirement by increasing their retained earnings (for nonprofits, fund balance), either over the most recent year or over a three-year annual average. Credit unions would have these options as well, with one important addition: CDCUs could use "the entire net capital that has been accumulated since the inception of the Applicant," provided that the credit union increased its deposits (shares) at a ratio of 4:1. At the National Federation, we viewed this concession as helping to level the playing field, even though it diluted the original vision of leveraging private-sector capital. In any case, the provision would apply to the first funding round; the fund anticipated reassessing the treatment of retained earnings or net capital for future rounds.

## Setting Parameters

Starting a new federal agency is no small task; the problem has been called "flying the plane while building it."[1055] A daunting task, certainly—but Fred Cooper, who came from the Enterprise Foundation to join the staff and served as an initial reviewer, remembered it as "so much fun—go create an agency! It called for a lot of inventiveness."[1056] On the other hand, Cooper recalled, there was little guidance from the Treasury Department, compared with—for example—the Department of Housing and Urban Development.

While the fund was busy developing its regulations, its selection process was still evolving: "The Fund is currently in the process of developing its review process. The Fund does not anticipate that decisions on the review process will be finalized prior to the application deadline."[1057] The legislation did provide general parameters that would guide the fund. It was not required to give preference to particular types of investment or lending activities, such as housing, small-business, or financial services.[1058] It would consider whether an applicant was an insured depository but would have no definite preference for these institutions. The authority to make decisions on applications was vested in the fund director; applicants should "be assured that applications will be reviewed by persons with substantial and appropriate expertise."[1059] (In fact, the fund's review process subsequently provoked criticism from CDFIs and a political backlash from congressional opponents, especially for the lack of a standard scoring approach, such as ones used by other federal agencies.)[1060]

The CDFI Fund's application for funding was rigorous and extensive. However, leaving the matter of funding aside, it was much simpler for an applicant to obtain certification as a CDFI by meeting the basic tests of eligibility—that is, demonstrating that it had a primary mission of promoting community development; that it served one or more investment areas or targeted populations; that it provided loans or equity investments and "development services"; that it maintained accountability to residents of the target area or population; and that it was not a government entity. There were practical benefits to becoming certified, as the fund noted, including "enhanced attractiveness to banks and thrifts subject to the Community Reinvestment Act" and banks and thrifts seeking BEA awards for their support of CDFIs, the highest priority of the fund.

## What Didn't Make the Cut

Various CDFIs, including particularly LISC, had urged the legislators to include a provision for institutions that provided liquidity to other CDFIs.* But in drafting the regulations, the fund's short response was: No.[1061]

Neither would the fund establish a set-aside for small, resource-poor organizations, as the National Federation had advocated. As early as September 1993, I had proposed "that the coalition formally endorse a 'developmental' set-aside, or 'small institutions window' within the CDFI Fund: a pool of $10 million, which would be available for equity grants of up to $100,000 per institution, with modified matching requirements."[1062] Although the fund now made a very limited provision for reduced matches for very small institutions, it did not agree to a carve-out or set-aside, mechanisms that had become increasingly unpopular with policymakers. (The National Federation persisted, however, and several years later, the fund did institute a "window" for Small and Emerging CDFI Assistance, or SECA.)

## The Bank Enterprise Award Act Program

Compared with the CDFI program, BEA was much less complex and prompted far fewer questions. The program provided cash awards to banks and thrifts, based on *prospective* increases in support for community development, which would be disbursed only after these were achieved. The fund elaborated its criteria and priorities in detail.

> First, Equity Investments in CDFIs serving Distressed Communities will be evaluated and funded. If any monies are still available, the Fund will then evaluate Equity Investments in CDFIs serving areas other than Distressed Communities. If any monies are still available, the Fund will then evaluate Eligible Development Activities.[1063]

There was a long list of eligible development activities, to be rated on a weighted scale. At the low end were deposits from residents (weighted at 1.0) and financial services, such as increasing the number of ATMs and consumer loans (1.2). Real estate loans and business loans were rated higher (1.6 to 1.9), and the highest weighting went to "grants used to support the operating costs of new origination (including refinancing) or loans to, or technical assistance provided to CDFIs."[1064]

There were, of course, no guarantees, but the structure of the BEA clearly prioritized directing bank investments into equity, the greatest single need of CDFIs: An equity investment could bring a cash award as much as 15 percent of the total invested, while other investments might bring as little as

---

\* An institution may provide liquidity to another by buying a portion of the latter's assets and thus freeing it to make additional loans or investments.

5 percent. In addition, a higher priority was accorded to equity investments in distressed communities with a 30 percent poverty rate—even higher than the 20 percent rate used for CDFI awards.[1065] The regulations did not require a BEA applicant to specify which organizations it would invest in at the time of application, although it required a list of potential investees and a description of investment criteria.[1066] Finally, CDFIs would be able to use any BEA investments they received to meet their matching requirement for fund awards.[1067]

Although mainstream banks had won a victory with the BEA, they did not very much appreciate the award process. "Carol J. Parry, a managing director at Chemical Bank and a member of the advisory board [of the fund], criticized the [BEA] application process as being extremely complicated," requiring a different tracking system than did CRA. In response, Kirsten Moy promised the fund would simplify the application procedure.[1068]

So the framework for both the CDFI financial awards and the BEA awards were made clearer. The fund had even prepared an application workbook to help applicants navigate the process. The CDFI Coalition found few surprises in the regulations, although it found the extensive requirements likely to deter some potential applicants. The fund "believes that it will *not* [emphasis in original] receive an overwhelming number of applications," reported Mark Pinsky. "[Moreover] demand for the $15.5 million in Bank Enterprise Award funds seems very limited."[1069] (In fact, this assessment proved accurate. In fall 1996, the fund reallocated unused BEA funds to supplement the first round of CDFI financial assistance awards.)

## A Budget Reprieve

By December 11, 1995, the heavy cloud of uncertainty about a second year of appropriations for the CDFI Fund was tentatively lifted. After negotiations, "the White House and Congressional budgeteers apparently reached a tentative agreement to provide $50 million for the CDFI Fund in fiscal 1996 (the second year), with a slim chance that there could be even more funds."[1070] Still, the budget process was not done; Congress patched together a series of continuing resolutions rather than finalizing the budget. The House and Senate versions differed on CDFI Fund appropriations; rather than the House version, which limited funding to $25 million and staffing to 10 full-time equivalents, Secretary Rubin wrote to Senator Patty Murray (D-WA) on March 26, 1996, urging that she support the Senate version at the minimum figure of $50 million. In the end, the Senate version prevailed at the $50 million level, which, as Rubin pointed out, "is merely the same level appropriated for FY 1995…[It is] a modest amount, but it does keep the initiative moving forward."[1071]

Finally, in late April 1996, Congress approved a deal that would end the continuing-resolution battles. As one of Clinton's top priorities, the CDFI Fund survived and emerged with a semblance of stability, even amid cuts in many other parts of the domestic budget. On May 5, 1996, CDFI Fund Director Kirsten Moy wrote a personal letter of thanks to Secretary Rubin.

I felt compelled to write to tell you not only what your unwavering commitment and support has meant to me and my staff (simply put, it has meant everything), but the impact of what you, as much as anyone has wrought.

The passage of the recent budget bill, which gave the Fund $45 million of two-year money with no FTE [full-time equivalent] caps, is transforming the perception *and reality* [emphasis in original] of the President's program from a one-time opportunity for a few organizations to get some money, to a multiple-year, multi-faceted community institution building initiative with the potential for enduring. ....

[In] the early stages of development of any program, each additional year of operation increases the likelihood of survival and success immeasurably. And the lifting of the FTE cap alleviates one of the greatest worries I have had since becoming the director of the CDFI fund.[1072]

## The Selection Process

Faced with a condensed deadline for the new fund's formidable application process, CDFIs received a brief reprieve, with dubious thanks to the federal budget crisis and a natural disaster. The 1995 fiscal year for the federal government ended on September 30 without a budget for the new year. The series of "continuing resolutions" to provide stop-gap funding to keep the government running began. One resolution expired on November 13, leading to a shutdown of all "non-essential" government operations from November 14 through the 19th; yet another stop-gap allowed operations to resume, but a second, longer shutdown began on December 16 and lasted through January 6, 1996.[1073] On January 10, 1996, the CDFI Fund blasted out a fax memo to the CDFI field: The CDFI and BEA program deadlines were extended to January 29, 1996. "Two extraordinary and unanticipated events have led to the decision to extend these deadlines. First, the snow storm of the century has shut down the Federal government during a critical period when many prospective applicants are seeking to get questions answered by the Fund. Second, while not affecting the CDFI Fund directly, the furlough of some Federal employees (which began on December 16, 1995 and ended just as the snow storm began), has adversely impacted the ability of prospective applicants to obtain data from some Federal agencies."[1074] Specifically, the U.S. Census Bureau and Labor Department—important sources for the data that applicants needed to provide—were closed down for most of January.

Meanwhile, the fund was laboring under severe staffing limitations—initially, six full-time equivalents—because of congressional concerns about administrative costs. To maximize administrative support, some staff members were hired for interim appointments of less than one year. Given the large volume of applications for the CDFI and BEA programs, it would have been impossible to make decisions and awards before the end of the fiscal year, September 30, 1996. Further complicating the process, this was a program unlike any other that the federal government had run. How would the fund assemble the specialized expertise to assess the applications from institutions as varied as the smallest microenterprise fund, to a credit union, to a full-fledged bank?

The answer was to turn to consultants who had worked in the emerging field, who knew (and in many cases, had worked for) applicants. It was a reasonable approach, but one that would provide fodder for the CDFI Fund's enemies. The fund would need "real experts" who understood the kinds of institutions it was dealing with.[1075] The team that was assembled included consultants with extensive experience and knowledge about community development, banking, and microlending—people like Nancy Andrews and Joyce Klein, who had been and would continue to be prominent CDFI practitioners and researchers. However, no one on the team had a significant background in credit unions.* The fund took care not to assign reviewers to the applications of any institution they had been affiliated with; consequently, instead of assigning Alan Okagaki, who had previous ties to ShoreBank and the others it had been advising, deputy director Steve Rohde personally reviewed bank applications that had ties to ShoreBank—ShoreBank itself, Southern Development Bank, Louisville, and Douglass.[1076]

What exactly was the selection process that would later bring the CDFI Fund under heavy congressional fire and politically damage it in its infancy? From the start, this was not going to be a typical government program. When Steve Rohde took his job as deputy director, his condition was that it *not* be run in a traditional way—which, in his view, involved a set scoring system and a potential for political manipulation. His philosophy, with which Moy agreed, was that "We're really reviewing institutions here." Did the applicant have a business plan that made sense? A competent management team? Good prospects for raising a match? The fund was to be in the business of *underwriting* applicants; it would need to speak to the principals of the organization, as well as anyone else in the industry who could provide context.

## Stretching the Dollars or Maximizing Impact?

The fund received 268 applications—far more than it could have funded with about $35 million, the scant residue of the original Clinton dream of $1 billion, and only two-thirds of the appropriation of $50 million, since one-third of the funding was set aside for the BEA. The fund's leadership made a strategic decision *not* to give out relatively small amounts to large numbers of institutions. Steve Rohde recalled:

> We went the other direction.... [I believed] that we were really at the forefront of something significant, we were really trying to create models, so that we should look

---

\* This was an ongoing concern of the National Federation of CDCUs, especially in the CDFI Fund's first decade: Through 2004, credit unions never exceeded 10 percent of the total awards. The percentage increased somewhat thereafter. Over 1996–2016, the average credit union share was 12.22 percent. (Analysis courtesy of Community Development Bankers Association, based on CDFI Fund data.)

for investments that could have a demonstrable impact, for institutions that would be significant and would do important stuff and really be highlighted as models going forward.[1077]

The fund established a two-step process. First, nine reviewers supervised by Rohde each reviewed applications for CDFIs in their respective areas of expertise. Screening out those that were not competitive left a pool of 60 finalists from the original 268. Rohde regarded this stage as preliminary. He made handwritten notes about the four community development banks that he reviewed personally, determining that each was clearly qualified to advance to the next round; because of his other responsibilities in the review process, he later stated, he "didn't have time" to do a formal write-up of his review.[1078]

Then the intensive work of final selection began. A panel of five was charged with reviewing each of the 60 applications: Director Moy, Rohde, Nancy Andrews, Fred Cooper, and Paul Pryde, who had not previously been a reviewer. Rohde describes the process as a "venture capital model": Each of the five reviewed each voluminous application. Representatives of the management teams of the 60 applicants were brought to Washington at the fund's expense and interviewed intensively, after which the review panel debriefed. It was a "grueling" but "exciting" process, Rohde recalled, lasting up to seven weeks.

Valerie Piper had an inside view of much of that process. Piper was working on special projects at HUD, including coordinating the first mixed finance public housing grant competition, before she was shifted over to Treasury on an interim appointment.[1079] She joined the fund early in 1996, in time for the second part of application review. Her work included massive amounts of note-taking by hand for the review and interview sessions. Later—sometimes significantly later—other staff would type up the notes, a process that contributed to the charges of backdating that emerged from the congressional investigation of the fund in 1997.

## Square Pegs, Round Holes

The CDFI transition team had found an unwelcoming atmosphere in Treasury, shaped by the perception that this new entity was not going to be around for long. As the fund became operational, many administrative processes had to be built from scratch. Piper remembered speaking with a senior executive who was trying to understand the fund's competitive selection and investment process as a federal procurement activity. There were, for example, no written procedures on how to handle a stock certification that a CDFI had submitted. As well, the fund had to create transaction documents for processing its awards. She recalled:

> You're doing something very specialized, that combines federal regulatory and private-sector transaction experience. You can't just plug any federal employee into it.

We had to invent the administrative foundation of the program as we went, and given our staffing constraints, we couldn't get very far ahead.[1080]

There were also technical challenges in dealing with the Office of Management and Budget (OMB) prior to announcing the winners of the competition. In a process that seems incredibly obscure to laymen—and did to the CDFI movement—OMB has to "credit-score" debt-based federal programs, to account for potential losses to the government. When OMB got to look at the actual transactions the fund was about to make, credit scores were adjusted, affecting the amounts of loans and investments that could be made with the appropriated money.[1081]

## The Specter of Politics

The process established by Rohde called for the five members of the review panel to reach a consensus on the award winners and their respective amounts, a process he has described as comparable to that used by venture capital investors. After all of the interviews were completed, the five members of the review panel gathered in a room for two days of discussions aimed at achieving unanimity. Each member of the review panel gave his or her initial view of each applicant: definitely fund, possibly fund, or definitely do not fund. Rohde later asserted that each panelist put all four of the community development banks with ties to ShoreBank in the "definite yes" category. The review panel then turned to applications where there was not initially a consensus whether to fund. After achieving unanimity on the winners, the panelists worked to achieve unanimity on the amounts and the form of award for each.

But what exposed the fund to attack was the Clinton connection. Not only was ShoreBank Bill Clinton's favorite model: He and Hillary Clinton had helped start Southern Development Bancorp in Arkansas. Hillary had served on its board, and her college friend, Jan Piercy, had worked for ShoreBank. Rohde maintained that he was the only member of the review panel who knew that Hillary Clinton had been on Southern's board, and that neither her name nor Jan Piercy's ever came up in discussions: "The idea that there was any sort of funny business… was absurd."[1082]

Piper, like others, rejected the notion that politics entered the picture: The process, she recalled, was "technical," based on very detailed business review of the applications.

> What I was most impressed by was the level of rigor that went into those selections… what the real balance sheet and projections for these businesses were telling the group about the impact that the organization could make with the investment, and what they had and hadn't thought of in terms of their market. They were really, really working very hard to set up not just a little program, but a set of institutions that could continue to play an intermediary role and aggregate capital for particular

uses. Just the nature of that analysis was something that I was just learning a huge amount from.

You know, it was a very private-sector model in terms of how you would do an investment of this sort. The way to find the experts who could perform with the necessary rigor was to buy talent. There aren't many federal programs that require this expertise even now. Honestly, it doesn't exist at a very high rate in the federal government still. It was just a really excellent job from my perspective. It was so rigorous and we kept missing deadlines because of the people saying, 'No, no. We really have to look at this again. We have to go back through this thing with a fine-tooth comb.'[1083]

Part of the underwriting approach was interviewing the principals, but as Piper said, that was out of the ordinary and "risky" for a government agency: "Interviewing applicants can lead to different things coming into focus in the conversation; even when you have a clear framework, different applicants will have different strength and weakness that you have to probe."[1084] On the other hand, she noted, *not* going through this process meant that as an investor, you might lack the essential information.

## The Dissertation Defense

For the applicants, Bill Luecht, longtime public affairs official of the fund, recalled that the interview process was extremely stressful.

Imagine you're defending your dissertation. You're walking in and there's a panel of experts. You had Kirsten, you had Steve Rohde, so you had the director and the deputy director reading the applications, and then you had [the other reviewers on the panel].... They would all focus on different things.... These experts, these thought leaders in the industry, were sitting down, pouring through those applications, studying them. Applicants were allowed to bring three people into the interview. Steve Rohde would be literally zeroing in saying, 'Okay, on page seven, on the second paragraph, go to the third line.' They *knew* these applications.

They knew that they needed to make the best decisions. They had to be getting the cream of the cream in this competition; the best had to be the ones funded, so that the program would continue. It had to be above-board. It had to be the best organizations, and this process, I think was intimidating for applicants. Basically, you're going to be defending your dissertation.[1085]

Excessively concerned about any appearance of political interference, the fund's leadership decided to circumvent a well-established tradition: notifying members of Congress in advance about announcements of federal awards going to their respective jurisdictions. As Piper pointed out:

You're just notifying. You've already made your decisions based on your criteria. You're just giving the member the opportunity to make a congratulatory phone call or an announcement. Steve was very much against doing it, because he felt that that created an implication of political influence, and he didn't want to have anything like that tainting this process. In the end, we called the applicants confidentially so that they knew that they had won based on the fund's decisions.

The irony of having someone like that, who is so committed to the apolitical nature of the selection process, being accused of influence… it just didn't seem fair.[1086]

## And the Winners Are...

At a ceremony on July 31, 1996, Treasury Secretary Robert Rubin announced the winners of the first round of CDFI funding. Some 268 applications had requested more than $300 million in assistance; of these, 31 organizations were awarded $35.5 million. This funding, Rubin announced, "is expected to leverage, in just the next two or three years, an additional $140 million in private sector investment and significantly more over time."[1087]

On October 1, 1996, Secretary Rubin announced that 38 banks and thrifts would be granted $13.1 million in Bank Enterprise Awards for increasing their support for community development. The BEA program, he stated, had "leveraged nearly $66 million in private sector equity investment and other financial support from these banks and thrifts to Community Development Financial Institutions. In addition, the program catalyzed $60 million in total direct lending and services provided by these banks and thrifts within the distressed neighborhoods they serve."[1088] Two-thirds of the awards went to recipients who increased their assistance to CDFIs, including more than $1 million in equity investments made into the Louisville startup community development bank (which also received more than $2 million in grant and technical assistance funds from the CDFI program).

# CHAPTER 20. CDFIs at the Dawn of the New Era

*My views as to reversing income inequality and dealing with the problems of the inner cities are not social judgments or moral judgments. They are hard-headed business judgment about the future economic and social health of our nation.*

*I want to focus in on two policy areas that can contribute to a reversal of income disparity—investing in human capital and access to financial capital.... One very powerful tool is the Community Reinvestment Act.... The second major element to improve capital access in our inner cities is the Community Development Financial Institutions Fund.*

*Treasury Secretary Robert E. Rubin*[1089]

The establishment of the CDFI Fund was a victory for President Clinton and the successful culmination of a long journey to credibility and recognition for the pioneering organizations that became known as CDFIs. Foundations, faith-based organizations, individual supporters, and—in the case of credit unions—low-income communities themselves had provided the capital to start these institutions and helped them grow to modest levels. What was the state of the movement before the CDFI Fund began supplying capital in amounts that would transform it?

## The Community Development Banks

Four institutions were cited in early community development banking legislation, dating back to 1992: South Shore Bank, Southern Development Bancorp, Community Capital Bank, and Self-Help.

## ShoreBank Expands—Amid Opposition

As the CDFI Fund was gearing up, ShoreBank was expanding. On the way, it confronted a fault line in the community development banking movement. Even an institution like ShoreBank, with the best intentions and a track record of lending to match, was not synonymous with African American economic empowerment. In 1995, ShoreBank moved to consummate a merger with Chicago's African

American-owned Indecorp, in a deal that would double its assets. The transaction painfully exposed race-related contradictions that would persist in the CDFI movement, if rarely so obviously.

Indecorp was the largest black-owned bank in the United States, although still a relatively small institution. Its holding company had two bank subsidiaries, Independence Bank (founded in 1964 at the height of the civil rights movement) and the venerable Drexel National Bank (founded in 1888). By 1993, the bank's two largest shareholders, Alvin J. Boutte and George E. Johnson, were in their sixties and contemplating retirement. "We understand the banking environment is changing dramatically," Boutte told the press. "It requires a different approach. We're going to have to meet all the standards of CRA and the communities."[1090] Reportedly, "regulators have told Independence it must improve its community lending—a situation suitors say is an embarrassment."[1091]

Indecorp began to explore ShoreBank's interest in acquiring the two banks. As Mary Houghton recalled, "It was ideal strategically, as the Indecorp bank branches were located geographically in a way to serve customers that were already buying and rehabbing apartment buildings southwest of ShoreBank. It allowed ShoreBank to continue a slow expansion further north, west, and south, and to increase its annual 'mission' loan originations dramatically."[1092]

That CRA would be a factor in the decline and disappearance of African American banks was ironic. But the record of minority banks in meeting the mortgage and other credit needs of their local communities was very uneven: For example, Woodstock Institute data from 1991 showed that Drexel had made only 19 mortgages and home improvement loans, while Independence had made 28 for $1.4 million—a very small percentage of its assets. South Shore Bank, on the other hand, had made 469 loans totaling $26.3 million in its service area.[1093] Often, African American banks invested their assets in government securities and credit lines for major corporations that were attempting to demonstrate diversity and support for minority-owned institutions.

In December 1994, a pending sale of Indecorp to Omnibanc Corporation fell through over differences in the sales price. Subsequently, there were efforts to line up African American purchasers, but ShoreBank, which had been in discussions with Indecorp, emerged as the prime bidder. Even before a deal was struck, opposition arose within the black community. "We've made it clear before that we oppose their selling to South Shore,' said Charles Gaines, a former state representative and an Independence founder.'"[1094] Congressman Bobby Rush, whose district included ShoreBank and who praised its record, walked a fine line: "I would be extremely careful and cautious about supporting a sale to any entity that has not provided the community with thorough plans and programs that would enhance the services provided by Indecorp."[1095]

On June 19, 1995, ShoreBank and Indecorp reached a deal. The opposition ramped up: Mark Allen, president of the Black Leadership Development Institute, told the press, "I received more than a dozen phone calls today from people in the community who feel let down. They want to preserve Indecorp as a black-controlled institution. None of ShoreBank's stockholders is black."[1096] In fact, the investors included foundations, corporations, religious organizations, and socially concerned individuals; none of the stockholders were black. However, as Joan Shapiro, ShoreBank's executive vice president and a prominent figure in the national socially responsible investment movement pointed out, the board of directors "is fully integrated."[1097] Jim Fletcher (then CEO of South Shore Bank) and Milton Davis (then chair of the board of South Shore Bank), both African Americans, were half of the ShoreBank management "quartet." Defending his decision to sell, Indecorp co-owner Alvin Boutte told the press, "We looked for an organization capable of carrying on [our] legacy. ShoreBank, because of its 22-year track record of economic development in our communities, was the ideal choice."[1098]

Consummating the deal required obtaining multiple regulatory approvals; surviving opposition from the African American community; and—not least—raising additional capital. ShoreBank needed to raise $15–$20 million in stock to support the expansion of its asset base to over $500 million with the Indecorp acquisition. It didn't make it easier that ShoreBank had suffered a loss in 1994 of some $580,000 from its real estate arm, City Lands Corporation.[1099] Moreover, some of ShoreBank's previous investors were banks that had since opened branches in the area, raising issues of competition.

The first hurdle was winning approval from federal regulators. Several community leaders filed a formal protest to block the acquisition. Rev. Al Sampson, head of the Metropolitan Area Black Churches, told the press, "We are asking that South Shore Bank…withdraw from this illicit sale and work with a group of us that would like to acquire the bank."[1100] However, the Chicago Federal Reserve Bank received dozens of letters supporting the acquisition, including from pastors of large South Side churches and from the African American U.S. Senator Carol Moseley-Braun, whose roots were on the South Side.

In October, the Federal Reserve Board approved the acquisition; ShoreBank's financial capacity, record of minority lending, and "outstanding" CRA record outweighed the concerns expressed by some community leaders. Protests continued: "The African-American community worked too hard and too long to build these black institutions to let them go without a fight," said Mark Allen, leader of the community coalition protesting the acquisition.[1101] Mattie Butler, director of the We Can community group, described the anguish that many South Shore residents felt: "We keep our account there. They're good people. But we're losing the biggest black bank in the country. They don't seem to understand what that means. It's a real blow for us and for the community.[1102]

Two regulatory hurdles remained: approval from the state banking regulator and the FDIC. By December 1995, ShoreBank cleared these and raised the capital it needed from new and existing investors. Mark Allen delivered a sad, bitter epitaph for the struggle, telling the press: "We're going to make the best of a bad situation. We'll move on. Unfortunately…federal regulators could care less about…the kind of community concerns that we are concerned with, especially the fight to retain black ownership."[1103]

It was, as a *Wall Street Journal* reporter wrote, "an emotional, nationally significant debate about race and economic empowerment."[1104] Even when black-owned banks underperformed in lending to their communities, the loss of institutions like Indecorp in Chicago and Freedom National Bank in New York City a few years before produced cries of pain. The loss of black-owned banks would continue nationally on a relentless trajectory for decades to come.

Doubling in size created management challenges for ShoreBank, as it would for most institutions. South Shore Bank's pre-tax income more than doubled between 1994 and 1996, although its profitability ratio, measured by return on equity, shrank immediately after the merger: Profits had to be spread over the larger capital base required by the merger. Early in 1996, ShoreBank consolidated two nonprofit subsidiaries—The Neighborhood Institute and the Austin Labor Force Intermediary on the West Side of Chicago—into the Chicago Neighborhood Institute.[1105] "If we succeed," Mary Houghton said, "we would hope to make the point that a banking institution can develop unusual partnerships both with employers and with residents."[1106] ShoreBank would contribute about $500,000 to the entity's $3 million operating budget and offer an innovative incentive to promote local employment: Companies that hired local residents were eligible to receive up to a 3 percent rebate on loans.[1107]

Beyond Chicago, the ShoreBank "family" included enterprises in Detroit, Cleveland, the Upper Peninsula of Michigan, and the Pacific Northwest (not to mention its relationship with Southern Development Bancorp). Richard Taub, who closely followed and wrote extensively about ShoreBank in its formative years, posed the question: "I think they're stretched out. It is only now that they're beginning to construct a management structure appropriate to the increased scope of the operation and hiring outside talent. I see them coming together, but who knows?"[1108]

By 1998, the merger with Indecorp appeared to be yielding fruit. South Shore Bank raised the loan-to-deposit ratio at the former Indecorp branches to about 70 percent. William Michael Cunningham, head of Creative Investment Research in Washington, which focused on minority financial institutions, told the press: "South Shore has done what it said it was going to do. For all of that controversy, minority individuals are better off than they were before the merger." Not everyone agreed. Rev. Al Sampson, a leader of the opposition to the merger, complained to the press that South Shore "is just as dangerous today as they were a few years ago," claiming that their lending in the Indecorp area was not benefiting low-income residents.[1109]

## Community Capital Bank (CCB)

By 1996, Community Capital Bank (CCB), the bank organized in Brooklyn by Lyndon Comstock—the third community development bank in the nation, but the first organized from scratch—was producing solid financial results.* By the end of 1996, management reported to stockholders that the bank's total deposits had reached $26.7 million, with assets totaling $31.4 million.[1110] It closed $7.5 million in new loans in 1996 and reached $16.7 million in outstanding loans, up 16 percent

---

\* Community Capital Bank obtained its charter from the New York State Banking Department and issued an initial public offering (IPO) for the bank's stock. Kerwin Tesdell, later with the Ford Foundation, served as the bank's lawyer while working for Debevoise & Plimpton LLC and later the Community Development Legal Assistance Center.

from the prior year. The bank was recording modest but increasing profits: $44,503 in 1995, increasing to $87,728 in 1996. In 1996, CCB won its first Bank Enterprise Award of $215,461 from the CDFI Fund.

No less than conventional banks, CCB had to meet the requirements of the Community Reinvestment Act (CRA). It did so enthusiastically: Management reported that 97 percent of its loans in 1996 were CRA-type loans, with an emphasis on affordable housing, small businesses, and nonprofit organizations. "When reviewing new loans from a community reinvestment standpoint, we consider factors such as the ownership and employment patterns of the business, as well as its purpose. Every loan includes a social purpose description within the credit analysis memorandum."[1111]

CCB was based in the downtown Brooklyn business district. Unlike ShoreBank, it did not have a focus in a single neighborhood, but rather lent across New York City (a reason that the Ford Foundation had declined to fund it several years before).[1112] CCB had a varied portfolio of commercial and other loans. Management proudly cited several examples: microloans for working capital for small businesses started by New York City public housing residents; participation with other banks in a construction loan for a church in Queens; and affordable housing projects in Brooklyn and the Bronx. It joined another CDFI, the Low Income Housing Fund, for one affordable housing loan and also partnered with the nonprofit Community Service Society.[1113]

CCB was the main financial engine but only one component of Comstock's vision of community economic development. He recalled, "I really wanted the bank to be a flagship organization for community economic development. For the term 'flagship' to be a meaningful term, there's got to be a rest of the fleet."[1114] In Brooklyn, the other "ship" in the CCB fleet was LEAP, a nonprofit organization that developed new training and enterprise-incubation programs in promising sectors, such as food service and training for commercial drivers. Comstock chaired LEAP—and in fact, his heart was there, much more than in the day-to-day operation of the bank.

The holding company model akin to ShoreBank's had captured the imagination of the Clinton team. But CCB of Brooklyn never did set up a true holding company.[1115] Although the bank and the nonprofit were integrated by vision, in practice, they were not. This did not make for a seamless relationship, and in fall 1996, Comstock wrote to the boards of the bank and LEAP, seeking to begin dialogue on establishing a holding company that he would chair, rather than chairing both the nonprofit LEAP and CCB. This strategy would not be successful. As Comstock later recalled:

> It did not work out that great in terms of the connection between the bank and the non-profit either at Community Capital Bank or at the Oakland Community Bank of the Bay.... [The boards felt] 'we've got our hands completely full trying to run this brand new startup bank with this unusual and challenging mission. Just what is it that you want us to be doing with this nonprofit over here on the side?' I couldn't really get them to focus on the nonprofit or see it as part of the mission.... The initial connection between the bank and LEAP in each case, rather than growing, seemed to erode.[1116]

Nonetheless, CCB continued its incremental progress. It won a BEA award in 1997 ($164,627) and in a half-dozen subsequent years. The BEA awards were relatively modest compared with the multimillion-dollar CDFI awards that Southern and other community development banks received from the CDFI Fund, a source of considerable irritation to Lyndon Comstock, who had fought so long for the fund. That BEA was the source of assistance for CCB was ironic, if not a bit embarrassing to Comstock, who had excoriated BEA's author, Rev. Floyd Flake, for siphoning money from the CDFI Fund.[1117] Comstock recalled:

> [Rev. Flake] later buttonholed me, and I meant that literally, he grabbed me by the suit lapel at a Fannie Mae event in DC and said that I shouldn't have opposed him on BEA. What could I do but shrug, because he was right, at least as far as CCB was concerned. BEA was very good for Community Capital Bank, and the main [CDFI assistance] program ended up being of no use for CCB. Of course, I had opposed BEA not because of CCB's narrowly defined self-interest but because that was a political decision made by our CDFI [Coalition]; I was part of that collective and supported the group's decisions on what was the best way to advance the entire CDFI movement of which CCB was a part.[1118]

For much of the early 1990s, as he was working to set up Community Bank of the Bay, Comstock lived a bicoastal life. For several years, "every weekend I was flying cross-country in one direction or another. I really wanted to continue being involved in New York, but I just couldn't do it, it was just too taxing. I stayed on the board [during the late 1990s], just going to board meetings by phone and so forth or occasionally flying to New York, and finally just stepped down from the board."[1119]

## Southern Development Bancorporation

By 1995, Southern had trimmed some of its affiliates to focus more on its core banking operation and its nonprofit lending program. George Surgeon, who was then serving as president and CEO of Southern, recalled: "By then, we had really gotten Southern Bank Corporation in adequate shape. We had integrated the back-office operations of the companies, and we had stabilized management. However, some of the non-bank companies were not performing as well as we had hoped."[1120] Among the less successful units were its Small Business Investment Corporation and its real estate development company, the Opportunity Lands Corporation. But, as Surgeon reported to shareowners and others on Southern Development Bancorp's progress in 1995, it had "generat[ed] $85 million development investments…[and] harvested our most successful year of financial returns as well by achieving record earnings of $489,272.… In 1995, for the first time, all the Southern companies were profitable in the same year."[1121]

To increase its impact in Arkansas, Southern looked to expand geographically. "The board and especially some or our key Arkansas investors were very interested in Southern being more involved in East Arkansas—the Delta. You really can't do that from Arkadelphia, which is in southwest Arkansas, a three-hour drive from Helena, in the eastern part of the state." He continued:

> We created a strategic plan in 1995. Basically, what it said was that the way for us to expand Southern Development Bank Corporation as a totality was by increasing partnerships with other active community development entities throughout the state. At the bank level, we really needed to buy another bank, and because of the banking regulations at that time in the state, we really needed to buy a bank in eastern Arkansas.[1122]

However, expansion would require substantial capital—some $10–$20 million dollars. Faced with such a hurdle, Southern's leadership raised the question of whether Southern should, in fact, become a subsidiary of ShoreBank, whose role up to that point had been supplying management services. "The board [of Southern] went through a very deliberate process," Surgeon recalled, "to decide whether they wanted to maintain Southern as an independent company or for Southern to become a subsidiary of ShoreBank. They decided to maintain Southern as an independent company, which I think, in hindsight was the right decision."[1123] Ron Grzywinski and Mary Houghton remained involved both in Southern and its nonprofit, the Arkansas Enterprise Group (AEG), and ShoreBank continued to provide advisory services, but the management role of ShoreBank's personnel role was reduced.[1124] Southern's decision "was also facilitated by [the fact that] we had a very excellent offer to buy what was then the First National Bank of Phelps County in Helena, Arkansas."[1125]

The launch of the CDFI Fund was timely for Southern. "We prepared a joint application, for our nonprofit and for the holding company," Surgeon recalled. "It turned out to be very complicated and cumbersome—a one-million-dollar equity investment in Southern Bank Corporation and a one-million-dollar capital grant to what was then the Arkansas Enterprise Group. In essence, we had to duplicate all the paperwork."[1126] The good news: The application was successful. The bad news: It provided fuel for Alabama Republican Rep. Spencer Bachus's investigation of the CDFI Fund in 1997.

## Self-Help

By its 15th anniversary year in 1995, the Center for Community Self-Help had grown dramatically. Headquartered in Durham, it had five branches around North Carolina. Its two financial engines worked seamlessly together: The Self-Help Credit Union raised funds through deposits and made a range of housing and small-business loans, while the Self-Help Ventures Fund provided higher-risk commercial financing and developed real estate projects. Cumulatively, Self-Help had loaned out $70 million in North Carolina, including one-thousand small-business loans. Reaching beyond small businesses, Self-Help launched its North Carolina Community Facilities Fund to provide financing for nonprofits, social service agencies, and child care centers, including those in rural areas.

Self-Help had initially focused on financing worker ownership. It had now become a major player in mortgage lending to low-income people in North Carolina, especially for minorities and single heads of households. In 1995, aided by investments from partners, including Metropolitan Life Insurance, Self-Help diversified its loan products by introducing a fixed-rate mortgage. But Self-Help made its biggest breakthrough to scale in October of that year, with its Secondary Market Demonstration Project—a $100 million partnership with five North Carolina banks and housing finance giant Fannie Mae. Without exaggeration, Self-Help described this as "the most nationally significant endeavor that we have ever undertaken. The partnership with Fannie Mae and the banks will expand home ownership on a scale far greater than Self-Help could achieve on its own."[1127]

By the end of 1996, Self-Help's assets had reached $94 million. Its secondary market program continued to grow, with additional support coming from the North Carolina General Assembly, Duke University, and other institutions. Like other CDFIs, Self-Help had received support for years from faith-based investors, especially women's orders and local congregations; now, it received investments from the General Board of Pension and Health Benefits of the United Methodist Church. Self-Help expanded its financing for supportive housing, home rehabilitation, charter schools, and residential real estate in its headquarters city of Durham. Its Staged Microlending Program enhanced access for small businesses with weak credit or little track record or collateral. Despite its innovative, sometimes high-risk lending, Self-Help managed to keep its loan loss rate to 0.5 percent.[1128]

Self-Help's growth was aided by an expanding, increasingly diverse set of funders. The Ford Foundation had provided grants and loans totaling $11 million since 1984.[1129] The Calvert Social Investment Foundation and other socially responsible investors, banks, regional foundations, federal agencies, and individuals had contributed to its growth. In 1996, Self-Help won a $3 million first-round award from the CDFI Fund.

Self-Help was unique among CDFIs in its strong emphasis on advocacy, both on major financial-systems issues, and locally, in defending and supporting the network of small, African American credit unions that struggled in rural North Carolina. Recognizing the extraordinary leadership of Self-Help's CEO, Martin Eakes, in 1996 the John D. and Catherine T. MacArthur Foundation awarded him its "genius" fellowship.

## Intermediaries: The CDFI Associations

As the CDFI Fund was becoming a reality, the two national associations that had formed and driven the CDFI Coalition strengthened and expanded their roles.

## National Association of Community Development Loan Funds (NACDLF)

By 1995, with the CDFI legislation passed and the fund becoming a reality, Martin Trimble decided to move on.

> I felt like I was becoming a banker. [We had gotten] that first million dollars for equity grants [in 1992], which we used as a way of imposing or enforcing performance standards. Then we got the PRIs from Ford and MacArthur and a bunch of other places. I looked up one day, and I was worried about loan-loss reserves.... [Meanwhile], I was living in the city that I loved, and it was imploding.
>
> I wanted to get back on the street. I understood, fundamentally, that the issue is power, and I left because I believed in the organizing work that the Industrial Areas foundation (IAF) was doing. I felt that that was really my strength.[1130]

Mark Pinsky succeeded Trimble as the association's executive director. From Trimble's perspective, the transition was a natural one: "He and I had developed a strong relationship through the CDFI Coalition work that he was doing for us. He just seemed like the logical person to take over. He had the drive and charisma to do it."[1131] Having served as a consultant for NACDLF and the CDFI Coalition on CDFI matters, Pinsky became the chair of the coalition's Steering Committee. As NACDLF raised larger amounts of funds for the coalition, NACDLF added staff to carry out the coalition's work, including Christine Gaffney and Laura Schwingel.

In 1995, NACDLF began collaborating with Citibank to develop a new capital product for nonprofit CDFIs: the Equity Equivalent investment, popularly known as "EQ2." On October 23, 1996, at NACDLF's annual conference in Chicago, the association and Citibank announced the bank's $1 million investment for the new product, to be followed with an additional $1 million after the first investment was deployed. Optimism ran high: "For the first time, banks are encouraged under CRA to invest in non-profit CDFIs,' said Mark Pinsky. 'We expect that this new product will bring tens if not hundreds of millions of new dollars into poor communities through CDFIs.'"[1132] EQ2 was a response to the limited supply of equity for nonprofits. It was not true equity, but rather deeply subordinated debt with a special structure. A typical EQ2 investment had 10-year rolling term, with automatic renewal for each of the first 10 years; thus, principal was repayable after 20 years (or more, depending on the investment). Because it was subordinate to all other claims on a CDFI, it enabled the CDFI to leverage additional debt.

EQ2 had a special appeal to banks. Because of its lengthy term and subordination, EQ2 was far riskier than an ordinary loan. But the tradeoff for bank investors was greater CRA credit: Rather than getting dollar-for-dollar credit when it made an ordinary loan to a CDFI, by making an EQ2 investment a bank could obtain CRA credit for a pro-rata share of the increase in a CDFI's *total* lending. Furthermore, a bank would get credit for an EQ2 investment as an "innovative" investment. In a June 27, 1996, letter to Citibank, the regulators wrote, "Like true equity interest, subordinated debt investments are fully subordinated to the claims of all debtors, are designed to raise revenue of the issuer, and have, in effect, an indeterminate term."[1133] In January 1997, NACDLF secured a favorable opinion of EQ2 from the Comptroller of the Currency: "This special debt investment is a precedent-setting community development debenture that will permit 'equity like' investments in not-for-profit corporations."[1134] The four bank regulatory agencies subsequently clarified that bank EQ2 investments could receive CRA credit either under the investment test or the lending test of CRA.[1135]

NACDLF continued the broad financial-sector advocacy that had been its hallmark. A main target was the "parallel banking industry"—the non-depositories, such as insurance companies and money-market funds, which aggregated larger and larger amounts of funds but, unlike banks, did not have CRA obligations.[1136] In requesting a grant from the MacArthur Foundation, NACDLF wrote that it "is committed to leading—in conjunction with others—a multiyear effort to make community reinvestment by parallel banks a front-burner issue."[1137] NACDLF also focused on another issue, the impact of modernization of the financial services industry on low-income communities and individuals. Such changes, prompted by global market trends, included "aggressively stripping away fire walls between the banking and securities industries."[1138]

NACDLF had allies in high places for its expansive vision of prodding reinvestment by the "parallel" banks. On July 15, 1997, Comptroller of the Currency Eugene A. Ludwig delivered an address to the Director's Roundtable in San Francisco.[1139] Ludwig commended the increase in CRA lending since the Clinton-driven reform of 1994: "In the past four years, banks have invested four times as much in community development projects as they did in the whole previous thirty years." He noted, though, that "CRA covers an ever-shrinking share of the financial services industry… [and that] nonbanks had a larger share of the nation's financial assets than commercial banks and thrifts combined." Gingerly but firmly, he argued, "We must begin now to seriously focus on this central question: to what degree should financial providers beside banks be asked to step up to the plate and participate in a CRA-like program as the banking industry has done?" Without offering a specific, "one-size-fits-all" CRA regulation for the nonbanks, he suggested that one way for nonbanks to further the public purpose was to "enter into partnerships with Community Development Financial Institutions in the same way that conventional institutions have done—through co-investments, contributions to lending pools, and so on. I have seen proposals for parallel banks to establish and fund a National Reinvestment Bank, which would provide a capital base for CDFIs."[1140] Such an approach would, of course, open access to vast amounts of capital for CDFIs. But it would have been an enormous political lift, inconceivable except under a Clinton administration—and ultimately, not even then.

## NACDLF and the CDFI Coalition

From the time that the CDFI Coalition began to seek funding for its operations, NACDLF served as its fiscal agent, raising money and providing staffing for the coalition, which was not separately incorporated. In its policy efforts, NACDLF was "working primarily through the CDFI Coalition to monitor the CDFI Fund, to advocate for the CDFI field generally, and to respond to interest from the Presidents of the Federal Home Loan Banks to increase FHLB involvement with and investment in CDFIs."[1141]

With Mark Pinsky serving both as the CDFI Coalition's chair and executive director of NACDLF, he and NACDLF increasingly became identified as the voice of the CDFI movement. Undeniably, NACDLF played an essential role in keeping the coalition going. But the increasing identification of the CDFI movement with NACDLF distressed the other CDFI sectoral associations, particularly the National Federation, which railed at references in the press to "CDFIs and credit unions"—as if many credit unions were not, in fact, CDFIs themselves. Compounding the tension, in 1995, NACDLF opened its membership to credit unions, banks, and venture capital funds, although it maintained its membership criterion: "Performance is the core value defining the CDLF industry and should be the chief characteristic of the national CDFI system."[1142]

By the close of 1996, NACDLF's membership numbered 46 organizations, including two community development credit unions. Some loan funds were primarily housing lenders, others small-business lenders, and some both; some served cities or metropolitan areas, while others were regional. A few invested nationally; the Lakota Fund, established in 1987, served the Pine Ridge Reservation.[1143] Collectively, the members had $286 million in total capital at year-end 1996; a year later, the membership would grow to 49, with a dramatic increase in capital under management to $475 million, some of which was attributable to awards from the CDFI Fund.[1144]

In 1997, NACDLF rebranded itself, changing its name to the National Community Capital Association (NCCA). Its stated purpose was

> to more accurately reflect our Member CDFIs, which, in addition to community development loan funds, include multi-purpose community development corporations, microenterprise loan funds, credit unions, community development venture capital organizations, and other types of financial intermediaries. As the field of community development finance evolves and CDFIs diversify their financing and capitalization activities, the distinctions among different types of organizations are blurring.[1145]

In fact, NCCA's membership continued to be overwhelmingly nonprofit loan funds, with only a sprinkling of credit unions and venture funds. The "blurring of distinctions" that undergirded NCCA's expansion caused friction with the other CDFI associations. The tension was manageable, but it did not go away—especially since loan funds systematically obtained the largest share of CDFI Fund awards.

## National Federation of Community Development Credit Unions

The successful campaign to create the CDFI Fund brought the National Federation to new heights. In 1996, 32 CDCUs from 18 states joined the federation, bringing its membership to a record high of 150 institutions. The federation, which had always prided itself on minority membership and governance, expanded its outreach to maximize diversity of the movement. It held its third National Church Credit Union Conference at the National Baptist World Center Headquarters in Nashville, TN, furthering its collaboration with this denominational organization and with the National Congress for Community Economic Development. The federation held a national conference for youth-serving credit unions. Seeking to replicate its success in reaching out to the sector of African American church-based credit unions, it launched the Latino Credit Union Network.[1146]

The federation's headquarters were literally on the margins of Wall Street, the last building at the eastern end of the street, overlooking the East River. It had a full-time staff of 15, with one employee stationed in Madison, WI, at the offices of the Credit Union National Association (CUNA), the federation's ally and supporter. As it had in the previous decade, in the 1990s it operated multiple programs to raise the profile of CDCUs and help its members increase their impact. It operated one of the largest AmeriCorps VISTA programs in the country, deploying these mostly young "volunteers" to credit unions around the country, helping them to expand their outreach and resources.[1147] The federation eagerly embraced the new Individual Development Account (IDA) anti-poverty strategy, a natural fit for the asset-building work of CDCUs. The federation provided technical assistance in CDCU operations, as well as support for groups organizing new credit unions. It launched a mortgage-lending assistance project. As it had done throughout its history, the federation devoted extensive effort to advocating with the federal regulator, the National Credit Union Administration (NCUA).

Meanwhile, the Capitalization Program for CDCUs, the intermediary that the federation launched in 1982 as a long-term strategy for organizational stability, was steadily realizing its promise. The federation closed 1996 with assets of $8.35 million under management, double the volume of five years earlier. Its net worth reached $598,133, compared with a scant $72,170 at the end of 1991. In 1996, striving to expand beyond simply providing insured deposits to local CDCUs, the federation created a new product to strengthen the credit unions' balance sheets: secondary capital.

A robust net worth (equity) position was fundamental to the survival of a financial institution. Banks could increase their equity capital by selling stock, but in general, credit unions could build equity only by incrementally generating and retaining the net earnings—"profit"—from their operations. (Very few CDCUs received grants.[1148]) Especially in a low-income community, building substantial equity took many years. Unlike loan funds, credit unions faced intense regulatory pressure to maintain an adequate net worth-to-assets ratio; failure to do so could bring liquidation or forced merger.

In fall 1995, inspired in part by NACDLF's success in devising EQ2 and encouraged by the support of its largest funder, the Ford Foundation, the National Federation began formulating a proposal for low-income-designated credit unions to raise secondary capital—long-term, subordinated debt that could, with conditions, be classified as net worth on a credit union's balance sheet. It was unprecedented in the credit union movement. In December 1995, a federation staff and board team made a presentation to NCUA Chairman Norman D'Amours at the regulator's headquarters in Alexandria, VA. D'Amours, a former New Hampshire Congressman and Clinton appointee, was a strong supporter of CDCUs, in stark contrast to his predecessors of the Reagan and Bush administrations. In record time of less than two months, on January 25, 1996, the Board of the NCUA issued a rule giving low-income credit unions the exclusive privilege of raising secondary capital.

In 1997, the federation obtained the capital that would make secondary capital investments in CDCUs possible. The Ford Foundation led the way, with grants and loans of $3.1 million in the spring. By September, the federation had obtained an additional $250,000 from the National Community Investment Fund, for placement in the market area of NationsBank. The federation applied to the CDFI Fund as a capital intermediary for its second funding round. In September, it was awarded $3.25 million, a major infusion of net worth that would enable it to greatly expand its high-risk secondary capital investments in CDCUs around the country. By the end of 1997, the federation had disbursed or committed $2.25 million in secondary capital to its members.[1149] The federation ended the year with $12.6 million under management, with $2.4 million in net worth and a budget of more than $2 million. We were well on our way to fulfilling the vision of sustainability that had given birth to our Capitalization Program for CDCUs 15 years earlier.

Meanwhile, bank consolidation and the continuing withdrawal of mainstream banks from low-income neighborhoods helped the National Federation raise the credit union profile—and open a second front in the effort to secure public-sector capital for CDFIs. On September 11, 1995, the *New York Times* published an article with a theme that had grown familiar over the past two decades. It featured the story of a small firm of lawyers trained in the Dominican Republic but without a credit history. Unable to finance their business with a bank loan, they borrowed $10,000 from a loan shark at 6 percent interest per week. "Their story is not unusual in poor and working-class neighborhoods in New York City and nationwide," the article continued, "where the consolidation of the banking industry has hit hard."[1150] The impending merger of two banking giants, Chemical Bank and Chase Manhattan, was likely to produce more local branch closings, and "to drive more people into a parallel universe of low-level finance." The article closed with my quote:

> We are looking at a quantum leap in the number of the poor and unbanked.... There are more examples than one might ever imagine of people piling their money under mattresses. It's not just a metaphor. It's reality.
>
> You have to reinvent the banking system for low-income neighborhoods. It has to be a whole new financial structure and delivery system.

Citibank was paying attention. As I told the *Credit Union News*, "They called me up and said, 'We think we should be doing more with you.' It was a fundraiser's dream."[1151] On February 22, 1996, the Citicorp Foundation awarded the federation a grant of $1.25 million to support our Neighborhood Banking 2000 Fund. The bulk of the grant—$1 million—was to be downstreamed as equity grants to member CDCUs in the five select markets served by Citibank, while the balance went for the federation's technical assistance and organizing of new CDCUs ($100,000) and to support our Capitalization Program ($150,000).[1152]

## Creating a State CDFI Fund

Well before the new CDFI Fund had put a single dollar out on the street, the prospect of the new federal source of capital had energized the movement. In February 1994, Lyndon Comstock of Community Capital Bank wrote to Clara Miller, executive director of the Nonprofit Facilities Fund in New York City, "Cliff Rosenthal and I have already been talking about trying to sit down with you and maybe a few other folks who work in our field. We really ought to try to have a New York CDFI caucus."[1153]

As the federal CDFI Fund was surmounting its last legislative hurdles, the federation revived a campaign it had first conceived in 1984 to establish a New York State CDFI Fund. On August 30, 1994, a month before the CDFI law was signed, I testified to a New York State Assembly Committee on Banks about the lack of banking services in poor neighborhoods. With an eye to the CDFI Fund's proposed requirement for nonfederal matching funds, I asked the state to commit $5 million annually for four years to help New York CDFIs compete for CDFI Fund awards. Errol Louis, formerly federation associate director and the manager of the new Central Brooklyn Federal Credit Union, testified: "With a $1 million injection of capital, I can guarantee you that my credit union will make $10 million of loans in central Brooklyn."[1154] The committee's chair, Assemblywoman Aurelia Greene from the Bronx, told the press that Rosenthal's proposal "warrants serious consideration."[1155]

The proposal proved fruitful, although not immediately, as the National Federation had envisioned. Rosenthal, Miller, and Comstock cofounded the New York State Coalition of CDFIs. After obtaining a grant from the Robert Sterling Clark Foundation, they hired Cathie Mahon as the coalition's full-time coordinator in July 1995 and soon counted 47 CDFIs as its members—mostly credit unions, but also loan funds, like the Leviticus 25:23 Alternatives Fund and Rural Opportunities, Inc.[1156] The coalition expanded its funding goal to $100 million in a combination of private and state funding.

The New York CDFI Coalition gained an opportunity to raise its profile when Chemical and Chase banks, both headquartered in New York City, announced merger plans to create a $300 billion bank, the largest in the United States. New York's congressional delegation, state and city legislators, and community groups joined the New York CDFI Coalition's call for a New York State CDFI Fund. Coalition representatives met repeatedly with Chase and Chemical officials. By November 1995, "Chemical Bank Chairman and CEO Walter Shipley affirmed that 'we have earmarked $25 million over five years for investment and loans to community development financial institutions, credit unions and nonprofit loan funds that focus on small business lending.'"[1157]

In fact, the merging banks' commitment to CDFIs was part of a much larger, multi-billion-dollar package that was both innovative and controversial. Chemical Bank had a top CRA grade and had previously made a major commitment when it merged with Manufacturers Hanover Bank in 1992. It now launched what one lawyer called a "pre-emptive strike": Rather than waiting for groups to launch a CRA protest, Chemical solicited input from 375 community groups about their needs, and it developed a package of community investment accordingly. "We don't want to submit to what has been seen in the past as C.R.A. blackmail,' Carol Parry, Chemical's top community reinvestment officer, said.'"[1158]

Parry's unfortunate "blackmail" quote provoked a backlash. Some advocates criticized the Chemical/Chase commitment as a cynical measure to buy off community groups. But John Taylor, executive director of the National Community Reinvestment Coalition, commented: "In the past, mergers were largely adversarial. Banks did not sit down and talk about community needs. Now we and the banks realize we're all in this together."[1159]

Though CDFI advocates could not take credit for the entire bank commitment to community development, the support they won validated the Clinton administration's goal of leveraging nonfederal capital for the nascent CDFI industry. The Chemical/Chase commitment did not go toward the establishment of a state fund; rather, it provided funding to New York CDFIs directly. Neither did the New York CDFI Coalition win the $100 million state CDFI Fund it had hoped for. But by 1997, it had achieved its public-sector breakthrough: The New York State legislature appropriated $1.5 million in grants for institutions certified as CDFIs by the federal fund. The funding did not establish a separate corporation, as the New York CDFI Coalition had hoped; rather, it was established as a program under the Empire State Development Corporation, whose mandate was to support lending for minority- and women-owned small businesses. It did not provide core institutional equity capital, as the federal CDFI Fund did. But having found a place in the budget, the program was renewed almost every year, providing $1–$1.5 million annually to New York CDFIs, sometimes with provisions that broadened its scope.

## Native American CDFIs

First Nations Development Institute was an early member of the CDFI Coalition. Community development finance was typically viewed as an urban issue, but rural areas were no less disadvantaged—and for Native American reservations and communities, the problems were both greater and more complex. Virtually no banks were located on reservations, and those in adjacent areas typically did not serve Native Americans. Poverty levels were astronomical. Some reservations were enormous—the Pine Ridge reservation was larger than Delaware and Rhode Island combined—and they lacked the population density that could provide a critical mass for organizing CDFIs. Businesses were scarce on reservations—and Native-owned businesses far scarcer. Tribal law codes were frequently incompatible with modern finance. Mortgage lending was impossible on some reservations because land was not privately owned. According to a history of the Lakota Funds, "Eighty-five percent of our clients never had a checking or savings account; seventy-five percent never had a loan; and ninety-five percent had no business experience."[1160] The War on Poverty had attempted to foster credit unions for Native American communities, but by the 1980s, there were only two substantial institutions, the First American Credit Union, formed in 1962 as Navajoland CU in Window Rock, AZ, and the Sisseton-Wahpeton Federal Credit Union in South Dakota. As Sherry Salway Black (Oglala Lakota) put it, in the 1980s "there were so many gaps and needs in Indian country. How do you move all these different pieces? You have to build so many things at the same time."[1161]

These were some of the challenges when Rebecca Adamson (Cherokee),[1162] an activist in the Indian-controlled-school movement, founded the First Nations Financial Project in 1980.[1163] The Ford Foundation was an early supporter, providing an initial seed grant of $25,000 and subsequent funding to help the organization grow, including a later Program-Related Investment of $500,000.[1164] Sherry Salway Black[1165] recalls that on her first day of work in 1985, she flew with Rebecca Adamson for a meeting in New York, where the Ford Foundation had brought in program officers from around the world to talk about different models of microlending, including the Grameen Bank.

In 1985, First Nations, along with Oglala Lakota College, began to facilitate the grassroots organizing effort that would give birth to the Lakota Fund in Pine Ridge, SD. They invited community development resource people, including Martin Eakes from Self-Help and Laura Henze from the Industrial Cooperatives Association (ICA). Black began spending a week each month in Pine Ridge. There was a year of planning, of board development, of selecting a business model. Although Ford had introduced First Nations to the Grameen model, Black stressed that "we did not have Circle [peer-group] banking as the first credit program.… We were not sure that would work. There were not a lot of people around. [Unlike Bangladesh] you can't find another person for miles."[1166] In fall 1986, the Lakota Fund made its first loans: $1,000 loans to individuals for businesses, not for consumers. (Later, with uneven success, it would try the peer-group lending approach as well.[1167]) Thus, it became the first reservation-based microenterprise lender in the country.

Trying to tackle the range of financial issues, in 1987 First Nations started a new project, Oweesta ("money," in the Mohawk language). In 1988, it held its first national conference, addressing community development finance but also the much larger matter of empowering tribal organizations to take over and manage trust funds. Access to capital and credit were an important part of First Nations' agenda, although not the only part, of First Nations' broad, varied mission of achieving self-determination.

Throughout the 1990s, First Nations—like the National Federation and the National Association of Community Development Loan Funds—raised funds from faith-based organizations, foundations, and others to reinvest in local organizations and projects. But because of its broad scope, First Nations was not itself a CDFI; it could not meet the test of being "primarily" engaged in lending and investment. Neither was it a trade organization. Even had it qualified, First Nations would likely not have accepted CDFI Fund money as an intermediary: Committed to breaking Native American dependency on the federal government, for its first 20 years First Nations did not accept any federal funding.[1168] But early in the CDFI legislative process, its advocacy had been reflected in legislative provisions specifying that reservations and Native Americans were to be eligible markets for CDFI Fund investments. First Nations was an early and important member of the CDFI Coalition. It had collaborated with the National Federation on the first Oweesta conference, and Rebecca Adamson was elected to the board of the Association for Enterprise Opportunity (AEO), among other linkages.

Only in 1999 would the Oweesta Program of First Nations become the "First Nations Oweesta Corporation, a wholly-owned subsidiary of First Nations that aids the development and capitalization of Native CDFIs."[1169] As it describes itself, the First Nations Oweesta Corporation's mission is as follows:

> to provide opportunities for Native people to develop financial assets and create wealth by assisting in the establishment of strong, permanent institutions and programs contributing to economic independence and strengthening sovereignty for all Native communities.... Oweesta is the only existing Native CDFI intermediary offering financial products and development services exclusively to Native CDFIs and Native communities. Specifically, Oweesta provides training, technical assistance, investments, research, and policy advocacy to help Native communities develop an integrated range of asset-building products and services, including financial education and financial products.[1170]

## Microenterprise: The Association for Enterprise Opportunity (AEO)

Connie Evans recalled the 1980s as "a time when people were saying women can't run businesses. That's for college-graduate white men to do. They said women were not credit-worthy, particularly low-income women."[1171] Evans, who is African American, knew otherwise: She had served as director of the first resident-managed project in public housing in Chicago—run by low-income women.

In 1986, Evans founded the Women's Self-Employment Project (WSEP) in Chicago, along with Mary Houghton from ShoreBank, who had consulted with Grameen Bank in Bangladesh, and women from local foundations. There were other organizations around the country run by and predominantly serving women: in Minnesota, the Women's Economic Development Corporation (WEDCO), a self-employment project run by Kathy Keeley, and in Arkansas, the Good Faith Fund, which was launched with the aid of Houghton and ShoreBank. But WSEP in Chicago became the first and largest urban microbusiness development organization in the United States, and the first adaptation of the Grameen Bank model to a United States urban setting. "There had not been anything done in an urban setting like Chicago," Evans recalled, "that had a lot of black women, low-income women."[1172]

Self-employment was integral to the origins of the microenterprise movement, owing in part to the work of the Corporation for Enterprise Development (CFED), founded by Bob Friedman. Focused on institutional racism since his undergraduate days—followed by law school, where he focused on affirmative action—Friedman's "threshold interest was job creation," as he describes it. In the eighties, he and several colleagues went on a study tour of Western Europe, visiting programs in the U.K. and France that enabled unemployed workers to start businesses using lump-sum payments, which would otherwise have funded income maintenance. In the late 1980s, with assistance from the Mott and Joyce foundations, he pioneered a multistate demonstration program, the Self Employment Investment Initiative, to test whether self-employment was a realistic option for mothers receiving welfare payments.[1173]

Self-employment programs and microenterprise funds began to spread. By 1991, Friedman recalled, "I knew most of the leaders, and thought, 'Well, maybe we needed a trade association, because there were clearly things burdening local programs that they can't do separately, but that they could do together, including policy advocacy, best-practices exchange, all the stuff that would be done in the other trade associations.'"[1174]

On February 27, 1991, some two-dozen practitioners, funders, researchers, and others came together for a planning meeting "to explore (not decide) the shape of consensus within a group of diverse actors in the field around key design issues surrounding the formation of an association to advance enterprise opportunity, and to make those decisions necessary to hold a truly representative organizing event."[1175] Organizationally, they were a diverse group: Some were standalone organizations, while others were housed within community development organizations, including CDCs like Coastal Enterprises, Inc. of Maine. The most prominent funder was the Charles Stewart Mott Foundation, whose program officer, Jack Litzenberg, supported microenterprise and self-employment initiatives for decades.

Although microenterprise funds shared core values and a commitment to providing credit, they were distinguished from the other emerging CDFIs in multiple dimensions:
- Their product—small loans that would be uneconomic for many other CDFIs
- Their intensive engagement in borrower training and support—which sometimes even overshadowed their financial activity
- Strong international influence—especially, but not only, of the Grameen Bank
- A strong focus on women, both in organizational leadership and as clients
- Linkage to self-employment—especially as a means to help borrowers escape poverty.

The group insisted that the association be practitioner-driven and inclusive; however, policy, research, and evaluation were also prominent purposes. AEO's member programs would be "open to all Americans, especially the one third of U.S. households with no assets, [but who should have] a reasonable opportunity to start and grow their own businesses."[1176] CFED, which had its charitable designation from the IRS, would "incubate" the new organization, serving as its fiscal sponsor.

On June 20–22, 1991, AEO held its official organizing event in Berkeley, CA, attended by 154 people representing 100 organizations from 30 states.[1177] Like the planning meeting, "It was very democratic, with a small 'd,'" Bob Friedman recalled. "Eventually, we ran the whole meeting through consensus."[1178] The meeting set out its first-year priorities, urged establishment of an electronic mailing list ("HandsNet"), and identified a number of federal legislative priorities. Workshops addressed issues of scale and sustainability, as well as assets and savings; the program included a presentation by Professor Michael Sherraden, whose pioneering work on Individual Development Accounts (IDAs) and emphasis on the ability and need for the poor to acquire assets would lead to a major shift in anti-poverty policies.

The new association elected its first board of 18, among whom were many prominent leaders not only of microenterprise, but of community development finance more generally: Rebecca Adamson, founder and president of First Nations Development Institute; Bill Bynum, then of the North Carolina Rural Development Center and later of Hope Enterprise Corporation of the Delta; Mary Houghton of ShoreBank; Bob Friedman; Jack Litzenberg, the Mott Foundation's stalwart supporter of microenterprise; Ron Phillips of Coastal Enterprises; and Peggy Clark, formerly of the Ford Foundation and then of the Aspen Institute's Self-Employment Learning Project. Elizabeth "Jing" Lyman, one of the founders of AEO, not only was active in microenterprise, but also made major contributions in women's causes locally and nationally, helping to found Stanford University's Institute for Gender Research, Women and Foundations/Corporate Philanthropy (WAFCP), and other organizations. By mid-August 1991, even without a membership recruitment campaign, AEO had over 200 members and had received $100,000 in renewable grant commitments from the Charles Stewart Mott Foundation and the Joyce Foundation.[1179]

Of all the types of CDFIs, microenterprise organizations were generally the smallest and least scalable. As Bob Friedman put it, "The micro-enterprise piece was a hard nut to crack because most micro-enterprise programs were more program than lending arm. There wasn't the scale, there was labor intensity."[1180] Even for those that did prioritize lending, the product itself—typically, a small loan of a few thousand dollars—made it hard to cover costs and achieve efficiency; low-income credit unions, perhaps the closest relative of microenterprise funds, at least had the ability to balance very small loans with larger ones, such as for home rehabilitation or mortgages.

Given the inherent challenges of the business model, it was important for microenterprise funds to find partners and/or sources of subsidy. Banks were an important potential ally: They had no interest in very small loans and would certainly not see microenterprise funds as competitors (as some banks viewed credit unions). Early on, Citibank became an important ally. Janet Thompson of Citibank learned of the work of Accion International from a fellow banker who had become acquainted with its work in South America and who convinced Thompson that the Accion concept was worth trying in the United States.[1181] Accion International had worked in the Americas since 1961, providing loans to microentrepreneurs using the "solidarity group" model of collective responsibility for borrowing. Thompson became one of the incorporators of Accion in the United States, which launched in New York City in 1991; by 1995, it had lent $2 million to microentrepreneurs throughout the city. In 1994, Accion had associated organizations in Albuquerque, San Antonio, Chicago, and San Diego, adding one in El Paso in 1995.[1182] Thompson's and Citibank's support for Accion's programs in various locations would continue for more than a quarter-century.

By asset size, lending volume, or other financial metrics, the microenterprise movement was a relatively small player in the CDFI world. But its importance to the field exceeded its size. Candidate Bill Clinton had not only promised 100 community development banks—he also envisioned 1,000 microenterprise programs. Hillary Clinton was, if anything, an even more avid supporter of microenterprise, having visited examples around the world and in the United States. It was her commitment, originating from the Fourth World Conference on Women held in Beijing, that led to the Presidential Awards for Excellence in Microenterprise Development, created in 1996.[1183]

AEO was an active member and cofounder of the CDFI Coalition as early as 1992. But its advocacy efforts had another focus beyond the CDFI Fund, which was—if anything—more crucial and productive for microenterprise organizations. In 1991, AEO drafted and worked to pass the original, five-year Small Business Administration Microloan Pilot Program, which became operational and began providing capital to microenterprise organizations in 1992. In 1993, AEO worked with Democratic Rep. Ron Wyden of Oregon and Democratic Senator Harris Wofford of Pennsylvania to pass the Unemployment Insurance/Self-Employment Assistance (SEA) Program. In 1997, with microenterprise in the spotlight through the presidential awards and the International Microcredit Summit, AEO successfully promoted the expansion and permanent reauthorization of the Microloan Pilot Program in the Small Business Reauthorization Act of 1997.[1184]

In the first round of CDFI awards in 1996, only two microenterprise funds won investments: Accion Texas, and FINCA, another U.S. progeny of an international microlender.

## CDCs: The National Congress for Community Economic Development

Long before "CDFI" was a recognizable name, policymakers, funders, and researchers were familiar with CDCs. These institutions—a preferred strategy for the Ford Foundation from the 1960s—numbered about 2,000 by the 1990s, varying in size from very small organizations that did a few one-off deals to large, sophisticated entities with multiple divisions or subsidiaries. But their trade association, the National Congress for Community Economic Development (NCCED), was not among the founding organizations of the CDFI Coalition, and the sector's path to engagement and subsequent history was not a smooth one.[1185]

The tensions surfaced at a meeting in Washington between coalition representatives, representatives of NCCED, and large CDCs in 1993. As Mark Pinsky and I reported back to the Steering Committee of the coalition, "The agenda collapsed under the weight of pent-up frustrations." David Lizárraga, CEO of TELACU, a prominent East Los Angeles CDC that owned a state-chartered thrift, "went on a verbal tear, suggesting that CDCs 'are where the rubber meets the road' and that 'I don't understand why all of you guys are ignoring us.'"[1186] Why indeed? The substantive reason, as the coalition saw it, was that most CDCs were not primarily in the business of providing finance; more typically, they packaged deals with "other people's money." Nothing wrong with that—but it was not a path to building sustainable financial institutions.

As tempers cooled, "the participants from the NCCED and large CDC side seemed to share our primary objectives—diversity of institutions, equity capital, human capital development, and rigorous guidelines for eligibility and performance. They also recognize, in varying degrees, that this program isn't intended for 2,000 CDCs." Consequently, the meeting ended with an outline of the key goals, objectives, eligibility, and issues, to be worked out by a joint task force that included representatives of the coalition, CDCs, and ShoreBank.[1187] The participants left with the understanding that NCCED would likely join the coalition.

Not so fast! The coalition and NCCED continued to wrangle. On July 6, 1993, the Coalition Steering Committee decided to use the term "CDC-based financial institutions" to designate those that were to be part of the CDFI universe. NCCED was not prepared to go along with this, maintaining still that eligibility should be "community development corporations" in general. Bob Rapoza, whose firm represented a group of the largest, most influential CDCs, informally named the "Eagles," threatened to pull his group out of the coalition. Mark Pinsky urged the coalition not to be bullied, but to stick with "community development corporation–based financial institutions."[1188] In the end, the coalition's accurate but awkward formulation gave way to, simply, "community development corporations" (CDCs). NCCED, despite its threats, would join the coalition.[1189]

As NCCED described its field, CDCs were a "a multi-disciplined and comprehensive institutional response to communities in need."[1190] CDCs were, in fact, engaged in a wide range of activities. Their original concept and hallmark had been comprehensive community development, and it was this aspect that had prompted South Shore Bank to develop its holding-company structure in the 1970s, recognizing that a CDC was able to engage in a host of community-building activities that the bank itself could not. To trace and compile data on the development of the CDC field, NCCED periodically conducted a census of the field. Its 1998 census, entitled "Coming of Age," was conducted by The Urban Institute and obtained responses from 1,200 organizations, which it estimated amounted to 33 percent of the CDC universe (which admittedly had somewhat fluid boundaries).[1191] CDCs were engaged in affordable housing production and increasing homeownership; commercial and industrial real estate development; workforce development; small and micro-business lending; and community building—which included services such as child care, education, training, counseling, transportation, health care, advocacy, senior and youth programs, tenant counseling, and more.

But above all, "housing remains the primary development activity for most CDCs."[1192] NCCED reported that over the decades, CDCs could take credit for creating 550,000 units of affordable housing. Some engaged in housing finance, but many others were working in housing production or management, acquisition, or rehabilitation.[1193] Accordingly, the U.S. Department of Housing and Urban Development (HUD) was the major source of federal funding, especially through the Community Development Block Grant (CDBG) and HOME Investment Partnership programs.[1194]

Although 333 respondents to the census identified themselves as CDFIs,[1195] HUD remained a far more important funder for the CDC field than the CDFI Fund; for most CDCs, the CDFI Fund was not, in fact, a game-changer. By 1997, however, "funding from community development intermediaries has become a more significant source for the CDC field," increasing from 27 percent in 1995 to 41 percent in 1998. LISC was by far the most prominent funding intermediary (22 percent of respondents), but the Neighborhood Reinvestment Corporation, Enterprise Foundation, and Housing Assistance Council each were cited by between 5 percent and 9 percent of respondents.[1196]

## Community Development Venture Capital Alliance (CDVCA)

Even more than limited access to credit, the lack of equity capital often constrained small businesses, especially in low-income communities, and especially if they were started by entrepreneurs with little of their own net worth to invest. Because equity investments do not require that a business produce cash to begin repaying principal and interest immediately, equity can be a powerful tool for business development and job creation. Debt alone is often insufficient to start a new company, expand a product line, or open a new facility; businesses often need flexible equity capital that can, in turn, make additional lending possible. In the 1960s and 1970s, a handful of foundations, including Ford, invested directly in businesses, hoping to create or expand employment opportunities. They had limited success, both in terms of financial return and social impact. Thus, the foundation turned instead to intermediaries, which yielded better results but did not necessarily solve the problem.[1197]

The idea of using the investment practices of venture capital as a tool for economic development in economically distressed communities was pioneered in the early 1970s by the Kentucky Highlands Investment Corporation (KHIC), a CDC operating in the heart of Appalachia in Southeastern Kentucky, one of the poorest regions of the nation. What was later named "community development venture capital (CDVC)" was first conceived by KHIC's then-president, Tom Miller, who would later be chosen to head the Ford Foundation's Office of Program-Related Investments. Miller recruited an experienced venture capitalist, Fred Beste, to run KHIC's venture capital investment program. Although other CDCS were using federal grants to run programs and pay salaries, KHIC invested them in businesses. The effort met with such financial success that when the Reagan administration slashed funding for CDCs in the early 1980s, KHIC continued its activities, funded exclusively through earned income. After several decades of investment, one-third of the jobs in the seven-county region where KHIC operated were in companies that KHIC had financed.

Beste eventually returned north to run a family of successful traditional venture capital funds, and L. Ray Moncrief, whom he had trained, carried on KHIC's venture capital activities. Moncrief had started his career with the Firestone company, moved on to other Fortune 500 companies, and started his own business in Kentucky. KHIC invested in his business and then recruited him to work for them. Equipped with "hard" business skills, Moncrief joined Kentucky Highlands on October 1, 1984, becoming its president and chief operating officer; by 1986, he was chief executive officer. He recalled the era this way.

> In those days, there was no one—*no one* that would invest in small business; there was just nothing else out there. Kentucky Highlands was a unique organization, one of the very few that used equity as a tool to invest in would-be companies to create employment in a highly distressed area. It had a sterling reputation because of its stick-to-itness. If they invested in a company that started sliding down or sideways, Kentucky Highlands would put somebody in there that could manage the company out of its difficulty. And quite frankly, that's where I really cut my teeth.[1198]

KHIC made a wide range of investments—"near equity," subordinated debt, convertible debt, and common stock.

Separately and without knowledge of each other, other CDCs began experimenting with business equity investment as a tool of economic development. Ron Phillips, president of Coastal Enterprises, Inc. (CEI), a leading CDC in Maine, built a small and successful portfolio of equity investments in area businesses using grant funds from the Ford and MacArthur foundations. He hired Nat Henshaw, who had worked for several traditional venture capital funds, and Henshaw ultimately raised four community development venture capital funds for CEI.

The first fund to be organized as a standalone, not in conjunction with an existing CDC or CDFI, was the Northeast Ventures Corporation. Nick Smith, a successful business lawyer and community leader, learned of the pioneering work of Kentucky Highlands and raised capital for Northeast Ventures to invest in businesses in the Iron Range of northern Minnesota, a region devastated by the decline of the iron mining and timber industries.

By the early 1990s, the Ford Foundation had built a small portfolio of developmental venture capital funds that had received Program-Related Investments from the foundation. Judy Samuelson, then director of Ford's Office of Program-Related Investments, and Kerwin Tesdell, then new to Ford, soon recognized in these funds the emergence of a new field aligned with Ford's values and goals. Although Ford had long worked with development lenders, Tesdell recalled, "these equity investors brought a new and powerful type of capital to the development process, which was (and still is) utterly lacking in economically distressed areas of the nation. Ford was interested in economic development and quality job creation, and equity capital is vital to the creation of new economic activity, whether by financing a startup or allowing an existing company to launch a new product line." It was not only capital: The venture funds could enhance job quality and achieve other social impacts by providing extensive entrepreneurial and managerial assistance and taking seats on company boards.[1199]

Samuelson and Tesdell convened the initial meetings of these funds with the consulting help of Woody Tasch, a former venture capitalist who was then experimenting with social purpose venture capital investments as the chair of the investment committee of the Jessie Smith Noyes Foundation. Thereafter, Smith took the lead in bringing structure to the group, expanding attendance, and organizing bi-annual meetings starting in 1993. The group's leaders focused on financing businesses owned by African Americans. They coined the term "community development venture capital" to describe what they did, and in 1995, they incorporated as a trade association, the Community Development Venture Capital Alliance (CDVCA), with Smith as its first president. After receiving a $25,000 grant from Ford, CDVCA expanded its activities and funding with the aid of two-year grants from the Ford and MacArthur foundations.

For five years, CDVCA operated as a member-led organization, run by Smith and his law firm's administrative assistant. In 1998, CDVCA decided to professionalize, hiring Tesdell as its first president and CEO (in which capacity he continues to serve). Tesdell had degrees in economics and law. In addition to early civil rights work with the NAACP Legal Defense and Education Fund and ACLU, he had worked with worker cooperatives at the Industrial Cooperative Association and did the legal work to organize the Community Capital Bank. After a stint with a large Wall Street law firm, he represented many emerging CDFIs and CDCs as director of the Community Development Legal Assistance Center. Using the other CDFI trade associations as a model, Tesdell quickly raised additional funding and expanded CDVCA's member services, industry research, and public policy advocacy. Like its peer organizations for credit unions and loan funds, CDVCA became a financial intermediary, investing in its member funds; however, unlike the other two, it also developed the capacity to make venture capital equity investments directly in businesses—usually, but not always, as co-investments with its member funds. It differed, as well, in that it had an international membership. CDVCA became an active member of the CDFI Coalition, for which Tesdell served as board chair for seven years.

In the CDFI Fund's first award round, only three equity-investing organizations received awards: Smith's Northeast Ventures Corporation; Moncrief's Kentucky Highlands Investment Corporation; and ShoreBridge Capital in Cleveland, OH, part of the ShoreBank family. The trend would continue for many years. Even though the job-creation mission of venture funds accorded very well with President Clinton's vision of community development banking, this CDFI sector regularly received only modest capital support from the CDFI Fund (with the prominent exceptions of KHIC and CDVCA, both of which received multiple financial assistance awards, as well as New Markets Tax Credit allocations). As Tesdell has explained, the structure of community development venture capital funds was incompatible with the CDFI Fund's understanding of a CDFI. Neither the CDFI Fund's certification process nor its award application forms were well suited to those funds.[*]

## The National Community Investment Fund (NCIF)

Although there were national intermediaries for community development credit unions and loan funds, none existed for community development banks when the CDFI Fund was created in 1994. That changed in 1995, when a $15 million trust—the National Community Investment Fund (NCIF)—was created with a lead investment from NationsBank. The seeds of the initiative were sown when ShoreBank's Ron Grzywinski met Hugh McColl of NationsBank at the White House Rose Garden ceremony on July 15, 1993. When NCIF was started, Margaret Cheap, who had joined ShoreBank from the National Cooperative Bank in Washington, became its fund adviser. The goal of the fund was to provide capital for high-impact, potentially sustainable CDFIs. Established as a 501(c)(4) charitable trust, NCIF itself was supposed to become sustainable; it would not be a source of grant capital, but rather would provide equity and subordinated debt investments to for-profit banks, and flexible, below-market loans to nonprofit CDFIs.

As the CDFI legislation was moving toward reality, several banks were emerging, including Albina in Portland, OR; City First in Washington, DC; and Community Bank of the Bay in Oakland, CA.

---

[*] For a further discussion of structural issues, see Chapter 24.

However, there was no real explosion of bank chartering. Startup (*de novo*) banks faced high entry barriers: high capital requirements, management and regulatory hurdles, and increasingly, competition by CRA-motivated banks that had increased their lending in low-income and minority communities, thus "moderat[ing] the perceived need for dedicated bank CDFIs."[1200]

In 1997, NCIF approached the MacArthur Foundation with a request to support a seed fund—"a separate portfolio of high-risk investment targeted at banks and complex community development financial institutions (CDFIs) in the early stages of forming or organizing to operate in distressed communities around the country." The foundation agreed to provide $500,000 to support NCIF's efforts to increase the number of bank CDFIs. MacArthur's staff remarked:

> While the number of bank CDFIs is limited (three in 1990 and ten today), their potential is significant. Through their deposit collecting function banks have tremendous ability to leverage resources and achieve a scale that is unparalleled in the CDFI industry. The recently created NCIF fund will facilitate the creation of additional bank CDFIs by providing a range of services to assist organizations in meeting the required regulatory and financial standards.[1201]

To supplement MacArthur's support, NCIF sought an investment of $750,000 from the Ford Foundation. NCIF's early investments in CDFIs included $250,000 in the Capitalization Program of the National Federation of CDCUs for its new secondary capital initiative.

## The CDFI Field and the CDFI Coalition

At the beginning of 1995, the CDFI Coalition claimed that the movement numbered 310 CDFIs in 45 states, managing more than $1 billion; coalition members had loaned out more than $3 billion. "The Coalition had a far greater influence than any of its individual sectors might have had alone," wrote Mark Pinsky at the time. Having CDFIs in 45 states proved critical, providing a geographically broad constituency, he observed: "Having a 'b' rather than an 'm' before the 'illion' added credibility to the industry, even though collectively it is about the size of a small bank."[1202] Pinsky emphasized the grassroots nature of the movement: "The Coalition firmly believed that hiring a lobbyist ran counter to the values of community-based organizations, yet it had few resources and knew that it would get rolled if it tried to stand toe-to-toe with banking industry lobbyists, who were vying to make the program fund their activities. Coalition members knew they could succeed only by having CDFI practitioners make the case in the communities where they lived and worked."[1203]

The coalition was not separately incorporated; it operated as an "independent project" of NACDLF.[1204] The relationship between NACDLF and the CDFI Coalition became strained once the CDFI Fund became a reality and the scope of the coalition's work grew. As Mark Pinsky wrote in June 1995, "Because the Coalition is preparing to undertake a new venture of significant size and scope in a new area and Coalition membership has grown and changed over the past six months, past informal agreements do not adequately address the mix of issues involved in the relationship between the CDFI Coalition and NACDLF, as host of and fiscal agent for the Coalition."[1205]

Both sides agreed on the need to define roles. "The steering committee acknowledged the substantial work the NACDLF has done in conducting the CDFI Coalition's projects," the coalition noted. "The NACDLF has taken on many responsibilities and it is greatly appreciated. However, the relationship between the NACDLF and the [coalition] steering committee must be more clearly defined."[1206] The prospect of additional investment capital flowing into the CDFI field only magnified the issue. "Attracting investment for the Coalition and member CDFIs is a concern for the Coalition," the Steering Committee noted. "NationsBank's National Community Investment Fund is a potential source of capital and a model for other trust funds."[1207] Nonetheless, "the coalition was in full agreement that the Coalition is not and will not be a financial intermediary. The Coalition should in no way compete with existing CDFIs and associations for scarce capital resources."[1208] That much was clear; the coalition would not become another capital intermediary. But it was not until 2002 that a bright line was drawn, when the coalition became an independent nonprofit charitable organization and elected its own board of directors.[1209]

With its enhanced stature and resources, the coalition wrestled with the question of membership. Although the coalition had a mailing list of several thousand, the "members" were, in fact, the Steering Committee. As spelled out in a document from the period, "members are either national or international organizations representing CDFIs or established CDFIs that are not represented by such organizations… [and that] represent a significant sector of the CDFI Industry."[1210] Thus, the national trade organizations were members, but individual institutions—like Community Capital Bank, Southern Development Bancorporation, and ShoreBank—were also members, since they did not at the time have a trade association. Uneven participation in the Steering Committee was beginning to be a concern. The expectations were modest: participate in conference calls, in annual or semi-annual meetings, and in task forces, and pay $500 in annual dues. Still, some organizations did not consistently participate. "If expectations are not met, steering committee members will consider discontinuing membership."[1211] Among other issues, "The steering committee is concerned with diversity within the coalition and will evaluate diversity at [its] semi-annual meeting."[1212]

The establishment of the CDFI Fund was a major victory, but its future remained uncertain in the face of congressional attacks. This made the CDFI Coalition cautious: "CDFIs should consider the Fund's uncertain tenure when developing a strategy to utilize the Fund…. In light of these political realities it is in CDFIs' best interest to hold off committing someone full-time to accessing the Fund," the coalition advised. As for the coalition itself, it made plans for "a coordinator [to be] hired to direct the Coalition's involvement in the CDFI Fund…. The person must be in Philadelphia [home of NACDLF] two to three days a week and have a solid understanding of the political system in Washington."[1213]

In 1995, the coalition established task forces to address the various field-building and CDFI Fund advocacy challenges it faced—outreach, training, and technical assistance, and intergovernmental relations. These task forces drew members beyond the CDFI Coalition's Steering Committee, including practitioners from individual CDFIs, researchers, training organizations, and funders. In 1995, with the support of the Ford Foundation, the coalition embarked on its major field-building project: the Training, Assessment and Demonstration Study, "to develop an industry-wide strategic plan to strengthen the training and human capacities of CDFIs."[1214] The coalition contracted with the Corporation for Enterprise Development (CFED); Andrea Levere (later CEO of CFED; from 2017, Prosperity Now) was the project director.

CFED conducted focus groups with practitioners and funders, surveyed more than 400 coalition members, and presented its preliminary findings at the Second National CDFI Institute on March 23, 1996. It identified several trends that characterized the CDFI field in the mid-1990s.

- CDFIs were growing in numbers, size, and sophistication; some had assets of $20 million or more.
- Funding sources were becoming deeper and more diversified. Increasingly, CDFIs were succeeding in expanding investments and credibility with private-sector institutions.
- There was growing awareness of the need to establish industry standards to evaluate operations and impact. The federal role "will bring increased public scrutiny and heightened expectations to the industry."[1215]
- The movement faced a challenge of clarifying its relationship to private capital markets: "Are CDFIs a niche industry or a parallel financial system? What level of standardization is necessary to access capital through the secondary markets?"[1216]
- Broadly, the field needed training on the context for economic development, financial skills, and organizational development.
- Possible roles for the coalition included:
    - Developing common definitions and standards for the field
    - "Some basic messages which emphasize commonality in the field"
    - Raising the profile of CDFIs
    - Serving as a broker of training services, in collaboration with the trade organizations
    - Raising funds to subsidize the cost of developing training materials and developing curricula that address common training needs, as well as coordinating or developing internship programs.[1217]

## A Funder Assesses the Field

Another important perspective on the state of the field at the dawn of the CDFI era emerged in a report to the John D. and Catherine T. MacArthur Foundation, which had been second only to the Ford Foundation as a supporter of CDFIs. After 15 years of making Program-Related Investments (PRIs) in CDFIs, the foundation commissioned a team of consultants to assess its results and strategy.[1218] The report by CDFI veteran and researcher Alan Okagaki and others observed that "in 1983, when the MacArthur Foundation made its first PRI, the community development finance industry in the United States was in its infancy.... Nearly two decades later, the industry is far more developed in every respect—a young adult, perhaps—and faces profound challenges." The foundation had been "a consistent and leading player in PRIs, averaging about $10 million a year in investments. It has supported pioneers in community development finance and helped build some of the largest and strongest community development financial institutions (CDFIs)—retailers—in the U.S."[1219] Among MacArthur's largest, repeat CDFI borrowers were LISC (10 PRIs, $14 million), the Enterprise Foundation (7 PRIs, $10 million), ShoreBank and its affiliates (8 PRIs, $8.9 million), and Self-Help Ventures (4 PRIs, $6 million). The foundation had experienced very few losses—in part, the report noted, because "PRIs have become heavily concentrated in 'blue chip' CDFIs." Consequently, "the portfolio does not seem to fully address critical, widespread issues facing the field of community economic development financing."[1220]

The problem was perpetuated by the fact that "most of the prospecting [for PRI recipients] involves going to industry association meetings where 'the usual suspects' congregate (e.g., the National Community Capital Association and the Community Development Venture Capital Alliance). Thus, it is unlikely for an organization to obtain a PRI if it did not have a previous relationship or connection to the Foundation staff."[1221] From one perspective, this was understandable. The development of the CDFI field had been uneven: "CDFI capacity is spread unevenly across the country. While there is much sophistication and capacity in some parts of the country, systems are lacking in others."[1222] Moreover, there was a big drop-off in quality between the "blue chips" of the CDFI movement; a relatively small "B" list; and a large, growing number of "C"-class CDFIs. These disparities were accentuated by the lack of "star quality" talent in the field, especially among the lower-tier organizations. It was not clear that the advent of the CDFI Fund would mitigate this problem: The consultants pointed out that "an increase in government funding for CDFIs has spawned the creation of many new, small organizations that may not be sustainable."[1223]

Although the CDFI Fund had laid out an "official" definition of a CDFI, the boundaries of the field were somewhat blurry (and in fact, contested, since many organizations did everything that the fund-certified institutions did, but did not seek certification). By the late 1990s, the total capitalization of CDFIs was in the range of $2–$4 billion—orders of magnitude greater than the early-stage movement. But in any case, the amount was dwarfed by the universe of "socially responsible investments" in mutual funds, which was estimated at about $50 billion,[1224] a market CDFIs had barely tapped. Banks, meanwhile, had begun making CRA commitments of billions of dollars, motivated by CRA; a modest but significant portion flowed into CDFIs. Although CDFIs could not match these other sources of socially or policy-motivated capital streams by volume, what they could offer a foundation like MacArthur was "very high targeting to social purposes" consistent with the foundation's mission.

How could foundations best help the field to grow? The report recommended that MacArthur "invest substantially in wholesale-intermediary organizations and activities that will attract capital for CDFIs from other investors."[1225] Wholesale intermediaries could help develop a more efficient infrastructure for the field, centralizing functions such as loan servicing, research and development, and advocacy. This, in turn, could help strengthen "retail" CDFIs, which needed to broaden their geographic reach and increase their efficiency and effectiveness.[1226] Implementing these strategies would require the foundation to double its investment from $10 million annually to $20 million; as well, the report urged internal reorganization to increase staffing and make PRIs a major, independent program—as well as a supportive "utility"—within the foundation.

The report highlighted what the National Federation of CDCUs had long argued was a gap in the conceptual framework of community development finance.

> CDFIs (with the exception of credit unions and a few microenterprise organizations) have only recently begun taking an interest in personal asset-building and savings strategies. Community development finance has historically been defined in terms of lending rather than savings. However, the changes in the financial services industry are likely to have as much detrimental impact on savings opportunities for low-income communities as on credit availability.[1227]

In the second half of the 1990s, the disparity in wealth—especially between African Americans and whites—had moved to the forefront of anti-poverty policy. Individual Development Account (IDA) programs spread among social-service agencies as well as CDFIs, with support from foundations, the federal government, and even state and local government. But the connection between household asset-building and broader community economic development was tenuous (and has remained so).

Undeniably, CDFIs had come a long way. "The amount of progress CDFIs have made in technical proficiency, capacity, production volume, portfolio quality, and resources leveraged over the last 15 years has been truly remarkable. The degree of success is under-appreciated," the assessment report summarized. But despite great success in nurturing the CDFI movement, after a decade of support, "funder fatigue is becoming an issue".[1228] Foundation funding was rarely perpetual; typically, foundations supported innovative initiatives for several years and then moved on. There were still significant, relevant opportunities and needs for foundation funding of the CDFI field; data collection and field-building continued to receive support from MacArthur and Ford. But to expand their capacity and impact, the report noted, CDFIs would have to look for other sources of capital, even beyond the new CDFI Fund—for example, the broader capital markets. Mega-mergers of the top-tier banks, like Citi and Bank of America, produced CRA commitments in the hundreds of millions of dollars, and a portion of the CDFI movement was well positioned to take advantage of these deals. But the socially responsible investment market was largely untapped. To access capital from this market, CDFIs needed wholesale intermediaries and standardized, familiar vehicles (other than simply deposits) that would appeal to social investors.

## A New Intermediary, A New Capital Product

How, then, could CDFIs reach this relatively untouched market? The Calvert Social Investment Funds (from 2007, Calvert Impact Capital) devised a product that would bridge the gap: Community Investment Notes, "a high-impact, fixed-income product that supports a diversified portfolio of non-profits, microfinance institutions, social enterprises, and loan funds that benefit underserved communities in the U.S. and around the world."[1229] Rebecca Adamson, the founder of First Nations and a board member of Calvert, and Laura Henze, who had assisted in starting the Lakota Fund, worked in the early 1990s to gain Calvert shareholders' approval for the new product. "It was considered radical by the mutual fund industry," Adamson recalls. "What our shareholders were concerned about was safety of principal. They did not want to lose their principal but were fine with very little return. We did it first through the Calvert mutual fund but quickly moved it to the Calvert Foundation. I wrote the business plan and got Ford, Mott, and MacArthur to fund it, so the investment principal was protected.... Community Investment Notes became an asset class."[1230]

Calvert's product was particularly helpful for unregulated nonprofit loan funds. South Shore Bank and credit unions, like Self-Help, offered a safe, easy way for individuals and organizations to invest in federally insured deposits; the National Federation served as a wholesale intermediary, raising funds and depositing them in local low-income credit unions. But it was more difficult for loan funds, which did not have federal deposit insurance, to raise funds from individuals, at least those beyond their local markets. There was interest among the investors in socially responsible mutual funds, but technical issues made it difficult for them to invest in nonprofit CDFIs. This was the issue that Calvert addressed.

In the early stages, Calvert's plans generated tension with the CDFI trade associations, especially the National Federation and NACDLF, who saw the creation of another intermediary—especially one funded by "their own" major foundation supporters—as a competitive threat, and an unnecessary one: Calvert would be an intermediary for intermediaries, they argued, just an added layer. But "really, our focus was to engage a broader retail investor base," as Justin Conway of Calvert described it. Calvert's Catherine Godschalk added, "We really see ourselves as interfacing with capital markets and normalizing, if you will, or standardizing a way in for investors to then channel the capital to the ground layer of intermediation."[1231]

Calvert was a leader in the socially responsible investment field. Through its own outreach and later through networks of brokerages and financial advisers, it was able to reach thousands of individual investors who otherwise might never have learned about CDFIs. In 2000, the Calvert Foundation itself became a certified CDFI.

## The New Generation

As the MacArthur Foundation's consultants put it, the early CDFIs were now "young adults." Meanwhile, a new generation was emerging.

## Chapter 20. CDFIs at the Dawn of the New Era

Community development credit unions (CDCUs) had suffered under the administration of George H.W. Bush (1989–93). The federal credit union regulator, NCUA, was all but overtly hostile to CDCUs, and no new CDCU charters were issued in 1990 or 1991; only one was issued in 1992. Meanwhile, NCUA aggressively pruned its official list of credit unions with low-income designation, which was required to raise outside capital in the form of nonmember deposits. In November 1993, the Clinton administration appointed a new, liberal chairman of the three-person NCUA board, former Congressman Norman E. D'Amours, and the atmosphere changed dramatically.

*Errol Louis (left) and Mark Winston Griffith (right), organizers of the Central Brooklyn Federal Credit Union, with Joyce Jackson (National Credit Union Administration) at celebration of the credit union's acquisition of a former bank branch. The tapestry was made by a credit union member. Courtesy of Errol Louis and Mark Griffith.*

Under D'Amours, the number of low-income-designated credit unions grew steadily. Four new CDCUs were chartered in 1993. Among these was the Central Brooklyn Federal Credit Union, which was founded in Brooklyn's Bedford-Stuyvesant neighborhood by two young African Americans and which gained unprecedented national publicity in the popular and African American media.[1232] There were five new CDCUs chartered in 1994, six in 1995, and 12 in 1996. It was not only the prospect of a new funding source that prompted the emergence of new CDCUs. Chartering credit unions was a lengthy, demanding process, typically taking several years. There was pent-up demand, released first by the shock of the South Central Los Angeles riots in 1992 and then sustained by the eased policies of a friendlier NCUA.

The upsurge in community development loan funds had not taken place by the time of the first CDFI Fund awards. NACDLF's membership rolls listed only about 10 new loan funds that had made their first loans from 1990 through 1994.[1233] (Of course, there were loan funds that were not members of NACDLF.) Among the 268 applicants to the first round of the CDFI Fund, there were also some organizations, like CDCs, that had repurposed or reorganized themselves, or more likely, had separated out a division or unit that was predominantly engaged in finance, a requirement to obtain CDFI certification. The number of CDFI-certified loan funds would grow steadily over the years.

With uneven success, a new cohort of community development banks was taking shape, inspired by South Shore, Southern, and Community Capital Bank and anticipating access to equity capital from the CDFI Fund. In November 1995, the proposed Community First Bank of the District of Columbia received its preliminary regulatory approval from the Office of the Comptroller of the Currency. But before it could open, a group led by proposed chairman John M. Hamilton needed to execute a private placement of $7 million. Raising capital wasn't easy, as the experience of Community Capital Bank's founder Lyndon Comstock had shown. By February 1996, the organizing group was still well short of its goal and had to delay its planned opening; only $1 million—a commitment from Georgetown University—had been obtained. Despite the buzz surrounding the CDFI Fund, the task was not easy. "We're going through tough times right now,' said Anthony Romero, DC's superintendent of banking and financial institutions. 'No one wants to throw a lot of money around right now, but I expect some money to come from some of the big banks. I think they [Community First] will be fully capitalized before long.'"[1234]

"Months of work paid off," *American Banker* reported, "when Albina Community Bank, the first community development bank in the West, opened its doors last week in Portland, Ore."[1235] The bank, which was to focus on serving northeast Portland, where 70 percent of the black population lived, had raised $4.75 million in capital from 77 investors, mostly from the Portland area (including Nike, which was located nearby) and Fannie Mae. There was one unique source for the original capitalization: It included $1.7 million because of an overcharging dispute involving the Pacificorp utility; the settlement money was to aid low- and middle-income neighborhoods.[1236]

Both Community Bank of the Bay and the Albina Community Bank had their grand openings in September 1996. As *American Banker* reported on August 5, "After three years of preparation, Community Bank of the Bay is ready to have a go at wiping away five decades of urban blight," having raised $7.7 million in capitalization. The bank would serve not only Oakland, but parts of San Francisco, Richmond, Berkeley, East Palo Alto, and San Rafael. Other new community development banks would soon follow, including Neighborhood National Bank in San Diego (1997) and Legacy Bank in Milwaukee (1999).

## Conclusion

The "era of CDFIs" had begun.

Faith-based organizations and foundations had provided the vital seed money for the new CDFI movement in the 1980s. The Ford and MacArthur foundations had invested hundreds of millions of dollars in PRIs. By the mid-1990s, when investment in CDFIs was explicitly recognized as a CRA-eligible activity, banks were supplanting foundations as the biggest private-sector funders of CDFIs. In 1996, the new federal fund made investments of up to $3 million, totaling $37 million in "financial assistance" awards to 32 CDFIs of every type, while Bank Enterprise Awards channeled additional funds into the field. New local CDFIs of various types began to appear, while the infrastructure of sectoral CDFIs—associations of community development credit unions, loan funds, banks, venture capital funds, microenterprise funds, and Native American organizations—and the CDFI Coalition were expanding and strengthening,

As Lisa Mensah, then a program officer at the Ford Foundation, recalled, "We claimed victory in an officers' meeting. We said, 'This is the picture-perfect course of action of foundation funding: When you invest in the prototype, the R & D money, and the federal government buys it.' I remember Kerwin Tesdell [a fellow program officer at Ford] saying, 'This is the brass ring. We just grabbed it!'"[1237]

# CHAPTER 21. The Class of 1996

> *Simply put, the United States will fall far short of its economic potential, for all of us, if we do not deal with the problems of our distressed rural communities and inner cities.*
> Robert Rubin, Secretary of the Treasury[1238]

The CDFI Fund had $50 million in appropriations to spend for the 1996 fiscal year ending on September 30. On July 31, 1996, Treasury Secretary Robert Rubin announced the selection of 31 community development organizations for $35.5 million in CDFI Fund financial and technical assistance awards.[1239] (Later in the year, when the Bank Enterprise Awards were undersubscribed, the fund awarded an additional $1.75 million in financial assistance to CDFIs, making one new award and supplementing two others, bringing first-year funding to $37.2 million.[1240])

The Treasury announcement reinforced key themes of the Clinton vision and the community development banking legislation.

- **Private-sector investment.** "These funds," Treasury announced, "will be leveraged with significant private funds and are expected to result, over time, in at least $350 million of lending and investing in distressed urban and rural communities." (The unscientific 10:1 ratio calculated by Treasury would prove a useful number for CDFI supporters in their lobbying with Congress.)
- **Geographic diversity.** CDFI funds would be deployed in 46 states and the District of Columbia.
- **Institutional diversity.** Recipients included community development banks, credit unions, loan funds, venture capital funds, and microenterprise funds, which would provide a wide range of financial products and services. Rubin briefly described three awardees of various types: the Louisville community development bank holding company, which was working with the city's Enterprise Community; the Santa Cruz Community Credit Union in California, which was expanding to serve a community with a large population of Latino farmworkers; and FINCA, a microlender based in Washington, DC.

In his remarks, Secretary Rubin declared that "over the next six years, the President's budget contains nearly $1.7 billion for CDFI funding, fully paid for, because of the great promise it holds for empowering communities. But as you all know too well, we've been in a great struggle with some in Congress to ensure adequate funding for CDFI going forward."[1241] In fact, as Rubin knew, the struggle would continue.

## Sectoral Distribution

Inspired by the Grameen Bank and ShoreBank, Bill Clinton called for 1,000 microenterprise organizations along with 100 community development banks. Only 2 microenterprise funds received awards, and only 4 banks and bank holding companies (existing and in formation) were funded. Nonregulated loan funds predominated. The CDFI Fund classified 13 awardees as "loan funds." However, it is arguably more descriptive to include as loan funds the organizations it classified either as "multi-faceted" (e.g., Self-Help), a "national intermediary" (LISC), microlenders, and a "Native American organization" (Tlingit-Haida Regional Housing), since they were non-depositories and used the funds for lending, rather than venture capital. Using this framework, 19 of the 32 recipients were loan funds, accounting for about 59 percent of funding, or about $22 million. Banks accounted for about 25 percent ($9.24 million); credit unions about 7 percent ($2.73 million); and venture capital organizations nearly 9 percent ($3.2 million).

| Table 1. First Awardees of CDFI Fund | |
|---|---|
| CDFI Type* | # of Awardees |
| Loan funds | 13 |
| Credit unions | 6 |
| Banks and bank holding companies | 4 |
| Venture capital funds | 3 |
| Microenterprise funds | 2 |
| Multi-faceted CDFIs | 2 |
| National intermediaries | 1 |
| Native American regional organizations | 1 |

*By CDFI Fund's classification

## Equity Funding Predominates

In the early years of the community development loan fund movement, there was considerable ambivalence about taking federal money, with all the strings that would entail. But as Julie Eades, CEO of the New Hampshire Community Loan Fund, recalled, "The beauty of the CDFI Fund was that it really was meant to infuse equity, to grow what we already were doing. We did not, really, want government restraint. But that money was shaped like no other federal money. It was really unique. On the institutional level, it was used to strengthen your balance sheet."[1242]

In fact, although the CDFI Fund had the option of investing in various ways, it prioritized equity investments or capital grants, which could be used in turn to leverage debt: Equity investments and grants totaled about $10.8 million and $18.7 million, respectively, nearly 80 percent of all funding; loans totaled about $6.7 million; and technical assistance awards (which were essentially grants) totaled $770,000. Given that CDFIs had emphasized the overarching need for equity capital or grants, it may appear surprising that some applicants applied for and received debt; it was likely because matching funds were required to be of like kind, and other sources of grant and equity capital were still quite limited.

The fund's like-for-like matching requirement posed an obstacle for credit unions, which, though nonprofit, were not charities and rarely received grants.* The National Federation had successfully argued that credit unions should be allowed to match CDFI grant funds with retained earnings, derived from the surplus generated through their operations and collectively owned by the entire membership; in effect, low-income communities themselves were providing the private-sector match.[1243] But a problem remained: Most low-income credit unions had limited amounts of retained earnings to match a fund investment. Building retained earnings or net worth was a slow, incremental process; unlike banks, credit unions could not raise capital by issuing stock. Consequently, given this limitation, credit unions generally received smaller awards than did loan funds. All but three loan funds received at least $1 million, while only two credit unions received awards that large: First American and Santa Cruz Community credit unions, which had been in operation for decades and had reached $33 million and $20 million in assets, respectively.

For the most part, banks received equity investments, sometimes with technical assistance funding added in. The exception was Southern Development Bancorporation, which received $1 million in equity and a $1 million grant for its nonprofit affiliate. On average, banks received the largest awards, somewhat over $2 million; the proposed ShoreBank, Detroit organization received the highest single amount, $3 million.

## Demographics

Most of the winners served local markets. But several had already set up operations in multiple cities or claimed a national market, although their penetration was scattered. The Low Income Housing Fund worked nationally, with emphasis on California, New York, and Washington, DC; the Nonprofit Facilities Fund had locations in Boston, Chicago, Philadelphia, and San Francisco; LISC, as a national community development intermediary, served organizations in many states. The rural CDFIs either operated in multiple states or large swaths of their home state: Appalbanc served several Appalachian states; Rural Community Assistance Corporation provided services in 12 western states; Enterprise Corporation of the Delta served 55 counties in Arkansas, Louisiana, and Mississippi; and Southern Development Bancorporation served southern and eastern Arkansas.

CDFIs were distributed unevenly across the United States and would long remain so. The major urban centers often had multiple CDFIs, whereas the Southeast, Mountain states, and Midwest were

---

* Federal credit unions are exempt from federal taxes under section 501(c)(1), and state-chartered credit unions are exempt under section 501(c)(14).

sparser. Proximity to urban centers brought distinct financial advantages: The major cities were hubs for philanthropy and large banks, which made it much easier for CDFIs in those markets to raise matching funds than it was for rural CDFIs, which often lay outside the target areas of foundations or the Community Reinvestment Act "footprint" of major banks.

Many awardees served predominantly African American populations, urban and rural, including 5 of the 6 credit unions selected. Only one African American-owned bank was funded, Douglass Bancorp, based in Kansas City. Accion and FINCA, the microlenders, served largely Latino customers, and Santa Cruz Community Credit Union received funds to establish a branch office serving migrant and seasonal farmworkers. It would be several years before a formal Native CDFI "window" would open at the CDFI Fund, but two institutions serving indigenous populations received awards. First American Credit Union, based in Window Rock, AZ, was the largest Native American-serving institution in the country, with $33 million in assets and a membership of 15,000 in Arizona, New Mexico, and Utah. Tlingit-Haida Regional Housing Authority was a Native American organization in Southeast Alaska that served remote rural villages. No predominantly Asian American CDFIs received awards in the first CDFI Fund round.

## Filling the Financial Gaps

Many award recipients focused on affordable housing: from organizations that specialized in homebuyer counseling and partnerships with local banks (Neighborhood Housing Services affiliates); to organizations like the New Hampshire Community Loan Fund, which lent for resident-owned manufactured housing projects; to the Low Income Housing Fund, which specialized in predevelopment and short-term gap financing; to Self-Help, with its innovative secondary market enterprise.

Gaps in financing for small business had been central to candidate Bill Clinton's vision for community development banking. Among the CDFI Fund's initial awardees, there was no shortage of organizations promising to stimulate job creation and engage the private sector. These ranged from microenterprise organizations, to some of the loan funds (Enterprise Corporation of the Delta, Cascadia Revolving Fund, and others), to banks and community development venture capital organizations. Two loan funds (the Illinois Facilities Fund, based in Chicago, and the Nonprofit Facilities Fund, headquartered in New York City) specialized in filling another niche: facilities and working-capital loans for nonprofit organizations. Santa Cruz Community Credit Union had established a national reputation as an innovative lender to nonprofits, cooperatives, sustainable agricultural operations, and small businesses.

The lack of banking services in low-income minority communities had been exposed dramatically in the 1992 riots in South Central Los Angeles, where check-cashers far outnumbered bank branches. The CDFI Fund chose six credit unions, all of which offered basic financial services, like savings accounts and small loans; several also offered self-employment or small-business loans that were badly needed in rural areas (Quitman County Federal Credit Union in the Mississippi Delta), the reservations of the Southwest (First American Credit Union), and minority urban neighborhoods (Bethex Federal Credit Union in New York City's South Bronx). The community development bank recipients of awards were not focused on the small savers, transactors, and borrowers who came into their lobbies—a costly clientele, as South Shore Bank had discovered early in its history. Rather, community development banks generally prioritized small-business lending and, in some cases, housing.

## Summing Up the First Round[*]

The first award round included both the young and emerging CDFIs, and the "legacy" institutions that exemplified the earlier stages of community development finance. Douglass Bancorp and School Workers Federal Credit Union were born in the 1940s, responding to racial segregation. First American Credit Union arose in the early 1960s, just before the dawn of the War on Poverty. The Kentucky Highlands Investment Corporation, launched in 1968, was one of the early community development corporations (CDCs) funded by the Office of Economic Opportunity. Santa Cruz Community Credit Union was established in 1977, the year that the Community Reinvestment Act became law. LISC was created in 1979 by the Ford Foundation to strengthen and expand the CDC movement.

The CDFI Fund checked off most of the boxes specified by its statute and regulations. Geographical distribution was one requirement. Awardees touched—if unevenly—more than 80 percent of the states and the District of Columbia. There were CDFIs in some of the very poorest urban and rural communities—the South Bronx, the Mississippi Delta, and Indian reservations. (Ironically, none were located in South Central Los Angeles, the site of the riots that had strengthened the initial case for the CDFI legislation in 1992.) All institutional types of CDFIs were represented—banks, credit unions, loan funds, microenterprise lenders, venture capital providers. But they were not represented equally: unregulated institutions—primarily nonprofit loan funds—predominated, gathering the most awards and the largest share of the funding (as they did in subsequent rounds). This was a far different outcome than envisioned either by candidate Clinton or in the legislative history, which prioritized whether an applicant was, or had plans to become, an insured depository institution—i.e., a bank or credit union. In addition to the four bank and bank holding company awardees, there were the two "multi-faceted" organizations that mirrored the holding company model, Appalbanc in Kentucky and Self-Help in North Carolina, each of which included a credit union, a nonregulated loan fund, and a nonprofit entity. Few, if any, of the loan fund awardees indicated plans to become banks or credit unions (and none of them subsequently did).

"This was the toughest thing I've ever applied for, and the hardest money to get," said Jacqueline Johnson, executive director of Tlingit-Haida Regional Housing, which had won an award of $1.25 million.[1244] Most applicants would have agreed. The award winners, naturally, were thrilled. For those small, often new organizations that won awards, a CDFI investment brought a measure of

---

[*] Please see Appendix 1 for profiles of all the first-round CDFI winners.

instant credibility. The board chairman of microlender Accion Texas, Alfonso Martinez-Fonts, joined Executive Director Janie Barrera in Washington at the first award ceremony. "Now you can really start making an impact," she recalls him saying, "because your balance sheet is strong."[1245] As Appalbanc CEO Dave Lollis recalled, its CDFI Fund award opened the door to other capital sources.

> It started to bring commercial banks into the picture. They didn't feel that we were competitors. They thought we were trying to help make their business work, to serve people they knew were in their community, but could never serve themselves. The fund came around right at the right time. And it was handled in a way that didn't polarize the traditional banking community and community lenders. We would create products that were advantageous to both.

It was not only the banks that came to support Appalbanc: The Appalachian Regional Commission gave it a grant of $400,000. "These things just kept coming, multiplying," Lollis recalled.[1246]

But 90 percent of the 268 applicants lost. Expectations and hopes for the CDFI Fund were high; how could they not have been, for a program that was years in the making and was so highly favored by the president? The responses from disappointed applicants ranged from resignation to disillusionment—and when the fund faced its first crisis a year later, there was a lack of support from some sectors of the CDFI field.

The fund's selection of banks drew fire from Lyndon Comstock, who had organized the first urban community development bank after ShoreBank (Community Capital Bank in Brooklyn) and had gone on to organize the emerging Community Bank of the Bay in Oakland, CA. Comstock told the press, "I can't fathom how they could have moved so far from the original purpose of the legislation.... The only two community development banks that opened (since 1994) didn't get funded,' referring to his own bank and Albina Community Bank in Portland. 'The selection they've come up with is almost entirely geared toward the longest-established institutions.'"[1247] Comstock's comments were followed up with a letter from six members of the California congressional delegation to CDFI Fund Director Kirsten Moy, copied to Treasury Secretary Rubin and John Emerson, special assistant to the president, demanding an explanation why the two startup banks were considered "less qualified for the CDFI Fund investment than those 30 well-established CDFIs" that received awards. They asked (unsuccessfully) for reconsideration of the Community Bank of the Bay for "any funding amount that may still be available."[1248] Fund Director Moy responded: "We funded generally one in 10 institutions. Community development banks did far better than that as a ratio."[1249] Only 14 of the 268 applicants were community development banks; four out of 14 bank applicants won, a ratio of nearly 30 percent.

Of the four banks selected, Douglass Bancorp of Kansas City, KS, was the only minority bank, an African American–owned institution with $63 million in assets. Two of the four bank winners were not yet fully operational—Detroit Development Bancorp and Louisville Community Development Bank Holding Company, both in formation. ShoreBank was not funded for its Chicago operation, but others in its extended family were. George Surgeon, then CEO of Southern Development Bancorporation, recalled:

> The CDFI Fund award kicked off Southern's expansion into the Mississippi Delta and the acquisition of First National Bank of Phillips County. The investment by the Fund was critical for ShoreBank's expansion to Detroit, in particular. I also recall everyone in Arkansas and Chicago being happy for Douglass and Louisville; both of those banks won awards on their own merits, but we felt the same way for all the other winners, as well.[1250]

Whether Southern and others were funded "on their own merits" rather than because they were allegedly Clinton "cronies" would become the focus of Rep. Bachus's investigation of the CDFI Fund in early 1997.

Community development credit unions were especially disappointed and sometimes embittered by their failure to win CDFI Fund support. The National Federation had written the original concept paper calling for a CDFI Fund, and it had cofounded the CDFI Coalition. Its member institutions were largely minority, especially African American; although they were mostly small, on average they had longer track records than other categories of applicants. Many had toiled for decades in obscurity, unrecognized and unaided, serving the segregated South and the redlined northern cities, or loaning to single mothers, whom no bank would touch. Why, CDCUs asked, did the "big guys" need $2 million or $3 million? Why couldn't the fund have given those institutions a little less and distributed more to the dozens of small institutions for whom $50,000 or $100,000 would have been so precious?

The fund's management had made a strategic choice: Make fewer but larger awards, with the expectation that these would produce greater impact. But that choice came with a potential political price. Martin Eakes of Self-Help recalled a conversation with the fund's leaders, Kirsten Moy and Steve Rohde.

> They were not badly intentioned. Their goal was to make sure that this not be a patronage distribution—that it be really focused on what they consider to the strongest and best CDFIs.
>
> As it turned out, their decision-making was very concentrated. It didn't include a lot of the minority-led credit unions at all. I remember an event [where] Kirsten was presenting. After the event was over, it was very tense. I remember sitting down and saying, 'You won't survive. You'll be pure and short-lived.'
>
> We also had the conversation, then and after, about how I felt credit unions were under-represented, and the diversity of the movement was underrepresented. There weren't enough organizations that specifically served communities of color included in the first round. [The Fund was] saying, 'We don't have enough staff to do a lot of

small grants.' [My] proposal…was that we should have intermediaries that could do grant-making to small institutions.[1251]

Although the fund's strategy rendered it unpopular in some sectors of the CDFI movement, this would not have threatened its survival. Rather, it was its awards to institutions with earlier links to the Clintons that would bring about the first crisis of the fledgling CDFI Fund in 1997.

## The Bank Enterprise Awards

Two months after Treasury made its first awards to CDFIs, it announced its other main program, the Bank Enterprise Awards (BEA), which would provide another channel for capital to flow to community development. The awards, announced on October 1, 1996, totaled $13.1 million to 38 institutions in 18 states and the District of Columbia. These awards were "designed to foster partnerships between banks and thrifts and CDFIs and [are] another way the Clinton Administration helps to ensure that residents of economically distressed neighborhoods have access to financial capital."[1252] The awards ranged from the minuscule (Stock Yards Bank & Trust company, Louisville, KY, $3,750) to many millions of dollars; Chase Manhattan Bank received the largest single award ($2,699,625), while Bank of America's various entities received a total of more than $2 million and NationsBank's received nearly $4 million. The fund calculated that nearly two-thirds of the BEA recipients had committed a total of nearly $66 million in support to CDFIs.[1253]

In the first round, the CDFI Fund was unable to award all the funds set aside for BEA, which amounted to one-third of the $50 million appropriation. Over time, the BEA became much better known and more popular among banks. CDFI banks, like ShoreBank and Community Capital, found the BEA to be much more accessible than the competitive financial assistance awards available from the CDFI Fund.

# CHAPTER 22. The First Crisis

Community development finance began 1997 on a high note. On January 30, dozens of its leading practitioners came to the White House for the inaugural presentation of the Presidential Awards for Excellence in Microenterprise Development. The initiative was "undertaken in conjunction with the Beijing Women's Conference...[to] recognize the important work of micro-enterprise lenders in the United States, give awardees greater credibility in obtaining private sector resources, and underscore for the American public the value and importance of micro-enterprise programs."[1254] President Clinton, Treasury Secretary Rubin, and CDFI Director Kirsten Moy officiated, but above all, it was First Lady Hillary Clinton's show. As she commented in a press briefing preceding the ceremony, microenterprise "is very important and near and dear to my heart."[1255]

Mrs. Clinton's commitment to microenterprise went back to the Clintons' days in Arkansas. As she wrote in her autobiography, "I had first learned about the Grameen Bank more than a decade earlier, when Bill and I invited the bank's founder, Dr. Muhammad Yunus, to Little Rock to discuss how microcredit lending programs might help some of the poorest rural communities in Arkansas."[1256] She had become a board member of Southern Development Bancorp; the Rose Law Firm, with which she was associated, performed legal work for Southern.

In March 1995, Mrs. Clinton took her first extended trip overseas without the president, accompanied by Jan Piercy, "my friend from Wellesley and U.S. Executive Director of the World Bank," who was also a link to the South Shore Bank.[1257] On September 5, in Beijing, China, she delivered her famous speech to the Plenary Session of the U.N. 4th World Conference on Women: "If there is one message that echoes forth from this conference, let it be that human rights are women's rights and women's rights are human rights once and for all."[1258] The economic empowerment of women was fundamental to her vision, and she visited many leading microenterprise organizations around the world, including the Grameen Bank, SEWA (the Self-Employed Women's Association in India), FINCA in Nicaragua and Chile, and Banco Sol in Bolivia.

> Around the world and here at home, many of us have seen first hand the power of microcredit to transform the lives of individual loan recipients, their families, and their communities....
>
> I've met with women in some of the most remote parts of India and some of the poorest barrios in South America, in places that have weathered civil wars and

earthquakes, and I have listened as they have told me how their lives were changed from destitution to inspiration because a community bank had given them the opportunity to start a small business, perhaps sewing clothes or selling auto parts or baking bread and pastries or weaving mosquito netting....

Too many citizens across our own country—people who work hard, who have little or no collateral who wish to secure a loan to start a business, know that it is but a distant dream today. As one woman at Mi Casa, a micro-lending project in Denver, told me, too many great ideas die in the parking lots of banks.[1259]

Mrs. Clinton acknowledged that translating international models or even ShoreBank more broadly was not automatic.

You cannot take what is done in Bangladesh and transfer it directly to Chicago or Arkansas or Washington, DC, but you can take the principles underlying what was done in Bangladesh and take those principles and begin to make them work in the American context. And that is what South Shore has done for a number of years, and what we did in working with them in Arkansas.[1260]

Closer to home, Mrs. Clinton had taken the opportunity to see the emerging shoots of community development banking not far from the White House. Several weeks before the conference, she had joined HUD Secretary Henry Cisneros in announcing the new community development bank in the District of Columbia, City First; a few days after the conference, she would visit the FINCA microenterprise project in Washington, DC, which won one of the first CDFI Fund awards.

As much as she valued microenterprise, Mrs. Clinton did not lose sight of the larger, private-sector vision advanced by then-candidate Bill Clinton years before.

What I would like to see is 5, 10 years from now, having community banks that are free-standing private banks—maybe they would be part of a larger holding company—back in neighborhoods, back on street corners—banks like I used to remember when I was growing up, with people being able, with advances in technology, to get small loans again.[1261]

Seven organizations received microenterprise awards the day of the conference: no cash, but enormously valuable recognition. They were commended for a variety of achievements: access to credit, excellence in program innovation, poverty alleviation, and public or private support for microenterprise development.[1262]

## The Fund Under Attack

Weeks later, the glow from the conference would dissipate under congressional attack.

Republican Rep. Spencer Bachus from Alabama had defeated Democrat Ben Erdreich and had ascended to the chair of the House Banking Committee's general oversight subcommittee, with jurisdiction over the CDFI Fund. On March 11, 1997, responding to complaints about the first-round selection process—for example, that only the "big players get noticed"[1263]—Bachus requested information from the fund about its management practices. The fund's responses indicated to him that it was not using an objective scoring system and that Director Moy and Deputy Director Rohde had "participated in making awards to firms with which they had been previously associated."[1264] (Moy had been an adviser to the Low Income Housing Fund, while Rohde had worked for LISC. Both organizations were first-round award recipients.) Bachus then requested that the subcommittee be permitted to review application files and other documents.

Thus began an investigation that would swirl around unsubstantiated charges that the new entity was a kind of "slush fund" for President Clinton to reward the institutions he and Hillary Clinton had long lauded. Meanwhile, President Clinton was under fire for alleged misdeeds in the Whitewater affair. As his opponents depicted it, the CDFI Fund fit into a persistent pattern of Clintonian corruption and self-dealing.

At the center of the storm were the awards to four applicants that were part of the ShoreBank circle.[1265] Strictly speaking, other than South Shore Bank itself, none of the other three were affiliates of ShoreBank, although to varying degrees, all had ShoreBank ties, whether through board relationships or consulting contracts with ShoreBank Advisory Services. The problem—which, to the subcommittee, was the "smoking gun"—was this: The fund's files contained evaluation memoranda on successful candidates from the initial round of reviews, but not for these four. More precisely: The memoranda were not there on the subcommittee's first visit to the fund but appeared in the files on a subsequent visit.

On their first visit, subcommittee staff did not find memos on the four in the file. They arranged to visit the fund on April 18 for a more intensive examination of the files. Learning of the visit, on April 17, Director Moy had called Rohde from Paris, where she was attending a conference, and instructed him to complete the first-round evaluation memos on the four banks. According to the subcommittee's narrative, Rohde then worked all night to complete the memos, which—contrary to the advice of Maurice Jones, the Fund's counsel—he left undated and had placed in the file. The subcommittee staff promptly examined these on April 18, 1997, and noted that they were written in the present tense, as if they had been prepared contemporaneously months before. The subcommittee concluded and Rep. Bachus subsequently declared that "Kirsten Moy and Steven Rohde wrote spurious documents in a blatant, calculated attempt to mislead Congress and obstruct the subcommittee's investigation."[1266]

Rohde had done the first-stage review of the four community development banks because another reviewer, Alan Okagaki, had a potential conflict of interest.* Rohde made handwritten notes about these applicants. He did not have them typed up, dated, and placed in the file; in an interview, he acknowledged that he "should have," that it was on his to-do list before the awards were announced, that Kirsten Moy had encouraged him to, but that the initial review was simply an early screening process, not the final selection stage.[1267] Rohde took responsibility for failing to properly paper the file, pleading a crushing work load: In the early screening process, he was supervising all of the reviewers, and during the final review panel stage he was reviewing all of the final 60 applications and also coordinating the work of the review panel. "I was literally working about 90 hours a week over a period of months, and since it was obvious that these four applications should not be screened out at that early stage, to my subsequent regret, I failed to take the time to take care of that."[1268]

By May, Bachus was ready to take his accusations public. "The Treasury has opened the system up to political favoritism and abuse," he charged.[1269] On May 9, Bachus wrote a letter to Treasury Secretary Rubin, claiming that the fund's process "raises many troubling issues."[1270] Although Southern and the ShoreBank connections were at the center of his target, another organization, the Low Income Housing Fund in San Francisco, was also singled out as an example of conflict of interest; in addition, Bachus questioned Rubin about a letter from President Clinton concerning Enterprise Corporation of the Delta that had been shown to reviewers.[1271]

The investigation attacked the fund on several grounds: the Clinton connection; the conflicts inherent in using consultants who had experience and connections in the CDFI field; and—most inflammatory—the alleged doctoring of files "for the purpose of misleading congressional investigators."[1272] Further inflaming the situation was the Treasury Department's delay in promptly responding to Bachus, who on May 15 had requested that Treasury provide documents by May 21. On May 27, Under Secretary Hawke wrote to Bachus explaining that the department was working on an "appropriate protocol" to protect the proprietary information of applicants; the Treasury Department's Office of Inspector General (OIG) would be conducting its own investigation.[1273] In a follow-up letter to Secretary Rubin on May 28, Bachus charged that "the department's failure to respond is simply the latest in a series of patent stalling tactics, designed to postpone answers to the subcommittee's questions."[1274]

## Treasury's Response: (Somewhat) Guilty, but Not as Charged

On July 11, Treasury's Inspector General, Valerie Lau, delivered her report to Treasury Undersecretary for Domestic Finance Hawke and to the Subcommittee. On July 14, Hawke wrote to Bachus, stating: "We are pleased that the Inspector General found no basis for concluding that the CDFI Fund improperly selected which applicants would receive funds. This confirms my strong conviction that

---

\* Please see Chapter 19.

the CDFI Fund's decisions with respect to awards were made solely on the merits." Hawke also stated that the report concluded that based on the investigation, there was no "conflict of interest on the part of a senior CDFI Fund official."[1275] (Inspector General Lau promptly issued a statement that the investigation had focused on the evaluation memoranda, and not the broader question of whether applicants were inappropriately chosen.[1276])

Hawke pleaded the novelty of the fund and its commitment to do better: "The CDFI Fund is, of course, in a startup phase and has only completed its first round of awards. It has worked diligently for many months to strengthen its procedures. The CDFI Fund has already begun implementing measures that address needed improvements."[1277] After the first round in 1996, Hawke reported, the fund had retained the firm of Ernst & Young "to assist in developing and strengthening its internal systems, controls, and procedures." The list of changes included refining criteria for selecting reviewers; developing written policies to address potential conflicts of interest; instituting a two-day training curriculum for reviewers; developing "a standardized form for reviewers' analysis of applications during the initial review stage" and a numeric worksheet; involving team leaders in the initial review stage to ensure consistency among reviewers; preparing a guide to standardize interview and due diligence procedures; and developing "policies and procedures for administration of the intake, review and award processes." The fund would hire additional staff in critical areas, including a new deputy director for operations and a chief financial officer.[1278]

Notwithstanding the extensive list of changes, on July 15, 1997, subcommittee members sent a letter to Secretary Rubin asking him to identify "what administrative or disciplinary actions the Department might contemplate to demonstrate…that it will not tolerate deceptive actions on the part of its senior officials."[1279] In a press interview of July 17, Bachus claimed that Kirsten Moy and Steve Rohde had "warped the rules" and should be fired.[1280] On August 6, Secretary Rubin informed the congressional oversight committee that Moy and Rohde had resigned. Moy was to leave in October, Rohde on August 30. Rubin acknowledged that Rohde's placement of the evaluation memoranda "was a serious error of judgment and inconsistent with the standards that should govern our relationship with Congress.… [He offered his] personal assurance that the Department will make it clear that such actions will not be tolerated."[1281]

For his part, Rohde strongly denied to the press that he was asked to resign, asserting that he had submitted his letter of resignation on June 4; that Treasury Undersecretary Hawke and others had tried to convince him to stay; that he agreed to delay the effective date of his resignation but not to rescind it; and that "any suggestion that I was asked to resign by the Treasury Department is completely untrue."[1282] He had decided to resign, he stated, because the Treasury Department was reacting to the controversy by changing from the underwriting or venture capital approach that Rohde employed to a more standardized federal procedure.[1283] Rohde further stated that Moy eventually resigned for similar reasons, despite Secretary Rubin's personally asking her not to resign.

In any case, the closing chapter of the Moy-Rohde administration was a painful one. As one person close to the fund put it, "Kirsten Moy was hung out to dry." She and those close to her complained that she had received no support, either internally or from the CDFI movement itself.

## Chapter 22. The First Crisis

### Shuttling Up the Hill

The investigation of the CDFI Fund had become broader public news, with anonymous congressional sources suggesting to the media that the program was a kind of "slush fund" for Clinton. Bill Luecht, who was serving as public affairs officer, recalls the tremendous stress that the Bachus inquiry put on the staff. "I remember the angst that came over the office during that time. It was like a pall over the office, because they would be constantly sending more letters and more requests in, and it just felt like you were guilty before you were ever found so."[1284] The alleged misdeeds of the CDFI Fund added fuel to the broader Republican attack on Clinton. It also reflected the political ambitions of the investigation's leader: "We happened to be Bachus's thing," Luecht recalled. "He could go after us and prove himself to his party and prove himself to his constituency that he was bringing home the bacon."[1285]

Maurice Jones, the fund's general counsel, was on the front lines of the CDFI Fund's defense. An African American graduate of Hampden-Sydney College with a master's degree from Oxford and a law degree from the University of Virginia, he was relatively new to government; he had joined the fund from the main Treasury staff, where he had been special assistant to the general counsel.[1286] "For the next few months," recalled Jones, "literally, I was locked away in a conference room going through thousands of pages of documents." Jones shuttled back and forth to Congress, hauling documents, responding to question after question. "Our goal at that time was to rebuild confidence, particularly on the Republican side, that we had the capability to run a very tight ship…that we were trying to be partners to these incredible community institutions… frankly, trying to make sure that we kept this enterprise alive."[1287] Jones recalled speaking to Bachus's staff every day—an inquisition that actually had its positive side. "As painful as the investigation was, and as taxing, it also gave us an opportunity to try to school them every day ….In the midst of us shuttling back and forth and answering congressional requests," Jones recalled, "we were also educating folks on the importance" of the CDFI Fund.[1288]

What made an enormous difference was that now—in contrast with the earlier attempts at defunding it before it opened its doors—the fund was actually operating and had invested money around the country. "The saving grace for us was that the knowledge of the impact that CDFIs were having all over the country was spreading," a message that was getting through to Congress thanks in part to the parallel work that the CDFI movement was spreading around the country. "This industry was working *everywhere*."[1289]

### Southern in the Crosshairs

ShoreBank had always been the foremost model held up by Clinton. But now, Bachus affirmed that "there is no allegation that ShoreBank did anything wrong or that there is anything wrong with the Community Development Financial Institutions Fund or those who support it."[1290] Instead, much of the attention focused on Southern Development Bancorp of Arkansas. The key target of the investigating committee was Hillary Clinton.

After serving earlier on the holding company's board and on several of its subsidiaries' boards, Hillary Clinton severed her ties to Southern Development Bancorp in 1992. Nonetheless, after Southern received a $2 million investment in the fund's first round, the troubled past of one of its subsidiaries, Southern Ventures Inc. (SVI), was raised. Clinton had not served on SVI's board, but the Rose Law Firm, where she was a partner until 1992, represented Southern. The *Wall Street Journal* reported that "Southern is also of interest to Whitewater Independent Counsel Kenneth Starr, in part because former Rose partner Webster Hubbell removed files on Southern from Rose's office in 1992, at the same time he took other files relating to Mrs. Clinton's legal work," which he claimed was to enable her to respond to press inquiries.[1291] SVI was obliged to surrender its Small Business Administration license after alleged regulatory violations.

Tom McRae had played an important role in establishing Southern when he headed the Winthrop Rockefeller Foundation. He had moved on to become vice president of Southern Development Bancorporation, and now he publicly responded to charges that Southern had unfairly benefited from the Clinton connection. "I don't see how they [could have conducted the grant] process and not funded us," he told the *Chicago Tribune*. "It's very unfair for us to get negative publicity. There never was any contact with the White House or anything.... [The application] is an exhaustive document going into the demographics of the area, our business plan, our strategy in dealing with it.... We did everything just like anybody else."[1292] George Surgeon, who had been CEO at Southern, was back at ShoreBank when Bachus conducted his investigation. "All of us at ShoreBank took the investigation very seriously," he recalled. "We hired a public relations firm to help us respond. We shared our story with our Congressional delegation. But in the final analysis, the investigation was a distraction for ShoreBank."[1293]

The Low Income Housing Fund (LIHF) was dragged into another front of the attack on the CDFI Fund. LIHF was not a member of the ShoreBank "family" or the Clinton circle, but charges of conflict of interest were leveled at it as well. Bachus claimed that LIHF's vice president, Daniel P. Lopez, was employed to review applications and that he used his position to reject another CDFI competitor, the Northern California Community Loan Fund. On July 2, 1997, *American Banker* printed a letter to the editor repudiating the charge, signed by Daniel M. Liebsohn, president of LIHF; Daniel B. Lopez (Daniel B. Lopez & Associates); and, importantly, Paul Sussman, executive director of the Northern California Community Loan Fund. Lopez "is not and has never been employed by the Low Income Housing Fund," the letter asserted, and he had no financial stake in the nonprofit organization; he worked as a paid consultant for the CDFI Fund. Moreover:

> It is important to note that the Northern California Community Loan Fund has no reason to believe that any possible conflict of interest adversely affected the review process of its application. Nor does it believe that Mr. Lopez's review of its application was tainted by any favoritism. Furthermore, the Northern California Loan Fund has never voiced any concern or complaint to anyone at the CDFI Fund or elsewhere

about unfair treatment or inappropriate action or behavior as a factor in the review of its application.

In closing, we wish to reiterate our own strong support for the mission of the CDFI Fund to assist in the revitalization of low-income communities across the country.[1294]

Thus, even an unsuccessful grant-seeker rejected the charge of conflict of interest.

## The Fund's Appropriation, Salvaged

While the Bachus subcommittee did its work, the Whitewater investigation continued to drag on. Meanwhile, there was still the matter of the budget to be resolved. The White House and the House had been negotiating for months on a bipartisan budget amendment. In June 1997, Treasury Secretary Rubin wrote to the Republican chairman of the House Committee on Ways and Means, Rep. Bill Archer, detailing the administration's dissatisfaction with aspects of the House budget proposal that do not "meet the test of fairness to working families and [have] other serious problems," including disproportionately distributing tax cuts to the top 5 percent of the income scale. "In addition," Rubin wrote, "no provision is included to stimulate investments in Community Development Financial Institutions to revitalize distressed neighborhoods around the country."[1295]

Nonetheless, the process advanced. By July 17, 1997, the *Washington Post* reported, "With the White House and Republican leaders close to agreement on the details of the balanced budget deal, there has been little appetite for the usual battles that stall spending bills and result in presidential vetoes or, as two years ago, partial government shutdowns."[1296] While other parts of the spending bill gained overwhelming bipartisan votes, Bachus and Republican Rep. Mark Foley from Florida attempted to freeze the CDFI Fund budget at $50 million, the previous year's level. The effort failed, and $125 million remained in the House version of the budget, pending the results of the investigation of the fund; President Clinton himself had made the case for the fund to GOP leaders.[1297] But the battle was not won: The Senate Appropriations Committee proceeded to zero out the fund.

Finally, on July 31, Congress passed the Balanced Budget Act of 1997, which had been negotiated with the White House. On August 5, President Clinton signed the legislation, which provided for the CDFI Fund to receive a total of $1 billion over the next five years. (Among the collateral casualties of the budget-balancing exercise was Medicare, which suffered billions of dollars of cuts.)

## Aftermath

The CDFI Fund survived the attack, but with casualties. The Bachus investigation brought charges of internal leaks and betrayals within the fund. For her part, Kirsten Moy felt bitterly abandoned by the field she had come to Washington to help, and which she had supported throughout her career. "Few

CDFIs came to the defense of the Fund" when it was attacked, she recalled. "That," she said, "told me something about the field. It was very sad."[1298] As for Rohde, he was embittered by what he felt was the erroneous implication in the press, based on the tone of Treasury statements, that he had been asked to resign; it caused him to lose respect for the department's leadership.

In December 1997, the Clinton administration named Ellen W. Lazar to head the fund. Lazar had extensive national experience in housing policy and had been head of the Enterprise Foundation's loan fund. She was popular in banking and CDFI circles alike. Carol Parry, executive vice president for community development at Chase Manhattan, commented that "Ellen will help bring credibility to the program among industry as well as Congress. She's smart and knows how government works."[1299] Lazar recalled, "I knew what I was getting into. It was very challenging. Bob Rubin said to me the first week I was there, 'Don't let this thing go awry.' We had to go rebuild the viability of the program with the Hill. We really had an uphill climb to make sure that we could keep the fund in place and get appropriations for it."[1300]

On June 4, 1998, a year after the investigation, the Bachus Subcommittee on General Oversight and Investigations delivered its majority (i.e., Republican) staff report to the House of Representatives Committee on Banking and Financial Services, chaired by Rep. Jim Leach. (The ranking Democratic member was Rep. Maxine Waters, who defended the program.) The report dealt only with the CDFI Fund financial assistance awards, because the BEA program was undersubscribed, and all BEA applicants received awards.[1301] In his letter of transmittal, Bachus pointed out that Kirsten Moy had declined to be interviewed; on the other hand, Bachus wrote, "I do wish to commend former Deputy Director Steve Rohde for his cooperation in the Subcommittee's review. Although Mr. Rohde has acknowledged he made a serious mistake of judgment in creating misleading documents and I consider that his approach to the first round to have been—in the best light—hopelessly naïve, his willingness to be interviewed at length by Subcommittee staff has demonstrated a true commitment to community development."[1302]

Although Bachus noted improvements made by the fund, he declared that

> the list of deficiencies is staggering and would be unacceptable for a government program in its infancy, much less one that has expended over $9 million in administrative expenses in its history.... The cavalier approach the Fund took in awarding taxpayer money was surpassed only by the laxity of its approach to spending taxpayer money.[1303]

In less vivid language, the report itself listed at length the problems with the fund's procedures—inadequate documentation, inconsistency in evaluations (especially of startups), inadequate conflict-of-interest policies, possible political considerations, and much more. Looking at the CDFI Fund's second round (1997), the report suggested that a "decline in quality of applications suggests industry saturation."[1304]

## Chapter 22. The First Crisis

Two weeks later, on June 17, 1998, the banking committee's Subcommittee on Financial Institutions and Consumer Credit held a hearing on H.R. 3617—Reauthorization of the Community Development Financial Institutions Fund. If adopted, the bill would provide permanent authorization of the CDFI Fund. But as Chairwoman Marge Roukema, Republican from New Jersey, introduced the hearing, she observed that "this government program has been, it seems, particularly identified as troubled."[1305]

Rep. Bruce Vento of the Democratic-Farmer-Labor Party of Minnesota urged putting in perspective all the sins attributed to the fund: "The fact is that on the learning curve, CDFI's every mistaken musical note has been so amplified as to lose the melody of the music.... What has been forgotten is what, after all, this program is supposed to do."[1306] Perhaps in this spirit, Bachus himself adopted a less adversarial tone in his statement.

> I traveled on an Amtrak train yesterday or the day before yesterday from Boston to Washington, and from the window of that train you could see a lot of communities in need of development that good, solid community development fund institutions could help.... This is not a goal we ought to abandon. Anybody that looks out a train window knows that there is a tremendous need for this. I think the only question is, how do we do it and how do we do it most effectively.... [There] was nothing in our review that said we should not be involved in community development, in encouraging these institutions, like South Shore, from doing good work, which they have done. There was nothing in that. I don't want to say anything today to slam them again. It would be piling on at this late point.
>
> The Secretary of the Treasury took a courageous stand.... I think we just got off to a bad start, maybe because this was a new program, and it does not mean we don't try again and keep trying until we get it right.[1307]

Bachus didn't "pile on." But he did float a suggestion that perhaps the BEA program should get two-thirds of any appropriation—that is, doubling the share that would go to banks, at the expense of awards to CDFIs directly.

Treasury Undersecretary Hawke returned Bachus's conciliatory comments by thanking him for his "very thoughtful statement.... There is nobody in the congress today who knows more about this program than Mr. Bachus."[1308] He made a strong case for the fund's disbursement of equity and grants, rather than limiting itself to loans, explaining how those investments—matched in kind from private sources—achieved greater leverage than debt. To illustrate the impact of the fund, he described his site visit to Durham, NC, where a micro-loan from Self-Help had enabled one borrower to expand his fresh and fast-food fish business.[1309] He also described Self-Help's work in rehabilitating a Durham neighborhood.

Secretary Rubin acknowledged the fund's "growing pains" to the House Appropriations Committee.[1310] Hawke listed a sample of the improvements the fund had made in its procedures, including a numeric scoring system, reviewer training, conflict-of-interest policies, and better documentation of the awards file. Ellen Lazar, the new director of the CFI Fund, promised that the fund would eliminate the material weaknesses audits had discovered, and that it would reduce its reliance on outside contractors. She highlighted various initiatives to increase the capacity of and support to small institutions, including technical assistance.[1311]

Southern Development Bancorporation did not escape scrutiny in the hearing. This time, it was ostensibly not because of the Clinton connection, but because it used half of its $2 million CDFI Fund award to acquire a bank in the Eastern Arkansas delta, specifically the bank headed by Bill Brandon, who subsequently moved to Southern. Hawke and Maurice Jones explained at length that this did not indicate this was a CDFI Fund strategy to facilitate bank mergers and acquisitions, but rather a cost-effective way to bring services to an underserved area without starting a new bank from scratch. Brandon, who succeeded Surgeon as head of Southern's bank holding company, became an effective advocate for community development banking, as Surgeon recalled.

> He spent time speaking very favorably about the CDFI Fund to members of the House and the Senate throughout the South—'This is really a good thing. You should really find out more about what we're doing.' Bill actually had a meeting with Rep. Spencer Bachus to try to talk him through [the program]: 'You know, we're a real organization serving the rural South. The decision to award funds to Southern didn't come because of people doing nefarious things behind people's backs. This was really being done on merit. This is a good program. Maybe [Southern] ought to come to Alabama?'[1312]

The hearing included testimony from the Office of the Inspector General of the Treasury, the General Accounting Office, and KPMG Peat Marwick. It closed with my testimony on behalf of the Coalition of CDFIs. The coalition, which then claimed to represent 350 CDFIs, urged reauthorization of the fund. Addressing the question of whether the market for CDFI funding was "saturated," as the Bachus committee report suggested, I pointed out that less than one-fifth of the CDFIs had received funding; of the 170 member credit unions of the National Federation of CDCUs, scarcely 10 percent had benefited. The CDFI Coalition acknowledged that "the Bank Enterprise Award indeed has done some significant good for our field," encouraging partnerships and increasing investment. It went on to say, "We do not think, however, that it is in any way a substitute for a strong, healthy, growing CDFI industry.... [The coalition acknowledged the] "terrific progress that we have seen in the CDFI Fund over the last couple of years. We understand the basis for some of the criticisms that were made, even though we would not necessarily agree with all of them."[1313] I used the opportunity to urge that the fund increase its investments in small institutions:

> We, as a coalition, would strongly like to recommend that the CDFI Fund, as a priority, create what we call an 'easy-access window' as part of its core component. This

window would be designed to increase the participation of smaller and emerging CDFIs by streamlining the application process and accordingly limiting the amount of capital that applicants could request, perhaps to a cap of $100,000 per applicant.[1314]

Chairwoman Roukema responded that the proposal "does not necessarily meet with what I believe to be in the best interests of the development of the program."[1315] However, two years later, the CDFI Fund would institute this approach through the Small and Emerging CDFI Access (SECA) program, fulfilling a longtime goal of the National Federation.

## Assessing the Investigation

The Bachus investigation confronted the newborn CDFI Fund with a series of issues. Some were wrapped in politically motivated conspiracy charges; some alleged more garden-variety conflicts; others questioned the nature of the selection process, which they viewed as unduly subjective.

Was it true that the files were not properly documented? Yes—Rohde admitted it.[1316] As Maurice Jones, the fund's counsel, recalled, "People worked day and night because we had a small skeleton staff. …. [There was no question that because of] the need for speed and inadequate capacity, there were some mistakes made."[1317]

Were unworthy candidates selected? As the *Wall Street Journal* reported, "No one, not even Bachus, has called into question the actions of the award recipients."[1318] Even critics were hard-pressed to deny that Southern was doing the kind of work community development banks were supposed to do.

Did an alleged Clinton connection influence the selections, as Bachus and his allies charged? Steve Rohde, who took over the review of ShoreBank-related institutions from Alan Okagaki to avoid the perception of conflict of interest, vigorously denies even mentioning the Clinton connection in his review discussions. All those involved in the early stage of the fund vehemently and consistently deny the charge. Okagaki described the reviewers and process as "the least politicized" imaginable… Steve (Rohde) didn't give a rip about the politics…"[1319] Rohde endured most of the attack on the alleged backdating of the memos, but according to Okagaki, it never crossed his mind to do anything other than look at the merits of the proposal. Rohde, he said, had a memory of each application that was "absolutely extraordinary. He just had it all in his head, it was just amazing."[1320]

Was the alleged backdating of review documents an attempt to enhance the likelihood of funding for the four development banks? Rohde asserted that the quality of these applications was such that it would have been unthinkable to screen out these four applicants prior to the review panel stage, as buttressed by the fact that each member of the review panel independently concluded at the beginning of the final review deliberations that these four should definitely be funded.[1321] The subcommittee never produced evidence, or even argued, that the banks were *less worthy* than other awardees.

Connected with this, was the insertion of a memo an attempt to mislead Congress? No, not in the sense that it was aimed at covering up misdeeds. Yes, in that it attempted to make it appear that the process—hastily constructed, understaffed, under pressure from an eager administration and an impatient CDFI movement—was more orderly than it was.

Were there rampant conflicts of interest among reviewers? The CDFI movement was still relatively small. Not everyone knew everyone—but there was a dense web of relationships; rarely were there as much as three degrees of separation between reviewers and applicants.

Was the process inherently flawed—too "subjective" or "narrative" for a federal agency, involving telephone calls and in-person interviews of the candidates, as well as collateral research? The administration had supported Kirsten Moy and Steve Rohde in choosing their approach of *underwriting institutions*—a "venture capital" approach—rather than imposing a typical "objective," points-based scoring system. Moy had been an underwriter, Rohde had underwritten projects for state government, and they "tried to use a private-sector underwriting process" at the fund. For example, if you were underwriting an investment in a financial institution, as Okagaki noted, "you'd call the applicant if you had a question," or call a third party.[1322]

Still, the new fund's way was certainly not the established "federal" way; it would prove politically untenable, and the fund soon modified its procedures. To her regret, Moy recalled, she learned that "there is no underwriting process in government."[1323] In retrospect, she acknowledged, "I probably should have hired a career administrative person"[1324]—that is, someone steeped in the ways of the Beltway bureaucracy. There was a "cultural mismatch."

To some degree, the mismatch was rooted in the DNA of the original community development banking concept and reinforced in successive legislative drafts. The goal was to build a network of CDFIs—not programs, but *sustainable institutions* with the potential to be self-sufficient, leveraging all-important private-sector support and surviving in the marketplace. The CDFI Fund was deliberately not conceived to be like HUD or other agencies, a dispenser of annual support to entities that would carry out the programs favored by the administration in power. But Washington was not yet ready to embrace an underwriting process that might be best suited to building a network of sustainable institutions.

The CDFI Fund had been created with extensive bipartisan support; apart from the BEA, it had been relatively uncontroversial. But, as Bill Zavarello, legislative director for Rep. Maxine Waters, recalled, the Bachus investigation changed that: "Sometimes if you say something about a program, it takes hold. And so all of a sudden, the CDFI program became 'controversial' when it hadn't been. After this played itself out, there were good times. The opponents weren't going kill it, but they weren't going to fund it very aggressively either. That was the best we could hope for. [Still], there was always a residual partisan impression of the 'CDFI president.'" There were congressmen, like Senator Shelby, with whom, Zavarello recalled, it was best never to bring up CDFI.[1325]

Reflecting on her three years directing the CDFI Fund, Ellen Lazar concluded that "the biggest accomplishment was to stabilize the fund and help develop respect for it within Treasury, and on the Hill. It needed to have policies and procedures in place. It needed to have a clean audit. It needed to be a government agency. I mean that wasn't what was originally conceived, but it's what ultimately the Gingrich crowd wanted. The only way to satisfy them was to make it a normal operating government agency."[1326]

## The Second Round

Amid the turmoil and stress, the CDFI Fund was attempting to continue its work of providing capital to the community development banking network. On April 4, 1997, the fund published in the *Federal Register* its Revised Interim Rule with Request for Comment, along with its second Notice of Funds Availability. Among changes in procedures, there was one especially significant for the field: the initiation of an "intermediary component."

The complaints of smaller institutions and their advocates, including the National Federation, led the fund to establish this mechanism for "wholesale" institutions to channel investments to organizations ill-equipped to compete against their larger, more sophisticated peers. By now, the fund had adopted some of the procedural changes demanded by its critics, including a more objective scoring system and greater attention to conflicts of interest. On September 30, 1997, the CDFI Fund announced $38.3 million in awards to 48 certified CDFIs. Among the winners was the National Federation. The fund's $3.25 million grant was transformative. It greatly expanded the federation's decade-old Capitalization Program, distributing equity grants to some of our poorest member institutions and funding the federation's new, high-risk, equity-like investment—secondary capital. With the fund's support, the federation launched the most extensive training and human-resources development effort in our history, the Community Development Credit Union Institute.[1327]

# PART VII.
# Community Development Financial Institutions in Historical Perspective

A quarter-century after the creation of the CDFI Fund, it is timely to assess where the community development banking initiative stands in the long line of efforts to broaden access to capital for people and communities on the economic margins. What is distinctive about the emergence of CDFIs? What has, and has not, ben transformative about community development banking? That it has been a public-policy success seems indisputable—but what is the nature of that success? How have the small, mission-driven organizations that came to be known as CDFIs evolved? How do we describe the universe of diverse institutions that bear that brand—now arguably the most valuable one in community development? Finally, what is the nature of the social phenomenon that we call community development finance?

# CHAPTER 23. Twenty Years After

One spring afternoon in 2016, I walked down Market Street toward San Francisco's Embarcadero to meet with Nancy Andrews, CEO of the Low Income Investment Fund (LIIF). The elevator sped me up to the 29th floor, where I was announced at the spacious reception area suitable for a corporate law firm.

Sitting in Nancy's office, looking out at the panorama of the bay, I recalled our first meeting nearly 20 years before, when I traveled to Washington to defend the National Federation's CDFI Fund application to Andrews and her fellow reviewers. Her career trajectory had tracked that of the CDFI movement, from her time at the Ford Foundation, which she joined in 1984, working in Program-Related Investments (PRIs) under Tom Miller.[1328] Andrews recalled an early experience at Ford.

> When I made the first PRI to ICE [the Institute for Community Economics], I remember taking it to the officers of the foundation. I was really trying to kind of pump it up—I wanted them to see that this was important. ... I wanted to *make it* important. I remember saying with a great deal of pride, there are 12 of these community loan funds around the United States and collectively they have 25 million dollars under investment. That seemed like a ton of money at that time.*
>
> Now look at this field! There are a thousand CDFIs. Billions of dollars that get placed every year. The Low Income Investment Fund makes $25 million investments routinely. [The movement has] gone from being a dozen organizations with 25 million dollars under management to having a hundred times that.[1329]

LIIF had come a long way from its origins, founded in 1984 by Dan Liebsohn as the Low Income Housing Fund. For years, Leibsohn recalled, he worked 85 or 90 hours a week until steady sources of

---

\* Michael Swack, who worked with Chuck Matthei of ICE on its proposal, recalled the less-than-formal closing process of this early investment. "I worked on a lot of the details. We had finally reviewed all the documents, and we were ready for a closing. Except Chuck was on the road. The only time and place where the three of us (Nancy Andrews, Chuck, and I) could meet was on a Sunday morning at my house. My wife was not impressed—we had just gotten married that year, and she was a little concerned about maintaining a balance between work and personal life. I still remember her words, 'Sunday morning? In our kitchen? Really? You're kidding, right?'" (Email correspondence to author, October 25, 2017)

earned income and, to a lesser extent, grants finally were sufficient to support operations.[1330] It was not an uncommon story.

## Growth of the CDFI Field

In 1996, 298 institutions applied to the CDFI Fund; the fund certified 196. By 2017, the CDFI field had grown to approximate Bill Clinton's original call for 100 community development banks and 1,000 microenterprise programs. The fund counted 1,094 certified CDFIs (although there were probably twice that many doing similar work that either had not sought to become certified or let their certification lapse, largely because they had not, or did not plan to, receive funding or because the reporting requirements outweighed the anticipated benefits).*

| Table 2. Certified CDFIs by Type (2017) | |
|---|---|
| Bank or thrift | 137 |
| Credit union | 297 |
| Depository institution holding company | 87 |
| Loan fund | 556 |
| Venture capital fund | 17 |
| Total number of CDFIs | 1,094 |

*Data as of March 31, 2017. Courtesy of CDFI Fund.*

Although early drafts of the CDFI Fund legislation explicitly envisioned higher award amounts for regulated depositories than for others, that preference was eliminated in the final legislation; all types of CDFIs were to be considered equally. Ostensibly, the playing field was level: banks, credit unions, loan funds, and venture capital funds all would compete for investment on an equal footing. It would have been reasonable to expect at least rough parity between the CDFI Fund's investments in depositories and nonregulated loan funds. Instead, from 1996 through 2016, nonprofit loan funds received 80 percent of CDFI Fund grants and investments, while typically banks and credit unions combined obtained less than 20 percent. (See Table 3.)

The dominance of loan funds was neither the policy nor the intent of the CDFI Fund; nonetheless, it was the outcome, at least through 2016. The result suggests a case of disparate impact: Unintentionally, the design and procedures of the fund inherently provided an advantage to nonregulated loan funds.

---

\* For example, although only 297 credit unions were certified as of early 2017, there were more than 2,000 credit unions that the National Credit Union Administration had designated as low-income, many of which would presumably have qualified for CDFI certification.

- **Raising matching funds.** Applicants were required to raise matching funds of "like kind and value." Loan funds had better access to philanthropic and corporate grants and investments than did banks and credit unions. Foundations gave primarily to 501(c)(3) charities—a status enjoined by most nonprofit loan funds, but neither by community development banks nor credit unions. Loan funds were the partners of choice for mainstream banks' corporate and CRA giving; they did not see loan funds—unlike community development banks and credit unions—as competitors.[1331]
- **The culture of grant-seeking.** Applying to the CDFI Fund was like a daunting grant competition. Nonprofit loan funds had the skilled grantwriters and culture to compete; by the nature of their business, banks and credit unions did not. Resource-poor communities—which many credit unions served—were especially disadvantaged (a point made by Rep. Lucille Roybal-Allard of Los Angeles at congressional hearings in 1993).[1332]
- **Structure of applications.** The fund's definitions, terminology, and data fields were derived from the universe of nonprofit loan funds; credit unions, banks, and venture funds struggled to fit their variously shaped pegs into the holes defined by the CDFI Fund. As Jeannine Jacokes, of the Community Development Bankers Association, has noted, "banks and credit unions were forced to go through the painstaking and expensive task of reclassifying their data to submit reports and applications designed for loan funds."[1333] As for venture funds, their very structure was largely incompatible with the fund's understanding of a CDFI.[1334]
- **Review procedures.** The CDFI Fund evaluated applicants in a single pool, rather than creating separate pools to evaluate each quite different CDFI subsector. As the representatives of CDFI credit unions and banks argued in a letter to congressional appropriators in 2017: "The 'one-size-fits-all' single-pool evaluation processes resulted in an imbalanced distribution of resources [among the various CDFI sectors].... The single-pool evaluation process creates unintended but real bias that plays to the strengths of unregulated CDFI sectors while ignoring the strengths of the regulated CDFIs. Placing the highly diverse organizations with different operating environments into a single applicant pool elevates the bias. Treasury officials acknowledge this challenge yet report they cannot change the evaluation process to accommodate the CDFI subsector differences without a clearer legislative directive from Congress."[1335]
- **Numerical preponderance of loan funds.** Especially in the CDFI Fund's early years, loan funds far outnumbered other types of applicants. The fund's practice of making awards in approximate proportion to the number of applicants from each subsector of the CDFI field yielded more loan fund winners.[1336]

From the fund's earliest days, loan funds (including microenterprise funds) dominated the roster of CDFIs numerically. The numerical predominance diminished somewhat over the years, especially after 2010, as the numbers of fund-certified banks and credit unions increased significantly. There were two primary reasons for this growth: First, the Treasury Department's Community Development Capital Initiative (CDCI) of 2010 offered certified banks and credit unions access to low-cost capital; and second, the Consumer Financial Protection Bureau (CFPB) gave CDFI banks and credit unions exemptions to certain mortgage rules. Consequently, although loan funds predominated numerically, as Table 4 shows, by January 2016, CDFI-held assets were heavily concentrated in banks, thrifts, and credit unions—approximately $93 billion of the $108 billion total.[1337]

| | Loan Fund | Venture Capital | Credit Union | Bank | Grand Total | CU+bank | CU only | Bank Only |
|---|---|---|---|---|---|---|---|---|
| 1996 | 20,802,500 | 1,700,000 | 2,727,500 | 9,989,500 | 35,219,500 | 36.11% | 7.74% | 28.36% |
| 1997 | 35,661,300 | | 3,893,000 | 4,265,000 | 43,819,300 | 18.62% | 8.88% | 9.73% |
| 1998 | 49,432,221 | 1,415,000 | 2,855,550 | 3,650,500 | 57,353,271 | 11.34% | 4.98% | 6.36% |
| 1999 | 65,350,930 | 4,615,000 | 4,811,440 | 5,551,435 | 80,328,805 | 12.90% | 5.99% | 6.91% |
| 2000 | 65,195,135 | 6,828,000 | 5,760,850 | 1,050,000 | 78,833,985 | 8.64% | 7.31% | 1.33% |
| 2001 | 48,692,100 | 3,080,000 | 3,932,050 | 2,085,000 | 57,789,150 | 10.41% | 6.80% | 3.61% |
| 2002 | 44,504,730 | 46,000 | 3,734,940 | 2,720,000 | 51,005,670 | 12.66% | 7.32% | 5.33% |
| 2003 | 20,120,320 | 2,565,000 | 1,131,191 | | 23,816,511 | 4.75% | 4.75% | 0.00% |
| 2004 | 50,461,342 | 71,425 | 4,295,340 | 5,120,449 | 59,948,556 | 15.71% | 7.17% | 8.54% |
| 2005 | 28,309,888 | 1,156,663 | 4,440,273 | 4,446,550 | 38,353,374 | 23.17% | 11.58% | 11.59% |
| 2006 | 26,050,171 | | 3,788,389 | 835,000 | 30,673,560 | 15.07% | 12.35% | 2.72% |
| 2007 | 24,022,899 | | 4,690,905 | 2,255,061 | 30,968,865 | 22.43% | 15.15% | 7.28% |
| 2008 | 56,070,659 | 543,664 | 4,598,827 | 1,193,270 | 62,406,420 | 9.28% | 7.37% | 1.91% |
| 2009 | 125,803,250 | 3,527,500 | 18,994,963 | 12,551,588 | 160,877,301 | 19.61% | 11.81% | 7.80% |
| 2010 | 98,133,039 | 1,500,000 | 12,588,984 | 2,870,173 | 115,092,196 | 13.43% | 10.94% | 2.49% |
| 2011 | 152,152,124 | 1,500,000 | 27,800,127 | 2,100,000 | 183,552,251 | 16.29% | 15.15% | 1.14% |
| 2012 | 158,125,994 | 2,907,612 | 17,437,011 | 8,072,836 | 186,543,453 | 13.68% | 9.35% | 4.33% |
| 2013 | 142,857,421 | 2,194,000 | 27,669,093 | 12,320,000 | 185,040,514 | 21.61% | 14.95% | 6.66% |
| 2014 | 153,717,290 | 2,000,000 | 28,291,024 | 11,444,666 | 195,452,980 | 20.33% | 14.47% | 5.86% |
| 2015 | 149,510,020 | 1,384,402 | 35,243,008 | 14,900,001 | 201,037,431 | 24.94% | 17.53% | 7.41% |
| 2016 | 141,280,695 | 1,000,000 | 33,352,151 | 9,375,000 | 185,007,846 | 23.09% | 18.03% | 5.07% |
| Total | 1,656,254,028 | 38,034,266 | 252,036,616 | 116,796,029 | 2,063,120,939 | 17.88% | 12.22% | 5.66% |
| Sector % | 80.28% | 1.84% | 12.22% | 5.66% | 100.00% | 17.88% | 12.22% | 5.66% |

Table 3. CDFI Fund Financial Assistance Awards by Sector (1996-2016)

*Banks include Bank Holding Companies*
*Source: CDFI Fund via Community Development Bankers Association*

The original concept for the CDFI Fund envisioned a network of self-sustaining community development banks and microenterprise organizations; the goal, as stated in the CDFI statute, was to support institutions "that will not be dependent upon assistance from the Fund for continued viability."[1338] From this perspective, loan funds' dominant share of CDFI Fund support appears paradoxical: Loan funds, which are typically nonprofits that depend on grant funding, received approximately 80 percent of all award dollars, while banks and credit unions, which by their very nature must be self-sustaining, received 20 percent or less over the fund's first 20 years. Although the CDFI Fund does not make multi-year awards, winning became virtually an annual event for some of the largest loan funds: For example, several awardees of the Class of 1996 received more than 30 grants and New Markets Tax Credit allocations over 1996–2016. (See Table 5.)

| Table 4. Asset Distribution by CDFI Sector (January 2016) | | | | |
|---|---|---|---|---|
| CDFI Type | Total Assets (billions) | Percentage of Assets | Average Assets (millions) | Median Assets (millions) |
| Bank or thrift | $37.93 | 35% | $318.72 | $215.79 |
| Credit union | 55.67 | 52 | 208.51 | 52.99 |
| Loan fund | 14.19 | 13 | 27.07 | 7.00 |
| Venture capital fund | 0.21 | - | 14.91 | 4.66 |
| Total | $107.99 | 100% | $116.88 | $19.73 |

*Courtesy of CDFI Fund.*

Using institutional and transaction-level data for 2015, the CDFI Fund analyzed the self-sufficiency, net assets, and leverage ratios for a sample of loan funds, credit unions, and bank awardees. It calculated that the median self-sufficiency ratio of CDFI loan funds was 60.7 percent, while banks (112.2 percent) and credit unions (109.0 percent) were fully self-sufficient.[1339] The Opportunity Finance Network (OFN), which compiles extensive annual statistics on its membership of more than 200 institutions, calculated that the aggregate self-sufficiency ratio of unregulated loan funds (which it defines as "the extent to which a CDFI is covering its expenses through earned revenue") was 70 percent for its sample. OFN determined that the self-sufficiency ratio varied widely, depending on the type of institution and its product line (e.g., business loans, housing loans to individuals, housing loans to organizations), from a top ratio of 87 percent for institutions specializing in financing housing for organizations, to a low of 24 percent for those financing consumers.[1340]

It is striking that many CDFI-certified loan funds have lofty levels of net assets, or equity. As calculated by the CDFI Fund, the median net-asset ratio was 49.1 percent for loan funds, compared with 12.4 percent for CDFI banks and 10.4 percent for credit unions. On average, loan fund balance sheets show a ratio far higher than most foundations and other private-sector investors require of CDFIs (typically 20 percent). High net-asset ratios correspond with low leverages on a balance sheet—that is, the proportion of debt to equity. The CDFI Fund calculated median balance-sheet leverage ratios at 1.0 for loan funds, 7.1 for banks, and 8.6 for credit unions. These figures confirm the conclusion of a study published in 2012 by Professor Michael Swack and his colleagues: "CDFI [loan funds] are generally not well leveraged."[1341]

The data suggests that some of the top-tier loan funds—particularly those specializing in housing loans to organizations—are now virtually self-sustaining. Although some of these funds are frequent winners of awards, they likely could operate successfully without the CDFI Fund's support, at least with respect to their core products and operations. It is reasonable to ask whether the CDFI Fund should continue to allocate its limited resources of equity to the most well-endowed loan funds, rather than requiring them to build their assets by obtaining additional debt. At the other end of the spectrum, as one loan fund veteran put it, some smaller CDFI loan funds are essentially dependent on year-to-year CDFI Fund support and would likely be hard-pressed to continue without it.

## Twenty Eventful Years

From 1996 to 2016, the economy went through several business cycles: the relative prosperity in the Clinton years, which produced a budget surplus; the dot-com bust of 2000–02; and of course, the Great Recession that produced failures of some of the largest banks and shook the world economy. The recession intensified the relentless trend of consolidations and mergers that reduced the numbers of banks and credit unions by about half over 20 years. CDFI banks and credit unions were not immune to this dynamic. On the other hand, in 2011, widespread outrage over growing inequality and the abuses of the largest banks erupted in the Occupy Wall Street movement, one result of which was a campaign to "move your money" to credit unions and community banks.*

The CDFI Fund went through its own cycles. In a rare piece of bipartisan legislation, the Community Renewal Tax Relief Act of 2000 was signed into law in the last few weeks of the Clinton administration, creating the New Markets Tax Credit (NMTC) program. It did not add to the CDFI Fund's supply of grants or equity for CDFIs. Rather, it is a highly competitive program through which CDFIs vie with other "Community Development Entities" (CDEs, among which are mainstream banks, developers, and other for-profit entities) for allocations of tax credits that are then sold or passed through to investors as incentives to finance qualified businesses and enterprises in low-income communities. The daunting complexity of the program put it out of reach for most CDFIs. But for those with the capacity to use it, as Elyse Cherry, CEO of Boston Community Capital put it, "The New Markets Tax Credit was an absolutely critical piece of what has enabled us to grow. If you asked me, 'What is the single most important factor in the growth of the organization?' I would say that it's fees from the tax credit, because it allowed us to create a balance sheet."[1342] A select few CDFIs won tens of millions of dollars or more of tax credits.

Despite this fleeting display of bipartisanship in the creation of the NMTC program, under the presidency of George W. Bush the CDFI Fund lost the favored status it had enjoyed under President Clinton. In 2005, the Bush administration tried to kill the fund through "consolidation" with other programs under a proposal euphemistically known as SACI, the Strengthening America's Communities Initiative. The CDFI Coalition called upon its supporters to "beat back SACI." The Bush initiative

---

\* It was estimated at the time that more than one million people moved their accounts to credit unions. It was a frustrating paradox that this was not always good news for some credit unions: An influx of deposits diluted their net-worth ratio, lowered their loan-to-assets ratio at a time when investment yields were low, and brought increased regulatory pressure.

took aim at many other popular federal programs, like Community Development Block Grants; the opposition was immediate and widespread, and SACI was promptly declared "dead on arrival" in Congress.* Nonetheless, the CDFI Fund's appropriation was reduced to $54 million for FY 2006 and $54.5 million for FY 2007—marginally more than the fund's startup budget of $50 million in FY 1995 and less than half of the $118 million in the final Clinton budget for FY 2001.

## CDFIs and the Great Recession

Officially, the Great Recession began in 2007 and lasted through 2009. But the full force of the economic disaster hit in fall 2008. On September 7, 2008, the giant government-sponsored housing secondary markets, Fannie Mae and Freddie Mac, were placed into conservatorship. On September 15, the venerable Lehman Brothers investment firm filed for bankruptcy. On October 3, amid widespread fears of global financial collapse, President Bush signed into law the Emergency Economic Stabilization Act of 2008, which created the Troubled Assets Relief Program (TARP) to purchase up to $700 billion in bank-owned "toxic assets" and to invest equity in these institutions.

Economic devastation was widespread, but low-income and minority communities were especially hard hit, through foreclosures, layoffs in the service sector, and tightened credit. In turn, as institutions created to serve those communities, CDFIs faced serious challenges, although the Great Recession affected the various sectors—loan funds, banks, credit unions, and microenterprise funds—in different ways.

For loan funds, the Great Recession brought a mix of challenges and benefits. Many loan funds depended on CRA-motivated grants and investments from banks. But some major bank supporters failed, including Washington Mutual and Wachovia, which were absorbed by J.P. Morgan Chase and Wells Fargo, respectively. Other banks reduced their CRA support or even dissolved their CRA units. Some loan funds faced a potential liquidity crisis: If the value of their portfolios declined because of troubled loans, they could find themselves in violation of their loan covenants with investors, which could have triggered a demand to accelerate repayment. Fortunately, this did not become a significant problem; banks generally exercised forbearance.

Amid the retrenchment of banks, there was also a bright side for CDFI loan funds. Banks were tightening their lending, denying loans even to their established, financially sound customers; they were shunning new projects that they now considered too risky. Over 2008–10, Opportunity Finance Network (OFN; formerly NCCA) conducted quarterly market surveys that traced the trends among its members at this tumultuous time. By the third quarter of 2008, they reported "feeling the negative impact of the nationwide economic slowdown, tightening credit markets, and declining confidence in financial institutions.... They generally experienced a decrease in competition as mainstream lenders

---

\* "My budget substantially reduces or eliminates more than 150 government programs that are not getting results or duplicate current efforts or do not fulfill essential priorities," President Bush declared in his February 2005 State of the Union Address.

pulled back due to the increasing turmoil in the credit markets, which is making all lenders more cautious, including CDFIs."[1343] Along with the decreased competition, many loan funds experienced an increase in loan demand. By the first quarter of 2009, "demand for CDFI financing continued to rise....New originations did not keep pace with demand due to liquidity constraints and intensified due diligence, among other reasons."[1344]

As the recession wore on, by the end of 2009, loan fund originations still could not keep up with demand. Many dealt with capital and liquidity constraints; they imposed tighter lending criteria, enhanced their due diligence, and increased loan workouts. A significant percentage of loan funds responded by freezing hiring or salaries; some 22 percent laid off staff.[1345] As 2010 went on, the stress of the recession began to ease. OFN members reported both increased originations and increased demand; troubled loans decreased, although loan restructuring increased. However, the effects of the recession were evident in other ways as well, as respondents began to report stress from the declines in state and municipal budgets: "There is still a risk to our overall portfolio due to the status of state and municipal budgets," one respondent noted.[1346]

The CDFI Fund played an important role in helping loan funds survive the Great Recession. Its grants during this difficult period helped loan funds maintain the liquidity they needed to keep lending. As well, the cumulative support from the CDFI Fund provided over a decade enabled the loan funds to build significant net worth. As Elyse Cherry, CEO of Boston Community Capital, later reflected:

> We've managed to dodge a bunch of bullets, and to build an organization that is sufficiently robust to carry us through bad times and good times.... We never flagged; we kept growing, because we had a balance sheet that allowed us to be confident enough to keep working with borrowers who might have been getting into real trouble. [We helped] in a way that kept them afloat, kept projects afloat, just because we had the financial strength to do it. If you have sufficient capital, it gives you a runway. You can weather storms.[1347]

But microenterprise funds had an especially difficult time, as the Aspen Institute's FIELD project reported.

> The recession and financial crisis have created dramatically different market conditions for microlending organizations. These conditions—a weaker economy, a highly stressed private financial sector, donors and investors with weaker endowments or corporate profits—have affected microlenders in varying ways. They affect existing borrowers, whose businesses may face declining sales. They have altered the profile of potential borrowers: lenders may see businesses that were formerly able to access financing from banks that have tightened their lending.... And, they affect microlenders' budgets, as many donors and investors have fewer resources.[1348]

Banks and credit unions that specialized in serving low-income communities faced a different dilemma than did loan funds. Their customer base—low-wage workers in the service sector, small property owners, minority and other small businesses—was hard hit. Home foreclosures were rampant; credit losses mounted. Although loan funds frequently found flexibility from their investors, banks and credit unions were accountable to increasingly nervous regulators, who demanded increased loan loss allowances and reserves, thus magnifying the stress on these financial institutions. Equity ratios, rather than liquidity, were the dominant concern.

To make matters worse for credit unions, multi-billion-dollar corporate or "wholesale" credit unions—U.S. Central Credit Union and Western Corporate Federal Credit Union—failed in spring 2009, as a result of their investments in subprime securities.* All federally insured credit unions had to pay premiums to replenish the NCUA federal deposit insurance fund. Like loan funds, credit unions began to see some improvement by the latter part of 2010. Aggregate figures showed that community development credit unions remained profitable, if at a reduced level—but these numbers reflected the weight of larger credit unions, which fared much better than small ones.[1349]

The Great Recession took a significant toll among regulated depositories of all kinds. In 2009, 140 banks and 31 credit unions failed; in 2010, the toll was 157 banks and 24 credit unions.[1350] CDFIs did not escape the damage altogether. However, a study of regulated institutions carried out for the CDFI Fund demonstrated that CDFIs "show no greater risk of institutional failure than similar 'mainstream' peer institutions."[1351] Another study found that "the CDFI industry has grown substantially, leveraging investment and increasing its lending activity even in the face of a recession and cataclysmic changes in the financial environment."[1352]

The CDFI Fund's support became ever more crucial for many institutions. President Obama was far more supportive of community development than his predecessor. On February 17, 2009, weeks after his inauguration, President Obama signed into law the American Recovery and Reinvestment Act of 2009 (ARRA), an economic stimulus package that added $100 million to the CDFI Fund's appropriation of $106.9 million for the FY 2009 funding round; the funding was fast-tracked, and it was awarded by the end of the fiscal year in September.† For FY 2010, the fund received a record total of $246.75 million, by far the largest amount in its history to that point.

Throughout Obama's two terms, the CDFI Fund would receive far larger appropriations than it had even in the Clinton years. Initially, the dramatic increase in the CDFI Fund's support was part of the federal response to the Great Recession, a tidal wave of economic destruction that would disproportionately damage low-income communities. CDFIs could not heal those communities; they could, at least, help mitigate the harm.

---

\* Corporate credit unions provided a range of liquidity, investment, and correspondent services to "retail," or "natural person" credit unions, which served individual members.

† The New Markets Tax Credit program was also supplemented by an additional $1.5 billion.

## TARP for CDFIs: The Community Development Capital Initiative (CDCI)

The federal investment of $700 billion in TARP funds, appropriated in the final months of President Bush's administration, overwhelmingly supported the largest financial institutions; credit unions and loan funds were not eligible, and only a few CDFI banks got access. For CDFIs, as for many ordinary citizens, it was glaringly unfair that the largest financial institutions received a "bail-out" from the federal government, to the exclusion of small, mission-driven institutions that did not cause the crisis. In fall 2009, an informal group of CDFI leaders began to advocate with the Treasury Department and the Obama administration for capital to help their afflicted low-income communities recover. Meanwhile, a subcommittee of the CDFI Fund Advisory Board was working hard on the term sheet and other features of the initiative.

In an apparent early success, on October 21, 2009, President Obama announced the outlines of a new program. This was no White House Rose Garden ceremony; the president spoke in a records-storage warehouse in the industrial suburbs of Washington, DC, chosen because it had received an SBA loan. CDFI representatives were disappointed; the proposal was too scant to make a real difference. For the next few months, CDFIs pressed for better terms. On February 3, 2010, at a small briefing with CDFI leaders in the Treasury Building, Secretary Timothy Geithner announced a revised, improved program: the Community Development Capital Initiative (CDCI).[1353] The initiative aimed to "[spur] economic development in the communities that have been hit hardest by the economic downturn."[1354]

Treasury did not place a hard ceiling on the program, although it estimated that outlays would not exceed $1 billion. The agency would not be providing grants, but rather equity-like loans and investments for CDFI credit unions and banks; the initial interest rate was set at 2 percent annually for eight years, then rising to 9 percent for an additional five years, to encourage institutions to depart the program.[1355] Only CDFI-certified depositories were eligible; CDFI loan funds and venture funds were not. The investments were conditioned by onerous regulations; restrictions on executive compensation had been designed to constrain the large banks receiving TARP money, but they were preposterously excessive for some of the smallest institutions, especially CDCUs, whose "staff" sometimes consisted of low-paid tellers or even volunteers. As Sheila Bair, then the head of the FDIC, wrote in her book, *Bull by the Horns*, large banks managed to reward their CEOs despite TARP limitations on executive compensation; meanwhile, small institutions wrestled mightily with the regulations or decided it was not even worth applying.* Amplifying the inequity, "Throughout the crisis and its aftermath, the smaller banks—which didn't benefit from all the government largesse—did a much better job of lending than the big institutions did."[1356] During spring and summer 2010, many banks and credit unions attracted by access to low-cost capital applied for CDFI Fund certification for the first time.

But CDFI certification was not enough. To qualify for a CDCI investment, an institution had to convince regulators that it was financially viable. CDFIs whose financial status was marginal could qualify by raising matching capital. One of these marginal institutions was ShoreBank. This iconic

---

\* The Lawyers Alliance of New York City, a longtime supporter of CDCUs, provided crucial pro bono legal assistance for many credit union applicants.

community development bank was heavily invested in urban areas devastated by the recession. It had been under a cloud from July 2009, when its weakened financial position triggered a "cease and desist" order from its regulators. During spring and summer 2010, it urgently sought private-sector matching capital. Former Comptroller of the Currency Eugene Ludwig and even former president Bill Clinton joined the effort, which successfully raised commitments of nearly $150 million from some of the largest banks and foundations in the country. Ludwig was optimistic: "In the end, the financial services industry stood together and got this done. ShoreBank is an international symbol of hope for low- and moderate-income citizens, and the banking industry recognizes that it is too important to allow its leadership role to wither away."* But it wasn't enough to win approval from the bank regulators who held its fate: ShoreBank was denied CDCI assistance. On August 20, 2010, ShoreBank was closed. Bank and foundation investors capitalized its successor, the newly formed Urban Partnership Bank, in a loss-sharing arrangement with the FDIC.[1357]

The closing of ShoreBank was contentious. In her book, Sheila Bair expressed her regret, describing the closure of ShoreBank as "heart-rending… a particular tragedy."[1358] One later article captured the bitter irony perceived by some in the CDFI world: "Too Good to Fail."[1359] But the sentiment among CDFIs was not universal: Some in the CDFI movement were convinced that ShoreBank's potential losses far exceeded management estimates and funding commitments (as in fact proved to be true). They believed that it would have been worse to use federal funds to salvage a financially untenable ShoreBank.

The failure of ShoreBank sent tremors through the CDFI field. Would the failure of this, the most prominent community development bank, discredit the CDFI concept and tarnish the CDFI brand? But there was no tsunami of destruction, no chain of CDFI dominoes falling. CDFIs and the CDFI Fund moved on. On September 30, 2010, the Treasury Department announced that the Community Development Capital Initiative (CDCI) would provide $570 million to 84 CDFIs; the most numerous recipients were credit unions (48 institutions), but most of the dollars (88 percent) went to banks.

For those that did win CDCI funding, it was virtually life-saving. In a 2015 interview, Alden J. McDonald, longtime CEO of the African American–owned Liberty Bank and Trust Company, headquartered in New Orleans, recalled:

> After Katrina, we knew we lost our customer-base. It was only a matter of time when they would begin to move their accounts to other institutions, wherever they relocated to; 80 percent of our customer-base was displaced and down, in different states. We were based in—guess what?—the community that nobody else wanted to be placed in, that flooded the most. We lost all of our facilities, and we lost all of our homes, and lost our employees. We had to literally rebuild the bank after 2005.

---

* John D. McKinnon and Dan Fitzpatrick, "ShoreBank Close to Raising $125 Million in Private Capital," *Wall Street Journal*, May 19, 2010, http://www.wsj.com/articles. At the time, Ludwig was CEO of the Promontory Financial Group. The investors included Goldman Sachs Group, Inc.; Citigroup, Inc.; J.P. Morgan Chase & Co.; Bank of America Corp.; and Morgan Stanley.

> TARP [CDCI] was great. Without the TARP money, we would not have been able to acquire and save financial services in the communities that were the hardest hit in the 2008 debacle and still have not recovered today.[1360]

Apart from CDCI, the CDFI Fund not only enjoyed an increase in its "regular" annual appropriation, but it also became the gateway to additional capital resources over 2009-11. The Capital Magnet Fund, established in July 2008 by the Housing and Economic Recovery Act, came on line in 2010, making $80 million in grants available to certified CDFIs and qualified nonprofit housing organizations to expand lending for affordable housing, economic development, and community facilities. The CDFI Bond Guarantee Program was enacted through the Small Business Jobs Act of 2010, providing government guarantees for bonds with a minimum denomination of $100 million and a maximum maturity of 30 years. In 2011, the Healthy Food Financing Initiative was launched, providing CDFIs with $25 million in grants for a program to address "food deserts"—areas with little access to fresh foods, a problem that had engaged First Lady Michelle Obama.

More than ever, "CDFI" became the most valuable brand in community development, an all-but-indispensable resource for institutions seeking to expand their capital and their impact. Twenty years after the establishment of the CDFI Fund, there were scores of institutions that had grown beyond their founders' dreams, and others that, even if they had not expanded as dramatically, had nonetheless managed to survive and serve poor communities despite the worst economic crisis since the Great Depression.

## The Class of 1996 Revisited

In 1996, the CDFI Fund made investments in 32 institutions. Some of the awardees were still in formation; only a minority had operating histories longer than a decade. In effect, the CDFI Fund was making educated bets, informed by strenuous underwriting of the applicants. Rather than spreading out its funds as broadly as possible, its strategy was to invest in institutions that it believed had the potential to make the greatest impact.

Over two decades, there were far too many externalities to criticize the CDFI Fund for any bad bets or congratulate it for its "wins." With that caveat, how did the CDFI Fund's 1996 bets turn out?*

## Twenty-Year Survival Rates

**Microenterprise Funds.** Two funds received awards in 1996. FINCA eventually discontinued its domestic operations, while its parent, FINCA International, continues to work around the world. Accion Texas was rebranded as the LiftFund in 2014, having grown to serve more than a dozen states in the Southeast.

---

\* Please see Appendix 2 for selected profiles of the original awardees after twenty years.

**Loan Funds.** Of the original community development loan fund awardees, only the Cascadia Revolving Fund in Seattle ceased to operate independently. Cascadia, which had received $3.8 million in four financial assistance awards from the CDFI Fund through 1999, merged in 2006 with ShoreBank Enterprise Pacific, creating ShoreBank Enterprise Cascadia (later rebranded as Craft3). Described as "the first merger of its kind in the country,"[1361] the action attracted much attention and support from funders, including Ford, MacArthur, and regional foundations. The merger was assisted by the Ford Foundation, which endorsed it, in the words of Frank DeGiovanni, director of Ford Foundation's Economic Development Unit, "because of its potential to address the region's growing, interconnected issues of poverty, social equity, economic vitality and environmental stewardship at significant scale."[1362]

**Community Development Venture Capital Funds.** Three institutions were selected in 1996. Over the years, Northeast Ventures Corporation in Duluth, MN, received three investments from the fund, totaling $3.4 million. It ceased investing and began to wind down its operations in 2006. After ShoreBank's failure in August 2010, ShoreBridge Capital in Cleveland, OH, separated from ShoreBank's successor, the Urban Partnership Bank. Kentucky Highlands Investment Corporation has continued to thrive.

**"Multi-faceted" Awardees.** The two institutions thus characterized by the fund in 1996 both changed their configurations. Self-Help, which in 1996 included its Ventures Fund and a state-chartered credit union, added a federal credit union under its umbrella and grew enormously. Appalbanc's depository component, the Central Appalachian People's Federal Credit Union, was merged into another, larger credit union, Appalachian Community Federal Credit Union.

**National and Regional Intermediaries.** Rural LISC, which received a CDFI Fund award in 1996, continues to operate under the auspices of its parent, the Local Initiatives Support Corporation. The Tlingit-Haida Regional Housing Corporation created the Haa Yakaawu Financial Corporation to manage its CDFI Fund award in 1996. The parent housing corporation still operates a variety of programs, although it is not currently a CDFI.

**Credit Unions.** Six credit unions were selected by the CDFI Fund in 1996, although two other recipients (Self-Help and Appalbanc) had credit unions as part of their multi-faceted structure, and one (Hope Enterprise) added a credit union later. Of these original six, four continued to serve their low-income communities through 2016.

**Banks.** Southern Development Bancorporation and Louisville Development Corporation both survived. Douglass and Detroit did not.

## The Dynamics of Growth

Microenterprise funds, which typically make small, high-touch loans, have an especially difficult challenge to achieve self-sufficiency; many, if not most, remain grant-dependent. The LiftFund overcame the challenge by developing and implementing an innovative technology platform that not only expedited underwriting, but also made it possible to capture extensive customer data from people who had lived largely in the cash economy. By 2017 Accion was at or near sustainability.

The greatest transformation among the awardees of the Class of 1996 took place among the non-regulated loan funds (see Table 5). Some had been well on their way by 1996: The Local Initiatives Support Corporation (LISC) had been seeded with $10 million in grants from the Ford Foundation and others in 1979; the Illinois Facilities Fund (later IFF) and Delaware Valley Community Reinvestment Fund (later TRF and subsequently RF) were the largest of their cohort in 1996, with more than $20 million each. But most loan funds, especially those with purely grassroots origins, were far smaller in 1996. Twenty years later, a half-dozen loan funds had assets of hundreds of millions of dollars on their balance sheets; some managed hundreds of millions more in off-balance-sheet funds.

The most dramatic financial growth was largely attributable to New Markets Tax Credit allocations, which contributed in multiple ways. Awards typically ranged from several tens of millions of dollars to more than $100 million. The tax credits did not remain on the balance sheets of the CDFIs, but management fees provided significant income and helped build the equity of the recipients. Tax credit allocations enabled these CDFIs to build capacity and credibility, add products, form partnerships, and attract additional debt and equity; several broke into the broader capital markets, winning credit ratings from Standard & Poor's. As they grew in sophistication, they added affiliates and limited liability corporations (LLCs) to manage various rounds of funds. Of the Class of 1996, seven CDFIs, all considered leaders in the field, each won more than $200 million in total CDFI Fund awards, including New Markets Tax Credit allocations: LISC; Boston Community Capital, Inc.; RF (initially, the Delaware Valley Community Reinvestment Fund); LIIF (initially, the Low Income Housing Fund); IFF (formerly the Illinois Facilities Fund); Self-Help; and NFF (the Nonprofit Finance Fund). Hope Enterprise Corporation was slightly behind the top winners, with $125 million in New Markets Tax Credit allocations and some $15 million in grant awards.

In addition to winning tax credits, most of the loan funds that became industry leaders used the full range of CDFI grant programs: the large, "core" financial assistance grants; Health Food Financing Initiative awards; and Capital Magnet Fund awards. Not only were these institutions the largest recipients of CDFI Fund awards—they were also the most frequent, some of them obtaining grants almost every year. As Table 5 shows, a dozen loan funds received between 12 and 32 awards over 1996–2016; except for the microlender, LiftFund, and Kentucky Highlands Investment Corporation, no other type of CDFI received as many as 10. It was not only the assets of the loan funds that grew. Their net worth, or equity base, grew to tens of millions of dollars, yielding ratios of 20 percent to more than 50 percent—far higher than any bank or credit union.

Many large CDFIs expanded their lending to charter schools, community facilities, groceries, and healthy food outlets. Some expanded into additional states, and the New Hampshire Community Loan Fund incubated a national affordable-housing CDFI, ROC USA, which financed the conversion of hundreds of manufactured housing developments into resident owned communities (ROCs). Some formed partnerships with other CDFIs or banks to finance larger projects. Several, including NFF, IFF, and LIIF, established consulting and advisory practices, which brought in additional income and staff while helping to build the CDFI field. Receiving an award in 1996 did not guarantee a leading role for a CDFI loan fund. But a list in 2016 of the leading CDFI loan funds would be heavily weighted to the Class of 1996.

None of the original credit union or bank awardees appear among the top 100 recipients of CDFI Fund investments, largely because they did not directly receive New Markets Tax Credit allocations, although some of their affiliates did. Some obtained multiple awards, but none achieved the frequency or dollar amounts of the leading loan funds. For some CDFI banks, the Bank Enterprise Act (BEA) program proved a far more accessible and productive source of capital than the CDFI Fund's financial assistance awards. (For example, ShoreBank in Chicago received more than $5 million in BEA awards; its operation in Cleveland received more than $1.5 million.)

CDFI depositories faced the challenge of surviving the relentless trend of mergers and consolidation, accelerated by the Great Recession and compounded by a growing compliance burden, which especially strained the capacity of small, understaffed institutions. Over 20 years, the surviving credit unions from the Class of 1996 grew substantially, though not meteorically. Santa Cruz Community Credit Union and First American Credit Union each grew to more than $100 million in assets, from around $20 million and $33 million, respectively; First Legacy Federal Credit Union (formerly School Workers Federal Credit Union) tripled to more than $30 million; and Faith Community United Credit Union in Cleveland grew to $14 million, while establishing a national reputation as a leader in providing alternatives to payday loan.

The greatest growth among credit unions came not from those selected in 1996, but rather those that operated under the "holding company" model. Self-Help expanded its family by chartering a federal credit union in California, which grew dramatically through a dozen mergers there and elsewhere, as well as through the acquisition of a former bank in Chicago. Hope Enterprise Corporation grew far beyond its Jackson, Mississippi roots, to reach parts of Alabama, Arkansas, Louisiana, Mississippi and Tennessee. Its credit union, which began by serving a single church in 1995, has grown to more than $200 million in assets. Self-Help and Hope have both played a vital role in providing financial services in communities which could no longer maintain independent credit unions or which had been abandoned by banks.

Two banks survived from the Class of 1996. The Louisville Development Bank (later Metro) grew modestly, to some $30 million in assets. Southern Bancorp, the Arkansas institution that inspired and won support from Governor Bill Clinton, grew robustly, to more than $1.2 billion in assets, aided by investments from corporations, foundations, and the Community Development Capital Initiative (CDCI). Its nonprofit arm provided volunteer tax assistance and helped build family assets through an Individual Development Account program. Strikingly, Southern's holding company was officially converted to a Public Benefit Corporation in 2017.

Kentucky Highlands Investment Corporation, the "legacy" community development venture capital organization with roots reaching back to the War on Poverty, has continued to play a prominent role in broad regional development efforts in Kentucky and beyond.

## Table 5. The Class of 1996: Twenty Years After

| | 1996 Award | FA Awards # | FA Awards ($ millions) | All Awards ($ millions) | Assets 2015 ($ millions) | Net Worth ($ millions) | Ratio |
|---|---|---|---|---|---|---|---|
| **Microenterprise Funds** | | | | | | | |
| Accion Texas (LiftFund) | $500,000 | 16 | $17.10 | $17.10 | $59.18 | $13.82 | 23.4% |
| FINCA | $450,000 | 1 | $0.45 | $0.45 | closed | -- | -- |
| **Loan Funds** | | | | | | | |
| *Low-Income Investment Fund (LIHF) | $2,500,000 | 32 | $43.73 | $501.73 | $280.62 | $91.25 | 32.5% |
| *Rural LISC (includes LISC) | $1,000,000 | 32 | $40.37 | $1,033.00 | $532.85 | $260.35 | 48.9% |
| *RF (Delaware Valley CRF) | $2,000,000 | 30 | $45.45 | $518.87 | $368.13 | $145.84 | 39.6% |
| *IFF (Illinois Facilities Fund) | $900,000 | 25 | $31.70 | $239.70 | $329.34 | $82.79 | 25.1% |
| *Boston Community Capital (incl. Boston CLF) | $1,000,000 | 22 | $23.44 | $546.45 | $142.05 | $39.49 | 27.8% |
| *NFF (Nonprofit Finance Fund) | $1,000,000 | 21 | $17.84 | $298.84 | $76.17 | $39.47 | 51.8% |
| New Hampshire Community Loan Fund | $1,000,000 | 16 | $25.47 | $25.47 | $113.05 | $23.01 | 20.4% |
| *Rural Community Assistance Corp | $1,700,000 | 16 | $19.29 | $27.29 | $98.22 | $34.57 | 35.2% |
| Community LF of Southwestern PA (Bridgeway) | $280,000 | 14 | $16.36 | $16.36 | $61.04 | $30.69 | 50.3% |
| *Hope Enterprise (Enterprise Corp. of the Delta) | $2,000,000 | 14 | $15.10 | $140.10 | $52.03 | $25.32 | 48.7% |
| Vermont Community Loan Fund | $167,500 | 13 | $9.86 | $9.86 | $35.75 | $9.80 | 27.4% |
| *Self-Help Ventures Fund | $3,000,000 | 12 | $12.00 | $340.00 | $674.06 | $426.50 | 63.3% |
| FAHE (Appalbanc) | $1,330,000 | 9 | $9.91 | $9.91 | $54.33 | $25.07 | 46.1% |
| Cascadia Revolving Fund | $600,000 | 4 | $3.80 | $3.80 | merged | -- | -- |
| Neighborhoods, Inc. | $1,350,000 | 3 | $2.41 | $2.41 | $4.72 | $4.31 | 91.3% |
| NHS of Richmond | $250,000 | 2 | $0.27 | $0.27 | $2.31 | $0.97 | 42.0% |
| Haa Yakaawu (Tlingit-Haida) | $1,025,000 | 1 | $1.03 | $1.03 | $91.91 | $71.31 | 77.6% |

| | | | | | |
|---|---|---|---|---|---|
| **Banks** | | | | | |
| Southern Development Bancorporation (1) | $2,000,000 | 8 | $9.90 | $1,178.13 | $122.56 | 10.4% |
| *Louisville Development Bancorp | $2,336,000 | 5 | $2.34 | $126.84 | $30.99 | $5.45 | 17.6% |
| Detroit Development Bancorp | $3,000,000 | 1 | $3.00 | closed | -- | -- |
| Douglass Bancorp | $1,903,000 | 1 | $1.90 | closed | -- | -- |
| **Credit Unions** | | | | | |
| Self-Help Federal Credit Union | | 7 | $14.55 | $611.88 | $32.82 | 5.4% |
| First Legacy FCU (School Workers) | $150,000 | 7 | $5.47 | $35.01 | $6.00 | 17.1% |
| Santa Cruz CU | $1,000,000 | 5 | $5.20 | $107.20 | $6.12 | 5.7% |
| Self-Help Credit Union | | 4 | $3.97 | $714.92 | $62.60 | 8.8% |
| Bethex FCU | $100,000 | 8 | $1.66 | merged | -- |
| First American CU | $1,000,000 | 1 | $1.00 | $111.08 | $8.37 | 7.5% |
| Faith Community CU | $350,000 | 1 | $0.35 | $13.19 | $2.60 | 19.7% |
| Quitman County FCU | $127,500 | 4 | $0.33 | merged | -- |
| **CD Venture Funds** | | | | | |
| *Kentucky Highlands | $450,000 | 15 | $14.09 | $78.28 | $57.53 | 73.5% |
| Northeast Ventures Corp | $1,250,000 | 3 | $3.30 | closed | -- |
| ShoreBridge Capital | $1,500,000 | 2 | $1.55 | merged | -- |

*FA includes Financial Assistance, Healthy Food Financing Initiative, Capital Magnet Fund*

*Total includes FA + New Markets Tax Credit allocations*

*Bank Enterprise Awards not included.*

\* Includes New Markets Tax Credits

\*\* Assets and net worth are from IRS 990 filings.

(1) Southern Bancorp figures are from Consolidated Balance Sheet. Net worth is total Shareholders' Equity.

# CHAPTER 24. Reflections on Democratic Finance

By 2017, there were more than 1,000 organizations in the United States certified by the United States Treasury Department as CDFIs. (Many more do similar work but either have not sought certification or let it lapse.) They are loan funds and credit unions, banks and venture funds. Some have hundreds of millions in assets (or more), do sophisticated deals, and work regionally or even across the country; others are small, local organizations with a modest number of clients or activities. All would describe themselves as "mission-driven" rather than simply profit-maximizing. But they use different tools and have different accountabilities, cultures, and challenges. Each type of institution has a trade association; they mostly go their parallel—sometimes competitive—ways. Beyond sharing the CDFI brand and a desire to maximize federal resources, what unites these institutions? Did they—do they—constitute a movement? An industry? A field?

Credit unions, an important sector of the CDFI world, began as a movement, and a populist one at that. As one key leader described it, it was a crusade, driven by organizers who spread the gospel of credit unions across the country to groups of working people hungry for the promise of equitable finance.[1363] Quasi-religious fervor inspired the credit union movement—and sometimes the impetus was literally religious. Indeed, the first credit union, St. Mary's Bank in New Hampshire, was based in a Catholic parish, as were many that followed. Some early leaders of the credit union movement expressly tied it to values of Christian brotherhood (although Edward Filene, the movement's philanthropic patron, was Jewish, as were some in his circle). Filene was far from a charismatic figure. But in January 1933, late in his life, when he addressed a gathering of more than 1,000 people in Chicago, he was surprised and overwhelmed by the rapturous response. As described by a journalist attending the meeting: "There was a spiritual fervor in the attitude of these folks from parishes and farms, from factories and stores, from railroads and shops, towards a man who, for the most part, had been almost a legendary figure in the background of a movement that promises to become a great economic force in this country."[1364] As President Franklin D. Roosevelt remarked in a tribute upon Filene's death in 1937, "He was a prophet who perceived the true meaning of these changing times."[1365]

The secular passion that drove the credit union movement was the commitment to democracy. Credit unions were fervently democratic—not only in their own governance, based on one member, one vote, but also in their political philosophy. Although Filene was not a socialist, he viewed credit unions as the schools for the masses so that they may be educated to establish financial democracy for themselves and free their jobs and themselves from the absolute control of those who ... are using money solely for their own profit, without the requisite understanding that they have no right to use money except for the common good and social interest of all the people, and that the wholly selfish use of it will bring with it radical movement[s], revolution and war.[1366]

The radical movements that troubled Filene in the 1930s were fascism and communism. Cooperativism, in contrast, was a profoundly democratic "third way." (Nonetheless, the anti-radical ethos of cooperativism did not spare credit unions from being labeled "communist" by their right-wing opponents.)

The single most powerful voice in the early development of CDFI loan funds was Chuck Matthei, founder of the Institute for Community Economics (ICE) and cofounder of the National Association of Community Development Loan Funds. Matthei was profoundly influenced by Gandhian philosophy and his years with Dorothy Day's Catholic Worker Movement. He forged an austerely communal lifestyle for ICE in Western Massachusetts, a kind of secular counterpart to a religious community. Matthei was an evangelist, first for community land trusts and then for community development loan funds, traveling with a powerful message of aligning investment with social values.[1367] But although faith-based organizations were absolutely crucial in capitalizing early CDFIs, and although significant faith-based CDFIs—like the Leviticus Fund and Partners for the Common Good—have been created, the CDFI field on the whole has always been ideologically and culturally secular, with the notable exception of many African American faith-based credit unions.

The CDFI movement was fed by multiple oppositional streams. The early founders came from campaigns against apartheid, redlining, nuclear power, poverty, and racial discrimination. The closest, most explicit ties to the civil rights movement were found in the South, where African Americans formed credit unions in economic self-defense, because they were excluded from banks whether because of general racism or specifically as punishment for fighting for the right to vote. CDFIs of various types shared a common commitment to rectify injustice and equalize opportunity. But there was no overarching philosophy—certainly, not socialism.

Barely five years after its founding in 1985, the 45 or 50 members of the National Association of Community Development Loan Funds were vigorously debating whether they constituted a movement at all—or rather, were they an industry? Clara Miller, founder of the Nonprofit Facilities Fund (later Nonprofit Finance Fund) who served later as chair of the National Association of Community Development Loan Funds (later OFN) characterized the debate this way: Are we going to be an organization that will focus on performance, and have the elite get resources and become real players, or be a big tent, a "marginal protest organization"?[1368] To Jeremy Nowak, founder of the Delaware Valley Community Reinvestment Fund, the answer was not "either/or," but rather "both": Loan funds constituted both an industry and a movement.

Successful movements evolve. The "movement vs. industry" question often becomes intertwined with the question of "mission drift." By the 1940s, the president of the Credit Union National Association (CUNA) was worried that many credit unions "don't want to be bothered with $50 or $100 loans for remedial purposes," a prime reason that credit unions were organized to begin with.[1369] This criticism only sharpened in the next decade. In May 1952, one national leader complained that some credit unions were losing sight of their original purposes: "They operate as a cross between a bank and a loan company. The members' welfare and benefit is not their chief purpose.... We find many credit unions that have none of the original board left, and somehow we have neglected to tell these new directors about the purpose of the credit union movement."[1370] The tensions became still more acute in the 1960s, when CUNA tried, with misgivings, to play a role in the ill-starred War on Poverty campaign to foster credit unions in low-income communities.[1371] Thereafter, the "mainstream" movement disengaged, which created the space and the demand for the formation of the National Federation of Community Development Credit Unions in 1974.

The advent of deposit insurance for credit unions was a turning point. Backed for the first time by a federal guarantee for member deposits, credit unions grew dramatically in size and complexity. The debate tilted decisively toward "industry," as credit unions developed an ecosystem of trade associations, consultants, vendors, a strong Washington lobbying arm, and political action committees. In 1980, there were more than 20,000 credit unions in the United States; by 2017, after decades of consolidation, there were 5,600 credit unions—fewer, but larger. Credit unions collectively had aggregate assets of more than $1.3 trillion and more than 110 million members; the largest credit union, Navy Federal Credit Union, had more than $90 billion in assets and served more than 7.5 million members. Credit unions were successful; they had reached scale. Undoubtedly, they were an industry, with scores of industry financial benchmarks closely watched and sometimes set by regulators. Within the credit union industry, there remained a *movement*—the 200 or so institutions dedicated to serving low-income and minority populations, the National Federation of Community Development Credit Unions.

Thirty years into their collective history, some CDFIs—loan funds, in particular—are confronting the question of mission drift. In the early 1990s, the National Association of Community Development Loan Funds put forth a broad critique of the banking system, coupled with demands to extend the Community Reinvestment Act (CRA) to nonbank financial institutions and government-sponsored entities. But by the mid-1990s, when the CDFI Fund was launched, banks had become the largest source of private-sector matching capital for CDFIs (at least those in the CRA "footprints" of banks—not so much in rural areas and the South).[1372] Banks invested in, with, and through CDFIs, through their foundations, corporate giving, and community development departments; Bank of America, for example, has provided more than $1.5 billion to CDFIs in loans, deposits, investments, and capital grants over the course of 20 years. Unquestionably, bank support has been a key element in the growth of the CDFI field.

However, certain tensions have come with the relationship. In a 2016 study for the Opportunity Finance Network (OFN), Jeremy Nowak wrote:

CDFIs emerged as critics of conventional finance, but are now overwhelmingly capitalized by the banking industry.... The dilemma of being both partner and critic reached its sharpest point during the run up to the Great Recession when many CDFI leaders criticized the practices of subprime lending, including the role of those banks that enabled it.[1373]

The tension has persisted. The Consumer Financial Protection Bureau, launched in 2011, has fined some of the largest bank supporters of CDFIs hundreds of millions of dollars for abusing customers; Wells Fargo, in particular, opened millions of phony accounts, deceptively sold unwanted insurance, and more.[1374]

In a 2015 interview by the author, Clara Miller expressed the hope that "we're not becoming a fig leaf for banks that have basically stopped serving the public."[1375] CDFI loan funds were born to take the credit risks that banks shunned. Questions are being voiced privately or sometimes publicly: Are they still on the margins, the cutting edge? Have they become more concerned with making the loans and deals that keep their financial performance strong enough to win awards in the next CDFI Fund round, rather than focusing on the most pressing societal needs? Miller, who moved to the F.B. Heron Foundation after her decades heading the Nonprofit Finance Fund, framed the question for philanthropy, but it resonates for CDFIs as well: "We foundations often refer to ourselves as 'risk capital for society,' but last year [2014] we were reminded often that the real risk of failure is not primarily borne by us, but by both the potential beneficiaries of the enterprises we finance and by those enterprises themselves."[1376] Sister Corinne Florek of the Adrian Dominicans—one of the earliest CDFI investors, which risked placing their retirement money in the hands of untried, small organizations at the dawn of the CDFI era—has powerfully raised the same question, not to criticize, but to remind and re-inspire CDFIs. As Mark Regier of Everence (formerly Mennonite Mutual Aid) has put it, the early faith-based investments were a "prophetic act," driven by the primacy of a vision of social justice. Regier, who has shepherded socially responsible investment for Everence for nearly 20 years and who is a board member of the Social Investment Forum, has characterized the challenge for CDFIs this way: "How do we professionalize that process, how do we move it from a prophetic act that's solely run on justice, to one that says, 'Now, wait a minute, justice without sustainability is a sort of fleeting experience.'"[1377]

In summary, how to characterize the multitude of institutions—banks, credit unions, loan funds, venture funds, microenterprise organizations? The various subsectors have their separate cultures, regulatory and accounting issues, and priorities. They share a common goal of preserving and expanding access to federal resources, especially the CDFI Fund. They all seek to channel capital to those who lack access. But they are not collectively advancing a broader societal critique or agenda for change. There are elements both of movement and of industry. But it is perhaps most accurate to describe CDFI simply as a field, composed of subsectors that are not mutually dependent. ShoreBank, the iconic community development bank, inspired the CDFI field but never led it (nor intended to). And when it failed in August 2010, its demise did not produce a tsunami discrediting the field and washing away scores of CDFIs, as some had feared.

In 2015, there were rumblings that certain CDFIs were considering refusing to repay loans to banks even though they had the capacity to do so. In cofounding the community development loan fund movement decades before, Chuck Matthei had written, "We have to understand that the performance of any one will ultimately reflect on all the others. None of us can afford serious mistakes on the part of the others. We will, in the old figure of speech, sink or swim together."[1378] That no longer seems an accurate description of the CDFI field.

## Democratizing Finance: The Limits of Empowerment

In an article published after ShoreBank's demise, its cofounder, Ron Grzywinski, summarized his bank's impact this way: "We have made it legitimate for ourselves and others to use the nation's banking system to advance the cause of development. More broadly, we have contributed … to democratizing the availability of private nongovernment credit to low income and otherwise disadvantaged people. And we have done that in many parts of the world."[1379] It is a major accomplishment, for which ShoreBank's founders are rightly honored throughout community development circles. CDFIs of various types have brought credit and financial services to people, businesses, and nonprofits who would otherwise have been excluded.

But what the community development banking initiative has *not* done is maximize community or democratic ownership of financial institutions. There was no legislative mandate for the CDFI Fund to do so, but there was explicit encouragement in the statute: The fund is to consider in its awards "the extent to which the applicant is, or will be, community-owned or community-governed."[1380] In practice, a weaker standard prevails, requiring a CDFI's "accountability" to its target community. However, the primarily accountability of banks—even CDFI banks—is to their shareholders, and of venture capital funds to their investors. Nonprofit loan funds generally are not bound by the same legal strictures, but they are also at some level accountable to their investors, which may include banks, foundations, the CDFI Fund itself, and sometimes, individuals; it is rare to find one that is governed or owned by a community or by its borrowers.[1381]

There are, in fact, CDFIs that are owned and governed by their members or communities. Credit unions, regardless of size, retain a strictly democratic structure: one member, one vote, regardless of the amount of a member's deposits in the institution; there are no outside shareholders. But on average, only a small portion of CDFI funding went to these institutions. The CDFI Fund has played a singularly important role in nurturing another type of community-owned institution: namely, Native American CDFIs, the only group for whom a "set-aside" in CDFI Fund awards was established. The First Nations Development Institute was instrumental in including "American Indian–specific language in the Community Development Financial Institutions Fund (CDFI Fund) legislation."[1382] Since 2000, some 73 Native CDFIs, primarily loan funds, have been established. For generations,

Native American communities have struggled to gain control of the assets held in trust and administered by the paternalistic Bureau of Indian Affairs. The defining innovation of the CDFI Fund—providing equity capital and grants without continuing federal control or supervision over their use—was an important step toward empowerment for Native CDFIs, most of which are predominantly or entirely controlled by members of their tribe, nation, or community. "Native Community Development Financial Institutions (Native CDFIs) offer a locally controlled, community-responsive resource for credit and other financial services to support asset-based development in Native communities," as the First Nations Development Institute has written.[1383] As Sherry Salway Black (Oglala Lakota) put it, "This has been an opportunity to really address some of the needs out there for access to capital and credit. And it came at a time when it was all about self-determination in communities, self-determination of the tribes, self-governance."[1384]

Notwithstanding the examples of credit unions and Native American CDFIs, much of the CDFI movement does not descend from the tradition of "maximum feasible participation" of the poor advanced in the War on Poverty of the 1960s. Rather, it reflects the other tendency of that era—community development directed and implemented by managers with technical and financial skills.[1385] These CDFIs are "for" the people; they do vital, challenging work in improving communities, but they are not "of" and "by" the people. In an interview several months before his retirement in 2016, Michael Rubinger, longtime CEO of LISC, reflected on the roles and limitations of CDFIs, particularly the largest community development loan funds: "I think [community development] needs CDFIs, because certainly we need conduits for capital. But you need a place to put the capital. I'm not being exclusive here. I'm not saying there's not a place for for-profit or regional CDFIs, but that should not be to the exclusion of neighborhood-based or more local kinds of organizations who really are representative of those communities in ways that the big CDFIs and the regionals are not."[1386]

These "big" CDFIs perform; they deliver capital and contribute significantly to improving the quality of life in poor communities. But they are not radically democratic institutions.* As Antony Bugg-Levine, who came from impact investing to head the Nonprofit Finance Fund, put it, "I feel like within the CDFI world, we have self-selected to be the non-radical, kind of wonky part of this broad spectrum of social justice imperatives. And we shouldn't be defensive sometimes and act like we can be the fire-brand radicals. We have our role."[1387]

Apart from structural issues in CDFI governance, Bugg-Levine and Ellis Carr have called attention to the composition of the leadership of CDFIs themselves. "Let's be blunt," they wrote, "Our industry's leadership is less racially diverse and gender balanced than we need to be.... [We need to

---

\* Hence, Mehrsa Baradaran's scathing contrast of the CDFI field with the origins of credit unions in the United States: "The CDBA [Community Development Banking Act] was not intended to change the business of banking to meet the needs of the poor but to fit the needs of the poor into the business of banking. Unlike the Progressive and the Populist movements that brought about the credit union and the savings and loan, the CDBA movement was rooted in the market ethos that defines modern banking." Source: Mehrsa Baradaran, *How the Other Half Banks* (Cambridge: Harvard University Press, 2015), 169.

focus] on not just the effects of the capital we provide but also who is empowered to provide it."[1388] Over the past several years, the topic has repeatedly emerged at CDFI conferences. A session at the 2018 CDFI Coalition conference was dedicated to exploring how "CDFIs must now look through a racial equity lens with the goal of cultivating more equitable opportunities for underbanked and underserved communities, including communities of color. People of color, and the places where they live, continue to experience higher rates of poverty and economic isolation, with few opportunities available to build the assets and access the capital required for them and their families to escape the cycle of poverty."

## The Shape of Success: The Banking Dilemma

"Community development banking" has been a public policy success—but more so in community development than in banking.

As of 2017, more than a thousand institutions are certified as CDFIs, with combined assets estimated to exceed $130 billion. CDFIs have played a valuable role in expanding the conventional boundaries of finance, creating hundreds of thousands of housing units and financing child care centers, health clinics, and other community facilities. "CDFI" has become the most valued brand in community development. Nationally, the U.S. Departments of Agriculture, Housing and Urban Development, and the Small Business Administration have opened their programs to certified CDFIs, thanks to the participation of federal agencies on the CDFI Fund Advisory Board. At the state level, the New York State Economic Development Corporation established a program for CDFIs. In the private sector, foundations and social investors have increased their investments in CDFIs.

But what of regulated depository institutions—the banks and credit unions that provide small-scale credit, savings, and retail services for minority and low-income communities? As Paul Weinstein, a key presidential adviser who helped develop the community development banking program, recalled, "What the President had in mind was full-service [institutions]. It wasn't just about investment, it was also about credit, and it was about banking services, because we were heavily focused on the unbanked. That was a big deal for us. We wanted more people to have access to banking services."[1389] In a 1997 speech celebrating microenterprise funds, First Lady Hillary Clinton, a longtime supporter of the CDFI initiative, shared her vision of a reinvigorated, locally oriented banking system: "What I would like to see 5 [or] 10 years from now, [is] community banks that are free-standing private banks…back in neighborhoods, back on street corners—banks like I used to remember when I was growing up, with people being able, with advances in technology, to get small loans again."[1390] When the CDFI Fund legislation was finalized, it directed the fund to consider "whether the applicant is, or will become, an insured community development financial institution"[1391]—that is, a bank or credit union.[1392] There is little evidence that this consideration has weighed heavily in the fund's investments.

What, in fact, has become of banking during the CDFI era? In particular, what has been the fate of minority banks and credit unions? Obviously, First Lady Hillary Clinton's dream of seeing banks "back in neighborhoods, back on street corners—banks like I used to remember"[1393] has not been realized. Rather, since the CDFI Fund was established in 1994, the numbers of banks and credit unions in the United States have each declined by about half. The trend has been especially bleak for African American–owned banks. Researchers for the Federal Reserve Bank of Chicago noted that "the disproportionate impact of the financial crisis and housing market shocks on racial and ethnic minority neighborhoods" was accompanied by "higher rates of failures and closures [of minority-owned community banks] relative to nonminority bank peers."[1394] Drawing on FDIC data, they counted 48 banks and thrifts identified as African American–owned or with majority African American boards of directors in 2001; by 2015, there were 27.[1395] Similarly, there was a marked decline in credit unions serving African American communities.[1396] Liquidations or forced mergers eliminated scores of African American credit unions. Historically black credit unions disappeared in the Deep South, where many traced their roots to the civil rights movement. In North Carolina, almost no African American credit unions remain where once there were dozens. The Northeast, Ohio, and other areas that have a long history of church-based credit unions have seen many fade away.

Banks and credit unions that serve predominantly minority, especially African American, low-income populations have always faced special challenges. They serve capital-poor communities, with costly labor-intensive customer bases of small depositors and borrowers; it is thus difficult to achieve profitability and build equity. Recognizing the dilemma, Congress included Section 308 in the Financial Institutions Reform, Recovery, and Enforcement Act (FIRREA) of 1989, which set regulatory goals, including preserving the number and character of minority depositories and promoting and encouraging the creation of new such institutions.[1397] As the CDFI legislation was taking shape in mid-1993, the National Bankers Association, which represented black-owned and other minority- and women-owned banks, wrote to Senate Banking Committee Chairman Don Riegle, calling attention to FIRREA and urging that these banks "should be given a preference, based on the specialized financial services that we already provide to economically disadvantaged communities."[1398] However, Congress did not choose to apply Section 308 to the CDFI Fund, which is not a regulator. Although many minority- and women-owned banks have become certified CDFIs, the fund did not prioritize investment in these significant yet vulnerable institutions, asserting that the CDFI statute would prohibit it from doing so.

Equity is crucial to growth; one dollar of equity enables a bank or credit union to raise multiple additional deposit dollars while remaining in compliance with regulatory capital-to-assets ratios.[1399] It is difficult for small banks in general, and African American banks in particular, to raise equity through the capital markets. The federal Minority Bank Deposit Program provides access to market-rate deposits, which can be helpful but are of limited value. Low-income credit unions, which cannot raise equity from capital markets, struggle to incrementally increase their equity or net worth year to year by retaining any earnings generated by their operations.

It is not surprising, then, that the establishment of the CDFI Fund—a unique source of equity—raised such elevated hopes for minority banks and community development credit unions. Those institutions that have won CDFI Fund investments have benefited greatly. For an African American–owned bank, like Liberty Bank and Trust in New Orleans, it was actually the Bank Enterprise Award (BEA) program, which provides cash awards, that proved the most helpful. Alden McDonald, its longtime CEO, remarked:

> the BEA program was very, very key to our ability to take more risks, because we knew we had that extra income to write off more loans. We always had more charge-offs than the marketplace. Low balance, high volume business killed us, right? It's still killing us today in operating these institutions. The BEA Award not only offset the additional risks that were being taken, but also the additional cost of operating a branch in the areas that others were leaving."[1400]

But neither minority banks nor credit unions fared well in competing against loan funds for CDFI Fund Financial Assistance ("FA") awards of grants and equity investments. Nor have they been among the greatest beneficiaries of the New Markets Tax Credit program, which turbocharged the growth of some loan funds. The trends dismayed McDonald. The fund's New Markets Tax Credit awards helped Liberty to cross-subsidize its high-cost, limited-return banking business by doing larger commercial deals. But "we don't get New Markets Tax Credits anymore," McDonald lamented. "The large banks with all of their resources are able to put a better package together for the application process, and probably show more leveraging, if that's what the CDFI folks are looking for. It has become more what I'm going to call an investment banking-type program. The New Markets Tax Credit has been out of reach."[1401]

There are two aspects to the FIRREA Section 308 policy: on the one hand, "preserving the number and character of minority depositories"; on the other, "promot[ing] and encourag[ing] creation of new minority depository institutions." Both tasks are difficult. Existing minority depositories struggle against the strong tide of market forces that have decimated the ranks of small depositories in general. Entry barriers for new institutions—regulatory, financial, and technological—have become ever more daunting. But if not the CDFI Fund, then what other entity could make a difference in helping ensure a future for minority banks and credit unions? As noted above, the fund asserts it does not have the statutory authority to prioritize this task; however, other interpretations of the legislation are plausible. Whether through legislative or policy changes, the CDFI Fund still has the potential to increase its impact on these vulnerable sectors of the financial marketplace. Saurabh Narain, CEO of the National Community Investment Fund, which was founded by ShoreBank and which works with many minority institutions, offered this perspective on African American–owned banks: "They're struggling, because they haven't evolved. From a public policy perspective, we need to save them. As an investor, we need to help them evolve."[1402]

## People and Place in Community Development

The case for expanding the CDFI Fund's support for credit unions and banks goes beyond achieving distributional balance. As Antony Bugg-Levine and Ellis Carr have framed it: "Our generation is called to answer a new question: How can community development finance make a measurable contribution to addressing the inequality and injustice that continue to undermine our national aspirations?"[1403] The question is not new; Treasury Secretary Robert Rubin himself raised it in 1995 in a forum on income disparity. But it is, if anything, more pressing. It is not only the lack of income that perpetuates poverty—it is also the lack of assets. Michael Sherraden powerfully advanced this argument in his seminal book, *Assets and the Poor: A New American Welfare Policy* (1991); Melvin Oliver and Thomas Shapiro deepened the discussion with *Black Wealth / White Wealth: A New Perspective on Racial Inequality* (1995).

There are two main streams of community development: place-based, typically reflected in physical development, and people-based. Several years after the establishment of the CDFI Fund, researchers noted this in a report to the John D. and Catherine T. MacArthur Foundation.

> CDFIs (with the exception of credit unions and a few microenterprise organizations) have only recently begun taking an interest in personal asset-building and savings strategies. Community development finance has historically been defined in terms of lending rather than savings. However, the changes in the financial services industry are likely to have as much detrimental impact on savings opportunities for low-income communities as on credit availability.[1404]

More recently, Bugg-Levine reflected on the "disconnect" in the CDFI world—the "idea that we define our success by physical places becoming better off rather than looking through the place to say, 'The people who were living there is the purpose of all this work.'"[1405] Frank DeGiovanni, who ran the Ford Foundation's Program-Related Investment and economic development units, questioned "whether CDFI [loan funds] really are focused on poverty alleviation or not. I see CDFIs as primarily about developing communities and not so much about reducing poverty."[1406] The Ford Foundation supported community development credit unions, ShoreBank, and other depositories "because they [help build] savings, and for us, savings are critical, because it's how you build assets. Most of our work now focuses on asset-building as a strategy for moving people out of poverty."[1407]

The growth of the asset-building movement from the 1990s offered a potential bridge between place-based and people-based community development. Sherraden's insights translated into federal, state, and private support for Individual Development Accounts (IDAs), Child Savings Accounts, and other asset-building initiatives. Bob Friedman, a founder of the microenterprise movement, has observed that "the growth of the asset-building movement has paralleled, and hopefully overlaps with, the CDFI movement."[1408] IDAs were eagerly adopted by segments of the CDFI movement, especially credit unions and microenterprise funds, although they have less been used by CDFI loan funds, with prominent exceptions like the Opportunity Fund in California.[1409]

The wealth gap, and especially the racial wealth gap, has stubbornly persisted, aggravated by the Great Recession; black families' median and mean net worth is less than 15 percent that of white families, and the figures for Hispanic families are only slightly higher.[1410] The Federal Reserve Board reported that "forty-four percent of adults say they either could not cover an emergency expense costing $400, or would cover it by selling something or borrowing money," while "twenty-six percent of all adults and 54 percent of non-Hispanic black adults are either unbanked or underbanked."[1411] Community development banks and credit unions cannot solve the problem themselves, but they are indispensable to preserving and building assets, both in providing basic banking services, access to affordable credit, and savings accounts—mundane services that are essential to an integrated strategy of community development and poverty alleviation.

## Building a Sustainable Network

The Trump administration's first budget, released early in 2017, called for eliminating program funding for the CDFI Fund; the second administration budget, in 2018, repeated that call. A divided Congress rejected both proposals, in an impressive display of bipartisan support for the CDFI Fund. But the specter of eliminating the fund, though banished at least temporarily, raised the question of a future for the CDFI field without the infusions of equity that the fund uniquely provides.

The challenge of self-sufficiency is greatest for microenterprise programs—the other half of Bill Clinton's envisioned network of "100 community development banks and 1,000 microenterprise programs." It is rooted in their business model of making high-touch self-employment and small-business loans, often accompanied by substantial support or, in the language of the CDFI Fund, "development" services. The LiftFund (formerly Accion Texas) has perhaps come the closest, with an innovative shared platform and automated underwriting. But even that organization has approached break-even by offering larger loans guaranteed by the Small Business Administration, which serve to essentially "cross-subsidize" LiftFund's core business of small-dollar lending.[1412] Few other standalone microlenders have reached that level (although microlending continues to be practiced successfully within other community development organizations).

The question of sustainability of CDFIs remains relevant even if congressional support has so far warded off the Trump administration's efforts to eliminate the CDFI Fund. Nonprofit loan funds, which depend on grants, are especially at risk, although some of the largest funds have substantial net worth that all but ensures their sustainability.* Some in the field believe that contraction or consolidation is likely—and perhaps inevitable. Nancy Andrews, CEO of the Low Income Investment Fund, one of the largest and most prominent CDFIs, believes that "we don't need 1,000 CDFIs. [Not] little,

---

\* Please see Chapter 23.

tiny CDFIs. We need a thousand really big CDFIs making big investments. But that's not going to happen without the federal subsidy or the state and local subsidy that supports the creation of affordable housing, early learning, and so forth."[1413] The culture and structure of the CDFI field have impeded it from achieving its potential. After two decades of the CDFI Fund, the field largely is populated by hundreds of vertically integrated small institutions, each with its own back office, human relations department, and underwriting and collections units. The loan fund sector, in particular, has made limited progress in developing shared infrastructure and common platforms. Michael Swack, one of the founders of the loan fund movement, believes that "some progress is now being made through, for example, [the Community Reinvestment Fund's] Spark platform which standardizes a lot of these operations on a platform. [But] I believe the future of CDFI sustainability will depend on creating CDFIs that really do collaborate—using technology to support shared operating platforms on the one hand, and building connections that allow us to serve more people with more products."[1414]

For the most part, the sustainability of CDFI banks and credit unions does not hinge on the CDFI Fund or federal funding in general. They are predicated on self-sufficiency and sustainability. Their ability to grow, deepen their services, and innovate might be limited by the loss of the CDFI Fund, but none would perish as a result. Rather, threats to their survival come from broader economic and regulatory trends. As to community development venture funds, they have never received a large portion of their capital from the CDFI Fund. Even if the CDFI Fund were to disappear, it would not profoundly impact the sector.

## Growth Prospects for the CDFI Field

Of the 1,094 certified CDFIs as of March 2017,* loan funds numbered 556, while credit unions had increased their ranks to 297 and banks and bank holding companies numbered 224. Only 17 certified institutions were community development venture capital funds. Although loan funds still represented about half of all CDFIs, their proportion has declined, especially since 2010, as banks and credit unions sought certification in order to access the Community Development Capital Initiative (CDCI) and, from 2013, to benefit from exemptions from certain Consumer Financial Protection Bureau (CFPB) mortgage lending regulations. The impressive growth in the aggregate assets of the CDFI field to more than $130 billion by 2017 came largely through additional certifications of credit unions and banks, among which were several institutions with billions in assets. As of 2016, banks and credit unions accounted for about 87 percent of all CDFI assets.[1415]

---

\* The figure varies month to month, as additional institutions have been certified and others have let their certification lapse, typically because they have not received or expect to receive funding. Because some apparently qualified institutions have never sought the designation, official figures underestimate the size of the CDFI universe.

For the most part, the increase in the ranks of CDFI banks and credit unions has *not* come through the founding of new institutions, but rather through existing institutions obtaining certification. Few new CDFI banks and credit unions have been chartered; in fact, chartering of banks and credit unions in general has been very limited over the past 20 years. From 1995 through 2017, 22 new community development banks were chartered.[1416] Over that period, 170 credit unions of all types were chartered, of which 110 were low-income; about 40 percent are still active. Since 2010, an average of about three new credit unions were chartered each year; a total of 14 low-income credit unions were chartered, including one in 2016 and three in 2017.[1417]

Community groups working to organize new community development credit unions have been disappointed that the CDFI Fund is not a source of startup capital. The barriers to chartering a new credit union have risen enormously since the early- to mid-twentieth century, when seven individuals each pledging five dollars could obtain a charter. Today, an applicant must provide a business plan demonstrating "economic viability" from the outset, a big challenge unless it can demonstrate firm commitments of equity contributions (not merely deposits). This capital is necessary to help a new credit union absorb operating losses, which are virtually inevitable during a credit union's first few years until it builds a substantial loan portfolio. To start any but a volunteer-run, limited-service credit union, an applicant typically must raise a half-million dollars or more in pledges of donated equity. It is common for community groups to work for three years or more to amass the necessary commitments—by which time many run out of organizing support and/or abandon their efforts. The CDFI Fund could have played a major role in incubating dozens of credit unions in low-income communities by providing advance commitments, even if those commitments were conditional on a group's obtaining a charter. But the fund's own regulations constrain it: An organizing group cannot receive investments or commitments from the fund because the credit union itself does not yet exist as a legal financial entity, and the group cannot give assurances with a high degree of certainty that it will obtain a charter.*

For those groups that have surmounted the barriers and obtained a charter, CDFI Fund awards have been enormously helpful. The Latino Community Credit Union, headquartered in Durham, NC, is the most successful startup in CDCU history. Started in 2000 with financial and in-kind assistance from Self-Help and the State Employees Credit Union of North Carolina, it has grown to more than $275 million in assets, serving a primarily immigrant membership of 75,000 with 11 branches.[1418] The CDFI Fund has been essential to its unprecedented growth, providing 15 grants for more than $15 million from 2000 through 2017. There are few similar stories. Local, cooperatively owned and democratically governed credit unions are enormously appealing to community groups hungry for empowerment. Movements like Occupy Wall Street and Black Lives Matter have rekindled interest

---

\* In contrast, an established organization that plans to become a CDFI is not excluded from funding.

in starting credit unions.* Unfortunately, they cannot count on the CDFI Fund for commitments of seed capital. A regulatory or technical legislative reform could change that.

In summary, if spawning a new generation of financial institutions seems unlikely, and if multiplication of small CDFIs is not a path to greater impact, then what is? The larger, stronger CDFIs have extended their reach geographically, as well as in terms of products, and they may continue to do so. Developing a common infrastructure for CDFIs, although difficult, would make a difference. Finally, "mission conversion" by existing institutions may prove a viable path for the expansion of community development finance. Some long-established, recently certified credit unions and banks serve hundreds of thousands of individuals. They have the potential to make "CDFIs" if not a household word, then nonetheless institutions with greater impact than the field has yet known.

## Conclusion

At the ceremony at the U.S. Treasury Department on October 1, 2014 marking the twentieth anniversary of the CDFI Fund, Gene Sperling† reflected: "CDFI was a minor story when it passed but look now: a thousand CDFIs. Look at the role the CDFIs play and the stability role they [provided] during the crisis, when other banks did far worse: the over 2 billion given out, the multiples of the loans, the lives that are changed because of that."[1419]

"CDFI" is an important success story, even if it has not come in quite the shape that some activists (the author included) and President Clinton envisioned. In its origins, it is a case study in institution-building made possible by small groups of risk-taking social entrepreneurs; by faith-based organizations that put their money where their beliefs were; by foundations that were willing to use new tools and partners; by legislators who were jolted into action by the flames of an urban uprising in South Central Los Angeles; and, of course, by a Southern governor running for president inspired by a singular bank in Chicago and one that provided loans to the impoverished population of Bangladesh.

"We never believed," said Martin Eakes of the Center for Community Self-Help, "that community development credit unions or community development financial institutions would ever be large enough as a sector to be an alternative delivery system to the U.S. banking system for development loans. What we did believe was that we could be engaged in real projects and learn what would work and not work, and translate that into social change through policy activities, through policy change."[1420]

---

\* After the killings of African Americans Jamar Clark (2015) and Philando Castile (2016) by the police in Minneapolis, the local Association for Black Economic Power and the nonprofit community organization Blexit decided to organize a black-led credit union in North Minneapolis. Camille Erickson, "Black-led credit union in North Minneapolis is 'the most important work' to drive economic vitality," *Twin Cities Daily Planet*, July 31, 2017. The name proposed for the credit union is Village Trust Financial Cooperative.

† Sperling served as deputy director (1993–96) and later as director of the National Economic Council under President Clinton.

If CDFIs have not achieved a wholesale transformation of the banking system, they have nonetheless shaped policy in various ways. Self-Help's nonprofit affiliate, the Center for Responsible Lending, has been an influential voice on predatory lending and other financial policies. RF (the Reinvestment Fund) created PolicyMap, a tool for identifying areas of need, such as "food deserts"; its work was instrumental in the development of the CDFI Fund's Healthy Food Financing Initiative. Hope Enterprise Corporation in Mississippi, IFF in Chicago, and Boston Community Capital, among others, advocate on statewide and national issues. CDFI leaders, some of whom sat on the CDFI Fund's Community Advisory Board, successfully helped shape the Community Development Capital Initiative, without which the Troubled Assets Relief Program (TARP) would not have reached the financial institutions serving communities most in need of help. CDFIs pioneered the introduction of new capital instruments: Community development credit unions obtained regulatory changes that enable low-income credit unions to obtain equity-like subordinated debt, while OFN obtained approval for an equity equivalent product, "EQ2," for loan funds. CDFIs won recognition from the Consumer Financial Protection Bureau, which provided them an exemption from certain new mortgage regulations.

Michael Barr, former senior Treasury official, put the CDFI Fund in perspective this way.

> When I look back over the last twenty years, if you think about the ability to establish the CDFI Fund from scratch in a quite challenging political environment, and to have it exist and sustain itself for [two decades], it's kind of stunning. The approach to community development that it embodied was novel, and in some ways still is novel—that the funding to the community from the CDFI Fund would not be programmatic; that it would not be dictated by the Fund, that it would not be dictated by the Congress; that the funds would flow not to units of state and local government or governmental creations, but directly to nonprofits and communities—I think it's kind of remarkable.[1421]

\* \* \*

# PART VIII. Epilogue

After eight years of generous support under the Obama administration, the advent of the Trump administration brought a new challenge to the CDFI field. The Office of Management and Budget (OMB) released a proposed budget on March 13, 2017, that called for eliminating appropriations for the CDFI Fund, except for certain ongoing program management tasks. The proposal bore the imprint of the conservative Heritage Foundation, which demanded, "Eliminate the Community Development Financial Institutions Fund. This proposal saves $238 million in FY 2017."[1422] It repeated its demand in its *Blueprint for Balance: A Federal Budget for Fiscal Year 2018*.[1423] The Heritage Foundation's rationale could only leave CDFI proponents scratching their heads: "The CDFI fund should be shut down because it amounts to corporate welfare. Furthermore, the grants hinder competition and distort private markets, ultimately leading to higher consumer prices and further justification for increased federal spending." OMB provided a less apocalyptic rationale: "The CDFI Fund was created more than 20 years ago to jump-start a now mature industry where private institutions have ready access to the capital needed to extend credit and provide financial services to underserved communities."[1424]

Notwithstanding the Trump administration's proposal, Congress passed a final CDFI budget for FY 2017 of $248 million, the largest appropriation in the fund's history. On September 19, 2017, the CDFI Fund announced one of the largest funding rounds in its history: $171.1 million in financial and technical assistance to 265 organizations in 46 states and the District of Columbia; $22 million for 13 CDFIs through the Healthy Food Financing Initiative financial assistance awards; and $15.6 million to 38 organizations through the Native American CDFI program. Demand was strong, possibly stimulated in part by the uncertain prospects for the fund's continuation: Some 434 eligible organizations had applied.

There was good news for banks and credit unions. The CDFI Fund had instituted a revised application "designed, in part, to make it easier for CDFIs to demonstrate the impact they'd be able to achieve with an award regardless of what type of financial institution they are. As a result, the percentage of the 224 CDFIs that received CDFI Program Financial Assistance awards in the FY 2017 round closely mirrored the percentage of institution types that applied."[1425] Consequently, credit unions and banks both exceeded their historical shares: A total of 55 credit unions received $39.4 million (23 percent), while 27 banks received $24.3 million (14 percent). Together, depositories accounted for $63.7 million, about 37 percent of the total, the greatest proportion depositories had received since the fund's first year. Representatives of the National Federation of Community Development Credit Unions and the Community Development Bankers Association were cautiously optimistic that the results heralded a new direction for the CDFI Fund, more responsive to the need to provide basic financial services to low-income and underserved populations.

As the Trump administration moved into its second year, its FY 2019 budget, released in February 2018, again called to eliminate appropriations for CDFI grant programs; once again, the rationale was that the CDFI industry was now "mature," and that "private institutions should have ready access to the capital needed to extend credit and provide financial services to underserved communities."[1426] As the CDFI Coalition pointed out, "All told, the budget would reduce federal outlays for community and regional development to…its lowest level as a share of GDP since at least 1962."[1427] Thus, CDFIs would be obliged to continue relying on the bipartisan support of Congress that they had impressively built up over the years.

# APPENDIX 1. Profiles of the "Class of 1996"

## Microenterprise Funds

The Grameen Bank of Bangladesh, founded by Muhammad Yunus, had inspired Governor Bill Clinton's call for 1,000 microenterprise programs, along with community development banks. In her travels to the Third World, First Lady Hillary Clinton had been inspired by her visits to microlending projects. Microenterprise was still a very young field in the United States, but the first family's enthusiasm would lead to the first Presidential Awards for Excellence in Microenterprise Development, presented in a White House ceremony on January 30, 1997—a major boost for the field's visibility.

**FINCA**, which received a $450,000 award, was established in 1984 with the concept of "village banking," a peer-group lending approach based on collective guarantees of groups of borrowers. An international organization that had begun in Latin America and the Caribbean, in 1994 FINCA launched a domestic operation in the Baltimore-Washington area and rural Minnesota, focusing on self-employment for low-income people. By the time of its CDFI award, FINCA had made 100 loans of $500–$6,000 to entrepreneurs, overwhelmingly to women (85 percent), nearly two-thirds of whom were the primary or sole income-earners in their households.[1428]

**Accion** Texas, also formed in 1994, "has adapted the lessons of Accion International's Latin American experience."[1429] Accion International's track record lent credibility to the organizations it started in several cities across the United States with large Hispanic populations. Based in San Antonio, Accion Texas served low-income and Hispanic entrepreneurs. Led by Janie Barrera, the organization proposed to use its $500,000 award to help it scale up: At the time of its application, its loan portfolio was $250,000, built with the aid of $125,000 in interest-free startup loans (Frost Bank, Wells Fargo, and Broadway Bank) and grants (Levi-Strauss, $50,000), which it obtained with the assistance of its board chair, Alfonso Martinez-Fonts, who was also chairman of the Greater San Antonio Chamber of Commerce and president of Texas Commerce Bank's San Antonio unit.[1430]

## Community Development Venture Capital Funds

**Kentucky Highlands Investment Corporation (KHIC)** was perhaps the most prominent organization of its type, working in a nine-county rural area of Southeast Kentucky, where poverty rates ranged from 30 percent to 45 percent. Launched in 1968 during the War on Poverty as Job Star Corporation, KHIC was one of the community development corporations (CDCs) funded by the Office of Economic Opportunity, and specifically, one of the first community development venture capital organizations.[1431] Over its 28-year history, it had made $40 million in risk capital investments, accounting for 40 percent of all the manufacturing jobs in the region. It received a grant of $450,000 from the CDFI Fund.

**Northeast Ventures Corporation,** based in Duluth, MN, won a $1.25 million equity award from the fund. Like Kentucky Highlands, it was rural, serving an area economically devastated by a shrinking mining industry. Formed in 1990, Northeast Ventures was part of the new generation of community development venture capital organizations, which invested in small, young enterprises dedicated to revitalizing the local economy. The corporation attracted shareholders from the Northwest Area Foundation, Blandin Foundation, and Minnesota Power; the Ford and MacArthur foundations also made Program-Related Investments. By the time of its CDFI Fund award, Northeast Ventures had attracted almost $8 million in investment capital and had invested in 14 companies, creating 161 full-time jobs in the Iron Range region.

**ShoreBridge Capital,** although part of the ShoreBank family, was a proposed community development venture capital fund rather than a bank. It was managed by Cleveland Enterprise Group, a nonprofit affiliate of Cleveland Development Bancorporation, a subsidiary of ShoreBank Corporation. It won an award of $1.5 million, half of which was to go for equity in ShoreBridge, with the balance to go as a grant to the Cleveland Enterprise Group. Its goal was to link labor force development with business development and expansion; it would operate in coordination with an Empowerment Zone—not a requirement of the CDFI Fund, but a linkage that the Clinton team had always sought to encourage.

## Community Development Banks

As governor, Bill Clinton had highlighted **Southern Development Bancorporation** as a model for community development banking. In making its award to Southern in 1996, the CDFI Fund noted that Southern was "demonstrating that a bank holding company, with appropriate affiliates and subsidiaries, can be profitable while achieving important community development objectives."[1432] The fund awarded $1 million for an equity investment in Southern and $1 million as a grant to its nonprofit Arkansas Enterprise Group. The award was to fund a major expansion of banking operations into the Arkansas Delta—a region where African American poverty rates exceeded 65 percent—as part of a "comprehensive program directed to commercial and housing lending, real estate development, small business expansion, venture capital and microenterprise lending."[1433]

**Douglass Bancorp,** founded in 1946, was the oldest African American–owned bank west of the Mississippi. The only minority bank among the CDFI Fund's awardees, "it is now focusing on becoming a community development bank," forging alliances with neighborhood organizations and expanding from its Kansas City, KS, base to Kansas City, MO. The fund made its award despite the bank's relatively recent financial troubles, declaring that Douglass had since "engineered a remarkable financial turnaround."[1434] The $1.903 million investment ($1.75 million in equity, $153,000 in technical assistance) was intended to enhance the capital of the bank's holding company.

**Louisville Development Bancorp** won an award package of $2.336 million, of which $2 million was equity. Not yet operational, this holding company would have three subsidiaries: a full-service bank emphasizing small-business lending, home improvement, and mortgages; a real estate development company; and a nonprofit enterprise development center. As early as 1992, the mayor of Louisville had convened local business, civic, and religious leaders to develop a comprehensive plan for the inner city, which brought the city designation as an Enterprise Community. The bank holding company was an integral part of the plan.

**Detroit Development Bancorporation** (later ShoreBank, Detroit) won the CDFI Fund's largest award, a $3 million equity investment that was to support a comprehensive new initiative on the east side of Detroit. A holding company would include a full-service bank; a for-profit real estate development company that would develop 500 homes; and a nonprofit enterprise development affiliate that would assist small manufacturers, create a labor force development strategy, and provide first-time homebuyer training and assistance. The holding company was to be a subsidiary of ShoreBank; the plan was to raise $20 million in capital.[1435]

## Community Development Credit Unions (CDCUs)

The fund selected six credit unions serving poverty communities from the South Bronx to the Navajo Nation. They served populations that had long been excluded from financial services by segregation and racial discrimination, redlining, geographic isolation, and denial of credit to women. As a group, CDCUs were by far the oldest of any awardees—the earliest started in 1941, and none later than 1981. Although bank awardees included startups and those still in the formative stage, no prospective credit unions were funded: Credit union organizing groups were ineligible because they did not yet constitute corporate entities. (This disparity would be a continuing frustration for the CDCU movement: Awards from the CDFI Fund could have greatly accelerated the chartering process for credit union organizing groups.)

Not only were the credit unions older and more established than most other recipients: They were also larger than almost all other awardees, except for some of the banks. First American Credit Union had $33 million in assets, and Santa Cruz Community Credit Union had $20 million; each of the member-owned cooperatives served thousands of members. Santa Cruz and First American each received $1 million awards; the other credit unions received awards that were generally below the CDFI Fund's average. In aggregate, CDCUs received $2.73 million, about 7.3 percent of the total funding. Awards came as grants, which the recipients matched with their retained earnings. With increased net worth, the credit unions were able to leverage their awards several times over with additional deposits, all the while maintaining the crucial net worth–to–total assets ratio their regulators required.

**Bethex Federal Credit Union** (chartered in 1970; $100,000 award) began life in a church basement in New York City's South Bronx. Founded by Joy Cousminer[1436] with students in her adult education classes, the credit union long operated on volunteer labor. It served single mothers and women receiving public assistance, who had a doubly difficult time accessing affordable credit in their own names; they typically relied on pawn shops, loan sharks, and check-cashers for their financial services. Located in one of the poorest congressional districts in the country—family income was about one-third of the New York–area median—the resource-poor credit union had been repeatedly forced to move around the South Bronx until it found permanent facilities.

**Faith Community United Credit Union** (1957; $200,000 grant, $150,000 in technical assistance) was founded as the Mount Sinai Baptist Church Credit Union. For decades, it served the predominantly African American community on the East Side of Cleveland with an unpaid staff, including Mrs. Rita Haynes, one of its first volunteers who later served as manager.[1437] Aided by grants from the Lilly Endowment, the Gund Foundation, and the Cleveland Foundation, in 1990 it expanded into the community and changed its name to reflect its broader mission. Faith Community United Credit Union was a beneficiary of the Community Reinvestment Act: When Key Bank was closing its branch in the neighborhood, the credit union, with the help of the WECO community organization, persuaded the bank to donate its facility. Thus, Faith completed its transition from a small, borrowed space in a church to a modern, standalone building complete with a parking lot and membership of 2,500.

**First American Credit Union** (1962; $1 million) began operations in a trailer in Window Rock, AZ, serving employees of the Navajo Nation. Later, it expanded to serve 15,000 Native Americans of tribes and reservations throughout Arizona and in parts of New Mexico and Utah. In addition to basic consumer financial services, the credit union provided small-business loans to agricultural ventures and Native American craft enterprises. With $33 million in assets, First American was the largest CDCU in the country. By assets and people served, it was also one of the largest recipients of CDFI funding of any kind.[1438] To better serve its vast, sparsely settled rural market, the credit union planned to use funding to install ATMs and explore purchasing a mobile branch.

**Quitman County Federal Credit Union** (1981; $100,000 grant, $27,500 in technical assistance) was founded in Marks, MS. It served the rural Mississippi Delta region, perpetually ranked among the poorest in the country. Its population, almost entirely African American and 56 percent below the poverty line, had long been denied access to credit by segregation; local banks were often owned by the descendants of plantation owners. The credit union's membership of 1,325 amounted to nearly half of Quitman County's black households. Led by Robert Jackson, the credit union operated in tandem with a community development corporation.[1439] It planned to expand financing for home improvement and residential construction.

**Santa Cruz Community Credit Union** (1977; $1 million grant) was located in a university community on the northern California coast. It was one of the largest CDCUs in the country, with $20 million in assets and more than 6,100 members. A full-service retail institution, it had topped $100 million in cumulative lending, $37 million of which had gone specifically for community development loans, including small businesses, nonprofits, cooperatives, and environmentally screened agricultural operations. In his press conference announcing the awards, Secretary Rubin highlighted one of the credit union's borrowers, the Odwalla juice company, which began with a $1,200 loan from Santa Cruz Community Credit Union and grew to become a publicly traded company. The CDFI Fund award was designated for opening a branch office serving a low-income, largely Latino farmworker community in Watsonville.

**School Workers Federal Credit Union** (1941; $150,000 grant) was founded in Charlotte, NC, during the era of segregation to serve African American employees who were excluded from the white teachers' credit union. North Carolina was the home of the country's largest cluster of credit unions owned and managed by African Americans, and School Workers Federal Credit Union was arguably the strongest of this group: by 1996, it had $10 million in assets and served 2,700 members, concentrated in Charlotte's low-income West Side neighborhood, which was underserved by traditional lenders.

## Multi-Faceted CDFIs

Two awardees were described as "multi-faceted community development financial institutions"—nonprofit organizations with multiple lending or investing units.

**Appalbanc,** based in Berea, KY, brought three components under a single umbrella in 1994: the Federation of Appalachian Housing Enterprises (FAHE); the Human Economic Appalachian Development Community Loan Fund (HEAD); and the Central Appalachian Peoples Federal Credit Union (CAPFCU). Appalbanc had a distinctive model for reaching a widespread market of some of the poorest areas of rural America: Working with a network of nonprofits, it served 85 counties of Central Appalachia, including parts of Kentucky, Tennessee, West Virginia, and Virginia. Its three-part structure, which included a regulated depository (the credit union) and nonprofit loan funds, enabled it to meet a range of credit needs, for housing, small business, and consumer loans. Through its affiliates, it had financed the development or rehabilitation of more than 20,000 homes. Appalbanc won a package of $1.33 million from the CDFI Fund: a grant of $370,000; a loan of $930,000; and $30,000 in technical assistance.

**Self-Help,** which was launched in 1980, referred to itself as a "statewide development bank." Its structure included the parent nonprofit, the Center for Community Self-Help; the state-chartered Self-Help Credit Union; and the Self-Help Ventures Fund, which, despite its name, primarily engaged in lending rather than equity investment. Self-Help won the CDFI Fund's largest award, $3 million, which it designated for its Ventures Fund. In making the award, the CDFI Fund noted particularly Self-Help's secondary market initiative—an innovative, scalable program to purchase mortgages from banks, thus freeing its resources to make additional loans to low-income homebuyers and "having significant impact in transforming conventional loan underwriting standards." Based in Durham, Self-Help had five regional offices in North Carolina.

## Community Development Loan Funds

Nonprofit community development loan funds were the most numerous of the awardees. Among their ranks were five founding members of the National Association of Community Development Loan Funds in 1985; several more had been formed over the following five years, while the youngest of the loan funds was formed in 1994.

As unregulated institutions, loan funds were unable to offer investors insured deposits; however, because they were generally incorporated as 501(c)(3) charities, they were eligible to obtain grants from foundations and offer tax deductions to individual donors. Several built their asset bases through hundreds of individual donations and loans from individuals, religious organizations, and local businesses. Foundation support had grown in the 1990s: The pioneering investors in CDFIs—Ford and MacArthur, especially—had been joined by many others, including the Pew Charitable Trusts, the W. K. Kellogg Foundation, the Chicago Community Trust, the Lilly Endowment, the Gund Foundation, and the Cleveland Foundation. CDFIs in New York, Philadelphia, Chicago, San Francisco, and other major cities increasingly obtained investments from banks; rural CDFIs in areas like the Southeast were rarely so fortunate.

Most of the loan funds focused on affordable housing. Their services ranged from homeowner counseling (a priority for the two affiliates of the NeighborWorks network), to financing home repair and rehabilitation; down-payment assistance; cooperative ownership conversion; and complex multi-family housing partnerships with banks. However, especially in rural areas and those that had suffered declines in manufacturing, lending for small business and entrepreneurship was also important.

**Boston Community Loan Fund (BCLF),** founded in 1984 with $3,500 in a grant from Old South Church plus loans from individuals, began as an affordable housing lender focused on neighborhoods in and around Boston. At the time of its 1996 CDFI Fund award of $1 million (half as a grant, half as a loan), BCLF had $6.8 million in assets and had expanded to serve communities in Eastern Massachusetts. It lent for housing for persons with special needs and community facilities, including daycare centers and health clinics.

**Cascadia Revolving Fund,** established in 1985, focused on economically distressed areas in Washington and Northwestern Oregon. By 1990, it had reached $500,000 in assets, lending to nonprofits, environmental businesses, and cooperatives, especially in communities whose workers had been displaced from forestry, fishing, or other natural-resource businesses.[1440] As of 1996, it had made a total of 100 loans. By partnering with other financial service providers, Cascadia enabled borrowers to access the loan programs of the Small Business Administration and other government agencies. Cascadia obtained a $600,000 grant from the CDFI Fund.

**Community Loan Fund of Southwestern Pennsylvania,** which won a grant of $250,000 and a technical assistance award of $30,000, was established in 1990 by the Religious Leadership Forum of the Pittsburgh area. It served low-income neighborhoods of Pittsburgh and 19 rural communities that had suffered from the demise of the steel industry. With its dramatically increased net worth from the CDFI Fund's award and nonfederal matching funds, the Community Loan Fund planned to ramp up its work stimulating local entrepreneurship.

**Delaware Valley Community Reinvestment Fund (DVCRF)** received a $2 million award, half as a grant and half as a loan. Based in Philadelphia, it served the most distressed neighborhoods in its metropolitan area: sections of Philadelphia itself, as well as Chester, PA, and Camden, NJ, where DVCRF had brought congressional staff on a site visit. The fund and its subsidiaries specialized in financing affordable housing, providing training and technical assistance to community development corporations, and making equity investments in businesses in distressed communities. Since its founding in 1985, it had attracted 700 investors and grown to $20.8 million in assets.[1441]

**Enterprise Corporation of the Delta,** headquartered in Jackson, MS, was a startup loan fund serving a 55-county market in the impoverished Delta counties of Arkansas, as well as Louisiana and Mississippi. The fund had been launched in 1994 with support from the Pew Charitable Trusts, Entergy Corporation, and the Walton Family Foundation. Agriculture had historically been central to the region's culture and its commercial lending, but the sector employed only a small percentage of the population. Creating employment was a pressing concern, given the high rate of poverty—as much as 40 percent in parts of Enterprise's market area. With a $2 million grant from the fund, Enterprise would focus its financing on small manufacturers and other businesses with the potential to create jobs for low-income people.

**Low Income Housing Fund (LIHF).** Founded 11 years earlier, LIHF received $2.5 million as a grant of $1.2 million and a loan of $1.3 million. By the time of its award, it had financed and/or provided technical assistance for the development of 15,000 units of affordable housing. Housing for persons with special needs—the frail low-income elderly, persons with disabilities, and people with AIDS—accounted for 40 percent of its portfolio. Headquartered in San Francisco, LIHF had added offices in Los Angeles and New York and had financed housing in 20 states. LIHF worked extensively with banks, both negotiating loans on behalf of nonprofit borrowers and managing three lending pools capitalized by nearly 40 financial institutions.[1442]

**New Hampshire Community Loan Fund (NHCLF).** Manufactured homes, typically found in mobile home parks, are a widespread, crucial source of affordable housing, especially for low-income people. Before the establishment of the New Hampshire Community Loan Fund in 1983, residents of these communities seeking to ensure a stable place to live found it virtually impossible to obtain bank financing. The New Hampshire Community Loan Fund perfected a financing model for converting the parks into resident-owned cooperatives. By 1996, it had closed 200 loans for more than $11 million. Its pioneering work encouraged commercial lenders in New England to enter the manufactured housing market. Capitalized by investments from hundreds of individuals, faith-based organizations, philanthropies, and businesses, NHCLF won a $1 million grant from the CDFI Fund in 1996.

**Vermont Community Loan Fund,** which received a grant of $150,000 and $17,5000 in technical assistance funding, was launched in 1987. One of its first loans was to the Brattleboro Community Land Trust for $5,075. Within three years, it had loaned $1 million for affordable housing; by 1991, it had broadened its lending to serve other community needs, including nonprofits and community facilities, and by 1996, it was loaning to small businesses.

**Neighborhoods, Inc.,** of Battle Creek, MI, received a $1.35 million grant in October 1996 when the CDFI Fund reallocated the unspent balance of the BEA program. Founded in 1981, with a priority on housing-related services, the nonprofit became a charter member of the NeighborWorks America network in 1991. In the five years leading up to its award, it had made $8.5 million in loans; approximately half of its 600 loans went for home purchases, the other half for home improvements. The W.K. Kellogg Foundation of Battle Creek was a major supporter of the organization, which also attracted investments from local corporations, banks, government, and community organizations.

**Richmond Neighborhood Housing Services,** founded in 1982, received a total of $250,000 (a grant of $120,000 and a loan of $130,000). The Virginia organization focused on the distressed Barton Heights neighborhood. Collaborating with local banks and city government, it developed programs for emergency repairs for low-income elderly homeowners; home improvement; and below-market second mortgages. Its Neighborhood Ownership Works program had enabled 100 families to become homeowners.

**Rural Community Assistance Corporation (RCAC),** founded in 1978 and based in Sacramento, CA, was one of several awardees that bridged eras in community development. RCAC had its roots in Self-Help Enterprises, an organization that specialized in organizing low-income farmworkers to build their own homes. As in the case of many organizations that became CDFIs, Self-Help Enterprises benefited from the support of a faith-based organization, the American Friends Service Committee. A $15,000 grant from the Rosenberg Foundation helped Self-Help Enterprises to spin off the Rural Community Assistance Corporation in October 1978; within a year, grants from three federal agencies established RCAC as a regional provider of technical assistance for rural community development.[1443] Responding to the needs of farmworker housing and other groups for financial as well as technical assistance, in 1988 RCAC established its loan program.[1444] In 1996, RCAC won a CDFI Fund award of $1.7 million, of which $900,000 was a grant and $800,000 was a loan.

Two CDFI loan funds with parallel histories served the needs of nonprofit organizations. Both were incubated by foundations, the Illinois Facilities Fund (IFF) by the Chicago Community Trust and the Nonprofit Facilities Fund (NFF) by the New York Community Trust; similarly, both had origins in energy conservation issues. "We really had to make the case that housing or housing plus health clinics were not the only positives,' recalls Clara Miller of NFF."[1445] "We were slightly problematic for the Fund, because we were different from other CDFIs," partly because NFF financed arts and other cultural organizations and because, like commercial lenders, it looked at income streams rather than real estate collateral. "We were constantly pushing the box."[1446]

# Appendix 1. Profiles of the "Class of 1996"

**Nonprofit Facilities Fund,** which was founded in 1980 in New York City as the Energy Conservation Fund, received a $1 million loan from the CDFI Fund. By 1996, it had made over $11 million in loans to arts and cultural facilities, community service centers, health facilities, and child care centers, with the support of a broad range of funders, including banks, insurance companies, foundations, and public agencies.[1447] The CDFI Fund's award was designated to assist NFF's work not only in New York City, but also in Boston, Chicago, Philadelphia, and San Francisco. In 1996, President Clinton appointed NFF's executive director, Clara Miller, to the U.S. Treasury's first Community Development Advisory Board for the CDFI Fund, which she later chaired.

**Illinois Facilities Fund (IFF)** was incorporated in 1988 and led by Trinita Logue, who had served as assistant director of the Chicago Community Trust. It made its first loans in 1990, aided by a $1.75 million grant from the Trust. By 1991, its loan portfolio was approaching $3 million, and it had established itself as a real estate consultant for nonprofits. By 1996, the fund had raised major foundation and bank grants and investments, including a $750,000 Program-Related Investment from the John D. and Catherine T. MacArthur Foundation. A $2 million grant from the Chicago Community Trust had enabled IFF to facilitate an innovative $18.6 million bond deal to construct child care centers in Illinois neighborhoods, some of which had not seen new construction for 25 years. An innovative pool funded by six banks provided for the purchase of up to $10 million in trust notes collateralized by IFF. By December 31, 1995, IFF reported total assets of $25.1 million, with net worth of nearly $9.0 million.[1448] In 1996, it received a $900,000 grant from the CDFI Fund.

**Rural LISC** was characterized in a category of its own by the CDFI Fund as "national financial and technical services community development intermediary." Rural LISC was formed in 1995 as a program of the Local Initiatives Support Corporation (LISC), the nation's largest community development support corporation. Rural LISC's parent, LISC, had been launched in 1979 with a $10 million grant from the Ford Foundation and several corporations to support community development corporations (CDCs).[1449] Although LISC's CDC constituency was primarily engaged in urban real estate development and operations, the CDFI Fund's $1 million grant in 1996 was designated for LISC's year-old effort to support dozens of CDCs in nonmetropolitan areas.

**Tlingit-Haida Regional Housing,** categorized as a Native American regional organization, was part of an organization whose history dated to 1973. It served communities so remote that many could be reached only by boat or airplane. Tlingit-Haida had provided affordable housing through purchase or rental assistance for more than 700 primarily Native American households. The CDFI award of $1.025 million ($1 million in a loan, $25,000 in technical assistance) went to the organization's startup enterprise, required because the parent organization prioritized development, not lending; the authority's new affiliate for lending was called Haa Yakaawu Financial Corporation, translated as "one who represents your face, or a trading partner for life."[1450] "Our affiliation with Native corporations and Indian country was important," Executive Director Jacqueline Johnson later noted. "We presented it as a model that we would like to replicate in Indian country in other areas."[1451] With its award, the organization would initiate affordable mortgage lending in the high-cost urban areas of Juneau, Ketchikan, and Sitka, AK.

# APPENDIX 2.
# Selected Profiles: The Class of 1996 Revisited

## Microenterprise: LiftFund/Accion Texas

For microenterprise lenders, scale and sustainability are daunting challenges, since their business is based on relatively small, labor-intensive loans to borrowers who often lack the sophistication of bank borrowers. Accion Texas found a successful path through technology. As CEO Janie Barrera described it, "From 1998, we have used technology to capture the data from our customers. We save that. Most customers take two or three loans with us before they 'graduate' and go to the bank. We report to credit bureaus. We have data on people who only use cash. We have people who don't use a credit card. We have data on startups."[1452]

Accion Texas, headquartered in San Antonio, received a $500,000 CDFI Fund award in 1996, when it was barely two years old, having made its first loan in June 1994. Over the next five years, organizations invited it to establish offices in El Paso, the Rio Grande Valley, Houston, Austin, and Dallas/Fort Worth. Its shared technology platform, which has evolved into a comprehensive, web-based underwriting platform, the Microloan Management Services® (MMS®), has enabled its broader expansion. After 2000, Accion Texas became a 13-state operation with a staff of more than 100. In 2008, it began offering its platform to outside organizations, and in 2014 it rebranded as the LiftFund. By 2016, LiftFund's annual lending volume reached $30 million; cumulatively, it had made nearly 20,000 small-business loans totaling more than $200 million.

No microenterprise fund has better addressed the challenge of self-sufficiency than LiftFund. By expanding its products to include larger loans, including Small Business Administration 7A loans, the fund neared break-even when its average loan size reached $19,000. The larger loans "cross-subsidize" the fund's traditional business of offering loans as small as $500. Janie Barrera, the former Sister of the Incarnate Word and Blessed Sacrament community (Corpus Christi, TX) who became Accion Texas's first executive director in 1994, has guided it through its dramatic growth ever since.

Appendix 2. Selected Profiles: The Class of 1996 Revisited

## The "Bank Holding Companies": Southern Bancorp, Self-Help, Hope Enterprise Corporation

Governor Bill Clinton's vision of community development banking was greatly influenced by the bank holding company model developed by South Shore Bank, which recognized early that it needed to add nonprofit and for-profit affiliates to fulfill its community development mission.

**Southern Bancorp** (previously Southern Development Bancorporation) in Arkansas, which Governor Clinton and ShoreBank helped start, grew robustly from 1996, aided by a total of $9.9 million in eight financial assistance awards from the CDFI Fund. With additional capital from corporations and foundations, Southern grew through acquisitions in economically distressed communities in rural South Arkansas, the Arkansas Delta, and later, throughout the Mississippi Delta. In 2010, Southern received a $33.8 million investment under the TARP Community Development Capital Initiative (CDCI), which it paid off with interest in November 2016.

By 2016, Southern Bancorp reached $1.2 billion in assets and 44 locations, serving over 65,000 customers across two states through its wholly owned subsidiary bank and its nonprofit, Southern Bancorp Community Partners (also a CDFI). In addition to its financial services, Southern has provided free income tax preparation to thousands of people through the VITA program; operated an Individual Development Account (IDA) program to promote family asset-building; and conducted public policy advocacy on issues such as the state minimum wage and payday lending. In March 2017, Southern Bancorp's shareholders approved the conversion of the bank holding company into a public-benefit corporation, which Delaware law defines as one "that balances the stockholders' pecuniary interests, the best interest of those materially affected by the corporation's conduct, and the public benefit or public benefits identified in its certificate of incorporation."[1453] Darrin L. Williams, today the CEO of Southern Bancorp, Inc., served as chief deputy attorney general for the State of Arkansas under Governor Clinton.

**Self-Help** was the model for a bank holding company without a bank. Although many original CDFI awardees—particularly loan funds—grew dramatically, none matched the increase in scale, scope, and outreach of Self-Help. Initially focused primarily on its home state of North Carolina, in 1998, its secondary market program expanded nationally with the aid of a $50 million grant from the Ford Foundation. In 2008, Self-Help took the unprecedented step of establishing a second credit union under its "holding company" umbrella: the Self-Help Federal Credit Union in Oakland, CA. The parent provided a major infusion of equity-like secondary capital, as well as primary capital, aided by a PRI of $30 million and a grant of $2 million in 2009 from the Ford Foundation.

Self-Help Federal Credit Union grew rapidly, largely through mergers with 12 other credit unions whose history and mission made them a good fit. In many cases, the institutions it acquired were casualties of the Great Recession. Without Self-Help's intervention, the low-income communities they served—many of which were majority Latino—likely would have been left with no affordable financial services. Among these institutions was a California credit union started in 1963 by the United Farm Workers (led by Cesar and Helen Chavez and Dolores Huerta). In southwest Chicago,

Self-Help acquired three branches from a closed bank that was originally founded to serve European immigrants and that had served Mexican immigrants for decades. In 2015, Self-Help took in a struggling Florida credit union founded by nuns that had served migrant and seasonal farmworkers for more than 30 years. By 2017, the two Self-Help credit unions served more than 125,000 members in North Carolina, California, Illinois, and Florida.

The various arms of Self-Help all won awards from the CDFI Fund. In the first round in 1996, the Self-Help Ventures Fund won a $3 million award. Over the course of two decades, the Ventures Fund received $328 million in New Markets Tax Credit allocations, as well as $12 million in financial assistance awards; the Self-Help Credit Union won nearly $4 million; and the Self-Help Federal Credit Union (chartered in 2008) won $14.6 million in financial assistance. In total, Self-Help received nearly $359 million in grants and tax credit allocations.

Along with two other CDFIs—Coastal Enterprises, Inc. and LISC—Self-Help was part of the original working group that helped draft the New Markets Tax Credit (NMTC) legislation. The NMTC greatly fueled Self-Help's growth and expanded its commercial lending capacity. In 2003, Self-Help received an allocation in the program's first round that enabled it to provide $40 million in financing to redevelop the campus of the American Tobacco factory in Durham, NC, thus catalyzing a dramatic revitalization of the city's long neglected downtown.

As of 2016, Self-Help controlled more than $2 billion in assets: $745 million in the original Self-Help Credit Union; $716 million in the Self-Help Federal Credit Union; and $676 million in the Self-Help Ventures Fund. Apart from its financial units, Self-Help started and supports a nationally prominent advocacy arm, the Center for Responsible Lending.

**Hope Enterprise Corporation** provides another powerful example of a nonprofit loan fund working in tandem with a credit union. The nonprofit loan fund received a $2 million grant in 1996; by the end of 2015, it had reached $52 million in assets. Like Self-Help, Hope's growth owed much to the $125 million it received in New Markets Tax Credit allocations. These capital infusions enabled Hope to expand the scope of its financing and provide services statewide in Arkansas, Louisiana, and Mississippi, and in southwest Tennessee. Its Hope Charter School Facilities Fund, which received seed funding from a Department of Education grant, helps build, equip, and modernize schools. Hope has used tax credits to finance the municipally owned Field Memorial Community Hospital (Centreville, MS), the only hospital in a 40-mile radius.

Hope Federal Credit Union (FCU) was born as Mississippi's only state-chartered, church-sponsored credit union, founded through the efforts of Anderson United Methodist Church. By 2000, the credit union had expanded its field of membership to 28 churches; then, in 2002, Hope Enterprise Corporation became the sponsor of this formerly volunteer-run operation. Between 2004 and 2007, fueled by Hope's innovative use of its initial New Markets Tax Credit allocation, the credit union grew from approximately $4 million to $48 million in assets, and from 4,000 to 9,000 members. Like Self-Help FCU, Hope FCU's growth was accelerated by mergers with other credit unions, including College Station Community FCU (Arkansas), which had deep roots in the civil rights movement and the War on Poverty, and American Savings Credit Union (Memphis, TN). In 2010, the credit union was awarded $4.52 million in secondary capital under the Community Development Capital Initiative. By 2016, the credit union had topped $200 million in assets, with a membership of 36,000; that year, it made nearly 2,500 loans for $40 million. Hope FCU has played a crucial role in preserving financial services in several Mississippi towns that were losing bank branches. It has also established new locations in Arkansas and mini-branches or computer kiosks in Jackson, MS, and New Orleans. Among CDCUS, it has been a leader in bringing mobile services to an underserved, low-income population.

Since 1994, the combined efforts of Hope's nonprofit and credit union have generated over $2.5 billion in financing, benefiting more than one million people in the Delta and other distressed communities. In addition to financial services, the organization's family includes the HOPE Policy Institute, which advocates on issues of social and economic justice, consumer protection, community reinvestment, housing, tax policy, and more. Bill Bynum, the organization's founder and CEO, came to Hope Enterprise after his early work at Self-Help and the North Carolina Rural Economic Development Center. He served terms as chairman of the Advisory Committee of the Community Development Financial Institutions Fund and of the Consumer Advisory Board of the Consumer Financial Protection Bureau.

## Community Development Venture Capital: Kentucky Highlands Investment Corporation (KHIC)

Kentucky Highlands Investment Corporation (KHIC), one of the earliest and most prominent community development corporations, has continued to play a significant role in virtually every major regional development effort in Kentucky. In July 1999, as President Clinton was traveling the country for his proposed New Markets Tax Credit initiative, he began his tour of Appalachia with a visit to Annville, KY, and the Mid-South Electrics Company, an investee of KHIC. By that time, KHIC's investments had generated 5,200 jobs, accounting for 40 percent of all manufacturing jobs in the region.[1454]

KHIC obtained 15 awards totaling more than $47 million from the CDFI Fund. In 2013, it helped form Appalachian Community Capital, a wholesale capital intermediary, which received investments from banks (Deutsche Bank and Bank of America); foundations (Calvert, Ford, Mary Reynolds Babcock, and others); and the Appalachian Regional Commission.[1455] On January 7, 2014, KHIC partnered with eight counties in southeastern Kentucky to implement the first rural Promise Zone in the nation, designated by President Obama; it coordinated an initiative that engaged 50 private, community-based, and government organizations.[1456] KHIC also participated in the Small Business Finance Collaborative, funded by Goldman Sachs's 10,000 Small Businesses initiative.

## Community Development Credit Unions (CDCUs)

The four surviving credit unions among the 1996 awardees represent a cross-section of the diverse movement serving low-income and minority communities. First American Credit Union (CU), headquartered in Arizona, serves multiple Native American tribes; Santa Cruz Community CU in California serves a substantial Latino population, including farmworkers; two credit unions serve largely African American memberships—Faith Community United CU in Cleveland and First Legacy FCU in Charlotte, NC. None of the credit unions obtained New Markets Tax Credits and thus have not achieved the dramatic growth of some loan funds; only two (First Legacy and Santa Cruz Community) received more than an initial award from the CDFI Fund. First American and Santa Cruz Community credit unions, both of which received $1 million in 1996, have each grown to more than $100 million in assets, while Faith Community CU and First Legacy FCU are mid-sized CDCUs, with $14 million and $35 million, respectively.

Despite its modest size, Faith Community United CU—the largest African American faith-based CDCU in the country—has been an innovator in providing credit to low-income borrowers who would otherwise be vulnerable to high-cost payday lending. As George Barany, then an organizer for WECO, put it, the CDFI award "was big. It really propelled them to the national level. It allowed Faith to be a significant player in probably the poorest neighborhoods on the East Side of Cleveland, where there were really no bank branches for miles around."[1457] The 70-year-old credit union on Cleveland's East Side won national recognition for its Grace Loan program, which helps its members avoid or recover from predatory loans.[1458]

Santa Cruz Community CU, which marked its 40th anniversary in 2017, works in tandem with its nonprofit affiliate, Santa Cruz Community Ventures, to provide financial counseling, low-interest loans for child care facilities, and assistance to immigrants, including loans to people under the Deferred Action for Childhood Arrivals (DACA) program. Long a national leader in lending to small businesses and cooperatives, Santa Cruz Community CU participates in lending programs of the Small Business Administration and the U.S. Department of Agriculture.[1459]

## Community Development Loan Funds

The cumulative impact claimed by loan funds reflects their growing scale: Boston Community Capital, for example, has helped finance over 20,000 affordable housing units, 2 million square feet of commercial real estate, and health care facilities serving over 129,000 patients annually. LIIF has invested over $1 billion in housing. IFF has financed 5,374 child care slots; 46,465 seats in charter schools; and 2,474 beds in supportive and homeless housing and facilities for persons with disabilities.[1460] By 2016, NFF had provided over $600 million in financing to support over $2.3 billion in projects for thousands of nonprofit organizations nationwide.[1461] Bridgeway Capital (formerly the Community Loan Fund of Southwestern Pennsylvania) has made more than 1,140 loans in a 15-county region totaling

## Appendix 2. Selected Profiles: The Class of 1996 Revisited

$145 million to entrepreneurs, startup and growing small businesses, and nonprofits; nearly 300 loans have gone to enterprises owned and led by African Americans, and 398 to enterprises owned and led by women.

Few organizations had a national or regional presence at the start of the CDFI era. One was the Rural Community Assistance Corporation, founded in 1979, which always worked regionally in the western states; another was LISC, which worked in multiple cities. Funded in 1996 for its rural expansion, LISC has moved beyond urban centers to develop partnerships with 77 community-based organizations in more than 2,000 rural counties in 44 states. Several CDFI loan funds now have offices in multiple states. IFF, which began as the Illinois Facilities Fund in Chicago, has regional offices in Indianapolis, Detroit, Minneapolis, St. Louis, Columbus, and Milwaukee. The LiftFund (formerly Accion Texas) has a presence in more than a dozen states in the Southeast. RF, originally the Delaware Valley Community Reinvestment Fund, has expanded its reach to invest in 20 states and the District of Columbia. It has established an office in Baltimore, where it has worked closely with its longtime community-organizing partner, the Industrial Areas Foundation, to rebuild the housing stock of East Baltimore's Oliver neighborhood. Even when loan funds do not maintain satellite offices, their tax credits and other funding have enabled some of them to do financing deals in other regions of the country; LIIF, for example, has calculated that its investments have touched 31 states.

Apart from their programmatic growth, loan funds are beginning to break into the broader capital markets: RF, for example, has received an AA issuer credit rating from Standard & Poor's. But the contributions of loan funds to the CDFI field have gone beyond their growing assets and sophistication. Unconstrained by bank or credit union regulations, they have been especially resourceful in innovating products and creating new markets.

- The New Hampshire Community Loan Fund was a pioneer in financing the conversion of manufactured housing (mobile home) parks into cooperatives. By 2017, it had financed more than 130 resident-owned communities in New Hampshire. In 2008, the loan fund joined forces with CFED (Prosperity Now) and Capital Impact Partners to establish ROC USA, which with its regional affiliates in the ROC USA network have helped finance more than 200 resident-owned communities (ROCs) across the country.
- RF developed PolicyMap, a vital resource for community developers that it describes as an "easy-to-use online mapping [tool] with data on demographics, real estate, health, jobs and more in communities across the US."[1462] Its work in identifying "food deserts"—areas lacking access to fresh food, like Camden, NJ—was instrumental in the development of the Healthy Food Financing Initiative.
- LIIF (Low Income Investment Fund) is a leader in financing transit-oriented development, a rapidly growing approach that brings affordable housing, businesses, and community services close to mass transportation with access to job markets; it has delivered $60 million in financing to projects in California, Massachusetts, and Washington, DC.
- Two CDFIs with deep roots in the nonprofit world have played roles in innovative Social Impact Bond ("Pay for Success") programs, an approach born in the United Kingdom in 2010

and initiated in the United States in 2012. IFF (Illinois Facilities Fund) has used this approach to expand childhood education services at Chicago public school sites. NFF (Nonprofit Finance Fund) has provided $4.3 million in grants from the Social Innovation Fund of the federal Corporation for National and Community Service to address homelessness, recidivism, and early childhood education.
- RCAC (Rural Community Assistance Corporation) specializes in infrastructure financing and development. It assists small municipalities, rural districts, tribal communities, farmworker and other organizations with water and waste-water planning and development.
- Collaborating with banks, public-sector agencies, and other CDFIs (including Hope Enterprise), LIIF has helped develop an integrated food outlet to serve a food desert in New Orleans.
- LISC has established a network of more than 75 Financial Opportunity Centers (FOCs), which provide an integrated "bundle" of three main services: employment counseling, financial coaching, and income-support counseling, building upon a model developed by the Annie E. Casey Foundation's Center for Working Families.[1463]
- Several loan funds have worked to expand the field by developing management consulting, training, and advisory services to help structure deals. Among these are LIIF, IFF, and NFF.

## Case Study: Boston Community Capital (BCC)

Since its early days in the 1990s as an affordable housing lender with less than $7 million in assets and a focus on Boston and surrounding communities, the Boston Community Loan Fund has grown and diversified enormously as part of Boston Community Capital (BCC). As of 2016, the combined assets of BCC and its affiliates were $278 million, of which $135 million was in the Boston Community Loan Fund. Total assets under management by BCC and its affiliates exceeded $1 billion.

In addition to the loan fund, BCC has expanded its scope through its family of affiliates. Its SUN (Stabilizing Urban Neighborhoods) initiative is a nationally recognized foreclosure relief program that has helped stabilize over 800 households facing foreclosure-related eviction. BCC Solar is a for-profit corporation that works to stabilize and reduce energy and utility costs for affordable housing, nonprofits, and municipal facilities by improving their energy efficiency and renewable energy use. BCLF Managed Assets Corporation develops new business initiatives and innovative funding vehicles for low-income communities and administers the BCC's New Markets Tax Credit awards. BCLF Ventures, Inc. makes equity investments in businesses that create social, environmental, and financial returns. WegoWise provides online, automated tracking and benchmarking of utility usage for affordable housing and other property managers, owners, and funders.

BCC has invested over $1.3 billion and leveraged over $6 billion in public and private investment in underserved communities. The organization's growth has been fueled by major capital injections from all the CDFI Fund programs: financial assistance awards (cumulatively $18.5 million); New

Markets Tax Credits ($523 million in allocations); Healthy Food Financing Initiative awards ($5.3 million); and the Capital Magnet Fund ($4.5 million).

The organization has enjoyed exceptional continuity in leadership over three decades. BCC Solar President DeWitt (Dick) Jones joined the loan fund in 1985 as its first executive director; CEO Elyse D. Cherry, a member of BCC's founding board, joined the staff full-time in 1997; and BCLF President Michelle Volpe joined BCC in 1995. In addition to its financing work, BCC has been extremely active in statewide policymaking, advising on foreclosure, food access, and more. Its housing advocacy and foreclosure work have received national attention, highlighting inequalities in the housing market.[1464]

# NOTES

## Preface

1. Paul Grogan, "The Future of Community Development." In *Investing in What Works for America's Communities: Essays on People, Place & Purpose*, edited by Nancy O. Andrews and David J. Erickson (San Francisco, CA: Federal Reserve Bank of San Francisco and Low Income Investment Fund, 2012), p. 188, https://www.frbsf.org/community-development/publications/special/investing-in-what-works-american-communities-people-place-purpose/.
2. Nancy O. Andrews and Christopher Kramer, "Coming Out as a Human Capitalist: Community Development at the Nexus of People and Place," *Community Development Investment Review* (San Francisco, CA: Federal Reserve Bank of San Francisco, 2009), p. 64, https://www.frbsf.org/community-development/publications/community-development-investment-review/2009/december/community-development-people-place/.
3. Douglas Jutte, "Community Development and Health," in *The Practical Playbook: Public Health and Primary Care Together* (New York: Oxford University Press, forthcoming).
4. For more detail on how a population-health business model and pay-for-success financing work, please see *What Matters: Investing in Results to Build Strong, Vibrant Communities* (San Francisco, CA: Federal Reserve Bank of San Francisco, 2017), https://www.investinresults.org/.

## Introduction

5. Memorandum from the NEC-DPC Interagency Working Group on Community Development and Empowerment, "Community Lending Proposal," April 10, 1993.
6. Robert M. Garsson and Claudia Cummins, "Clinton Unveils Plan for Community Loans," *American Banker*, July 16, 1993, 18.
7. Paul Weinstein, interview by author, Washington, DC., February 22, 2016.
8. White House Office of the Press Secretary, "Remarks of the First Lady, Secretary of the Treasury Bob Rubin and AID Administrator Brian Atwood in Press Briefing," January 30, 1997.

## Chapter 1

9. Reprinted in Walter Isaacson, *Benjamin Franklin: An American Life* (New York: Simon & Schuster, 2004), 389.
10. Ford Foundation, *Investing for Social Gain: Reflections on Two Decades of Program-Related Investments* (New York: Ford Foundation, December 1991), 6.
11. Isaacson, ibid., 389.
12. Ibid.
13. Ibid., 390.

## Notes

14. Ibid., 475.
15. Ibid.
16. Ibid.
17. Dan Immergluck, *Credit to the Community: Community Reinvestment and Fair Lending Policy in the United States* (Armonk, NY: M.E. Sharpe, 2004), 54; quoted from Juliet Walker, *The History of Black Business in America: Capitalism, Race and Entrepreneurship* (New York: Macmillan Library Reference USA, 1998).
18. Immergluck, 55.
19. Citing Carl R. Osthaus, *Freedmen, Philanthropy, and Fraud: A History of the Freedman's Savings Bank* (Urbana, IL: University of Illinois Press, 1976).
20. It also is often spelled as "Freedmen's," including by Frederick Douglass.
21. Reginald Washington, "The Freedman's Savings and Trust Company and African American Genealogical Research," *Federal Records and African American History* 29 (2) (Summer 1997), quoting Walter L. Fleming, *The Freedman's Savings Bank: A Chapter in the Economic History of the Negro Race* (1927). http://www.archives.gov/publications/prologue/1997/summer/freedmans-savings-and-trust.html.
22. Philip S. Foner, ed., *Frederick Douglas: Selected Speeches and Writings* (Chicago: Lawrence Hill Books, 1975).
23. Immergluck, 56, quoting Walker.
24. "Report of the Commissioners of the Freedman's Savings and Trust Company," 43rd Congress, 2nd Session, 1.
25. Frederick Douglass, *The Life and Times of Frederick Douglass* (Mineola, NY: Dover Publications, 2003), 293.
26. Ibid., 292.
27. Ibid., 293–94.
28. Ibid., 295–96.
29. "Report of the Commissioners," 59.
30. Ibid., 4.
31. Ibid., 6–7.
32. Washington, ibid.
33. "Report of the Commissioners," 9–10.
34. The Washington headquarters of the bank was torn down in 1899. Twenty years later, the U.S. Treasury Department built its new Annex building on the same spot. To honor the bank's legacy, on January 7, 2016, the Treasury Department commemorated the 150th anniversary of the Freedman's Bank by renaming the Treasury Annex the Freedman's Bank Building. https://www.treasury.gov/about/education/Pages/Lasting-Impact-of-the-Freedman%27s-Bank.aspx, accessed February 26, 2018.
35. Douglass, 292.
36. Ibid., 293.
37. Ibid., 295.
38. W. E. B. Du Bois, *The Souls of Black Folk* (New York: Barnes & Noble Classics, 2003), 32. (First published in 1903. Punctuation as printed.)
39. Washington, ibid.
40. J. Carroll Moody and Gilbert C. Fite, *The Credit Union Movement. Origins and Development, 1850–1970* (Lincoln: University of Nebraska Press, 1971), 7. In 1850, he founded the first cooperative credit society, which started with $140 in initial capital contributed by a group of friends but required regular contributions of capital from members.
41. Ibid., 13.
42. Ibid., 14.
43. Ibid., 19.
44. Ibid., 22
45. Desjardins presentation to the House of Commons, quoted in Moody and Fite, 25.
46. Ibid., 24.
47. Ibid., 36. See also https://www.stmarysbank.com/nav/about-us/history.

48  Ibid., 27.
49  Ibid.
50  Ibid, 30.
51  Ibid., 44.
52  Ibid. Many of the early pioneers of credit union development in Boston were Jewish, as they were in New York City. Despite their philanthropic intentions, they worried that their efforts would be hindered because of the historic association of Jews with usury.
53  Ibid., 61.
54  Ibid., 43.
55  Quoted in Moody and Fite, 43.
56  Quoted in Moody and Fite, 50.
57  Ibid., 66. The early days of credit unions recall the proliferation of microenterprise funds and, to some degree, non-regulated loan funds in the United States of the late twentieth century.
58  Ibid., 70, 72–73.
59  Ibid., 87.
60  Ibid., 92–93.
61  Ibid., 144. The Russell Sage Foundation, which played a prominent early role in pressing for uniform small loan legislation with a 42 percent ceiling, was not an active financial supporter for credit unions by about 1930. Filene and CUNEB had an uneasy, sometimes tense, and often competitive relationship with the Russell Sage Foundation, including (but not only) turf battles over the movement in New York State.
62  Ibid., 126. The credit unions collectively totaled $45 million in assets and were providing short-term loans at a rate of $60 million a year.
63  Quoted in Moody and Fite, 147.
64  Ibid., 159.
65  Ibid., 1208, 224.
66  Jessica Gordon Nembhard, *Collective Courage. A History of African American Cooperative Economic Thought and Practice* (University Park: The Pennsylvania State University Press, 2014), 146.
67  Ibid, 176. North Carolina continued to be the largest concentration of African American credit unions for more than a half-century. In the past 20 years, their ranks were decimated. First Legacy Credit Union in Charlotte, chartered in 1941, is one survivor; it was one of the original CDFI Fund awardees and now has assets of more than $30 million. Several other African American credit unions, facing liquidation by the regulators, were merged by Self-Help Credit Union.
68  Clyde G. Atwell, *A Passion to Survive: A Credit Union Grows in Brooklyn. A documentary 1939–1969* (New York: Pageant-Poseidon Press Ltd., 1976), 2.
69  F. Lord Levi, Preface in Atwell, 1. Levi was a founder and treasurer-manager of the credit union.
70  Quoted in Moody and Fite, 236, from "Dictation by Edward A. Filene Concerning His Work and Objectives," New York, May 19, 1937, typescript. Filene summarized his view of income tax policy this way: "Why shouldn't the American people take half my money from me? I took all of it from them." https://www.forbes.com/quotes/2467/
71  Ibid., 264.
72  Paul Deaton, chairman of the CUNA Dues Committee, Quoted in Moody and Fite, 307.
73  Ibid., 319.
74  Ibid., 291.

## Chapter 2

75  Esther Peterson, Introduction to David Caplovitz, *The Poor Pay More* (New York: The Free Press, 1967).

## Notes

76  As Caplovitz noted, "It [the title of the book] seems to have a life of its own and has become much better known than the book itself." It was used for a documentary on National Education Television. "Preface to the 1967 edition," *The Poor Pay More* (New York: Glencoe Free Press, 1967), xxvii.
77  Quoted in David Zarefsky, *President Johnson's War on Poverty: Rhetoric and History* (Birmingham: University of Alabama Press, 1986), 9.
78  Shriver, the brother-in-law of President John Kennedy, was a passionate, lifelong anti-poverty advocate. The Sargent Shriver National Center on Poverty Law in Chicago honors his memory.
79  Zarefsky, xvii–xviii. The birth of the CDFI Fund, like that of OEO, was initially relatively bipartisan. But in each case, within three years, this harmony gave way to partisan battles.
80  Zarefsky, xix.
81  Ibid.
82  Caplovitz, 14.
83  Ibid., 30.
84  Ibid., 155.
85  The CFPB, created by the Dodd-Frank law of 2010 and launched in 2011, has a broad mandate to identify and root out "unfair, deceptive, and abusive acts and practices" (UDAAP). From the reselling of debt, to unwanted or inappropriate add-on credit card products, to arbitration clauses, the bureau has addressed a wide range of anti-consumer practices that differ in form but inflict similar harm on the consumers of today, compared with those of 50 years ago.
86  Caplovitz, 26. In the following decades, subprime lending and rampant, irresponsible securitization funded by Wall Street grew enormously, fueling the Great Recession.
87  Bureau of Federal Credit Unions, "1964 BFCU report," 49.
88  CUNA president, H. B. Yates, quoted in Moody and Fite, 319, on the "great chasm between the rich and the poor" and the potential of credit unions to "permanently solve this problem of unequal distribution by enabling man to help himself and permanently improve his condition."
89  Moody and Fite, 338, drawn from abridged minutes of CUNA directors.
90  Crear rose through the ranks of the movement to become executive vice president of CUNA, the first and only African American to reach that position, and later the CEO of the World Council of Credit Unions.
91  Crear, interview by author, telephone, March 14, 2016.
92  Ibid.
93  Comptroller General of the United States, "Progress Being Made and Difficulties Being Encountered by Credit Unions Serving Low-Income Persons." Report to the Congress (June 17, 1971), 10.
94  Ibid., 49.
95  Ibid., 50. The CDFI Fund established a separate window for Native American CDFIs in 2002. Persons with disabilities were recognized as an "other target population" years later, in response to advocacy efforts.
96  Bureau of Federal Credit Unions, "Federal Credit Union Program. Annual Report 1965" (Washington, DC, FCU-561), 12.
97  Ibid., 12.
98  Ibid., 36.
99  Ibid.
100  Ibid.
101  Bureau of Federal Credit Unions, "Federal Credit Union Program. Annual Report 1966," inside cover.
102  Ibid., 1.
103  Ibid., 3. In addition to federal charters, there would have been hundreds of additional state-chartered credit unions, which BFCU did not supervise.
104  Ibid., 3.
105  Bureau of Federal Credit Unions, "Annual Report of the Bureau of Federal Credit Unions, 1967," 3.

106 U.S. Department of Health, Education, and Welfare, "Project Moneywise: Role of the Credit Unions in the War on Poverty," Text, March 1967, http://texashistory.unt.edu/ark:/67531/metapth595318/, accessed May 1, 2016, University of North Texas Libraries, "The Portal to Texas History," http://texashistory.unt.edu, crediting Texas Southern University, Houston, TX. Many of the insights and language of Caplovitz's book appear here, including the finding that local merchants and their salesmen cultivated personalized, informal relationships to appeal to low-income consumers.

107 Vice President Humbert Humphrey is shown presenting a check to make a share deposit in a credit union helped by Project Moneywise. He is quoted as saying, "Some of us fortunate enough not to be poor join this credit union because we want to be a part of that community effort and to devote a share of our resources to the common 'pot.'" Ibid., 7.

108 Barbara C. Jordan, "Speech Notes," Text, no date, http://texashistory.unt.edu/ark:/67531 /metapth595078, accessed May 1, 2016, University of North Texas Libraries, "The Portal to Texas History," http://texashistory.unt.edu, crediting Texas Southern University, Houston, TX. Ms. Jordan was the first African American elected to the Texas Senate after Reconstruction. She was later the first black woman from the South elected to the U.S. House of Representatives.

109 One such leader who emerged was Annie W. Vamper from Alabama. She participated in Project Moneywise; was hired by the National Credit Union Administration (NCUA); and in 1983 left NCUA to join the National Federation of Community Development Credit Unions, where she worked as associate director until her death in 1990.

110 Ibid., 3.

111 Ibid., 6.

112 Comptroller General of the United States, "Progress Being Made," ibid. This GAO report was based on the activities of eight credit unions.

113 Ibid., 7.

114 Moody and Fite, 340, quoting articles from *Credit Union Magazine,* October 1967, and CUNA's *Frontline,* January 12, 1968, 1, 4.

115 Caplovitz, xviii–xix.

116 Popularly known as the Kerner Commission report, the report was issued in 1968 by The National Advisory Commission on Civil Disorders, chaired by former Illinois governor Otto Kerner.

117 "Progress Being Made," 1. The report did not include data on 19 state-chartered credit unions.

118 Moody and Fite, 340.

119 Caplovitz, xxiv.

120 "Progress Being Made," 2, 6. The bureau's 1967 report found that delinquent loans represented 8.0 percent of total loans for limited-income credit unions, compared with 3.3 percent for all federal credit unions. A total of 0.47 percent of loans had been charged off.

121 Ibid., 2.

122 Ibid., 50.

123 Moody and Fite, 340. Quote drawn from CUNA's *Frontline,* June 13, 1969, and CUNA's *Briefs,* December 12, 1969, 1. Orrin Shipe, who held the title of managing director of CUNA, equivalent to CEO, was the father of Robert Shipe, who over three decades took the Navajoland Credit Union (initially Navajo Tribal Employees Credit Union; later First American Credit Union) from a broken-down trailer on the reservation to the largest indigenous credit union in the country. First American Credit Union was one of the first recipients of a CDFI award in 1996.

124 "Progress Being Made," 5.

125 Bob Shipe, interview by author, telephone, April 29, 2016.

126 "Progress Being Made," 2–3.

127 Moody and Fite, 341, quoting CUNA's *Frontline,* November 25, 1970, 1.

128 "Progress Being Made," 2–3.

129 Ibid., 24.

## Notes

130  Interview of John Earnest Johnson in videotape, National Federation of Community Development Credit Unions, *Dollar by Dollar* (New York, 1999).
131  Ibid. Johnson worked for decades for the Federation of Southern Cooperative/Land Assistance Fund. He served as a board member of the National Federation of Community Development Credit Unions and as a technical assistance consultant. In 1999, Johnson was inducted into the national Cooperative Hall of Fame.
132  Carol Zippert and John Zippert, interview by author, Washington, DC, May 4, 2017.
133  Interview in videotape, *Dollar by Dollar*.
134  Ibid.
135  Ylvisaker worked at Ford from 1955 to 1971. That his title was "Public Affairs" should not be taken to mean that public-relations concerns motivated the effort. It would be years before Ford had divisions such as economic development or urban poverty.
136  Mitchell Sviridoff, ed., *Inventing Community Renewal: The Trials and Errors That Shaped the Modern Community Development Corporation* (New York: New School University, Milano Graduate School, 2004), 28.
137  Sviridoff, 3.
138  Ibid., 30.
139  Sviridoff, quoting Lou Winnick, public affairs director of Ford, 29.
140  Robert Cohen, in Sviridoff, 41.
141  Patricia Rosenfield and Rachel Wimpee, *The Ford Foundation: Constant Themes, Historical Variations* (Tarrytown, NY: Rockefeller Archive Center, 2015), 13.
142  Ibid.
143  Sviridoff, 57.
144  Rosenfield and Wimpee, 13.
145  The Twentieth Century Fund, "CDCs: New Hope for the Inner City," New York, 1971, 66.
146  The Paragon Federal Credit Union, which was founded by Caribbean immigrants and served this community for many years, was located on Fulton Street, close to what became the headquarters of Bedford-Stuyvesant Restoration.
147  Sviridoff, 67–68. Pratt Institute Center for Community and Environmental Development, under Shiffman's leadership for many years, was a major resource and advocate for community development planning in New York City, as well as training generations of community development leaders. When, for example, the community wanted to take over a former Manufacturers Hanover Bank building on Manhattan's Lower East Side to convert it to a credit union, Pratt staff carried out feasibility studies of the facility.
148  Shiffman became one of the most prominent New York City and national leaders in the field of community economic development.
149  Quoted in Sviridoff, 68.
150  Ralph Blumenthal, "Brooklyn Negroes Harass Kennedy," *New York Times,* February 5, 1966, 17.
151  Sviridoff, 71.
152  Steven V. Roberts, "Redevelopment Plan Set for Bedford-Stuyvesant," *New York Times,* December 11, 1966, 1.
153  Ibid.
154  Ibid.
155  Editorial, "Remaking Brooklyn's Slums," December 12, 1966, 46.
156  Ibid.
157  Sviridoff, 75.
158  Quoted by William P. Ryan in Sviridoff, 76.
159  Eric John Abrahamson, *Resonance. A History of the Taconic Foundation, 1958–2013* (Rapid City, SD: Vantage Point Historical Services, 2016), 12.
160  Rosenfield and Wimpee, 15.
161  Ibid.

162  Ford Foundation, "Investing for Social Gain: Reflections on Two Decades of Program-Related Investments" (New York: Ford Foundation, 1991), 6.
163  Ibid., 18.
164  Abrahamson, 226.
165  Other early participants included the Field, New York, New World, Norman, Ellis L. Phillips, and Sachem foundations. In the mid-1970s, the Rockefeller Brothers Fund joined with a $1 million investment.
166  Ibid., 228.
167  Council on Foundations. *Legal Aspects of Program-Related Investments* (Washington, DC: Council on Foundations, 1991).
168  Abrahamson, 230.
169  Adolfo Alayon, interview, in videotape, National Federation of Community Development Credit Unions, *Dollar by Dollar* (New York, 1999).
170  "Progress Being Made," 15.
171  Ibid.
172  Ibid., 23.
173  See Chapter 17.

## Chapter 3

174  Immergluck, 52.
175  Michael Westgate and Ann Vick-Westgate, *Gale Force* (Cambridge, MA: Harvard Bookstore, 2011), 36–37, drawn from Amy E. Hiller article in *Journal of Urban History* 29: 394–420.
176  Hull House was the first "settlement house," a social service agency that served immigrants and others. Hull House, like Union Settlement, University Settlement, and others, incubated credit unions from the 1950s.
177  Westgate and Vick-Westgate, 5. Few writers could resist commenting on Cincotta's striking appearance. Martin Mayer, the author of many books on banking, described her as "a very large housewife in a Mother Hubbard, with a round red face under an aureole of curly white hair—and (on the rare occasions when there is no cigarette between the lips) the most glorious politician's smile of the 1970s." *Gale Force,* 93, quoting Martin Mayer, *The Builders: Houses, People, Neighborhoods, Governments, Money* (New York: Norton, 1978).
178  Westgate and Vick-Westgate, 13, quoting from Cincotta's c.v.
179  Immergluck, 141; Westgate and Vick-Westgate, 42. Reaching the top management of a bank was eased by the fact that there was "unit banking," i.e., the bank was not part of a branch system with layers of hierarchy stretching up to a holding company.
180  Westgate and Vick-Westgate, 53.
181  Ibid., 54.
182  Ibid., 63, quoting Kathy Desmond, program officer for the national Campaign for Human Development. Msgr. Baroni was a national figure, recognized by *TIME* magazine in its July 15, 1974, issue as "one of 200 faces to watch for the future," 73.
183  Ibid., 61, quoting Justin McCarthy.
184  Ibid., 112.
185  Ibid., 152.
186  Quoted in Westgate and Vick-Westgate, 233.
187  Ibid., 236, quoting Shel Trapp.
188  Ibid., 271.
189  Ibid., 274.
190  Immergluck, 162.
191  Westgate and Vick-Westgate, 95.
192  Ibid., 166.

## Notes

193   Ted Wysocki, interview by author, telephone, March 25, 2016.
194   Westgate and Vick-Westgate, 156, quoting case study by Kirk Hallahan of November 7, 1991.
195   Bruce Gottschall, "ShoreBank's Legacy and Vision Continue: A Practitioner's Reflections," *Cascade* (Winter 2011).
196   Grzywinski, interview by author, Chicago, April 8, 2015. Unless otherwise noted, subsequent quotes from Grzywinski are from this interview.
197   See Chapter 3.
198   Grzywinski interview.
199   In Chicago's racially polarized finance sector, a partnership team composed of two white members (Ron Grzywinski and Mary Houghton) and two African Americans (Milton Davis and Jim Fletcher) was indeed extraordinary. Their unique partnership lasted until the 1990s. Fletcher died from complications of lymphoma on September 16, 1998, at the age of 63. In 1998, State Senator Barack Obama participated in a ceremony naming a Chicago street after Davis (1932–2005), who retired in 1999.
200   Grzywinski recalled, "I had an office in Robie House, Frank Lloyd Wright's masterpiece. My office was the former maid's bathroom."
201   Richard P. Taub, *Community Capitalism: Banking Strategies and Economic Development* (Boston: Harvard Business School Press, 1988), 19. Taub, a sociologist at the University of Chicago, observed, interviewed, and collaborated with South Shore Bank from 1973.
202   Taub, 19–20, 53.
203   Grzywinski interview.
204   Ibid.
205   Stanley Hallett (1930–98) was a prolific urban planner and civil rights activist who cofounded the Center for Neighborhood Technology and the Woodstock Institute in Chicago.
206   Grzywinski interview; also, Taub, 21.
207   Grzywinski interview.
208   Grzywinski interview.
209   Ibid. Such a structure was similar in many respects to the Equity Equivalent (EQ2) investment that the National Association of Community Development Loan Funds devised 20 years later for its nonprofit members.
210   Taub, 22. James E. Post and Fiona S. Wilson, draft for "Too Good to Fail," *Stanford Social Innovation Review* (Fall 2011): 66–71, http://search.proquest.com/docview/886036880?accountid=12261, accessed March 24, 2015.
211   Taub, 41–42.
212   Ibid., 42.
213   For example, community development credit unions (CDCUs) consistently show average balances below the industry norms, which often brings pressure from their examiners.
214   Houghton, interview by author, Chicago, April 8, 2015.
215   Taub, 44–45, 48.
216   Ibid., 54.
217   Ibid., 61.
218   Taub, 4. Chart from the Woodstock Institute, "Evaluation of the Illinois Neighborhood Development Corporation."
219   Taub, 118.

## Chapter 4

220   At the time of the book, he was a fellow at the Institute of Politics at the Kennedy School of Harvard. Among his career achievements, he was a founder of the Economic Policy Institute.
221   "CDCs: New Hope," 25.
222   The "Kerner Commission" was the author of the *Report of the National Advisory Commission on Civil Disorders*. The report received mass dissemination: 2 million copies were sold.

223 "CDCs: New Hope," 8.
224 Ibid., 4.
225 Ibid., 7.
226 Ibid., 114.
227 Ibid., 115.
228 Ibid., 11.
229 See Chapter 16.
230 CDFI Act of 1994, Sec. 107, (a)(11).
231 There was debate early in the CDFI legislation process about whether a special charter should be created for community development banks. Neither the CDFI field nor the banking industry supported the idea, which died. See Chapter 12.
232 Sviridoff, 98.
233 P.L. 91-468.
234 The National Credit Union Administration (NCUA) succeeded the Bureau of Federal Credit Unions. It was charged with chartering, regulating, and supervising federal credit unions, as well as administering the National Credit Union Share Insurance Fund (NCUSIF) for credit union deposits. Many states continued to charter credit unions, and in some of these, separate deposit insurance funds were established.
235 The GAO report of June 1971 included several innovative ideas to enhance the viability of low-income credit unions. Among these were incentives to institutions to encourage deposits and mechanisms to "guarantee credit unions against loss on loans made to low-income persons," or "rediscount a portion of the notes held by credit unions" (25). These ideas—which would likely be considered innovative even today—were not implemented.
236 Today, more than 90 percent of credit unions are federally insured, even if they are state-chartered. A small number of state-chartered credit unions continue to be privately insured.
237 Credit Union National Association (CUNA), "The Growth and Prospects of Community Development Credit Unions" (Madison, WI:1974), 1. Included in National Federation of Community Development Credit Unions, *The Community Development Credit Union: A Proposal for Strengthening and Expanding the Impact of This Effective Low Income Community Development Agent* (Brooklyn, NY: 1975?). Hereafter, "Proposal for Strengthening and Expanding the Impact."
238 "Proposal for Strengthening and Expanding the Impact," 1.
239 Ibid., 5.
240 CUNA, "The Growth and Prospects," 14.
241 "Proposal for Strengthening and Expanding the Impact," 9.
242 Alayon interview, *Dollar by Dollar*.
243 "Proposal for Strengthening and Expanding the Impact," 1.
244 Ibid., 2-3.
245 Ibid., 11.
246 Low-income recipients had to purchase their allotment of food stamps with cash at a percentage of their face value. Banks were reluctant to have their lobbies filled with people seeking to obtain food stamps.
247 Ibid., 12.
248 Ibid., 10.
249 Ibid., 13-15.
250 Ibid., 23. It would take several decades for the federal government to fully implement direct deposit through electronic funds transfer (EFT).
251 Ibid., 11.
252 Ibid., 32.
253 Undated memo to the membership, November 1978 (?). Courtesy of National Federation of Community Development Credit Unions.

## Notes

254 Jimmy Carter, "National Urban Policy Message to the Congress," March 27, 1978, http://www.presidency.ucsb.edu/was/?pid=30567
255 Ibid.
256 Ibid.
257 Ibid.
258 Ibid.
259 Jim Clark, memo to the board, March 31, 1978. Courtesy of National Federation of Community Development Credit Unions.
260 Jim Clark, undated memo to the board. Courtesy of National Federation of Community Development Credit Unions.
261 Alayon interview, ibid.
262 Ibid.
263 Ibid.
264 Consumer Action Program of Bedford-Stuyvesant (CABS), "CABS Demonstration Federal Credit Union: A Proposal for Inducing Asset Growth Through Procurement of Non-Member Deposits" (Brooklyn, NY: 1973?), 29. (Hereafter "CABS"). Included in "Proposal for Strengthening and Expanding the Impact."
265 Although nonmember depositors enjoyed insurance on their funds, they were not able to borrow or to vote for credit union officials. Thus, contrary to concerns sometimes expressed by the regulators or "mainstream" credit unions, democratic governance of the credit unions was preserved; a large outside depositor could not control a credit union (although a withdrawal of substantial funds could create liquidity issues for the credit union).
266 National Center for Urban Ethnic Affairs (NCUEA), "Community Development Credit Union Organizing Handbook: A Tool for Rebuilding Urban America" (Washington, DC: December 1981), 16.
267 The "New York Four" were located in Brooklyn (CABS Demonstration Federal Credit Union in Bedford-Stuyvesant) and in Manhattan (Lower East Side Federal Credit Union; Union Settlement House Federal Credit Union in East Harlem; and the Upper West Side Federal Credit Union).
268 LESEDAC, "Plan for SBA Guaranteed Business Loans and for Growth Thru Non-Member Deposits, April 1974." Included in "Proposal for Strengthening and Expanding the Impact."
269 Ibid., 2. LESEDAC was the credit union's partner nonprofit. The Lower East Side Federal Credit Union (FCU) of this era eventually went out of business; its successor, the Lower East Side People's FCU was chartered in 1986. (See Chapter 8).
270 Consumer Action Program of Bedford-Stuyvesant (CABS), "CABS Demonstration Federal Credit Union," 2, included in "Proposal for Strengthening and Expanding the Impact."
271 All three credit unions still operate. As of December 31, 2016, Santa Cruz Community CU had $113 million in assets, and Alternatives had $101 million; both received significant CDFI Fund investments. North Side FCU ($7.9 million) has gained national recognition for its alternatives to payday lending.
272 See, for example, Professor Hyman Minsky's proposal in 1992 (Chapter 12).
273 Even in the early stages of the credit union movement, its leaders recognized the need for a backup or central financial facility: In 1929, Roy Bergengren wrote that the "most serious problem confronting credit unions of the future will have to do with investment of resources not needed for loans to their members." Quoted in Jim Jerving, *The Central Finance Facility: A guide to development and operations* (Dubuque, Iowa: Kendall/Hunt Publishing Company, 1987), 3.
274 Attracta Kelly, OP, in Adrian Dominican Sisters Portfolio Advisory Board, *Celebrating 40 years of socially responsible investing* (Adrian, MI: 2015), 2.
275 Ibid., 2.
276 Ibid., 4.
277 Ibid., 6.
278 Ibid., 10.
279 Ibid., 7.

280 Ibid., 10.
281 Houghton interview.
282 Kelly, OP, in *Celebrating 40 years*, 2.
283 Council on Foundations, *Program Related Investment Primer* (Written by the staff of the Piton Foundation; revised by Brody & Weiser, 1993), 57.
284 Letter of December 4, 1975 (Rockefeller Archive Center).
285 Edward Lawrence, Executive Director, Veatch Program North Shore Unitarian Society, June 14, 1976, letter from John Simon, Taconic Foundation records (FA407), Series 1: Grants, File: Cooperative Assistance Fund, File: Correspondence, 1977–79, Box 35, Folder 363, Rockefeller Archive Center.
286 Bolling letter from Simon.
287 Ibid.
288 See Chapter 3.
289 Ford Foundation, "Investing for Social Gain: Reflections on Two Decades of Program-Related Investments" (New York: December 1991), 8.
290 Rosenfield and Wimpee, 24.
291 12 CFR Part 1002.1 b.
292 Houghton interview.

## Part IV and Chapter 5

293 President Carter was famously and erroneously cited as describing the condition of America as "malaise." He never actually used the term.
294 At the time, Vidal was director of the Community Development Research Center, New School for Social Research.
295 Avis C. Vidal, *Rebuilding Communities: A National Study of Urban Community Development Corporations. Executive Summary* (New York: New School for Social Research, 1992), 3.
296 Ibid., 6.
297 Ibid., 3.
298 Ibid., 8.
299 Ibid., 15. Vidal found that in 22 of 29 cities with CDCs, their numbers had increased over the previous five years—regardless of region or size of city.
300 Ford Foundation Records, Asset Building and Community Development Program (ASSETS), Human Development and Reproductive Health (HDRH), Office Files of Virginia Davis Floyd (FA513), Series III: Subject Files, Mature CDC Initiative, 1994, Box 4, Attachment A, "Funding History of Foundation-Supported Mature CDCs." In addition to Bedford-Stuyvesant Restoration Corporation and MACE, Chicanos por La Causa, Mexican American Unity Council, Inc., Spanish Speaking Unity Council, and Watts Labor Community Action Committee were among the mature CDCs receiving repeated, major grants and investments from Ford. The largest ($3.4 million) and one of the early PRI guarantees was to Bedford-Stuyvesant Restoration Corp.
301 Ibid., program officer comments, 3.
302 Ibid.
303 Vidal, 20.
304 Michael Rubinger, interview by author, New York, NY, April 7, 2016. Sviridoff joined the Ford Foundation as vice president of its National Affairs division in 1966.
305 Ibid. Rubinger left Ford around 1974 and returned in 1980 to work with Sviridoff on LISC. He worked at LISC until 1989, leaving for the Pew Charitable Trusts. He served as CEO of LISC from 1999 through 2016.
306 Ibid.
307 Ibid.
308 William P. Ryan, in Sviridoff, 98.

## Notes

309 Ibid., 100.
310 Rubinger interview.
311 Chuck Matthei, "ICE Board of Trustees Orientation Packet" (Fall 1985). Courtesy of DeWitt Jones. (Hereafter "Orientation Packet.")
312 Kirby White, "An Interview with Bob Swann," *Community Economics* (Summer 1992), 3–5.
313 The two-hour interview was videotaped by Michael Swack. Quotes and references that follow come from that interview, unless otherwise noted.
314 President Richard Nixon later chose Rumsfeld to begin the work of gutting the Office of Economic Opportunity. Rumsfeld held a number of top-level posts in Republican administrations, ultimately serving as Secretary of Defense.
315 Matthei interview by Swack.
316 "Catholic Workers live a simple lifestyle in community, serve the poor, and resist war and social injustice." From catholicworker.org/communities/director.html. As a young woman, Dorothy Day was arrested and jailed with Alice Paul in 1917 for picketing the White House in support of women's suffrage. She founded the *Catholic Worker* newspaper in 1933 and edited it until her death.
317 Joanne Sheehan, "Chuck Matthei, 1948–2002," *Nonviolent Activist* (November–December 2002).
318 "Orientation Packet."
319 Matthei interview by Swack.
320 Ford Foundation Records, Program officer summary, 6, Grants H-K, 22759, Microfilm Reel 6673, Grant PA-850-0719, Rockefeller Archive Center. (Hereafter ICE 1985 Proposal.)
321 Ibid.
322 Ibid., staff summary, 9.
323 The data and quotations are gathered from the foundation's grant file, ibid.
324 "ICE 1985 Proposal," 7.
325 Ibid.
326 Ibid.
327 Institute for Community Economics, Inc. "*Revolving Loan Fund Policies and Procedures,*" as revised and approved at the September 21, 1985 Board of Trustees meeting. Courtesy of DeWitt Jones.
328 "Orientation Packet," 6.
329 "ICE 1985 Proposal," 11.
330 Ibid., 7.
331 Ramm, interview by author, telephone, February 3, 2016.
332 "Orientation Packet," 7.
333 Collins, interview by author, New York, May 11, 2016. Collins worked for ICE from 1983 to 1992, fulfilling several roles, including providing technical assistance to aspiring resident-owned mobile home parks. Currently a senior scholar at the Institute for Policy Studies in Washington, DC, where he directs the Program on Inequality and the Common Good, Collins's most recent book (2016) is *Born on Third Base: A One Percenter Makes the Case for Tackling Inequality, Bringing Wealth Home, and Committing to the Common* Good (White River Junction, VT: Chelsea Green Publishing, 2016).
334 Ramm interview.
335 Ibid.
336 Ann Monroe, *Wall Street Journal,* June 28, 1985, 25.
337 Nicholas D. Kristoff, *New York Times,* August 17, 1985.
338 Institute for Community Economics, "A Proposal for Communication and Cooperation among Community Loan Funds," Submitted by the Institute for Community Economics for consideration at the First National Conference of Community Loan Funds (Greenfield, MA; no date). Courtesy of DeWitt Jones.
339 Chuck Matthei, "Who We Are, What We've Learned, Where We're Going" (Greenfield, MA: Institute for Community Economics, 1985).

340  Ibid.
341  Ibid.
342  Ibid.
343  Carol Watson, who represented the Housing Fund of the Archdiocese of New York, was also the lead organizer of the Lower East Side community team that negotiated the commitment from Manufacturers Hanover Trust to invest in the startup of the Lower East Side People's FCU. (See Chapter 8.)
344  "Profile of Community Loan Fund Activity," compiled by ICE. Undated; prior to the conference.
345  Chuck Collins, ICE, Letter to Facilitators, October 8, 1985.
346  Institute for Community Economics, Inc. "A Proposal for Communication and Cooperation among Community Loan Funds," (Greenfield, MA; undated).
347  ICE, Memorandum to Conference Participants, November 19, 1985.
348  National Association of Community Development Loan Funds (NACDLF), "Building the Foundation for Economic, Social and Political Justice. A 5-year Profile of the Membership of the National Association of Community Development Loan Funds, 1986–1990" (Philadelphia, PA: July 1991).
349  Chuck Matthei, "The Spirit of Work. Economics as If Values Mattered, Part 3." http://equitytrust.org/2011/09/the-spirit-of-work. First published in *Sojourrners Magazine* (February 1994).
350  Ramm interview.
351  Rebecca Dunn, interview by author, telephone, December 23, 2014.
352  Juliana Eades, interview by author, telephone, November 10, 2015.
353  DeWitt (Dick) Jones, interview by author, telephone, June 18, 2015.
354  NACDLF, "Report to the Membership," October 1987; "1988 Annual Report to the Membership of NACDLF," October 1988; "1989 Annual Report to the Membership of NACDLF," October 1989.
355  "Report to the Membership," October 1987, 3.
356  Ibid., 4. The investment was actually received in April 1989. ("NACDLF Annual Report," October 1989).
357  [50] Martin Paul Trimble, interview by author, Washington, DC, October 3, 2014.
358  Ibid. His dismissal came with the advent of a new administration at Pew.
359  Ibid.
360  National Association of Community Development Loan Funds, "Annual Report to the Membership of the National Association of Community Development Loan Funds. October 1989," 5.
361  Clara Miller, interview by author, telephone, May 20, 2017.

## Chapter 6

362  The Illinois Neighborhood Development Corporation was the regulated bank holding company that served as the umbrella for South Shore Bank and its associated nonprofit and for-profit development organizations. Hereafter, references to "South Shore Bank" typically refer to the retail banking operation, while "ShoreBank" is used to describe the overall entity; however, for many years, "South Shore" remained in common usage.
363  Houghton interview. ShoreBank was often used for the bank holding company, which included South Shore Bank in Chicago and various affiliates and subsidiaries.
364  Ibid.
365  In the late 1980s, the National Federation of Community Development Credit Unions collaborated with the Woodstock Institute of Chicago to organize Austin/West Garfield Federal Credit Union. There were loose contacts between ShoreBank and the credit union, but no systematic partnership.
366  Grzywinski interview.
367  Houghton interview.
368  Taub, 114. In credit unions serving low-income communities, the staff-to-asset ratio is frequently high, which conventionally (and in the eyes of examiners) stigmatizes them as "inefficient" institutions.

## Notes

369 Houghton interview.
370 Ibid.
371 Taub, 118–22.
372 Taub, 122–26.
373 Winthrop Rockefeller (1912–73), a third-generation Rockefeller, was the 37th governor of Arkansas (1966–70) and the first Republican since Reconstruction. Tom McRae IV served as president from 1975 to 1989. He later joined Southern Development Bank.
374 Walter Smiley, Darrin Williams, Dominik Mjartan (Southern Development Bank), interview by author, Little Rock, AR, April 16, 2015. Thomas Chipman McRae IV (1938–2004), the great grandson of a governor of Arkansas, served in the Peace Corps in Nepal and later in the Office of Economic Opportunity (OEO) in Washington. After leaving the Winthrop Rockefeller Foundation in 1989, he later served as vice president of Southern Development Bank and CEO of the Mountain Association for Community Economic Development (MACED) in Berea, KY, www.ruebelfuneralhome.com/archivedobits/2004/McRae, accessed July 13, 2015.
375 Grzywinski interview. Rev. Dr. David Ramage Jr. (1930–2010) had a long career that bridged and connected many of the streams that formed the community economic development movement. An ordained minister, he served on the board of Saul Alinsky's Industrial Areas Foundation, national church bodies, and later as president of the Center for Community Change. http://www.legacy.com/obituaries/bostonglobe/obituary.aspx?pid=139787670, accessed July 14, 2016. As the head of the New World Foundation in New York (1975–85), he played a critical role in the resurrection of the National Federation of Community Development Credit Unions in 1983, as described in Chapter 8.
376 Smiley interview.
377 Grzywinski interview.
378 Houghton interview.
379 Piercy, interview by author, telephone, October 6, 2014. Piercy later worked in the Clinton White House as deputy director of Presidential Personnel, after which she was appointed to the World Bank.
380 Grzywinski interview.
381 Surgeon, interview by author, Chicago, April 8, 2015.
382 Ibid.
383 Ibid.
384 Ibid.
385 Smiley et al. interview.
386 Hillary Rodham Clinton, *Living History* (New York: Scribner, 2003), 284.
387 Piercy interview.
388 In September 1995, Vindasius was named a White House Fellow, taking leave of the Good Faith Fund.
389 Smiley interview.
390 Press Release (Contact: George Stephanopoulos), September 16, 1992, "Creating Jobs, Helping entrepreneurs and building Communities. The Clinton Community Development Plan."
391 Lyndon Comstock, interview by Judith Karpova, 1989.
392 Ibid.
393 Ibid.
394 Ibid. Comstock recalls his early meeting with South Shore Bank this way: "They were polite but had no real interest in engaging with me." Email to author, November 3, 2015.
395 Karpova, ibid.
396 Lyndon Comstock, interview by author, Berkeley, CA, March 16, 2016.
397 Comstock, email to author, November 3, 2015.
398 Ibid.
399 I met Lyndon Comstock at a presentation I made about social investment in the mid-1980s when he was still employed as a banker. Subsequently, I served on the advisory board for Comstock's organizing effort.

400  Lyndon Comstock, letter from Ford Foundation Program Investment Officer Judith F. Samuelson, January 19, 1990. Courtesy of Lyndon Comstock.
401  "Synopsis of the Three Community Development Banks in the U.S.," March 26, 1994. Description of shareholders from memo to Rockefeller Brothers Files by WFM, June 15, 1991. An affiliate of the International Brotherhood of Electrical Workers (IBEW) was the largest single shareholder, owning 10 percent of all outstanding shares. Comstock, email to author, August 9, 2016.
402  Ibid.
403  Ibid. In 2000, Leap, Inc. merged with the Fifth Avenue Committee to form Brooklyn Workforce Innovations, which has become one of the most prominent workforce development organizations in New York City. Its program, Red Hook on the Road, has successfully trained unemployed public housing residents for commercial driving careers.
404  In summer 1983, three months into my role as CEO of the National Federation of CDCUs, I made my first field trip to North Carolina, at which time I met Martin Eakes. With his wife and partner, Bonnie Wright, I reviewed the business plan for Self-Help's proposed new credit union.
405  Subsequently, the requirements to charter a credit union became increasingly stiffer. Typically, regulators require prospective credit unions to provide firm, documented commitments of hundreds of thousands of grants and donations.
406  In the following decades, the Self-Help family would expand to include the Center for Responsible Lending, a major advocacy organization; a second credit union, Self-Help Federal Credit Union in California; a former bank in Chicago; and more.
407  See Chapter 8. The National Federation vigorously fought the restriction, which was gradually softened but not eliminated.
408  Schall, interview by author, Durham, NC, June 30, 2015.
409  Memo, "Organizations That Have Received Self-Help Credit Union Loans," December 1, 1985. Courtesy of the Center for Community Self-Help.
410  Schall interview.
411  When Self-Help went to the White House for the announcement of CDFI legislation in July 1993, one of the featured speakers was Tim Bazemore of the Workers Owned Sewing Company of Windsor, NC, which had received financing both from the Venture Fund and the credit union. (See Chapter 16.)
412  Schall interview.
413  "News from the Self-Help Credit Union," Fall 1989.
414  Newsletter, "Loan Report: 1988 Wrap-up, 1989 Goals."
415  "News from the Self-Help Credit Union," ibid.
416  Ibid.
417  This chronology comes from Self-Help's "Highlights from the First Ten Years."
418  Martin Eakes, email to author, June 3, 2015.
419  "The Future for Development Banking," delivered November 7, 1992.
420  Self-Help's scale has been adjusted to increase compensation for staff in high-cost areas, including California and Washington, DC.

## Chapter 7

421  Paul Lingenfelter, "Program Related Investments in Intermediary Organizations," January 1991, excerpt reprinted in Christie I. Baxter, *Program-Related Investments: A Technical Manual for Foundations* (New York: John Wiley & Sons, Inc., 1997), 271–77, 279.
422  Lingenfelter, interview by author, telephone, February 17, 2015.
423  Ibid.
424  Ibid. This lesson also impressed itself on Lingenfelter in the process of making a loan to LISC to finance multifamily housing on the West Side of Chicago, which weighed in at 15 inches of paperwork. "We decided we never again would make a loan that had recourse" except to the organization, he recalled.

## Notes

425  Lingenfelter, ibid., 1.
426  Ibid., 7–8.
427  "Table 1, John D. and Catherine T. MacArthur Foundation Program Related Investments (1983 through 1990)," Exhibit 5-1 in Lingenfelter article.
428  Adams-Morgan in Northwest DC in the 1970s was a heavily low-income area with a substantial and growing immigrant Latino population. Jubilee Housing, which later inspired James Rouse to create the Enterprise Foundation, was one of the organizations serving Adams-Morgan.
429  Tom Miller, interview by author, telephone, November 20, 2014.
430  Ibid.
431  Ibid.
432  Ibid.
433  Ibid.
434  "Equity Grant Review. Prepared for Ellen Arrick," Ford Foundation Records, Program Related Investments, Administrative Files (FA686), Series II: Consultant Files, Brody & Weiser, August 1988, Report #019942, Rockefeller Archive Center, 3. Page numbers cited in the text refer to this report.
435  Ibid., 52.
436  Ibid., 8.
437  Ibid., 13.
438  Ibid., 17.
439  Ibid., 4.
440  Ibid., 22.
441  Ibid., 34.
442  Ibid., 10.
443  In 1989, along with Peter Kinder and Steve Lydenberg, she began work on the Domini 400 Social Index, an index of mostly large-cap U.S. corporations with holdings selected on a range of social and environmental standards. In 2005, Amy Domini was named one of *TIME* magazine's 100 of the world's most influential people. https://www.domni.com/why-domini/our-team/amy-domini, accessed December 12, 2014.
444  Amy Domini, interview by author, telephone, December 12, 2014.
445  Formally, the Domestic and Foreign Missionary Society of the Protestant Episcopal Church in the United States of America, often referred to as "The Society," for short, in church documents.
446  Courtesy of Amy Domini. (Hereafter "Letter.")
447  "Letter," reproduced in The Joint Advisory Council on Alternative Investments, "Alternative Investments: An Analysis of Issues, Prepared to the Executive Council of the General Convention of the Episcopal Church and the Board of Trustees of the Church Pension Fund," June 11, 1990, ii.
448  "Letter," xx.
449  "Report to the Executive Council to the Domestic and Foreign Missionary Society of the Protestant Episcopal Church in the United States of America by the Committee on Trust Funds on Strategies Related to Alternative Investments," November 13, 1992.
450  "Alternative Investments," ibid.
451  Ibid., 5.
452  Ibid., 3.
453  Ibid., 4.
454  Ibid.
455  Ibid., 3.
456  Domini interview.
457  Eades interview.

458 The Mercy Loan Fund is a certified CDFI. Its 2015 annual report noted that it ended the year with $46 million in loans outstanding. Source: Mercy Housing, "2015 Mercy Loan Fund Annual Report."
459 Sarah Smith, interview by author, telephone, January 21, 2016.
460 A certified CDFI, the Leviticus Fund has long been a leader of the New York State Coalition of CDFIs. By June 30, 2016, its lending pool had reached $31.7 million, including $8.5 million in equity. It had loaned $65 million and created more than 3,000 affordable housing units. Source: www.leviticusfund.org, accessed August 3, 2016.
461 Carol Coston, OP, "Women Religious Invest in Their Values." In *Journey in Faith and Fidelity,* edited by Nadine Foley, OP (New York: Continuum, 1999), 231.
462 Coston, 230.
463 Ibid., 232. Ultimately, the zoning permit was obtained after an economic boycott by African Americans. See also Chapter 13, testimony by Robert Jackson of Quitman County FCU to Congress.
464 Coston, 234.
465 Ibid., 235.
466 Tim Smith, interview by author, telephone, January 27, 2016. Smith served as executive director of ICCR until 2000, transitioning to a position at a social investment firm, Walden Asset Management (later a division of Boston Trust and Investment Management Company), directing shareholder engagement. For five years, he served as board chair of the Social Investment Forum. Ron Phillips, who went on to run Coastal Enterprises, Inc., a leading CDC and CDFI, was director of ICCR's Corporate Information Center in the 1970s.
467 According to Tim Smith, the clearinghouse functioned until about 1990, when it was discontinued in a restructuring. By this time, Smith recounts, "the world of community development had become more sophisticated," and there were other channels through which investors and CDFIs could connect. Ibid.
468 Social Investment Forum, "The Social Balance Sheet: Executive Summary," April 25, 1985, citing ICCR.
469 Among mutual funds active in the social investment arena were Calvert, Dreyfus, Parnassus, Pax World, and New Alternatives, while Working Assets and Calvert operated screened money market funds. Ibid.
470 Fenton Communications, "Social Investment Forum Adds Bank to Social Balance Sheet. South Shore Bank's 'Social Paper' Outperforms the Average." Press release (undated).
471 Ibid.
472 The "Social Balance Sheet" cited Cooperative Fund of New England, Fund for an Open Society, ICE, the Industrial Cooperative Association, the MACED Cumberland Fund, the Massachusetts Urban Revitalization Advisory Group Revolving Loan fund, and the Self-Help Association for a Regional Economy as recipients of social investment. MACED was the largest, with $3.5 million in assets.
473 Social Investment Forum, "Survey of Alternative Investments" (September 1989), 3. Prepared by Beate Klein Becker and Shirley Selhub. Chuck Matthei (ICE) and Joan Shapiro (South Shore Bank) were both on the Project Advisory Group. "Alternative investments" were typically those in organizations focused on affordable housing, small business, cooperatives, land trusts, environmental initiatives, or economic opportunity for low- and moderate-income people.
474 Ibid., 1. The 114 respondents ("members and friends" of SIF) included financial professionals (investment managers, brokers, and others), individual and institutional investors, and "development lenders"—primarily loan funds, but also several banks and credit unions.
475 Ibid., 2.
476 Ibid., 4. The authors refrained from emphasizing the obvious. Clearly, CDFIs had a limited capacity to absorb social investment funds even if all other barriers were removed. To some degree, this conundrum has persisted to the present.
477 Ibid., 5–6.
478 Ibid., 9.
479 Ibid., 12.
480 Ibid., 29.

# Notes

## Chapter 8

481  National Federation of Community Development Credit Unions, *Tenth Anniversary Journal,* November 1981.
482  Ibid., 5.
483  Leander J. Foley III, a partner in Moss, McGee, Bellmon, Bradley, Ushio & Foley, was a strong advocate for community development and anti-poverty programs for decades. On numerous occasions, he provided pro bono counsel and assistance to the National Federation; later, he also advised the CDFI Coalition.
484  Market interest rates were, in fact, very high in the early 1980s; the federal prime rate hit an all-time high of 21.50 percent on December 19, 1980. By August 18, 1982, it was 14.0 percent. Only by May 20, 1985, did it fall back to 10 percent. http://www.fedprimerate.com/wall_street_journal_prime_rate_history .htm#primeratealltimehigh>, accessed August 19, 2016. When the CDCU Revolving Loan Fund was eventually reactivated in 1984, interest rates would be 7.5 percent (Source: National Federation of Community Development Credit Unions, *25th Anniversary Journal*). Many of the credit unions that chose to accept these funds soon failed.
485  Letter of August 31, 1982. Courtesy of National Federation of Community Development Credit Unions.
486  "Proposal to NFCDCU Board of Directors from Capitalization Fund Issue Forum Participants. NFCDCU Sixth Annual Meeting—Nov. 20, 1981." Courtesy of National Federation of Community Development Credit Unions.
487  Jim Williams, President, CUNA, letter from Jim Clark, August 9, 1982. Courtesy of National Federation of Community Development Credit Unions.
488  See Chapter 6 on Ramage's role with respect to Southern Development Bank.
489  Similarly, the federation was unsuccessful in obtaining support from the Equitable Life Assurance Society's Urban Initiatives Division, then headed by Kirsten Moy. (Letter to Kirsten Moy from Jim Clark, December 7, 1982).
490  National Federation of Community Development Credit Unions, press release, November 18, 1982.
491  When the federation launched its Capitalization Program in 1982–83, it accepted loans at up to 8 percent from religious organizations, which it reinvested in CDCUs at rates that peaked at 10 percent. Although high by recent standards, the rate was still below-market. Yield was important to the women's orders, because they depended on the income for their retirement.
492  National Federation of Community Development Credit Unions, *CDCU Report*, March 1985.
493  National Federation of Community Development Credit Unions, *News Bulletin,* Vol. 2, Issue 11, August/September 1982.
494  "History of Impact," https://ncb.coop/default.aspx?id=5084. The Office of Self-Help was incorporated as a District of Columbia nonprofit called the Consumer Cooperative Development Corporation in 1982. By 1985, it had become the NCB Development Corporation (NCBDC). In 2004, NCBC won an allocation of $75 million under the New Markets Tax Credit Program to help charter schools and health centers in economically distressed communities. In 2006, NCBDC became NCB Capital Impact, and in 2011 it became an independent CDFI, no longer an affiliate of NCB.
495  Board of Federation, letter from Jim Clark, April 25, 1980.
496  The figures are from audited financial statements by Misthal and Schwartz, May 10 and May 11, 1983.
497  The Community Credit Union Job Training Program developed out of the experience that CDCUs had in training their members in credit union operations and, frustratingly, seeing them snatched up by banks or other employers. The federation's program was led by Joy Cousminer, an adult educator by background who founded and for more than four decades managed the Bethex Federal Credit Union in the South Bronx. Many of the graduates moved on to positions in the credit union industry, including Pablo DeFilippi, a Chilean immigrant who later became the manager of the Lower East Side People's FCU and, eventually, a senior staff member of the National Federation of CDCUs.
498  Robert A. Bennett, "Deregulation Alters Banking," *New York Times,* December 5, 1983, Late Edition.
499  In retrospect, it may be surprising that some banks indeed provided these kinds of services to low-income people. In fact, on January 27, 1984, the day before my presentation, a *New York Times* article cited Manufacturers Hanover

Trust (MHT)'s plans to stop cashing welfare checks and distributing food stamps at more than 100 branches. MHT was virtually the last major bank to provide these services. MHT's plans to abandon its branch spurred the campaign to organize the Lower East Side Peoples Federal Credit Union in 1984.

500   Clifford N. Rosenthal, "The New Era in Financial Services: Implications for Low- and Moderate-Income Neighborhoods." Courtesy of the National Federation of Community Development Credit Unions.

501   Clifford N. Rosenthal and Joseph Schoder, *"People's Credit": A Study of the Lending of the Lower East Side People's Federal Credit Union, 1986–89* (New York: National Federation of Community Development Credit Unions, 1990).

502   Although an 18-month process of obtaining a charter may appear unduly long, the process became far longer in later decades—typically three or four years, a formidable barrier for any community group aspiring to start a credit union.

503   Carlyle C. Douglas, "Banking Makes Return to Ave. B.," *New York Times*, May 2, 1986, 1.

504   National Federation of Community Development Credit Unions, "Community Reinvestment Breakthrough: Lower East Side Group Obtains Major Bank Commitment," *CDCU Report*, March 1986, 6.

505   This account is drawn from "People's Credit," i–iii. I participated in the meetings of October 1985 at the Federal Reserve Bank. By the mid-1980s, the National Credit Union Administration (NCUA) was issuing barely 50 new federal charters a year in the whole United States, compared with several hundred a year in the 1970s. By the first decade of the 21st century, NCUA issued fewer than 10 new charters a year—and in some years, none at all.

506   National Federation of Community Development Credit Unions, *CDCU Report*, Fall 1985, 1, 6. Even after raising the cost of its loans to credit unions to 7.5 percent, the National Credit Union Administration made continuing efforts to abolish the Community Development Revolving Loan Fund altogether (National Federation of Community Development Credit Unions, *25th Anniversary Journal*, 13.) Once again, the federation and its allies managed to defeat OMB's efforts (*CDCU Report*, ibid., 1).

507   The Community Development Revolving Loan Fund for Credit Unions resided within the Department of Health and Human Services, which had little knowledge of and less interest in the program. Reluctantly, given the federation's longstanding opposition to placing the program in the hands of the regulator, NCUA, we supported transferring the program to that agency. This was accomplished through the Community Development Credit Union Revolving Loan Fund Transfer Act of 1986—"the only piece of banking legislation to pass the 99th Congress" ("Annual Report of the National Federation of CDCUS," 1986, 2). It still took several years for the program to become operational, but ultimately, it survived and expanded greatly at NCUA.

508   *CDCU Report*, Fall 1985.

509   RCA, an industrial electronics firm rather than a financial company, was not an obvious candidate to invest. Its investment was made possible by a family contact with a senior RCA executive. Programmatically, RCA had an interest in Indianapolis, where it had an operation. The federation had two member CDCUs there that aligned with the company's interests.

510   *CDCU Report*, March 1986, 1,7.

511   The federation's annual CPA audit showed a fund balance of $20,505—approximately 2 percent of assets. (DeFino, D'Elia & Co., "Years ended December 31, 1987 and 1986," 4.)

512   National Federation of Community Development Credit Unions, "Annual Report, 1986," 5.

513   Clifford Rosenthal, "Memo to the Board of Directors and Alternates," April 19, 1986; "Annual Report, 1986," 12–13.

514   Downloading and processing the data was far beyond the federation's capacity. We were assisted by The Fund for the City of New York.

515   Prepared by Ward Smith, president, NFCDCU; Clifford Rosenthal, executive director, NFCDCU; and Harold Gore, Department of Health and Human Services, Office of Community Services. Hereafter cited as "Report to the White House."

516   "Report to the White House," 11.

517   Ibid., 13, 15, 16.

518   Memo to the Board of Directors and Alternates from Cliff Rosenthal, October 4, 1986.

519   "Report to the White House," 107–11.

## Notes

520  "White House Briefing Highlights Federation's Annual Meeting," *CDCU Report*, June 1987, 1.
521  Ibid., 11.
522  Mary Reardon, quoted in Thomas E. McGrath, "A Tale of CDCUs," *Credit Union News* (May 7, 1987): 3.
523  Memo to Community Banking Advocates from Cliff Rosenthal, executive director, NFCDCU, Re: "Creation of a 'Neighborhood Banking Corporation' (NBC)," March 8, 1988.
524  NFCDCU, "Proposal to Establish the Neighborhood Banking Corporation: Overview," March 8, 1988, 1.
525  Ibid.
526  Ibid., 2.
527  Memo to Ellen Arrick, Program-Related Investments, Ford Foundation, from Cliff Rosenthal, executive director, NFCDCU, "Update on Community Development Credit Unions (CDCUs)." In fact, most of these objectives would be fulfilled over the next decades. The federation pioneered secondary capital in 1996; created the CDCU Institute in 1999; and developed a secondary market for CDCU housing loans in the early 2000s.
528  Memorandum to the Board of Directors, November 3, 1988. Courtesy of the National Federation of Community Development Credit Unions.
529  Quoted in "NCUA Loan Program Halted," *CDCU Report*, Spring/Summer 1988.
530  Michael Casey and Rick Hornung, "King of Omaha," *Village Voice*, February 29, 1989, 29. The *Village Voice* for many years was a New York City newspaper renowned for its investigative reporting.
531  Ibid.
532  Ibid.
533  Rick Atkinson, "Omaha's Hurricane of Scandal: Larry E. King Jr., in the Eye of the Storm Over Fraud, Restitution," *Washington Post,* April 1, 1990, F2. The publisher of the *Omaha World-Herald,* for example, was one of King's biggest supporters and raised money for the remodeling of Franklin's office.
534  Casey and Hornung, 30.
535  Ibid., 31. These charges were never proved, and they were not the ones for which Lawrence King pleaded guilty.
536  Atkinson, F1.
537  *Wall Street Journal,* Section B, 8. Retrieved from LexisNexis® Academic, August 28, 2016.
538  "Chronology of Events Linked to Franklin Credit Union," *Omaha World-Herald,* July 25, 1990, 14.
539  Memo to the Board of Directors and Alternates from Cliff Rosenthal, "Franklin Community FCU Liquidation," November 21, 1988. Courtesy of National Federation of Community Development Credit Unions.
540  Typically, NCUA drafts rules, solicits extensive public comments, and then issues final rules, a process that may take as long as 18 months. In this case, NCUA provided no advance written notice whatsoever to credit unions. The NCUA Board met on December 14 and passed an Interim Final Rule, effective five days later. (NFCDCU press release, "New Federal Regulation Strikes Blow at Low-Income Financial Institutions" (Undated, January 1989).
541  National Federation of Community Development Credit Unions, *5th Anniversary Journal,* 12.
542  DeFino, D'Elia & Co., Certified Public Accountants, Independent Auditor's Report for 1990 and 1989, 2, 4.

## Chapter 9

543  NACDLF, "1989 Annual Report," 5.
544  Trimble.
545  NACDLF, "1991 Year End Report," 4.
546  Ibid., 6.
547  NCUA was an independent agency, but its three-person board consisted of two Senate-confirmed members of the party in power and one from the other party. Terms are six years and are not synchronized with presidential elections. The Republican-dominated NCUA would eventually switch to a Democratic two-to-one majority board after the 1992 elections.
548  National Federation of Community Development Credit Unions, *25th Anniversary Journal,* 14.

549 Rep. Flake, along with Rep. Thomas Ridge, had already begun pressing for the Bank Enterprise Award (BEA) program. (See Chapters 10, 16, and 17.)

550 "Agreement between Credit Union National Association, Inc. and National Federation of Community Development Credit Unions," signed February 26, 1991. Courtesy of National Federation of Community Development Credit Unions.

551 Although the federation's board of directors was always autonomous, for five years I was simultaneously a vice president for association services of CUNA and executive director of the federation. The dual reporting arrangement was inherently unstable and contributed to the ultimate dissolution of the arrangement between the two organizations.

552 Louis, who had done much of the feasibility work for the federation's Ford-funded demonstration project, later became a prominent columnist for the *Daily News* in New York City, a commentator on CNN, and the host of a popular nightly cable television show devoted to New York and national politics. Robert Jackson, the CEO of the Quitman County Development Corporation and founder of its credit union, was a county commissioner in Marks, MS, and later the first African American state senator for his district, which he has represented from 2004 to the present (2018).

553 Memo to the Board of Directors and Alternates from Cliff Rosenthal, "Board Meeting Follow-Up," March 5, 1991.

554 March 18, 1991, memo to the board, ibid.

555 NACDLF, "1991 Year End Report," 7–8.

556 Ibid., 8.

557 Lyndon Comstock letter to the author, November 13, 1991. This and subsequent memoranda and letters: courtesy of Lyndon Comstock.

558 Lyndon Comstock letter to Jeremy Nowak and Martin Trimble, December 27, 1991, "CDFI Educational Program." Nearly a quarter-century later, the CDFI Fund launched a "capacity-building initiative" that would draw upon the various sectors.

559 Lyndon Comstock letter to Martin Trimble, November 29, 1991.

560 Lyndon Comstock letter to Jeremy Nowak and Martin Trimble, November 18, 1991.

561 NACLDF, "1991 Year End Report," 8.

562 Ibid., 8–9.

## Chapter 10

563 Center for Community Change, "Action Alert," May 28, 1991. Courtesy of National Federation of Community Development Credit Unions.

564 Paulette Thomas, "House Panel Clears Measure Covering Low-Income Loans," *Wall Street Journal*, June 21, 1991, Eastern edition, A2.

565 Ibid.

566 Ridge was later elected governor of Pennsylvania. Subsequently, he served as director of the Office of Homeland Security.

567 Center for Community Change, ibid.

568 Zavarello, interview by author, Washington, DC, March 10, 2016.

569 As of 2016, according to the church's website, "The church and its subsidiary corporations operate with an annual budget of over $34 million. The church also owns expansive commercial and residential developments; a 600-student private school founded by Flake and his wife, Elaine; and various commercial and social service enterprises, which has placed it among the nation's most productive religious and urban development institutions. The corporations, church administrative offices, school, and ministries comprise one of the Borough of Queens' largest private sector employers." http://allencathedral.org/about-us/allen-ame-floyd-flake/

570 The church had sponsored a credit union, but it was tiny in comparison with the church's development needs and, in any case, was an independent, conservative entity. Rev. Flake was widely admired in the African American church

## Notes

world; he was a prominent speaker both at the federation's first national church credit union conference in 1992 and at the federation's 25th anniversary celebration, launched at Trinity Church in June 1999.

571 Email from Stein to author, September 23, 2016. Erdreich lost his election in 1992 as a result of redistricting to Republican Spencer Bachus, who later became a leading critic of the CDFI Fund.

572 Rep. Tom Ridge, "Bank Enterprise Act Coauthor Disappointed by Coverage," *American Banker*, letter to the editor, January 7, 1992, 4.

573 Immergluck, 268.

574 Sec. 232(c), Availability of Funds.

575 F. Simon Tolbert and Richard K. Kneipper, "Comment: Instead of Complaining, Banks Should Look on the Bright Side of CRA," *American Banker*, August 23, 1993, 18.

576 Zavarello interview, ibid.

577 Letter to Jeannine Jacokes, Senate Banking Committee (cc: Victoria Stein, Stacy Hayes of House Banking Subcommittee on Policy Research and Insurance), from Clifford N. Rosenthal, executive director, NFCDCU, March 17, 1992.

578 Jacokes, email to author, October 17, 2016.

579 Mr. Don Winn, Office of Congressional Affairs, Board of Governors, Federal Reserve System, letter from Steven B. Harris, staff director and chief counsel, Committee on Banking, Housing, and Urban Affairs, July 8, 1992.

580 "Traditional and Non-Traditional Lenders' Role," 1. Subsequent page references are to this document.

581 Ibid., 55–56.

582 Ibid., 3–4.

583 Ibid., 65.

584 Ibid., 4–5.

585 Ibid., 6.

586 Ibid., 73.

587 Ibid., 6–7.

588 Ibid., 22.

589 Ibid., 8.

590 Ibid., 46.

591 Ibid., 193.

592 Ibid., 27.

593 Ibid., 133–34.

594 Ibid., 33–34.

595 Ibid., 35–36.

596 Ibid., 37–38.

597 Ibid., 172.

598 In fact, this proposed trust structure was similar to one suggested by the National Federation of CDCUs.

599 Ibid., 117–9.

600 Ibid., 10.

601 Ibid., 121.

602 Ibid., 11.

603 Ibid., 123.

604 Ibid., 46–49.

605 Ibid., 211.

606 Ibid., 206.

607 Ibid., 211.

608 Ibid., 38.

609 Ibid., 157.

610 Ibid., 30–32.
611 Ibid., 158–9.
612 Ibid., 69–70.
613 Ibid., 84.
614 Ibid., 76.
615 Ibid., 39.
616 Ibid.
617 Ibid., 33.
618 Ibid., 175.
619 Ibid., 20.
620 Ibid., 84.
621 Ibid., 13.
622 Ibid., 83.
623 Ibid., 85.
624 Memorandum from Lingenfelter, August 17, 1992, 163.
625 Ibid., 40.
626 Ibid., 175.
627 "Traditional and Non-Traditional Lenders," 18.
628 Ibid., 41.
629 Ibid., 15–16.
630 Ibid., 18.
631 H.R. 5334 (102nd): Housing and Community Development Act of 1992, https://www.govtrack.us/congress/bills/102/hr5334, accessed September 29, 2016.
632 Sections (a)(1) and (a)(2) of H.R. 5334 provided $3 million each for "a nonprofit community-based public benefit corporation which was created in response to the civil disturbances of April 29, 1992, through May 6, 1992" and a nonprofit public benefit corporation to be established by the mayor of Los Angeles and governor of California. (Subsequent section numbers refer to this bill.)
633 Sec. 853, A and B.
634 Sec. 853, D and E.
635 Sec. 853, (3)(D)(I), (II); (ii), (iii)
636 Ibid.
637 Sec. 853, (7) Capital Assistance, (ii) and (iii)
638 Sec. 853, (4) Selection Criteria, (G)
639 John T. Woolley and Gerhard Peters, *The American Presidency Project,* http://www.presidency.ucsb.edu/ws/print.php?pid=21697, accessed September 29, 2016.
640 Jacokes email to author.

## Chapter 11

641 *The Arsenio Hall Show,* June 3, 1992.
642 Gwen Ifill, "The 1992 Campaign: Youth Vote; Clinton Goes Eye to Eye with MTV Generation," *New York Times,* June 17, 1992, http://www.nytimes.com/1992/06/17/us/the-1992-campaign-youth-vote-clinton-goes-eye-to-eye-with-mtv-generation.html.
643 Jon Meacham, "The Grace of George H.W. Bush," *New York Times,* October 16, 2016, 46.
644 Gerhard Peters and John T. Woolley, "1992 Democratic Party Platform," *The American Presidency Project,* July 13, 1992, http://www.presidency.ucsb.edu/ws/?pid=29610.

## Notes

645 Press Release (Contact: George Stephanopoulos), September 16, 1992, "Creating Jobs, Helping entrepreneurs and building Communities. The Clinton Community Development Plan." Fax copy, September 21, 1992, courtesy of National Federation of Community Development Credit Unions. Hereafter: Press Release, "Creating Jobs."

646 Other related points in the press release call for the establishment of Individual Development Accounts (IDAs), an asset-building strategy later embraced enthusiastically by many CDFIs, including especially CDCUs and microenterprise funds; and the creation of 75 to 125 "comprehensive enterprise zones." IDAs were a central part of strategies developed by Professor Michael Sherraden (*Assets for the Poor*) and the Corporation for Enterprise Development (CFED).

647 Ibid.

648 Ibid.

649 Martin Eakes, email to author, June 3, 2015.

650 Press Release, "Creating Jobs."

651 Ibid.

652 Hunter S. Thompson, "Mr. Bill's Neighborhood," *Rolling Stone*, September 17, 1992. Along with Thompson, the interviewers included the novelist P.J. O'Rourke; *Rolling Stone*'s publisher, Jann S. Wenner; and William Greider, with whom NACDLF had developed a close relationship. (See Chapter 9.) Hereafter: *Rolling Stone* interview.

653 Although Jan Piercy is often described as Hillary's "roommate," she explained to me that they were not exactly roommates, but rather close neighbors in the dormitory hall. (Jan Piercy, interview by author, telephone, October 6, 2014.)

654 *Rolling Stone* interview. The Good Faith Fund actually was affiliated with Southern Development Bank.

655 *Rolling Stone* interview.

## Chapter 12

656 CDFIs included Community Capital Bank, the Enterprise Foundation, ShoreBank, Self-Help, Southern Development Bancorpration, the National Federation of CDCUs, LISC, the Woodstock Institute, and the National Association of Community Development Loan Funds. Chase and Chemical were consulted, as well as the Independent Bankers of America and the American Bankers Association. Among advocates, ACORN, the Center for Community Change, and the Center for Study of Responsive Law were polled. The Michigan State Housing Development Authority and the National Association of Lenders to Low- and Moderate-Income Housing rounded out the list, along with a member of the Clinton Transition Team.

657 Memo to Senate Banking Committee staff—Matt Roberts, Jeannine Jacokes, Rick Carnell, and Konrad Alt—from Lyndon Comstock, November 20, 1992.

658 Ibid.

659 Ibid.

660 Center for Community Self-Help, "Response to Senate Banking Committee Questions Regarding Community Development Banks," November 30, 1992, 3.

661 Ibid., 5.

662 Ibid., 6.

663 Ibid., 10, 14, 18.

664 Ibid., 10.

665 "Concept Paper: The National Neighborhood Finance Corporation (NNFC)," July 9, 1992, 2.

666 Clifford Rosenthal and Errol T. Louis, "Concept Paper, Executive Summary," 1.

667 The National Federation had consistently criticized the reluctance of the National Credit Union Administration (NCUA) to charter new credit unions in low-income areas. For several years, the federation had assisted a South Central Los Angeles organizing group in applying—unsuccessfully—for a charter. Only after the riots in April 1992 did NCUA move expeditiously to grant a charter.

668 Memorandum to Senate Banking Committee staff (Roberts, Jacokes, Carnell, Alt), "Community Development Banks," from Martin Paul Trimble (NACDLF) and Mark Pinsky (NACDLF), November 18, 1982.
669 Ibid., 2.
670 Ibid.
671 Ibid.
672 https://umc-gbcs.org/about-us/the-united-methodist-building, accessed October 31, 2016.
673 Memorandum to meeting participants from Pinsky and Trimble, November 17, 1992.
674 Author's meeting notes, November 20, 1992. Courtesy of National Federation of Community Development Credit Unions.
675 Presidential Transition Domestic Policy Staff. Cover memo prepared by Al From and Bruce Reed. *History of the Domestic Policy Council and Clinton Administration History Project,* "Domestic Policy Council – Documentary Annex II [6]," Clinton Digital Library, accessed November 17, 2016, http://clinton.presidentiallibraries.us/items/show/4577, 1.
676 Ibid.
677 Ibid., 2.
678 Ibid., 3.
679 Ibid., 6.
680 Ibid., 4.
681 Ibid., 5–6.
682 Ibid., 13.
683 Ibid., 15.
684 Letter to Christopher Edley Jr. from author, December 7, 1992. Courtesy of National Federation of Community Development Credit Unions.
685 I recall that Martin Trimble was in favor of storming the office, but we managed to restrain ourselves.
686 Courtney Ward, interview by author, telephone, November 2, 2016.
687 The account of the meeting with Courtney Ward on December 10, 1992, which I attended, comes from my notes, courtesy of National Federation of Community Development Credit Unions.
688 Ibid.
689 "CU representative at Clinton's Economic Summit foresees larger role," *Credit Union Times,* January 13, 1993.
690 Caryl Stewart conference call with author and Martin Eakes, December 16, 1992. Author's notes, courtesy of National Federation of Community Development Credit Unions.
691 Hyman P. Minsky, Dimitri B. Papadimitriou, Ronnie J. Philips, and L. Randall Wray, "Community Development Banks," Working Paper No. 83 (Annandale-on-Hudson, NY: Levy Economics Institute of Bard College, December 1992). Hyman P. Minsky, "Community Service and Development Banks: A Concept Paper," Hyman P. Minsky Archive, Paper 279 (January 12, 1993), http://digitalcommons.bard.edu/hm_archive/279.
692 Minsky et al., unpaginated.
693 Minsky, January 12 concept paper, 2.
694 Ibid., 19.
695 Ibid., 29–30.
696 Jerry Knight, "Banker Groups Endorse Clinton Idea," *Washington Post,* December 20, 1992, A18.
697 Meeting with Ken Robinson, CEO (NAFCU), Bill Donovan (NAFCU), and Martin Eakes, Arlington, VA, December 9, 1992, author's notes.
698 See Chapter 9.
699 Letter to Bill Clinton from Ralph S. Swoboda, president of CUNA, December 3, 1992, sent to author, December 7, 1992. Also reported in Bureau of National Affairs, Inc. *Regulation, Economics, and Law,* December 7, 1992.
700 Robert Pear, "A Lending Plan for the Distressed," *New York Times,* January 18, 1993, D. 1.
701 Knight.

Notes

702  Ibid.
703  Pear, ibid.
704  See Chapter 23.

## Chapter 13

705  Neil R. Peirce, "Clinton's Risky Plan for Development Banks," *Washington Post*, January 16, 1993, F26.
706  Following contentious negotiation, NCCED joined after a March 26 meeting with coalition representatives in Chicago. A group of leading CDCs had pressed for 2,000 of their peers to be eligible for the new CDFI Fund. The coalition successfully argued that only those with affiliates or units engaged primarily in financing should be considered CDFIs. Memorandum to NACDLF Public Policy Committee from Mark Pinsky, Re: NACDLF's Public Policy Project, May 12, 1993. Courtesy of National Association of Community Development Loan Funds.
707  "Principles of Community Development Lending & Proposals for Key Federal Support," 4. Emphasis added throughout the listing of key principles.
708  Ibid., 5.
709  Ibid., 5-6.
710  Ibid., 6. Here, too, the coalition was arguing against the kind of strategy that was employed in the War on Poverty, when the OEO attempted to foster the emergence of hundreds of new low-income credit unions.
711  Ibid., 7. In formulating the "Principles," the National Federation and Woodstock Institute were concerned with avoiding the problems of the War on Poverty. In fact, the dangers of "fraud and abuse" in the failings of the War on Poverty were, at least with respect to CDCUs, overstated compared with the failings of management capacity and government policy. (See Chapter 2.)
712  Ibid.
713  See Chapter 4.
714  "Principles," 2.
715  Ibid., 4.
716  Ibid., 8.
717  Ibid., 9.
718  Ibid., 10.
719  Lyndon Comstock, Memorandum, February 12,1993, "Congressional Hearings and Congressional Briefing on Community Development Financial Institutions, February 2-3, 1993." Courtesy of Lyndon Comstock.
720  Ibid.
721  "Update on CDFI Coalition Activities," from Mark Pinsky, February 19, 1993.
722  Memo to Community Capital Bank Board of Directors, "Federal support for community development banks," from Lyndon Comstock, January 23, 1993. The Ben & Jerry's franchise featured prominently in the Rose Garden ceremony of July 15. Courtesy of Lyndon Comstock.
723  Robert B. Cox, *Banking Week*, February 1, 1993, 11.
724  NNC was led at the time by Bud Kanitz, a veteran CRA advocate and ally of Gale Cincotta during his days in Chicago.
725  Author's meeting notes. Courtesy of National Federation of Community Development Credit Unions.
726  Comstock memo, February 12, 1993, distribution list unspecified. Courtesy of Lyndon Comstock. Later, the committee heard testimony from bank regulators, the National Cooperative Bank, ACORN, Ralph Nader, Chase Community Development Corporation, and banking trade associations.
727  See Chapter 3.
728  Marcy Kaptur testimony to Hearing before the Subcommittee on Financial Institutions (typescript), February 2, 1993, 6-7, 10. Courtesy of National Federation of Community Development Credit Unions.

729　Also participating were Kathy Tholin of the Woodstock Institute; Connie Evans of AEO; Brian Hassel of Self-Help; Robert Jackson of Quitman County Federal Credit Union; Jeremy Nowak of the Delaware Valley Community Reinvestment Fund; and Michael Swack of Southern New Hampshire University.

730　Author's notes. Courtesy of National Federation of Community Development Credit Unions.

731　Ibid.

732　"Problems in Community Development Banking, Mortgage Lending Discrimination, Reverse Redlining, and Home Equity Lending." Hearings before the Committee on Banking, Housing, and Urban Affairs, 103rd Cong., February 3, 1993, "Community Development Banking," 1–3.

733　Ibid., 4–5.

734　Memorandum to Banking Committee Members, Banking Committee Staff and LAs, and Housing and Urban Affairs from Jeannine Jacokes and Matt Roberts, January 29, 1993. Courtesy of Jeannine Jacokes.

735　Ibid., 7–8.

736　Ibid., 9.

737　Ibid., 17–19.

738　Ibid., 23.

739　Ibid., 31.

740　Ibid., 37.

741　Ibid., 40.

742　Ibid., 34.

743　Ibid., 41.

744　Ibid., 59.

745　Jackson was a county supervisor (commissioner) in Quitman County, and later, the first African American state senator elected to Mississippi's District 11.

746　Ibid., 49–50.

747　Ibid., 54.

748　Ibid., 177–79.

749　Ibid., 181–82.

750　Ibid., 131–32.

751　Ibid., 134.

752　Ibid., 198.

753　Ibid., 207.

754　Ibid., 199–200.

755　Letter to President William J. Clinton from Paul S. Sarbanes and Donald W. Riegle Jr., March 8, 1993. Courtesy of Jeannine Jacokes.

## Chapter 14

756　http://www.american-presidents.com/bill-clinton/1993-state-of-the-union-address/, accessed May 31, 2016.

757　The NEC was created by executive order on January 25, 1993. The Domestic Policy Council was established informally in January and formally by executive order on August 16, 1993. See Shambaugh and Weinstein, 35, 39.

758　Memo to the President (cc: Mack, Rubin, Rasco), from John Podesta, February 15, 1993. Clinton Presidential Library.

759　Paul Weinstein Jr., interview by author, Washington, DC, February 22, 2016. When the Clinton administration entered office, Weinstein first served as a senior policy analyst; later, he moved up to become special assistant to the president for domestic policy, and in Clinton's second term, he served as chief of staff of the Domestic Policy Council.

760　The "War Room" had nothing to do with war but, as Weinstein remarked, with rapid response. The term later became established in the political lexicon. A documentary about the Clinton campaign with that name was made by Chris Hegedus and D.A. Pennebaker and released in 1993. It was nominated for an Academy Award in 1994.

## Notes

761 Ibid.

762 "Cisneros Says Community Development Plan Will Use Banks, Thrifts, Credit Unions." Quoted in *Regulation, Economics, and Law,* March 4, 1993, No. 41, A-12.

763 Senator Bill Bradley, Floor Speech to Senate, "Statement on Urban Community-Building Initiative. March 18, 1993." Fax copy courtesy of National Federation of Community Development Credit Unions.

764 Ibid. Chartered in 1984, by 2016 the credit union today served more than 3,000 members with assets of more than $3 million.

765 Subcommittee on General Oversight, Investigations, and the Resolution of Failed Financial Institutions, "The Bank Enterprise Act's Ability to Catalyze Community Development Banking." Press release (April 21, 1993).

766 Text of speech, received by CDFI Coalition. Courtesy of National Federation of CDCUs.

767 Ibid.

768 Memorandum to Ad Hoc Coalition of CDFIs, "White House & CDC Meetings (and related events)," from Mark Pinsky and Cliff Rosenthal, March 29, 1993. Also: handwritten notes by the author. Courtesy of National Federation of CDCUs.

769 Ibid. In a follow-up letter the week after meeting with Weinstein, the coalition emphasized its support for strengthening CRA, affirming that bank lending and CDFIs were not an "either/or" proposition, but rather "both/and." Draft letter to Paul Weinstein from the Coalition of Community Development Financial Institutions, April 1, 1993. Courtesy of National Federation of CDCUs.

770 Pinsky and Rosenthal, March 29 memo.

771 Memorandum for the President, "Economic Empowerment Agenda," from Bruce Reed and Gene Sperling, April 19, 1993. *History of the Domestic Policy Council and Clinton Administration History Project,* "Domestic Policy Council – Documentary Annex II [3]," Clinton Digital Library, accessed November 3, 2017, https://clinton.presidentiallibraries.us/items/show/4574.

772 Although Riegle's Community Investment Corporation Demonstration (CICD) was signed into law, the Clinton initiative superseded the $30 million pilot program.

773 Memorandum to the CDFI Coalition, "President's Enterprise/Empowerment Zones Proposal & CDFIs," from Mark Pinsky, May 5, 1993.

774 Memorandum to NACDLF Public Policy Committee, "NACDLF's Public Policy Project," from Mark Pinsky, May 12, 1993. Provided by NACDLF member.

775 McKee later served as the first interim director of the CDFI Fund.

776 Memorandum to Mark Pinsky, Jeremy Nowak, and Martin Trimble; Errol Louis and Cliff Rosenthal; Bob Rapoza and Vicki Stein; Frank DiGiovanni and Lisa Mensah, from Kate McKee and Bryan Hassel (Self-Help). Courtesy of National Federation of Community Development Credit Unions.

777 Weinstein interview. ACORN was the acronym for the Association of Community Organizations for Reform Now, one of most prominent national, multi-issue advocacy groups.

778 Ibid.

779 Pear.

780 Memorandum for the President, "Community Development Banks and the Commerce Department," from Ronald H. Brown, February 4, 1993. (Forwarded to Carol Rasco by John Podesta, assistant to the president and staff secretary, February 15, 1993). Brown, the first African American Secretary of Commerce, died with 34 others in a plane crash in Croatia in 1996. Domestic Policy Council, Carol Rasco, and Subject Series, "Community Development Banks [2]," Clinton Digital Library, accessed November 3, 2017, https://clinton.presidentiallibraries.us/items/show/21979.

781 Weinstein interview, ibid.

782 Ibid.

783 Memorandum for the President Through Bruce Reed and Gene Sperling, "Community Banking Proposal," from the NEC-DPC Interagency Working Group on Community Development and Empowerment, April 20, 1993. Clinton Presidential Library, *History of the Domestic Policy Council and Clinton Administration History Project,* "Domestic

784 Ibid., 4.
785 Ibid., 7.
786 Ibid., 8.
787 Ibid., 7.
788 Memorandum to Bruce Reed and Gene Sperling, "Legislative Strategy on Community Development Financial Institutions Proposal," from Paul Weinstein, May 10, 1993. Domestic Policy Council, Bruce Reed, and Subject Files, "Community Development Banks [2]," Clinton Digital Library, accessed October 26, 2017, https://clinton.presidentiallibraries.us/items/show/31262.
789 Jerry Knight, "White House Scales Back Community Lending Plan," *Washington Post,* May 19, 1993, F1.
790 Weinstein memo to Reed and Sperling.
791 Ibid. Bruce Reed wrote a note to Weinstein on the memo, "Good Work. Sarbanes makes me tired. Hang in there."
792 Ibid.
793 Bureau of National Affairs, "Draft Community Bank Bill Would Provide Matching Funds," *Regulation, Economics and Law,* May 19, 1993, A-17.
794 Knight, "White House Scales Back."
795 Claudia Cummins, "President Plans $382 Million Community Lending Fund," *American Banker,* May 19, 1993, 1, 18.
796 Ibid.
797 Knight, "White House Scales Back."
798 Memorandum to Chris Edley from Paul Dimond, "Structure for CDFI Fund," May 25, 1993. Domestic Policy Council, Bruce Reed, and Subject Files, "Community Development Banks [2]," Clinton Digital Library, accessed October 26, 2017, https://clinton.presidentiallibraries.us/items/show/31262.
799 Memorandum to Paul Dimond, NEC, "Re: Draft 'Community Development Financial Institutions Act.'"
800 See Chapters 2 and 4.
801 Memorandum to Dimond, 4–7.
802 Ibid., 7. It was precisely the predominance of larger, more sophisticated competitors that later drove the National Federation of CDCUs to advocate for a separate funding track for small institutions. In 2000, its efforts finally paid off, when the CDFI Fund started the Small and Emerging CDFI Access program (SECA).
803 Ibid., 8–9.
804 Ibid.
805 See Chapter 10.
806 Draft memo to CDFI Coalition for Discussion Purposes Only, "Re: Draft Cdfi Legislation Dated June 4, 1993," June 1993 (undated).
807 Memorandum to All [CDFI Coalition], "Draft of White House Legislation," from Mark Pinsky, PageMark Communications, July 1, 1993. Courtesy of OFN.
808 A federal program was established in 1998 through the Assets for Independence Act (AFIA). IDAs became an important tool for many CDFIs. Credit unions were well-suited, eager adopters of IDA accounts, but other nondepository CDFIs also established IDA programs. One of the largest and most successful was the IDA program of the Opportunity Fund of Northern California, which harnessed IDAs to its microenterprise strategy.
809 Memorandum to Shirley Sagawa from Paul Weinstein, June 20, 1993, "Community Development Banks and National Service," Domestic Policy Council, Bruce Reed, and Subject Files, "Community Development Banks [2]," Clinton Digital Library, accessed October 26, 2017, https://clinton.presidentiallibraries.us/items/show/31262. Sagawa became the first chief operating and policy officer of the Corporation for National and Community Service.
810 Ibid.

## Chapter 15

811  Memorandum for the President, "Tomorrow's CD Bank/CRA Reform Event," from Gene Sperling and Bruce Reed, July 14, 1993. *History of the Domestic Policy Council and Clinton Administration History Project*, "Domestic Policy Council – Documentary Annex II [4]," Clinton Digital Library, accessed October 26, 2017, https://clinton.presidentiallibraries.us/items/show/4575.

812  Memorandum for Gene Sperling and Bruce Reed, "Presidential Announcement of the CDFI and CRA Initiatives," from Paul Dimon, Paul Weinstein, and Sheryll Cashin, June 22, 1993, Domestic Policy Council, Bruce Reed, and Subject Files, "Community Development Banks [1]," Clinton Digital Library, accessed October 26, 2017, https://clinton.presidentiallibraries.us/items/show/31261.

813  Zavarello, interview by author, Washington, DC, March 10, 2016.

814  Ibid.

815  Memorandum to CD Bank Team, from Paul Carey, June 30, 1993, Domestic Policy Council, Bruce Reed, and Subject Files, "Community Development Banks [1]," Clinton Digital Library, accessed October 26, 2017, https://clinton.presidentiallibraries.us/items/show/31261.

816  Memorandum to David Gergen, Howard Paster, George Stephanopoulos, Marcia Hale, and Mark Gearan, "Presidential Announcement of the CDFI and CRA Initiatives," from Bruce Reed, Gene Sperling, Paul Dimon, Paul Weinstein, and Sheryll Cashin, June 24, 1993. Domestic Policy Council, Bruce Reed, and Subject Files, "Community Development Banks [1]," Clinton Digital Library, accessed October 26, 2017, https://clinton.presidentiallibraries.us/items/show/31261.

817  Draft—For CDFI Coalition Discussion Purposes Only, "What's New in Washington & What Do We Have to Say About It," undated, 1. Courtesy of Opportunity Finance Network.

818  Memorandum to the CDFI Coalition Steering Committee, from Mark Pinsky, June 28, 1993.

819  "CDFI Coalition Work Plan, As of Monday, June 28, 1993," included with Mark Pinsky memo, ibid.

820  Sperling and Reed, "Memorandum to the President," July 14.

821  Memorandum for the President, through Gene Sperling, "Background on CRA Reform, CDFI Initiative," from Bruce Reed, Paul Dimon, Paul Weinstein, and Sheryll Cashin, July 14, 1993.

822  Ibid.

823  Errol T. Louis, interview by author, New York, NY, February 29, 2016.

824  Sperling and Reed, "Memorandum to the President," July 14.

825  Louis interview.

826  Anita Nager, interview by author, August 7, 2015. The invitees were informed that "business dress" would be appropriate. Like many, Nager wondered: "What do I wear? I remember going to Lord and Taylor and assembling an outfit from floor to floor. Even though I worked for a foundation, I was casual. I definitely need a suit, and once you have the suit you need shoes. The next day I got a phone call from Lord and Taylor saying, 'We just want to make sure that you really wanted this, making these purchases, because you don't usually use your card.'"

827  Except where noted, all quotes from the White House ceremony were as transcribed by the author from a video of the event.

828  White House Television (WHTV), "President Clinton Announcing Community Development Banking and Finance Initiative (1993)," *Clinton Digital Library*, https://clinton.presidentiallibraries.us/items/show/15736. Transcription by author.

829  Ibid.

830  Mary Adamski, "Isles a stopover and vacation spot for presidents," *Honolulu Star-Bulletin*, October 22, 2003.

831  Grzywinski, Houghton, and Surgeon, interview by author, Chicago, IL, April 8, 2015.

832  Robert Weissbourd, interview by author, Chicago, IL, April 8, 2015.

833  Louis interview.

834  Mark Winston Griffith, interview by author, Brooklyn, NY, February 26, 2016.

835 Louis interview.
836 Matthew Davis, "Clinton praises credit union," *Raleigh News & Observer*, July 16, 1993.
837 Grzywinski et al. interview.
838 Coalition of Community Development Financial Institutions, "Coalition Supports President Clinton's Community Development Finance Legislation." Press release (July 15, 1993).
839 "Clinton Announces Community Finance Bill," *CDCU Report. Special Edition: Legislative & Regulatory News,* July 1993, 1-2.
840 Consumer Federation of America, "CFA Hails Clinton Initiative on Community Development Banks." Press release (July 15, 1993).
841 Ted Wysocki, "Community bank bill remakes urban debate," *Crain's Chicago Business,* August 2-8, 1993.
842 Robert M. Garsson and Claudia Cummins, "Clinton Unveils Plan for Community Loans," *American Banker,* July 16, 1993, 18.
843 Ibid.
844 Robert M. Garsson, "Community Development Plan Excludes Banks, S&Ls," *American Banker,* July 13, 1993, 1.
845 Garsson and Cummins, 18.
846 Jonathan R. Macey, "Porkbarrel banking," *Wall Street Journal,* Eastern edition. July 19, 1993, A10.
847 Dave Skidmore, "Urban-rural loan proposal dwindles," *Washington Times,* July 13, 1993.
848 Editorial, "Banking on the Inner City," *Washington Post,* July 19, 1993, A14.

## Chapter 16

849 Weinstein et al., July 14 memorandum.
850 Sec. 3(b).
851 Faxed letter to Paul Dimond from the Coalition of Community Development Financial Institutions, signed by Mark Pinsky, July 19, 1993.
852 Memo to CDFI Coalition Steering Committee, "Re: Conversation with Jeannine Jacokes," from Mark Pinsky, July 20, 1993.
853 Associated Press, "President unveils program for community lending," *Mobile Register,* July 16, 1992, 8-B.
854 Ibid.
855 "The Community Development Banking and Financial Institutions Act of 1993" Hearings on H.R. 2666 before the Committee on Banking, Finance, and Urban Affairs, House of Representatives, 103rd Cong., July 21, 1993, 102. Henry Gonzalez was a legendary figure, representing a district that included San Antonio, TX, from 1961 to 1998. He was a vigorous, influential opponent of discrimination, from the poll tax to segregation. The National Community Reinvestment Coalition has named an award after Gonzalez. (Hereafter "Hearing Report, July 21.")
856 Ibid., 3.
857 Ibid., 3.
858 Ibid., 23.
859 Ibid., 7.
860 Ibid., 8.
861 Ibid., 9-10.
862 Ibid., 62.
863 Ibid., 20.
864 Ibid., 66.
865 Ibid., 47-48.
866 Ibid., 20, 22.
867 Ibid., 18.
868 Ibid., 23-24.

869  Ibid., 24.
870  Ibid., 29.
871  Ibid., 26.
872  "Opening Statement for Representative Bobby L. Rush for House Banking, Finance, and Urban Affairs Hearing to Receive the Clinton Administration's 'Community Development Banking and Financial Institutions Act of 1993,'" *Hearing Report,* July 21, 1943, 45.
873  Ibid., 36.
874  Ibid., 37.
875  Ibid., 46.
876  Ibid., 31.
877  Robert M. Garsson, "GOP Rebuffed in Effort to Win Community Loan Funds for Banks," *American Banker,* July 22, 1993, 2.
878  Ibid., 32-33.
879  Ibid., 35.
880  Weinstein et al. memo, July 14.
881  Andrew Taylor, "Community Lending Proposal Challenges Clinton Plan," *Congressional Quarterly,* July 31, 1993, 2029, http://search.proquest.com/libproxy.newschool.edu/wallstreetjournal/printviewfile?accountid=12261, accessed November 29, 2014.
882  National Federation of Community Development Credit Unions, "Community Development Banking: The Credit Union Option. A Proposal to the Clinton Administration," June 9, 1993. Courtesy of National Federation of Community Development Credit Unions.
883  Taylor, ibid.
884  Ed Castell, telephone conversation with author, August 3, 1993. Courtesy of National Federation of Community Development Credit Unions.
885  "Community Development Financial Institutions Act of 1993," Hearings on S. 1275 before the Committee on Banking, Housing, and Urban Affairs, 103rd Cong., September 8, 1993, 160-161, http://hdl.handle.net/2027/pst.000022377050, accessed January 20, 2017.
886  Ibid., 148–49.
887  Ibid., 140–41.
888  Memo to Leon Panetta and Alice Rivlin from Christopher Edley Jr., "Re: Financial Sector Reform," September 11, 1993. Domestic Policy Council, Bruce Reed, and Subject Files, "Community Development Banks [1]," Clinton Digital Library, accessed October 26, 2017, https://clinton.presidentiallibraries.us/items/show/31261.
889  Unclassified faxed memo to Jeannine Jacokes from Fé Morales Marks, Department of the Treasury, September 15, 1993. Courtesy of Jeannine Jacokes.
890  Albert Karr, "Community-Development Lending Bill Clears Senate Banking Unit on 18–1 Vote," *Wall Street Journal,* September 22, 1993, A4.
891  Ibid.
892  S. REP. 103-169. *The Community Development, Credit Enhancement, and Regulatory Improvement Act of 1993,* Report of the Committee on Banking, Housing, and Urban Affairs, United States Senate, to Accompany S. 1275 together with Additional Views (United States Government Printing Offices, Washington, 1993).
893  Robert M. Garson, "D'Amato Is Close to Supporting Clinton Development Bank Plan," *American Banker,* September 9, 1993, 2.
894  Ibid.
895  "Community Bank Bill Launched," *Banking Policy Report* 12 (19) (October 4, 1993): 1–2.
896  One consolation in the House bill for CDCUs—and their regulator, NCUA, which had pressed for it—was a proposed $15 million increase over four years to the Community Development Revolving Loan Fund run by NCUA. The Senate had proposed $4 million. This funding would be separate from CDFI funding.

897 Memorandum to CDFI Coalition Steering Committee from Mark Pinsky, November 11, 1993. One result of the House committee's action was that H.R. 2666 became H.R. 3474, the designation under which it would subsequently be known.
898 Robert M. Garsson, "Panel Backs Incentive for Low-Income Loans," *Banking Week,* November 15, 1993, 1.
899 On December 10, *American Banker* published a generally complimentary full-page profile of me by James B. Arndorfer, "Credit Union Activist Brings '60s Idealism to Community Work," 8. It cites an unidentified House Banking Committee staff member who criticized my "unwillingness to compromise" in my opposition to the BEA carve-out, saying, "He only wants things one way. That could hurt him in the long run."
900 Memorandum for the President, "Community development bank and financial institutions legislation," from Paul Weinstein (DPC), Paul Dimon (NEC), Sheryll Cashin (NEC), November 21, 1993. *History of the Domestic Policy Council and Clinton Administration History Project,* "Domestic Policy Council – Documentary Annex II[4]," Clinton Digital Library, accessed November 17, 2016. http://clinton.presidentiallibraries.us/items/show/4575.
901 NACDLF communicated its performance standards to Senate Banking Committee staff in March and then again in a letter from Martin Paul Trimble, its executive director, to Jeannine Jacokes, on September 29, 1993. Courtesy of OFN.
902 Memorandum to Jeannine Jacokes, Senate Banking Committee, "CDFI Legislation and CDCUs," from Kathryn Tholin, vice president, Woodstock Institute, October 25, 1993.
903 Ibid.
904 The "Keating Five" were five senators including Riegle who were implicated in intervening in 1987 on behalf of Charles H. Keating, Jr., Chairman of the Lincoln Savings and Loan Association, which was the target of a regulatory investigation by the Federal Home Loan Bank Board (FHLBB). Lincoln was closed in 1989, at a cost that ultimately exceeded $3 billion. The Senate Ethics Committee held hearings in 1990-91 and criticized Riegle for acting improperly.
905 "Riegle Exits Amid A Dearth of Tears from Bankers," *Banking Policy Report* 12 (20) (October 18, 1993): 2.
906 Memorandum for Carol Rasco, Gene Sperling, and Bruce Reed, "Subject: Additional Budget Authority for Community Development Banks and Financial Institutions (CDBFIs)," from Paul Weinstein, December 17, 1993. Domestic Policy Council, Bruce Reed, and Subject Files, "Community Development Banks [1]," Clinton Digital Library, accessed October 26, 2017, https://clinton.presidentiallibraries.us/items/show/31261.
907 Ibid.

## Chapter 17

908 Memo to Carol Rasco, Bob Rubin, Bruce Reed, Gene Sperling, and Paul Dimond, "Update on Community Development Banks and Financial Institutions," from Paul Weinstein, January 24, 1994. Domestic Policy Council, Bruce Reed, and Subject Files, "Community Development Banks [1]," Clinton Digital Library, accessed October 26, 2017, https://clinton.presidentiallibraries.us/items/show/31261.
909 *CDFI News,* Vol. II, No. 1, January 11, 1994, 1.
910 Memorandum to NACDLF Board Members, "Washington Update," February 4, 1994. Courtesy of OFN.
911 *Federal Register,* December 21, 1993.
912 *CDFI News,* 2.
913 Domestic Policy Council, Bruce Reed, and Subject Files, "Community Development Banks [1]," Clinton Digital Library, accessed October 26, 2017, https://clinton.presidentiallibraries.us/items/show/31261.
914 Quoted in *CDFI News,* Vol. II, No. 2, February 1994, 1.
915 Faxed memorandum to members of the CDFI Steering Committee, from Mary Mountcastle, Self-Help, November 11, 1993. A primary organizer of the conference, Mountcastle had worked on planning it since summer 1993, and Self-Help provided significant human and financial resources toward the conference. Courtesy of National Federation of Community Development Credit Unions.

## Notes

916    Text provided to author by Lingenfelter.

917    Lingenfelter, interview by author, telephone, February 17, 2015.

918    Letter and proposal to the Ford Foundation (Frank DeGiovanni, Roland Anglin, and Lisa Mensah), from the CDFI Coalition, February 24, 1994.

919    Ibid.

920    Letter to Mark Pinsky (coordinator, CDFI Coalition), from Lisa Mensah (deputy director, Rural Poverty and Resources Program), Frank DeGiovanni (deputy director, Program Related Investments), and Roland Anglin (program officer, Urban Poverty Program), April 13, 1994. Courtesy of National Federation of Community Development Credit Unions.

921    Letter to the Federal Reserve, Office of the Comptroller of the Currency, Office of Thrift Supervision, and FDIC, from the CDFI Coalition (signed by all eight members), March 17, 1994. Courtesy of OFN.

922    Memorandum for Gene Sperling, "Community Development Bank and Financial Institutions Legislation," from Paul Weinstein, Paul Dimon, and Sheryll Cashin, March 3, 1994. Domestic Policy Council, Bruce Reed, and Subject Files, "Community Development Banks [1]," Clinton Digital Library, accessed October 26, 2017, https://clinton.presidentiallibraries.us/items/show/31261.

923    Ibid.

924    Memorandum to Mark Pinsky from author, "Rosenthal Amendment," January 27, 1994. Courtesy of National Federation of Community Development Credit Unions.

925    Memorandum to the CDFI Coalition Steering Committee, "The 'Wofford' (née Rosenthal) Amendment to S. 1275, the CDFI Legislation," from Mark Pinsky. Courtesy of National Federation of Community Development Credit Unions.

926    Memorandum to National Federation of Community Development Credit Union, files from author, March 8, 1994.

927    Robert M. Garsson, "Regulatory Relief Added to Community Banking Bill," *American Banker*, March 17, 1994, 3.

928    Ibid., 1–2.

929    Robert M. Garsson and Robyn Meredith, "Bank Issues Don't Look Vulnerable to Whitewater Fallout," *American Banker*, March 21, 1994, 3.

930    *BNA's Banking Report,* March 21, 1994. "Whitewater" referred to a land deal in the Ozark Mountains in which the Clintons had invested during the 1970s. The issue became conflated with the failure of the Madison Guaranty Savings and Loan institution that the Clintons' investment partner, James McDougal, had purchased.

931    *CDFI News,* Vol. II, No. 3, March 1994, 1.

932    *BNA's Banking Policy Report,* 6.

933    April 4, 1994, Vol. 13, No. 7, 4.

934    The article noted that the House was likely to drop one provision that had roused opposition, namely that CDFIs be allowed to borrow from the Federal Home Loan Bank System without buying bank stock or becoming a member of the system. Ibid.

935    Faxed memo to CDFI Coalition Steering Committee, "Conference Committee Strategy," from Mark Pinsky and John Coulter, March 30, 1994. Courtesy of National Federation of Community Development Credit Unions.

936    Ibid.

937    *BNA's Banking Report,* May 16, 1994, 862.

938    Memorandum to NACDLF Members, Associates, and Colleagues, from Mark Pinsky (coordinator of public policy, NACDLF), April 8, 1994 (copied to National Federation of Community Development Credit Unions). Courtesy of National Federation of Community Development Credit Unions.

939    Robert M. Garsson, "Lawmakers Aim to Wrap Up Two Banking Bills Next Week," *American Banker*, July 15, 1994, 1.

940    *CDFI News,* Vol. II, No. 4, June [sic] 1994, 1. (The issue actually came out in July and was mislabeled.)

941    Robert M. Garsson, "Bottleneck in Congress for Two Major Banking Bills," *American Banker,* July 21, 1994, 1.

942    Robert M. Garsson, "Industry Wins Big as Senate Approves Lending Bill," August 11, 1994, 1.

943    Robert M. Garsson, "D.C. Breakthrough on Branching Bill," *American Banker,* June 13, 1994, 1.

944 Quoted in Robert M. Garsson, "Interstate Bill Faces Big Delay If Conferees Don't Act This Week," *American Banker*, July 12, 1994, 2.
945 Garsson, "Bottleneck in Congress," 1.
946 Robert M. Garsson, "Negotiators Report Out Banking Bill—With a Hitch," *American Banker*, July 26, 1994, 1.
947 Quoted in Robert M. Garsson, "Leach's Point Man Relishes Role as Coalition Builder," *American Banker*, July 25, 1994, 2A.
948 Garsson, "Industry Wins Big," 1.
949 Quoted in Robert M. Garsson, "Bankers Hail Legislative Package as Return to Reasonable Regulation," *American Banker*, July 27, 1994, 1.
950 Letter to The Honorable Barbara Mikulski, chairperson, VA, HUD, and Independent Agencies Subcommittee, Senate Committee on Appropriations; and The Honorable Louis Stokes, chairperson, VA, HUD, and Independent Agencies Subcommittee, House Committee on Appropriations, from Sen. Donald W. Riegle Jr., August 5, 1994.
951 The White House, Office of the Press Secretary, "Statement of the President," August 10, 1994.
952 White House Television (WHTV), "Riegle Community Development and Regulatory Improvement Act of 1994," Clinton Digital Library, accessed November 3, 2017, https://clinton.presidentiallibraries.us/items/show/15782.
953 https://www.govinfo.gov/app/content/pkg/PPP-1994-book2/pdf/PPP-1994-book2-doc-pg1596-2.pdf, 1596–99, accessed November 24, 2016.
954 Lawson comments courtesy of Lyndon Comstock.
955 Lollis, interview by author, telephone, March 16, 2017.
956 White House Television (WHTV), "Riegle Community Development."
957 Rev. Reggie White (1961–2004) was an ordained Baptist minister, which, combined with his football prowess, earned him the nickname "Minister of Defense." "They [he and his wife] founded the Alpha & Omega Ministry to sponsor a community development bank in Knoxville. 'I'm trying to build up black people's morale, self-confidence and self-reliance to show them that the Jesus I'm talking about is real,' White explained in *Ebony*." http://biography.jrank.org/pages/2548/White-Reggie.html, accessed November 23, 2016. Richard Dent started the Make A Dent Foundation in 1989, to assist children and young adults in getting an education. http://www.makeadentfoundation.org/about/about-make-a-dent/
958 In a memo of September 21 to presidential speechwriter Carter Willkie, Paul Weinstein Jr. noted that First Interstate, Wells Fargo, and Union Bank had pledged $1.5 million to start a community development bank in San Diego, slated to open later that year, and that First America had committed $1 million toward the startup of a community development bank in Detroit.
959 Zavarello interview.
960 "The Week Ahead," September 19, 1994, 2.
961 Quoted in Robyn Meredith, "Few Incentives for Banks in Community Development Law," *American Banker*, September 26, 1994, 3.
962 NACDLF, "Loan Fund Network Model for National Legislation," Press release (September 23, 1994). Courtesy of OFN.
963 Meredith, "Few Incentives."
964 Memorandum for Frank Newman, Paul Weinstein; CC: Gene Sperling, Ellen Seidman, Sheryll Cashin, Bruce Reed. Domestic Policy Council, Bruce Reed, and Subject Files, "Community Development Banks [1]," Clinton Digital Library, accessed October 26, 2017, https://clinton.presidentiallibraries.us/items/show/31261.
965 Ibid.

## Chapter 18

966 See Chapter 17.

## Notes

967 Memorandum for the President, August 17, 1994. *History of the Department of the Treasury and Clinton Administration History Project* "[History of the Department of the Treasury – Supplementary Documents] [23]," Clinton Digital Library, accessed October 30, 2017, https://clinton.presidentiallibraries.us/items/show/5401.
968 Robert M. Garsson, "CRA, Red Tape Lead Lobbying Agenda. Optimism Reigns in Aftermath of GOP's Congressional Landslide," *American Banker,* November 30, 1994, 3.
969 *CDFI News,* Vol. II, No. 5, October 1994, 2.
970 Robert M. Garsson, in *American Banker,* December 7, 1994, p. 3.
971 McKee, interview by author, Washington, DC, October 1, 2014.
972 Katharine McKee, associate director, Self-Help. Testimony before the U.S. House of Representatives Committee on Small Business, Subcommittee on Regulation, Business Opportunities, and Technology, June 7, 1993. Courtesy of Katharine McKee.
973 Courtesy of Katharine McKee.
974 McKee interview.
975 Ibid.
976 Jeannine Jacokes, interview by author, Washington, DC, February 22, 2016.
977 Katherine McKee, interview by Mark Pinsky, in "CDFIsMakingHistory.OFN.org," August 5, 2014. Courtesy of OFN.
978 Memorandum to Leon Panetta from Carol H. Rasco, in "Weekly Report – January 13–20, 1995." January 20, 1995, "Carol Rasco – Miscellaneous Series – Domestic Policy Council – Collection Finding Aid," Clinton Digital Library, accessed November 3, 2017, https://clinton.presidentiallibraries.us/items/show/36307.
979 McKee interview.
980 Olaf de Senerpont Domis, "Community Development Funds Targeted for Cut," [name of publication?] February 28, 1995, 3.
981 Quoted in Domis.
982 Jacokes interview.
983 Courtesy of National Federation of Community Development Credit Unions.
984 Memorandum to CDFI Coalition, CDFI Practitioners, and Colleagues, "Urgent! Action Alert: Help Save the CDFI Fund," from Mark Pinsky and Laura Schwingel, CDFI Coalition, February 27, 1995.
985 Olaf de Senerpont Domis, "House Expected to Ax $125 Million for Community Development Banks," *American Banker,* March 15, 1993, 3.
986 Ibid., 3.
987 Memorandum to CDFI Coalition Members and Colleagues, "Urgent Action Alert Re: Key Senate Vote on CDFI Fund," from Laura Schwingel, CDFI Coalition Program Associate, March 20, 1995.
988 Carol Rasco, "Weekly Report—April 28 through May 5, 1995." "Carol Rasco – Miscellaneous Series – Domestic Policy Council – Collection Finding Aid," Clinton Digital Library, accessed November 3, 2017, https://clinton.presidentiallibraries.us/items/show/36307.
989 Quoted in Olaf de Senerpont Domis, "In Focus: With a GOP Congress, Development Fund Is on Shaky Ground," *American Banker,* May 22, 1995, 4.
990 Ibid.
991 Memorandum to Leon Panetta, "Weekly Report—April 28 through May 5, 1995, Update on Key Initiatives," from Carol H. Rasco. "Carol Rasco – Miscellaneous Series – Domestic Policy Council – Collection Finding Aid," Clinton Digital Library, accessed November 3, 2017, https://clinton.presidentiallibraries.us/items/show/36307.
992 Quoted in Domis, March 15, 4.
993 Quoted in Olaf de Senerpont Domis, "House Spares Development Banks from Budget Ax," *American Banker,* July 3, 1995, 1.
994 Ibid.
995 Michael Barr, interview by author, Detroit, MI, May 15, 2014.

996   Ibid.
997   Ibid.
998   Robert Rubin, presentation to the 20th anniversary celebration of the CDFI Fund, Treasury Department, Washington, DC, October 2, 2014.
999   McKee interview.
1000  Ibid.
1001  Ibid.
1002  Jacokes interview, ibid.
1003  See Chapter 10.
1004  Jeff Wells, interview by author, telephone, March 31, 2017.
1005  Ibid.
1006  Ibid.
1007  Draft notes of CDFI Fund Meeting, January 26, 1995 (author unspecified). Courtesy of National Federation of Community Development Credit Unions.
1008  Memorandum to Veronica Biggins, "Administrator of the Community Development Bank and Financial Institutions Fund," from Carol Rasco and Paul Weinstein, March 2, 1994.
1009  The book was the product of President Reagan's Task Force on Private Sector Initiatives. Kirsten Moy was loaned to it from the Equitable, where she was manager of the office of social initiatives investments.
1010  https://www.congress.gov/nomination/104th-congress/232?q=%7B%22search%22%3A%5B%22Kirsten+Moy%22%5D%7D&r=1, accessed January 3, 2017.
1011  Memorandum, Paul J. Weinstein, Jr. to Carol H. Rasco, May 4, 1995, Domestic Policy Council, Carol Rasco, and Meetings, Trips, Events Series, "Kristen Moy Meeting 5 May 1995 10:30 - 10:50," *Clinton Digital Library*, accessed March 20, 2018, https://clinton.presidentiallibraries.us/items/show/20466. Rasco was one of the trusted senior advisors to Governor Clinton who joined the Administration in Washington.
1012  Ibid.
1013  Rohde interview by author, telephone, January 26, 2016.
1014  Ibid.
1015  Mark Pinsky, previously the coordinator of the coalition, had become executive director of NACDLF.
1016  Memorandum to Elgie Holstein, National Economic Council, from Mark Pinsky, CDFI Coalition, September 29, 1994. Courtesy of National Federation of Community Development Credit Unions.
1017  Memorandum to CDFI Coalition Steering Committee Members, "Strategic Issus Discussion Memo," from Mark Pinsky, NACDLF, June 20, 1995.
1018  Minutes of the CDFI Coalition Steering Committee Meeting, June 27, 1995, New York, NY. Courtesy of National Federation of Community Development Credit Unions.
1019  Ibid.
1020  Ibid.
1021  "Building the CDFI Field through Training & Human Capacity Building: A Proposal to the Ford Foundation," May 24, 1995. Courtesy of National Federation of Community Development Credit Unions.

## Chapter 19

1022  Memorandum to the CDFI Coalition Steering Committee and Colleagues, "RE: CDFI Fund Status & Application Preparation," from Mark Pinsky and Laura Schwingel, August 10, 1995.
1023  Moy's nomination had been submitted to the Senate in February for confirmation. However, once it was decided to place the CDFI Fund in Treasury rather than have it operate as an independent agency, Senate confirmation was no longer required; Moy was a Treasury employee reporting to Treasury hierarchy. Source: Jeannine Jacokes.
1024  Pinsky and Schwingel.

## Notes

1025 *Federal Register,* October 19, 1995, Part III. Department of the Treasury, Community Development Financial Institutions Fund, 2 C.F.R. Chapter XVIII et al., Vol. 60, No. 202.
1026 Ibid., 54110.
1027 Ibid., 54111.
1028 Ibid., 54113. "Depository institutions" here means banks and thrifts; credit unions were not eligible under BEA. Had they been, it is possible that low-income credit unions could have accessed substantial funding from large "mainstream" credit unions.
1029 Letter from The White House, signed by Bill Clinton, October 19, 1995, addressed "Dear Friend."
1030 Letter of Robert E. Rubin, Secretary of the Treasury, addressed to "Dear Applicants," October 20, 1995.
1031 Letter of Kirsten S. Moy, director, Community Development Financial Institutions Fund, addressed to "Dear Friends," October 19, 1995.
1032 Quoted in Olaf de Senerpont Domis, "Development Fund Wounded, But Surviving," *American Banker*, November 7, 1995, 3.
1033 *Federal Register,* Vol. 60, No. 236, December 8, 1995, 63120.
1034 Pinsky and Schwingel.
1035 "CDFI Fund Issues Regulations, Applications Due December 22," *CDFI News,* Vol. 3, No. 2, October 20, 1995.
1036 Hereafter, "Questions-and-Answers."
1037 Ibid., Question 5, 4–5.
1038 See Chapter 20.
1039 "Questions-and-Answers," Question 8, 5.
1040 Ibid., Questions 14–16, 6–7.
1041 Ibid., Question 35, 12.
1042 Ibid., Question 17, 7.
1043 Ibid., Question 23, 9.
1044 Ibid., Question 24, 9.
1045 In fact, federal credit union regulations do not specify any particular amount of required capital; the requirement is that a proposed credit union demonstrate its economic viability—that is to say, that it would not have negative net worth in its early years. Since a startup credit union with staff and expenses could not reasonably be expected to break even for several years, a new credit union would typically need to raise or obtain in-kind support from a sponsor amounting to several hundred thousand dollars. See Clifford Rosenthal and Linda Levy, *Organizing Credit Unions: A Manual* (New York: National Federation of CDCUs, 1995).
1046 Ibid., Question 33, 11.
1047 See Chapter 22.
1048 Ibid., Question 12, 6.
1049 Ibid, Question 163, 36.
1050 Ibid., Question 188, 41.
1051 Ibid., Question 249, 53.
1052 Ibid., Question 152, 34.
1053 Ibid., Question 134, 29–31.
1054 Ibid.
1055 This was the metaphor commonly used when I joined the Consumer Financial Protection Bureau (CFPB), then one year old, in 2012.
1056 Fred Cooper, interview by author, telephone, July 9, 2014.
1057 "Questions-and-Answers," Question 303, 44.
1058 Ibid., Question 206, 44.
1059 Ibid., Question 262, 56.
1060 See Chapter 22.

1061 "Questions-and-Answers," Question 277, 58.
1062 Memorandum to Members of CDFI Coalition, "Senate Banking Committee Bill of 9/21/93: Matching Requirements," from author, September 29, 1993. Courtesy of National Federation of Community Development Credit Unions.
1063 "Questions-and-Answers," "BEA Questions," 9, 60.
1064 *Federal Register,* Vol. 60, No. 202, October 19, 1995, 54128; also, "Questions-and-Answers," Question 32, 65.
1065 "Questions-and-Answers," Question 33, 65.
1066 Ibid., Question 27, 64.
1067 Ibid., Question 35, 66.
1068 Olaf de Senerpont Domis, "Community Development Program Has $300M in Applications, and $31M to Spend," *American Banker,* February 6, 1996, 4.
1069 Memorandum to NACDLF Members, "Re: CDFI Fund Application Process Update," November 14, 1995.
1070 Memorandum to CDFI Coalition Steering Committee, "CDFI Fund Extends Application Deadlines," from Mark Pinsky, executive director, December 12, 1995.
1071 Letter to Senator Patty Murray, from Treasury Secretary Robert E. Rubin, March 26, 1996. *History of the Department of the Treasury and Clinton Administration History Project,* "[History of the Department of the Treasury – Supplementary Documents] [23]," Clinton Digital Library, accessed October 30, 2017, https://clinton.presidentiallibraries.us/items/show/5401.
1072 *History of the Department of the Treasury and Clinton Administration History Project,* "[History of the Department of the Treasury – Supplementary Documents] [23]," Clinton Digital Library, accessed October 30, 2017, https://clinton.presidentiallibraries.us/items/show/5401.
1073 Notoriously, it was during these shutdowns that President Clinton engaged in—as he ultimately admitted—an "improper physical relationship" with White House intern Monica Lewinsky.
1074 Memorandum, "Extension of CDFI and BEA program application deadlines," from Kirsten Moy, director, CDFI Fund, January 10, 1996.
1075 Ibid.
1076 Rohde, interview by author, telephone, January 26, 2016.
1077 Ibid.
1078 Ibid.
1079 Valery Piper, interview by author, Washington, DC, February 24, 2016.
1080 Ibid.
1081 Ibid.
1082 Rohde interview.
1083 Piper interview.
1084 Ibid.
1085 Bill Luecht, interview by author, Washington, DC, February 26, 2016.
1086 Piper interview.
1087 CDFI Coalition, "Treasury Secretary Rubin Announces First CDFI Fund Awards," *CDFI News,* Vol. 4, No. 3, August 10, 1996, 1.
1088 Department of the Treasury, "Secretary Rubin Announces $13.1 Million in Bank Enterprise Awards," *Treasury News,* October 1, 1996.

## Chapter 20

1089 Department of the Treasury, Remarks of Treasury Secretary Robert E. Rubin, "Schumer/Bradley Income Disparity Forum," *Treasury News,* December 6, 1995.
1090 Barbara Rose, "New banking era jolts African-American lenders," *Crain's Chicago Business,* July 19, 1993, 3.

## Notes

1091  Beth Healy, "Shorebank Again Eyes Indecorp," *Crain's Chicago Business,* March 27, 1995, 1.
1092  Email from Mary Houghton to author, March 17, 2017.
1093  Cited in Rose, ibid.
1094  Healy, "Shorebank Again Eyes Indecorp," 1.
1095  Ibid.
1096  William Gruber, "Black-Owned Banks to Be Acquired; Shorebank Gets Drexel, Independence," *Chicago Tribune,* June 20, 1995, 1.
1097  Ibid.
1098  Lisa Holton, "Shorebank Corp. Buying Indecorp. Largest Black-Owned Bank Had Sought Deal," *Chicago Sun-Times,* June 20, 1995, 39.
1099  Beth Healy, "Shorebank's Indecorp Hurdles," *Crain's Chicago Business,* June 26, 1995, 4.
1100  Barbara F. Bronstein, "Shorebank, a Community Lending Model, Takes Heat Over Bid for Black-Owned Bank," *American Banker,* August 10, 1996, 1.
1101  Barbara F. Bronstein, "Chicago Protesters Step Up Fight to Halt Sale of Biggest Black-Owned Bank in U.S.," *American Banker,* October 25, 1995, 7, http://search.proquest.com.libproxy.newschool.edu/printviewfile?accountid=12261.
1102  John R. Wilke, "Power Struggle: Plan to Sell Black Bank to a White One Stirs Protests in Chicago—South Shore Is Criticized for Bid to Buy Indecorp Despite Inner-City Loans – At Issue: Self Determination," *Wall Street Journal,* Eastern Edition, November 13, 1995, A1.
1103  Barbara F. Bronstein, "Shorebank Buys Indecorp in Deal That Spurred Challenges Over End to Minority Ownership," *American Banker,* December 20, 1995, 6.
1104  Wilke.
1105  Beth Healy, "Two Development Units Merged by Shorebank," *Crain's Chicago Business,* April 8, 1996, 14.
1106  Quoted in Barbara F. Bronstein, "Shorebank Forms Subsidiary to Both Create and Fill Jobs in Two Chicago Neighborhoods," April 10, 1996, 6, http://search.proquest.com.libproxy/printviewfile?acccountid=12261.
1107  Ibid.
1108  Steven R. Strahler, "Growing Pains for Shorebank," *Crain's Chicago Business,* August 19, 1996, 1.
1109  Laura Pavlenko Lutton, "Chicago's South Shore Says Buyout of Black Bank Has Paid Off for Community," *American Banker,* April 13, 1998, 11.
1110  "Letter to the Stockholders," from Lyndon Comstock, chairman, and Merton Corn, president and CEO, February 28, 1997. Courtesy of Lyndon Comstock.
1111  Ibid.
1112  See Chapter 6.
1113  Ibid.
1114  Comstock, interview by author, Berkeley, CA, March 24, 2016.
1115  See Chapter 13.
1116  Comstock interview.
1117  See Chapter 17.
1118  Comstock, email to author, February 23, 2017.
1119  Comstock interview.
1120  George Surgeon, interview by author, Chicago, IL, April 8, 2015.
1121  George Surgeon, Letter to Shareowners and Friends, "A Time to Plant. A Time to Harvest," May 31, 1996.
1122  Surgeon interview.
1123  Ibid.
1124  Surgeon, "A Time to Plant."
1125  Surgeon interview.
1126  Ibid.
1127  Self-Help, "Update 1995." Courtesy of Center for Community Self-Help.

1128  Self-Help, "Annual Report 1996." Courtesy of Center for Community Self-Help.
1129  Robert B. Rackleff, "Going Where Other Banks Fear to Tread: Self-Help provides a national model for connecting struggling communities to capital," *Ford Foundation Report,* Summer 1997, 15.
1130  Trimble, interview by author, Washington, DC, October 3, 2014.
1131  Ibid.
1132  "New CRA Investment Tool to Direct Millions to Distressed Communities Through CDFIs," *The Free Library,* 1996. As part of its policy agenda, NACDLF sought, though unsuccessfully, a tax credit tied to the Equity Equivalent Investment (EQ2). https://www.thefreelibrary.com/New+CREA+Investment+Tool+To+Direct+Millions+To+Distressed+Communities ...-a018794401
1133  Quoted in "New CRA Investment Tool."
1134  Comptroller of the Currency, Administrator of National Banks, concerning Citibank's Equity Equivalent Investment in National Community Capital Association, January 23, 1997.
1135  Beth Lipson, "Equity Equivalent Investments," *Community Investments,* March 2002, 10–13.
1136  In November 1996, NACDLF issued a paper, "The Parallel Banking System and Community Reinvestment," written by Mark A. Pinsky and Valerie L. Threlfall.
1137  Letter to Greg Ratliff, director, Program Related Investments, John D. and Catherine T. MacArthur Foundation, from Allyson Randolph, NACDLF, October 17, 1997. Courtesy of OFN.
1138  Ibid.
1139  https://www.ots.treas.gov/news-issuances/speeches/1997/pub-speech-1997-65.pdf.
1140  Ibid.
1141  "Letter to Greg Ratliff."
1142  Memorandum to NACDLF Members, "Board Decisions on NACDLF Strategic Plan: 1995–2000," from NACDLF Board, September 28, 1994. Courtesy of OFN. NACDLF subsequently rebranded as National Community Capital Association (NCCA) and later, Opportunity Finance Network (OFN).
1143  Data from cdfihistory.ofn.org/archive, accessed March 14, 2017. Among its membership was one international organization, the Montreal Community Loan Association. Courtesy of OFN.
1144  National Community Capital Association, "Charting CDFI Progress: Report on the Membership," August 1998, 2.
1145  Ibid., 1.
1146  National Federation of Community Development Credit Unions (NFCDCU), "Report to the Membership. 1996–97." Courtesy of NFCDCU.
1147  "VISTA" stands for Volunteers in Service to America, often described loosely as a domestic Peace Corps. It was a program under the Corporation for National and Community Service, started by the Clinton administration. The work of the federation-sponsored VISTA workers (who received a federal stipend and other benefits) resembled that envisioned by White House staff for building the human resources of the CDFI field (see Chapter 15). In fact, some VISTA workers went on to become employees and managers of CDCUs and related organizations.
1148  Credit unions are nonprofit, under sections 501(c)(1) or 501(c)(14) of the IRS code, but they are not charities. Consequently, few foundations are able and willing to provide grants to credit unions, even those that were certified as serving low-income populations.
1149  Clifford Rosenthal, "Report to the Membership: The National Federation of CDCUs, 1997–98," May 15, 1998. Courtesy of the National Federation of Community Development Credit Unions.
1150  Matthew Purdy and Joe Sexton, "Bank-Poor Communities are Forced to Improvise," *New York Times,* September 11, 1995, A1.
1151  "Citibank makes $1.25k Grant to CDCUs" [sic], *Credit Union News,* March 22, 1996, 4.
1152  Grant Letter to Cliff Rosenthal, executive director, NFCDCU, from Paul M. Ostergard, president, Citicorp Foundation, February 22, 1996.
1153  Letter to Miller from Comstock, February 28, 1994. Courtesy of Lyndon Comstock.
1154  Quoted in Christine Dugas, "Giving the Poor Credit," *New York Newsday,* August 31, 1994. .

## Notes

1155  Ibid.

1156  After working at the National Federation of Community Development Credit Unions for about five years, Mahon became a consultant and later, deputy commissioner of the Department of Consumer Affairs of New York City, in charge of the city's innovative Office of Financial Empowerment. In 2012, after I departed the federation to work for the Consumer Financial Protection Bureau, Mahon returned to the National Federation as CEO.

1157  Letter to NFCDCU, State Senator Franz Leichter, and other officials and community groups, November 1, 1995, quoted in National Federation of Community Development Credit Unions, "New York CDFI Fund Sought," *CDCU Report*, November 1995, 6.

1158  Saul Hansell, "Two Big Banks in Merger Set Aid for Poor," *New York Times*, November 1, 1995, D1.

1159  Ibid.

1160  www.lakotafunds.org/mission.htm, accessed March 14, 2017.

1161  Sherry Salway Black, interview by author, telephone, March 31, 2017.

1162  Adamson initiated numerous projects and served on the boards of many organizations domestically, including the Calvert Social Investment Fund. In 1997, she founded First Peoples Worldwide, furthering her advocacy on the rights of indigenous people across the globe. *Ms.* magazine named her one of its seven "Women of the Year" in 1997. https://en.wikipedia.org/wiki/Rebecca_Adamson

1163  In 1990, it rebranded as the First Nations Development Institute. Sherry Salway Black emphasizes that "the word 'project' has real connotations to it. We're ten years old, we don't want to be seen as the 'Indian project.'" See also B. Thomas Vigil, chairman, Board of Directors, First Nations Development Institute, "From the 2015 Annual Report," http://www.firstnations.org/about/chairman_letter, accessed March 15, 2017.

1164  Siobhan Oppenheimer-Nicolau, a Ford Foundation program officer, was a strong supporter of First Nations for many years and joined its board of directors. Vigil, ibid.

1165  Black served for 19 years as the senior vice president of First Nations. She has served on numerous boards and advisory committees, including the Hitachi Foundation, Trillium Asset Management, the National Community Reinvestment Coalition, the Harvard "Honoring Excellence in the Governance of Tribal Nations" program, and the American Indian Head Start program.

1166  Sherry Salway Black interview.

1167  Ibid.

1168  Rblauvelt, "First Nations Development Institute: A Look Back to the Beginning," September 20, 2015, http://indiangiver.firstnations.org/nl150910-01/?_ga=2.161248509.1716437296.1525729818-1054700573.1525729818

1169  Vigil, ibid.

1170  www.oweesta.org/about, accessed March 15, 2017.

1171  Connie Evans, interview by author, Washington, DC, March 9, 2016.

1172  Ibid.

1173  Robert Friedman, interview by author, San Francisco, CA, March 23, 2016.

1174  Ibid.

1175  "Summary of Major Points of Discussion and Agreement at AEO Planning Meeting," February 27, 1991. Courtesy of AEO.

1176  Ibid.

1177  "Report on the Organizing Event of the Association for Enterprise Opportunity, June 20–22, 1991, Berkeley, California," 1.

1178  Friedman interview.

1179  "Report on the Organizing Event," 3.

1180  Friedman interview.

1181  Thompson, interview by author, New York, NY, September 25, 2014.

1182  Gabriela Romano, Accion International, posting of October 17, 1995, on Community Development Banking listserv. Courtesy of OFN.

1183  See Chapter 23.
1184  Association for Enterprise Opportunity, "Twenty-Five Years of Achievements," *EconoCon25: AEO's 25th National Conference and Anniversary Celebration,* May 2016, 16.
1185  NCCED was the earliest of the CDFI trade organizations, founded in 1970. See Chapter 4.
1186  Memorandum to Steering Committee, Ad Hoc Coalition of CDFIs, "White House & CDC Meetings (and related events)," from Mark Pinsky and Cliff Rosenthal, March 29, 1993.
1187  Ibid.
1188  Memorandum to the CDFI Coalition Steering Committee, "Coalition Description of CDC-based Financial Institutions," from Mark Pinsky, July 7, 1993.
1189  National Congress for Community Economic Development (NCCED) dissolved in 2006. Dee Walsh and Robert Zdenek, former officials of NCCED, described the developments of the mid- to late 1990s that "started the slow decline of NCCED." Factors included the organization's emphasizing special projects and initiatives outside its core mission, which made the organization less relevant to its members; financial challenges; and the growth of Latino and Asian American community development organizations that "felt they were not being well represented by NCCED" and formed their own organizations. Dee Walsh and Robert Zdenek, "Coming Together," posted February 12, 2010, in http://www.shelterforce.org/article/1851/coming_together/PO/.
1190  National Congress for Community Economic Development (NCCED), "Coming of Age," (1999?), 21.
1191  Ibid., 1.
1192  Ibid., 11.
1193  Ibid., 12.
1194  Ibid., 16.
1195  Ibid., 7.
1196  Ibid., 17.
1197  See Chapter 5.
1198  Moncrief, interview by author, telephone, April 11, 2017.
1199  Email correspondence with author, February 14, 2018.
1200  John D. and Catherine T. MacArthur Foundation, Program on Human and Community Development, "Resolutions for Board Consideration," November 13, 1997. Courtesy of the John D. and Catherine T. MacArthur Foundation.
1201  Ibid.
1202  Mark A. Pinsky, "Coalition Organizes to Shape Law," *Shelterforce,* January/February 1995, 20.
1203  Ibid., 20–21.
1204  Ibid.
1205  Memorandum to CDFI Coalition Steering Committee, "Draft Memorandum of Understanding between the National Association of Community Development Loan Funds and the Steering Committee of the Coalition of Community Development Financial Institutions & Its Members," June 27, 1995, from Mark Pinsky, NACDLF.
1206  Ibid.
1207  Ibid.
1208  Ibid.
1209  CDFI Coalition, "History and Mission," http://www.cdfi.org/about-cdfi-coalition/history/, accessed March 25, 2017. I became the first elected chairman of the coalition at that time.
1210  The Coalition of Community Development Financial Institutions, "Membership in the CDFI Coalition," undated.
1211  "Minutes from the Coalition of Community Development Fund [sic] Institutions," May (?) 1995.
1212  Ibid.
1213  Ibid.
1214  CFED, "Setting a Training and Capacity-Building Agenda for the CDFI Industry. Preliminary Findings from the Community Development Financial Institutions Coalition's Training Assessment and Demonstration Study (TADS)," March 23, 1996, 1. Courtesy of Kate McKee.

# Notes

1215 Ibid., 8.
1216 Ibid., 9.
1217 Ibid., 18–21.
1218 Alan Okagaki, Peter Plastrik, Marc de Sousa-Shields, and Antonia de Sousa-Shields, "MacArthur Foundation Program Related Investments: Assessment and Strategy. Final Report," revised February 11, 2000. Courtesy of John D. and Catherine T. MacArthur Foundation.
1219 Ibid., i.
1220 Ibid., ii.
1221 Ibid., 15.
1222 Ibid., 21.
1223 Ibid., 26.
1224 Ibid., 6.
1225 Ibid., iv. The examples the authors cited included LIMAC (a LISC-sponsored secondary market for affordable rental housing); the Self-Help Ventures Fund secondary market for housing loans; the Community Reinvestment Fund; Neighborhood Housing Services of America; and the Calvert Social Investment Foundation (14).
1226 Ibid., iv.
1227 Ibid., 22
1228 Ibid.
1229 http://www.calvertfoundation.org/invest, accessed April 6, 2017. By 2017, 18,000 investors had collectively invested $1.4 billion.
1230 Adamson, email to author, April 6, 2017.
1231 Justin Conway and Catherine Godschalk, Calvert Foundation, interview by author, Bethesda, MD, March 8, 2016.
1232 See Chapter 16, describing their participation in the White House Rose Garden ceremony of July 15, 1993.
1233 Cdfihistory.ofn.org/archive, accessed March 14, 2017. Courtesy of Opportunity Finance Network.
1234 Quoted in Janine S. McDonald and Christopher Rhoads, "Community Development Start-Up Too Short of Capital to Open Doors," *American Banker,* February 1, 1996, 10.
1235 R. Kevin Dietrich, "Development Bank Opens in Portland, Ore.," *American Banker,* December 27, 1995, 6.
1236 Ibid.
1237 Mensah, interview by author, Washington, DC, December 30, 2014. At the time, Kerwin Tesdell was also a program officer at Ford. Shortly after, he became the CEO of the Community Development Venture Capital Alliance.

## Chapter 21

1238 U.S. Department of the Treasury, "Remarks of Treasury Secretary Robert E. Rubin. CDFI Fund Awards Announcement." Washington, DC, July 31, 1996.
1239 Department of the Treasury, "Rubin Awards $35.5 Million to Community Development Institutions." Press release (July 31, 1996).
1240 In this subsequent action, Neighborhoods, Inc., of Battle Creek, MI, received a new award of $1.35 million, while initial awards to two organizations were increased: Northeast Ventures by $250,000 and Douglass Bank by $150,000.
1241 "Remarks of Treasury Secretary Robert E. Rubin."
1242 Eades, interview by author, ibid.
1243 See Chapter 20.
1244 Quoted in Rose Ragsdale, "Juneau Group Wins Questioned Funding," *Alaska Journal of Commerce,* 21 (1997), 37.
1245 Janie Barrera, interview by author, telephone, March 29, 2017.
1246 Lollis, interview by author, telephone, March 16, 2017.
1247 Barbara F. Bronstein, "Losers Hit Treasury on Community Lending Grants," *American Banker,* August 7, 1996, 6.

1248 Letter to Kirsten Moy, from George Miller, Barbara Boxer, Ron Dellums, Lynn Woolsey, Anna Eshoo, and Tom Lantos, September 19, 1996. Courtesy of Lyndon Comstock.

1249 Bronstein.

1250 Surgeon, email to author, March 17, 2017.

1251 Martin Eakes and David Beck, Self-Help, interview by author, Durham, NC, June 29, 2015. In fact, the fund came around to precisely this position for its second round, when it began making awards to intermediaries.

1252 Department of the Treasury, "Secretary Rubin Announces $13.1 Million in Bank Enterprise Awards," press release, October 1, 1996.

1253 Message from Director Kirsten S. Moy, Community Development Financial Institutions Fund, "Annual Report, Fiscal Year 1996," undated, no page number.

## Chapter 22

1254 Memorandum for the President from Carol Rasco and Laura Tyson, "Memorandum directing the Secretary of the Treasury to coordinate all micro-enterprise programs," August 24, 1995, Domestic Policy Council, Carol Rasco, and Subject Series, "Micro-Enterprise Awards Coordinate," Clinton Digital Library, accessed November 3, 2017, https://clinton.presidentiallibraries.us./items/show/22127.

1255 White House Office of the Press Secretary, "Remarks of the First Lady, Secretary of the Treasury Bob Rubin and AID Administrator Brian Atwood in Press Briefing," January 30, 1997.

1256 Hillary Clinton, *Living History* (New York: Scribner, 2003), 284.

1257 Ibid., 268.

1258 http://www.americanrhetoric.com/speeches/hillaryclintonbeijingspeech.htm.

1259 Office of the Press Secretary, The White House, "Remarks by the First Lady and Secretary of the Treasury Robert Rubin at Microenterprise Awards Ceremony," January 30, 1997. As Mrs. Clinton was speaking from the podium, we saw a beaming President Clinton reminding her to include some point. I recall that she responded somewhat testily, "I know that."

1260 "Remarks of the First Lady," press briefing, January 30, 1997.

1261 Ibid.

1262 The winners were the Accion US Network of Accion International; Cascadia Revolving Fund; North Carolina Rural Economic Development Center; Working Capital; Women's Self-Employment Project; Nebraska Microenterprise Partnership Fund; and the Self-Employment Learning Project of the Aspen Institute.

1263 "Treasury: CDFI Fund Mixed Up," *NCUA Watch*, June 2, 1997, 1.

1264 "Review of Management Practices at the Treasury Department's Community Development Financial Institutions Fund." Majority staff report prepared for the Subcommittee on General Oversight and Investigations of the Committee on Banking and Financial Services, June 1998, 2. (Hereafter "Review of Management Practices.") The majority of the subcommittee was, of course, Republican at this time. As the report indicates, "This report has not been officially adopted by the Committee on Banking and Financial Services or its General Oversight and Investigations Subcommittee, and may not therefore necessarily reflect the views of their members."

1265 South Shore Bank in Chicago did not receive funding. Fred Cooper remembered that it had ample capital and that the fund would not be adding much value, compared with investing in the affiliated banks in Detroit and Cleveland. Cooper interview, ibid.

1266 Anonymous, "CDFI officials resign," *National Mortgage News*, August 11, 1997, 48.

1267 Steven Rohde, interview by author, telephone, January 26, 2016.

1268 Rohde, email to author, February 2, 2018.

1269 Olaf de Senerpont Domis, "Conflicts of Interest Plague Community Development Fund, House Prober Says," *American Banker*, May 19, 1997, 2:1.

1270 Ibid.

## Notes

1271  "Review of Management Practices," 21.
1272  Domis, "Conflicts of Interest," ibid.
1273  Quoted in in Olaf de Senerpont Domis, "Capital Briefs: Treasury Accused of Blocking House Probe," *American Banker*, May 30, 1997, 4:4.
1274  Ibid.
1275  Letter to The Honorable Spencer Bachus, chairman, Subcommittee on General Oversight and Investigations, Committee on Banking and Financial Services, from John D. Hawke Jr., Under Secretary (Domestic Finance), July 14, 1997. (Hereafter "Hawke letter.") Courtesy of National Federation of Community Development Credit Unions.
1276  "Review of Management Practices," 26.
1277  "Hawke letter."
1278  Ibid.
1279  "Review of Management Practices," 26.
1280  Nancy Millman and William Gruber, "Firings Urged in Treasury Program," *Chicago Tribune*, July 18, 1997, 3,1:6.
1281  Letter from Rubin to Committee Chair James Leach, August 6, 1997, and letter to Subcommittee Chairman Spencer Bachus, August 6, 1997, quoted in "Review of Management Practices," 27.
1282  Karen Gullo, "Two Treasury Officials Quitting Over Bank Grants," *Washington Post*, August 7, 1997, A14.
1283  Rohde interview.
1284  Luecht, interview by author, Washington, DC, February 23, 2016.
1285  Ibid.
1286  Jones later served as deputy director for policy and programs from February 1998 to October 2000, and then briefly, as director of the fund, from October 2000 to January 2001. After a career as a newspaper publisher and a senior official in Virginia state government, in 2016 he was named CEO of the Local Initiatives Support Corporation.
1287  Jones, interview by author, telephone, March 12, 2015.
1288  Ibid.
1289  Ibid.
1290  Millman and Gruber, "Firings Urged in Treasury Program."
1291  Glenn R. Simpson, "U.S. Loans to Firms with Clinton Ties Are Questioned," *Wall Street Journal*, May 15, 1997, A24.
1292  Nancy Millman, "Cronyism Charges Unfair, Development Banker Says," *Chicago Tribune*, July 27, 1997, 5 1:1.
1293  George Surgeon, email to author, March 17, 2017.
1294  Daniel M. Leibsohn, Paul Sussman, and Daniel B. Lopez, "Conflict of Interest? Not in This Case," *American Banker*, July 2, 1997, 9.
1295  Letter to The Honorable Bill Archer, chairman, Committee on Ways and Means, June 11, 1997, Clinton Presidential Records, Office of Speechwriting and Jonathan Prince, "1997 – Treasury – CDFI Fund," Clinton Digital Library, accessed November 3, 2017, https://clinton.presidentiallibraries.us/items/show/34409.
1296  Associated Press, "House, Senate Quickly Approve Domestic Spending Measure," *Washington Post*, July 17, 1997, A14.
1297  Glenn R. Simpson, "Treasury Aides Trumped Up Papers to Defend Awards as Probe Drew Near," *Wall Street Journal*, July 16, 1997, A4.
1298  Moy interview.
1299  Bill McConnell, "Community Lending Czar Aims to Expand Program," *American Banker*, February 5, 1998, 2.
1300  Ellen Lazar, interview by author, Washington, DC, September 30, 2014.
1301  "Review of Management Practices at the Treasury Department's Community Development Financial Institutions Fund," June 2, 1988, http://archives.financialservices.house.gov/banking/cdfitoc.html.
1302  Ibid., v.
1303  Ibid., xi, xiii.
1304  Ibid., xxi.

1305   *Reauthorization of the Community Development Financial Institutions Fund: Hearing on H.R. 3617, before the Subcommittee on Financial Institutions and Consumer Credit of the Committee on Banking and Financial Services*, 105th Cong. (1998), June 17, 1998, 1.
1306   Ibid., 3.
1307   Ibid., 4–5.
1308   Ibid., 6.
1309   Ibid., 7.
1310   Michael Selz, "Financing Small Business: Treasury's Fund Proposal for Poor Areas Faces Hurdles," *Wall Street Journal,* March 10, 1998, B2.
1311   Ibid., 11.
1312   Ibid.
1313   Ibid., 31–32.
1314   Ibid., 32.
1315   Ibid., 33.
1316   Rohde, interview by author, telephone, January 26, 2016.
1317   Jones, interview by author, telephone, March 12, 2015.
1318   Millman, ibid.
1319   Okagaki, interview by author, telephone, February 17, 2015.
1320   Okagaki interview.
1321   Rohde interview.
1322   Okagaki interview.
1323   Moy, interview by author, New York, NY, June 19, 2014.
1324   Ibid.
1325   Zavarello interview.
1326   Lazar interview.
1327   "Report to the Membership: The National Federation of CDCUs, 1997–98," 4.

## Chapter 23

1328   See Chapter 7.
1329   Nancy Andrews, interview by author, San Francisco, CA, March 25, 2016.
1330   Daniel Liebsohn, email correspondence with author, March 9–11, 2017.
1331   In their headquarter cities, the giant top-tier banks were less concerned about competition. In New York City, for example, they provided significant assistance to Community Capital Bank and community development credit unions.
1332   See Chapter 17; also, see Chapter 16, which describes the same point raised by community, consumer, and anti-poverty advocates, as well as community development credit unions.
1333   Jeannine Jacokes, email correspondence with author, September 8, 2017.
1334   As Kerwin Tesdell of the Community Development Venture Capital Alliance has described it, part of the issue was that these funds were in the business of providing equity rather than debt. More important, traditionally structured venture funds raise all their capital at the beginning of their lives and then invest and obtain the return of capital over 10 years. Unlike loan funds, where a single legal entity raises capital continuously, when a venture capital organization needs more capital, it forms a new fund, with a new legal identity, legally separate from the "parent" organization that manages the funds.
1335   On June 26, 2017, the National Federation of Community Development Credit Unions and the Community Development Bankers Association, supported by five national trade associations for banks and credit unions, sent a letter to House and Senate appropriators, urging them "to include legislative and report language that explicitly reaffirms Congressional intent that the US Treasury Department's Community Development Financial Institutions (CDFI) program support the entire diverse CDFI sector" [emphasis in original]. Other signatories included the

## Notes

American Bankers Association; the Credit Union National Association; the Independent Community Bankers of America; the National Association of Federally-Insured Credit Unions; and the National Bankers Association.

1336  After 2010, the numerical advantage of loan funds shrank as more credit unions and banks obtained CDFI certification. However, the predominance in funding continued.

1337  Ibid., citing sources: CDFI Fund certification database; CDFI Fund Community Investment Impact System (CIIS); NCUA data 2Q2015; FDIC call report data 4Q2015. It is a notable success of the CDFI Fund that there are 70 certified CDFIs (78 percent of which are loan funds) that primarily serve Native American populations.

1338  Riegle Community Development and Regulatory Improvement Act of 1994, Sec. 105 (b)(A).

1339  CDFI Fund, Financial Strategies and Research, "CDFI Program and NACA Program Awardees: A Snapshot in 2015," August 2017, accessed from www.cdfifund.gov, September 26, 2017. The report provided averages; subsequently, the CDFI Fund provided the author with medians by email.

1340  Opportunity Finance Network, "Opportunity Finance Institutions Side by Side: Fiscal Year 2015 OFN Member Data Analysis" (Philadelphia, PA: Opportunity Finance Network, 2016). The low rate of self-sufficiency for institutions financing consumers obviously does not reflect credit unions and banks.

1341  Michael Swack, Jack Northrup, and Eric Hangen, "CDFI Industry Analysis: Summary Report" (Manchester, NH: Carsey Institute, Spring 2012), 10. The report, based on a study of a large sample of CDFIs from 2005 to 2010, was conducted under contract to NeighborWorks America and the U.S. Department of the Treasury's CDFI Fund.

1342  Elyse Cherry, interview by author, Brookline, MA, July 21, 2014.

1343  Opportunity Finance Network (OFN), "Findings from the Third Quarter 2008 Market Conditions Survey," October 2008."

1344  OFN, "CDFI Market Conditions Report. First Quarter 2009," June 2009.

1345  OFN, "CDFI Market Conditions Report. Fourth Quarter 2009," March 2010.

1346  OFN, "CDFI Market Conditions. Fourth Quarter 2010. Report I – Results and Analysis," March 2011.

1347  Cherry interview.

1348  FIELD (Aspen Institute), "Surviving the Recession: How Microlenders Are Coping with Changing Demand, Risk and Funding," *FIELD Trendline Series* (1) (July 2010) 1.

1349  For a detailed account of this period, see Clifford Rosenthal, "Credit Unions, Community Development Finance, and the Great Recession," Working paper 2012-01 (San Francisco: Federal Reserve Bank of San Francisco, February 2012), http://frbsf.org/cdinvestments.

1350  http://www.bankrate.com/banking/list-of-failed-banks/

1351  Gregory B. Fairchild and Ruo Jia, "Risk and Efficiency Among CDFIs: A Statistical Evaluation Using Multiple Methods," Research conducted for Office of Financial Strategies and Research, Community Development Financial Institutions Fund, U.S. Department of the Treasury, August 2014.

1352  Michael Swack, Eric Hangen, and Jack Northrup, "CDFIs Stepping into the Breach: An Impact Evaluation—Summary Report," The Carsey School of Public Policy, University of New Hampshire, August 2014, 5. (Research conducted for Office of Financial Strategies and Research, Community Development Financial Institutions Fund, U.S. Department of the Treasury.)

1353  For a more detailed account of the CDCI program, see Rosenthal, "Credit Unions, Community Development Finance," ibid.

1354  U.S. Treasury Department, "Treasury Announces Special Financial Stabilization Initiative Investments of $570 Million in 84 Community Development Financial Institutions in Underserved Areas," September 30, 2010, https://www.treasury.gov/press-center/press-releases/Pages/tg885.aspx, accessed May 21, 2017.

1355  CDFI banks that had previously participated in the Capital Purchase Program under TARP were allowed to exchange that funding, which bore a rate of 5 percent, for CDCI funding at 2 percent. In addition, the rate increase to 9 percent was slated for eight years for the CDCI program, compared with five years for the Capital Purchase Program.

1356  Sheila Blair, *Bull by the Horns: Fighting to Save Main Street from Wall Street and Wall Street from Itself* (New York: Simon & Schuster, 2012), 199-200.

1357   The Urban Partnership Bank, capitalized by nearly $150 million from Wall Street banks, as well as foundations, took over the remnants of ShoreBank, retaining some companies but dropping others. Although the FDIC had agreed to share losses on a portion of the ShoreBank loans Urban had purchased, as Urban's president and CEO, William Farrow, acknowledged in 2016, "Resolving the acquired ShoreBank portfolio has been more expensive and time-consuming than expected due to, among other things, its condition and complexity." After accumulating losses that drained its net worth, in August 2016, the Urban Partnership Bank announced a new campaign to raise capital.

1358   Bair, 284.

1359   James E. Post and Fiona S. Wilson, "Too Good to Fail," *Stanford Social Innovation Review* (Fall 2011): 66–71.

1360   Alden McDonald, interview by author, New Orleans, LA, June 9, 2015.

1361   *Business Wire,* September 29, 2006.

1362   Business Wire, ibid.

## Chapter 24

1363   Roy Bergengren entitled the history of the movement he helped create *Crusade: The Fight for Economic Democracy in North America, 1921–1945* (Hicksville, New York: Exposition Press, 1952).

1364   The quote comes from a first-hand report by a local newspaper reporter. See Chapter 1.

1365   Quoted in CUNA Mutual Insurance Group, *The Debt Shall Die with the Debtor. The Story of CUNA Mutual Insurance Society* (Madison, WI: CUNA Mutual Insurance Group, 1991), 23.

1366   Quoted in Moody and Fite, 236, from "Dictation by Edward A. Filene Concerning His Work and Objectives," New York, May 19, 1937, typescript. See also Chapter 1.

1367   I first met Matthei in the late 1970s, when I brought him to a conference I organized for advocates for migrant and seasonal farmworkers.

1368   Clara Miller, interview by author, January 7, 2015.

1369   Moody and Fite, 264.

1370   Paul Deaton, chairman of the CUNA Dues Committee, quoted in Moody and Fite, 307.

1371   See Chapter 2.

1372   Darrin Williams, CEO of Southern Bancorp in Arkansas, framed the question sharply: "The CRA money has done nothing for Southern over the years. Zero, because we don't have any big banks in our footprint. Most CDFIs are capitalized with CRA money." Interview of Walter Smiley, Darrin Williams, and Dominik Mjartan, by author, ibid.

1373   Jeremy Nowak, "CDFI Futures: An Industry at a Crossroads" (Philadelphia, PA: Opportunity Finance Network, March 2016), 47.

1374   Wells Fargo Bank has been one of the most prominent supporters of CDFIs, including through its support of the NEXT award program, operated by the Opportunity Finance Network. After investigations by the Consumer Financial Protection Bureau, Wells Fargo admitted to opening unauthorized bank and credit accounts over a period of years; the initial estimate of 2.1 million accounts was raised to 3.5 million on August 31, 2017. It paid approximately $150 million in compensation and remediation to victims. https://newsroom.wf.com/press-release/wells-fargo-reports-completion-expanded-third-party-review-retail-banking-accounts, accessed September 1, 2017. The bank also has come under scrutiny for forced placement of automobile insurance, unauthorized changes to mortgage repayment terms in bankruptcy, and other issues. In February 2018, the Board of Governors of the Federal Reserve Board restricted its growth and forced the removal of several of the bank's directors. In its press release of February 2, Board Chair Janet L. Yellen stated: "We cannot tolerate pervasive and persistent misconduct at any bank, and the consumers harmed by Wells Fargo expect that robust and comprehensive reforms will be put in place to make certain that the abuses do not occur again."

1375   Miller interview.

1376   Clara Miller, "President's Letter: A Look Back at 2014, Part II" (New York: F.B. Heron Foundation, June 4, 2015), http://heron.org/2015/06/04/presidents-letter-part-ii/, accessed June 12, 2015.

## Notes

1377 Mark Regier, interview by author, Detroit, MI, September 24, 2015.
1378 Chuck Matthei, "Who We are, What We've Learned, Where We're Going" (Washington, DC: Institute for Community Economics, 1985).
1379 Post and Wilson, "Too Good to Fail."
1380 CDFI Act of 1994, Sec. 107, (a)(11).
1381 The CDFI Fund's position is that by virtue of satisfying the certification requirement of demonstrating "accountability" to its target community, a CDFI is community-owned. There is, as the fund points out, no statutory definition of community ownership or community governance.
1382 First Nations Development Institute, "Native Community Development Financial Institutions (CDFIs)." In *Integrated Asset Building Strategies for Reservation-Based Communities: A 27-Year Retrospective of First Nations Development Institute* (2007), 129. The CDFI Fund's statute mandated a study of the limited access to capital of Native communities. The CDFI Fund conducted the Native American Lending Study (NALS), which was issued in 2001. This landmark study was the first national report of its kind.
1383 Ibid., 125.
1384 Sherry Salway Black, interview by author, telephone, March 31, 2017.
1385 See Chapter 2 for a discussion of the different concepts of community development in the 1960s and 1970s—specifically, the discussion of Community Progress, Inc., in New Haven, CT, a Ford Foundation–funded "Gray Areas" project, generally acknowledged as the foremost project of its kind and led by Mitchell Sviridoff, later executive director of LISC. "Sviridoff and his associates spurned such unruly and ill-defined goals as 'community organizing' and 'citizen participation.'" Source: Robert Cohen, in Mitchell Sviridoff, ed., *Inventing Community Renewal: The Trials and Errors That Shaped the Modern Community Development Corporation* (New York: New School University, Milano Graduate School, 2004), 41.
1386 Michael Rubinger, interview by author, New York, NY, April 7, 2016.
1387 Bugg-Levine, interview by author, New York, NY, July 23, 2015.
1388 Antony Bugg-Levine and Ellis Carr, "Community development finance has shown we can invest in low-income communities and get repaid. It's time to do more." <https://medium.com/@ABLImpact/community-development-finance-has-shown-we-can-invest-in-low-income-communities-and-get-repaid-123cdaae59d2> October 23, 2016. Carr is CEO of Capital Impact Partners, a CDFI.
1389 Paul Weinstein, interview by author, Washington, DC, February 22, 2016.
1390 "Remarks of the First Lady," press briefing, January 30, 1997.
1391 CDFI Act of 1994, Sec. 107, Selection of Institutions, (a)(9).
1392 The fund has acknowledged that it does not prioritize insured depositories in evaluating applicants. However, it has provided technical assistance grants to at least one organization, the Lakota Fund, which chartered a federal credit union.
1393 See Chapter 23.
1394 Maude Toussaint-Comeau and Robin Newberger, "Minority-Owned Banks and Their Primary Local Market Areas," Federal Reserve Bank of Chicago, *Economic Perspectives* 41 (4) (2017): 1, accessed from the Internet, August 22, 2017.
1395 Ibid., 3.
1396 There was no NCUA data field indicating minority characteristics of credit unions until 2011.
1397 Section 308. It instructs regulators to: "Preserve the number of minority depository institutions; Preserve the minority character in cases of merger or acquisition; Provide technical assistance to prevent insolvency of institutions not now insolvent; Promote and encourage creation of new minority depository institutions; and Provide for training, technical assistance, and educational programs." Federal Deposit Insurance Corporation, FDIC Laws, Regulations, Related Acts, 5000 – Statements of Policy. Policy Statement Regarding Minority Depository Institutions. The policy covers not only depositories owned by African Americans, but also those owned by Asian Americans, Hispanic Americans, and Native Americans. https://www.fdic.gov/regulations/laws/rules/5000-2600.html.

1398 National Bankers Association, letter of May 18, 1993, accompanying "Position Paper on Community Development Banks," signed by Jessie H. Turner Jr., national chairman, and Samuel L. Foggie Sr., president. Courtesy of Jeannine Jacokes.

1399 Twenty years after FIRREA, Robert Cooper, chairman of the National Bankers Association (NBA), stated, "To be honest, we have not seen much benefit from FIRREA Section 308." Quoted in Mehrsa Baradaran, *The Color of Money. Black Banks and the Racial Wealth Gap* (Cambridge, MA: Belknap Press of Harvard University, 2017), 265.

1400 McDonald, interview by author, New Orleans, LA, June 9, 2015.

1401 Ibid.

1402 Saurabh Narain, interview by author, telephone, March 12, 2018.

1403 Bugg-Levine and Carr, ibid.

1404 Okagaki et al., "MacArthur Foundation Program Related Investments," ibid., 22.

1405 Bugg-Levine, interview by author, New York, NY, July 23, 2015.

1406 Frank DeGiovanni, interview by author, New York, NY, June 25, 2015.

1407 Ibid.

1408 Bob Friedman, interview by author, San Francisco, CA, March 23, 2016.

1409 Based in San Jose, CA, the Opportunity Fund has developed one of the largest IDA programs in the country.

1410 The Federal Reserve Bank's Survey of Consumer Finances for 2016 showed that "the long-standing and substantial wealth disparities between families of different racial and ethnic groups…have changed little in the past few years…. Black families' median and mean net worth is less than 15 percent that of white families. Source: Lisa J. Dettling, Joanne W. Hsu, Lindsay Jacobs, Kevin B. Moore, and Jeffrey P. Thompson, with assistance from Elizabeth Llanes, "Recent Trends in Wealth-Holding by Race and Ethnicity: Evidence from the Survey of Consumer Finances," *FEDS Notes*, September 27, 2017, https://www.federalreserve.gov/econres/notes/feds-notes/recent-trends-in-wealth-holding-by-race-and-ethnicity-evidence-from-the-survey-of-consumer-finances-20170927.htm.

1411 Board of Governors of the Federal Reserve System, "Report on the Economic Well-Being of U.S. Households in 2016. May 2017" (Washington, DC: Board of Governors of the Federal Reserve System, 2017), 2.

1412 See Chapter 23.

1413 Andrews, interview by author, San Francisco, CA, March 25, 2016.

1414 Michael Swack, email to author, October 25, 2017.

1415 See Chapter 23.

1416 Source: Community Development Bankers Association, "List of Certified CDFI Banks and Thrifts as of November 30, 2017."

1417 From 1994 through 2017, 130 new federal charters were issued (86 low-income) and 52 federally insured credit unions (34 low-income), for a total of 182, of which 120 were low-income (55 percent). By 2018, 49 of the low-income credit unions were active, about 41 percent of those chartered in this time span. After 1997, there was no year when as many as 10 new federal credit unions were chartered; in 2016, there were none, and in 2017, 3. Source: National Credit Union Administration.

1418 Latino Community Credit Union, "2017 Year in Review," *Growing Together* (electronic newsletter), January 2018.

1419 Transcription of audio recording by author.

1420 Eakes, interview by author, Durham, NC, June 29, 2015.

1421 Michael Barr, interview by author, Detroit, MI, May 15, 2014.

## Epilogue

1422 The Heritage Foundation, "Blueprint for Balance: A Federal Budget for 2017" (Washington, DC: The Heritage Foundation, 2016), 56.

1423 The Heritage Foundation, "Blueprint for Balance: A Federal Budget for Fiscal Year 2018" (Washington, D.C.: The Heritage Foundation, 2017), 80.

## Notes

1424  Office of Management and Budget, "America First. A Budget Blueprint to Make America Great Again," 37, https://www.whitehouse.gov/sites/whitehouse.gov/files/omb/budget/fy2018/2018_blueprint.pdf.
1425  Amber Kuchar-Bell, "Program Notes: A Deeper Look at the FY 2017 CDFI Program and NACA Program Award Round," https://www.cdfifund.gov/impact/Pages/BlogDetail.aspx?BlogID=39, accessed October 27, 2017.
1426  Quoted in CDFI Coalition, "President's FY 2019 Budget Again Proposes to Eliminate CDFI Fund Grant Programs," February 12, 2018.
1427  Ibid.

## Appendix 1

1428  Treasury Secretary Robert E. Rubin Press Conference, "CDFIs Selected for Funding under the CDFI Fund Program," July 31, 1996 (transcribed from an audio recording by Alderson Reporting Company, Inc.), 19–20. "FINCA" stood for the Foundation for International Community Assistance.
1429  Department of the Treasury, "Profiles of Organizations Selected for Funding Under the 1996 Community Development Financial Institutions Program." Except where noted, descriptions of the awardees are drawn from this document.
1430  http://www.liftfund.com/about/history/, accessed March 27, 2017.
1431  Jerry Ricketts and Brenda McDaniels, Kentucky Highlands Investment Corporation, interview by author, Washington, DC, February 2015.
1432  Community Development Financial Institutions (CDFI) Fund, "Annual Report, Fiscal Year 1996," undated, 13.
1433  "Profiles of Organizations Selected."
1434  Ibid.
1435  CDFI Fund, "Annual Report, Fiscal Year 1996," 7.
1436  Cousminer, who was inducted into the National Cooperative Business Association's Hall of Fame, also received the highest awards from the National Credit Union Foundation and the National Federation of Community Development Credit Unions.
1437  Mrs. Haynes, who served the credit union for more than a half-century, received the highest awards from the National Federation of Community Development Credit Unions, which she chaired from 2001 to 20016; the National Credit Union Foundation; and in 2017, the National Cooperative Business Association, joining its Hall of Fame.
1438  The credit union was managed by Robert Shipe, son of Orrin Shipe, who headed the Credit Union National Association in the 1960s. See Chapter 2.
1439  Robert Jackson had testified to Congress in hearings to establish the CDFI Fund in 1993. See Chapter 14.
1440  Terry Lawhead, "Cascadia Revolving Fund—Nonprofit Fund Fuses Investors, Values to Aid Communities," *Seattle Times*, April 2, 1990.
1441  CDFI Fund, "Annual Report, Fiscal Year 1996," 6.
1442  Ibid., 9.
1443  Stanley Keasling, email to author, May 27, 2017.
1444  Department of the Treasury, "Rubin Awards $35.5 Million to Community Development Institutions," press release, July 31, 1996.
1445  Clara Miller, interview by author, telephone, May 10, 2017.
1446  Clara Miller, interview by author, New York, NY, July 7, 2015.
1447  "Rubin Awards $35.5 Million."
1448  "A Different Kind of Lender," http://iff.org/resources/content/4/3/7/documents/DiffLender.pdf.
1449  See Chapter 5.
1450  Ragsdale, "Juneau Group Wins."
1451  Ibid.

## Appendix 2

1452  Barrera, interview by author, telephone, March 28, 2017.
1453  http://delcode.delaware.gov/title8/c001/sc15/
1454  "President Clinton's New Markets Tour Highlights CDFIs," *CDFI Fund Quarterly* 2 (2) (Fall 1999): 6.
1455  L. Ray Moncrief, retired KHIC executive vice president, served as board chairman of Appalachian Community Capital. Before his retirement, he had served as elected chairman of the CDFI Coalition.
1456  Kentucky Highlands Investment Corporation, press release, "A Year of Promise: More than $175 million in funding announced," June 2015, 1.
1457  Barany, interview by author, Washington, DC, May 3, 2017.
1458  See earlier footnote about Mrs. Haynes, who received top awards from credit union and cooperative organizations and served as chair of NFCDCU from 2001 to 2006.
1459  https://www.scccu.org/
1460  http://iff.org/performance-and-results.
1461  NFF website.
1462  https://www.policymap.com/about/
1463  http://www.urban.org/research/publication/assessment-local-initiatives-support-corporations-financial-opportunity-centers/view/full_report.
1464  See the op-ed piece by Elyse Cherry, "Where the Housing Crisis Continues," June 3, 2015, www.nytimes.com/2015/06/03/opinion/where-the-housing-crisis-continues.html.

# BIBLIOGRAPHY

Adams, James Ring. *The Big Fix: Inside the S&L Scandal* (New York: John Wiley & Sons, Inc., 1990).

Aspen Institute (FIELD). "Surviving the Recession: How Microlenders Are Coping with Changing Demand, Risk and Funding," *FIELD Trendline Series* 1 (July 2010).

Atwell, Clyde G. *A Passion to Survive: A Credit Union Grows in Brooklyn* (New York: Pageant-Poseidon Press Ltd., 1976).

Bair, Sheila. *Bull by the Horns: Fighting to Save Main Street from Wall Street and Wall Street from Itself* (New York: Simon & Schuster, 2012).

Baradaran, Mehrsa. *How the Other Half Banks: Exclusion, Exploitation, and the Threat to Democracy* (Cambridge, MA: Harvard University Press, 2015).

Baradaran, Mehrsa. *The Color of Money: Black Banks and the Racial Wealth Gap* (Cambridge, MA: Belknap Press of Harvard University Press, 2017).

Baxter, Christie I. *Program-Related Investments: A Technical Manual for Foundations* (New York: John Wiley & Sons, Inc., 1997).

Benjamin, Lehn, Julia Sass Rubin, and Sean Zielenbach. "Community Development Financial Institutions: Current Issues and Future Prospects," *Journal of Urban Affairs* 26 (2), 2004: 177-95.

Bovenzi, John F. *Inside the FDIC: Thirty Years of Bank Bailouts, Failures, and Regulatory Battles* (Hoboken, NJ: John Wiley & Sons, Inc., 2015).

Bureau of Federal Credit Unions. "Annual Report of the Bureau of Federal Credit Unions" (Washington, DC: Bureau of Federal Credit Unions, 1967).

Bureau of Federal Credit Unions. "Federal Credit Union Program: Annual Report 1966" (Washington, DC: Bureau of Federal Credit Unions, 1967?).

Caplovitz, David. *The Poor Pay More*. Introduction by Esther Peterson. (New York: Free Press, 1967).

Chestnut, J. L., Jr., and Julia Cass. *Black in Selma: The Uncommon Life of J. L. Chestnut, Jr.* (New York: Farrar, Straus and Giroux, 1990).

Clinton, Hillary Rodham. *Living History* (New York: Scribner, 2003).

Comptroller General of the United States. "Report to Congress: Progress Being Made and Difficulties Being Encountered by Credit Unions Serving Low-Income Persons." B-164031(4) (Washington, DC: Comptroller General of the United States, June 17, 1971).

Council on Foundations. *Legal Aspects of Program-Related Investments* (Washington, DC: Council on Foundations, 1991).

Council on Foundations. *Program Related Investment Primer.* Revised by Brody & Weiser, 1993. (Washington, DC: Council on Foundations, July 1991).

CUNA Mutual Insurance Group. *The Debt Shall Die with the Debtor: The Story of CUNA Mutual Insurance Society* (Madison, WI: CUNA Mutual Insurance Group, 1991).

Douglass, Frederick. *Selected Speeches and Writings*. Edited by Philip S. Foner (Chicago: Lawrence Hill Books, 1975).

Du Bois, W. E. B. *The Souls of Black Folk.* 1903 edition (New York: Barnes & Noble Classics, 2004).

Erickson, David J. *The Housing Policy Revolution: Networks and Neighborhoods* (Washington, DC: Urban Institute Press, 2009).

Fairchild, Gregory B., and Ruo Jia. "Risk and Efficiency Among CDFIs: A Statistical Evaluation Using Multiple Methods." Research conducted for Office of Financial Strategies and Research, Community Development Financial Institutions Fund, U.S. Department of the Treasury, August 2014.

"Financial Institutions and Black Churches: Forging a Partnership to Empower the African-American Community." Hearing before the Subcommittee on General Oversight, Investigations, and the Resolution of Failed Institutions of the Committee on Banking, Finance, and Urban Affairs, U.S. House of Representatives, 103rd Cong., Second Session (September 16, 1994). H.R. Rep. 103-164.

Foner, Eric. *Reconstruction: America's Unfinished Revolution, 1863–1877* (New York: Harper & Row, 1988).

Ford Foundation. *Investing for Social Gain: Reflections on Two Decades of Program-Related Investments* (New York: Ford Foundation, December 1991).

Gilbert, Abby L. "The Comptroller of the Currency and the Freedman's Savings Bank," *Journal of Negro History* 57 (April 1972).

Gottschall, Bruce. "Shorebank's Legacy and Vision Continue: A Practitioner's Reflections," *Cascade* 76 (Winter 2011).

Greer, James L., and Oscar Gonzales. *Community Economic Development in the United States: The CDFI Industry and America's Distressed Communities* (New York: Palgrave MacMillan, 2017).

# Bibliography

Immergluck, Dan. *Credit to the Community: Community Reinvestment and Fair Lending Policy in the United States* (Armonk, NY: M.E. Sharpe, 2004).

Isaacson, Walter. *Benjamin Franklin: An American Life* (New York: Simon & Schuster, 2004).

Isbister, John. *The Community Development Credit Union Movement in the United States* (Davis, CA: University of California Center for Cooperatives, 1994).

Jerving, Jim. *The Central Finance Facility: A Guide to Development & Operations* (Dubuque, IA: Kendall/Hunt Publishing Company, 1987).

Klein, Joyce A., and Alan Okagaki. "The Promise of Shared Platforms for the Microenterprise Industry: Lessons for Platform Users," *FIELD at the Aspen Institute* (April 2017).

Lowry, Sean. "Community Development Financial Institutions (CDFI) Fund: Programs and Policy Issues." 7-7500 (Washington, DC: Congressional Research Service, October 3, 2012), www.crs.gov, R42770.

Mayer, Martin. *The Bankers* (New York: Ballantine Books, 1974).

Moody, J. Carroll, and Gilbert C. Fite. *The Credit Union Movement: Origins and Development, 1850–1970* (Lincoln, NE: University of Nebraska Press, 1971).

Munnell, Alicia H., Lynne E. Browne, James McEneaney, and Geoffrey M. B. Tootell. "Mortgage Lending in Boston: Interpreting HMDA Data." Working paper no. 92-7 (Boston, MA: Federal Reserve Bank of Boston, October 1992).

National Center for Urban Ethnic Affairs. "Community Development Credit Union Organizing Handbook: A Tool for Rebuilding Urban America." Edited by Sydney P. Earle and Steve Schanback. (Washington, DC: National Center for Urban Affairs, December 1981).

Nembhard, Jessica Gordon. *Collective Courage. A History of African American Cooperative Economic Thought and Practice* (University Park, PA: Pennsylvania State University Press, 2014).

Nowak, Jeremy. "Shore Bank." Case study written for Development Finance Forum, September 2004 meeting.

Peirce, Neal R., and Carol F. Steinbach. *Corrective Capitalism: The Rise of America's Community Development Corporations* (New York: Ford Foundation, 1987).

Post, James E., and Fiona S. Wilson. "Too Good to Fail," *Stanford Social Innovation Review* (Fall 2011): 66–71, http://search.proquest.com/docview/886036880?accountid=12261, accessed March 23, 2015.

Robinson, Jackie. *I Never Had It Made.* Originally published 1972. As told to Alfred Duckett. (New York: HarperCollins Publishers, 1995).

Rosenfield, Patricia, and Rachel Wimpee. *The Ford Foundation: Themes, 1936–2001* (Sleepy Hollow, NY: Rockefeller Archive Center, 2015).

Rosenthal, Clifford N. *Community Banking Partnerships: Legal Structures That Work* (London: New Economics Foundation, 2005).

Rosenthal, Clifford N. "Credit Unions, Community Development Finance, and the Great Recession." Working paper 2012-01 (San Francisco, CA: Federal Reserve Bank of San Francisco, February 2012), http://frbsf.org.cdinvestments.

Rosenthal, Clifford N., and Linda Levy. *Organizing Credit Unions: A Manual* (New York: National Federation of Community Development Credit Unions, 1995).

Rosenthal, Clifford N., and Joseph Schoder. *"People's Credit": A Study of the Lending of the Lower East Side People's Federal Credit Union, 1986–89* (New York: National Federation of Community Development Credit Unions, 1990).

Sviridoff, Mitchell, ed. *Inventing Community Renewal: The Trials and Errors That Shaped the Modern Community Development Corporation* (New York: New School University, Milano Graduate School, 2004).

Swack, Michael, Eric Hangen, and Jack Northrup. "CDFIs Stepping into the Breach: An Impact Evaluation—Summary Report" (Durham, NH: University of New Hampshire, Carsey School of Public Policy, August 2014).

Swack, Michael, Jack Northrup, and Eric Hangen. "CDFI Industry Analysis: Summary Report" (Durham, NH: University of New Hampshire, Carsey School of Public Policy, 2012).

Taub, Richard P. *Community Capitalism: Banking Strategies and Economic Development* (Boston, MA: Harvard Business School Press, 1988).

Thompson, Paul. *Development of the Modern U.S. Credit Union Movement 1970–2010* (Morrisville, NC: Lulu.com, 2012).

Twentieth Century Fund Task Force on Community Development Corporations. *CDCs: New Hope for the Inner City* (New York: Twentieth Century Fund, 1971).

Vidal, Avis C. *Rebuilding Communities: A National Study of Urban Community Development Corporations. Executive Summary* (New York: Community Development Research Center, Graduate School of Management and Urban Policy, New School for Social Research, 1992).

Washington, Reginald. "The Freedman's Savings and Trust Company and African American Genealogical Research," *Federal Records and African American History* 29 (2) (Summer 1997), http://www.archives.gov/publications/prologue/1997/summer/freedmans-savings-and-trust.html.

Witzeling, Ruth. *People Not Profit: Story of the Credit Union Movement* (Madison, WI: Credit Union National Association, Inc., 1993).

Zarefsky, David. *President Johnson's War on Poverty: Rhetoric and History* (Birmingham, AL: University of Alabama Press, 1986).

# INDEX

*Note:* Page references followed by *f* or *t* refer to figures or tables, respectively. Page references containing "n" refer to endnotes.

## A

Accion International, 165, 311
Accion Texas (LiftFund)
   CDFI Fund award to, 312, 329, 331, 366*t*, 385
   current presence of, 399
   as LiftFund, 362
   sustainability of, 364, 378, 394
ACORN (Association of Community Organizations for Reform Now), 205–206, 212, 216–217, 242
   ACTION-Pittsburgh, 37
Adamson, Rebecca, 308–309, 311, 322, n1162
Addams, Jane, 48
Ad Hoc Coalition of Public Purpose Lenders. *See* CDFI Coalition
Adrian Dominican Sisters, 73–74, 121–122, 130, 371, n463
AEG (Arkansas Enterprise Group), 102, 172, 299, 386
AEO (Association for Enterprise Opportunity), 157, 195, 204, 309–312
AFIA (Assets for Independence Act), 209, n808
African American CDFIs. *See also names of individual institutions*
   in the 1950s, 25–26
   African American ownership, 16–17, 374–376, 386, 387
   CDCI funding and, 361–362
   CDFI Coalition and, 332
   CDFI Fund awards, 329, 331, 387, 398–399
   Center for Community Self-Help and, 108, 226–227
   church-based, 154, 304, 369, 388, 398
   civil rights movement and, 369
   "The Color of Money", xv, 79–80, 112, 159
   community development banks, 386–387
   community development venture capital and, 315–316
   Cooperative Assistance Fund and, 75
   CRA and decline of, 293–295
   Freedman's Savings and Trust Company, 1, 6–11, 7*f*, n20,n34
   Freedom National Bank, New York, 11, 19
   Good Faith Fund, 100, 102, 166, 179, 309
   gradual decline in number of, 375, n67
   in the Great Depression, 16–17
   King (Lawrence, Jr.) scandal and, 144–147
   mergers with white-owned banks, 293–295
   mutual aid groups, 6
   The Neighborhood Institute, 59–60, 98–99, 296
   in North Carolina, n67
   OEO and, 30–32, 36–37
   Saving Fund and Land Association, 6
   South Shore Bank and, 52–55, 54*f*, 96
   WOSCO story and, 226–227
African Americans. *See also* African American CDFIs; Bedford-Stuyvesant, Brooklyn
   after Katrina, 361–362
   after the Civil War, 6–11
   backlash from King scandal, 146–147
   Bush, George H. R., and, 144–145
   civil rights and credit unions, 33–35, 146, 369, 381
   distrust of banks, 11
   Individual Development Accounts and, 321
   legacy of slavery, 203
   lending discrimination against, 112, 159, 201, 203, 214–217, n802
   protest against ShoreBank-Indecorp merger, 293–296
   redlining and, 47, 50, 177
   rural access to capital, 217, 226–227, 386–389
   self-employment and microenterprise projects, 309–312

wealth disparities of, 377–378, n1410
African Insurance Company, 6
African Union Society, 6
agricultural credit unions, 13, 15
Alayon, Adolfo "Al", 42, 67, 70, 126, 126f, 131
Albina Community Bank, 316, 324
Alinsky, Saul, 48
Allen, Mark, 294–295
Alt, Konrad, 181
Alternatives FCU, 72
Altman, Frank, 169–170, 172
Alvord, John W., 6
American Friends Service Committee, 392
American National Bank, 57
American Recovery and Reinvestment Act of 2009 (ARRA), 359
American Savings Credit Union, 396–397
AmeriCorps VISTA, 304, n1147
Andrews, Nancy, ix, 91, 288–289, 351
Annie E. Casey Foundation, 400
Appalachian Community Capital, 397
Appalachian Community FCU, 363
Appalachian Regional Commission, 397
Appalbanc, 259, 330–331, 363, 366t, 389
Archer, Bill, 341
Arkansas Enterprise Group (AEG), 102, 172, 299, 386
ARRA (American Recovery and Reinvestment Act of 2009), 359
Arrick, Ellen, 143, n527
Assets for Independence Act (AFIA), 209, n808
Association for Enterprise Opportunity (AEO), 157, 195, 204, 309–312
Association for Black Economic Power, 381
Astor Foundation, 40
Atwell, Clyde, 17
Austin Labor Force Intermediary, 296
Ayers, Eddie, 35

## B

Bachus, Spencer, 336–339, 341–344
Bair, Sheila, 360–361
Balanced Budget Act of 1997, 341
Baltimore Community Investment Company, 41
Bank Enterprise Act (BEA) of 1991
  award selection criteria, 285–286
  award winners, 292, 298, 325, 326, 333, 365
  banks and, 239–241
  CDFI bill and, 186, 199, 235, 244, 255–257, n934
  Flake and, 160–162, 210, 237, n549
  funding of, 279, 343–344
  origins of, 159–162
  shortage of award applicants, 286
Bank Holding Company Amendments of 1970, 55, 59
banking industry. *See also* Savings and Loan scandal
  in 1992 House hearings, 165–166
  bank holding company concept, 55, 59, 165, 183, 395–397
  bank within a bank model for inner-city markets, 166
  on BEA awards to distressed communities, 285–286
  on CDFI bill, 231–232, 239–241
  on community reinvestment legislation, 50–51, 252–254
  on interstate bank branching, 256
  mega-mergers of banks, 306–307, 321
  new bank chartering, 317, 380–381, n231
  partnerships with CDFIs, 228
Bank of America, 333, 370
Baradaran, Mehrsa, 373
Barany, George, 398
Baroni, Msgr. Geno, 49, 71, n182
Barr, Michael, 271, 382
Barrera, Janie, 331, 394
Barth, James R., 265
Bavaria, Joan, 91
Bazemore, Timothy, 226, 236, 421n411
BCC (Boston Community Capital), 364, 366t, 382, 398, 400–401
BCC Solar, 400–401
BCLF (Boston Community Loan Fund), 390, 400
BCLF Managed Assets Corporation, 400
BCLF Ventures, Inc., 400
BEA. *See* Bank Enterprise Act (BEA) of 1991
Bedford-Stuyvesant, Brooklyn, 17
  1964 riots in, 37
  Consumer Action Program, 67, 71–72
  Paragon Association, 17
  Robert Kennedy and, 37–39
Bedford-Stuyvesant Restoration Corporation, 37–40, 83, n300
Beijing Women's Conference, 334
Ben & Jerry's, 227, n722
Bennett, Michael, 55
Bennett, Robert, 201–202
Bentsen, Lloyd M., 233, 236–237, 239, 258, 265–266
Bereiter, Doug, 238

# Index

Bergengren, Roy F., 14–15, n273, n1363
Beste, Fred, 314
Bethex FCU, 367t, 388
Bhargava, Deepak, 216, 242
Black, Sherry Salway, 308, 373, n1163, n1165
Black Americans. *See* African Americans
Blexit, 381
block busting, 47–48
"The Blue Book", 67
Bolling, Landrum R., 75
Borgacz, Sister Louise, 74
Boston Community Capital (BCC), 364, 366t, 382, 398, 400–401
Boston Community Capital Solar, 400–401
Boston Community Loan Fund (BCLF), 390, 400
Boutte, Alvin J., 294–295
Bowles, Erskine, 258
Bradford, Cal, 49
Bradley, Bill, 209–210, 211–212, 221, 233
Brandon, Bill, 102, 344
Braun, Carol Moseley, 215, 295
Bridgeway Capital, 398–399. *See also* Community Loan Fund of Southwestern Pennsylvania
Brody & Weiser, 116
Brooklyn Ecumenical Cooperatives, 105
Brooklyn Workforce Innovations, n403
Brown, Ronald, 213, 233, n780
Brumbaugh, R. Dan, Jr., 265
Bryant, John, 260
Bugg-Levine, Antony, 373–374, 377
Bundy, McGeorge, 37, 40–41
Bureau of Federal Credit Unions, 24, 25–28, 43
Burns, Arthur, 50
Bush, George H. R., administration of, 153, 159, 175, 323
Bush, George W., administration of, 356–357
Butera, Jim, 231
Butler, Mattie, 295
Bynum, Bill, 311, 397

## C

CAAs (community action agencies/programs), 21, 23–24, 62, 281
CABS FCU, 71–72,
CAF (Cooperative Assistance Fund), 41, 75, 138
Calvert Social Investment Fund, 153, 300, 322
CAMEL rating system, 141

Campaign for Human Development, 49, 71, 73
CANDO (Chicago Association of Neighborhood Development Organizations), 231
CAPFCU (Central Appalachian People's FCU), 72, 259, 363, 389
capital access, role of
   Bill Clinton on, vi
   CDFI Fund and, 62–66
   Comstock on, 104–105
   CRA and, vii
   Franklin on, 5
   in low-income areas, 35, 42, 64–67, 171, 250–251, 281–282
   in nineteenth-century cooperatives, 11–12
   raising private capital, 71–72, 75–76, 191–192, 243, 326–327
   in War on Poverty, 42
Capital Impact Partners, 399
Capitalization Program (NFCDCU)
   assets in the late 1990s, 304–305, 320
   CDFI Fund and, 347
   CDRLF seeking control of funds, 127
   impact of King scandal on, 146–147
   interest rates in, 127,
   investments in, 114–115, 121–123, 128–131, 138–139, 153–154, 317
   origins of, 128–129, 131–132, 138
   Self-Help Credit Union and, 111
Capital Magnet Fund, 362, 364, 401
Capital Purchase Program (TARP), n1355
Caplovitz, David, 23, 24–25, 31–32, n76, n106
CAPs (community action agencies/programs), 21, 23–24, 62, 281
Carnell, Rick, 181
Carr, Ellis, 373–374, 377
Carter, Jimmy, administration of, 69–70, 79, 293
Cascadia Revolving Fund, 363, 366t, 390–391
Cashin, Sheryll, 209, 212
Catherine McAuley Housing Foundation, 120, 139, n458
Catholic Charities, 49
Catholic Church
   Adrian Dominican Sisters, 73–74, 121–122, 130, 371, n463
   Campaign for Human Development, 49, 71, 73
   Catholic Charities, 49
   Catholic Worker, 89, 369, n316
   in Chicago community reinvestment, 49

women's orders, 73–74, 77, 100, 120–121, 130, 139, 146–147 (*See also names of individual orders*)
CCB. *See* Community Capital Bank
CDBs. *See* community development banks
CDCI (Community Development Capital Initiative), 360–362, 365, 379, 382, 397, n1355
CDCs. *See* community development corporations
CDCUs. *See* community development credit unions
CDFI Bond Guarantee Program, 362
CDFI Coalition
  Capital Campaign, 275
  CDFI Fund relationship to, 263, 277
  on CDFI legislation, 210–212, 216, 221–222, 230–232, 241, n769
  on CDFI legislation reconciliation, 248–249, 256
  CDFI transition team and, 270–272
  "CDFI Woodstock" conference (1994), 249–251
  Clinton's transition team and, 188–191
  community development banks and, 312–313
  dialogue with legislators, 171–173, 272
  on domestic policy agenda (1992), 181, 187–190
  federal appropriations role in equity, 196–198
  on Federal Bank for Community Development Banks, 191
  First Nations in, 308
  funding and staffing proposal to Ford Foundation (1994), 251–252
  future goals of (1994), 275–277
  "Key Principles" position paper (1993), 194–195, 204, 230–232, n710, n711
  on matching requirements, 283–284
  NACDLF and, 151–152, 156–157, 276, 302–303, 317–318
  NCCED in, 195, 312, n706, n1185
  on need versus performance, 245
  origins of, 156–158, 187–188
  on private-sector funding, 191–192
  at release of Clinton's CDFI bill, 226–227, 230
  second national conference, 275
  at Senate hearings (1993), 201–204
  size of (1995), 317
  steering committee, 275–276
  on technical assistance and training, 196, 252
  Training, Assessment and Demonstration Study, 319
CDFI depositories, 237, 360, 365
CDFI Fund. *See also* CDFI Fund winners (1996)
  on accountability to the community, 282
  administrative costs, 237–239, 266–267, 287
  application process, 113–114, 279–280, 383–384, n424
  Bachus investigation of, 336–344, n1264
  Bond Guarantee Program and, 362
  budget crisis (1995) and, 286–287
  budget for FY 2017, 383
  Capital Magnet Fund and, 362
  CDFI Coalition relationship to, 277
  Clinton connection to applicants, 290–291, 345
  in Clinton's final bill, 235, 238–239
  Community Reinvestment Act and, 51
  consultants hired for selection, 288
  credit scores of applicants, 290
  democratizing finance, 372–373
  drafting regulations, 278–280
  eligibility criteria, 280–282, n1045
  equity capital investment in, 43
  faith-based investments and, 73–74
  Financial Assistance awards, 376
  funding appropriation for, 260–261, n958
  funding rescinded from CDFI legislation, 253, 263, 268–270
  in George W. Bush administration, 356–357
  Great Recession and, 356–358
  Healthy Food Financing Initiative and, 362
  increasing disparity in CDFIs, 320–321
  as information clearinghouse, 43, 216, 219
  interim rule (1995), 278–279
  lack of small institutions provision, 285
  minority-owned CDFIs and, 375–376
  model legislation for (1984), 137–138
  Moy and Rohde as leadership of, 273–274
  Native American Lending Study, n1382
  nonprofit loan fund advantages in, 352–354
  origin of, vi, 42–43, 151, 173, n78
  private sources of capital in, 75–76, 326–327
  reauthorization of (1998), 341–345
  regulation writing, 273
  Republican Revolution and, 266, 269
  selection process, 282, 287–289, 291–292
  self-assessment after Bachus investigation, 345–347
  South Shore Bank and, 54–55
  state CDFI Funds, 306–307
  structure of, 214–215, 218–219
  transition team, 266–273
  in Treasury Department, 213–214, 265, 268, 270–273, 289–290, 337–338
  Trump on eliminating funding, 378, 383

wholesale-intermediary organizations, 320–321, 347, n1225
CDFI Fund winners (1996)
   age of CDFIs in, 330, 331
   analysis of, 352–356, 352*t*, 356*t*, 357*t*, n1335
   criticism of process, 331–333
   demographics of, 328–330
   deposit insurance and, 218, 219, 220, 234, 284, 330
   documentation issues, 336–337, 345
   equity funding for, 327–328
   growth of, 366*t*–367*t*
   institutional diversity in, 326
   nonprofit loan funds in, 352–356, 352*t*, 354*t*, 355*t*
   sectoral distribution of, 327
CDFI legislation. *See also* Senate Banking Committee
   administration release of bill, 224–228
   administration final bill, 215–220
   administrative costs, 237–239
   aftermath of signing, 260–261
   approval and reconciliation, 255–257
   BEA and, 235–236, 239–241, 244, n896
   Bradley initiative, 209–212
   CDFI Coalition on, 194–196, 210–212
   Clinton transition team on, 188–193
   Clinton vision for, 176–180
   community empowerment and, 216–218
   Community Investment Corporation Demonstration and, 175, 181, 182, n772
   competitive funding and disparate impact, 217–218, n802
   CRA and, 210–211, 212–213
   first reactions to release of, 230–232
   Flake-Ridge-Leach initiative, 239–241
   funding options, 214–215
   in historical context, 242
   House Banking Committee hearing (July 1992), 164–175
   House Banking Committee hearing (July 1993), 236–241, 244
   Individual Development Accounts and, 221
   insured vs. uninsured depositories, 237
   Leach bill, 210
   location of CDFI Fund, 213–214
   national service apprenticeships and, 221
   need vs. performance criteria in, 245
   OEO credit unions vs. CDFIs, 246–247
   private-sector secondary market, 243
   role of banks in, 235–236

Rose Garden ceremony (1993), vi, 221–222, 223–230, 236, 239, 316
Rush bill, 210
in the Senate, 233–236, 241–242, 244–245
Senate Banking Committee hearings (1993), 181–188, 198–207, 233–236
Senate pilot CDB legislation (early 1992), 163–164
signing of, 257–260, 258*f*
source of federal support in, 196–198
Waters bill, 210
White House strategy, 242–243
CDFIs (community development financial institutions)
   capital initiative for, 353, 360–362, 365, 379, 382, 397
   defining characteristics of, vii, 233
   as financial intermediaries, 252, 282
   as "fringe lenders", 198
   funding, 173
   in the Great Recession, 357–359
   growth of, by type, 352–356, 352*t*, 354*t*, 355*t*, 379–381
   increasing disparity in, 320–321
   insured vs. uninsured depositories, 237, 360
   leadership demographics, 373–374
   low-income housing tax credit, 171
   multi-faceted, 327, 327*t*, 330, 363, 389–390
   national convention, 157–158
   on need for secondary market instruments, 169–170
   "new" CRA and, 252–254
   new generation in, 322–324
   ownership of, 205, 234, 372–373, n1381
   reflections on influence of, viii–ix
   relationship with mainstream banks, 200–202, 205–206
   sustainability of, 378–379
   technical assistance from, 196
   wholesale intermediaries, 320–321, 347
CDRLF. *See* Community Development Revolving Loan Fund
CDVCA (Community Development Venture Capital Alliance), 314–316
CEI (Coastal Enterprises, Inc.), 166–167, 171, 203, 396
Center for Community Change, 159, 216–217, 249
Center for Community Self-Help
   CDFI Fund awards, 330, 343
   Center for Responsible Lending, 382, n407
   growth of, 299–300, 363–364
   managing, 112
   McKee resignation from, 267
   as model for CICD legislation, 178, 184–186

North Carolina Community Facilities Fund, 300
Self-Help Credit Union (*See* Self-Help Credit Union)
Self-Help FCU, 396, n406
Self-Help model, 111, 178, 184–186, 395–396
Self-Help Partnership Lending program, 110–111
Self-Help Ventures Fund (*See* Self-Help Ventures Fund)
Central Appalachian People's FCU (CAPFCU), 72, 259, 363, 389
Central Brooklyn Coordinating Council, 37–38
Central Brooklyn FCU, 306, 323*f*
CFA (Consumer Federation of America), 205, 216–217, 231
CFED (Corporation for Enterprise Development), 144, 277, 309–310, 319, 399
CFPB (Consumer Financial Protection Bureau), 353–354, 371, 379, n85, n1374
Chafkin, Sol, 84
Charles Stewart Mott Foundation, 60, 98, 310, 311
Chase Bank, 306–307
Chase Manhattan Bank, 333
Chavez, Cesar and Helen, 395
Cheap, Margaret, 316
Chemical Bank, 147, 306–307
Cherry, Elyse, 356, 358, 401
Chicago. *See also* community reinvestment movement
 community reinvestment movement, 47–51, 107
 early bank protests, 48–49
 government/industry alliances in, 26
 mortgage lending discrimination in, 48, 50
 ShoreBank in the 1980s, 96–97
Chicago Association of Neighborhood Development Organizations (CANDO), 231
Chicago Community Trust, 60, 98, 390
Chicago Neighborhood Institute, 296
CICD (Community Investment Corporation Demonstration), 175, 181, 182, n772
Cincotta, Gale, vii, 48, 49–52, 81, n177
Cisneros, Henry, 241, 335
Citibank, 301–302, 305–306, 311
City First, 316
City Lands Corporation, 59, 99
civil rights, credit unions and, 33–35, 146, 369, 381
Clark, James N., 67–70, 127–129, 131
Clark, Peggy, 311
class struggle, accusations of, 24
Cleary, Barbara, 91
Cleveland Foundation, 390
Clinton, Bill. *See also* CDFI legislation

on bank holding company model, 183, 395
campaign platform of 1992, vi, xiv–xv, 43, 63–64, 176–180
on CDFI Fund, 149, 227–228, 279, 286
on community development bank networks, xiv–xvi, 43, 63–64, 103, 181–182
on Community Reinvestment Act, 212–214, 228
criticism of CDFI Fund awards connection, 290–291, 332, 337, 339
domestic policy agenda (1992), 188–190
Domestic Policy Council, 208–209
Economic Summit (Little Rock, 1992), 190–191
Good Faith Fund and, 166
on Individual Development Accounts, 221
legislative proposals on CDFIs (1993), 209–222
Lewinsky scandal, n1073
Little Rock economic summit (1992), 190–191
on microlending, 149, 200, 204, 311, 327, 378
National Economic Council and, 208–209
on a national service corps, 196
*Putting People First*, 176–177, 209, 216
at release of CDFI bill, 227–228
*Rolling Stone* interview, 179
on Self-Help model, 178, 184–185
ShoreBank and, 99, 101, 290
signing of CDFI legislation, 257–260, 258*f*
Southern Development Bank and, 101–102, 386, 395
during transition, 181–193
transition team, 188–193
veto threat for CDFI Fund rescission package, 270, 274
Waters and, 163
White House Rose Garden ceremony (1993), vi, 221–222, 223–230, 236, 239, 316
Whitewater investigation, 254–255, 335, 340–341, n930
Clinton, Hillary
 on community development banks, 179, 374–375
 criticism of CDFI Fund connection, 336–337, 339–340
 Elkhorn Bank of Arkansas and, 227
 on microenterprise, xvii, 311–312, 334–335, 385, n1259
 national service at CDFIs and, 221
 Southern Development Bank and, 101–102, 290
 Whitewater investigation, 254–255, 340–341, n930
CNVA (Community for Nonviolent Action), 93
Coastal Enterprises, Inc. (CEI), 166–167, 171, 203, 396
Cole, Tony, 257
College Station Community FCU, 396
Collins, Chuck, 86, 104, n333
"The Color of Money", xv, 79–80, 112, 159

# Index

Common Space, 85
community action agencies/programs (CAAs/CAPs), 21, 23–24, 62, 281
community banking bill (1992), 163–164, 224–225
Community Bank of the Bay, 108, 259, 298, 316, 324
Community Capital Bank (CCB)
   BEA and, 298
   capital raising for, 105–108, 106f
   chartering, 182–184
   loan to Joseph Holland, 227
   organizing for, 103–105
   profile of (1996), 296–298
   at Senate hearings (1993), 200
Community Capital Partnership Act of 1993, 209–212
Community Corporation Act of 1970, 62, 77
Community Credit Union Job Training Program, 132, n497
community development banking bill of 1992, 174–175
community development banks (CDBs). *See also* CDFIs; Center for Community Self-Help; ShoreBank; Southern Development Bank
   basic banking services and, 63–64
   Capital Purchase Program under TARP and, n1355
   CDCs and, 63
   Clinton on network of, 63–64, 176–178, 185
   Clinton's proposed reforms to, 224–225
   Community Capital Bank, 103–108, 106f
   difficulties in chartering new banks, 380–381, n231
   early banks, 293
   Federal Bank for, 191
   growth of, 363, 367t
   minority-owned, 374–376, 386–387
   national, 64, n231
   new generation of, 324
   ownership of, 64, n1381
   rural, 99–102
   Self-Help and, 184–185
Community Development Block Grant funding, 69, 82, 313, 357
Community Development Capital Initiative (CDCI), 353, 360–362, 365, 379, 397, n1355
Community Development Venture Capital Alliance, 157
community development corporations (CDCs), 313
   in 1992 House hearings, 166–167
   in Bedford-Stuyvesant, 38–40
   CDFI Coalition and, 312–313
   cultural shift in 1980s, 81–82
   dilemma of mature, 83

   Enterprise foundation, 85
   LISC and, 83–85
   power to raise capital in, 62–63
   in the Reagan years, 81–82
   Robert Kennedy and, 37–38
   theory of change in, 67–68
   top-down development vs. maximum feasible participation, 61–62
Community Development Credit Union Demonstration Project, 143–144
Community Development Credit Union Institute, 347
community development credit unions (CDCUs). *See also* National Federation of Community Development Credit Unions
   in 1992 House hearings, 168–169
   in 1996 CDFI awards, 387–389, 398
   in congressional hearings (1992), 168–169
   deposit insurance for, 33, 64–65, 138, 172–173, 370
   difficulties becoming chartered, 136–137, n502, n505, n1417
   growth of, 313, 363, 367t
   impact of OEO failure on, 42–43
   minority owned, 374–376
   nonmember deposits in, 71–72, 109, 146, 216, n265
   origins of, 18, 368–372, 377–378, n40
   raising private capital, 71–72
   scandal and embezzlement impact, 144–147
   in Self-Help model, 184–186
Community Development Finance Authority of New Hampshire, 204
Community Development Financial Institution Coalition. *See* CDFI Coalition
Community Development Financial Institution Fund. *See* CDFI Fund
community development financial institutions. *See* CDFI Coalition; CDFI Fund; CDFIs
community development loan funds. *See also* National Association of Community Development Loan Funds
   in 1992 House hearings, 167–168
   in CDFI Fund applications, 352–356, 352t, 354t, 355t, n1331, n1336
   in CDFI Fund awards, 303, 326–330, 327t, 390–393, 398–400
   Community Investment Notes and, 324
   equity importance in, 117–118, 124, 152
   First National Conference of Community Loan Funds, 91–92

Franklin on, 3–6
Great Recession and, 357–359
growth of, 363, 366t, 376, 379
ICE and, 88–90, 92–93
for low-income neighborhoods, 167–168, 185, 390–392
Matthei and origins of, 85–88, 93–95, 369
mission drift in, 370–374, 377
in multi-faceted CDFIs, 389
NACDLF formation, 92–93, 95
profiles of, 390–393, 398–401
sustainability of, 352–356, 352t, 354t, 355t, 362–365, 366t
venture funds compared to, n1334
Community Development Revolving Loan Fund (CDRLF)
under Carter, 199
under Clinton, 233, 261
creation of, 71, 125–128
funding of, 186, n896
interest rates and, 127, n484
moved to NCUA, 140–141, 144, 153, nn506–507
Neighborhood Banking Corporation and, 142, 155
Reagan's efforts to terminate, 130, 138, 147
Community Development Venture Capital Alliance (CDVCA), 314–316, n1335
community development venture capital funds
in CDFI Fund awards, 367t, 379
CDVCA on, 315–316, n1335
dynamics of growth in, 363–364
Kentucky Highlands Investment Corporation, 314–315, 386, 397
Northeast Ventures Corporation, 315, 386
ShoreBridge Capital, 386
community empowerment
business-driven approach and, 38
in CDCU concept, 132
CDFI Coalition on, 196
in Clinton plans, 188, 209, 216–217
South Shore Bank and, 58
in War on Poverty, 43, 61, 64, 216
Community First Bank, 324
Community for Nonviolent Action (CNVA), 93
Community Investment Corporation Demonstration (CICD), 175, 181, 182, n772
Community Investment Notes, 322
Community Loan Fund of Southwestern Pennsylvania, 366t, 391, 398–399
Community Progress, Inc., New Haven, 36, n1385
Community Reinvestment Act (CRA) of 1977
in 1992 House hearings, 169–170
African American banks and, 293–295
attack on, under George H. W. Bush administration, 159
bank mergers and, 306–307, 321
Bill Clinton campaigning on, 177
in CDFI legislation, 212–214, 236–237, 248–249
CDFIs and weakening of bank requirements, 198, 205–206, 210, 250
Clinton's proposed reforms to, 224–225
EQ2 and, 301–302
FDIC administration of, 270
in the Great Recession, 357
Lower East Side People's FCU, 135–137, 136f
New York Corporation for Community Banking, 137–138, 147
origin of, 49–51, 76, 79
revisions to (1994), 252–254
as "safe harbor" for banks, 160, 205–206, 211, 235, 240, 243
Spark platform, 379
Community Reinvestment Fund (CRF), 169–170
community reinvestment movement (Chicago)
CDFI initiative and, 107
community advocacy and development, 51–52
disclosure in, 50
early bank protests, 48–49
mortgage lending discrimination and, 47–48
National People's Action (NPA), 49–50
reinvestment legislation, 50–51
South Shore Bank, 52–60
Community Renewal Tax Relief Act of 2000, 356
Community Self-Determination Act (proposed, 1968), 62–64
Community Services Administration (CSA), 69, 79, 82, 125–126
Comstock, Lyndon
background of, 103–104
on CDFI Coalition, 156–157
on Clinton's network proposal, 182–184
Community Bank of the Bay and, 259
Community Capital Bank and, 105–108, 106f, 182–184, 296–298, 306, 324
criticism of CDFI Fund selection, 331
fact-finding visits to CDFIs by, 198
on Flake-Ridge-Leach initiative, 240
at House hearings (1993), 198–199
at ICE, 104–105
at LEAP, 297

New York State Coalition of CDFIs, 306
   at Senate hearings (1993), 200–201, 206
   South Shore Bank and, n394
   on training needs, 197, 297
congressional hearings (1992)
   Bank Enterprise Act, 159–162
   community development and mainstream banks, 165–166
   community development corporations, 166–167
   community development credit unions, 168–169
   community development loan funds, 167–168
   dialogue in, 171–173
   on federal role in community development, 173
   first community development banking bill, 174–175
   in the House, 164
   key messages in, 168, 174
   on philanthropy role, 170–171
   secondary market need, 169–170
   in the Senate, 163–164
   South Central Los Angeles riots and, 162–163
Congress on Racial Equality (CORE), 30
Consumer Advisory Council of the Federal Reserve System, 147
Consumer Cooperative Development Corporation, 87, 138, n494
Consumer Federation of America (CFA), 205, 216–217, 231
Consumer Financial Protection Bureau (CFPB), 353–354, 371, 379, n85, n1374
Consumer Service Organization, 145–146
Conway, Justin, 322
Cooper, Fred, 284, 289, n1265
Cooper, Robert, n1399
Cooperative Assistance Fund (CAF), 41, 75, 138
cooperative credit society (1850), n40
Cooperative Fund of New England, 85
Cooperative League (Filene), 15
cooperativism, 11–13, 369
CORE (Congress on Racial Equality), 30
Corporate FCU, 359
Corporation for Enterprise Development (CFED), 144, 277, 309–310, 319, 399
Corporation for National and Community Service, 221
Coston, Sister Carol, 121–122
Cousminer, Joy, 388
CRA. *See* Community Reinvestment Act (CRA) of 1977
Crear, Pete, 25–26, n90
Credit Union Development Fund, 68
Credit Union National Association (CUNA)

   alliance to keep federal tax exemption for credit unions, 26
   Capitalization Program request to, 129
   consumer education, 28–29
   demonstration projects of, 26
   difficulties becoming chartered, 136–137, n502
   formation of, 16
   low-income credit unions, 25–26, 32, 66
   mission drift in, 18, 25–28
   CUNA Mutual Insurance Group, 129
   opposition to NFCDCU 1986 proposals, 141
   on time to become self-supporting, 42
   on wealth inequality, n88
Credit Union National Extension Bureau (CUNEB), 14–15, 25, n61
credit unions
   agricultural, 13
   bookkeeping in, 26
   civil rights and, 33–35, 146, 369, 381
   credit and poverty, 24–25
   difficulties becoming chartered, 136–137, n502, n505, n1417
   federal deposit insurance (*See* deposit insurance)
   Filene on role of, 17–18
   mission drift in, 18, 25–26, 370
   municipal power structure and, 24–25
   national system of, 16
   origins of, 11–12, n40, n52
   ownership of, 29, 372, n1381
   for persons with disabilities, 26–27
   rapid growth of, 13–15
   U.S. Central Credit Union, 73, n273
   during World War II, 18
CRF (Community Reinvestment Fund), 169–170
CSA (Community Services Administration), 69, 79, 82, 125–126
C.S. Mott Foundation, 276
Cummins Engine Foundation, 56
CUNA. *See* Credit Union National Association
CUNEB (Credit Union National Extension Bureau), 14–15, 25, n61
Cunningham, William Michael, 296

## D

DACA (Deferred Action for Childhood Arrivals), 398
D'Amato, Alfonse
   on bank incentives, 232, 236

on CRA safe harbors, 200–201, 205–206, 235
on NFCDCU management of CDRLF, 127
on secondary markets for small-business loans, 241, 243–244, 254
D'Amours, Norman, 305, 323
Davis, Milton, 54, 54*f*, 58–59, 98, 199–201, 206, 295
Davis, Susan, 58
Day, Dorothy, 86, 369
Dedmon, Bill, 159
Deferred Action for Childhood Arrivals (DACA), 398
DeGiovanni, Frank, 363, 377
de Haas, Jacob, 13
Delaware Valley Community Reinvestment Fund (DVCRF), 171–172, 198, 364, 366*t*, 391, 399
Demopolis FCU, 35
Dent, Richard, 259
deposit insurance. *See also* Federal Deposit Insurance Company
  administrative requirements for, 244
  Capitalization Program and, 128
  in CDFI bill (1993), 237, 245
  in CDFI Fund awards, 218, 219, 220, 234, 284, 330
  cooperative concept and, 65
  credit union growth and, 370
  Federal Credit Union Act (1970), 33, 65
  in the Great Recession, 359
  for low-income credit unions, 33, 65–66
  in matching requirements, 254
  for nonmember deposits, 71–72, 109, 146, 216, n265
  ratio of equity to assets and, 58, 65–66
  in Self-Help model, 184
Desjardins, Alphonse, 12–13
Detroit Development Bancorp, 331, 363, 387
Development and Services Corporation (D&S), 38–40
Dick, Edison, 56
Dillon, Douglas, 38
Dimond, Paul
  on the CDFI Fund, 216, 224, 235
  in CDFI Fund transition, 268
  in CDFI legislation reconciliation, 249
  on CRA, 212
  on Flake amendment to include BEA, 244
  on goals after CDFI law signing, 261
  at the NEC, 209–210
Dinkins, David, 136
disabilities, credit unions for persons with, 26–27
Dodd, Christopher J., 256

Domenici, Pete, 202–203, 269–270
Domestic Policy Council (DPC), 208, n757
Domini, Amy, 95, 118, 120, n443
Dominican Sisters of Springfield, 147
Doughton, Morgan, 139, 141
Douglass, Frederick, 7–10, 8*f*
Douglass Bancorp, 329–331, 363, 367*t*, 387
DPC (Domestic Policy Council), 208, n757
Drexel National Bank, 294
D&S (Development and Services Corporation), 38–40
DuBois, W. E. B., 10
Dunn, Rebecca, 93
DVCRF (Delaware Valley Community Reinvestment Fund), 171–172, 198, 364, 366*t*, 391, 399

# E

Eades, Julie, 86, 91, 93–95, 120, 327
Eakes, Martin
  on CDFI Fund selection process, 332
  Center for Community Self-Help founding, 108
  First Nations and, 308
  "genius" fellowship of, 300
  Self-Help credit union, 111–112, n404
  on success of CDFI movement, 381
  telling Bill Clinton about Self-Help, 178
East Alabama FCU, 33
Eastern Carolina Council, 17
economic inequality. *See also* poverty
  in the 1950s, 25
  credit union movement on, 18, 377–378
  Federal Reserve Bank survey (2016), n1410
  wealth gap, 18, 25, 377–378
"Economic Justice and the Christian Conscience" (Urban Bishops Coalition), 118–119
Economic Opportunity Act of 1964, 23–25
Economic Summit (Little Rock, 1992), 190–191
Edelman, Marian Wright, 190
Edley, Christopher, Jr., 189, 242–243
Elk Horn Bank & Trust Co., 165, 171–172
Empire State Development Corporation, 307
Energy Conservation Fund, 393
Entergy Corporation, 391
Enterprise Community Partners, 83, 85
Enterprise Corporation of the Delta, 328, 337, 391
Episcopal Church, 56, 95, 118–119, 129, 153
Episcopal Community Investment Fund, 95

## Index

EQ2 (Equity Equivalent investment), 301–302, 382, n209
Equal Credit Opportunity Act of 1974, 76–77
Equitable insurance company, 273–275
equity grants, 116–118
equity to assets ratio, 58, 65–66, 116–117
Erdreich, Ben, 161, 164, 171–172
Espy, Mike, 233, 236, 258
Evans, Connie, 249–250, 309
Everence, 371
Evers, Medgar, 259

### F

FAHE (Federation of Appalachian Housing Enterprises), 91, 259, 389
faith-based investments. *See also names of individual investors*
   in the 1970s, 72–74
   in the 1980s, 118–123, 129–131
   Adrian Dominican Sisters, 73–74, 121–122
   African American church-based credit unions, 154
   in Community Capital Bank, 105
   Episcopal Church, 56, 95, 118–119, 129, 153
   Interfaith Center on Corporate Responsibility, 74, 118, 122–123
   Leviticus 25:23 Alternative Fund, Inc., 121
   Methodist Church, 123, 129, 139, 187, 396
   Presbyterian Church (U.S.A.) Foundation, 123, 146
   as "prophetic act", 371
   Sisters of Mercy, 120–121
   socially responsible investment, 123–124, 320–321
   women's orders/congregations, 73–74, 77, 100, 120, 130, 139
Faith Community United Credit Union, 154, 365, 367t, 388, 398
Fannie Mae, 211, 300, 357
Farrow, William, n1357
Faux, Geoffrey, 61–62
F.B. Heron Foundation, 371
FDIC. *See* Federal Deposit Insurance Company
Federal Bank for Community Development Banks proposal, 191
Federal Credit Union Act, 16, 33, 65
Federal Deposit Insurance Company (FDIC)
   BEA and, 159–160, 162, 240, 256, 270
   CRA and reduction in premiums, 160–162, 186, 240, 255–256
   Freedom National Bank and, 11, 19
   impact on credit union growth, 370
   ShoreBank and, 295, 361, n1357
Federal Housing Administration (FHA), 47
Federal Housing Finance Board (FHFB), 166
Federal Reserve Bank, n1410
Federal Reserve Board, 172, 295
Federation of Appalachian Housing Enterprises (FAHE), 91, 259, 389
Federation of Greene County Employees FCU (FOGCE FCU), 34–35, 72
Federation of Limited Income Credit Unions, 66, 67
Fenlon, Sister Maureen, 122
FHA (Federal Housing Administration), 47
FHFB (Federal Housing Finance Board), 166
Filene, Edward A., 12–18, 15f, 61, 368–369, n61, n70
Financial Democracy Campaign, 156
Financial Institutions Reform, Recovery, and Enforcement Act (FIRREA) of 1989, 375–376, n1397, n1399
Financial Opportunity Centers (FOCs), 300
FINCA microenterprise project, 329, 335, 366t, 385
FIRREA (Financial Institutions Reform, Recovery, and Enforcement Act of 1989), 375–376, n1397, n1399
First American Credit Union (Navajoland CU), 308, 365, 367t, 387–388, 398, n123
First Legacy FCU, 365, 367t, 398, n67. *See also* School Workers FCU
First National Bank of Phelps County, 299
First National Conference of Community Loan Funds (1985), 85
First Nations, 116
First Nations Development Institute, 195–196, 204, 307, 372–373, n1163
First Nations Financial Project, 308
First Nations Oweesta Corporation, 309
First Peoples Worldwide, n1162
Flake, Rev. Floyd
   on BEA program, 160–162, 210, 237, n549
   in CDFI legislation, 215, 227, 229, 236, 239–241
   in CDFI legislation reconciliation and signing, 248, 255–257, 260
   Comstock and, 298
   at first faith-based credit union conference, 154
   at Greater Allen A.M.E. Church, 160, nn560–570
Fletcher, James, 54, 54f, 98, 295, n199
Florek, Sister Corinne, 122, 371
Foley, Leander J., III, n483
Foley, Mark, 341

food deserts, xvii, 362, 382, 399–400
Ford, Gerald, 76
Ford Foundation
   application paperwork for, 113–114, 279–280, 383–384, n424
   capital to back secondary capital investments, 305
   Community Capital Bank and, 107
   on community development corporations, 37, 39–40
   developmental venture capital funds, 315
   equity grants of, 116–118
   on Gray Areas, 35–36
   human capacity grant from, 276–277
   ICE and, 87–89
   intermediary formation, 83–85
   mature CDCs and, 83
   NFCDCU support by, 142–144, n527
   PRI programs, 40–41, 115–116, 124, 153–154, 308, n300
   seed fund for starting new banks, 317
   Self-Help and, 109, 110
   Southern Development Bank and, 100–101
   South Shore Bank and, 56
Frank, Barney, 189
Franklin, Benjamin, 3–6
Franklin Community FCU, 144–146
Freddie Mac, 211, 357
Freedman's Savings and Trust Company
   costs of failure of, 9–10
   operation and closure of, 1, 6–9, 7f
   relationship to government, 10
   spelling of name, n20
   Treasury Annex named for, n34
Freedmen's Bureau, 6, 10
Freedom National Bank, New York, 11, 19
Friedman, Bob, 309–311, 377
Friend, Amy, 255
Full Circle Fund, 165
Fund for an OPEN Society, 85
Funding Exchange, 94, 152

## G

Gaffney, Christine, 275, 301
Gaines, Charles, 294
GAO (Government Accounting Office), 31, 33, n120
Garsson, Robert, 266
Geithner, Timothy, 360
Gerbode Foundation, 139

Germany, early credit unions in, 11–12
Gingrich, Newt, 266
Gleason, Georgianna, 105–106, 158
"God Box" (Interfaith Center on Corporate Responsibility), 74, 118, 122–123, nn466–467
Godschalk, Catherine, 322
Gonzalez, Henry B., 190, 236, 239, 244, n855
Goode, Wilson, 6
Good Faith Fund, 100, 102, 166, 179, 309
Gore, Al, 226, 229
Gottschall, Bruce, 51, 52
Government Accounting Office (GAO), 31, 33, n120
Gramdan land reform and lending, 86
Grameen Bank, Bangladesh
   influence on Clintons, 102–103, 229, 258, 327, 334, 385
   influence on others, 86, 165–166, 178–179, 204, 308, 310
   as peer-group lending, 4
   on serving the poverty population, 200, 229
   ShoreBank and, 97, 309
Gramm, Phil, 243
grantwriting, 353
Gray Areas project, 35–36, n1385
Great Depression, 15–17
Greater Allen A.M.E. Church, 160, nn560–570
Great Recession, 357–359
Greene, Aurelia, 306
Greenlining Bill, 166, 186. *See also* Bank Enterprise Act (BEA) of 1991
Gregg, Judd, 269
Greider, William, 179
Griffith, Mark Winston, 229, 323f
Grogan, Paul, viii, 85, 242
Grzywinski, Ron
   at the Adlai Stevenson Institute, 55, n182
   Grameen Bank and, 97–98
   National Community Investment Fund and, 316
   at release of CDFI bill, 228–230
   on ShoreBank importance, 372
   at Southern Development Bancorp, 299
   technical and design assistance, 100
Guenther, Kenneth A., 231
Gund Foundation, 390

## H

Haa Yakaawu Financial Corporation, 363, 366t, 393
Hallett, Stanley, 56, 411n205

# Index

Hamilton, John M., 324
Harlem Ark of Freedom, 227
Harrington, James, 101
Harrington, Michael, 23, 36
Harris, Patricia, 69
Harris, Steven B., 163–164
Hassel, Bryan, 189, 198, 212, n729
Hawke, John D., 337–338, 343–344
Haynes, Rita, 154, 388
HEAD (Human Economic Appalachian Development Community Loan Fund), 259, 389
healthcare, CDFI impact on, viii–ix
Healthy Food Financing Initiative, 362, 364, 382, 383, 399, 401
Heller, Walter, 23
Henderson, Irwin, 228
Henze, Laura, 308, 322
Heritage Foundation, 383
F.B. Heron Foundation, xii, 371, n1376
Hispanic communities. *See* Latino communities
HMDA (Home Mortgage Disclosure Act of 1975), 50, 76–77
Hohlt, Richard F., 260
holding company model
  in Appalbanc, 330
  in CDFI Fund winners, 330, 395–397
  in Community Capital Bank, 297
  growth of credit unions using, 365
  in Self-Help, 330, 365
  in ShoreBank, 108, 199–201, 274, 297, n363
  in Southern Development Bank, 102–103, 183
Holland, Joseph, 227
HOME Investment Partnership, 313
Home Mortgage Disclosure Act (HMDA) of 1975, 50, 76–77
Home Owners Loan Corporation, 47
Hope Charter School Facilities Fund, 396
Hope Enterprise Corporation, 364–365, 366*t*, 382, 396–397
Hope FCU, 396
HOPE Policy Institute, 397
Houghton, Mary
  in 1992 congressional hearings, 171–173
  on bank holding company model, 165
  in the Clinton transition, 190–191
  Good Faith Fund and, 309
  Interfaith Center on Corporate Responsibility and, 74
  ShoreBank expansions, 294, 296
  ShoreBank in the 1980s, 96–98
  ShoreBank origins, 54, 54*f*, 58–59, 77, n199
  at Southern Development Bancorp, 100, 299
  WSEP and, 309, 311
House, CDFI approval and reconciliation, 255–257
House Appropriations Committee rescission, 269–270
House Banking Committee
  Clinton staff meeting with staff of, 215–216
  hearing on CDFI bill (July 1993), 236–241
  hearing on lenders in development (July 1992), 164–175
  House bill (H.R. 3474), 244
Housing and Community Development Act of 1992, 174–175
Hubbell, Webster, 340
Huerta, Dolores, 395
Hull House, 48, 410n176
human capital, 197
Human Economic Appalachian Development (HEAD) Community Loan Fund, 259, 389
Humphrey, Hubert, 62, n107
Hurricane Katrina, 361–362
Hyde Park Bank, 53, 57

## I

ICCR (Interfaith Center on Corporate Responsibility; the "God Box"), 74, 118, 122–123, nn466–467
ICE. *See* Institute for Community Economics
ICE Revolving Loan Fund, 87–89, 91
IDAs. *See* Individual Development Accounts
Illinois Facilities Fund (IFF), 364, 366*t*, 382, 392–393, 398–400
Illinois Neighborhood Development Corporation (INDC). *See also* ShoreBank
  City Lands Corporation, 59, 99
  as holding company, 55, 59, 98, n362
  Neighborhood Fund, 59
  The Neighborhood Institute, 59–60, 98–99, 296
Immergluck, Dan, 47
INDC. *See* Illinois Neighborhood Development Corporation
Indecorp, 293–296
Independence Bank, 294
Independent Bankers Association of America, 243
Individual Development Accounts (IDAs)
  in the 1990s, 321, 377–378, n808
  Clinton on, 221, n646
  Corporation for Enterprise Development and, 144

NFCDCU on, 304
at Opportunity Fund of Northern California, n808
Sherraden on, 310–311, 366, n646
Industrial Areas Foundation, 48, 399, n375
Industrial Cooperative Association, 116, 119
inequality. *See* civil rights, credit unions and; economic inequality; poverty
Institute for Community Economics (ICE)
building capacity, 89–90
growth of, 351
NACDLF and, 92–95
National Conference of Community Loan Funds and, 90–92
organization and culture of, 89, 93
origin and core values of, 85–86
as Revolving Loan Fund, 87–89, 91
Institute for Gender Research, Women and Foundations/Corporate Philanthropy (WAFCP), 311
Interagency Working Group on Community Development and Empowerment, 208, 214–215, 223
Interfaith Center on Corporate Responsibility (ICCR; the "God Box"), 74, 118, 122–123, nn466–467
International Independence Institute, 86
Isaacson, Walter, 5

## J

Jackson, Joyce, 323*f*
Jackson, Rev. Jesse, Sr., vi, 227
Jackson, Robert, 155, 203–204, 389, n745
Jacobs, Eli, 40
Jacokes, Jeannine
on application structure, 353
on Banking Committee staff, 163
on CDFI Fund transition team, 267, 269, 272
in CDFI legislation talks, 181, 188, 212, 235–236, 246, 255
at CDFI Woodstock, 250
on CICD, 175
fact-finding visits to CDFIs by, 198
Jaffe, Jan, 113
Javits, Jacob K., 38–39
Jay, Pierre, 12
Jennette, Jo Ellen, 28–29
Jepsen, Roger, 146
Jessie Smith Noyes Foundation, 315
John D. and Catherine T. MacArthur Foundation
assessment of PRI investments, 319–321

Capitalization Program and, 139
genius fellowships, 300
PRI programs, 113–115, 139, 153, 170–171, 393
seed fund to help new banks, 317
Self-Help and, 110
wholesale-intermediary organizations, 320–321
Johnson, Earnest, 33–35, 34*f*, n131
Johnson, George E., 294
Johnson, Jacqueline, 330, 393
Johnson, Lyndon B., administration of, 23–24, 31, 47
Joint Committee on Internal Revenue Taxation, 41
Jones, DeWitt (Dick), 91, 93, 401
Jones, Maurice, 336, 339, 344, 345, n1286
Jones, Thomas R., 38
Jordan, Barbara C., 28, n108
Jordan, Vernon, 187
Joyce Foundation, 56, 310–311
J.P. Morgan & Co., 106
Jubilee Housing, 85, n428
Jutte, Douglas, ix

## K

Kanjorski, Paul E., 237
Kaptur, Marcy, 199
Keating Five, 246, 260, n904
Keeley, Kathy, 309
W.K. Kellogg foundation, 390, 392
Kennedy, John F., 23
Kennedy, Joseph P., 227, 238
Kennedy, Robert, 37–39
Kennington, Rev. John, 136
Kentucky Highlands Investment Corporation (KHIC), 314–316, 330, 363–365, 367*t*, 386, 397
Kerner Commission, on 1968 Detroit riots, 30
Kerry, John, x
Kinder, Peter, n443
King, Lawrence, Jr., 144–146, n535
Klein, Joyce, 288
Kovner, Sarah, 189

## L

La Caisse Populaire de Levis, 12
land contract installment sale, 47
Latino communities
Accion Texas and, 385

# Index

CDFI Fund awards and, 329, 380
CUNA demonstration projects, 26
farmworkers and, 326, 329, 389, 395–396, 398
Ford Foundation and, 83
housing, n428
Latino Credit Union Network, 304
NCCED and, n1189
NFCDCU and, 154
Section 308 and, n1397
Self-Help and, 395
wealth gap and, 378
Latino Community Credit Union, 380
Latino Credit Union Network, 304
Lau, Valerie, 337–338
Lawson, Rev. Philip, 258–259
Lazar, Ellen W., 342, 344, 346–347
Leach, Jim, 210, 236, 240–241, 257, 342
LEAP, Inc., 107, 157, 183, 201, 297, n403
Legacy Bank, 324
Legal Aid Society of Chicago, 57
Legal Services Corporation, 82
LESEDAC program, 72, n269
Levere, Andrea, 319
Leviticus 25:23 Alternative Fund, Inc., 120–121, 306, 369, n460
Levy, Michael B., 237
Lewis, Chris, 231
Lewis, Jerry, 272–273
Lewis, John L., 17
Liberty Bank and Trust Company, 361–362, 376
Liebsohn, Daniel, 91, 340, 351–352
LiftFund, 363–364, 366t, 378, 399. *See also* Accion Texas
LIHF. *See* Low Income Housing Fund
LIIF (Low Income Investment fund), 351–352, 398–400
Lilly Endowment, 390
Linder, Msgr. William, 210
Lindsay, John, 38
Lingenfelter, Paul
    on Ford application size, 113–114, n424
    Ford PRIs and, 113–114, 170–173, n424
    on "half-truth" of CDFIs, 250–251
    on lack of access to capital, 250–251
    on NFCDCU Capitalization Program, 139
LISC. *See* Local Initiatives Support Corporation
Litan, Robert, 191–192
Litzenberg, Jack, 310–311
Lizárraga, David, 312

Local Initiatives Support Corporation (LISC)
    CDFI Fund and, 282, 285, 327–328, 366t
    Financial Opportunity Centers of, 400
    Ford Foundation and, 83–85, 330, 364
    as intermediary to CDCs, 83–85, 282, 285, 313
    MacArthur Foundation and, 320
    Rural LISC, 363, 393, 399
    at Senate hearings on CDFIs (1992), 242
Logue, Trinita, 393
Lollis, David, 91, 258–259, 331
Lopez, Daniel B., 340–341
Lopez, Steven, 201
Louis, Errol T., 323*f*
    CDCU briefing of congress, 155
    CDCU study by, 143
    in community development banking Senate panel, 199
    as news commentator, n552
    on nonmember deposits, 163
    on NY State CDFI Fund, 306
    at Rose Garden ceremony, 225, 229
Louisville Community Development Bank Holding Company, 331
Louisville Development Bank, 365, 367t, 387
Louisville Development Corporation, 363
Lower East Side People's FCU, 134–137, 135*f*, 136*f*, 147, n269
low-income credit unions. *See also* community development banks; community development credit unions; poverty
    in the 1950s, 25–26
    basic banking services in, 68, 191, 205, 214, 242, n246
    in Carter's vision, 69–71
    CDFI Fund and
        awards, 352–356, 352t, 354t 355t, 387–389, 398
        eligibility for, 281–282
        low-income housing, 328–329
        matching requirements, 328
        need versus performance in, 218–220
    chartering, 282, n405, n1417
    civil rights and, 33–35, 34*f*, 146
    in Clinton's vision, 176–180
    Community Investment Notes for, 322
    debanking of New York City neighborhoods, 133
    deposit insurance in, 65, 66, 146, nn234–236
    discrimination in lending to, 216–217
    equity importance in, 35, 42, 64–67, 304–305, 314–316, 328

Gray Areas project, 35–36, n1385
in the Great Recession, 359
during George H. W. Bush administration, 153
increasing disparity in CDFIs, 320–321
Lower East Side People's FCU formation, 134–137, 135f, 136f
matching requirements for, 218–219, 253–254, 283–284
microenterprise and, 309–312
modernization impacts on, 302
National Neighborhood Banking Corporation proposal and, 163
NCUA pruning of, 323
net worth crisis in, 65–66
NFCDCU formation and, 67–69
NFCDCU on national fund for, 163–164
nonmember deposit restrictions, 71–72, 109, 145–146, 155, 216, n265
Office of Economic Opportunity and, 29–33, 42–43
Project Moneywise, 28–29, n107
raising secondary capital, 304–305
during Reagan administration, 133–134
service delivery systems, 36
South Shore Bank, 52–60
staff-to-asset ratio, n368
venture capital for, 314–316
Low Income Housing Fund (LIHF)
CDFI Fund awards to, 328–329, 361, 364
Community Capital Bank and, 297
investigation of CDFI Fund regarding, 336–337, 340
low-income housing tax credit, 171
Low Income Investment fund (LIIF), 351–352, 398–400
Low-Income Opportunity Act of 1987, 141
Ludwig, Eugene, 233, 242, 250, 302
Luecht, Bill, 291, 339
Luzzatti, Luigi, 11–12
Lydenberg, Steve, n443
Lyman, Elizabeth "Jing", 311

# M

MacArthur Foundation. *See* John D. and Catherine T. MacArthur Foundation
Macey, Jonathan R., 232
Mack, Connie, 200, 243, 254
MAHA (Metropolitan Area Housing Alliance), 49
Mahon, Cathie, xii, 306, n1156

Manufacturers Hanover Trust (MHT), 134–136, 135f, 307, n499
Martin, Mahlon, 249, 273
Marwick, Peat, 344
Mary Reynolds Babcock Foundation, 87, 108
Massachusetts Credit Union (MCU), 13
matching requirements, 218–219, 239, 253–254, 328, 353
Mather, Cotton, 6
Mathis, Bryan, 250
Matthei, Chuck, 86f
background of, 86, 369, n1367
Comstock and, 104
Equity Trust, Inc., 93
at ICE, 86, 90–93, 351
legacy of, 85, 93–94, 372
at NACDLF, 93–94, 151–152
Social Investment Forum and, 123
"maximum feasible participation", 61, 217, 220, 282, 373
McColl, Hugh, 228–230, 231, 316
McDonald, Alden J., 361–362, 376
McGrady, David, 267
McKee, Kate, 212, 249, 267, 268–272, 275
McKnight, Father A. J., 34
McNamara, Edward H., 201
McRae, Tom, IV, 99–100, 102, 340, 373–374
MCU (Massachusetts Credit Union), 13
Mensah, Lisa, xii, 325
Mercy Loan Fund, n458
Mercy Partnership Fund, 120
Methodist Church, 123, 129, 139, 187, 396
Metropolitan Area Housing Alliance (MAHA), 49
Metropolitan Life Insurance, 300
Meyer, Andre, 38, 40
Mfume, Kweisi, 215
MHT (Manufacturers Hanover Trust), 134–136, 135f, 307, n499
microenterprise lending
Beverly Ross and, 226–227
Bill Clinton on, 149, 200, 204
in CDFI Fund winners, 327, 394
differences from other CDFIs, 310
First Nations and, 308
Franklin and, 3–4
in the Great Recession, 226–227, 358
growth dynamics of, 362–365, 366t
Hillary Clinton on, 311–312, 334–335, 385, n1259
LiftFund, 363–364

Presidential Awards for, 334–335, n1262
for self-employment, 309–310
sustainability of, 378–379
twenty-year survival rates, 362
for women, 309
MICRO fund, 165
Microloan Management Services (MMS), 394
Mid-South Electrics Company, 397
Mikulski, Barbara, 257
Miller, Clara, 95, 306, 369, 371, 392–393
Miller, Tom, 113, 115–116, 143, nn429-433
Minority Bank Deposit Program, 374
minority communities. *See also* African Americans; Latino communities; Native American CDFIs
    CD credit unions and banks owned by, 374–376
    discrimination in lending to, 214, 216–217
    Ford funding in, n300
    Section 308, FIRREA (1989) and, 375–376, n1397, n1399
    wealth gap and, 378
Minsky, Hyman, 73, 191, 216, 220
mission drift, 18, 25–26, 32, 370
MMS (Microloan Management Services), 394
Moncrief, L. Ray, 314–316
Moore, Thad, 110, 230
Morales Marks, Fé, 267, 270
Moran, Jim, 174
Morena, Lucia, 154
Moses, Bob, 259
C.S. Mott Foundation, 276
Mountcastle, Mary, n915
Mount Sinai Baptist Church Credit Union, 388. *See also* Faith Community United Credit Union
Moy, Kirsten
    background of, 273–274, n1009
    on BEA application process, 286
    CDFI Fund and, 278–279, 286–289, n1023
    in criticism of CDFI Fund selection, 331–333, 336–338, 346
    at National Conference of Community Loan Funds, 91
    resignation of, 338, 341–342
Mulvaney, Mick, 137
Murray, Patty, 286
Murray, Terrance, 231–232
Muskie, Edmund, 62
mutual aid groups, 6
mutual funds, socially responsible, 320–321

## N

NACDLF. *See* National Association of Community Development Loan Funds
Nader, Ralph, 243
NAFCU (National Association of Federal Credit Unions), 140–141, 154, 192
Nager, Anita, 225–226, n826
NALS (Native American Lending Study), n1382
Narain, Saurabh, 376
Nash, Bob J., 238
National Association of Community Development Loan Funds (NACDLF)
    CDFI Coalition and, 151–152, 156–157, 276, 302–303, 317–318
    on CDFI Fund, 186–187, 269, 390
    Central Fund, 152
    in congressional hearings (1992), 167–168
    on CRA, 370
    EQ2 and, 301–302
    formation of, 92
    growth of, 93–95
    on insurance and money-market funds, 302
    model of, 92–93, 95
    name change of, 303
    on nature of CD loan funds, 369–370
    in Senate hearings (1993), 204
    under Trimble, 151–152
National Association of Federal Credit Unions (NAFCU), 140–141, 154, 192
National Center for Urban Ethnic Affairs (NCUEA), 71–72, 125
National Church Credit Union Conference (1996), 304
National Community Capital Association (NCCA), 303
National Community Corporation Certification Board, 63, 64
National Community Development Bank, 69, 77
National Community Development Trust proposal, 188–189
National Community Economic Partnership Act, 173
National Community Investment Fund (NCIF), 230, 305, 316–318, 376
National Community Reinvestment Coalition (NCRC), 228
National Conference of Community Loan Funds (1985), 90–92
National Congress for Community Economic Development (NCCED), 195, 312, n706, n1185

National Consumer Cooperative Bank (NCCB), 125, 130–131
National Council of La Raza, 216–217
National Council of the Churches of Christ, 71, 139
National Credit Union Administration (NCUA)
  on CD Central, 138
  on chartering new credit unions, 141, 186, 323–324, n505, n667, n1417
  on corporate central credit union, 130
  deposit insurance and, 65–66, 109, 359, n234
  in the Great Recession, 359
  low-income credit unions and, 141, 153, 169, 305, 323–324, n540
  makeup of, n547
  on nonmember deposits, 71–72, 109, 146, 163, n540
  power grab from NFCDCU, 70–71
  responsibilities of, n234, 429
National Credit Union Share Insurance Fund (NCUSIF), n234
National Economic Council (NEC), 208, n757
National Federation of Community Development Credit Unions (NFCDCU)
  capital breakthroughs (1989), 153–154
  Capitalization Program
    assets in the late 1990s, 304–305, 320
    CDFI Fund and, 347
    CDRLF seeking control of funds, 127
    impact of King scandal on, 146–147
    interest rates in, 127, n491
    investments in, 114–115, 121–123, 128–131, 138–139, 153–154, 317
    origins of, 128–129, 131–132, 138
    Self-Help Credit Union and, 111
  Carter's support for, 69–70
  CDCU Demonstration Project, 154
  CDCU Management Institute proposal, 143
  on CDFI Fund selection process, 332
  on Clinton's CDFI legislation (1993), 216, 231
  Community Capital Bank and, 106
  on community-controlled capital, 67–69, 77
  Community Credit Union Job Training Program, 132
  Community Development Central proposal, 131–132, 138, 140, 143
  Community Development Credit Union Demonstration Project, 143–144
  on federal tax exemption for credit unions, 154–155
  formation of, 370
  funding sources in the 1980s, 132–133, 142–144
  King scandal and, 144–147
  lobbying Senate for national fund, 163–164
  Lower East Side People's FCU formation, 134–137, 135f, 136f
  on matching requirements, 253–254, 328
  National Neighborhood Financial Corporation proposal, 140–142, 185–186
  National Service Corporation proposal, 140
  NCUA hijacking of, 70–71
  Neighborhood Reinvestment Corporation proposal, 140
  on nonmember deposit restrictions, 71–72, 109, 146, 155–156, 163, n265
  on personal asset-building and savings, 321, 377–378
  position paper on low-income communities, 169
  Reagan administration and, 125–127, 139–141, 147
  revolving loan fund, 125–128, 126f
  Small and Emerging CDFI Access (SECA) program, 345, n802
  Vamper and, 131–132, n109
  wholesale-intermediary organizations, 321–322, 347
National Negro Convention, New York (1855), 6
National Neighborhood Banking Corporation, 155–156, 163, 211
National Neighborhood Coalition, 198
National Neighborhood Financial Corporation proposal, 140, 185–186, 231
National People's Action (NPA), 49–50
National Training and Information Center (NTIC), 49–50, 51
NationsBank, 228, 230, 316, 333
Native American CDFIs
  in CDFI Coalition Steering Committee, 275
  CDFI Fund and, 281, 327, 327t, 372–373, n95, n1337
  challenges of, 307–308
  First American Credit Union (Navajoland CU), 308, 365, 367t, 387–388, 398, n123
  First Nations Development Institute, 195–196, 204, 372–373, n1163
  First Nations Oweesta Corporation, 204, 309
  in the House hearings (1993), 238
  Lakota Fund, 303, 308, n1392
  Sisseton-Wahpeton FCU, 72
  Tlingit-Haida Housing of Alaska, 282, 329–330, 363, 393
Native American Lending Study (NALS), n1382
Navajoland CU, 308
Navy FCU, 370

# Index

NCB Development Corporation, 426n494
NCCA (National Community Capital Association), 303
NCCB (National Consumer Cooperative Bank), 125, 130–131
NCCED (National Congress for Community Economic Development), 195, 312, n706, n1185
NCIF (National Community Investment Fund), 230, 305, 316–318, 376
NCISIF (National Credit Union Share Insurance Fund), n234
NCO (Northwest Community Organization), 48–49
NCRC (National Community Reinvestment Coalition), 228
NCUA. *See* National Credit Union Administration
NCUEA (National Center for Urban Ethnic Affairs), 71–72, 125
Neal, Stephen, 256
NEC (National Economic Council), 208, n757
Neighborhood Banking 2000 Fund, 305–306
Neighborhood Fund, 59
Neighborhood Housing Services (NHS), 51, 82, 366*t*
Neighborhood Institute, The (TNI), 59–60, 98–99, 296
Neighborhood National Bank, 324
Neighborhood Reinvestment Corporation (Chicago), 51–52
Neighborhoods, Inc., 366*t*, 392, n1240
NeighborWorks American network, 392, n1341
Nembhard, Jessica, 18–19
New Communities, Inc., 86, 199, 209–210
New Community FCU, 210
New Hampshire Community Loan Fund, 329, 364, 366*t*, 391–392, 399
New Lanark community, 11
Newman, Frank N., 215–238, 237, 239, 241–242
New Markets Tax Credit (NMTC), 355–356, 359, 364–365, 366*t*, 376, 396
New Mexico Community Development Loan Fund, 202–203
New World Foundation, 129, 142
New York Community Trust, 133, 137
New York Corporation for Community Banking, 137–138, 147
New York Foundation, 133
"New York Four" credit unions, 72, n267
New York State CDFI Fund, 306
New York State Coalition of CDFIs, 306, n460
NFCDCU. *See* National Federation of Community Development Credit Unions
NFF (Nonprofit Facilities Fund), 328, 392–393

NFF (Nonprofit Finance Fund), 364, 366*t*, 373, 400
NHS (Neighborhood Housing Services), 51, 82, 366*t*
Nixon, Richard M., 32, 76
NMTC (New Markets Tax Credit), 355–356, 359, 364–365, 366*t*, 376, 396
Nolan, Amy, 106*f*
nonmember deposit restrictions, 71–72, 109, 145–146, 155, 216, n265
Nonprofit Facilities Fund (NFF), 328, 392–393
Nonprofit Finance Fund (NFF), 364, 366*t*, 373, 398, 400
Norman Foundation, 129
North Carolina Community Facilities Fund, 300
North Carolina Rural Economic Development Center, 397
North Country Loan Fund, 85
Northeast Ventures Corporation, 315–316, 363, 367*t*, 386
Northern California Community Loan Fund, 340–341
North Side Community FCU, 72
Northwest Community Organization (NCO), 48–49
Nowak, Jeremy
    on CDFIs and the banking industry, 200, 371
    at CDFI Woodstock, 250
    in Delaware Valley Community Reinvestment Fund, 157, 167, 171–173, 203
    in NACDLF, 94–95, 167–168
    on nature of CD loan funds, 369
    in Senate hearings (1993), 200, 203–204, 241
NPA (National People's Action), 49–50
NTIC (National Training and Information Center), 49–50, 51
Nunez-Morales, Pauline, 202–204

## O

OBA (Organization for a Better Austin), 48
Obama, Barack, administration of, 359, 360
Obama, Michelle, 362
Occupy Wall Street movement, 137, 356, 380
OCS (Office of Community Services), 79, 82, 126
Odwalla juice company, 272–273, 389
OFC (Opportunity Funding Corporation), 75
Office of Community Services (OCS), 79, 82, 126
Office of Economic Opportunity (OEO)
    failure of, 42
    financial support for credit unions, 29–30
    government/industry alliances, 26–27
    low-income credit unions, 26–28, 32
    ownership of credit unions, 29

Project Moneywise, 28–29
waning support after 1968, 30–32, n120
War on Poverty and, 21, 23–24
Office of Management and Budget (OMB), 290, 383
Office of Self-Help and Technical Assistance, 130–131
OFN (Opportunity Finance Network), 355, 370–371
Oglala Lakota College, 308
Okagaki, Alan, 288, 319–321, 337, 345–346
Okagaki report (1995), 319–321
Oliver, Melvin, 377
OMB (Office of Management and Budget), 290, 383
Omnibanc Corporation, 294
ONE (Organization for a New Equality), 229
Operation Grassroots "Rally on the Mall", 155
Oppenheimer-Nicolau, Siobhan, n1164
Opportunity Finance Network (OFN), 355, 370–371
Opportunity Funding Corporation (OFC), 75
Opportunity Fund of Northern California, n808
Opportunity Lands Corporation, 100, 102, 298
Organization for a Better Austin (OBA), 48
Organization for a New Equality (ONE), 229
Oweesta Program of First Nations, 196, 308–309
Owen, Robert, 11

## P

Paragon Association, 17
Paragon FCU, 409n146
Parkside Partnership, 99
Parry, Carol J., 286, 307, 342
payday lending, 24–25, 67
Pear, Robert, 192, 213
peer group lending, 4
Peirce, Neal, 167, 194
Perkins, William C., 166
Peterson, Esther, 23, 28
Pew Charitable Trusts, 94–95, 390, 391
Phillips, Ron
    in Association for Enterprise Opportunity, 311
    in CDFI Coalition origins, 157
    in Coastal Enterprises, Inc., 166–167, 171
    on community development corporations, 173
    on community development venture capital funds, 315
    at Senate Banking Committee hearing, 203–204
Pierce, Samuel, 145
Piercy, Jan, 97, 101, 290, 334, n379, n656
Pillsbury, George, 91

Pilsen Neighbors FCU, 26
Pinsky, Mark
    as CDFI Coalition coordinator, 252, 301, 303, 312–313, 317–318
    on CDFI Fund funding, 220, 235–236, 260
    in CDFI legislation negotiations, 210–212, 220, 224, 244, 248
    as NACDLF executive director, 301, 303
    as NACDLF newsletter editor, 152
Piper, Valerie, 289–292
PolicyMap, 382, 399
Poor People's Campaign, 31
Portfolio Advisory Board (PAB), 73–74
poverty. *See also* economic inequality; low-income credit unions
    BEA awards to distressed communities, 285–286
    capital access impact on, viii, 42
    in CDFI Fund applicants, 43
    computerized credit scoring and, 133
    credit dilemma and, 24–25, 133
    distrust of credit unions and, 32
    early credit unions and, 13
    Franklin's loan fund applicants and, 5
    "half-truth" of CDFIs and, 250–251
    low-income credit unions and, 25–28, 32, 35
    OEO credit unions and, 29
    personal asset building and, 321, 377–378
    rediscovery of, in the 1960s, 23–24
    search for root causes of, 67–68
    War on Poverty, 23–25, 30–32, 41–43, 123, 216, 246–247
Powell, Adam Clayton, 37
Prairie-Halsted Federated Churches Credit Union, 26
Pratt Institute Center for Community and Environmental Development, 37–38, n147
Presbyterian Church (U.S.A.) Foundation, 123, 146
private capital, raising, 71–72, 75–76, 191–192, 243, 326–327
program-related investments (PRIs)
    first foundations using, 75–76
    by Ford Foundation, 113–114, 170–173, n424
    by MacArthur Foundation, 113–115, 139, 153, 170–171, 319–321, 393
    mission-related investments, 118
    Okagaki report evaluation of, 319–321
    origin of, 40–41
    tax status of loans, 41
Progress Enterprises, Philadelphia, 37
Project Moneywise, 28–29, n107

Promise Zone, 397
Proxmire, William, 50
Pryde, Paul, 289
*Putting People First* (Bill Clinton), 176–177, 209, 216

## Q

quasi-public entities, CDFI Fund and, 281
Quitman County FCU, 203, 367t, 388–389

## R

Ramage, Rev. David, Jr., 100, 127, 129, n375
Ramm, Gregg, 89–90, 92–93
Rapoza, Bob, 313
Rasco, Carol, 268, 270, 274
Ratliff, Greg, 187
RCAC (Rural Community Assistance Corporation), 328, 329, 366t, 399–400
RCA Corporation, 138, n509
Reagan, Ronald, administration of
  CDCs under, 82
  CDRLF under, 71, 125–128, 130, 138, 141
  debanking of low-income neighborhoods, 133–134
  NFCDCU 1986 recommendations to, 139–141
  transfer of Community Services Administration, 79
redlining, 47, 50, 177
Reed, Bruce, 209, 215–216, n791
Regier, Mark, 371
Reid, William, 18
Reinvestment Fund (RF), 382, 399. *See also* Delaware Valley Community Reinvestment Fund (DVCRF)
Revolving Loan Fund. *See* Cascadia Revolving Fund; Community Development Revolving Loan Fund; ICE Revolving Loan Fund; NACDLF
Richmond Neighborhood Housing Services, 392
Ridge, Tom, 159, 166, 236, 239–241, 257
Riegle, Donald
  in CDFI legislation and signing, 215, 246, 256, 260
  as Housing and Community Development bill sponsor, 174–175, 189–190
  in Savings and Loan scandal, n904
  in Senate Banking Committee hearing, 199–200, 202, 206
Riegle Community Development and Regulatory Improvement Act of 1994. *See* CDFI legislation
Riegle-Neal Community Development and Financial Modernization Act of 1994. *See* CDFI legislation

Rimbey, Judy, 122
Roberts, Matt, 181, 188, 198
Robert Sterling Clark Foundation, 306
Robinson, Jackie, 11
Rochdale Principles, 11
Rochdale Society of Equitable Pioneers, 11
Rockefeller Brothers Fund, 75, 106
Rockefeller Foundation, 40
ROC USA, 364, 399
Rohde, Steve
  Bachus investigation and, 336–338, 345
  background of, 274
  in CDFI Fund selection process, 288–289, 332–333, 346
  resignation of, 338, 342
Romero, Anthony, 324
Roosevelt, Franklin D., 16
ROSCAs (rotating savings and credit associations), 6
Rosenberg Foundation, 392
Rosenthal, Clifford N., 106*f*
  background of, 125
  on Barth-Brumbaugh concept, 265
  at CDFI Fund reauthorization hearing (1998), 344
  in CDFI legislation meetings (1993), 189, 210–211, n769, n899
  Charles Revson Foundation Fellowship of, 131
  on community development banks, 312–313
  on Comstock advisory board, n399
  on Consumer Advisory Council of the Federal Reserve System, 147
  as CUNA vice president, n551
  on the early movement, v–vi
  at First National Conference of Community Loan Funds, 91
  meeting Lingenfelter, 139
  meeting Matthei, n1367
  New York State CDFI Fund and, 306
  New York State Coalition of CDFIs, 306
  as NFCDCU director, 131–132, n404, n551
  on NFCDCU objectives, 143, n527
  on reduced matching for small institutions, 285
  Rosenthal Amendment, 253–254
Rosenwald, Julius, 13
Ross, Beverly, 226–227
rotating savings and credit associations (ROSCAs), 6
Roukema, Marge, 343, 345
Rouse, James, 85, n428
Rouse-Maxwell National Housing Task Force, 164

Roybal-Allard, Lucille, 238, 353
Rubin, Robert
    on addressing distressed communities, vi, 279
    on CDFI Fund improvements needed, 343–344
    on CDFI Fund winners, 292, 326
    drafting CDFI legislation, 215, 274
    on funding CDFI Fund, 286–287, 341
    Interagency Working Group and, 208
    as Treasury Secretary, 266, 271
Rubinger, Michael, 84–85, 373, n305
Rumsfeld, Donald, 32, n314
Rural Community Assistance Corporation (RCAC), 328, 329, 366*t*, 399–400
Rural Opportunities, Inc., 306
Rush, Bobby
    CDFI initiative and, 223, 227, 233, 236, 260
    at CDFI Woodstock, 250
    CRA bill and, 240–241
    ShoreBank and, 239, 294
Russell Sage Foundation, 13, n61

## S

SACI (Strengthening America's Communities Initiative), 356–357
Sagawa, Shirley, 221
Sampson, Rev. Al, 295–296
Samuelson, Judy, 250, 315–316
Santa Cruz Community Credit Union
    after the 1989 earthquake, 199
    as business lender, 72, 168
    CDFI Fund awards to, 328–330, 387–389, 398
    growth of, 365, 367*t*
    Latino farmworkers and, 326, 329, 389, 398
    loss rate of, 171
    Odwalla juice company and, 272–273, 389
Santa Cruz Community Ventures, 398
Sarbanes, Paul, 202, 206, 215
Saving Fund and Land Association, California, 6
Savings and Loan scandal
    bailout of, 160
    BEA bill after, 162
    CDCU movement after, 169, 190
    CDFI Fund linked to bailout, 187
    Franklin Community FCU and, 144–146
    Keating Five, 246, 260, n904
    losses from, 79, 112

SBA Microlending Demonstration Program, 102
Schall, Bob, 109–110
Schlesinger, Tom, 156
Schmidt, Benno, 40
School Workers FCU, 330, 365, 367*t*, 389. *See also* First Legacy FCU
Schosberg, Paul, 192–193, 209
Schultze, Charles L., 24
Schumer, Charles E., 190, 216
Schwingel, Laura, 275, 301
Sculley, John, 190
SECA (Small and Emerging CDFI Access) program, 345, n802
Secondary Market Demonstration Project, 300
Section 308, FIRREA (1989), 375–376, n1397, n1399
Self-Employment Investment Initiative, 310
Self-Help. *See* Center for Community Self-Help
Self-Help Credit Union
    Clinton on, 227
    founding of, 108–109
    growth of, 299, 367*t*, 389, 395–396
    NFCDCU Capitalization Program and, 111
Self-Help FCU, 421n406
Self-Help model, 111, 178, 184–186, 395–396
Self-Help Partnership Lending program, 110–111
Self-Help Ventures Fund
    CDFI Fund award, 363, 366*t*, 389–390, 396
    founding of, 109–110, 111
    growth of, 299, 366*t*
    WOSCO and, 226
Senate, CDFI bill approval and reconciliation, 254–257
Senate Appropriations Committee, 269–270
Senate Banking Committee
    on bank holding company structure, 183
    on CDCUs and banking deficits, 185–186
    on CDFI Fund, 186–187
    CDFI Senate bill, 241–245
    Community Capital Bank of Brooklyn and, 182–184
    on community development banking, 198–204
    CRA regulations and CDFIs, 201–202
    hearing from CDFI leaders (fall 1992), 181–188
    hearing on CDFI legislation (early 1993), 198–207, 215, 243
    hearing on Clinton's final bill (July 1993), 206–207, 233–236
    Housing and Community Development Act of 1992, 174–175

## Index

on national fund for low-income CDCUs, 163–164
pilot CD banking legislation (early 1992), 163–164
position papers presented, 204–206
on role for banks in CDFI bill, 200–202, 205–206, 235–236
on Self-Help model, 184–186
symposium on low-income credit sources, 181–182
service delivery systems, 36
Seton Enablement Fund, 139
Shapiro, Joan, 91, 123, 294–295
Shapiro, Thomas, 377
Shaw, Karen, 256
Shelby, Richard, 202, 243, 254, 266, 346
Sherraden, Michael, 310–311, 377
Shiffman, Ron, 38, nn147–148
Shipe, Orrin, 25, 32, n123
Shipe, Robert, n1438
Shipley, Walter, 306
Shockley, Brenda, 190
ShoreBank. *See also* South Shore Bank
   in CDFI Fund selection, 331, 336, 339
   Clintons and, 99, 101, 290
   closure of (2010), 360–361, n1357
   in congressional hearings (1992), 97–98, 165
   on CRA, 52
   Enterprise Cascadia, 363
   expansion of (1995), 293–296
   holding company model of, 199–201, 274, 297, n363
   importance of, 371–372
   international work of, 97–98
   Southern Development Bank and, 99–100
   South Shore Bank relationship to, n363
   stability of, in the 1980s, 96–97
ShoreBridge Capital, 363, 367*t*, 386
Shriver, Sargent, 23, 27, n78
SIF (Social Investment Forum), 123–124, nn473–476
Silby, Wayne, 90
Simon, John, 40–41, 75
Sisseton-Wahpeton FCU, 72, 308
Sisters, Servants of the Immaculate Heart of Mary, 130
Sisters of Mary Reparatrix, 130
Sisters of Mercy, 120–121, 130
Sisters of St. Francis, 130
Sisters of St. Joseph, Nazareth, MI, 130
Sisters of the Presentation of the Blessed Virgin Mary, 146
S&L scandal. *See* Savings and Loan scandal

Small and Emerging CDFI Access (SECA) program, 345, n802
Small Business Administration, 378
Small Business Finance Collaborative, 397
Smiley, Walter, 99–101
Smith, Nick, 157, 275, 315
Smith, Sarah, 94, 120
Smith, Tim, 122, n466
Snowden, Gail, 166, 173
Social Impact Bond (Pay for Success), 399–400
Social Investment Forum (SIF), 123–124, nn473–476
socially responsible investment (SRI), 123–124, 320–321
South Central Los Angeles and riots (1992), vi, xv, 63, 160, 162, 166, 168,162, 174, 176, 179, 188, 190, 194, 195, 200, 208, 227, 161, 271, 324, 329, 330, 381, n667
Southern Agricultural Corporation, 75
Southern Development Bank
   Arkansas Enterprise Group, 102, 172, 299, 386
   as CDFI Fund winner, 328, 332
   Clintons and, 101–102, 290, 339–341, 386, 395
   Community Partners, 395
   CRA and, n1372
   criticism of use of award funds, 344
   Elk Horn Bank & Trust Co., 165, 171–172
   Ford's equity-like loan to, 117–118
   growth of, 298–299, 365, 395
   holding company model in, 102–103, 183, 386
   in House Banking Committee hearing (1992), 165–166
   Opportunity Lands Corporation, 100, 102, 298
   ShoreBank and, 99–100, 172
   Southern Ventures, Inc., 171, 340
   on technical assistance and loss rate, 171
   twenty-year survival of, 363, 367*t*
Southern Ventures, Inc., 171, 340
South Shore Bank, 52–60. *See also* ShoreBank
   in Bachus investigation, 336, n1265
   on credit/underwriting standards, 171–172
   filling out the holding company, 59–60, 77
   as proof of concept, 51
   raising startup capital, 55–57, 74, 119,9n412
   retail banking vs. development, 58–59
   ShoreBank relationship to, n363
   socially responsible investment and, 123–124
   "South Shore Quartet", 54–55, 54*f*, n199
   sustainability of, 57–58
Spanish Speaking Unity Council, 101
Sperling, Gene, 209, 260, 381

SRI (socially responsible investment), 123–124, 320–321
Staged Microlending Program (Self-Help), 300
Starr, Kenneth, 340
St. Bridget's-St. Leo's FCU, 28
Stein, Vicky, 161
Steinbach, Carol, 167
Stevenson, Adlai, III, 53
Stewart, Caryl, 190, 192
Stith, Charles, 229
St. Mary's Cooperative Credit Association (St. Mary's Bank), 368
Stockman, David, 82, 127
Stock Yards Bank & Trust company, 333
Stokes, Louis, 257
St. Paul FCU, 34
Strengthening America's Communities Initiative (SACI), 356–357
Sullivan, Rev. Leon, 37
Sumner, Charles, 6
SUN (Stabilizing Urban Neighborhoods) initiative, 400
Surdna Foundation, 276
Surgeon, George
  on CDFI Fund selection process, 332, 340
  at the CDFI Woodstock, 249
  in Clinton's transition, 189
  Elk Horn Bank and Trust Company and, 101–102, 165–166
  at Southern Development Bancorporation, 298–299
  on technical assistance and loss rate, 171
Sussman, Paul, 340–341
*su su* (Caribbean), 6
Sviridoff, Mitchell "Mike", 35–36, 61, 84–85, n304, n1385
Swack, Michael, 94, 203–204, 351, 355, 379
Swann, Bob, 86, 192
Swoboda, Ralph, 192

## T

Taconic Foundation, 40–41, 75, 138
TARP (Troubled Assets Relief Program), 357, 382, 395, n1355
Tasch, Woody, 315
Tate, Juanita, 271
Taub, Richard, 57, 58, 296, n201
Taylor, John, 213, 307
TELACU, 312
Tesdell, Kerwin, 296, 315–316, 325, n1240, n1334

The Neighborhood Institute (TNI), 59–60, 98–99, 296
Theuner, Douglas E., 120
Thomas, Franklin A., 39, 61, 115
Thomas, Norman, 17–18
Thompson, Janet, 311
Tlingit-Haida Housing of Alaska, 282, 329–330, 363, 393
TNI (The Neighborhood Institute), 59–60, 98–99, 296
Towns, Edolphus, 155
Trapp, Shel, 49–50
Treasury Department
  CDFI Fund in, 213–214, 265, 268, 270–273, 289–290, 337–338
  Community Development Capital Initiative, 353
Trimble, Martin Paul
  on bank policy reforms, 156–157
  on CDFI Fund funding, 260
  in Clinton's transition, 189
  on community development banking bill, 189, n685
  leaving NACDLF, 276, 301
  as NACDLF executive director, 94, 151–152, 187–188
  November 20, 1992 meeting, 187–188
  at Senate hearing (1993), 198
Trinity Church, 105, 154, 158
Trinity Group, 158, 275. *See also* CDFI Coalition
Troubled Assets Relief Program (TARP), 357, 382, 395, n1355
Trump, Donald, administration of, 378, 383–384
Tuskegee FCU, 34
Twentieth Century Fund, 15, 61–62

## U

Union Settlement FCU, 41, 132, 134
unit banking, 410n179
United Church of Christ, 56, 122
United Farm Workers, 395
Urban Development Action Grants, 171
Urban Partnership Bank, 363, n1357
U.S. Central Credit Union, 73, 359

## V

Vamper, Annie, 131–132, n109
Veatch Program North Shore Unitarian Society, 75
Velazquez, Nydia, 239, 241
Vento, Bruce, 238, 343
Vermont Community Loan Fund, 366*t*, 392

Vermont Development Credit Union, 190
Vernon, Raymond, 35
Vidal, Avis, 81–82, n299
Vieth, Harvey R., 126–127
Village Trust Financial Cooperative, 381
Vindasius, Julia, 102, n388
VISTA (AmeriCorps), 304, n1147
VITA program, 395
Volpe, Michelle, 401

## W

WAFCP (Institute for Gender Research, Women and Foundations/Corporate Philanthropy), 311
Walsh, David I., 13
Walsh, Robert, 250
Walton, Rob, 101
Walton Family Foundation, 99, 391
Ward, Courtney, 189–190, 255
War on Poverty, 23–25, 30–32, 41–43, 125, 216, 246–247
Waters, Maxine
    on CDFI legislation, 210, 215, 223, 227, 236–237, 260
    defense of CDFI Fund, 342
    South Central Los Angeles violence, 162–163
Watson, Thomas, Jr., 38
Watts, Los Angeles, uprising of 1965, 30
wealth gap, 18, 25, 377–378
WEDCO (Women's Economic Development Corporation), 309
WegoWise, 400
Weinstein, Paul, Jr.
    on CD banking program, 374
    on CDFI Fund rescission, 268–269
    on CDFI legislation, 247, 248–249
    in Clinton administration, 208–215, nn759–760, n769
    on national service at CDFIs, 221
    on threatened CDFI Fund rescission, 268–270
Weissbourd, Bob, 189, 229
Wells, Jeff, 168–169, 172–173
Wells Fargo Bank, 371, n1374
Westgate, Michael, 49, 51
White, Reggie, 259–260, n957
White House Rose Garden ceremony (1993), vi, 221–222, 223–230, 236, 239, 316
Whitewater investigation, 254–255, 335, 340–341, n930
Whitley, Larry, 102
wholesale intermediaries, 320–321, 359, n1225

Wieboldt Foundation, 56
Williams, Darrin L., 395
Williams, Ed, 51
Winnick, Lou, 40–41, 84
Winthrop Rockefeller Foundation, 99–101, 117, n373
W.K. Kellogg foundation, 390, 392
Wofford Amendment, 253–254
Wolf, Sister Patricia, 120–121
Women's Economic Development Corporation (WEDCO), 309
Women's Self-Employment Project (WSEP), 165, 250, 309
Woodstock Institute, 158, 188, 204, 246, n365, n711
Workers Owned Sewing Company (WOSCO), 226, n411
Wright, Bonnie, 108, 110, 112, n404
Wysocki, Ted, 51–52, 231

## Y

Yates, H. B., 18, n88
Yingling, Edward L., 192, 257
Ylvisaker, Paul, 35, n135
Yunus, Muhammad
    Clintons and, vi, xv, 102, 179, 229, 334–335, 385
    presentation at Senate briefing, 200
    ShoreBank and, 97, 229

## Z

Zavarello, Bill, 160, 163, 223, 260, 346
Zelin, Karen, 155
Zippert, Carol, 34–35
Zippert, John, 35
Z. Smith Reynolds Foundation, 110–111

# ABOUT THE AUTHOR

After his early career as a Russian historian and translator, Clifford Rosenthal worked developing food cooperatives for Native American and migrant farmworker organizations. He joined the National Federation of Community Development Credit Unions in 1980 and served as its president and CEO for more than thirty years. He cofounded the national Coalition of CDFIs and served in its leadership for two decades. In 2012 he was appointed as the first director of the Office of Financial Empowerment of the federal Consumer Financial Protection Bureau, where he served until 2014.

He has received the highest honors of the National Credit Union Foundation and the Opportunity Finance Network, as well as the Lawyers Alliance of New York City and the Insight Center for Community Economic Development. The Clifford N. Rosenthal Community Center in the St. Claude community of the Upper Ninth Ward of New Orleans honors his assistance in helping the ASI Federal Credit Union recover from Hurricane Katrina. He was inducted into the African-American Credit Union Hall of Fame in 2019, the first non-African-American so honored. He lives in Brooklyn, New York, with his wife Elayne Archer, a writer and editor.

For more information about his consulting services and availability for speaking engagements, please visit:

www.archer-rosenthal.com
https://linkedin.com/in/cliff-rosenthal-479bb16/

CPSIA information can be obtained
at www.ICGtesting.com
Printed in the USA
LVHW051324031222
734484LV00011B/270